The Hamlyn A-Z of

CRICKET RECORDS

HAMLYN

LONDON · NEW YORK · SYDNEY · TORONTO

The Hamlyn A-Z of
CRICKET RECORDS

Peter
Wynne-Thomas

First published in 1983 by
The Hamlyn Publishing Group Limited
London · New York · Sydney · Toronto
Astronaut House, Feltham, Middlesex, England

Printed and bound by Graficromo s.a., Cordoba, Spain

The pictures in the preliminary pages are as follows:

ENDPAPERS
A 'grand national cricket match' played in the outer domain,
Sydney, between eleven players of New South Wales and eleven of
Victoria on 14, 15 and 16 January, 1857.

HALFTITLE
P Holmes and H Sutcliffe posing before the scoreboard which
records the highest partnership in English first-class cricket, 555 for
the Yorkshire first wicket against Essex in 1932.

TITLE PAGE
Geoffrey Boycott on his way to a double century against Essex in
1971. Boycott has the highest aggregate of runs in Test matches and
is the only batsman to average over 100 runs in an English season
twice.

Photographic Acknowledgements
BBC Hulton Picture Library: 15, 44 below, 45 top, 48, 49 top left, 73,
74–75, 86 below, 88, 93 below, 101, 109 top right, 111 below, 116 below,
117 below, 144, 148 below, 172 below, 174 top, 179 top, 179 below, 182;
Central Press, London: 8, 13, 49 top right, 49 centre, 69 below, 72 below, 78
top, 96 top, 109 below left, 115, 120 left, 122 below, 143 below, 145, 149
below left, 172 top; Colour Library International: 86 top, 143 top left, 150
below; Patrick Eagar: title-spread, 11 top right, 37 top, 38, 39, 47 top left, 50
top, 51 left, 69 top, 76 right, 80 below, 84, 87, 90 top, 91 top, 92, 95, 96
below, 98 top, 99 top, 102 top, 106, 107 top, 110, 117 top, 120 top, 120
right, 125, 128, 139, 143 top right, 146 top, 147, 150 top, 177 top, 180, 183,
184, 185; Mary Evans Picture Library: 123; Hamlyn Group Picture Library:
7, 12, 16, 35, 36, 37 below, 42 top left, 43, 44 top left, 44 top right, 45
below, 47 below right, 50 below, 71, 75 top, 76 left, 79 left, 81, 89, 90
below, 98 below, 100, 104, 105 left, 108, 111 top, 113 left, 121, 140, 148,
top, 168, 177 below left, 187; Ilford and Redbridge Post:142 left; Mansell
Collection, London: Endpapers, 91 below, 93 top, 107 top left, 107 below,
122 top, 124, 138, 142 right, 177 below right; Don Morley, Morden: 46, 47
top right, 181 top; Nottinghamshire County Cricket Club: 9, 10, 11 top left,
11 below, 14, 41, 42 right, 47 below left, 49 below, 51 right, 52, 68, 70, 72
top, 74 top, 77, 78 below, 79 right, 80 top, 97, 99 below, 103, 105 right, 109
top left, 112, 113 right, 116 top 118, 119, 146 below, 149 below right, 181
below; Popperfoto, London: 131, 132, 174 below; Press Association, London:
137; Sport and General Press Agency: 102 below, 149 top.

Introduction

With each season that passes, cricket 'records' become steadily more divorced from the matches out of which the statistics are culled.

The multitude of figures now have a life of their own, hypnotising those who tinker with them. What began in the middle of the nineteenth century as a simple exercise to evaluate the relative skills of batsmen has, 130 years later, developed to the point where anyone who studies these things can prove anything. To some this is a highly satisfactory state of affairs, but I feel the time has come when it is necessary to make it quite clear to the average cricket follower that most of the comparative 'tables' so accurately compiled and published in so many modern 'record books' give a totally misleading picture of the merits of the players who feature in them.

It is highly gratifying for a statistical buff to compile a complete list of first-class double centuries, but the publication of such a list invites the ordinary reader to think that here is a list of the greatest innings ever played, when nothing is further from the truth. A detailed inspection of each double century in the context of the match and circumstances of its making would quickly reveal that in many, perhaps most cases, the innings was made on an easy wicket against innocuous bowling and that many a fifty was worth more than quite a number of the 200s.

An analysis of most of the other tabulations that are nowadays looked upon with awe would reveal similar findings.

In compiling this book I have shunned such tabulations, save for the leading season-by-season averages, and I have tried to confine myself to THE RECORDS and to give a little of the background behind those records and the history leading up to them, so that the numerous events can be seen in perspective and not as is usual in a mathematical abstraction.

First-class Records

The problems of the exact definition of a 'first-class match' have bedevilled cricket record keepers for many years. The Association of Cricket Statisticians was formed to remove these problems.

In this book, the first-class records are confined to those matches listed as 'first-class' in the various Guides published by the Association.

It should be pointed out that the records in this book are complete to September 15 1981.

Acknowledgements

I wish to express my thanks to Philip Bailey for his continuous assistance throughout the compilation of this work and particularly for providing the season-by-season averages, and to Derek West, who compiled the index. My thanks are also due to the following who have helped in various ways: Peter Arnold, Dennis Lambert, S S Perera, Bob Normandale, Philip Thorn, Ken Trushell, Ernest Gross and Keith Warsop.

It would of course have been impossible to compile this work without the aid of the researches of all the cricket historians and statisticians who have preceded it. I must therefore humbly acknowledge my debt to Arthur Haygarth and every one of his successors – Thank you.

Peter Wynne-Thomas DECEMBER 1981

The Records

Abandoned

Three Test matches have been abandoned without a ball being bowled due to adverse weather conditions. The first abandoned match should have been played at Old Trafford on Aug 25, 26 and 27, 1890, the second at Old Trafford on July 8, 9, 11 and 12, 1938 and the third at Melbourne on Dec 31, 1970 and Jan 1, 2, 4 and 5, 1971. All three matches were between England and Australia. In the case of the last-named match an additional Test was added to the series, replacing MCC *v* Victoria.

The worst first-class English season as regards abandoned matches was 1979, when no less than 10 three-day fixtures were totally washed out – by odd coincidence the worst season ever for wet weather is reputed to be 1879: 'Rain, pitiless and persistent, made the four months of the cricket year cheerless for players, altogether uninviting and dismal for spectators, and no one of either class could possibly have been truly sorry when the last day of August brought the game to a standstill.'

In 1974 Hampshire appeared almost certain to win the County Championship, but their last match – *v* Yorkshire at Bournemouth – was abandoned without a ball being bowled.

Players selected to represent the All-England Eleven in the 'matches of the north' in 1847. From left to right: Guy, Parr, Martingell, A Mynn, W Denison, Dean, Clarke, N Felix, O C Pell, Hillyer, Lillywhite, Dorrinton, Pilch, Sewell.

Airedale and Wharfedale League

Championship winners

1936 Yeadon	1952 Ilkley	1967 Guiseley
1937 Otley	1953 North Leeds	1968 Hall Park
1938 Ilkley	1954 DP & E	1969 Guiseley
1939 Otley	1955 Ilkley	1970 Gargrave
1940 Hall Park	1956 North Leeds	1971 Guiseley
1941 Earby	1957 Guiseley	1972 North Leeds
1942 Otley	1958 Guiseley	1973 Guiseley
1943 Otley	1959 Ilkley	1974 Otley
1944 Burley	1960 Hall Park,	1975 Knaresborough
1945 Skipton	Horsforth	1976 Knaresborough
1946 Ilkley	1961 DP & E	1977 Knaresborough
1947 Guiseley,	1962 North Leeds	1978 Knaresborough
Ilkley	1963 DP & E	1979 Knaresborough
Rawdon	1964 Burley	1980 Knaresborough
1948 North Leeds	1965 Guiseley,	1981 Ilkley
1949 Ilkley	Illingworth	1982 Otley
1950 Menston	1966 Guiseley,	
1951 North Leeds	Otley	

All England Eleven

Formed in 1846 by William Clarke, this touring team contained for several years the best English cricketers of the day. Because of its strength the Eleven generally played sides composed of twenty-two men, though these odds were reduced when opposed to such sides as Sheffield, Manchester and some county teams. In 1852, several players set up the United All England Eleven as a rival to the AEE and from 1857–66 the annual match between these two teams was perhaps the most important contest of the English season – certainly judged by the quality of the players. The AEE lasted until 1880.

In all matches G Parr with 10,404 runs (av 16.78) was the leading batsman for the side and W Clarke took most wickets (2,385).

All-round Feats

In a season

Traditionally the target for an all-rounder is to achieve the record of scoring 1,000 runs and taking 100 wickets in the same season. This combination of records is known as the 'Double'. First cricketers to achieve the milestones of 1,000 runs and 100 wickets, 2,000 runs and 100 wickets are as follows:

1,000 runs and 100 wickets In 1874, W G Grace scored 1,664 runs (av 52.00) and took 140 wickets (av 12.71) playing in only 21 first-class matches. There is a web of deception surrounding this record, which makes an interesting story. In 1873 a journalist fiddled W G Grace's batting figures in order to give the great player the honour of scoring 2,000 runs in the season. Some very unimportant matches were added to his other 'first-class' appearances to bolster his run total. Then years later another statistician added the wickets Grace took in the minor matches to increase his wickets to 101; this then resulted in Grace scoring over 2,000 runs and taking over 100 wickets in 1873. Only in recent years has the muddle been unravelled and the true picture emerged. In 1873 Grace actually hit 1,805 runs and took only 75 wickets, so the double was first performed in 1874. Once a common feat – it has been performed over 300 times – the introduction of one-day cricket has made it a rarity nowadays: it was last done by F J Titmus of Middlesex in 1967.

2,000 runs and 100 wickets Ignoring the bogus record by Grace in 1873, this feat was first performed in 1876, W G Grace being the record-breaker again. He hit 2,622 runs (av 62.42) and dismissed 130 batsmen (av 18.90). In all this feat has been achieved 20 times, the last occasion being by T E Bailey of Essex in 1959.

2,000 runs and 200 wickets This outstanding feat has been accomplished just once in the history of first-class cricket. G H Hirst of Yorkshire in 1906 returned the following figures:

	M	I	NO	Runs	HS	Avge	100s
Batting	35	58	6	2385	169	45.86	6

	M	Overs	M	Runs	Wkts	Avge
Bowling	35	1306.1	271	3434	208	16.50

3,000 runs and 100 wickets Not perhaps quite such a landmark as the one achieved by Hirst, this feat also has only been achieved by one cricketer in first-class matches: J H Parks of Sussex in 1937. Parks was an opening batsman for his county and not an all-rounder in the class of Hirst; in fact he only achieved the target of 1,000 runs and 100 wickets on one other occasion. His record in 1937 reads:

	M	I	NO	Runs	HS	Avge	100s
Batting	35	63	4	3003	168	50.89	11

	Overs	M	Runs	Wkts	avge
Bowling	1047.3	265	2609	101	25.83

1,000 runs and 200 wickets This feat, confined to bowlers who can bat, has been performed on six occasions (excluding Hirst's much greater feat of 1906), but by only three players. A E Trott became the first player to reach the targets in 1899 and repeated it the following year. A S Kennedy of Hampshire did it in 1922, then in the three following years, M W Tate of Sussex reached the targets.

Earliest date in a season to reach 'Double' This, as one would suspect, belongs to G H Hirst in 1906. Having already hit 1,000 runs, Hirst took his 100th wicket on June 28 v Essex at Leyton, when he bowled F L Fane before lunch on the first day of the match. He was the first man to take 100 wickets in 1906, but it was a very close thing – his county colleague, S Haigh, took his 99th wicket in the same match!

Fred Titmus, the Middlesex all-rounder, the last player to score 1,000 runs and take 100 wickets in a season, in 1967.

The last player to score 2,000 runs and take 100 wickets in a season was Trevor Bailey of Essex in 1959.

IM PARKS

G HIRST

Far left *Jim Parks of Sussex achieved the unique double of 3,000 runs and 100 wickets in 1937.*

Left *The greatest all-round feat achieved in a season is also unique – the performance of George Hirst in 1906 in scoring 2,000 runs and taking 200 wickets.*

In a Match

A century and ten wickets in an innings (in an eleven-a-side match) In first class cricket this incredible feat has been performed only three times, including once in India, when F A Tarrant scored 182* and took 10–90 for the Maharajah of Cooch Behar's XI v Lord Willingdon's XI, Poona, 1918–19. Of the two feats accomplished in England, one was by W G Grace in 1886 for MCC v Oxford University, but the other is really the most outstanding of the three, considering the quality of the match. V E Walker, the Middlesex amateur, performed it for England v Surrey at the Oval on July 21, 22 and 23, 1859. A report on the game notes:

'Mr Walker obtained all the wickets in the first innings of Surrey, and four in the second. He got out in one four-ball over, with his first, third and last ball, Burbidge, Caffyn and Stephenson. He gave no chance in his innings of 108. Altogether, considering his age (only 22), this must be considered one of THE most wonderful cricketing feats on record; and his brilliant fielding must also be taken into consideration.'

In minor cricket the feat has been performed about 50 times so far as is known throughout the world. It would seem that E M Grace, brother of W G, stands alone in performing it on three occasions, namely: Lansdown v Clifton in 1861, MCC v Gents of Kent in 1862 and Thornburn v Clifton Victoria in 1881.

The only recorded instance of a player hitting 200 and taking all 10 wickets was L O S Poidevin in a school match in Sydney, Australia in 1887–88 – Poidevin went on to play for New South Wales, and then, coming to England to study medicine, he qualified for Lancashire, appearing for his adopted county for 5 seasons.

A century in each innings and five wickets in each innings G H Hirst playing for Yorkshire against Somerset at Bath on August 27, 28 and 29, 1906 hit 111 and 117 not out and took 6 for 70 and 5 for 45. He only performed this feat – an unique record – by courtesy of the Yorkshire captain, Ernest Smith, who declined to enforce the follow on when Somerset were 243 runs behind on the first innings. Yorkshire instead batted a second time and treated the Somerset bowling with scant respect, scoring 280 before declaring with only one wicket down. Yorkshire won by 389 runs.

A double century and 16 wickets G Giffen hit 271 and took 9 for 96 and 7 for 70 for South Australia against Victoria at Adelaide on November 7, 9, 10 and 11, 1891. It must be mentioned that Victoria were represented by a very second-rate eleven. The feat has not been accomplished in English first-class cricket.

A century in each innings and 10 wickets At Lord's for Middlesex against Sussex on May 25, 26 and 27, 1905, B J T Bosanquet hit 103 and 100 not out and also had bowling returns of 3 for 75 and 8 for 53.

A hundred runs in a match and 10 wickets This feat is the equivalent of the season's double and though not quite so common in first-class cricket has been performed about 200 times. The only player to accomplish it more than ten times is W G Grace, whose tally is 17. The feat is rarely seen in English first-class cricket these days, though there is no intrinsic reason why it should be rare – in the last 10 years it has only occurred however as follows: K D Boyce (*Essex*) 1975, Imran Khan (*Worcs*) 1976, M J Procter (*Gloucs*) 1977 and 1980, D S Steele (*Northants*) 1978, I A Greig (*Sussex*) 1981. I T Botham also performed it for England in the Jubilee Test v India, at Bombay, 1979–80.

In a Career

10,000 runs and 1,000 wickets The great all-rounders are usually measured by whether or not they have reached 10,000 runs and taken

9

George Giffen scored 271 and took 16 wickets for South Australia against Victoria in 1891.

B J T Bosanquet scored a century in each innings and took ten wickets playing for Middlesex against Sussex in 1905.

1,000 wickets in their first-class career, but since it requires some ten seasons to achieve, there are many notable all-rounders who, due to early retirement, or illness, have not reached both targets; on the other hand a number of 'ordinary' couny players, whose career has stretched to 15 years with few breaks for illness, have accomplished the feat. Over 60 players in all are contained in the complete list.

W G Grace was easily the first to reach both figures. He took his 1,000th wicket in 1877, having reached 10,000 runs in 1873.

20,000 runs and 2,000 wickets   As with the previous feat, W G Grace was the first cricketer to reach both targets, which he did in the mid-1880s. Only nine cricketers have accomplished the feat and there can be no doubt that they are a very select band indeed. Details are as follows:

		BATTING		BOWLING	
		runs	avge	wkts	avge
W E Astill (*Leics*)	1906–1939	22731	22.64	2431	23.78
T E Bailey (*Essex*)	1945–1967	28642	33.42	2082	23.13
W G Grace (*Gloucs*)	1865–1908	54211	39.45	2809	18.15
G H Hirst (*Yorks*)	1891–1929	36356	34.13	2742	18.73
R Illingworth (*Yorks, Leics*)	1951–1982	24063	28.37	2041	20.12
W Rhodes (*Yorks*)	1898–1930	39969	30.81	4204	16.72
M W Tate (*Sussex*)	1912–1937	21717	25.01	2784	18.16
F J Titmus (*Middx, Surrey*)	1949–1982	21588	23.11	2830	22.36
F E Woolley (*Kent*)	1906–1938	58959	40.77	2066	19.87

10,000 runs and 1,000 catches as a fielder   F E Woolley of Kent is the only cricketer to achieve both targets and since he features in the list of nine above, he is indeed an outstanding all-rounder. He took 1,020 catches in addition to his 58,959 runs and 2,066 wickets. It must however be pointed out that close to the wicket fieldsmen have much more opportunity of notching up a large total of catches – Woolley generally fielded in the slips.

30,000 runs and 1,000 dismissals as wicket-keeper   Two cricketers have realised these targets:

		BATTING		DISMISSALS
		runs	avge	
L E G Ames (*Kent*)	1926–1951	37248	43.51	1123 (706c, 417st)
J M Parks (*Sussex, Som*)	1949–1976	36673	34.76	1182 (1089c, 93st)

Both Ames and Parks were on many occasions played purely as batsmen and took many catches in the field, rather than as wicket-keeper. Parks is the son of J H Parks, who took 100 wickets and scored 3,000 runs in 1937.

Amateurs

The distinction between amateurs and professionals was abolished in England after the 1962 season. The last time a first-class county fielded an all-amateur eleven in a County Championship match was on June 30, July 1 and 2, 1887 when Gloucestershire played an all-amateur eleven against Yorkshire at Gloucester.

Two all-rounders with outstanding career records: Wilfred Rhodes (above) and wicket-keeper-batsman Leslie Ames (below).

Colin Cowdrey of Kent and England has played most often in Test matches – 114 between 1954 and 1975.

Annuals

The first known cricket 'annual' was published by Samuel Britcher, the scorer at Lord's, and covered the season of 1790. This annual ran for 15 issues and lasted until 1805.

The earliest 'county annual' to publish scores of matches was issued by Shropshire in 1865, but did not survive long. Of the present county annuals the one with the longest run belongs to Kent, this being established in 1877. The oldest cricket annual dealing with English cricket as a whole is Wisden's Cricketers' Almanack, which commenced in 1864.

Appearances

W Rhodes of Yorkshire, whose career ran from 1898 to 1930, made the most appearances in first-class cricket, his total number of matches being 1,111.

Rhodes also holds the record for most appearances in County Championship cricket with 763 matches to his name.

The record for most Test appearances belongs to M C Cowdrey, with 114 matches for England between 1954 and 1975.

Argentina

The first reference to cricket in Argentina occurred in 1806. The first match by Argentina took place in 1868 v Uruguay. All authorities date first-class cricket in Argentina from the M C C tour of 1911–12 and first-class status should be given to representative Argentine sides from that date until 1937–38.

The highest total in important cricket by Argentina is 612 for 6 dec v Chile at Belgrano in 1930.

The best individual innings is 256 not out by D Ayling for North v South in 1939.

The record wicket partnership is 242 for the 2nd wicket by D Ayling and R L Stuart v Chile at Belgrano in 1930.

The best bowling in an innings is 9–20 by D A Cavanagh v S A C T (Hurlingham) in 1956–57.

Argentina took part in the 1979 I C C Trophy, but failed to win a match – played 4, lost 3, drawn 1.

Army

The first first-class match in England involving a representative Army side took place at Lord's on May 30 and 31, 1912 against the Royal Navy. Matches by the Army were recognised as first-class from then until 1939, the final first-class match being against Cambridge University. It should be noted however that the Navy and Army Combined were first-class from 1910.

The highest total in first-class cricket by the Army is 589–5 dec v Navy at Lord's in 1928 and in the same innings E S B Williams made the highest individual score of 228, hit in 270 minutes.

The best bowling performance in an innings for the Army is 8 for 46 by A C Gore against the Navy at Lord's in 1925.

The highest individual innings in any military match is 402 not out by A H Du Boulay for the School of Military Engineering versus Royal Navy and Royal Marines at Chatham on July 12, 1907. He batted 225 minutes. Du Boulay had some outstanding successes in army cricket and in a single week in July 1906 made scores of 204, 153 and 175 for the Royal Engineers. Another remarkable batting feat in army cricket was performed on October 30 and 31, 1901 in an inter-company match of the Hampshire Regiment. Capt A C Richards hit 101* out of an all out total of 114 in the first innings and then 185 out of 221 in the second, the next highest individual score being 6.

ASDA Trophy *see* Fenner Trophy

Ashes, The

After Australia defeated England by 7 runs at the Oval on August 29, 1882, a mock memorial notice in remembrance of English cricket was published in *The Sporting Times* with the intimation that the body would be cremated and the Ashes taken to Australia. Ivo Bligh, who was captaining a team to Australia the following winter, announced at a dinner, before leaving England, that he would recover 'those Ashes'. Bligh's team duly beat the Australians and some ladies in Melbourne burnt the bails used in the deciding match and placed the ashes in an urn. That urn is now in a glass case at Lord's, where it remains, regardless of which side wins 'The Ashes'.

Assumed Names

During the 19th century it was relatively common for amateurs to appear in county cricket under an assumed name. R B Halliwell played in first-class matches under no less than five aliases – R Tessib, B Richards, H Brown, O N E More and Mr Allen – which seems to be a record for first-class cricket.

The most notorious change of name was by Trooper Dale, who had deserted from the Royal Horse Guards in 1873 and in 1880 arrived back in England as captain of the Canadian touring team, using the name Jordan. He was arrested during the Canadians' match with Leicestershire and sent to prison. The tour more or less collapsed after this.

One of the last players in first-class county cricket to use an alias was G N Bignell, who appeared for Hampshire in 1919 as 'G Newcombe'. A serving officer, it is presumed he did not have the necessary permission to play.

Attendances

On a single day The record crowd to attend a single day's play is 90,800, being the number on the Melbourne Cricket Ground on February 11, 1961 to watch the second day's play in the match between Australia and West Indies. The English record is 38,847 on July 25, 1938 during the England v Australia Test Match at Headingley.

Attendances in excess of 30,000 have been recorded on Whit Monday and August Bank Holiday Monday at matches between Lancashire and Yorkshire and Nottinghamshire and Surrey, but because the number of members watching the games has been estimated rather than counted, the total attendance figures cannot be exact. 36,000 were estimated to have watched Lancs v Yorks on Aug 4, 1924 at Old Trafford and the same number attended the same fixture at Old Trafford on June 1, 1925. 35,000 are estimated to have watched Notts v Surrey at Trent Bridge on May 17, 1948.

For a whole match The game between India and England at Eden Gardens, Calcutta on January 1, 2, 3, 5, 6, 1982 was reported to be watched by a total of more than 425,000.

The Australian record is 350,534 for the match between Australia and England played on Melbourne Cricket Ground on January 1, 2, 4, 5, 6 and 7, 1937.

The record in England stands at 158,000 at Headingley on July 22, 23, 24, 26 and 27, 1948, England playing Australia.

The record for a county championship match is 80,000 at the Oval on July 26–28, 1906 for W S Lees' benefit match, Surrey v Yorkshire.

Test Match Series 943,000 attended the five Tests between Australia and England in 1936–37. The highest for a series in England is 549,650 during the five Tests of the 1953 England v Australia series.

August

W R Hammond holds the record for the most runs scored in first-class cricket during the month of August. His details for August 1936 read:

M	I	NO	R	HS	Avge	100s
9	16	3	1281	317	98.53	4

Eight of his matches were for Gloucestershire and one for England. Hammond broke the long-standing record of 1,278 runs set by W G Grace in 1876.

Most wickets in the month are 86 by A P Freeman in 1933.

Australia

(*see also under* Sheffield Shield)

The first reference to cricket occurs in the *Sydney Gazette* of January 1804 which states: 'The late intense weather has been very favourable to the amateurs of cricket who have scarce lost a day for the last month.'

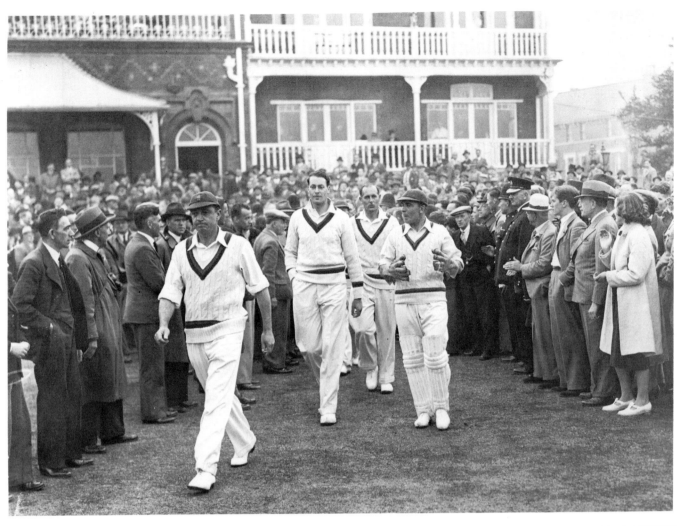

Above   *Walter Hammond leading out the England team at Trent Bridge in 1938. In 1936 Hammond scored a record total of runs for the month of August. Farnes, Verity and Ames are also in the picture.*

Left   *The highest individual innings in Australasian cricket is 566, scored by C J Eady in 1902.*

Right   *Bill Woodfull and Bill Ponsford, Australia's opening batsmen, each scored centuries in the highest team total in cricket, Victoria's 1,107 against New South Wales in 1926.*

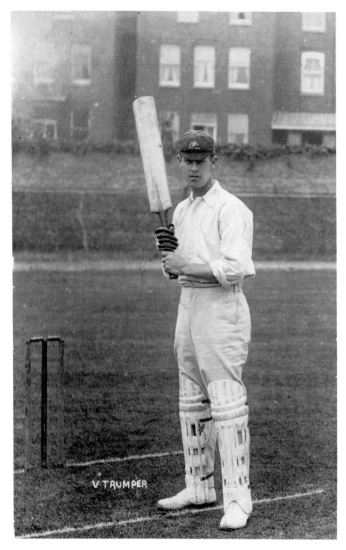

Victor Trumper, the great Australian opening batsman, who shares the record eighth-wicket partnership in Australian first-class cricket.

Clem Hill shares the oldest of the Australian wicket partnership records – 232 for the ninth wicket in 1900–01.

This is the first definite reference to the game in Australia, though it would seem that cricket was played for some time prior to that.

First-class cricket   The first inter-colonial match took place at Launceston between Tasmania and Victoria on February 11 and 12, 1851 and this is regarded as the initial 'first-class' match in Australia.

Highest team total   The record of 1,107 in a single innings was hit by Victoria against New South Wales on Melbourne Cricket Ground on December 24, 27 and 28, 1926. The innings lasted only 630 minutes, W H Ponsford scored 352, J Ryder 295, W M Woodfull 133 and H S T L Hendry 100. The bowler to suffer most was A A Mailey who conceded 362 runs off 64 overs.

Lowest team total   The lowest total in first-class matches is 15 by Victoria against MCC on Melbourne Cricket Ground, February 9, 1904. W Rhodes took 5 wickets for 6 runs and E G Arnold 4 for 8. One batsman – V S Ransford – could not bat due to illness and the innings lasted 45 minutes.

Highest individual innings   C J Eady scored 566 in 7 hours, 53 minutes for Break o' Day v Wellington in a match to decide the Champion Club of Southern Tasmania. Eady began his innings on Saturday, March 15, 1902 and continued it on Saturday, March 21, when, by close of play, he was 419 not out. The last day's play was on Wednesday, April 2, and he took his total to 566 before being stumped. The last day's play was little more than a farce, since only 8 of the Wellington side turned up.

The highest score in first-class cricket is 452* by D G Bradman for

New South Wales v Queensland on January 4 and 6, 1930. He batted 415 minutes and hit 49 fours. Remarkably the match was not a high scoring one, apart from Bradman's innings. NSW were dismissed for 235 and Queensland for 227. NSW made 761–8 dec in their second innings and then dismissed Queensland for 84. The match took place on Sydney Cricket Ground.

Best bowling in an innings   T W Wall returned figures of 12.4-2-36-10 for South Australia v New South Wales on Sydney Cricket Ground, February 3, 1933. NSW made 87 for 2 before lunch, then after the interval Wall took 8 wickets for 5 runs, including dismissing Fingleton, McCabe, Rowe and Cummins in a single over.

Best bowling in a match   Only one bowler has achieved the distinction of taking 17 wickets in a first-class match in Australia. G Giffen returned the following analysis for South Australia v Victoria at Adelaide on March 11, 12, 14, 15, 1886:

116.2 overs   21 mdns   201 runs   17 wkts

Wicket Partnerships

First-class records

1st	456	W H Ponsford, E R Mayne. Victoria v Queensland (*Melbourne*) 1923–24
2nd	378	L A Marks, K D Walters. NSW v S Australia (*Adelaide*) 1964–65
3rd	390*	J M Wiener, J K Moss. Victoria v W Australia (*Melbourne*) 1981–82

4th 424 I S Lee, S O Quin. Victoria *v* Tasmania (*Melbourne*) 1933–34

5th 405 S G Barnes, D G Bradman. Australia *v* England (*Sydney*) 1946–47

6th 346 J H W Fingleton, D G Bradman. Australia *v* England (*Melbourne*) 1936–37

7th 335 C W Andrews, E C Bensted. Queensland *v* NSW (*Sydney*) 1934–35

8th 270 V T Trumper, E P Barbour. NSW *v* Victoria (*Sydney*) 1912–13

9th 232 C Hill, E Walkley. S Australia *v* NSW (*Adelaide*) 1900–01

10th 307 A F Kippax, J E H Hooker. NSW *v* Victoria (*Melbourne*) 1928–29

The record partnership for any match in Australia is:

3rd 641 T Patton, N Rippon. Buffalo *v* Whorouly (*Gapsted, Victoria*) 1913–14

Records for the first-class States

NEW SOUTH WALES
Highest team total 918 *v* S Australia (*Sydney*) 1900–01
Lowest team total 37 *v* Victoria (*Sydney*) 1868–69
Highest innings 452* D G Bradman *v* Queensland (*Sydney*) 1929–30
Best bowling 9–41 W J O'Reilly *v* S Australia (*Sydney*) 1937–38

QUEENSLAND
Highest team total 687 *v* New South Wales (*Brisbane*) 1930–31
Lowest team total 40 *v* Victoria (*Brisbane*) 1902–03
Highest innings 283 P J P Burge *v* NSW (*Brisbane*) 1963–64
Best bowling 10–61 P J Allan *v* Victoria (*Melbourne*) 1965–66

SOUTH AUSTRALIA
Highest team total 821–7 dec *v* Queensland (*Adelaide*) 1939–40
Lowest team total 23 *v* Victoria (*Melbourne*) 1882–83
Highest innings 369 D G Bradman *v* Tasmania (*Adelaide*) 1935–36
Best bowling 10–36 T W Wall *v* NSW (*Sydney*) 1932–33

TASMANIA
Highest team total 505–9 dec *v* Queensland (*Hobart*) 1979–80
Lowest team total 18 *v* Victoria (*Melbourne*) 1868–69
Highest innings 274 C L Badcock *v* Victoria (*Launceston*) 1933–34
Best bowling 8–31 W Brown *v* Victoria (*Hobart*) 1857–58

VICTORIA
Highest team total 1107 *v* New South Wales (*Melbourne*) 1926–27
Lowest team total 15 *v* MCC (*Melbourne*) 1903–04
Highest innings 437 W H Ponsford *v* Queensland (*Melbourne*) 1927–28
Best bowling 9–2 G Elliott *v* Tasmania (*Launceston*) 1857–58

WESTERN AUSTRALIA
Highest team total 615–5 dec *v* Queensland (*Brisbane*) 1968–69
Lowest team total 38 *v* Victoria (*Melbourne*) 1892–93
Highest innings 243 C Milburn *v* Queensland (*Brisbane*) 1968–69
Best bowling 10–44 I J Brayshaw *v* Victoria (*Perth*) 1967–68

Geoff Boycott sweeps. Boycott is the only batsman to have a first-class average of over 100 in two English seasons.

Alfred Shaw of Notts in 1880 had the best average of any bowler taking 100 wickets in a season.

Averages

Batting

Best in an English first-class season Of those players who have had a minimum of 10 innings in a season, the highest average has been attained by D G Bradman (Australia) in 1938 when his record was:

20 matches   26 inns   5 not outs   2429 runs   278 hs   115.66 av

There have been only three other instances of batsmen exceeding an average of 100 in a season. G Boycott performed the feat in 1971 (av 100.12) and in 1979 (av 102.53) and W A Johnston (Australia) recorded 102.00 in 1953. The last however was a 'freak' figure since Johnston was not out in 16 of his 17 innings.

Best in a Test series Only one player has exceeded an average of 200 in a Test series, having appeared in at least four Tests in the series. The record was created by D G Bradman for Australia v South Africa in 1931–32, his figures being:

5 matches   5 inns   1 not out   806 runs   299* hs   201.50 av

Best in a first-class career D G Bradman's record in his career far exceeds the next batsman of those who scored over 10,000 runs. His figures are:

Career	I	NO	R	HS	Avge	100s
1927–28 to 1948–49	338	43	28067	452*	95.14	117

Best in a Test career D G Bradman (Australia) also holds the record for the best average in a Test career for those who appeared in 10 or more matches. His figures are:

52 matches   80 inns   10 not outs   6996 runs   334 hs   99.94 av

Best in an overseas season The record for the highest average in a season outside the British Isles in first-class matches with a minimum of 1,000 runs is held by V S Hazare in India in 1943–44. His figures read:

11 inns   3 not outs   1423 runs   309 hs   177.87 av

Bowling

Best in an English first-class season The lowest average obtained by a bowler taking at least 100 wickets was achieved by A Shaw (*Notts*) in 1880. His figures read:

2133 overs   1257 mdns   1589 runs   186 wkts   8.54 av

Since 1945 the lowest average has been achieved by H L Jackson (*Derbyshire*) in 1958, his figures being:

829 overs   295 mdns   1572 runs   143 wkts   10.99 av

Several bowlers have obtained very low averages whilst playing in a handful of matches. The most remarkable in recent years for any bowler with 10 or more wickets was attained by J A Bailey (*MCC*) in 1966, his record being:

51.3 overs   29 mdns   57 runs   13 wkts   4.38 av

Best in a Test series Of those bowlers who have taken 25 wickets or more in a series, the lowest bowling average has been attained by G A Lohmann for England against South Africa in 1895–96, his figures being:

104 overs   38 mdns   203 runs   35 wkts   5.80 av

Best in a first-class career The lowest average obtained by a bowler with at least 1,000 first-class wickets was achieved by A Shaw (*Notts* and *Sussex*), whose figures are:

Career	Runs	Wkts	Avge
1864–1897	24579	2027	12.12

Best in a Test career Of those bowlers who have taken at least 75 wickets in their Test career, the best record is by G A Lohmann (*England*), his figures being:

1205 runs   112 wkts   10.75 average

Best in an overseas season The record for the lowest average in a season outside the British Isles in first class matches with a minimum of 50 wickets is by R K Oxenham for the Australian touring side in Ceylon and India in 1935–36, his figures being:

323.3 overs   149 mdns   586 runs   86 wkts   6.81 av

First-class averages in English cricket 1864 to date

The leading 20 batsmen and bowlers are given for each English season from 1864, except for the years 1915–1918 and 1940–1944, when no first-class cricket was played. The qualification for inclusion is 10 innings for batsmen and for bowlers the taking of 10 wickets.

In seasons when Test matches were played, the English players to represent their country are denoted by a dagger and those players who played for England, but are not in the tables, are given in a footnote.

The bowling analyses for some matches played before 1880 are unobtainable. Where one of the bowlers involved in these matches is featured in the averages, the wickets he took are shown thus: (+2).

First-class averages: 1864

BATTING	M	I	NO	Runs	HS	Avge	100s
G Anderson (*Yorks*)	6	11	5	255	99*	42.50	0
H H Stephenson (*Surrey*)	18	25	4	824	119	39.23	2
W Mortlock (*Surrey*)	18	25	0	855	105	34.20	1
T Hayward (*Cambs*)	8	12	0	355	66	29.58	0
G Wells (*Mx/Sx*)	9	14	2	340	82	28.33	0
R Carpenter (*Cambs*)	8	11	1	270	52	27.00	0
R Daft (*Notts*)	11	20	1	498	80	26.21	0
T Humphrey (*Surrey*)	14	24	1	602	94	26.17	0
T B Case (*O U/Middx*)	9	13	0	339	116	26.07	1
H Jupp (*Surrey*)	16	28	3	647	110	25.88	1
John Lillywhite (*Mx/Sx*)	9	14	2	301	64	25.08	0
J Caesar (*Surrey*)	9	13	2	267	132*	24.27	1
C Smith (*Sussex*)	8	13	2	255	95	23.18	0
T Hearne (*Middx*)	18	28	3	562	125	22.48	1
John Berry (*Yorks*)	8	14	1	266	42	20.46	0
L Greenwood (*Yorks*)	5	10	1	183	65	20.33	0
C H Ellis (*Sussex*)	13	18	1	333	54	19.58	0
G Griffith (*Surrey*)	17	27	2	489	86*	19.56	0
T Lockyer (*Surrey*)	16	21	1	375	108*	18.75	1
J Thewlis (*Yorks*)	10	20	1	348	77	18.31	0

BOWLING	M	O	M	R	W	Avge	
E F Dyke (*CU*)	1	47.1	21	41	10	4.10	
W Catling (*Middx*)	6	82	23	131	16	8.18	
G F Tarrant (*Cambs*)	8	402	141	590	67	8.80	
A S Teape (*OU*)	5	86.1	26	114	11	10.36	(+1)
F R Reynolds (*Cambs*)	4	147.2	66	185	17	10.88	
J Grundy (*Notts*)	18	866.2	383	1109	98	11.31	(+1)
T Hayward (*Cambs*)	8	92	32	163	14	11.64	
W F Maitland (*OU*)	6	268.1	72	485	41	11.82	(+7)
V E Walker (*Middx*)	8	263.2	37	511	42	12.16	
T S Curteis (*CU*)	2	151.1	81	162	13	12.46	
H Arkwright (*MCC*)	3	121	31	279	21	13.28	
E Willsher (*Kent*)	16	871.2	344	1069	80	13.36	
Jas Lillywhite (*Sussex*)	12	807.3	264	1139	83	13.72	
R C Tinley (*Notts*)	9	231.2	36	508	35	14.51	
F G Pelham (*CU*)	2	124.1	47	175	12	14.58	
R Iddison (*Yorks*)	13	252	37	546	37	14.75	
G Wootton (*Notts*)	20	869	329	1277	85	15.02	(+2)
A Shaw (*Notts*)	8	144.2	47	219	14	15.64	
T Lockyer (*Surrey*)	16	132.2	40	238	15	15.86	
W H Fryer (*Kent*)	10	292.2	108	416	26	16.00	

First-class averages: 1865

BATTING	M	I	NO	Runs	HS	Avge	100s
W Oscroft (*Notts*)	9	13	1	518	107	43.16	1
R A H Mitchell (*O U*)	7	11	1	390	80	39.00	0
C G Lyttelton (*MCC*)	7	11	0	418	129	38.00	1
R Daft (*Notts*)	7	12	1	359	78	32.63	0
G Parr (*Notts*)	8	11	0	353	78	32.09	0
A J A Wilkinson (*Mx/Yks*)	7	10	1	288	84*	32.00	0
T Hayward (*Cambs*)	8	14	1	394	112	30.30	1
T Humphrey (*Surrey*)	23	42	1	1223	106	29.82	1
C Brampton (*Notts*)	7	10	0	291	86	29.10	0
C F Buller (*Middx*)	16	28	5	666	105*	28.95	1
G M Kelson (*Kent*)	9	15	0	416	89	27.73	0
J Caesar (*Surrey*)	16	25	2	583	82	25.34	0
C Payne (*Kt/Sx*)	12	22	3	478	76	25.15	0
R D Walker (*O U/Mx*)	19	32	1	770	103	24.83	1
T Hearne (*Middx*)	13	22	1	521	77	24.80	0
H Jupp (*Surrey*)	22	40	1	963	115	24.69	2
H H Stephenson (*Surrey*)	21	37	5	788	110	24.62	1
M A Troughton (*Kent*)	7	13	1	289	87	24.08	0
G Bennett (*Kent*)	14	26	0	622	100	23.92	1
John Lillywhite (*Sussex*)	11	20	3	405	61	23.82	0

BOWLING	M	O	M	R	W	Avge	
J C Shaw (*Notts*)	6	373.3	182	471	44	10.75	
J Jackson (*Notts*)	10	276.1	124	342	29	11.79	
G Wootton (*Notts*)	18	631.1	257	977	82	11.91	(+2)
S C Voules (*O U*)	6	71.3	22	123	10	12.30	
T Hearne (*Middx*)	13	263	127	370	30	12.33	
J Southerton (*Hants*)	3	168	48	270	21	12.85	
Jas Lillywhite (*Sussex*)	14	990	476	1147	87	13.18	
A Shaw (*Notts*)	10	212.3	103	239	18	13.27	(+1)
W G Grace (*Gents*)	5	157.2	64	268	20	13.40	
G Figg (*Sussex*)	5	285.1	117	395	29	13.62	
G F Tarrant (*Cambs*)	7	438.1	161	566	41	13.80	(+5)
E M Grace (*MCC*)	7	309.2	126	474	33	14.36	
W F Maitland (*O U*)	6	186	49	360	25	14.40	(+11)
R Iddison (*La/Yks*)	7	157	24	337	23	14.65	(+1)
G Wells (*Sussex*)	9	155	47	220	15	14.66	
J Grundy (*Notts*)	18	891.2	473	947	64	14.79	(+8)
T Humphrey (*Surrey*)	23	391.1	91	520	34	15.29	
W Mortlock (*Surrey*)	20	404.1	103	740	49	15.51	
T Hayward (*Cambs*)	8	141	38	264	17	15.52	(+6)
A J A Wilkinson (*Yks/Mx*)	7	273.1	98	412	26	15.84	

First-class averages: 1866

BATTING	M	I	NO	Runs	HS	Avge	100s
R Carpenter (*Cambs*)	8	10	4	367	97*	61.16	0
W G Grace (*Gents*)	8	13	2	581	224*	52.81	2
V E Walker (*Middx*)	14	18	4	550	79	39.28	0
O Spencer-Smith (*O U/Hts*)	7	11	1	354	98	35.40	0
C Payne (*Kt/Sx*)	10	16	2	471	135*	33.64	1
H Jupp (*Surrey*)	20	38	2	1140	165	31.66	1
A H Winter (*C U.Mx*)	9	17	0	519	121	30.52	1
T Hearne (*Middx*)	20	33	2	946	146	30.51	2
C F Buller (*Middx*)	18	32	2	826	106	27.53	1
C Smith (*Sussex*)	6	11	1	273	53	27.30	0
J Smith (*Cambs*)	8	14	0	371	62	26.50	0
T Hayward (*Cambs*)	7	12	0	312	78	26.00	0
G Holgate (*La/Yks*)	6	10	1	226	65	25.11	0
F G Pelham (*C U/Sx*)	7	13	1	297	78	24.75	0
R D Walker (*Middx*)	20	31	1	742	90	24.73	0
W Oscroft (*Notts*)	7	12	1	271	86	24.63	0
H A Richardson (*C U/Kt*)	6	10	0	245	92	24.50	0
G Tarrant (*Cambs*)	8	12	0	291	108	24.25	1
C Brampton (*Notts*)	5	10	2	189	89	23.62	0
John Lillywhite (*Sussex*)	7	10	0	218	59	21.80	0

BOWLING	M	O	M	R	W	Avge
R Lipscomb (*Kent*)	4	115.3	57	164	19	8.63
A S Teape (*O U*)	3	115.4	49	146	16	9.12
J C Shaw (*Notts*)	7	361.2	174	430	40	10.75
W H Parnell (*MCC*)	4	70.2	26	125	10	12.50
Jas Lillywhite (*Sussex*)	13	849.2	462	911	71	12.83
E Willsher (*Kent*)	11	578.1	272	689	52	13.25
G F Tarrant (*Cambs*)	8	545.1	229	809	61	13.26
J Southerton (*Hants*)	4	243	80	435	32	13.59
G Wootton (*Notts*)	22	1168	507	1677	119	14.09
G Howitt (*Mx/Nts*)	9	459.1	192	706	50	14.12
E M Grace (*Gents*)	7	246.1	85	347	24	14.45
G W S Lyttelton (*C U*)	5	137.3	45	236	16	14.75
T Hayward (*Cambs*)	7	252	98	371	25	14.84
E S Carter (*O U*)	6	253.2	121	291	19	15.31
T Hearne (*Middx*)	20	575.3	265	775	50	15.50
W G Grace (*Gents*)	8	317.1	123	483	31	15.58
C E Green (*C U*)	6	271.3	84	390	25	15.60
G Bennett (*Kent*)	10	532	189	906	58	15.62
G R Atkinson (*Yorks*)	3	152	64	174	11	15.81
J Grundy (*Notts*)	20	918	455	1067	67	15.92

First-class averages: 1867

BATTING	M	I	NO	Runs	HS	Avge	100s
R Daft (*Notts*)	6	12	5	377	111*	53.85	1
G W S Lyttelton (*C U*)	6	10	1	341	114	37.88	1
R Iddison (*Yks/La*)	10	17	3	460	71*	32.85	0
B B Cooper (*Middx*)	6	10	1	288	86	32.00	0
T Hayward (*Cambs*)	7	13	3	300	55*	30.00	0
C E Green (*C U*)	6	10	4	178	60*	29.66	0
V E Walker (*Middx*)	14	20	5	444	87*	29.60	0
H R J Charlwood (*Sussex*)	7	12	1	316	81*	28.72	0
C Payne (*Kt/Sx*)	15	27	4	608	137	26.43	1
T Humphrey (*Surrey*)	20	38	2	946	144	26.27	1
D Hayward (*Cambs*)	5	10	3	155	58*	22.14	0
W Mortlock (*Surrey*)	17	31	2	634	84	21.86	0
J Ricketts (*Lancs*)	9	15	1	305	195*	21.78	1
R Carpenter (*Cambs*)	7	13	1	259	46	21.58	0
I D Walker (*Middx*)	12	22	4	380	53	21.11	0
J Round (*MCC*)	10	14	1	273	142	21.00	1
H A Richardson (*C U/Kt*)	12	21	4	357	76	21.00	0
E Pooley (*Surrey*)	20	37	3	690	85	20.29	0
A H Winter (*C U/Mx*)	10	19	0	370	78	19.47	0
C E Boyle (*O U*)	6	12	0	232	53	19.33	0

BOWLING	M	O	M	R	W	Avge	
W G Grace (*Eng*)	4	195.3	96	293	39	7.51	
T Emmett (*Yorks*)	7	238.2	76	368	48	7.66	
G Freeman (*Yorks*)	8	564.2	300	552	66	8.36	
G F Tarrant (*Cambs*)	5	351	181	383	44	8.70	
L Greenwood (*Yorks*)	8	303.1	148	368	34	10.82	
G Wootton (*Notts*)	19	1233.2	561	1644	142	11.58	
A Shaw (*Notts*)	19	738.2	339	873	74	11.79	
F G Pelham (*C U/Sx*)	7	222.2	85	292	24	12.16	(+2)
D Buchanan (*GtsNth*)	3	221.2	46	351	27	13.00	
C A Absolom (*C U*)	6	328.2	122	490	37	13.24	(+1)
A Appleby (*Lancs*)	6	344.3	144	519	38	13.65	
J Bristow (*Surrey*)	2	100	36	167	12	13.91	
J Southerton (*Hts/Sx/Sy*)	15	1222.1	391	1867	132	14.14	
J C Shaw (*Notts*)	6	516.1	289	628	44	14.27	
W Watts (*Cambs*)	4	211.2	69	314	22	14.27	
E M Kenney (*O U*)	5	264	76	357	25	14.28	
E Willsher (*Kent*)	13	605.3	272	755	51	14.80	
Jas Lillywhite (*Sussex*)	13	741.3	385	816	54	15.11	
R Lipscomb (*Kent*)	12	699	278	973	64	15.20	
T Hayward (*Cambs*)	7	155	63	221	14	15.78	

First-class averages: 1868

BATTING	M	I	NO	Runs	HS	Avge	100s
W G Grace (*Gents*)	7	11	2	588	134*	65.33	3
I D Walker (*Middx*)	13	24	5	661	165	34.78	1
Jas Lillywhite (*Sussex*)	13	24	3	631	126*	30.04	1
H A Richardson (*C U/Mx/Kt*)	10	16	1	431	143	28.73	1
G Savile (*C U/Yks*)	7	11	0	294	105	26.72	1
R Daft (*Notts*)	7	13	0	335	94	25.76	0
H Jupp (*Surrey*)	23	42	3	965	134	24.74	2
W B Money (*C U*)	9	15	0	367	89	24.46	0
J W Dale (*C U*)	7	11	0	237	76	21.54	0
T Humphrey (*Surrey*)	22	39	0	835	103	21.41	2
C F Buller (*Middx*)	9	16	0	326	75	20.37	0
J Thewlis (*Yorks*)	7	11	1	203	108	20.30	1
R Iddison (*La/Yks*)	13	21	3	360	57	20.00	0
J Ricketts (*Lancs*)	10	20	2	359	54	19.94	0
M A Troughton (*Kent*)	9	17	3	275	69*	19.64	0
W Mortlock (*Surrey*)	10	19	2	324	66*	19.05	0
C A Absolom (*C U/Kt*)	10	15	1	263	40*	18.78	0
C Payne (*Kt/Sx*)	15	29	3	483	90	18.57	0
C H Smith (*Sx*)	6	12	1	204	47*	18.54	0
C E Green (*C U/Mx*)	10	17	0	296	59	17.41	0

BOWLING	M	O	M	R	W	Avge
T Hearne (*Middx*)	12	229.1	112	279	33	8.45
A Shaw (*Notts*)	7	121.2	69	111	13	8.53
T Emmett (*Yorks*)	8	407	209	528	60	8.80
G Freeman (*Yorks*)	7	390	195	454	46	9.86
E Willsher (*Kent*)	16	999.3	529	1128	113	9.98
G Howitt (*Mx/Nts*)	12	562.3	265	734	71	10.33
G Smith (*Cambs*)	2	120	61	163	15	10.86
R Iddison (*La/Yks*)	13	232	64	439	37	11.86
J C Shaw (*Notts*)	7	445.2	224	547	45	12.15
E L Fellowes (*O U*)	5	275	124	392	32	12.25
E M Kenney (*O U*)	5	235	103	284	22	12.90
G Wootton (*Notts*)	17	935.3	426	1422	106	13.41
D Buchanan (*Gents*)	3	137.2	33	258	19	13.57
J Southerton (*Sy/Sx*)	18	1096.3	334	2079	150	13.86
W B Money (*C U*)	9	232.3	79	479	34	14.08
W G Grace (*Gents*)	7	327	116	639	44	14.52
E Rutter (*Middx*)	5	254.3	70	499	33	15.12
C A Absolom (*C U/Kt*)	10	432.1	148	740	48	15.41
R Lipscomb (*Kent*)	13	666.2	243	1155	73	15.82
V E Walker (*Middx*)	13	105	30	176	11	16.00

First-class averages: 1869

BATTING	M	I	NO	Runs	HS	Avge	100s
W G Grace (*MCC*)	15	24	1	1320	180	57.39	6
R Daft (*Notts*)	9	14	4	494	103*	49.40	1
R Iddison (*La/Yks*)	9	15	5	353	112	35.30	1
H Jupp (*Surrey*)	22	41	5	1129	106*	31.36	2
I D Walker (*Middx*)	12	18	0	540	90	30.00	0
H R J Charlwood (*Sussex*)	10	18	1	483	155	28.41	1
C I Thornton (*C U/Kt*)	14	25	0	671	124	26.84	2
H Killick (*Sussex*)	5	10	0	262	78	26.20	0
W Yardley (*C U/Kt*)	9	16	3	319	65	24.53	0
F Wild (*Notts*)	7	12	1	265	54	24.09	0
J Rowbotham (*Yorks*)	8	14	1	313	101	24.07	2
W Oscroft (*Notts*)	9	15	3	282	48*	23.50	0
E A White (*Kent*)	5	10	2	181	32	22.62	0
E Lockwood (*Yorks*)	8	15	1	316	103	22.57	1
B Pauncefote (*O U/Mx*)	9	16	0	349	123	21.81	1
T Bignall (*Notts*)	10	16	1	322	116*	21.46	1
W Price (*Notts*)	12	19	2	364	57	21.41	0
B B Cooper (*Kent*)	13	21	1	427	101	21.35	1
E Pooley (*Surrey*)	21	38	1	780	88	21.08	0
T Emmett (*Yorks*)	9	11	5	117	47*	19.50	0

BOWLING	M	O	M	R	W	Avge
C J Brune (*C U/Mx*)	8	154	83	162	20	8.10
T Hearne (*Middx*)	14	303.2	191	439	47	9.34
G Freeman (*Yorks*)	8	540.2	298	584	60	9.73
R F Miles (*O U*)	3	176.2	66	268	24	11.16
J Grundy (*MCC*)	4	164.2	94	158	14	11.28
R D Walker (*Middx*)	4	121.2	26	181	16	11.31
W Hickton (*Lancs*)	5	330.1	124	448	39	11.48
T Emmett (*Yorks*)	9	552.1	286	721	59	12.22
J C Shaw (*Notts*)	9	661.1	363	808	65	12.43
G Howitt (*Mx/Nts*)	5	284.1	148	338	27	12.51
G Wootton (*Notts*)	20	1167	582	1519	121	12.55
A Appleby (*Lancs*)	7	293.2	138	393	30	13.10
D Buchanan (*Gents*)	3	261.2	74	361	26	13.88
J Southerton (*Sx/Sy*)	22	1384.3	518	2090	136	15.36
A F Walter (*O U*)	3	117.1	52	172	11	15.63
E Willsher (*Kent*)	15	816.3	418	1023	64	15.98
C A Absolom (*C U*)	6	275.2	98	438	27	16.22
W G Grace (*MCC*)	15	784.2	327	1189	73	16.28
B Pauncefote (*O U/Mx*)	9	107.3	31	245	15	16.33
G Bennett (*Kent*)	9	321	105	690	38	18.15

First-class averages: 1870

BATTING

	M	I	NO	Runs	HS	Avge	100s
W G Grace (*Gloucs*)	21	38	5	1808	215	54.78	5
R Daft (*Notts*)	9	15	4	565	117	51.36	1
W B Money (*C U*)	7	12	1	548	134	49.81	2
I D Walker (*Middx*)	13	25	3	820	179	37.27	1
B Pauncefote (*O U*)	7	14	1	363	116*	27.92	1
W Yardley (*C U/Kt*)	13	25	1	643	100	26.79	1
C J Ottaway (*O U/Kt*)	9	18	2	427	69	26.68	0
R Iddison (*La/Yks*)	12	18	2	377	77	23.36	0
J Smith (*North*)	8	13	1	277	96	23.08	0
E Pooley (*Surrey*)	27	52	5	1084	94	23.06	0
H R J Charlwood (*Sussex*)	9	18	1	387	61	22.76	0
G F Grace (*Gloucs*)	11	19	2	349	189*	20.52	1
J W Dale (*C U*)	13	25	0	510	90	20.40	0
H Jupp (*Surrey*)	28	52	2	1013	92	20.26	0
C E Green (*Middx*)	8	16	1	297	51	19.80	0
W H Hadow (*O U/Mx*)	6	12	0	232	58	19.33	0
J Rowbotham (*Yorks*)	11	17	0	323	35	19.00	0
C I Thornton (*C U/Kt*)	14	25	2	435	75	18.91	0
E B Rawlinson (*Yorks*)	9	15	1	264	52	18.85	0
E Lockwood (*Yorks*)	11	18	0	308	44	17.11	0

BOWLING

	M	O	M	R	W	Avge
G Freeman (*Yorks*)	10	482.2	247	484	68	7.11
W Hickton (*Lancs*)	4	155.3	69	202	26	7.76
R F Miles (*Gloucs*)	3	136.1	52	208	24	8.66
F R Reynolds (*Lancs*)	3	80.3	38	100	11	9.09
G M Kelson (*Kent*)	7	86.1	35	132	14	9.42
F H Farrands (*MCC*)	5	214	100	281	28	10.03
E E Ward (*C U*)	3	156	76	203	20	10.15
J C Shaw (*Notts*)	12	826.1	443	990	96	10.31
R O Clayton (*Yorks*)	3	101.1	51	117	11	10.63
F Tate (*Hants*)	2	72.2	24	139	13	10.69
W H Anstead (*Surrey*)	5	275.3	104	424	39	10.87
E Bray (*Surrey*)	5	112	29	193	16	12.06
E Willsher (*Kent*)	17	919.1	491	1066	84	12.69
G Howitt (*Mx/Nts*)	10	361.3	164	519	40	12.97
E M Grace (*Gloucs*)	5	232.2	96	286	22	13.00
A Shaw (*Notts*)	20	1171.3	629	1272	94	13.53
R Iddison (*La/Yks*)	12	130.1	24	289	21	13.76
T Emmett (*Yorks*)	10	441	181	757	54	14.01
W McIntyre (*Notts*)	8	354	178	508	36	14.11
Jas Lillywhite (*Sussex*)	12	376.3	180	468	32	14.62

First-class averages: 1871

BATTING

	M	I	NO	Runs	HS	Avge	100s
W G Grace (*Gloucs*)	25	39	4	2739	268	78.25	10
R Daft (*Notts*)	12	19	4	565	92	37.66	0
R Carpenter (*Cambs*)	9	16	4	446	87*	37.16	0
G F Grace (*Gloucs*)	14	24	4	716	98	35.80	0
W H Hadow (*O U/Mx*)	14	22	2	694	217	34.70	1
H R J Charlwood (*Sussex*)	10	16	0	494	81	30.87	0
E Lockwood (*Yorks*)	12	22	1	612	89	29.14	0
F E R Fryer (*C U*)	7	13	1	348	76	29.00	0
G R C Harris (*O U/Kt*)	8	14	1	377	107	29.00	1
W Yardley (*C U/Kt*)	9	18	1	492	126*	28.94	1
C E Green (*Middx*)	7	10	1	260	57*	28.88	0
E F S Tylecote (*O U*)	6	10	1	231	83*	25.66	0
T Bignall (*Notts*)	8	14	1	330	96	25.38	0
G Strachan (*Mx/Gloucs*)	12	18	5	324	38*	24.92	0
C I Thornton (*C U/Kt*)	17	30	0	746	111	24.86	1
I D Walker (*Middx*)	17	26	2	594	68	24.75	0
H Jupp (*Surrey*)	24	46	2	1068	85	24.27	0
E Pooley (*Surrey*)	22	40	1	926	125	23.74	1
B Pauncefote (*O U/Mx*)	8	12	1	258	94*	23.45	0
R Humphrey (*Surrey*)	19	37	3	786	116*	23.11	1

BOWLING

	M	O	M	R	W	Avge	
D Gregory (*Derbys*)	2	98.3	34	144	17	8.47	
W M Rose (*MCC*)	2	101	28	179	21	8.52	
A Hill (*Yorks*)	3	152.3	64	201	19	10.57	
S E Butler (*O U*)	6	251	108	377	35	10.77	(+2)
G Freeman (*Yorks*)	4	265	124	330	29	11.37	
T Emmett (*Yorks*)	7	375.2	153	625	50	12.50	
W N Powys (*C U*)	6	157.1	35	313	25	12.52	
E Willsher (*Kent*)	13	756.1	403	935	70	13.35	
G Bennett (*Kent*)	7	238.1	65	465	34	13.67	
A Appleby (*Lancs*)	7	459.3	215	639	46	13.89	
F H Farrands (*Notts*)	14	809.2	388	1111	79	14.06	(+1)
A Shaw (*Notts*)	21	1387.1	743	1463	101	14.48	
C J Brune (*Middx*)	9	123.3	51	220	15	14.66	
R O Clayton (*Yorks*)	7	326.3	140	492	33	14.90	
F R Reynolds (*Lancs*)	6	209	63	322	21	15.33	
W Hickton (*Dby/La*)	6	353.3	164	541	35	15.45	
J Southerton (*Sx/Sy*)	24	1633.1	643	2375	151	15.72	
E Bray (*C U/Sy*)	7	360.2	91	640	39	16.41	
W G Grace (*Gloucs*)	25	771	255	1345	79	17.02	
G Wootton (*Notts*)	11	308	146	485	28	17.32	

First-class averages: 1872

BATTING

	M	I	NO	Runs	HS	Avge	100s
W G Grace (*Gloucs*)	20	29	3	1485	170*	57.11	6
J Selby (*Notts*)	8	13	4	377	128*	41.88	1
R Daft (*Notts*)	13	20	3	589	102	34.64	1
W Yardley (*C U*)	11	19	3	529	130	33.06	1
A N Hornby (*Lancs*)	7	10	0	314	80	31.40	0
H R J Charlwood (*Sussex*)	16	27	4	651	80	28.30	0
F E R Fryer (*C U*)	9	15	0	405	91	27.00	0
F Wild (*Notts*)	8	13	1	321	104	26.75	1
E Lockwood (*Yorks*)	21	38	4	871	121	25.61	1
W Oscroft (*Notts*)	12	19	1	455	68	25.27	0
R Fillery (*Sussex*)	8	12	2	245	46*	24.50	0
R Humphrey (*Surrey*)	27	49	4	1072	96	23.82	0
H Jupp (*Surrey*)	28	48	1	1017	82	21.63	0
T G Matthews (*Gloucs*)	7	10	0	213	85	21.30	0
T Bignall (*Notts*)	11	17	0	350	74	20.58	0
G F Grace (*Gloucs*)	18	26	5	431	115*	20.52	1
R Carpenter (*North*)	10	15	1	278	67	19.85	0
T Hearne (*Middx*)	13	22	2	383	91	19.15	0
C J Ottaway (*O U*)	8	15	0	274	48	18.26	0
G H Longman (*C U*)	6	10	0	180	80	18.00	0

BOWLING

	M	O	M	R	W	Avge
W McIntyre (*Lancs*)	4	214.1	108	232	41	5.65
A Watson (*Lancs*)	4	144	57	178	20	8.90
G Wootton (*MCC*)	5	289.3	137	359	37	9.70
D Buchanan (*Gents*)	4	302.2	148	374	35	10.68
A W Ridley (*O U*)	7	210.3	70	332	31	10.70
G Howitt (*Middx*)	7	307	152	427	38	11.23
J West (*Yorks*)	8	118.2	59	150	13	11.53
E A Brice (*Gloucs*)	3	110.3	46	189	16	11.81
E Harvey (*C U/Mx*)	4	100.2	40	143	12	11.91
A Shaw (*Notts*)	17	984.2	489	1108	92	12.04
W G Grace (*Gloucs*)	20	427.2	166	678	56	12.10
S E Butler (*O U*)	5	136.2	65	280	22	12.72
J Southerton (*Sy/Sx*)	26	1570.1	629	2209	169	13.07
W N Powys (*C U*)	8	346.2	167	514	38	13.52
A Appleby (*Lancs*)	4	181	99	222	16	13.87
Jas Lillywhite (*Sussex*)	17	938	395	1305	94	13.88
R Daft (*Notts*)	13	96	22	217	15	14.46
E Lockwood (*Yorks*)	21	470.2	163	723	49	14.75
F Silcock (*South*)	5	123.2	49	178	12	14.83
J Street (*Surrey*)	12	634.1	275	907	60	15.11

First-class averages: 1873

BATTING

	M	I	NO	Runs	HS	Avge	100s
W G Grace (*Gloucs*)	20	32	7	1805	192*	72.20	6
R Daft (*Notts*)	8	12	2	416	161	41.60	1
A N Hornby (*Lancs*)	7	10	0	348	128	34.80	2
I D Walker (*Middx*)	11	20	3	587	64	34.52	0
C J Ottaway (*O U*)	6	10	1	304	82	33.77	0
G F Grace (*Gloucs*)	15	22	3	593	165*	31.21	1
E M Grace (*Gloucs*)	7	13	0	381	76	29.30	0
W Oscroft (*Notts*)	17	30	1	758	96	26.13	0
C E B Nepean (*O U/Mx*)	7	11	1	253	50	25.30	0
H Jupp (*Surrey*)	24	45	3	1052	94	25.04	0
J Rowbotham (*Yorks*)	12	19	2	411	113	24.17	1
T Emmett (*Yorks*)	16	31	5	608	104	23.38	1
T Latham (*C U*)	7	13	1	264	48	22.00	0
W Yardley (*Kent*)	13	22	2	426	51	21.30	0
A Greenwood (*Yorks*)	18	32	1	659	89	21.25	0
C H Longman (*C U*)	10	16	0	336	49	21.00	0
A F Smith (*Yorks*)	13	23	3	408	89	20.40	0
F Wild (*Notts*)	13	24	4	405	51	20.25	0
N Morris (*Surrey*)	7	13	0	262	64	20.15	0
W H Hadow (*Middx*)	10	15	1	276	50	19.71	0

BOWLING

	M	O	M	R	W	Avge
W McIntyre (*Lancs*)	8	378.2	162	528	63	8.38
G E Coles (*Kent*)	2	59.2	19	98	11	8.90
A Watson (*Lancs*)	7	278.3	92	445	48	9.27
I D Walker (*Middx*)	11	95.1	25	190	20	9.50
C W Boyle (*O U*)	5	190	53	285	30	9.50
A Rylott (*MCC*)	9	443	197	664	69	9.62
F Morley (*Notts*)	7	308.3	154	375	35	10.71
W Mycroft (*Derbys*)	2	89	42	108	10	10.80
J Maude (*O U*)	5	180.2	68	255	23	11.08
J Fellowes (*Kent*)	3	97.1	40	135	12	11.25
D Buchanan (*Gents*)	4	286.3	60	396	35	11.31
G Ulyett (*Yorks*)	6	137	56	211	16	13.18
T Hearne (*Middx*)	5	81	30	160	12	13.33
Jas Lillywhite (*Sussex*)	17	1054.2	471	1470	110	13.36
A Hill (*Yorks*)	14	810.2	305	1195	88	13.57
R D Walker (*Middx*)	4	128.2	3	233	17	13.70
A Shaw (*Notts*)	21	1351.3	666	1675	121	13.84
E Willsher (*Kent*)	8	379	191	473	34	13.91
J Southerton (*Surrey*)	22	1543.3	703	2067	148	13.96
W G Grace (*Gloucs*)	20	546	201	1093	75	14.57

First-class averages: 1874

BATTING

	M	I	NO	Runs	HS	Avge	100s
W G Grace (*Gloucs*)	21	32	0	1664	179	52.00	8
H Jupp (*Surrey*)	21	37	2	1275	154	36.42	3
G F Grace (*Gloucs*)	18	27	4	649	103	28.21	1
A N Hornby (*Lancs*)	8	15	2	365	72	28.07	0
H R J Charlwood (*Sussex*)	16	30	5	701	100	28.04	1
Lord Harris (*O U/Kt*)	7	11	0	306	58	27.81	0
F E R Fryer (*South*)	7	12	1	300	88*	27.27	0
J M Cotterill (*Sussex*)	5	10	1	240	61	26.66	0
E Lockwood (*Yorks*)	21	39	1	1000	96	26.31	0
J Phillips (*Sussex*)	11	21	1	498	58	24.90	0
J Rowbotham (*Yorks*)	13	23	2	510	70	24.28	0
A W Ridley (*O U*)	7	12	0	279	81	23.25	0
R Fillery (*Sussex*)	12	21	3	392	105	21.77	1
R Daft (*Notts*)	12	21	0	453	102	21.57	1
C I Thornton (*Kent*)	10	18	1	357	82	21.00	0
Martin McIntyre (*Notts*)	13	23	0	480	77	20.86	0
G H Longman (*C U*)	9	16	0	332	73	20.75	0
C J Ottaway (*Middx*)	5	10	0	206	40	20.60	0
A Chandler (*Surrey*)	7	12	0	231	58	19.25	0
I D Walker (*Middx*)	18	33	2	583	60	18.80	0

BOWLING

	M	O	M	R	W	Avge	
W Hickton (*Derbys*)	2	103.2	42	144	17	8.47	
W H Hadow (*Middx*)	8	127.3	49	211	23	9.17	
T W Lang (*O U/Gloucs*)	7	337.3	157	395	35	11.28	
Martin McIntyre (*Notts*)	13	203	65	408	36	11.33	
A W Ridley (*O U*)	7	170.3	57	273	24	11.37	
W Draper (*Kent*)	4	151.3	78	206	18	11.44	
A Hill (*Yorks*)	16	766.3	267	1156	101	11.44	(+4)
T Emmett (*Yorks*)	18	947.2	401	1243	107	11.61	
W Mycroft (*Derbys*)	4	191	76	245	21	11.66	
G Strachan (*Surrey*)	11	161.3	62	251	21	11.95	
J Southerton (*Surrey*)	17	1214.1	543	1576	128	12.31	
E Willsher (*Kent*)	7	298.1	139	434	35	12.40	
W N Powys (*C U*)	7	175.3	67	338	27	12.51	(+3)
W G Grace (*Gloucs*)	21	1009	342	1778	140	12.70	
W McIntyre (*Lancs*)	7	332.1	119	460	36	12.77	
A Watson (*Lancs*)	5	226.2	63	415	32	12.96	
J Flint (*Derbys*)	4	127	41	238	18	13.22	
A Shaw (*Notts*)	23	1463	726	1762	133	13.24	
J Fellowes (*Kent*)	3	140	60	241	18	13.38	
G Ulyett (*Yorks*)	12	334	158	649	48	13.52	

First-class averages: 1875

BATTING

	M	I	NO	Runs	HS	Avge	100s
Lord Harris (*Kent*)	13	22	3	682	92	35.89	0
J M Cotterill (*Sussex*)	7	12	0	430	191	35.83	1
F Penn (*Kent*)	9	16	2	477	101	34.07	1
W G Grace (*Gloucs*)	26	48	2	1498	152	32.56	3
R G Barlow (*Lancs*)	7	12	2	321	87	32.10	0
W W Read (*Surrey*)	5	10	2	247	98	30.87	0
A N Hornby (*Lancs*)	13	22	1	646	78*	30.76	0
W Blacker (*C U*)	8	12	1	315	64*	28.63	0
G F Grace (*Gloucs*)	22	39	4	978	180*	27.93	3
E Lockwood (*Yorks*)	22	39	4	968	74	27.65	0
G H Longman (*C U/Hts*)	10	18	1	460	80	27.05	0
A J Webbe (*O U/Mx*)	15	28	2	696	120	26.76	1
H M Sims (*C U/Yks*)	8	13	1	319	71	26.58	0
F F J Greenfield (*C U/Sx*)	11	19	0	501	79	26.36	0
E Lyttelton (*C U*)	7	10	0	249	63	24.90	0
A Greenwood (*Yorks*)	22	39	3	837	93	23.25	0
C F Buller (*Middx*)	7	13	0	287	54	22.07	0
A P Lucas (*C U/Sy*)	13	22	2	440	63	22.00	0
A W Ridley (*O U/Hts*)	11	20	2	385	64	21.38	0
H R J Charlwood (*Sussex*)	16	27	1	534	117	20.53	1

BOWLING

	M	O	M	R	W	Avge	
W Mycroft (*Derbys*)	9	612.3	242	665	90	7.38	
T Armitage (*Yorks*)	9	166	5	167	22	7.59	
F F J Greenfield (*C U/Sx*)	11	148	62	194	21	9.23	(+1)
A Shaw (*Notts*)	22	1755.1	1023	1495	160	9.34	
G G Hearne (*Kent*)	6	171.3	69	273	28	9.75	
E M Grace (*Gloucs*)	4	102.2	47	147	15	9.80	
J G Galpin (*Hants*)	3	145.2	88	150	14	10.71	
A Rylott (*MCC*)	2	91	42	133	12	11.08	
A Watson (*Lancs*)	7	234.1	75	331	28	11.82	
W B Clarke (*Notts*)	10	229.3	108	281	23	12.21	
W G Grace (*Gloucs*)	26	1691.1	647	2473	191	12.94	
R O Clayton (*Yorks*)	14	391.3	157	549	42	13.07	
A W Ridley (*O U/Hts*)	11	403.3	171	497	38	13.07	
W H Hadow (*Middx*)	11	417.2	187	538	41	13.12	
J Southerton (*Surrey*)	19	1525	740	1818	136	13.36	
A H P Snow (*Middx*)	3	213.1	104	272	20	13.60	
Jas Lillywhite (*Sussex*)	16	814.3	341	1201	88	13.64	
W R Gilbert (*South*)	8	170	68	219	16	13.68	
E Lockwood (*Yorks*)	22	392.1	150	511	37	13.81	
T W Lang (*Gloucs*)	5	264.2	101	338	24	14.08	

First-class averages: 1876

BATTING	M	I	NO	Runs	HS	Avge	100s
W G Grace (*Gloucs*)	26	46	4	2622	344	62.42	7
W W Read (*Surrey*)	9	17	3	588	106	42.00	1
A W Ridley (*Hants*)	11	19	3	585	105*	36.56	3
W R Gilbert (*Gloucs*)	17	27	2	907	205*	36.28	2
R Daft (*Notts*)	18	30	2	976	99	34.85	0
W H Game (*O U/Sy*)	7	11	1	336	141	33.60	2
E Lockwood (*Yorks*)	25	44	5	1261	108*	32.33	1
Lord Harris (*Kent*)	17	30	1	916	154	31.58	1
H R J Charlwood (*Sussex*)	13	23	2	662	123	31.52	2
A J Webbe (*O U/Mx*)	14	25	2	722	109	31.39	1
A N Hornby (*Lancs*)	19	33	2	965	72	31.12	0
A P Lucas (*C U/Sy*)	16	30	3	818	105	30.29	1
F Townsend (*Gloucs*)	9	14	1	386	88	29.69	0
D Q Steel (*C U/La*)	9	16	0	463	82	28.93	0
E Lyttelton (*C U*)	7	12	1	316	72*	28.72	0
I D Walker (*Middx*)	16	28	0	799	110	28.53	1
G F Grace (*Gloucs*)	19	33	5	780	95	27.85	0
A Lyttelton (*C U*)	9	15	1	383	83	27.35	0
W Yardley (*Kent*)	8	15	0	408	92	27.20	0
A Shrewsbury (*Notts*)	15	28	5	603	118	26.21	1

BOWLING	M	O	M	R	W	Avge	
W McIntyre (*Lancs*)	10	688	278	1016	89	11.41	
W Hickton (*Derbys*)	4	154	58	259	22	11.77	
A Penn (*Kent*)	1	138.1	65	173	14	12.35	
A Watson (*Lancs*)	10	540.2	253	640	51	12.54	
W Mycroft (*Derbys*)	14	776.3	322	1211	95	12.74	
A W Ridley (*Hants*)	11	474.2	178	705	53	13.30	
Lord Harris (*Kent*)	17	101	35	215	16	13.43	
A Shaw (*Notts*)	28	2631.2	1528	2601	191	13.61	
A Smith (*Sussex*)	3	213.1	78	346	25	13.84	
C K Francis (*Middx*)	5	247.2	123	319	23	13.86	
W S Patterson (*C U/La*)	8	521.3	207	769	52	14.78	
T Armitage (*Yorks*)	12	285.1	62	667	45	14.82	
Jas Lillywhite (*Sussex*)	16	1163.2	543	1384	89	15.55	
R O Clayton (*Yorks*)	18	383.2	176	588	37	15.89	
J B Hide (*Sussex*)	5	90.2	30	165	10	16.50	
R F Miles (*Gloucs*)	7	297	151	365	22	16.59	
G G Jones (*Surrey*)	12	298	110	496	29	17.10	
G G Hearne (*Kent*)	11	392.3	158	634	37	17.13	
W Foord-Kelcey (*Kent*)	11	571	218	952	55	17.30	
A Hill (*Yorks*)	25	1257.1	498	1984	114	17.40	(+1)

First-class averages: 1877

BATTING	M	I	NO	Runs	HS	Avge	100s
F M Buckland (*O U/Mx*)	7	11	2	412	117*	45.77	2
W G Grace (*Gloucs*)	24	40	3	1474	261	39.83	2
W W Read (*Surrey*)	7	11	0	399	140	36.27	1
A P Lucas (*C U/Sy*)	15	28	4	832	115	34.66	2
E M Grace (*Gloucs*)	7	11	1	327	89	32.70	0
W H Game (*Surrey*)	6	10	1	280	81*	31.11	0
F Penn (*Kent*)	19	33	3	930	148*	31.00	2
A N Hornby (*Lancs*)	18	29	3	787	144	30.26	2
L A Shuter (*Surrey*)	6	10	2	238	89	29.75	0
C Booth (*Hants*)	7	14	3	326	77	29.63	0
I D Walker (*Middx*)	17	29	2	788	95	29.18	0
A Lyttelton (*C U/Mx*)	13	22	1	611	101	29.09	2
W Lindsay (*Surrey*)	6	12	1	319	74	29.00	0
J M Cotterill (*Sussex*)	9	15	0	428	92	28.53	0
J T B D Platts (*Derbys*)	10	19	1	478	115	26.55	1
G F Grace (*Gloucs*)	22	37	5	840	134	26.25	1
A J Webbe (*O U/Mx*)	16	27	2	651	100	26.04	1
L K Jarvis (*C U*)	7	12	2	256	47	25.60	0
R Daft (*Notts*)	15	30	2	699	96	24.96	0
H Jupp (*Surrey*)	19	35	3	795	93	24.84	0

BOWLING	M	O	M	R	W	Avge
A Shaw (*Notts*)	2	207.1	147	131	16	8.18
A Appleby (*Lancs*)	3	126.3	63	167	19	8.78
A H Heath (*O U*)	4	48.3	19	108	10	10.80
W McIntyre (*Lancs*)	11	699	306	949	85	11.16
R F Miles (*Gloucs*)	8	263.2	143	258	23	11.21
T Armitage (*Yorks*)	10	356	155	490	42	11.66
H G Tylecote (*O U*)	6	229	90	362	31	11.67
G G Hearne (*Kent*)	18	899.1	425	1281	108	11.86
W Mycroft (*Derbys*)	22	1374	659	1927	157	12.27
W G Grace (*Gloucs*)	24	1801	772	2293	179	12.81
A Watson (*Lancs*)	15	1036.2	522	1233	96	12.84
W Hickton (*Derbys*)	7	339.2	137	522	40	13.05
F M Buckland (*O U/Mx*)	7	376	165	525	40	13.12
W S Patterson (*C U/La*)	11	939.3	555	1061	80	13.26
L Bury (*C U/Hts*)	8	112.2	38	229	17	13.47
R Henderson (*Middx*)	8	524.3	219	732	54	13.55
W E Midwinter (*Gloucs*)	9	451.1	255	426	31	13.74
A P Lucas (*C U/Sy*)	17	372.2	176	470	34	13.82
F Morley (*Notts*)	27	1647.1	838	2028	146	13.89
T Emmett (*Yorks*)	22	628.2	255	1020	69	14.78

First-class averages: 1878

BATTING	M	I	NO	Runs	HS	Avge	100s
J Selby (*Notts*)	21	31	1	938	107	31.26	1
E Lyttelton (*C U/Mx*)	16	26	0	779	113	29.96	1
W G Grace (*Gloucs*)	24	42	2	1151	116	28.77	1
F Penn (*Kent*)	12	20	1	534	160	28.10	1
G Ulyett (*Yorks*)	28	51	4	1270	109	27.02	1
L Hall (*Yorks*)	9	16	3	351	82*	27.00	0
A Lyttelton (*C U/Mx*)	13	20	1	476	72	25.05	0
G F Grace (*Gloucs*)	23	39	5	836	73*	24.58	0
T S Pearson (*Middx*)	6	10	1	219	84	24.33	0
Lord Harris (*Kent*)	17	29	0	703	106	24.24	1
A J Webbe (*O U/Mx*)	17	32	0	761	118	23.78	2
J Shuter (*Surrey*)	13	24	2	512	98	23.27	0
W W Read (*Surrey*)	8	15	3	278	80	23.16	0
A H Stratford (*Middx*)	11	16	3	301	48*	23.15	0
A N Hornby (*Lancs*)	22	35	0	801	100	22.88	1
A G Steel (*C U/La*)	18	27	3	537	78	22.37	0
H R Webbe (*O U/Mx*)	11	20	2	402	53	22.33	0
A Shrewsbury (*Notts*)	24	39	5	724	74*	21.29	0
P H Morton (*C U*)	8	11	4	148	39	21.14	0
C Bannerman (*Austr*)	15	28	1	566	61	20.96	0

BOWLING	M	O	M	R	W	Avge
A Rylott (*MCC*)	7	486	255	451	53	8.51
H Wood (*C U*)	4	89	36	117	13	9.00
E M Grace (*Gloucs*)	14	95.2	48	108	12	9.00
P H Morton (*C U*)	8	234.2	107	327	36	9.08
A G Steel (*C U/La*)	18	1115.1	453	1547	164	9.43
H F Boyle (*Austr*)	14	361.3	143	484	51	9.49
T W Garrett (*Austr*)	15	260.2	130	318	32	9.93
W Mycroft (*Derbys*)	18	1046.1	571	1196	116	10.31
A Shaw (*Notts*)	30	2630	1586	2201	201	10.95
F R Spofforth (*Austr*)	15	668.1	250	1067	97	11.00
D Buchanan (*Gents*)	2	169	86	185	16	11.56
R G Barlow (*Lancs*)	18	334.2	138	489	42	11.64
W Bates (*Yorks*)	20	857.1	347	1157	99	11.68
T Emmett (*Yorks*)	26	953.1	447	1260	107	11.77
A Watson (*Lancs*)	14	535.2	272	586	49	11.95
F Morley (*Notts*)	29	1996.3	1054	2386	197	12.11
H W Tate (*Hants*)	5	194.1	84	253	20	12.65
A Hill (*Yorks*)	20	531.1	244	680	53	12.83
W Foord-Kelcey (*Kent*)	9	313.1	121	450	35	12.85
G F Grace (*Gloucs*)	23	193	92	196	15	13.06

First-class averages: 1879

BATTING	M	I	NO	Runs	HS	Avge	100s
W G Grace (*Gloucs*)	18	28	3	880	123	35.20	2
A N Hornby (*Lancs*)	17	22	2	606	64*	30.30	0
A Lyttelton (*C U/Mx*)	16	27	3	688	102	28.66	1
A G Steel (*C U/La*)	15	23	3	553	93	27.65	0
W Oscroft (*Notts*)	19	31	2	763	140	26.31	1
W H Scotton (*Notts*)	13	19	3	409	84	25.56	0
A P Lucas (*Surrey*)	10	18	1	423	70	24.88	0
I D Walker (*Middx*)	13	23	3	476	60*	23.80	0
A J Webbe (*Middx*)	12	23	0	532	122	23.13	1
G Ulyett (*Yorks*)	22	41	3	868	98	22.84	0
W R Gilbert (*Gloucs*)	11	17	1	363	99	22.68	0
F Penn (*Kent*)	16	28	1	589	134	21.81	1
T Foster (*Derbys*)	7	13	0	269	68	20.69	0
D Q Steel (*C U/La*)	10	12	1	221	52	20.09	0
I F W Bligh (*C U/Kt*)	21	35	3	614	113*	19.18	1
R G Barlow (*Lancs*)	14	23	1	414	50	18.81	0
E Lockwood (*Yorks*)	19	32	4	520	68*	18.57	0
H J Whitfeld (*C U/Sx*)	11	19	2	305	38*	17.94	0
C I Thornton (*Middx*)	9	16	0	279	72	17.43	0
F Townsend (*Gloucs*)	9	14	1	225	71	17.30	0

BOWLING	M	O	M	R	W	Avge
A Hill (*Yorks*)	8	206	111	204	29	7.03
A Rylott (*MCC*)	7	307.2	171	291	37	7.86
J T B D Platts (*Derbys*)	7	82.2	28	116	14	8.28
W Mycroft (*Derbys*)	14	774	445	738	88	8.38
J Flint (*Derbys*)	2	73	32	92	10	9.20
A Shaw (*Notts*)	25	1595.1	934	1278	133	9.60
T Emmett (*Yorks*)	22	479.2	209	622	63	9.87
Jas Lillywhite (*Sussex*)	5	274.2	164	230	23	10.00
W Bates (*Yorks*)	18	738.2	328	883	87	10.14
G Hay (*Derbys*)	7	332	178	334	32	10.43
W Flowers (*Notts*)	20	370	190	403	38	10.60
F Morley (*Notts*)	24	1385	681	1573	147	10.70
R G Barlow (*Lancs*)	14	391	188	469	43	10.90
D Buchanan (*Gents*)	2	143	88	149	13	11.46
A F J Ford (*C U/Mx*)	12	538.2	273	604	51	11.84
H Wood (*C U/Yks*)	15	524.1	244	642	54	11.88
A H Evans (*O U*)	8	350.3	137	496	41	12.09
A G Steel (*C U/La*)	15	895.3	423	1134	93	12.19
G G Hearne (*Kent*)	18	533.3	264	611	50	12.22
J Southerton (*Surrey*)	10	541.3	302	556	45	12.35

First-class averages: 1880

BATTING	M	I	NO	Runs	HS	Avge	100s
†W G Grace (*Gloucs*)	16	27	3	951	152	39.62	2
R T Ellis (*Sussex*)	10	20	3	569	103	33.47	1
†Lord Harris (*Kent*)	16	26	2	772	123	32.16	1
A J Webbe (*Middx*)	14	24	1	708	142	30.78	1
I F W Bligh (*C U/Kt*)	21	38	5	1013	105	30.69	1
†W Barnes (*Notts*)	28	47	4	1220	143	28.37	2
†F Penn (*Kent*)	14	25	2	648	88	28.17	0
P S McDonnell (*Austr*)	9	15	1	391	79	27.92	0
W O Moberly (*Gloucs*)	7	10	1	251	99	27.88	0
R S Jones (*C U/Kt*)	13	21	1	553	124	27.65	1
H R J Charlwood (*Sussex*)	9	16	1	413	67	27.53	0
†A Lyttelton (*Middx*)	11	19	2	451	120	26.52	1
W W Read (*Surrey*)	6	12	0	306	93	25.50	0
G. Ulyett (*Yorks*)	24	43	5	929	141	24.44	1
W L Murdoch (*Austr*)	9	15	1	339	153*	24.21	1
A N Hornby (*Lancs*)	19	36	3	779	126	23.60	1
E Lockwood (*Yorks*)	25	42	1	950	70	23.17	0
F Taylor (*Lancs*)	7	13	1	275	66	22.91	0
I D Walker (*Middx*)	15	27	1	590	94	22.69	0
†A G Steel (*C U/La*)	14	22	0	496	118	22.54	1

BOWLING	M	O	M	R	W	Avge
F R Spofforth (*Austr*)	5	207	74	336	40	8.40
†A Shaw (*Notts*)	28	2133	1257	1589	186	8.54
F G G Jellicoe (*O U/Hts*)	6	261.1	115	301	32	9.40
G Nash (*Lancs*)	8	368.1	174	471	49	9.61
N Maclachlan (*O U*)	4	78	30	101	10	10.10
A Rylott (*MCC*)	6	290.2	143	394	39	10.10
R G Barlow (*Lancs*)	22	609.3	334	639	62	10.30
A Watson (*Lancs*)	15	910	470	947	88	10.76
C R Young (*Hants*)	4	188.1	82	224	20	11.20
W Mycroft (*Derbys*)	13	711.3	374	919	80	11.48
G E Palmer (*Austr*)	9	795.3	278	772	66	11.69
F Hearne (*Kent*)	12	94.2	42	142	12	11.83
F F J Greenfield (*Sussex*)	3	62	14	142	12	11.83
E Peate (*Yorks*)	22	1314.3	581	1662	138	12.04
†F Morley (*Notts*)	27	1841	936	2257	184	12.26
J Wootton (*Kent*)	6	326	146	474	38	12.47
†A G Steel (*C U/La*)	14	906	396	1210	92	13.15
A H Evans (*O U*)	7	364	128	662	50	13.24
G C Harrison (*O U*)	5	248	95	373	28	13.32
P H Morton (*C U*)	6	311.2	133	480	35	13.71

†Played for England but not featured above: E M Grace, G F Grace and A P Lucas.

First-class averages: 1881

BATTING	M	I	NO	Runs	HS	Avge	100s
A N Hornby (*Lancs*)	25	38	0	1534	188	40.36	3
W G Grace (*Gloucs*)	13	22	1	792	182	37.71	2
C F H Leslie (*O U/Mx*)	13	23	2	741	111*	35.28	2
G Ulyett (*Yorks*)	24	40	2	1243	112	32.71	1
W W Read (*Surrey*)	16	30	1	931	160	32.10	1
L C Docker (*Derbys*)	8	15	1	447	107	31.92	1
C T Studd (*C U/Mx*)	19	31	5	819	113	31.50	1
G B Studd (*C U/Mx*)	15	23	2	647	106*	30.90	1
A G Steel (*C U/La*)	20	33	4	848	106*	29.24	1
A P Lucas (*Surrey*)	14	27	2	712	142	28.48	1
W H Patterson (*O U/Kt*)	15	28	3	705	107*	28.20	1
W A Bettesworth (*Sx*)	9	18	3	423	77	28.20	0
E Lockwood (*Yorks*)	26	44	4	1111	109	27.77	1
J Selby (*Notts*)	11	18	0	473	80	26.27	0
J Cranston (*Gloucs*)	9	14	2	317	63	26.19	0
E M Grace (*Gloucs*)	10	15	1	353	77	25.21	0
A Shaw (*Notts*)	12	18	5	324	78*	24.92	0
G F Vernon (*Middx*)	24	38	2	897	119	24.91	1
W Lindsay (*Surrey*)	8	16	2	342	50	24.42	0
W A Thornton (*O U*)	5	10	0	241	54	24.10	0

BOWLING	M	O	M	R	W	Avge
J Crossland (*Lancs*)	7	66.3	23	93	13	7.15
A Rylott (*MCC*)	4	209.2	101	249	28	8.89
A Hill (*Yorks*)	10	345.1	154	437	43	10.16
G Nash (*Lancs*)	13	456.2	225	555	52	10.67
H Evans (*Derbys*)	3	107	44	189	16	11.81
A Watson (*Lancs*)	15	876	511	816	69	11.82
R G Barlow (*Lancs*)	20	747	380	940	79	11.89
T Emmett (*Yorks*)	28	616.2	275	919	76	12.09
A Penn (*Kent*)	4	211	76	352	29	12.13
A Shaw (*Notts*)	12	978.2	530	975	78	12.50
E Peate (*Yorks*)	27	1712	760	2195	173	12.68
A G Steel (*C U/La*)	20	1304	553	1744	130	13.41
F Morley (*Notts*)	16	926.2	434	1315	91	14.45
G G Jones (*Surrey*)	10	568.3	310	664	45	14.75
W Mycroft (*Derbys*)	15	997	479	1379	93	14.82
W Flowers (*Notts*)	12	476	211	709	47	15.08
W Barnes (*Notts*)	18	466.2	219	646	41	15.75
W R Gilbert (*Gloucs*)	9	185	76	321	20	16.05
G G Hearne (*Kent*)	16	761.1	352	1099	68	16.16
W Bates (*Yorks*)	28	1350	564	1971	121	16.28

First-class averages: 1882

BATTING	M	I	NO	Runs	HS	Avge	100s
S C Newton (*Som*)	5	10	1	310	80	34.44	0
C T Studd (*C U/Mx*)	25	43	5	1249	126*	32.86	4
Lord Harris (*Kent*)	14	24	0	787	176	32.79	2
†A P Lucas (*Surrey*)	15	25	3	707	145	32.13	2
W L Murdoch (*Austr*)	32	55	5	1582	286*	31.64	2
W Newham (*Sussex*)	6	12	1	334	101	30.36	1
A J Webbe (*Middx*)	16	28	6	660	108*	30.00	1
†A G Steel (*Lancs*)	18	30	2	818	171	29.21	1
F Taylor (*Lancs*)	8	11	1	290	62	29.00	0
†A N Hornby (*Lancs*)	30	53	4	1383	131	28.22	2
†W Barnes (*Notts*)	27	44	1	1194	130	27.76	3
†G Ulyett (*Yorks*)	33	60	4	1542	138	27.53	2
†R G Barlow (*Lancs*)	28	51	9	1138	68	27.09	0
E F S Tylecote (*Kent*)	13	24	3	561	100*	26.71	1
A Shrewsbury (*Notts*)	14	22	2	533	207	26.68	1
W E Midwinter (*Gloucs*)	23	40	9	823	137*	26.54	2
†W G Grace (*Gloucs*)	22	37	0	975	88	26.35	0
J Shuter (*Surrey*)	19	34	2	832	93	26.00	0
W W Read (*Surrey*)	19	35	1	882	117	25.94	1
J S Russel (*MCC*)	9	15	2	335	83	25.76	0

BOWLING	M	O	M	R	W	Avge
C E Currie (*Hants*)	1	40.2	13	82	10	8.20
J Crossland (*Lancs*)	22	795	354	1127	112	10.06
J Parnham (*UEE*)	1	50	12	126	12	10.50
G Nash (*Lancs*)	14	409.3	172	656	62	10.58
H H Armstrong (*Hants*)	2	98.3	46	107	10	10.70
†R G Barlow (*Lancs*)	28	895	481	1009	92	10.96
T Emmett (*Yorks*)	30	732.1	350	1044	95	10.98
†E Peate (*Yorks*)	30	1562.1	864	2466	214	11.52
A Shaw (*Notts*)	17	1195.2	713	1042	88	11.84
F Morley (*Notts*)	17	1051.3	541	1297	109	11.89
A Rylott (*MCC*)	5	218.3	111	265	22	12.04
H F Boyle (*Austr*)	27	1101.2	488	1523	125	12.18
R Peel (*Yorks*)	7	304.3	135	370	29	12.75
A Watson (*Lancs*)	21	966.2	532	993	77	12.89
F R Spofforth (*Austr*)	30	1470	646	2079	157	13.24
W Flowers (*Notts*)	26	1199.1	586	1388	103	13.47
W H Fowler (*Som*)	10	86	29	165	12	13.75
C E Horner (*Surrey*)	8	436.3	206	617	44	14.02
T W Garrett (*Austr*)	30	1167.3	474	1694	118	14.35
J Richardson (*Derbys*)	5	153	60	263	18	14.61

†Played for England but not featured above: A Lyttelton, C T Studd and J M Read.

First-class averages: 1883

BATTING	M	I	NO	Runs	HS	Avge	100s
W W Read (*Surrey*)	22	39	6	1573	168	47.66	2
C T Studd (*C U/Mx*)	20	34	5	1193	175*	41.13	2
W G Grace (*Gloucs*)	22	41	2	1352	112	34.66	1
L Hall (*Yorks*)	26	44	9	1180	127	33.71	2
A P Lucas (*Surrey*)	12	23	3	664	97	33.20	0
H J Whitfeld (*Sussex*)	10	17	4	425	74	32.69	0
I D Walker (*Middx*)	14	26	3	750	145	32.60	2
G Ulyett (*Yorks*)	29	50	1	1562	84	31.87	0
Lord Harris (*Kent*)	17	31	2	919	118	31.68	1
A G Steel (*Lancs*)	8	14	2	370	68	30.83	0
J G Walker (*O U*)	7	13	0	386	93	29.69	0
A Shrewsbury (*Notts*)	24	40	2	1117	98	29.39	0
W O Moberly (*Gloucs*)	7	13	1	351	121	29.25	1
E Sainsbury (*Som*)	7	13	0	363	116	27.92	1
W Barnes (*Notts*)	30	51	4	1308	120	27.82	1
J Selby (*Notts*)	10	14	2	328	100	27.33	1
J W Mansfield (*C U*)	7	12	2	264	117	26.40	1
A G G Asher (*O U*)	6	11	0	284	182	25.81	1
E J Diver (*Surrey*)	13	22	1	541	98	25.76	0
W E Roller (*Surrey*)	22	35	1	860	142	25.29	1

BOWLING	M	O	M	R	W	Avge
A Watson (*Lancs*)	19	940.2	463	1135	96	11.82
A Shaw (*Notts*)	15	1062	649	840	67	12.53
J Crossland (*Lancs*)	20	553.3	208	934	72	12.97
G P Harrison (*Yorks*)	21	785.3	326	1326	100	13.26
G E Robinson (*O U*)	6	253.3	97	474	35	13.54
T Emmett (*Yorks*)	26	497.3	220	784	55	14.25
E Peate (*Yorks*)	27	1376.3	665	1753	120	14.60
A J Fothergill (*Som*)	11	323	110	545	37	14.72
W Flowers (*Notts*)	30	1243	551	1699	113	15.03
G Nash (*Lancs*)	17	409	148	775	51	15.19
R G Barlow (*Lancs*)	23	1241.2	595	1664	106	15.69
E Mills (*Notts*)	13	259	122	346	22	15.72
C E Currie (*C U/Hts*)	3	105.3	47	158	10	15.80
J W Juniper (*Sussex*)	12	555.5	282	763	48	15.89
W G Dible (*Hants*)	6	208.2	114	448	28	16.00
A Rylott (*MCC*)	10	549	292	635	39	16.28
C R Young (*Hants*)	5	246.2	90	458	28	16.35
W A Woof (*Gloucs*)	17	990.2	429	1541	94	16.39
S Christopherson (*Kent*)	7	365.3	165	633	38	16.65
W A Tester (*Sussex*)	10	170.3	49	320	19	16.84

First-class averages: 1884

BATTING	M	I	NO	Runs	HS	Avge	100s
E O Powell (*C U/Hts*)	6	11	1	441	140	44.10	1
†A G Steel (*Lancs*)	16	28	3	967	148	38.68	2
W W F Pullen (*Gloucs*)	8	13	2	396	161	36.00	1
†W H Scotton (*Notts*)	19	31	5	897	134	34.50	2
†W G Grace (*Gloucs*)	26	45	5	1361	116*	34.02	3
†Lord Harris (*Kent*)	25	47	5	1417	112*	33.73	2
W Newham (*Sussex*)	12	23	0	741	137	32.21	2
W L Murdoch (*Austr*)	31	50	5	1381	211	30.68	2
†G Ulyett (*Yorks*)	30	46	1	1334	146*	29.64	3
†W W Read (*Surrey*)	27	46	3	1256	135	29.20	2
W Blackman (*Sussex*)	11	21	5	454	77*	28.37	0
†A Shrewsbury (*Notts*)	20	34	2	908	209	28.37	2
I D Walker (*Middx*)	15	27	3	674	83	28.08	0
†W Barnes (*Notts*)	27	43	4	1092	105*	28.00	1
G H Longman (*Hants*)	7	13	0	362	78	27.84	0
†T C O'Brien (*O U/Mx*)	24	46	4	1150	119	27.38	2
L Hall (*Yorks*)	25	40	1	1058	135	27.12	4
W H Patterson (*Kent*)	10	19	1	485	73*	26.94	0
J Shuter (*Surrey*)	22	38	2	968	125	26.88	2
C T Studd (*Middx*)	10	18	3	398	141*	26.53	1

BOWLING	M	O	M	R	W	Avge
A F J Ford (*Middx*)	2	77.2	43	102	10	10.20
A Shaw (*Notts*)	14	742	434	744	71	10.47
E H Buckland (*O U*)	6	101.1	50	149	13	11.46
T Emmett (*Yorks*)	26	1031	559	1250	107	11.68
W Attewell (*Notts*)	18	1150	659	1217	101	12.04
J Crossland (*Lancs*)	14	525	201	893	71	12.57
F R Spofforth (*Austr*)	32	1577	653	2654	207	12.82
W Flowers (*Notts*)	24	916.2	463	1163	90	12.92
†R G Barlow (*Lancs*)	26	1361	686	1714	130	13.18
†E Peate (*Yorks*)	30	1565	788	1868	137	13.63
G Collins (*Kent*)	3	67	21	142	10	14.20
C E Horner (*Surrey*)	20	998	449	1602	107	14.97
G Burton (*Middx*)	14	623.1	301	877	58	15.12
J T Rawlin (*Yorks*)	7	91.1	46	155	10	15.50
R Peel (*Yorks*)	21	471.3	222	667	43	15.51
A J Fothergill (*Som*)	4	109	52	174	11	15.81
W R Gilbert (*Gloucs*)	11	181.2	57	373	23	16.21
H O Whitby (*O U*)	9	457.2	153	941	58	16.22
P H Morton (*Surrey*)	3	94	41	164	10	16.40
G E Palmer (*Austr*)	31	1248.3	457	2169	132	16.43

†Played for England but not featured above: A P Lucas, Hon A Lyttelton, A N Hornby, R Pilling and S Christopherson.

First-class averages: 1885

BATTING	M	I	NO	Runs	HS	Avge	100s
F M Lucas (*Sussex*)	7	10	2	554	215*	69.25	1
A Shrewsbury (*Notts*)	16	24	4	1130	224*	56.50	4
W W Read (*Surrey*)	27	42	0	1880	163	44.76	6
W Newham (*Sussex*)	11	19	2	740	141*	43.52	3
W G Grace (*Gloucs*)	25	42	3	1688	221*	43.28	4
W H Patterson (*Kent*)	9	14	1	548	143	42.15	1
G B Studd (*Middx*)	7	13	3	405	104	40.50	1
W Gunn (*Notts*)	27	43	3	1451	203	36.27	1
S W Scott (*Middx*)	6	11	3	288	135*	36.00	1
J M Read (*Surrey*)	24	35	2	1137	186*	34.45	1
F Lee (*Yorks*)	21	32	3	901	101	31.06	1
R T Thornton (*Kent*)	10	16	1	460	79	30.66	0
W E Roller (*Surrey*)	16	24	0	729	204	30.37	2
R G Barlow (*Lancs*)	17	32	4	816	117	29.14	2
G Ulyett (*Yorks*)	28	47	1	1337	91	29.06	0
A J Webbe (*Middx*)	15	26	2	667	82*	27.79	0
J Briggs (*Lancs*)	20	33	2	857	186	27.64	2
O G Radcliffe (*Som*)	7	13	0	359	101	27.61	1
F H Sugg (*Derbys*)	10	19	2	462	187	27.17	1
E O Powell (*Hants*)	7	14	1	348	73	26.76	0

BOWLING	M	O	M	R	W	Avge
A Rylott (*MCC*)	2	112.2	57	123	17	7.23
W Gunn (*Notts*)	27	153.2	57	235	20	11.75
A G Steel (*Lancs*)	5	179.3	79	273	21	13.00
J W Juniper (*Sussex*)	6	209.3	107	289	22	13.13
J Briggs (*Lancs*)	20	649	326	921	67	13.74
W Attewell (*Notts*)	22	1301	776	1218	87	14.00
G A Lohmann (*Surrey*)	24	1253.1	588	2040	142	14.36
A Hearne (*Kent*)	13	643.2	284	928	64	14.50
W E Roller (*Surrey*)	16	417.2	217	537	37	14.51
A J Webbe (*Middx*)	15	121.1	57	146	10	14.60
W Cropper (*Derbys*)	11	337.1	146	514	35	14.68
W Flowers (*Notts*)	27	1312.3	718	1395	94	14.84
A Shaw (*Notts*)	12	479.3	267	450	30	15.00
J Wootton (*Kent*)	15	873.1	376	1358	90	15.08
A Watson (*Lancs*)	15	1235.2	713	1344	88	15.37
H Rotherham (*Gents*)	2	125	47	200	13	15.38
W Barnes (*Notts*)	27	1025.2	497	1508	97	15.44
A H J Cochrane (*O U*)	7	320.3	147	473	30	15.76
G Ulyett (*Yorks*)	28	300	125	426	27	15.77
G Burton (*Middx*)	13	877	443	1000	62	16.12

First-class averages: 1886

BATTING	M	I	NO	Runs	HS	Avge	100s
†A Shrewsbury (*Notts*)	24	38	5	1404	227*	42.54	3
†W W Read (*Surrey*)	28	46	3	1825	120	42.44	4
†A G Steel (*Lancs*)	9	12	2	418	83	41.80	0
A J Webbe (*Middx*)	8	13	0	518	103	39.84	1
†W G Grace (*Gloucs*)	33	55	3	1846	170	35.50	4
J M Read (*Surrey*)	26	43	4	1364	186	34.97	2
S W Scott (*Middx*)	10	19	2	556	94*	32.70	0
Lord Harris (*Kent*)	12	20	0	644	76	32.20	0
G Kemp (*C U*)	10	18	2	497	125	31.06	2
F M Lucas (*Sussex*)	10	17	1	474	121	29.62	1
C I Thornton (*MCC*)	7	13	1	350	107*	29.16	1
R Abel (*Surrey*)	27	47	5	1221	144	29.07	2
G G Hearne (*Kent*)	25	45	6	1125	126	28.84	2
A E Stoddart (*Middx*)	13	24	1	640	116	27.82	1
J G Walker (*Middx*)	17	32	2	819	79	27.30	0
W A Humphreys (*Sussex*)	19	35	8	735	68*	27.22	0
L Hall (*Yorks*)	22	41	4	1005	92	27.16	0
G Giffen (*Austr*)	35	61	8	1424	119	26.86	1
W Gunn (*Notts*)	20	31	3	752	83	26.85	0
†W H Scotton (*Notts*)	26	39	2	979	110*	26.45	1

BOWLING	M	O	M	R	W	Avge
A Teggin (*Lancs*)	6	137.2	61	175	16	10.93
A Watson (*Lancs*)	20	1188	701	1109	99	11.20
S Wade (*Yorks*)	12	240.1	115	371	33	11.24
F Martin (*Kent*)	7	295.2	156	327	29	11.27
T Emmett (*Yorks*)	23	1276.3	647	1591	124	12.83
H O Whitby (*O U*)	7	307.2	149	424	33	12.84
W Attewell (*Notts*)	20	1273.1	726	1246	96	12.97
T Bowley (*Surrey*)	19	973.3	497	1219	88	13.85
†W Barnes (*Notts*)	24	744	387	936	67	13.97
†R G Barlow (*Lancs*)	27	1238.1	653	1525	105	14.52
†E Peate (*Yorks*)	20	980.2	542	1027	70	14.67
†G A Lohmann (*Surrey*)	26	1715	809	2425	160	15.15
J Beaumont (*Surrey*)	19	880.3	441	1165	76	15.32
C W Rock (*C U*)	14	926.2	424	1193	77	15.49
A Shaw (*Notts*)	14	630.2	371	523	33	15.84
J Wootton (*Kent*)	25	1618.1	715	2281	143	15.95
A H J Cochrane (*O U/Dby*)	8	309	134	479	30	15.96
†J Briggs (*Lancs*)	27	1176	612	1471	92	15.98
W Wright (*Notts*)	10	502	277	528	33	16.00
W Cropper (*Derbys*)	13	537.2	259	739	46	16.06

†Played for England but not featured above: G Ulyett, E F S Tylecote and R Pilling.

First-class averages: 1887

BATTING	M	I	NO	Runs	HS	Avge	100s
A Shrewsbury (*Notts*)	17	23	2	1653	267	78.71	8
W G Grace (*Gloucs*)	24	46	8	2062	183*	54.26	6
A J Webbe (*Middx*)	18	31	5	1244	243*	47.84	3
W W Read (*Surrey*)	23	36	2	1615	247	47.50	5
K J Key (*O U/Sy*)	24	44	5	1684	281	43.17	2
W E Roller (*Surrey*)	10	12	0	490	120	40.83	3
L Hall (*Yorks*)	23	36	4	1240	160	38.75	4
G Ulyett (*Yorks*)	26	41	2	1487	199*	38.12	4
W Robinson (*Lancs*)	14	21	4	604	111*	35.52	1
W Gunn (*Notts*)	20	30	3	958	205*	35.48	1
W C Bridgeman (*C U*)	7	11	2	313	162*	34.77	1
F F Thomas (*C U/Sx*)	9	17	1	554	114	34.62	1
J Eccles (*Lancs*)	14	22	2	677	113	33.85	1
W Barnes (*Notts*)	22	30	1	957	160	33.00	3
J Shuter (*Surrey*)	18	27	0	871	111	32.25	2
Walter Quaife (*Sussex*)	15	30	1	926	111	31.93	1
A M Sutthery (*C U*)	8	14	1	391	73	30.07	0
F Lee (*Yorks*)	14	20	0	591	165	29.55	2
S W Scott (*Middx*)	7	13	1	354	99	29.50	0
L Martineau (*C U*)	7	11	4	206	109	29.42	1

BOWLING	M	O	M	R	W	Avge
G G Jones (*Surrey*)	8	233	125	282	24	11.75
H Richardson (*Notts*)	13	570.2	322	613	45	13.62
W Attewell (*Notts*)	19	1330.1	810	1238	89	13.91
A Watson (*Lancs*)	17	1532.2	937	1482	100	14.82
J T Rawlin (*MCC*)	9	538	277	675	45	15.00
G A Lohmann (*Surrey*)	25	1634.2	737	2404	154	15.61
J Beaumont (*Surrey*)	14	684.1	326	1072	64	16.75
A D Pougher (*MCC*)	10	541	267	780	46	16.95
W Flowers (*Notts*)	23	885	422	1171	68	17.22
E Peake (*Gloucs*)	3	157.1	67	293	17	17.23
R Peel (*Yorks*)	25	1097	507	1472	85	17.31
N K Stephen (*C U*)	4	209.3	95	261	15	17.40
A E Leatham (*MCC*)	4	88	30	177	10	17.70
J Briggs (*Lancs*)	20	1592.1	831	2018	114	17.70
E Mills (*Surrey*)	5	208	110	253	14	18.07
E A Nepean (*O U/Mx*)	15	476.2	124	1091	60	18.18
G Burton (*Middx*)	12	722.2	334	1004	55	18.25
W Cropper (*Derbys*)	7	312	139	503	27	18.62
J M Preston (*Yorks*)	20	533.2	233	974	52	18.73
R G Barlow (*Lancs*)	17	727	374	994	53	18.75

First-class averages: 1888

BATTING	M	I	NO	Runs	HS	Avge	100s
†W W Read (*Surrey*)	28	41	2	1414	338	36.25	4
†W G Grace (*Gloucs*)	33	59	1	1886	215	32.51	4
†R Abel (*Surrey*)	29	44	2	1323	160	31.50	1
W H Patterson (*Kent*)	10	17	1	425	84	26.56	0
†T C O'Brien (*Middx*)	11	18	1	450	79*	26.47	0
J Eccles (*Lancs*)	16	28	2	660	184	25.38	1
J M Read (*Surrey*)	23	32	1	786	109	25.35	1
†J Shuter (*Surrey*)	24	34	1	834	95	25.27	0
K J Key (*Surrey*)	25	38	3	875	108	25.00	1
G Kemp (*C U/La*)	8	15	1	331	64	23.64	0
M P Bowden (*Surrey*)	19	26	4	514	189*	23.36	1
P S McDonnell (*Austr*)	35	58	1	1331	105	23.35	1
C J M Fox (*Kent*)	13	23	2	490	93	23.33	0
C I Thornton (*MCC*)	7	11	2	210	48*	23.33	0
F J N Thesiger (*O U/Mx*)	8	12	0	276	88	23.00	0
W Newham (*Sussex*)	19	36	3	746	128	22.60	2
W W F Pullen (*Gloucs*)	11	19	1	401	70	22.27	0
O G Radcliffe (*Gloucs*)	20	35	1	754	99	22.17	0
J A Dixon (*Notts*)	14	26	2	527	83	21.95	0
S W Scott (*Middx*)	9	17	2	326	121*	21.73	1

BOWLING	M	O	M	R	W	Avge
J J Hulme (*Eng XI*)	1	42	21	50	10	5.00
W Chatterton (*MCC*)	7	124.2	69	127	14	9.07
J R Napier (*Lancs*)	2	43.2	14	102	11	9.27
†A G Steel (*Lancs*)	5	81.3	28	140	15	9.33
†John Briggs (*Lancs*)	26	1450.2	763	1679	160	10.49
Jos Briggs (*Notts*)	6	102.1	40	147	14	10.50
A Hearne (*Kent*)	15	687.2	339	786	73	10.76
F Martin (*Middx*)	15	753.2	404	791	73	10.83
†G A Lohmann (*Surrey*)	29	1649.1	783	2280	209	10.90
J Phillips (*MCC*)	6	299.3	145	393	35	11.22
F R Spofforth (*Gents*)	1	69	29	124	11	11.27
T Emmett (*Yorks*)	3	96	44	125	11	11.36
H Richardson (*Notts*)	17	534.1	303	535	47	11.38
W C Hedley (*Kent*)	6	279	131	440	38	11.57
C T B Turner (*Austr*)	36	2427.2	1127	3307	283	11.68
†R Peel (*Yorks*)	31	1648.1	830	2091	171	12.22
G Burton (*Middx*)	15	847	370	1135	92	12.33
W A Woof (*Gloucs*)	9	607	313	680	55	12.36
W Flowers (*Notts*)	24	824	451	857	66	12.98
S P Jones (*Austr*)	12	68.3	19	134	10	13.40

†Played for England but not featured above: F H Sugg, W Barnes, W Gunn, R Pilling, H Wood, G Ulyett and M Sherwin.

First-class averages: 1889

BATTING	M	I	NO	Runs	HS	Avge	100s
W Gunn (*Notts*)	26	40	5	1319	118	37.68	1
A Shrewsbury (*Notts*)	12	16	2	522	104	37.28	1
L Wilson (*Kent*)	7	10	0	360	132	36.90	1
W Barnes (*Notts*)	27	40	4	1249	130*	34.69	3
J M Read (*Surrey*)	17	27	2	847	136	33.88	1
W G Grace (*Gloucs*)	24	45	2	1396	154	32.46	3
T C O'Brien (*Middx*)	14	26	1	784	100*	31.36	1
J Cranston (*Gloucs*)	15	26	3	709	130	30.82	2
K J Key (*Surrey*)	23	40	5	1070	176*	30.57	2
A Ward (*Lancs*)	21	31	4	822	114*	30.44	1
A G Steel (*Lancs*)	8	11	0	329	65	29.90	0
F Marchant (*Kent*)	14	23	0	669	176	29.08	1
R Abel (*Surrey*)	25	43	5	1095	138	28.81	2
H J Mordaunt (*C U/Mx*)	7	12	0	338	127	28.16	1
W H Patterson (*Kent*)	9	16	1	422	115	28.13	1
F H Sugg (*Lancs*)	20	30	2	747	89	26.67	0
L Hall (*Yorks*)	21	39	2	975	86	26.35	0
W W Read (*Surrey*)	20	33	1	805	115	25.15	1
A E Stoddart (*Middx*)	18	35	2	817	78*	24.75	0
F G J Ford (*C U/Mx*)	12	20	0	495	123	24.75	2

BOWLING	M	O	M	R	W	Avge
F L Shand (*Gents*)	2	66	35	90	10	9.00
W Attewell (*Notts*)	26	1364.2	673	1635	149	10.97
W Price (*Lpl*)	2	110.1	60	111	10	11.10
J Briggs (*Lancs*)	23	1040.3	447	1646	140	11.75
A W Mold (*Lancs*)	18	679	262	1207	102	11.83
A Watson (*Lancs*)	18	850.3	438	1139	90	12.65
W Flowers (*Notts*)	22	477	57	698	55	12.69
W Wright (*Kent*)	20	863.2	308	1466	114	12.85
C J M Fox (*Kent*)	14	129.2	52	207	16	12.93
H Richardson (*Notts*)	19	716	373	869	65	13.36
G A Lohmann (*Surrey*)	27	1614.1	646	2714	202	13.43
J W Sharpe (*Surrey*)	12	274	130	416	30	13.86
F Martin (*Kent*)	20	980.4	404	1484	106	14.00
R G Barlow (*Lancs*)	13	113	44	183	13	14.07
F J Shacklock (*Notts*)	19	554.1	177	1168	80	14.60
E M Grace (*Gloucs*)	10	55	9	158	10	15.80
R Peel (*Yorks*)	26	1289.2	506	2131	130	16.39
W A Woof (*Gloucs*)	10	548	182	1068	65	16.43
L Whitehead (*Yorks*)	15	396.4	188	613	37	16.56
J Beaumont (*Surrey*)	20	716.3	274	1452	87	16.68

First-class averages: 1890

BATTING	M	I	NO	Runs	HS	Avge	100s
†A Shrewsbury (*Notts*)	25	43	5	1568	267	41.26	2
†W Gunn (*Notts*)	30	53	6	1621	228	34.48	3
W H Patterson (*Kent*)	7	12	2	342	123*	34.20	1
R Abel (*Surrey*)	20	31	1	914	151*	30.46	2
†J Cranston (*Gloucs*)	21	37	3	978	152	28.76	2
A J Webbe (*Middx*)	19	36	1	995	134	28.42	1
†W G Grace (*Gloucs*)	30	55	3	1476	109*	28.38	1
R N Douglas (*C U/Sy*)	13	22	0	619	84	28.13	0
W C Hedley (*MCC*)	6	10	3	194	70	27.71	0
W D Llewellyn (*O U*)	9	18	2	439	116	27.43	1
A G Paul (*Lancs*)	11	16	2	375	71*	26.78	0
F G J Ford (*C U/Mx*)	11	21	2	503	191	26.47	1
†W W Read (*Surrey*)	30	48	2	1169	94	25.41	0
J R Painter (*Gloucs*)	16	28	1	683	119	25.29	1
E C Streatfeild (*C U/Sy*)	15	26	3	563	145	24.47	1
W L Murdoch (*Austr*)	33	59	2	1394	158*	24.45	2
W Chatterton (*MCC*)	11	20	1	459	75	24.15	0
J E Barrett (*Austr*)	32	58	7	1226	97	24.03	0
W H Lockwood (*Surrey*)	16	23	0	548	102	23.82	1
L A H Hamilton (*Kent*)	12	22	1	489	117*	23.18	1

BOWLING	M	O	M	R	W	Avge
G P Harrison (*Yorks*)	4	216.3	105	323	31	10.41
E A Nepean (*Middx*)	4	193.3	62	395	34	11.61
W Chatterton (*MCC*)	11	101.4	26	203	17	11.94
J Briggs (*Lancs*)	26	1113.2	456	1950	158	12.34
W Attewell (*Notts*)	28	1581.2	820	1874	151	12.41
†J W Sharpe (*Surrey*)	22	1053.2	455	1754	139	12.61
W A Woof (*Gloucs*)	8	440.3	174	814	63	12.92
†R Peel (*Yorks*)	33	1552.4	714	2239	172	13.01
†F Martin (*Kent*)	29	1702.2	711	2480	190	13.05
S M J Woods (*C U*)	12	360.4	120	775	59	13.13
†G A Lohmann (*Surrey*)	32	1545.1	628	2657	186	14.28
E Wainwright (*Yorks*)	19	461	171	812	59	13.76
C T B Turner (*Austr*)	31	1501.1	655	2544	179	14.21
J J Ferris (*Austr*)	30	1545.1	628	2657	186	14.28
A W Mold (*Lancs*)	23	893.4	300	1737	118	14.72
J Phillips (*Middx*)	5	201.4	78	357	24	14.87
B C Bolton (*Yorks*)	3	110.1	53	179	12	14.91
W C Hedley (*MCC*)	6	221	83	480	32	15.00
F Needham (*Notts*)	3	95	45	150	10	15.00
†W Barnes (*Notts*)	24	411	166	697	46	15.15

†Played for England but not featured above: J M Read, G MacGregor and G Ulyett.

First-class averages: 1891

BATTING	M	I	NO	Runs	HS	Avge	100s
A Shrewsbury (*Notts*)	17	25	3	1071	178	48.68	3
W Gunn (*Notts*)	23	37	5	1336	169	41.75	4
R Abel (*Surrey*)	24	35	1	1139	197	33.50	2
T C O'Brien (*Middx*)	22	33	4	936	113	32.27	2
E C Streatfeild (*C U/Sy*)	8	13	4	279	98	31.00	0
G Bean (*Sussex*)	21	38	5	1002	145*	30.36	2
A Ward (*Lancs*)	19	29	1	841	185	30.03	1
S M Crosfield (*Lancs*)	11	14	3	320	82*	29.09	0
A E Stoddart (*Middx*)	20	32	1	857	215*	27.64	1
F Marchant (*Kent*)	16	26	2	660	123	27.50	1
J B Challen (*Som*)	10	18	3	394	89	26.26	0
J M Read (*Surrey*)	19	29	1	722	135	25.78	1
G Ulyett (*Yorks*)	25	44	1	1068	118	24.83	2
R N Douglas (*C U/Sy*)	10	18	0	447	131	24.83	1
R Peel (*Yorks*)	25	44	4	971	150	24.27	2
W Newham (*Sussex*)	20	35	2	799	134*	24.21	2
L C H Palairet (*O U/Som*)	18	35	1	821	100	24.14	1
L Hall (*Yorks*)	20	37	3	786	67	23.11	0
G A Lohmann (*Surrey*)	25	36	1	809	61	23.11	0
W W Read (*Surrey*)	24	36	0	831	77	23.08	0

BOWLING	M	O	M	R	W	Avge
T Smith (*Lpl*)	1	51	14	100	10	10.00
J T Hearne (*Middx*)	18	791.4	301	1449	129	11.23
G A Lohmann (*Surrey*)	25	1189.3	445	2065	177	11.66
J T Rawlin (*Middx*)	17	516	202	849	69	12.30
W H Lockwood (*Surrey*)	15	280.2	99	581	47	12.36
A W Mold (*Lancs*)	19	942.2	335	1724	138	12.49
G Davidson (*MCC*)	3	80	28	144	11	13.09
J Briggs (*Lancs*)	21	973.4	376	1693	128	13.22
F Martin (*Kent*)	22	1147.2	443	1873	140	13.37
A P Smith (*Lancs*)	11	173.2	82	243	18	13.50
J W Sharpe (*Surrey*)	21	726.2	260	1495	108	13.84
W Attewell (*Notts*)	28	1514.3	706	2132	153	13.93
F Needham (*Notts*)	4	105.3	54	160	11	14.54
W Murch (*Gloucs*)	7	170.1	52	436	29	15.03
F G Roberts (*Gloucs*)	15	383	145	733	48	15.27
J J Ferris (*MCC*)	14	592	232	1090	70	15.57
A Watson (*Lancs*)	14	394.4	177	610	38	16.05
G W Hillyard (*MCC*)	4	168.4	63	341	21	16.23
J Phillips (*Middx*)	15	153.3	38	428	26	16.46
A Hearne (*Kent*)	16	401.3	157	701	42	16.69

First-class averages: 1892

BATTING	M	I	NO	Runs	HS	Avge	100s
A Shrewsbury (*Notts*)	22	34	4	1260	212	42.00	5
W H Patterson (*Kent*)	9	14	1	511	114	39.30	1
S W Scott (*Middx*)	17	31	5	1015	224*	39.03	1
H T Hewett (*Som*)	24	42	2	1407	201	35.17	1
W W Read (*Surrey*)	23	37	5	1088	196*	34.00	3
L C H Palairet (*O U/Som*)	26	46	4	1343	146	31.97	2
A E Stoddart (*Middx*)	26	47	2	1403	130	31.17	1
W G Grace (*Gloucs*)	21	37	3	1055	99	31.02	0
W Gunn (*Notts*)	25	39	2	1120	103	30.27	1
W L Murdoch (*MCC*)	9	17	2	443	83	29.53	0
R Henderson (*Surrey*)	21	29	5	694	74	28.91	0
P H Latham (*C U*)	5	10	1	254	69	28.22	0
R Abel (*Surrey*)	26	41	1	1108	117	27.70	1
A C MacLaren (*Lancs*)	13	21	1	548	135	27.40	2
A P Smith (*Lancs*)	16	25	1	650	111	27.08	1
A Hearne (*Kent*)	19	32	2	810	116*	27.00	1
E Smith (*Yorks*)	13	23	1	590	122	26.81	1
H B Daft (*Notts*)	12	16	6	266	43*	26.60	0
J Le Fleming (*Kent*)	6	10	0	260	134	26.00	1
R W Rice (*O U/Gloucs*)	14	25	2	592	67	25.73	0

BOWLING	M	O	M	R	W	Avge
F Parris (*Sussex*)	5	124.4	50	196	17	11.52
J H J Hornsby (*MCC*)	2	42	8	142	12	11.83
W H Lockwood (*Surrey*)	22	890.2	292	2054	151	13.60
A W Mold (*Lancs*)	19	766.4	253	1636	120	13.63
J Briggs (*Lancs*)	22	1045	438	1706	124	13.75
R Abel (*Surrey*)	26	170.3	40	429	31	13.83
W Attewell (*Notts*)	26	1453.1	701	2017	144	14.00
W Oakley (*Lpl*)	1	82	26	142	10	14.20
A Watson (*Lancs*)	18	596.1	293	901	61	14.77
A D Pougher (*MCC*)	6	195.4	74	396	26	15.23
E J Tyler (*Som*)	19	656.1	191	1548	101	15.32
G A Lohmann (*Surrey*)	23	1213.4	431	2316	151	15.33
J T Hearne (*Middx*)	25	1360.3	527	2510	163	15.39
W Flowers (*Notts*)	20	585.4	227	1098	71	15.46
W C Hedley (*Som*)	15	301.2	92	709	45	15.75
G B Nichols (*Som*)	19	486.3	192	909	57	15.94
E Wainwright (*Yorks*)	23	820.4	289	1695	104	16.29
W Chatterton (*MCC*)	13	119	49	229	14	16.35
R Peel (*Yorks*)	26	1302.3	552	2034	121	16.80
S M J Woods (*Som*)	25	1055.4	319	2576	153	16.83

First-class averages: 1893

BATTING	M	I	NO	Runs	HS	Avge	100s
†W Gunn (*Notts*)	30	51	3	2057	156	42.85	7
†A E Stoddart (*Middx*)	28	50	1	2072	195*	42.28	4
†F S Jackson (*C U/Yks*)	21	36	4	1328	123	41.50	4
†A Shrewsbury (*Notts*)	25	43	4	1586	164	40.66	5
W Rashleigh (*Kent*)	7	14	1	482	101*	37.07	1
†A Ward (*Lancs*)	24	43	3	1435	140*	35.87	2
†W G Grace (*Gloucs*)	28	50	5	1609	128	35.75	1
J A Dixon (*Notts*)	13	23	0	756	139	32.86	3
G Brann (*Sussex*)	19	34	5	941	159	32.44	3
†W W Read (*Surrey*)	28	46	3	1377	147*	32.02	1
H T Hewett (*Som*)	21	38	2	1092	120	30.33	2
W L Murdoch (*Sussex*)	25	46	5	1228	96	29.95	0
G L Wilson (*Sussex*)	17	30	1	865	117	29.82	2
W Newham (*Sussex*)	21	39	4	1003	97	28.65	0
G Bean (*Sussex*)	25	47	2	1277	186	28.37	2
K J Key (*Surrey*)	14	24	4	563	100	28.15	1
J J Lyons (*Austr*)	29	50	1	1377	149	28.10	1
F J W Marlow (*Sussex*)	15	30	2	775	126	27.67	1
J Douglas (*C U/Mx*)	14	26	2	642	102	26.75	1
L C H Palairet (*O U/Som*)	19	34	1	871	91	26.39	0

BOWLING	M	O	M	R	W	Avge
W Hearne (*Kent*)	6	319.4	128	545	46	11.84
W Mead (*MCC*)	3	178.1	57	348	26	13.38
C T B Turner (*Austr*)	26	1049	413	2018	148	13.63
C M Wells (*C U/Sy*)	13	453.3	139	1049	73	14.36
G H Hirst (*Yorks*)	23	828.1	348	1425	99	14.39
A D Pougher (*MCC*)	3	127.4	54	216	15	14.40
†R Peel (*Yorks*)	27	1135.3	459	1829	126	14.51
E Wainwright (*Yorks*)	26	907	304	1833	125	14.66
W Brockwell (*Surrey*)	22	496.3	183	1047	68	15.39
†T Richardson (*Surrey*)	23	993.4	288	2680	174	15.40
C J Kortright (*MCC*)	2	82.3	16	269	17	15.82
†J Briggs (*Lancs*)	28	1364	488	2639	166	15.89
H B Daft (*Notts*)	18	82.3	21	196	12	16.33
J T Hearne (*Middx*)	29	1741.4	667	3492	212	16.47
H Trumble (*Austr*)	29	832.1	274	1794	108	16.61
†W H Lockwood (*Surrey*)	27	931.2	267	2517	150	16.78
T A Wardall (*Yorks*)	13	225.2	109	287	17	16.88
†A W Mold (*Lancs*)	25	1282.4	426	2817	166	16.96
W A Humphreys (*Sussex*)	21	813.4	122	2598	150	17.32
H R Bromley-Davenport (*C U*)	10	228.1	61	560	32	17.50

†Played for England but not featured above: W Flowers, E Wainwright, G MacGregor, J M Read and W Brockwell.

First-class averages: 1894

BATTING	M	I	NO	Runs	HS	Avge	100s
W Brockwell (*Surrey*)	32	45	6	1491	128	38.23	5
L C Docker (*Warw*)	8	12	2	372	85*	37.20	0
G J Mordaunt (*O U*)	10	19	1	662	100	36.77	1
W Rashleigh (*Kent*)	9	17	0	620	106	36.47	1
J E Hill (*Warw*)	9	10	2	290	139*	36.25	1
R Abel (*Surrey*)	31	47	5	1447	168*	34.45	4
H T Hewett (*MCC*)	11	18	1	579	110	34.05	1
K S Ranjitsinhji (*C U*)	8	16	4	387	94	32.25	0
J M Read (*Surrey*)	17	23	2	640	86	30.47	0
J T Brown snr (*Yorks*)	31	51	5	1399	141	30.41	3
A E Stoddart (*Middx*)	24	39	0	1174	148	30.10	1
W Gunn (*Notts*)	21	38	1	1112	121*	30.05	2
T C O'Brien (*Middx*)	9	16	3	390	110*	30.00	1
H G P Owen (*Essex*)	8	16	1	447	109	29.80	1
W G Grace (*Gloucs*)	27	45	1	1293	196	29.38	3
L C H Palairet (*Som*)	18	34	1	969	181	29.36	2
H K Foster (*O U*)	9	18	3	435	80	29.00	0
H C Stewart (*Kent*)	6	11	1	290	90	29.00	0
F S Jackson (*Yorks*)	24	39	3	1028	145	28.55	2
H W Bainbridge (*Warw*)	17	25	2	645	65*	28.04	0

BOWLING	M	O	M	R	W	Avge
J Ellis (*Lancs*)	1	41.2	12	76	11	6.90
G Porter (*Derbys*)	4	80	42	115	14	8.21
A D Pougher (*Leics*)	11	323.2	140	524	56	9.35
J A Dixon (*Notts*)	18	544	19	111	11	10.09
T Richardson (*Surrey*)	23	936.3	293	2024	196	10.32
A T H Newnham (*Gloucs*)	6	110.1	36	226	20	11.30
H J Pallett (*Warw*)	15	522	175	938	79	11.87
A W Mold (*Lancs*)	28	1288.3	456	2548	207	12.30
A Shaw (*Sussex*)	7	422.3	201	516	41	12.58
E Wainwright (*Yorks*)	32	1087.3	413	2114	166	12.73
F Parris (*Sussex*)	12	436.4	150	804	63	12.76
G Davidson (*Derbys*)	19	829.2	384	1266	97	13.05
W Hearne (*Kent*)	18	805	283	1542	116	13.29
R Peel (*Yorks*)	30	1265.2	505	1949	145	13.44
J Briggs (*Lancs*)	23	1084.1	380	2006	145	13.83
F E Smith (*Surrey*)	26	747.4	254	1325	95	13.94
J T Hearne (*Middx*)	31	1486	600	2739	195	14.04
R Moorhouse (*Yorks*)	16	149.1	54	270	19	14.21
J T Rawlin (*Middx*)	20	904.1	375	1512	104	14.53
G B Raikes (*O U*)	6	104	44	204	14	14.57

First-class averages: 1895

BATTING	M	I	NO	Runs	HS	Avge	100s
L H Gwynn (*Dublin U*)	5	10	2	455	153*	56.87	2
A C MacLaren (*Lancs*)	16	24	0	1229	424	51.20	4
W G Grace (*Gloucs*)	29	48	2	2346	288	51.00	9
K S Ranjitsinhji (*Sussex*)	21	39	3	1775	150	49.30	4
L C H Palairet (*Som*)	15	29	1	1313	165	46.89	3
R Abel (*Surrey*)	32	50	4	2057	217	44.71	5
A Ward (*Lancs*)	27	45	3	1790	163	42.61	2
W G Druce (*C U*)	10	16	3	546	129	42.00	1
G O Smith (*O U*)	8	13	3	412	100*	41.20	1
H K Foster (*O U*)	9	16	1	599	121	39.93	1
T C O'Brien (*Middx*)	19	32	4	1079	202	38.53	3
A Shrewsbury (*Notts*)	10	18	1	647	143	38.05	2
A E Stoddart (*Middx*)	25	43	0	1622	150	37.72	2
N F Druce (*C U/Sy*)	20	31	3	985	199*	35.17	3
A F A Lilley (*Warw*)	23	41	1	1399	158*	34.97	3
Walter Quaife (*Warw*)	20	37	2	1219	105	34.82	1
A E Street (*Surrey*)	15	19	3	551	161*	34.43	1
S M J Woods (*Som*)	22	41	0	1405	215	34.26	3
H W Bainbridge (*Warw*)	19	35	1	1162	142	34.17	3
F C Holland (*Surrey*)	22	28	3	832	171	33.28	2

BOWLING	M	O	M	R	W	Avge
W C Hedley (*Som*)	8	320	116	669	48	13.93
C L Townsend (*Gloucs*)	14	746.1	178	1827	131	13.94
G A Lohmann (*Surrey*)	12	496.2	166	904	64	14.12
T Richardson (*Surrey*)	31	1690.1	463	4170	290	14.37
W Mead (*Essex*)	25	1206	390	2605	179	14.55
R Peel (*Yorks*)	31	1693.1	714	2695	180	14.97
J R Painter (*Gloucs*)	12	238.1	96	412	27	15.25
R G Hardstaff (*Notts*)	3	119.4	38	261	17	15.35
H Baldwin (*Hants*)	18	1010.4	386	1798	114	15.77
C J Kortright (*Essex*)	17	468	105	1203	76	15.82
A W Mold (*Lancs*)	27	1629	598	3400	213	15.96
J W Bennett (*Derbys*)	12	261.1	104	465	29	16.03
J. Briggs (*Lancs*)	23	1109.3	412	2073	129	16.06
T W Hayward (*Surrey*)	30	281.2	83	663	41	16.17
G Davidson (*Derbys*)	28	1383.4	591	2317	138	16.78
W Attewell (*Notts*)	26	1486	685	2246	133	16.88
G Porter (*Derbys*)	15	725.4	258	1322	78	16.94
J Phillips (*Middx*)	13	350	75	822	48	17.12
C M Wells (*Middx*)	6	167.4	34	415	24	17.29
G L Jessop (*Gloucs*)	16	460.3	194	873	50	17.46

First-class averages: 1896

BATTING	M	I	NO	Runs	HS	Avge	100s
†K S Ranjitsinhji (*Sussex*)	29	55	7	2780	171*	57.91	10
†E G Wynyard (*Hants*)	13	23	2	1038	268	49.42	4
†W Gunn (*Notts*)	21	38	7	1383	207*	44.61	3
W N Roe (*Som*)	7	12	2	434	106	43.40	1
†W G Grace (*Gloucs*)	30	54	4	2135	301	42.70	4
†R Abel (*Surrey*)	35	55	3	2218	231	42.65	5
W Storer (*Derbys*)	24	36	5	1313	142*	42.35	5
†F S Jackson (*Yorks*)	27	42	3	1618	117	42.25	3
L C H Palairet (*Som*)	20	35	2	1362	292	41.27	4
W H Patterson (*Kent*)	8	13	1	492	181	41.08	1
H D G Leveson-Gower (*O U/Sy*)	10	17	2	606	93	40.40	0
W Chatterton (*Derbys*)	22	35	4	1193	111	38.48	2
F E Lacey (*Hants*)	6	11	2	346	75*	38.44	0
T C O'Brien (*Middx*)	19	30	1	1087	137	37.48	1
H K Foster (*O U*)	6	12	1	406	72	36.90	0
A C MacLaren (*Lancs*)	17	27	2	922	226*	36.88	1
C J Burnup (*C U/Kt*)	22	39	3	1295	101	35.97	1
H B Hayman (*Middx*)	12	22	3	679	152	35.73	1
†J T Brown snr (*Yorks*)	35	60	7	1873	203	35.33	4
W Rashleigh (*Kent*)	8	15	0	528	163	35.20	2

BOWLING	M	O	M	R	W	Avge
E R Bradford (*Hants*)	3	47	25	68	11	6.18
F R Spofforth (*MCC*)	3	127.2	35	256	28	9.14
T R McKibbin (*Austr*)	22	647.1	198	1441	101	14.26
†J T Hearne (*Middx*)	35	2003.1	818	3670	257	14.28
S Haigh (*Yorks*)	15	586.4	201	1289	84	15.34
W Attewell (*Notts*)	28	1388.3	654	2128	135	15.70
H Trumble (*Austr*)	30	1140.1	380	2340	148	15.81
F G Bull (*Essex*)	16	503.2	145	1360	85	16.00
E Jones (*Austr*)	29	887.3	282	1940	121	16.03
†G A Lohmann (*Surrey*)	23	766.4	258	1512	93	16.25
†T Richardson (*Surrey*)	34	1656.2	526	4015	246	16.32
F H E Cunliffe (*O U*)	8	471.4	168	984	60	16.40
†T W Hayward (*Surrey*)	34	645	202	1541	91	16.93
†R Peel (*Yorks*)	31	1275.1	485	2240	128	17.50
A W Mold (*Lancs*)	27	1161	373	2719	150	18.12
C M Wells (*Middx*)	7	253.4	78	527	29	18.17
F G Kitchener (*Hants*)	7	144.3	48	329	18	18.27
A Hearne (*Kent*)	24	641.1	214	1338	73	18.32
E Smith (*Yorks*)	14	246.3	80	588	32	18.37
A W Hallam (*Lancs*)	21	661	246	1304	70	18.62

†Played for England but not featured above: A E Stoddart, A F A Lilley, A C MacLaren and J Briggs.

First-class averages: 1897

BATTING	M	I	NO	Runs	HS	Avge	100s
F G J Ford (*Middx*)	10	18	3	805	150	53.66	2
N F Druce (*Sy/C U*)	14	20	2	928	227*	51.55	3
A C MacLaren (*Lancs*)	14	21	2	974	244	51.26	2
K S Ranjitsinhji (*Sussex*)	26	48	5	1940	260	45.11	5
R Abel (*Surrey*)	32	50	3	2099	250	44.65	6
William Quaife (*Warw*)	19	28	5	1020	178*	44.34	3
J A Dixon (*Notts*)	16	26	1	1100	268*	44.00	2
W Gunn (*Notts*)	20	32	3	1266	230	43.65	4
A J Turner (*Essex*)	10	17	3	590	111	42.14	1
J T Brown snr (*Yorks*)	30	48	5	1809	311	42.06	3
H W Bainbridge (*Warw*)	17	26	2	998	162	41.58	2
J Douglas (*Middx*)	7	13	1	480	110	40.00	2
W G Grace (*Gloucs*)	25	41	2	1532	131	39.28	4
F E Lacey (*Hants*)	7	12	2	385	121	38.50	1
T W Hayward (*Surrey*)	28	39	3	1368	130	38.00	1
F Mitchell (*C U/Yks*)	10	15	0	570	133	38.00	1
D L A Jephson (*Surrey*)	12	17	2	568	102	37.86	1
A Shrewsbury (*Notts*)	17	28	3	944	125	37.76	1
C J Burnup (*C U/Kt*)	11	18	2	597	108	37.31	1
J A Lester (*Phil*)	15	26	2	891	92	37.12	0

BOWLING	M	O	M	R	W	Avge
A E Trott (*MCC*)	8	273.4	75	693	50	13.86
C E M Wilson (*C U/Yks*)	10	271	94	458	33	13.87
T Richardson (*Surrey*)	30	1603.4	495	3945	273	14.45
S Webb (*Middx*)	2	99.1	33	213	14	15.21
E H L Nice (*Surrey*)	4	105.2	41	198	13	15.23
W R Cuttell (*Lancs*)	29	1121.4	442	1974	120	16.45
J Briggs (*Lancs*)	28	1288	381	2560	155	16.51
C Heseltine (*Hants*)	15	307.1	78	709	41	17.29
J T Hearne (*Middx*)	26	1619.3	647	3066	173	17.72
G L Jessop (*C U/Gloucs*)	26	983.3	296	2071	116	17.85
H W de Zoete (*C U/Ex*)	11	261	67	686	38	18.05
A W Mold (*Lancs*)	21	838.4	283	1769	98	18.05
F W Stocks (*O U/Lei*)	11	453	168	994	55	18.07
T W Hayward (*Surrey*)	28	832.3	244	2073	114	18.18
A W Hallam (*Lancs*)	29	1042	449	1820	100	18.20
S Haigh (*Yorks*)	26	786.4	260	1713	91	18.82
R Peel (*Yorks*)	22	764	275	1405	72	19.51
F H E Cunliffe (*O U/Mx*)	13	655.4	212	1413	75	19.64
W Attewell (*Notts*)	22	1194	521	2029	102	19.89
C J Kortright (*Essex*)	17	505.1	118	1442	71	20.30

First-class averages: 1898

BATTING	M	I	NO	Runs	HS	Avge	100s
William Quaife (*Warw*)	17	28	8	1219	157*	60.95	3
C B Fry (*Sussex*)	19	37	4	1788	179*	54.18	6
R Abel (*Surrey*)	30	45	3	2053	219	48.88	7
F A Phillips (*Som*)	6	10	2	390	83	48.75	0
W Gunn (*Notts*)	22	36	5	1484	236*	47.87	4
A E Stoddart (*Middx*)	15	26	4	1038	157	47.18	2
A Shrewsbury (*Notts*)	20	34	7	1219	154*	45.14	3
T W Hayward (*Surrey*)	26	38	2	1523	315*	42.30	3
W G Grace (*Gloucs*)	26	41	5	1513	168	42.02	3
W Storer (*Derbys*)	24	42	5	1548	109	41.83	3
L C H Palairet (*Som*)	17	29	2	1126	179*	41.70	4
F S Jackson (*Yorks*)	29	43	5	1566	160	41.21	5
J Tunnicliffe (*Yorks*)	30	49	5	1804	243	41.00	4
J Douglas (*Middx*)	9	13	2	451	153	41.00	2
S P Kinneir (*Warw*)	8	13	3	402	78*	40.20	0
F G J Ford (*Middx*)	20	31	2	1152	135	39.72	4
J R Mason (*Kent*)	23	40	1	1531	152	39.25	2
W Brockwell (*Surrey*)	30	46	2	1686	152	38.31	6
C M Wells (*Middx*)	9	10	0	382	101	38.20	1
F W D Quinton (*Hants*)	7	13	2	414	101*	37.63	1

BOWLING	M	O	M	R	W	Avge
E Smith (*Yorks*)	4	77	34	123	13	9.46
J J Hulme (*Derbys*)	2	100	36	152	12	12.66
J T Hearne (*Middx*)	30	1802.2	781	3120	222	14.05
W Rhodes (*Yorks*)	33	1230	482	2249	154	14.60
E Wainwright (*Yorks*)	27	515.3	185	1032	69	14.95
G Davidson (*Derbys*)	20	956.4	458	1403	91	15.41
W Roche (*MCC*)	6	163.4	51	469	30	15.63
F S Jackson (*Yorks*)	29	904	360	1630	104	15.67
H Baldwin (*Hants*)	14	472.1	155	975	59	16.52
W H Lockwood (*Surrey*)	25	1002	297	2228	134	16.61
W Reeves (*Essex*)	7	92.2	41	184	11	16.72
W Mead (*Essex*)	26	1038	382	2049	117	17.51
T Lancaster (*Lancs*)	4	141	57	263	15	17.53
H R Bromley-Davenport (*Mx*)	6	88.3	32	196	11	17.81
A E Hind (*C U*)	10	365.1	145	627	35	17.91
A E Trott (*Middx*)	19	1004.1	354	2333	130	17.94
G E Winter (*C U*)	7	115.1	17	309	17	18.17
S Haigh (*Yorks*)	31	873	305	1880	102	18.43
F Geeson (*Leics*)	12	362.3	98	820	44	18.63
B T J Bosanquet (*O U*)	10	250	74	561	30	18.70

First-class averages: 1899

BATTING	M	I	NO	Runs	HS	Avge	100s
R M Poore (*Hants*)	12	21	4	1551	304	91.23	7
C M Wells (*Middx*)	8	11	3	523	244	65.37	1
†K S Ranjitsinhji (*Sussex*)	36	58	8	3159	197	63.18	8
†T W Hayward (*Surrey*)	35	49	4	2647	273	58.82	7
R Abel (*Surrey*)	35	53	3	2685	357*	53.70	7
A Shrewsbury (*Notts*)	17	26	2	1257	175	52.37	4
†C L Townsend (*Gloucs*)	30	54	7	2440	224*	51.91	9
F L Fane (*Essex*)	9	16	0	746	207	46.62	2
P A Perrin (*Essex*)	21	36	4	1491	196	46.59	6
†F S Jackson (*Yorks*)	28	44	3	1847	155	45.04	5
†A O Jones (*Notts*)	23	38	2	1609	250	44.69	4
†C B Fry (*Sussex*)	31	55	1	2366	181	43.81	5
†William Quaife (*Warw*)	27	48	9	1703	207*	43.66	6
†J T Brown snr (*Yorks*)	21	35	1	1443	192	42.44	3
E G Wynyard (*Hants*)	18	32	1	1281	225	41.32	2
J Darling (*Austr*)	35	56	9	1941	167	41.29	5
V F S Crawford (*Surrey*)	8	10	2	330	129	41.25	1
S M J Woods (*Som*)	18	33	1	1291	146	40.34	3
A J Turner (*Essex*)	13	22	2	804	124	40.20	2
C J Burnup (*Kent*)	23	42	3	1565	171	40.12	3

BOWLING	M	O	M	R	W	Avge
J I'Anson (*Lancs*)	2	50	17	120	11	10.90
A Woodcock (*Leics*)	7	208.3	58	474	32	14.81
H Griffin (*Som*)	3	119	41	217	14	15.50
J L Ainsworth (*Lancs*)	4	146	56	289	18	16.05
A E Trott (*Middx*)	32	1772.4	587	4086	239	17.09
†W Rhodes (*Yorks*)	34	1518.4	543	3062	179	17.10
†W Mead (*Essex*)	28	1378.2	515	2634	146	18.04
H Trumble (*Austr*)	32	1249.1	431	2618	142	18.43
A J Paish (*Gloucs*)	22	1095.4	304	2540	137	18.54
A W Mold (*Lancs*)	25	766.4	299	2149	115	18.68
†W M Bradley (*Kent*)	25	1257	414	2981	156	19.10
C M Wells (*Middx*)	8	217.3	64	459	24	19.12
J Briggs (*Lancs*)	14	667.1	247	1150	60	19.16
†W H Lockwood (*Surrey*)	27	860.3	228	2284	117	19.52
J R Mason (*Kent*)	22	795.3	319	1635	83	19.69
J T Brown jnr (*Yorks*)	12	434.3	124	1131	57	19.84
A E Fernie (*C U*)	3	99	20	279	14	19.92
F Martin (*Kent*)	17	410.3	125	940	46	20.43
E G Bromley-Martin (*Worcs*)	9	72.4	19	205	10	20.50
F Davidson (*Derbys*)	5	114	32	226	11	20.54

†Played for England but not featured above: A F A Lilley, A C MacLaren, J T Tyldesley, J T Hearne, G L Jessop, W G Grace, H I Young, W Gunn, W Storer, W Brockwell and G H Hirst.

First-class averages: 1900

BATTING	M	I	NO	Runs	HS	Avge	100s
K S Ranjitsinhji (*Sussex*)	26	40	5	3065	275	87.57	11
C B Fry (*Sussex*)	26	41	3	2325	229	61.18	9
R Abel (*Surrey*)	31	49	3	2592	221	56.34	12
T W Hayward (*Surrey*)	38	57	7	2693	193	53.86	10
J R Mason (*Kent*)	24	36	2	1828	147	53.76	4
L Whitehead (*Yorks*)	9	12	6	321	67*	53.50	0
R E Foster (*O U/Worcs*)	23	37	2	1807	171	51.62	7
S P Kinneir (*Warw*)	19	30	7	1131	156	49.17	2
William Quaife (*Warw*)	25	38	9	1383	223*	47.68	2
E W Dillon (*Kent*)	6	10	1	429	108	47.66	1
P F Warner (*Middx*)	23	39	1	1727	170	45.44	5
W G Grace (*Lon/MCC*)	18	31	1	1277	126	42.56	3
D L A Jephson (*Surrey*)	38	57	10	1952	213	41.53	5
G H Hirst (*Yorks*)	36	56	8	1960	155	40.83	4
J H G Devey (*Warw*)	14	20	2	729	246	40.50	1
A E Stoddart (*Middx*)	7	11	1	402	221	40.20	1
G L Jessop (*Gloucs*)	31	58	3	2210	179	40.18	6
T L Taylor (*C U/Lancs*)	26	43	6	1461	147	39.48	2
C J B Wood (*Leics*)	28	51	4	1841	147	39.17	3
P A Perrin (*Essex*)	20	32	2	1138	205	37.93	4

BOWLING	M	O	M	R	W	Avge
A R Sladen (*Lancs*)	2	44.1	11	127	10	12.70
C M Wells (*Middx*)	9	212	66	468	36	13.00
A W Hallam (*Lancs*)	5	78	32	138	10	13.80
W Rhodes (*Yorks*)	35	1553	455	3606	261	13.81
A W Mold (*Lancs*)	18	560.3	153	1359	97	14.01
S Haigh (*Yorks*)	33	958.3	259	2416	163	14.82
F H Humphrys (*O U*)	3	60.4	9	180	12	15.00
S Webb (*Lancs*)	18	509	146	1102	72	15.30
L Whitehead (*Yorks*)	9	68.5	24	165	10	16.50
J S Munn (*O U*)	4	82.4	14	218	13	16.76
W Mead (*Essex*)	27	1022.2	342	2286	131	17.45
J Briggs (*Lancs*)	28	1162.2	433	2254	127	17.74
J H Young (*Derbys*)	12	128.4	38	330	18	18.33
H White (*O U*)	9	214.1	55	497	27	18.40
C Blythe (*Kent*)	22	842.1	232	2106	114	18.47
T G Wass (*Notts*)	18	747.2	180	2026	108	18.75
A D Pougher (*Leics*)	8	104.4	27	283	15	18.86
S Santall (*Warw*)	8	344.5	99	873	46	18.97
C J Kortright (*Essex*)	20	393	70	1266	65	19.47
J R Mason (*Kent*)	24	604.3	174	1678	86	19.59

First-class averages: 1901

BATTING	M	I	NO	Runs	HS	Avge	100s
C B Fry (*Sussex*)	29	43	3	3147	244	78.67	12
G Brann (*Sussex*)	8	10	3	518	130	74.00	3
K S Ranjitsinhji (*Sussex*)	27	40	5	2468	285*	70.51	8
W Smith (*Lancs*)	8	11	2	577	143	64.11	1
L C H Palairet (*Som*)	18	34	1	1906	194	57.75	5
William Quaife (*Warw*)	21	30	6	1360	177	56.66	6
J T Tyldesley (*Lancs*)	35	60	5	3041	221	55.29	9
R Abel (*Surrey*)	38	68	8	3309	247	55.15	7
S P Kinneir (*Warw*)	19	27	1	1354	215*	52.07	4
T W Hayward (*Surrey*)	36	58	8	2535	181	50.70	2
R E Foster (*Worcs*)	25	44	2	2128	136	50.66	6
C P McGahey (*Essex*)	24	43	5	1838	145*	48.36	5
A O Jones (*Notts*)	29	51	2	2292	249	46.77	5
E I M Barrett (*Hants*)	6	10	0	467	111	46.70	1
F L Fane (*Essex*)	13	25	2	1048	195	45.56	2
P F Warner (*Middx*)	22	39	2	1680	197*	45.40	3
F Mitchell (*Yorks*)	31	45	4	1807	162*	44.07	7
J Iremonger (*Notts*)	19	33	7	1108	133	42.61	4
G H Hirst (*Yorks*)	36	50	4	1950	214	42.39	3
C J B Wood (*Leics*)	28	52	3	2033	156	41.48	3

BOWLING	M	O	M	R	W	Avge
W Rhodes (*Yorks*)	37	1565	505	3797	251	15.12
G H Hirst (*Yorks*)	36	1135.3	261	2999	183	16.38
A Bird (*Worcs*)	17	366.2	106	882	48	18.37
W Mead (*Essex*)	27	1050.1	136	2407	129	18.65
T Soar (*Hants*)	8	157.3	43	415	22	18.86
E E Steel (*Lancs*)	8	313.1	68	849	44	19.29
A W Mold (*Lancs*)	15	381.2	70	1142	59	19.35
F W Tate (*Sussex*)	27	1135.5	329	2769	142	19.50
T W Hayward (*Surrey*)	36	195.5	39	613	30	20.43
J R Mason (*Kent*)	27	906	229	2413	118	20.44
B Cranfield (*Som*)	20	852	197	2534	122	20.77
R D Burrows (*Worcs*)	22	656.4	127	2020	96	21.04
S Hargreave (*Warw*)	19	1003.2	295	2324	110	21.12
S Haigh (*Yorks*)	22	417.3	87	1199	56	21.41
J H Sinclair (*Lon/SA*)	17	460.4	72	1698	79	21.49
A D Pougher (*Leics*)	8	154.5	40	435	20	21.75
W H Lockwood (*Surrey*)	23	579.3	122	1697	78	21.75
W G Grace (*London*)	19	459.1	128	1111	51	21.78
A E Trott (*Middx*)	29	1289.1	289	3835	176	21.78
W C Smith (*Surrey*)	8	283.1	90	728	33	22.06

First-class averages: 1902

BATTING	M	I	NO	Runs	HS	Avge	100s
A Shrewsbury (*Notts*)	22	32	7	1250	127*	50.00	5
V T Trumper (*Austr*)	36	53	0	2570	128	48.49	11
†K S Ranjitsinhji (*Sussex*)	18	26	2	1106	234*	46.08	3
†R Abel (*Surrey*)	41	64	8	2299	179	41.05	9
William Quaife (*Warw*)	27	38	5	1339	153*	40.57	3
†J T Tyldesley (*Lancs*)	33	51	3	1934	165	40.29	4
J Iremonger (*Notts*)	24	36	2	1358	146	39.94	4
J Douglas (*Middx*)	7	12	0	474	180	39.50	1
C J Burnup (*Kent*)	33	55	3	2048	161	39.38	6
E M Ashcroft (*Derbys*)	16	25	1	912	162	38.00	2
T L Taylor (*Yorks*)	28	43	3	1517	142*	37.92	5
W G Grace (*London*)	22	35	3	1187	131	37.09	2
R E Foster (*Worcs*)	10	17	2	551	109	36.73	1
†C B Fry (*Sussex*)	30	48	2	1625	159*	35.32	3
W Gunn (*Notts*)	17	24	1	807	120	35.08	3
P A Perrin (*Essex*)	22	38	6	1119	121	34.96	1
C A Ollivierre *Derbys*)	10	15	0	524	167	34.93	1
J A Dixon (*Notts*)	12	18	2	552	123	34.50	2
C P McGahey (*Essex*)	25	42	6	1240	126	34.44	2
†G L Jessop (*Gloucs*)	28	49	3	1562	126	33.95	4

BOWLING	M	O	M	R	W	Avge
G H Littlewood (*Lancs*)	2	83.2	27	228	21	10.85
H J Knutton (*Eng XI*)	1	45.2	13	117	10	11.70
S Webb (*Lancs*)	8	105.3	26	336	28	12.00
S Haigh (*Yorks*)	34	799	219	1984	158	12.55
†W Rhodes (*Yorks*)	37	1306.3	405	2801	213	13.15
T Marlow (*Leics*)	5	137.1	38	306	23	13.30
H Trumble (*Austr*)	20	912	292	1921	137	14.02
J Bean (*Sussex*)	6	82.5	34	163	11	14.81
C Blythe (*Kent*)	25	847	243	1965	127	15.47
†F W Tate (*Sussex*)	27	1183.2	359	2828	180	15.71
T G Wass (*Notts*)	21	803.2	188	2225	140	15.89
W Harrington (*Ireland*)	4	202	75	341	21	16.23
A Woodcock (*Leics*)	9	226.2	74	537	32	16.78
J R Mason (*Kent*)	28	628.5	218	1495	89	16.79
J V Saunders (*Austr*)	25	710	160	2085	123	16.95
S Santall (*Warw*)	18	386.1	148	816	48	17.00
†W H Lockwood (*Surrey*)	30	741.1	147	2142	124	17.27
E Robson (*Som*)	19	273	74	729	42	17.35
S Hargreave (*Warw*)	23	983.4	314	2021	115	17.57
A Hearne (*Kent*)	28	424.1	141	913	51	17.90

†Played for England but not featured above: F S Jackson, G H Hirst, A C MacLaren, L C Braund, L C H Palairet, A F A Lilley, T W Hayward and S F Barnes.

First-class averages: 1903

BATTING	M	I	NO	Runs	HS	Avge	100s
C B Fry (*Sussex*)	25	40	7	2683	234	81.30	9
K S Ranjitsinhji (*Sussex*)	28	41	7	1924	204	56.58	5
G H Hirst (*Yorks*)	30	44	5	1844	153	47.28	5
A J L Hill (*Hants*)	7	12	1	515	150	46.81	3
J Iremonger (*Notts*)	19	31	1	1380	210	46.00	4
A E Knight (*Leics*)	27	46	6	1834	229*	45.85	5
P A Perrin (*Essex*)	20	36	4	1428	170	44.62	4
J T Tyldesley (*Lancs*)	28	50	6	1955	248	44.43	2
A C MacLaren (*Lancs*)	30	52	8	1886	204	42.86	4
William Quaife (*Warw*)	21	30	4	1113	130	42.80	1
J R Gunn (*Notts*)	27	42	3	1665	294	42.69	3
H K Foster (*Worcs*)	22	41	3	1596	216	42.00	4
C M Wells (*Middx*)	9	13	4	371	82*	41.22	0
A O Jones (*Notts*)	23	38	2	1422	296	39.50	3
P F Warner (*Middx*)	21	33	4	1141	149	39.34	3
J A Lester (*Phil*)	13	23	3	786	126*	39.30	1
G L Jessop (*Gloucs*)	22	36	0	1382	286	38.38	2
G Brann (*Sussex*)	14	17	0	652	135	38.35	2
L O S Poidevin (*London*)	12	19	1	688	172*	38.22	1
W Gunn (*Notts*)	17	29	1	1011	139	36.10	2

BOWLING	M	O	M	R	W	Avge
J Hallows (*Lancs*)	8	119.4	33	304	26	11.69
W E Coleman (*MCC*)	3	43	7	125	10	12.50
W Ringrose (*Yorks*)	14	195.5	51	485	36	13.47
W Mead (*Essex*)	22	971.3	355	1791	131	13.67
C Blythe (*Kent*)	22	925.4	292	1953	142	13.75
W T Langford (*Hants*)	7	241.3	72	586	42	13.95
S Hargreave (*Warw*)	20	922.1	282	1879	134	14.02
C J Kortright (*Essex*)	16	118.2	18	398	28	14.21
W Rhodes (*Yorks*)	36	1378	425	2813	193	14.57
G H Hirst (*Yorks*)	30	817.5	230	1913	128	14.94
C J Posthuma (*London*)	5	107.2	22	346	23	15.04
J T Hearne (*Middx*)	26	906.1	313	2001	130	15.39
F Moorhouse (*Warw*)	18	373.1	115	870	55	15.81
H Wilson (*Worcs*)	2	56.3	12	159	10	15.90
J B King (*Philad*)	12	451.3	106	1253	78	16.06
F G Roberts (*Gloucs*)	17	595	184	1380	84	16.42
S Haigh (*Yorks*)	33	775.2	225	1854	112	16.55
A Hearne (*Kent*)	23	389.2	124	848	51	16.62
C M Wells (*Middx*)	9	176.4	35	448	26	17.23
H I Young (*Essex*)	20	389.2	102	897	52	17.25

First-class averages: 1904

BATTING	M	I	NO	Runs	HS	Avge	100s
K S Ranjitsinhji (*Sussex*)	23	34	6	2077	207*	74.17	8
C B Fry (*Sussex*)	29	42	2	2824	229	70.60	10
J T Tyldesley (*Lancs*)	30	44	5	2439	225	62.53	8
A O Jones (*Notts*)	21	34	5	1756	187	60.55	5
J Iremonger (*Notts*)	21	34	1	1983	272	60.09	6
T W Hayward (*Surrey*)	36	63	5	3170	205	54.65	11
G H Hirst (*Yorks*)	36	50	4	2501	157	54.36	9
P A Perrin (*Essex*)	19	32	4	1486	343*	53.07	5
William Quaife (*Warw*)	23	38	5	1689	200*	51.18	5
W H B Evans (*O U/Hts*)	11	19	1	861	115	47.83	2
F H Gillingham (*Essex*)	8	13	1	558	201	46.50	2
F S Jackson (*Yorks*)	17	25	2	1037	158	45.08	2
R H Spooner (*Lancs*)	31	46	3	1688	215	43.93	5
H K Foster (*Worcs*)	20	38	0	1635	119	43.02	5
J F Marsh (*C U*)	8	16	3	548	172*	42.15	2
A J L Hill (*Hants*)	11	18	1	698	117	41.05	2
L J Tancred (*SA*)	21	35	4	1269	113	40.93	4
P F Warner (*Middx*)	22	39	5	1390	163	40.88	3
J Douglas (*Middx*)	9	16	2	572	153	40.85	2
J R Mason (*Kent*)	15	24	3	853	138	40.61	4

BOWLING	M	O	M	R	W	Avge
W Huddleston (*Lancs*)	2	70	26	135	12	11.25
E Humphreys (*Kent*)	24	208.3	69	496	30	16.53
J N Crawford (*Surrey*)	9	262.5	79	745	44	16.93
W C Smith (*Surrey*)	15	400	102	1146	64	17.90
R O Schwarz (*SA*)	21	313.2	33	1187	65	18.26
E F Field (*Warw*)	6	96	24	277	15	18.46
J T Hearne (*Middx*)	32	1153.3	330	2732	145	18.84
A Hearne (*Kent*)	23	266	85	626	33	18.96
J E B B P Q C Dwyer (*Sussex*)	1	59	14	193	10	19.30
J Hallows (*Lancs*)	25	904.3	280	2092	108	19.37
C Blythe (*Kent*)	24	1024.2	274	2705	138	19.60
E G Dennett (*Gloucs*)	19	1018.4	282	2541	129	19.69
S Haigh (*Yorks*)	34	896.1	234	2402	121	19.85
J J Kotze (*Lon/SA*)	24	779.1	162	2403	121	19.85
C M Wells (*Middx*)	9	205	38	540	27	20.00
W R Cuttell (*Lancs*)	25	1021.2	345	2100	105	20.00
H Myers (*Yorks*)	30	572.5	119	1592	78	20.41
W Brearley (*Lancs*)	21	622	100	1978	95	20.82
A Warren (*Derbys*)	22	780	139	2597	124	20.94
G H Hirst (*Yorks*)	36	1033	219	2785	132	21.09

First-class averages: 1905

BATTING	M	I	NO	Runs	HS	Avge	100s
R E Foster (*Worcs*)	7	12	3	679	246*	75.44	1
†C B Fry (*Sussex*)	26	44	4	2801	233	70.02	10
William Quaife (*Warw*)	30	52	14	2060	255*	54.21	6
G H Hirst (*Yorks*)	35	52	10	2266	341	53.95	6
J G Greig (*Hants*)	10	18	2	804	187*	50.25	3
W W Armstrong (*Austr*)	29	45	7	1902	303*	50.05	4
E W Dillon (*Kent*)	16	28	1	1310	141	48.51	4
M A Noble (*Austr*)	30	46	2	2053	267	46.65	6
A J L Hill (*Hants*)	9	17	2	698	124	46.53	3
E W Mann (*C U*)	10	19	2	783	157	46.05	2
†T W Hayward (*Surrey*)	36	64	6	2592	129*	44.68	5
P F Warner (*Middx*)	19	35	0	1537	204	43.91	5
H K Foster (*Worcs*)	18	29	2	1164	180	43.11	2
C J B Wood (*Leics*)	26	44	3	1765	225*	43.04	4
L G Colbeck (*C U*)	8	15	2	552	120	42.46	2
†D Denton (*Yorks*)	37	60	3	2405	172	42.19	8
L G Wright (*Derbys*)	23	44	0	1855	195	42.15	4
A E M Whittle (*Warw*)	8	12	2	416	77*	41.60	0
E M Sprot	16	30	1	1206	141	41.58	2
J Douglas (*Middx*)	10	19	4	622	116*	41.46	1

BOWLING	M	O	M	R	W	Avge
A E Bailey (*Som*)	5	191.3	60	444	29	15.31
†S Haigh (*Yorks*)	37	831.5	220	1983	129	15.37
W C Smith (*Nrthts*)	15	378.5	82	998	59	16.91
†W Rhodes (*Yorks*)	38	1241.3	310	3085	182	16.95
G J Thompson (*Nrthts*)	22	734	155	2215	126	17.57
G G Napier (*C U/Mx*)	11	384.1	84	1146	64	17.90
W S Lees (*Surrey*)	34	1388.2	387	3476	193	18.01
F Laver (*Austr*)	26	848.1	245	2092	115	18.19
W W Armstrong (*Austr*)	29	1001.2	298	2221	122	18.20
J N Crawford (*Surrey*)	13	306.5	72	868	47	18.46
W Ringrose (*Yorks*)	20	447.4	82	1402	73	19.20
†W Brearley (*Lancs*)	25	1049.4	191	3486	181	19.25
H Myers (*Yorks*)	34	465	90	1399	72	19.43
E G Martin (*O U*)	8	2302	56	625	32	19.53
W Cook (*Lancs*)	10	272.3	48	900	46	19.57
J W Keene (*Worcs*)	4	74	9	217	11	19.72
†G H Hirst (*Yorks*)	35	781.4	167	2194	110	19.94
J T Hearne (*Middx*)	26	689.1	207	1701	85	20.01
W P Howell (*Austr*)	19	497	148	1215	68	20.29
A Cotter (*Austr*)	28	735.1	121	2429	119	20.41

†Played for England but not featured above: F S Jackson, J T Tyldesley, R H Spooner, A C MacLaren, E G Arnold, B T J Bosanquet, A F A Lilley, A O Jones, J R Gunn, A Warren, G L Jessop and C Blythe.

First-class averages: 1906

BATTING	M	I	NO	Runs	HS	Avge	100s
C J Burnup (Kent)	13	21	3	1207	179	67.05	4
T W Hayward (Surrey)	37	61	8	3518	219	66.37	13
K L Hutchings (Kent)	21	34	4	1597	176	53.23	4
E G Arnold (Worcs)	21	39	4	1767	166	50.48	6
J Iremonger (Notts)	23	43	6	1794	200*	48.48	4
P A Perrin (Essex)	23	43	3	1893	150	47.32	5
J T Tyldesley (Lancs)	31	52	3	2270	295*	46.32	4
G H Hirst (Yorks)	35	58	6	2385	169	45.86	6
E G Hayes (Surrey)	35	56	5	2309	218	45.27	7
F H Gillingham (Essex)	10	17	2	679	102	45.26	1
A O Jones (Notts)	21	39	3	1560	105	43.33	1
E W Dillon (Kent)	9	15	2	562	85	43.23	0
W B Burns (Worcs)	18	32	4	1206	165	43.07	3
P F Warner (Middx)	17	33	2	1299	137	41.90	2
T S Fishwick (Warw)	16	23	1	919	135	41.77	2
J H G Devey (Warw)	20	34	4	1237	110*	41.23	2
D Denton (Yorks)	36	60	4	2287	157*	40.83	7
J B Hobbs (Surrey)	31	53	6	1913	162*	40.70	4
J R Mason (Kent)	12	18	2	649	88	40.56	0
C S Baker (Warw)	18	25	4	848	144	40.38	2

BOWLING	M	O	M	R	W	Avge
W Huddleston (Lancs)	9	234.1	65	613	50	12.26
W R Cuttell (Lancs)	16	442.1	170	909	67	13.56
S Haigh (Yorks)	36	971.3	209	2540	174	14.59
N R Udal (O U)	5	146.1	53	434	29	14.96
G H Hirst (Yorks)	35	1306.1	271	3434	208	16.50
A W Hallam (Notts)	24	937.1	302	2133	168	16.56
E G Dennett (Gloucs)	22	1145.5	256	3096	175	17.69
W R Gregson (Lancs)	5	151.1	27	428	24	17.83
C Baker (Nrthts)	3	50.4	9	198	11	18.00
W Bestwick (Derbys)	20	776.1	186	2123	115	18.46
J Burrough (Grace's XI)	1	59	19	186	10	18.60
T G Wass (Notts)	18	609.2	130	1888	100	18.88
A F Morcom (C U)	7	255.4	57	700	37	18.91
H J Goodwin (C U)	5	78.2	12	286	15	19.06
F A Tarrant (Middx)	25	626	135	1740	91	19.12
G Deyes (Yorks)	4	64.3	14	192	10	19.20
A Kermode (Lancs)	20	592.2	149	1724	89	19.37
W Brearley (Lancs)	6	253.4	36	878	45	19.51
A E E Vogler (Middx)	11	374.1	67	1234	63	19.58
F Harry (Lancs)	27	648.1	200	1708	87	19.63

First-class averages: 1907

BATTING	M	I	NO	Runs	HS	Avge	100s
†C B Fry (Sussex)	19	34	3	1449	187	46.74	4
F H B Champain (Gloucs)	6	11	1	466	149	46.60	1
P F Warner (Middx)	27	47	6	1891	149	46.12	3
†T W Hayward (Surrey)	34	58	6	2353	161	45.25	7
A E Lawton (Derbys)	12	21	1	835	129	41.75	3
G N Foster (O U/Worcs)	18	33	4	1182	163	40.75	2
H K Foster (Worcs)	19	33	3	1127	152	37.56	3
J B Hobbs (Surrey)	37	63	6	2135	166*	37.45	4
A J L Hill (Hants)	11	20	1	711	116	37.42	1
P A Perrin (Essex)	20	34	2	1194	117	37.31	3
†R E Foster (Worcs)	16	25	1	888	174	37.00	2
J T Tyldesley (Lancs)	34	63	5	2132	209	36.75	5
†G L Jessop (Gloucs)	28	48	0	1754	240	36.54	3
B T J Bosanquet (Middx)	6	10	0	358	78	35.80	0
E G Hayes (Surrey)	32	53	1	1857	202	35.71	3
F L Bowley (Worcs)	15	23	1	784	110	35.63	2
Jas Seymour (Kent)	29	46	1	1548	204	34.40	2
J Vine (Sussex)	29	52	5	1580	112	33.61	3
E M Sprot (Hants)	22	40	2	1272	125	33.47	2
R H Spooner (Lancs)	9	14	0	462	134	33.00	1

BOWLING	M	O	M	R	W	Avge
S G Smith (Nrthts)	1	35.5	8	83	10	8.30
R O Schwarz (SA)	26	711.3	153	1616	137	11.79
A W Hallam (Notts)	24	937.1	302	2133	168	12.69
S Haigh (Yorks)	22	591.3	146	1308	102	12.82
J T Newstead (Yorks)	5	156.2	54	310	24	12.91
T G Wass (Notts)	22	885	218	2328	163	14.28
W Huddleston (Lancs)	19	452.3	116	1092	76	14.36
G C White (SA)	25	276.5	51	824	56	14.71
R G Barnes (O U)	6	86.4	24	180	12	15.00
†G H Hirst (Yorks)	36	1167.4	269	2859	188	15.20
†C Blythe (Kent)	27	1136.1	291	2822	183	15.42
H A Gilbert (O U)	8	285.4	99	683	44	15.52
W Rhodes (Yorks)	32	1067.1	231	2757	177	15.57
A E E Vogler (SA)	25	592	127	1859	119	15.62
F A Tarrant (Middx)	32	1085.5	244	2874	183	15.70
G A Faulkner (SA)	25	386.5	82	1013	64	15.82
E G Dennett (Gloucs)	26	1216.2	305	3227	201	16.05
A Fielder (Kent)	29	977.3	197	2773	172	16.12
F Harry (Lancs)	24	645.1	218	1393	84	16.58
S Santall (Warw)	20	738	192	1679	101	16.62

†Played for England but not featured above: L C Braund, A F A Lilley, J T Tyldesley, J N Crawford and N A Knox.

First-class averages: 1908

BATTING	M	I	NO	Runs	HS	Avge	100s
B J T Bosanquet (Middx)	14	22	2	1081	214	54.05	3
C B Fry (Sussex)	13	20	1	1000	214	52.63	3
H K Foster (Worcs)	14	24	1	1105	215	48.04	2
T W Hayward (Surrey)	37	52	1	2337	175	45.82	5
P F Warner (Middx)	29	45	5	1822	120	45.55	5
K S Ranjitsinhji (Sussex)	18	28	3	1138	200	45.52	3
J T Tyldesley (Lancs)	26	45	2	1891	243	43.97	6
G L Jessop (Gloucs)	26	48	3	1885	164	41.88	4
F A Tarrant (Middx)	33	49	7	1724	157	41.04	5
A Marshal (Surrey)	33	50	2	1931	176	40.22	5
F H Gillingham (Essex)	20	29	3	1033	194	39.73	4
A J L Hill (Hants)	10	17	2	588	110*	39.30	1
G H Hirst (Yorks)	35	50	9	1598	128*	38.97	1
J Douglas (Middx)	9	14	1	501	109	38.53	1
A C S Glover (Warw)	17	28	7	807	117*	38.42	2
J R Mason (Kent)	9	14	2	459	112	38.25	1
L J Moon (Middx)	16	25	1	918	135	38.25	2
D Denton (Yorks)	36	57	6	1925	133	37.74	3
J B Hobbs (Surrey)	36	53	2	1904	161	37.33	6
J Sharp (Lancs)	26	45	2	1598	136	37.16	3

BOWLING	M	O	M	R	W	Avge
J B King (Philad)	10	338.3	103	958	87	11.01
T C Ross (Ireland)	2	42.4	10	127	10	12.70
W Ringrose (Scotld)	1	47	10	146	11	13.27
S Haigh (Yorks)	26	623.2	176	1380	103	13.39
G H Hirst (Yorks)	35	1121.5	290	2445	174	14.05
S E Busher (Sy/Worcs)	3	104.3	16	292	20	14.60
A S Kennedy (Hants)	4	67.5	17	162	11	14.72
E C Kirk (Surrey)	5	206	63	470	30	15.66
W C Smith (Surrey)	15	374	107	895	57	15.70
G L Jessop (Gloucs)	26	141	40	348	22	15.81
W Rhodes (Yorks)	36	804.3	233	1855	115	16.13
W Brearley (Lancs)	20	856.2	165	2636	163	16.17
J A Lester (Philad)	10	48.4	7	164	10	16.40
J T Newstead (Yorks)	36	1045.3	287	2311	140	16.50
F A Tarrant (Middx)	33	1124.2	297	2819	169	16.68
C Blythe (Kent)	28	1366.4	386	3326	197	16.88
F E Woolley (Kent)	30	526.5	139	1355	80	16.93
F Harry (Lancs)	10	236.2	86	531	31	17.12
W Huddleston (Lancs)	14	431.1	126	1014	59	17.26
F R Foster (Warw)	5	170.5	44	397	23	17.26

First-class averages: 1909

BATTING	M	I	NO	Runs	HS	Avge	100s
J R Mason (Kent)	14	14	2	783	179*	65.25	3
W Bardsley (Austr)	33	49	4	2072	219	46.04	6
F B Roberts (Gloucs)	7	11	0	486	129	44.18	1
A P Day (Kent)	20	24	1	1014	177	44.08	3
W W Armstrong (Austr)	29	41	8	1451	110*	43.96	3
V S Ransford (Austr)	32	44	4	1736	190	43.40	6
†T W Hayward (Surrey)	20	37	4	1359	204*	41.18	3
†J B Hobbs (Surrey)	31	54	2	2114	205	40.65	6
†W Rhodes (Yorks)	37	59	7	2094	199	40.26	5
H E W Prest (C U/Kt)	7	10	1	360	57	40.00	0
†C B Fry (Hants)	14	25	3	834	132	37.90	1
†J Sharp (Lancs)	29	46	4	1580	183	37.61	5
C P Mead (Hants)	24	41	2	1459	114	37.41	1
C V L Hooman (O U)	10	17	0	633	117	37.23	2
E Humphreys (Kent)	30	43	4	1437	208	36.84	2
D Denton (Yorks)	35	55	3	1897	184	36.48	5
R R Relf (Sussex)	32	49	3	1672	272*	36.34	3
William Quaife (Warw)	23	41	8	1199	147*	36.33	2
†K L Hutchings (Kent)	35	48	1	1697	155	36.10	3
J Vine (Sussex)	32	50	7	1549	121	36.02	1

BOWLING	M	O	M	R	W	Avge
R T Crawford (L G XI)	1	44	13	108	11	9.81
†G L Jessop (Gloucs)	12	53	13	119	10	11.90
W C Smith (Surrey)	18	516.5	142	1181	95	12.43
J S Heap (Lancs)	15	246.2	78	557	40	13.92
†S Haigh (Yorks)	32	844.2	205	1702	122	13.95
†C Blythe (Kent)	32	1273.5	343	3128	215	14.54
†G J Thompson (Nrthts)	26	905.5	228	2392	163	14.67
F Laver (Austr)	17	479.5	158	999	68	14.69
H A Gilbert (O U)	11	407.5	128	928	61	15.21
†S F Barnes (Eng)	6	250.3	83	537	34	15.79
†W Rhodes (Yorks)	37	873.1	205	2241	141	15.89
F H Turner (O U)	5	79.2	14	272	17	16.00
T Rushby (Surrey)	23	709	171	1914	119	16.08
A E Lewis (Som)	14	455.5	124	1207	74	16.31
W W Armstrong (Austr)	29	858	274	1854	113	16.40
†W Brearley (Lancs)	17	622.5	95	2000	121	16.52
W Huddleston (Lancs)	26	696.4	227	1393	83	16.78
H Dean (Lancs)	22	702.1	199	1745	102	17.10
C G Macartney (Austr)	28	480.5	139	1143	64	17.85
J H B Lockhart (C U)	7	256	26	881	49	17.97

†Played for England but not featured above: A F A Lilley, R H Spooner, J T Tyldesley, A O Jones, A C MacLaren, G H Hirst, G Gunn, E G Hayes, J H King, A E Relf, P F Warner, D W Carr and F E Woolley.

First-class averages: 1910

BATTING	M	I	NO	Runs	HS	Avge	100s
J T Tyldesley (Lancs)	35	51	2	2265	158	46.22	7
K L Hutchings (Kent)	29	42	2	1654	144	41.35	5
P F Warner (Middx)	27	44	4	1646	150*	41.15	5
D C Collins (C U)	10	15	4	443	72*	40.27	0
C J B Wood (Leics)	19	35	2	1250	99	37.87	0
J Sharp (Lancs)	33	45	2	1626	150	37.81	4
F H Knott (Kent)	6	10	1	332	114	36.88	1
A Hartley (Lancs)	32	47	4	1585	234	36.86	3
H K Foster (Worcs)	16	28	0	1032	126	36.85	3
James Seymour (Kent)	29	46	4	1546	193	36.80	3
E Humphreys (Kent)	29	46	2	1618	200*	36.77	3
F A Tarrant (Middx)	26	41	2	1425	142	36.53	3
A C Johnston (Hants)	21	37	5	1158	130	36.18	1
C Charlesworth (Warw)	20	36	2	1196	216	35.17	3
R H Spooner (Lancs)	13	22	4	631	200*	35.05	1
G N Foster (Worcs)	20	35	4	1067	129*	34.41	2
G Curgenven (Derbys)	7	11	0	371	109	33.72	2
A O Jones (Notts)	21	35	1	1144	121	33.64	3
G L Jessop (Gloucs)	21	36	2	1142	165	33.58	4
E G Arnold (Worcs)	23	41	2	1305	215	33.46	2

BOWLING	M	O	M	R	W	Avge
J T Hearne (Middx)	21	752	253	1523	119	12.79
W C Smith (Surrey)	36	1423.3	420	3225	247	13.05
F H Hunt (Worcs)	3	52.4	14	136	10	13.60
D W Carr (Kent)	10	309.2	72	895	63	14.20
C Blythe (Kent)	25	1041.3	274	2497	175	14.26
F E Woolley (Kent)	31	731.3	177	1973	136	14.50
G H Hirst (Yorks)	36	1021.2	252	2426	164	14.79
H Dean (Lancs)	29	966.3	279	2113	137	15.42
P R Le Couteur (O U)	14	331.5	50	1151	72	15.98
F A Tarrant (Middx)	26	932.3	270	2169	134	16.18
J Iremonger (Notts)	21	618.3	192	1358	79	17.18
J R Mason (Kent)	9	74.3	14	208	12	17.33
W J Fairservice (Kent)	18	256.4	60	652	37	17.62
C P Buckenham (Essex)	24	658.1	112	2085	118	17.66
John Seymour (Nrthts)	20	194.1	34	607	34	17.85
G J Thompson (Nrthts)	25	829.5	181	2304	129	17.86
G J W Platt (Surrey)	14	303.5	72	913	51	17.90
W Huddleston (Lancs)	28	700.4	196	1561	87	17.94
J S Heap (Lancs)	21	414	116	1032	57	18.10
W Mead (Essex)	21	642.2	154	1604	88	18.22

First-class averages: 1911

BATTING	M	I	NO	Runs	HS	Avge	100s
C B Fry (Hants)	15	26	2	1728	258*	72.00	7
C P Mead (Hants)	29	52	5	2562	223	54.51	9
R H Spooner (Lancs)	26	45	0	2312	224	51.37	7
P A Perrin (Essex)	15	27	2	1281	114	51.24	6
S P Kinneir (Warw)	20	36	3	1629	268*	49.36	6
T W Hayward (Surrey)	30	51	6	2149	202	47.75	5
P F Warner (Middx)	31	51	5	2123	244	46.15	5
F A Tarrant (Middx)	29	48	4	2030	207*	46.13	5
J Hardstaff snr (Notts)	21	40	6	1547	145	45.50	5
C J B Wood (Leics)	23	44	7	1614	117*	43.62	5
Jas Seymour (Kent)	28	48	6	1825	218*	43.45	5
A P Day (Kent)	12	22	5	730	135*	42.94	2
J W Hearne (Middx)	27	41	3	1627	234*	42.81	4
J R Gunn (Notts)	21	35	3	1368	160	42.75	3
F R Foster (Warw)	23	40	2	1614	200	42.47	3
G L Jessop (Gloucs)	26	49	4	1907	153	42.37	7
D Denton (Yorks)	33	57	4	2232	137*	42.11	6
J B Hobbs (Surrey)	36	60	3	2376	154*	41.68	4
E S Litteljohn (Middx)	9	12	2	414	110	41.40	3
H S Bush (Surrey)	12	19	2	703	135	41.35	2

BOWLING	M	O	M	R	W	Avge
W Huddleston (Lancs)	5	156.2	53	321	29	11.06
A E Trott (MCC)	2	51.4	10	175	12	14.58
R T Crawford (Leics)	3	117	35	328	22	14.90
E Smith snr (L G XI)	2	53.5	6	194	13	14.92
J F Ireland (C U)	8	147.1	51	405	27	15.00
E Humphreys (Kent)	29	178.5	31	534	33	16.18
J H B Lockhart (C U)	6	144.1	27	498	30	16.60
G J Thompson (Nrthts)	22	735.5	199	1889	113	16.71
W East (Nrthts)	17	441.1	135	988	59	16.74
A P Day (Kent)	12	209.5	37	583	34	17.14
S Haigh (Yorks)	31	674.3	124	1684	97	17.36
H Dean (Lancs)	28	1295.5	324	3191	183	17.43
J T Hearne (Middx)	24	1041	345	2134	122	17.49
A R Litteljohn (Middx)	7	335.1	72	904	51	17.72
D W Carr (Kent)	9	303	52	985	55	17.90
A J Evans (O U/Hts)	9	218	75	575	32	17.96
P M Fairclough (Lancs)	7	164.2	34	414	23	18.00
J B Hobbs (Surrey)	36	162.1	29	523	28	18.67
J S Denton (Nrthts)	18	122	13	461	24	19.20
F A Tarrant (Middx)	29	860.1	196	2135	111	19.23

First-class averages: 1912

BATTING	M	I	NO	Runs	HS	Avge	100s
†C B Fry (*Hants*)	23	31	3	1592	203*	56.85	5
A C Johnston (*Hants*)	14	20	1	1044	175	54.94	3
W Bardsley (*Austr*)	36	52	6	2365	184*	51.41	8
C P Mead (*Hants*)	34	52	14	1933	160*	50.86	7
C G Macartney (*Austr*)	33	49	1	2187	208	48.06	6
J Sharp (*Lancs*)	24	34	3	1375	211	44.35	4
E S Litteljohn (*Middx*)	6	10	1	389	141*	43.22	1
K S Ranjitsinhji (*Sussex*)	19	28	2	1113	176	42.80	4
D Denton (*Yorks*)	38	54	4	2127	221	42.54	6
†R H Spooner (*Lancs*)	33	49	3	1939	130	42.15	7
†F E Woolley (*Kent*)	35	49	5	1827	117	41.52	2
E I M Barrett (*Hants*)	32	44	10	1381	138*	40.61	3
†E G Hayes (*Surrey*)	31	46	1	1812	143*	40.26	4
P A Perrin (*Essex*)	16	28	2	1009	245	38.80	3
†J B Hobbs (*Surrey*)	38	60	6	2042	111	37.81	3
J T Tyldesley (*Lancs*)	24	32	1	1147	174	37.00	3
G E V Crutchley (*O U/Mx*)	10	15	2	478	99*	36.76	0
William Quaife (*Warw*)	23	40	8	1163	134	36.34	1
†J W Hearne (*Middx*)	33	52	10	1502	123*	35.76	1
A W Nourse (*SA*)	35	55	5	1762	213*	35.24	4

BOWLING	M	O	M	R	W	Avge
A Morris (*M Co*)	2	41.5	14	80	10	8.00
C K Langley (*Warw*)	8	70.2	21	197	19	10.36
E C Baker (*C U/Sx*)	4	110	27	232	22	10.54
M Falcon (*MCC*)	5	89.1	25	237	22	10.77
†S F Barnes (*Eng*)	11	386.4	137	782	69	11.33
D W Carr (*Kent*)	11	258.5	47	733	61	12.01
C Blythe (*Kent*)	28	719.3	241	2183	178	12.26
†S Haigh (*Yorks*)	37	813.4	245	1541	125	12.32
S G Smith (*Nrthts*)	22	559	165	1269	100	12.69
H C McDonnell (*Hants*)	8	60.3	10	194	15	12.93
†H Dean (*Lancs*)	27	1060	356	2216	162	13.67
†F E Woolley (*Kent*)	35	706	187	1802	126	14.30
F A Tarrant (*Middx*)	31	940.4	261	2070	140	14.78
H J B Preston (*Kent*)	3	83.2	21	165	11	15.00
W C Hands (*Warw*)	11	114.3	37	257	17	15.11
S J Pegler (*SA*)	34	1286.5	352	2885	189	15.26
G A Faulkner (*SA*)	36	1015.1	207	2514	163	15.42
E G Dennett (*Gloucs*)	18	881.1	245	2129	137	15.54
J T Hearne (*Middx*)	25	696.2	248	1211	77	15.72
W Huddleston (*Lancs*)	23	678.3	194	1495	95	15.73

†Played for England but not featured above: W Rhodes, F R Foster, E J Smith, G L Jessop, P F Warner, J W H T Douglas, J W Hitch and W Brearley.

First-class averages: 1913

BATTING	M	I	NO	Runs	HS	Avge	100s
C P Mead (*Hants*)	32	60	8	2627	171*	50.51	9
J B Hobbs (*Surrey*)	32	57	5	2605	184	50.09	9
G Gunn (*Notts*)	22	39	5	1697	170	49.91	6
E L Kidd (*Middx*)	14	24	3	1041	150	49.57	3
L H Tennyson (*Hants*)	10	19	1	832	116	46.22	3
F E Woolley (*Kent*)	29	45	6	1760	224*	45.12	4
R B Lagden (*C U*)	11	20	1	847	153	44.57	3
J W Hearne (*Middx*)	29	49	3	2036	189	44.26	6
J R Gunn (*Notts*)	21	38	6	1405	126	43.90	3
G N Foster (*Worcs*)	7	12	0	500	175	41.66	2
H T W Hardinge (*Kent*)	32	56	7	2037	168	41.57	7
F A Tarrant (*Middx*)	26	42	2	1630	142	40.75	3
H S Harrison (*Surrey*)	24	41	9	1293	138*	40.40	1
F L Bowley (*Worcs*)	21	38	0	1508	201	39.68	4
William Quaife (*Warw*)	25	46	5	1595	129*	38.90	6
J T Tyldesley (*Lancs*)	25	43	1	1634	210	38.90	4
P R Johnson (*Som*)	10	20	1	734	105	38.73	2
Jas Seymour (*Kent*)	35	60	6	2088	124	38.66	5
S G Smith (*Nrthts*)	24	43	2	1522	133	37.12	4
P F Warner (*Middx*)	20	31	2	1072	125	36.96	3

BOWLING	M	O	M	R	W	Avge
S F Barnes (*Players*)	4	147.1	50	351	35	10.02
E B Alletson (*Notts*)	19	54.2	14	120	10	12.00
H L Simms (*Sussex*)	6	126.3	27	369	24	15.37
B G V Melle (*O U*)	9	350.2	105	875	55	15.90
R W Sievwright (*Scot*)	2	91	15	240	15	16.00
C Blythe (*Kent*)	34	1120.2	289	2729	167	16.34
N J Holloway (*Sussex*)	12	336.5	81	931	55	16.92
A Drake (*Yorks*)	32	818	225	1965	116	16.93
F A Tarrant (*Middx*)	26	986.3	246	2323	136	17.08
S G Smith (*Nrthts*)	24	860	273	1915	111	17.25
W C Smith (*Surrey*)	13	462.2	125	1127	65	17.33
G J Thompson (*Nrthts*)	23	978.4	254	2569	148	17.35
M W Tate (*Sussex*)	4	71	22	193	11	17.54
A E Relf (*Sussex*)	34	1220.1	408	2552	141	18.09
D W Carr (*Kent*)	11	302.1	47	1102	60	18.36
H Dean (*Lancs*)	21	962.5	247	2260	123	18.37
M W Booth (*Yorks*)	35	1156.5	185	3342	181	18.46
J W Hitch (*Surrey*)	30	958.4	169	3228	174	18.55
F E Woolley (*Kent*)	29	627.5	176	1542	83	18.57
A Morton (*Derbys*)	16	498.1	136	1151	61	18.86

First-class averages: 1914

BATTING	M	I	NO	Runs	HS	Avge	100s
J W Hearne (*Middx*)	26	43	8	2116	204	60.45	8
J B Hobbs (*Surrey*)	29	48	2	2697	226	58.63	11
C P Mead (*Hants*)	31	53	5	2476	213	51.58	7
J R Gunn (*Notts*)	20	34	5	1358	154*	46.82	3
F A Tarrant (*Middx*)	26	44	4	1879	250*	45.82	3
F E Woolley (*Kent*)	31	52	2	2272	160*	45.44	6
R R Relf (*Sussex*)	15	24	1	989	130	43.00	3
S G Smith (*Nrthts*)	21	34	2	1373	177	42.90	1
A Ducat (*Surrey*)	25	38	6	1370	118	42.81	4
J T Tyldesley (*Lancs*)	26	47	5	1754	253	41.76	4
G H Hirst (*Yorks*)	30	46	6	1670	146	41.75	3
D J Knight (*O U/Sy*)	20	31	2	1204	130	41.51	3
P A Perrin (*Essex*)	20	34	2	1261	126	39.40	2
J Hardstaff snr (*Notts*)	19	34	4	1178	213*	39.26	3
W P Robertson (*Middx*)	11	17	2	580	130	38.66	1
H T W Hardinge (*Kent*)	29	48	1	1768	183	37.61	4
E H Hendren (*Middx*)	22	30	4	968	133*	37.23	3
S Coe (*Leics*)	23	39	5	1258	252*	37.00	3
A P Day (*Kent*)	11	18	1	620	108	36.47	1
F H Gillingham (*Essex*)	9	15	2	472	121*	36.30	1

BOWLING	M	O	M	R	W	Avge
E Smith jnr (*Yorks*)	3	48	10	126	10	12.60
C Blythe (*Kent*)	29	1008.4	280	2583	170	15.19
A Drake (*Yorks*)	31	1017.2	283	2418	158	15.30
C H Parkin (*Lancs*)	6	202.4	53	535	34	15.73
S Santall (*Warw*)	10	117	29	299	19	15.73
F S Gough-Calthorpe (*C U*)	8	164.3	40	417	26	16.03
S G Smith (*Nrthts*)	21	687.1	208	1707	105	16.25
J Horsley (*Derbys*)	13	320.1	80	915	56	16.33
J C White (*Som*)	13	615.2	167	1409	85	16.57
M Falcon (*Gents*)	2	78.4	15	287	17	16.88
H C McDonnell (*Hants*)	8	167.2	20	609	35	17.40
J Burrough (*Army*)	2	55	6	246	14	17.57
M W Booth (*Yorks*)	31	983.5	178	2803	157	17.85
W Rhodes (*Yorks*)	31	840.4	214	2157	118	18.27
A G Slater (*Derbys*)	20	477.2	125	1264	69	18.31
C P Buckenham (*Essex*)	5	133.5	15	477	26	18.34
A Callington (*Leics*)	10	119.5	26	314	17	18.47
F R Foster (*Warw*)	25	879.2	214	2272	123	18.47
A Jaques (*Hants*)	28	926.4	244	2187	117	18.69
F A Tarrant (*Middx*)	26	1132.1	270	2601	138	18.84

First-class averages: 1919

BATTING	M	I	NO	Runs	HS	Avge	100s
G Gunn (*Notts*)	15	25	2	1451	185*	63.08	5
E H Hendren (*Middx*)	23	34	7	1655	214	61.29	5
J N Crawford (*Surrey*)	8	12	4	488	144*	61.00	1
J B Hobbs (*Surrey*)	30	49	6	2594	205*	60.32	8
C P Mead (*Hants*)	23	38	7	1720	207	55.48	3
A Ducat (*Surrey*)	23	35	3	1695	306*	52.96	4
J W Hearne (*Middx*)	21	35	7	1380	218*	49.28	4
W R D Payton (*Notts*)	15	20	6	671	84*	47.92	0
H T W Hardinge (*Kent*)	17	26	3	1101	172*	47.86	2
J R Gunn (*Notts*)	15	24	5	903	111*	47.52	2
J H Naumann (*C U*)	7	10	1	413	134*	45.88	1
A E Dipper (*Gloucs*)	19	34	5	1329	169*	45.82	4
D R Knight (*O U/Sy*)	23	38	3	1588	146	45.37	7
H Sutcliffe (*Yorks*)	31	45	4	1839	174	44.85	5
C A G Russell (*Essex*)	19	33	2	1387	160	44.74	4
P A Perrin (*Essex*)	15	24	5	850	126	44.73	3
J W H Makepeace (*Lancs*)	25	45	4	1814	171	44.24	4
G E Tyldesley (*Lancs*)	24	40	3	1635	174*	44.18	3
P Holmes (*Yorks*)	32	48	5	1886	140	43.86	5
J S F Morrison (*C U*)	9	12	0	524	168	43.66	1

BOWLING	M	O	M	R	W	Avge
N Hardy (*Som*)	4	81.5	16	234	18	13.00
W Rhodes (*Yorks*)	33	1048.3	305	2365	164	14.42
J C White (*Som*)	19	880	243	1913	128	14.94
C H Parkin (*Lancs*)	6	256	58	661	41	16.12
E F Field (*Warw*)	5	137.2	32	378	23	16.43
H L Collins (*AIF*)	27	728.5	164	1755	106	16.55
F E Woolley (*Kent*)	20	956.2	277	2196	128	17.15
S T Freeman (*Foster*)	3	55	6	173	10	17.30
J S Heap (*Lancs*)	16	440.4	105	1147	66	17.37
E R Wilson (*Yorks*)	11	321.5	108	699	40	17.47
V W C Jupp (*Sussex*)	10	105.2	16	342	19	18.00
J M Gregory (*AIF*)	25	830	124	2384	131	18.19
R Kilner (*Yorks*)	32	377	124	824	45	18.31
L Cook (*Lancs*)	6	242.2	73	557	30	18.56
J Horsley (*Derbys*)	12	205	39	669	36	18.58
W Wells (*Nrthts*)	7	266.5	49	670	36	18.61
W Bestwick (*Derbys*)	15	564.4	97	1676	90	18.62
A Waddington (*Yorks*)	20	718.1	186	1874	100	18.74
A C Williams (*Yorks*)	9	160.2	32	472	25	18.88
H A Gilbert (*Gents*)	5	181.5	41	540	28	19.28

First-class averages: 1920

BATTING	M	I	NO	Runs	HS	Avge	100s
E H Hendren (*Middx*)	30	47	6	2520	232	61.46	6
J B Hobbs (*Surrey*)	31	50	2	2827	215	58.89	11
H Ashton (*C U/Ex*)	8	14	2	691	236*	57.58	2
J W Hearne (*Middx*)	30	46	7	2148	215*	55.07	6
F H Gillingham (*Essex*)	8	15	2	671	151	51.61	2
P Holmes (*Yorks*)	34	51	6	2254	302*	50.08	7
C P Mead (*Hants*)	26	44	6	1887	178*	49.65	6
C A G Russell (*Essex*)	33	56	1	2432	197	44.21	3
G Brown (*Hants*)	27	45	2	1889	232*	43.93	6
G W Stephens (*Warw*)	9	15	1	612	111	43.71	1
H W Lee (*Middx*)	23	39	4	1518	221*	43.37	5
J R Gunn (*Notts*)	20	35	5	1299	131	43.30	4
J W H Makepeace (*Lancs*)	28	45	3	1762	152	41.95	3
G E Tyldesley (*Lancs*)	29	43	4	1604	244	41.12	3
F E Woolley (*Kent*)	31	50	3	1924	158	40.93	5
A P F Chapman (*C U*)	14	24	2	873	118	39.68	3
A Sandham (*Surrey*)	27	45	2	1694	167*	39.39	2
A Ducat (*Surrey*)	23	38	5	1245	203	37.72	3
Jas Seymour (*Kent*)	24	40	5	1291	123	36.91	2
A E Dipper (*Gloucs*)	21	35	2	1210	123	36.66	2

BOWLING	M	O	M	R	W	Avge
J B Hobbs (*Surrey*)	31	83	21	201	17	11.82
W Rhodes (*Yorks*)	34	1028.4	291	2123	161	13.18
C S Marriott (*C U/La*)	9	339.2	100	687	52	13.21
E R Wilson (*Yorks*)	12	530	210	886	64	13.84
M B Burrows (*O U*)	5	48.5	8	155	11	14.09
F E Woolley (*Kent*)	31	1135.4	315	2633	185	14.23
P T Mills (*Gloucs*)	20	308.2	74	748	52	14.38
L Cook (*Lancs*)	29	1069.4	275	2322	156	14.88
C W L Parker (*Gloucs*)	20	861.1	274	1974	125	15.79
J C White (*Yorks*)	23	1045	286	2216	138	16.05
H Dean (*Lancs*)	27	892.4	232	2004	124	16.16
J Bridges (*Som*)	20	553.4	164	1400	86	16.27
M L Hambling (*Som*)	6	93.5	20	249	15	16.60
A Waddington (*Yorks*)	29	972	264	2368	141	16.79
C H Parkin (*Lancs*)	10	391.1	77	1111	64	17.35
D R Jardine (*O U*)	8	71.3	17	226	13	17.38
W J Fairservice (*Kent*)	26	847.3	211	1973	113	17.46
A P Freeman (*Kent*)	27	672.3	181	1790	102	17.54
G R Cox (*Sussex*)	32	873.4	246	1936	110	17.60
R H B Bettington (*O U*)	12	355.2	73	1094	62	17.64

First-class averages: 1921

BATTING	M	I	NO	Runs	HS	Avge	100s
†C P Mead (*Hants*)	33	52	6	3179	280*	69.10	10
C G Macartney (*Austr*)	31	41	2	2317	345	59.42	8
†C A G Russell (*Essex*)	25	44	3	2236	273	54.53	8
W Bardsley (*Austr*)	30	41	4	2005	209	54.18	8
T F Shepherd (*Surrey*)	26	40	4	1907	212	52.97	6
†H T W Hardinge (*Kent*)	29	52	7	2339	207	51.97	9
J L Bryan (*C U/Kt*)	24	40	3	1858	231	50.21	5
†G E Tyldesley (*Lancs*)	29	46	8	1880	165	49.47	5
†A Sandham (*Surrey*)	30	48	5	2117	292*	49.23	5
†J W Hearne (*Middx*)	22	36	1	1721	202	49.17	7
†A Ducat (*Surrey*)	27	43	3	1881	290*	47.02	5
†C Hallows (*Lancs*)	28	47	5	1894	227	45.09	4
N V H Riches (*Glam*)	15	28	3	1080	177*	43.20	1
†F E Woolley (*Kent*)	31	50	1	2101	174	42.87	6
R A Haywood (*Nrthts*)	25	46	1	1909	198	42.42	8
A Jeacocke (*Surrey*)	14	26	1	1056	170*	42.24	3
†E H Hendren (*Middx*)	30	53	5	2013	113	41.93	7
A T Sharp (*Leics*)	12	23	2	879	150	41.85	4
W W Armstrong (*Austr*)	30	37	8	1213	182*	41.82	3
E Oldroyd (*Yorks*)	28	40	4	1469	144	40.80	3

BOWLING	M	O	M	R	W	Avge
E R Wilson (*Yorks*)	10	370	170	571	51	11.19
†W Rhodes (*Yorks*)	32	963	316	1872	141	13.27
W W Armstrong (*Austr*)	30	736.1	271	1444	100	14.44
†F E Woolley (*Kent*)	31	1163.1	367	2697	167	16.14
E A McDonald (*Austr*)	26	808.2	158	2284	138	16.55
J M Gregory (*Austr*)	27	655.4	126	1924	116	16.58
W Bestwick (*Derbys*)	19	935.4	200	2458	147	16.72
†J C White (*Som*)	24	1147.5	351	2442	143	17.07
†H Howell (*Warw*)	20	624.2	110	1780	104	17.11
G G Macaulay (*Yorks*)	27	651.2	140	1751	101	17.33
†C W L Parker (*Gloucs*)	25	1178.5	381	2893	164	17.64
H Dean (*Lancs*)	15	462.2	120	1059	59	17.94
W Wells (*Nrthts*)	19	429.3	80	1291	70	18.42
A J Nash (*Glam*)	18	695.4	192	1690	91	18.57
A P Freeman (*Kent*)	25	1017.2	217	3086	166	18.59
W S Hacker (*Glam*)	6	198.5	53	543	29	18.72
R Kilner (*Yorks*)	30	589.1	203	1147	61	18.80
A Waddington (*Yorks*)	26	679.3	124	1987	105	18.92
R K Tyldesley (*Lancs*)	30	592.2	142	1527	80	19.08
A A Mailey (*Austr*)	28	800	103	2595	134	19.36

†Played for England but not featured above: Hon L H Tennyson, G Brown, J W H T Douglas, V W C Jupp, D J Knight, C H Parkin, H Strudwick, A G Dipper, F J Durston, A J Evans, P G H Fender, N Haig, J W Hitch, P Holmes, T L Richmond and J B Hobbs.

First-class averages: 1922

BATTING	M	I	NO	Runs	HS	Avge	100s
E H Hendren (*Middx*)	27	38	7	2072	277*	66.83	7
J B Hobbs (*Surrey*)	29	46	5	2552	168	62.24	10
C P Mead (*Hants*)	32	50	10	2391	235	59.77	8
H T W Hardinge (*Kent*)	30	48	8	2207	249*	55.17	7
C A G Russell (*Essex*)	32	50	3	2575	172	54.78	9
H Ashton (*C U/Ex*)	19	27	5	1128	164*	51.27	2
J W Hearne (*Middx*)	28	44	6	1835	221*	48.28	3
Jas Seymour (*Kent*)	26	41	5	1727	170	47.97	6
H Sutcliffe (*Yorks*)	34	48	5	2020	232	46.97	4
A Sandham (*Surrey*)	28	45	5	1875	195	46.87	5
F E Woolley (*Kent*)	33	47	3	2022	188	45.95	5
J Hardstaff snr (*Notts*)	29	40	10	1307	117*	43.56	2
E Oldroyd (*Yorks*)	33	45	6	1690	151*	43.33	5
C A F Fiddian-Green (*C U/Wa*)	21	32	7	1057	120	42.28	3
G E Tyldesley (*Lancs*)	34	57	5	2168	178	41.69	4
J W H Makepeace (*Lancs*)	31	50	1	1983	169	40.46	4
C Hallows (*Lancs*)	30	49	5	1765	178*	40.11	4
W Rhodes (*Yorks*)	37	46	8	1511	110	39.76	4
A W Carr (*Notts*)	32	45	1	1749	135	39.75	4
H L V Day (*Hants*)	17	27	0	1062	107	39.33	1

BOWLING	M	O	M	R	W	Avge
W Rhodes (*Yorks*)	37	814.1	312	1451	119	12.19
D V Norbury (*Lancs*)	6	62.5	16	138	11	12.54
F B R Browne (*C U/Sx*)	12	322.4	105	716	55	13.01
C W L Parker (*Gloucs*)	31	1294.5	445	2712	206	13.16
T L Richmond (*Notts*)	28	862.2	209	2279	169	13.48
W S Cornwallis (*Kent*)	6	65.4	7	169	12	14.08
A P Freeman (*Kent*)	28	1101.1	270	2839	194	14.63
G G Macaulay (*Yorks*)	34	863.4	218	1952	133	14.67
R Kilner (*Yorks*)	36	1081.1	409	1797	122	14.73
J C White (*Som*)	23	1119.2	378	2282	146	15.63
G O B Allen (*C U/Mx*)	20	441.3	131	1119	71	15.76
E R Wilson (*Yorks*)	11	258	105	412	26	15.84
G M Louden (*Essex*)	9	344.2	80	933	58	16.08
A Waddington (*Yorks*)	35	906.4	200	2139	133	16.08
F H Barnard (*O U*)	8	81.5	16	243	15	16.20
F Barratt (*Notts*)	26	730.5	203	1781	109	16.33
W S Hacker (*Glam*)	8	225.2	55	571	34	16.79
A S Kennedy (*Hants*)	35	1346.4	366	3444	205	16.80
M B Burrows (*Army*)	2	61	12	222	13	17.07
E W Clark (*Nrthts*)	7	120.5	28	342	20	17.10

First-class averages: 1923

BATTING	M	I	NO	Runs	HS	Avge	100s
E W Hendren (*Middx*)	31	51	12	3010	200*	77.17	13
C P Mead (*Hants*)	33	52	8	2604	222	59.18	7
G Challenor (*W I*)	20	35	5	1556	155*	51.86	6
J W H Makepeace (*Lancs*)	33	53	6	2310	203	49.14	6
J W Hearne (*Middx*)	21	36	4	1519	232	47.46	5
L G Crawley (*C U/Worcs*)	13	20	2	801	161	44.50	2
W R D Payton (*Notts*)	27	43	7	1570	154	43.61	3
C Hallows (*Lancs*)	24	40	7	1438	179*	43.57	4
J L Bryan (*Kent*)	14	23	1	940	236	42.72	2
A Sandham (*Surrey*)	32	52	6	1894	200	41.17	4
H Sutcliffe (*Yorks*)	38	60	6	2220	139	41.11	3
F E Woolley (*Kent*)	34	56	5	2091	270	41.00	5
A E Dipper (*Gloucs*)	30	57	6	2048	252*	40.15	3
P Holmes (*Yorks*)	36	54	3	2001	199	39.23	3
A Ducat (*Surrey*)	27	44	2	1626	134	38.71	5
D R Jardine (*O U/Sy*)	18	28	4	916	127	38.16	2
J B Hobbs (*Surrey*)	34	59	4	2087	136	37.94	5
J R Gunn (*Notts*)	23	34	3	1173	116*	37.83	1
G E Tyldesley (*Lancs*)	39	60	6	2040	236	37.77	4
W Hill-Wood (*Derbys*)	18	30	0	1082	116	36.06	2

BOWLING	M	O	M	R	W	Avge
S Ellis (*Lancs*)	2	36.2	12	89	11	8.09
E A McDonald (*Rest*)	1	41.4	6	109	12	9.08
W Rhodes (*Yorks*)	37	929	345	1547	134	11.54
N S M Atkinson (*Middx*)	2	75.3	26	147	12	12.25
R Kilner (*Yorks*)	36	1259.5	507	2040	158	12.91
J G W Hyndson (*Army*)	1	51.3	16	133	10	13.30
G G Macaulay (*Yorks*)	35	1042.4	246	2297	166	13.83
M W Tate (*Sussex*)	36	1608.5	331	3061	219	13.97
F C Matthews (*Notts*)	25	575.5	115	1760	115	15.30
J C White (*Som*)	24	1111.4	365	2294	148	15.50
R K Tyldesley (*Lancs*)	31	945.4	303	2174	140	15.52
G N Francis (*W I*)	15	505.5	119	1278	82	15.58
E Robinson (*Yorks*)	35	748.3	222	1499	96	15.61
J Horsley (*Derbys*)	17	447	142	1019	63	16.17
W Bestwick (*Derbys*)	19	669.2	168	1483	91	16.29
R H B Bettington (*O U*)	11	303.4	60	1010	61	16.55
A P Freeman (*Kent*)	30	990	262	2642	157	16.82
C H Parkin (*Lancs*)	35	1356.2	356	3543	209	16.94
R C Robertson-Glasgow (*O U/Som*)	23	670.4	146	1980	108	17.40
A E R Gilligan (*Sussex*)	36	1075.4	235	2853	163	17.50

First-class averages: 1924

BATTING	M	I	NO	Runs	HS	Avge	100s
†A Sandham (*Surrey*)	24	37	2	2082	169	59.48	7
†J B Hobbs (*Surrey*)	30	43	7	2094	211	58.16	6
†E H Hendren (*Middx*)	35	48	11	2100	142	56.75	5
†F E Woolley (*Kent*)	34	49	2	2344	202	49.87	8
G J Bryan (*Kent*)	8	13	0	644	229	49.53	2
†H Sutcliffe (*Yorks*)	36	52	8	2142	255*	48.68	6
W W Whysall (*Notts*)	27	44	4	1852	151	46.30	6
N V H Riches (*Glam*)	11	15	1	624	170	44.57	1
†G E Tyldesley (*Lancs*)	34	48	6	1824	148*	43.42	4
K G Blaikie (*O U*)	8	13	1	507	120	42.25	2
H W Taylor (*S Africa*)	34	53	8	1898	126	42.17	4
C P Mead (*Hants*)	29	45	6	1644	154	42.15	3
†J C W MacBryan (*Som*)	27	41	2	1608	132	41.23	3
†J W Hearne (*Middx*)	29	43	6	1508	116	40.75	4
D R Jardine (*Surrey*)	27	38	7	1249	122	40.29	2
P Holmes (*Yorks*)	36	55	6	1954	202*	39.87	5
A E Dipper (*Gloucs*)	28	48	2	1825	247	39.67	5
A W Nourse (*S Africa*)	35	54	5	1928	147*	39.14	4
T F Shepherd (*Surrey*)	26	38	4	1301	192	38.26	4
G T S Stevens (*Middx*)	15	22	2	724	114	36.20	1

BOWLING	M	O	M	R	W	Avge
R H B Bettington (*F F*)	3	69	15	183	16	11.43
†G G Macaulay (*Yorks*)	35	1220.4	343	2514	190	13.23
†R Kilner (*Yorks*)	34	1159.4	464	1927	145	13.28
†C H Parkin (*Lancs*)	34	1162.5	357	2735	200	13.67
†M W Tate (*Sussex*)	36	1469.5	465	2818	205	13.74
†R K Tyldesley (*Lancs*)	36	1075.3	346	2574	184	13.98
C W L Parker (*Gloucs*)	30	1303.5	411	2913	204	14.27
F P Ryan (*Glam*)	24	680.1	165	1812	126	14.37
W Rhodes (*Yorks*)	38	746.3	240	1576	109	14.46
W Wells (*Nrthts*)	23	452.1	125	953	64	14.89
A P Freeman (*Kent*)	30	1035.2	250	2518	167	15.07
F J Durston (*Middx*)	25	469.5	132	1023	67	15.26
J C White (*Som*)	24	1099.4	357	2248	147	15.29
C S Marriott (*Kent*)	12	286	69	727	46	15.80
A E Thomas (*Nrthts*)	20	703.2	253	1209	75	16.17
C F Root (*Worcs*)	26	1007.3	281	2508	153	16.39
F B R Browne (*Sussex*)	6	173.1	45	412	25	16.48
†G Geary (*Leics*)	26	956.5	329	1960	116	16.89
P A Wright (*C U/Nrthts*)	12	424.1	130	986	58	17.00
A C Wright (*Kent*)	24	500.2	119	1170	68	17.20

†Played for England but not featured above: A E R Gilligan, A P F Chapman, P G H Fender, H Strudwick, G E C Wood, J W H T Douglas, G Duckworth and H Howell.

First-class averages: 1925

BATTING	M	I	NO	Runs	HS	Avge	100s
J B Hobbs (*Surrey*)	30	48	5	3024	266*	70.32	16
E H Hendren (*Middx*)	33	50	6	2601	240	59.11	8
P Holmes (*Yorks*)	37	52	9	2453	315*	57.04	6
F E Woolley (*Kent*)	29	43	4	2190	215	56.15	5
A Sandham (*Surrey*)	30	47	6	2255	181	55.00	5
H Sutcliffe (*Yorks*)	36	51	8	2308	235	53.67	7
C Hallows (*Lancs*)	34	51	6	2354	163	52.81	8
A W Carr (*Notts*)	30	49	4	2338	206	51.95	8
C A G Russell (*Essex*)	28	47	4	2081	150	48.39	7
G E Tyldesley (*Lancs*)	16	24	3	1010	114	48.09	3
C P Mead (*Hants*)	29	45	4	1942	213*	47.36	4
W R D Payton (*Notts*)	23	37	11	1212	140*	46.61	3
H J Enthoven (*C U/Mx*)	15	24	4	900	129	45.00	1
A Ducat (*Surrey*)	8	13	0	564	128	43.38	1
G T S Stevens (*Middx*)	14	24	2	954	129	43.36	2
J L Bryan (*Kent*)	14	21	2	823	182	43.31	2
J W Hearne (*Middx*)	29	45	3	1799	118	42.83	4
W Rhodes (*Yorks*)	37	43	9	1391	157	40.91	2
M Leyland (*Yorks*)	35	43	4	1572	138	40.30	3
G E B Abell (*O U/Worcs*)	9	17	4	513	124	39.46	1

BOWLING	M	O	M	R	W	Avge
A C Gore (*Army*)	2	46.1	13	137	11	12.45
J H Lockton (*Surrey*)	4	103.3	30	224	16	14.00
S G Hearn (*Kent*)	11	77.3	20	170	12	14.16
F M Sibbles (*Lancs*)	11	269.3	78	641	44	14.56
C W L Parker (*Gloucs*)	32	1512.3	478	3311	222	14.91
M W Tate (*Sussex*)	35	1694.3	472	3415	228	14.97
W Bestwick (*Derbys*)	7	258.1	89	525	35	15.00
P Havelock-Davies (*Army*)	3	107.3	26	277	17	15.11
R K Tyldesley (*Lancs*)	35	934	285	2206	144	15.31
G G Macaulay (*Yorks*)	35	1338.2	307	3268	211	15.48
H Storer (*Derbys*)	2	92	29	157	10	15.70
J C White (*Som*)	24	1023.4	367	2001	121	16.53
C S Marriott (*Kent*)	11	427.4	136	875	51	17.15
C F Root (*Worcs*)	29	1493.2	416	3770	219	17.21
A P Freeman (*Kent*)	27	1072.2	314	2544	146	17.42
T L Richmond (*Notts*)	27	673.3	129	2045	116	17.62
F P Ryan (*Glam*)	28	924.2	228	2454	139	17.65
A E Thomas (*Nrthts*)	13	379.5	144	654	37	17.67
G Geary (*Leics*)	26	864.4	272	1921	108	17.78
E W Clark (*Nrthts*)	19	612	137	1495	84	17.79

First-class averages: 1926

BATTING	M	I	NO	Runs	HS	Avge	100s
†J B Hobbs (*Surrey*)	30	41	3	2949	316*	77.60	10
†H Sutcliffe (*Yorks*)	35	47	9	2528	200	66.52	8
†G E Tyldesley (*Lancs*)	35	51	7	2826	226	64.22	10
†E H Hendren (*Middx*)	36	53	11	2643	213	62.92	9
C P Mead (*Hants*)	29	45	8	2326	177*	62.86	10
W M Woodfull (*Austr*)	27	34	5	1672	201	57.65	8
N V H Riches (*Glam*)	7	11	1	542	239*	54.20	2
C G Macartney (*Austr*)	27	33	4	1561	160	53.82	6
†J W Hearne (*Middx*)	21	31	4	1384	151*	51.25	3
†A P F Chapman (*Kent*)	22	31	4	1381	159	51.14	4
J W H Makepeace (*Lancs*)	36	54	6	2340	180	48.75	5
W R D Payton (*Notts*)	26	44	5	1864	133	47.79	6
H T W Hardinge (*Kent*)	30	52	5	2234	176	47.53	7
W Bardsley (*Austr*)	27	33	3	1424	193*	47.46	5
C A G Russell (*Essex*)	30	49	8	1906	180*	46.48	6
†F E Woolley (*Kent*)	32	50	3	2183	217	46.44	6
A Ducat (*Surrey*)	22	30	3	1245	235	46.11	4
D R Jardine (*Surrey*)	26	36	4	1473	176	46.03	3
A Sandham (*Surrey*)	31	44	2	1905	183	45.35	4
E Oldroyd (*Yorks*)	25	30	3	1197	135	44.33	3

BOWLING	M	O	M	R	W	Avge
N J Holloway (*F F*)	1	58.5	9	140	10	14.00
R G W Melsome (*Gloucs*)	4	144.1	31	367	26	14.11
†W Rhodes (*Yorks*)	33	892.4	315	1709	115	14.86
T H Dixon (*D U*)*	2	54	15	160	10	16.00
J Mercer (*Glam*)	28	986.2	226	2239	136	16.46
R K Tyldesley (*Lancs*)	36	963.5	324	2159	128	16.86
C H Parkin (*Lancs*)	11	285	85	721	42	17.16
†M W Tate (*Sussex*)	28	1261.4	365	2575	147	17.51
C V Grimmett (*Austr*)	24	834.3	251	1857	105	17.68
†G G Macaulay (*Yorks*)	34	1115.4	296	2383	134	17.78
C G Macartney (*Austr*)	27	559.3	242	873	49	17.81
†H Larwood (*Notts*)	31	974.1	217	2509	137	18.31
C W L Parker (*Gloucs*)	33	1739.5	556	3920	213	18.40
E W Clark (*Nrthts*)*	29	905.1	211	2268	122	18.58
A C Wright (*Kent*)	26	820.2	186	1920	102	18.82
†G Geary (*Leics*)	28	1160.4	367	2359	124	19.02
F P Ryan (*Glam*)	25	874.1	166	2163	112	19.31
A A Mailey (*Austr*)	27	816	153	2437	126	19.34
L G Irvine (*C U*)	12	291.1	39	1019	52	19.59
T O Jameson (*Hts/Ire*)	5	141.4	37	373	19	19.63

*Overs and maidens missing for one match.

†Played for England but not featured above: G T S Stevens, A W Carr, R Kilner, H Strudwick and C F Root.

First-class averages: 1927

BATTING	M	I	NO	Runs	HS	Avge	100s
D R Jardine (*Surrey*)	11	14	3	1002	147	91.09	5
C Hallows (*Lancs*)	33	44	13	2343	233*	75.58	7
C P Mead (*Hants*)	28	41	9	2385	200*	74.53	8
E H Hendren (*Middx*)	35	43	5	2784	201*	73.26	13
W R Hammond (*Gloucs*)	34	47	4	2969	197	69.04	12
A P F Chapman (*Kent*)	16	23	2	1387	260	66.04	4
A Sandham (*Surrey*)	33	46	6	2315	230	57.87	7
P Holmes (*Yorks*)	35	47	9	2174	180	57.21	6
H Sutcliffe (*Yorks*)	35	49	6	2414	227	56.13	6
T F Shepherd (*Surrey*)	30	45	6	2145	277*	55.00	8
E H Bowley (*Sussex*)	23	41	3	2062	220	54.26	4
J B Hobbs (*Surrey*)	23	32	1	1641	150	52.93	7
J W Hearne (*Middx*)	33	38	7	1632	245*	52.64	6
G E Tyldesley (*Lancs*)	33	39	4	1756	165	50.17	7
J H Parsons (*Warw*)	30	42	8	1700	225	50.00	5
A E Dipper (*Gloucs*)	31	53	8	2246	212	49.91	7
G T S Stevens (*Middx*)	8	10	1	436	89	48.44	0
F E Woolley (*Kent*)	31	41	2	1804	187	46.25	5
W W Whysall (*Notts*)	32	50	5	2069	184	45.97	5
C S Dempster (*N Z*)	24	37	5	1430	180	44.68	3

BOWLING	M	O	M	R	W	Avge
T W Durnell (*Warw*)	3	58.1	7	179	14	12.78
T H Dixon (*Ireland*)	1	59.5	22	130	10	13.00
R A D Brooks	2	72.1	10	197	14	14.07
H Howell (*Warw*)	8	223.3	51	505	30	16.83
H Larwood (*Notts*)	22	629.2	147	1695	100	16.95
C F Root (*Worcs*)	29	1265.4	450	2597	145	17.91
G G Macaulay (*Yorks*)	34	1110.2	288	2375	130	18.26
A P Freeman (*Kent*)	30	1220.1	269	3330	181	18.39
J C White (*Som*)	27	1212.2	475	2097	113	18.55
G M Lee (*Derbys*)	25	631.1	175	1339	72	18.59
F B R Browne (*Sussex*)	8	227	80	454	23	19.23
L F Townsend (*Derbys*)	25	738.3	274	1357	70	19.38
G Geary (*Leics*)	28	735	236	1595	82	19.45
J Mercer (*Glam*)	24	814	198	1961	100	19.61
H J Palmer (*Essex*)	9	235.3	47	628	32	19.62
C J Capes (*Kent*)	14	311.1	97	668	34	19.64
C W L Parker (*Gloucs*)	32	1727.4	540	3849	193	19.94
R K Tyldesley (*Lancs*)	34	969.1	352	2002	100	20.02
F P Ryan (*Glam*)	21	499.4	94	1423	71	20.09
E Robinson (*Yorks*)	33	848.1	304	1551	77	20.14

First-class averages: 1928

BATTING	M	I	NO	Runs	HS	Avge	100s
†D R Jardine (*Surrey*)	14	17	4	1133	193	87.15	3
†J B Hobbs (*Surrey*)	28	38	7	2542	200*	82.00	12
†G E Tyldesley (*Lancs*)	35	48	10	3024	242	79.57	10
†H Sutcliffe (*Yorks*)	34	44	5	3002	228	76.97	13
C P Mead (*Hants*)	30	50	10	3027	180	75.67	13
†E H Hendren (*Middx*)	35	54	7	3311	209*	70.44	13
J W Hearne (*Middx*)	12	19	4	988	223*	65.86	3
†W R Hammond (*Gloucs*)	35	48	5	2825	244	65.69	9
†C Hallows (*Lancs*)	33	46	5	2645	232	64.51	11
C A G Russell (*Essex*)	27	42	7	2243	182	64.08	8
F B Watson (*Lancs*)	33	46	4	2583	300*	61.50	9
F E Woolley (*Kent*)	36	59	4	3352	198	61.03	12
H T W Hardinge (*Kent*)	29	46	5	2446	263*	59.65	5
A Sandham (*Surrey*)	32	47	4	2532	282*	58.88	8
P Holmes (*Yorks*)	33	43	5	2220	275	58.42	6
R E S Wyatt (*Warw*)	32	52	10	2408	177	57.33	6
A Ducat (*Surrey*)	24	33	3	1660	208	55.33	5
A E Dipper (*Gloucs*)	31	49	6	2365	188	55.00	7
†M Leyland (*Yorks*)	30	37	4	1783	247	54.03	5
W W Whysall (*Notts*)	34	51	2	2573	166	52.91	9

BOWLING	M	O	M	R	W	Avge
S F Barnes (*Wales*)	2	97	29	205	20	10.02
R E G Fulljames (*RAF*)	2	98.3	34	231	19	12.15
W E Bowes (*MCC*)	2	62	20	157	11	14.42
†H Larwood (*Notts*)	31	834.5	204	2003	138	14.51
T H Dixon (*Ireland*)	3	143.2	39	343	20	17.15
C P Mead (*Hants*)	30	80.1	20	245	14	17.50
†A P Freeman (*Kent*)	37	1976.1	423	5489	304	18.05
R K Tyldesley (*Lancs*)	31	807.5	235	1983	104	19.06
†M W Tate (*Sussex*)	35	1584.2	491	3184	165	19.29
A W Speed (*Warw*)	6	136.1	30	388	20	19.40
W Rhodes (*Yorks*)	33	1163.2	403	2258	115	19.63
†J C White (*Som*)	25	1336.3	445	2720	138	19.71
E A McDonald (*Lancs*)	34	1254.1	266	3754	190	19.75
V W C Jupp (*Nrthts*)	32	1023	192	3345	166	20.15
C S Marriott (*Kent*)	11	418.3	103	1068	53	20.15
W E Hazelton (*Gents*)	3	99.3	22	332	16	29.75
E D Blundell (*CU*)	13	424.5	119	1152	54	21.33
S J Staples (*Notts*)	29	1016	248	2394	110	21.76
C W L Parker (*Gloucs*)	29	1474.2	470	3602	162	22.23
W E Astill (*Leics*)	33	1278.1	365	2904	130	22.33

†Played for England but not featured above: A P F Chapman, V W C Jupp, G Duckworth, H Elliott and H Smith.

First-class averages: 1929

BATTING	M	I	NO	Runs	HS	Avge	100s
†J B Hobbs (*Surrey*)	24	39	5	2263	204	66.55	10
†W R Hammond (*Gloucs*)	28	47	9	2456	238*	64.63	10
†F E Woolley (*Kent*)	35	55	5	2804	176	56.08	11
C P Mead (*Hants*)	21	38	7	1733	233	55.90	5
J W H Makepeace (*Lancs*)	12	16	3	698	163*	53.69	2
†R E S Wyatt (*Warw*)	34	55	6	2630	161*	53.67	10
†K S Duleepsinhji (*Sussex*)	29	51	3	2545	246	53.02	8
†H Sutcliffe (*Yorks*)	31	46	4	2189	150	52.11	9
A Sandham (*Surrey*)	31	52	2	2565	187	51.30	6
W W Whysall (*Notts*)	36	56	3	2716	244	51.24	7
A E Dipper (*Gloucs*)	30	50	3	2218	153	47.19	3
F B Watson (*Lancs*)	32	50	4	2137	207	46.45	6
G O B Allen (*Middx*)	9	15	3	544	155	45.33	1
W R D Payton (*Notts*)	27	41	10	1396	169	45.03	3
G E Tyldesley (*Lancs*)	27	39	4	1575	187	45.00	4
†J O'Connor (*Essex*)	32	54	3	2288	168*	44.86	9
E T Killick (*CU/Mx*)	17	32	1	1384	201	44.64	4
†E H Bowley (*Sussex*)	33	57	3	2360	280*	43.70	5
†M Leyland (*Yorks*)	36	50	5	1931	134	42.91	3
J Iddon (*Lancs*)	32	47	6	1739	222	42.41	4

BOWLING	M	O	M	R	W	Avge
W R Gouldsworthy (*Gloucs*)	2	52.2	12	142	10	14.20
A G Penfold (*Surrey*)	3	88.4	24	201	13	15.46
R K Tyldesley (*Lancs*)	31	1114.3	350	2399	154	15.57
†J C White (*Som*)	30	1556.1	631	2648	168	15.76
S F Barnes (*Wales*)	5	237.4	83	465	29	16.03
T W J Goddard (*Gloucs*)	31	1285.1	357	3015	184	16.38
R W Sievwright (*Scotland*)	2	71	14	197	12	16.41
E L Armitage (*MCC*)	4	102.4	15	305	18	16.94
W Voce (*Notts*)	30	894.2	253	2043	120	17.02
C W L Parker (*Gloucs*)	25	1066.1	307	2403	138	17.41
A W Shipman (*Leics*)	26	488.2	136	1050	59	17.79
H J Enthoven (*Middx*)	9	65	11	178	10	17.80
A S Kennedy (*Hants*)	29	1178.5	344	2773	154	18.00
D V Hill (*Worcs*)	3	122	38	289	16	18.06
†A P Freeman (*Kent*)	33	1670.5	381	4879	267	18.27
C A G Russell (*Essex*)	20	172	49	348	19	18.31
J C Clay (*Glam*)	14	301	90	684	37	18.48
†M W Tate (*Sussex*)	32	1420.1	393	2903	156	18.60
W Rhodes (*Yorks*)	30	1017.3	390	1870	100	18.70
W E Bowes (*Yorks*)	15	567.4	140	1241	65	19.09

†Played for England but not featured above: E H Hendren, E T Killick, H Larwood, L E G Ames, F Barratt, E W Clark, A W Carr, G Duckworth, P G H Fender, G Geary and R W V Robins.

First-class averages: 1930

BATTING	M	I	NO	Runs	HS	Avge	100s
D G Bradman (*Austr*)	27	36	6	2960	334	98.66	10
†H Sutcliffe (*Yorks*)	29	44	8	2312	173	64.22	6
A F Kippax (*Austr*)	23	32	7	1451	158	58.04	4
W M Woodfull (*Austr*)	23	26	1	1434	216	57.36	6
†K S Duleepsinhji (*Sussex*)	29	48	3	2562	333	56.93	9
†W R Hammond (*Gloucs*)	27	44	6	2032	211*	53.47	5
E Oldroyd (*Yorks*)	27	33	8	1285	164*	51.40	3
†J B Hobbs (*Surrey*)	30	43	2	2103	146*	51.29	5
†M Leyland (*Yorks*)	33	50	7	2175	211*	50.58	6
A Sandham (*Surrey*)	35	50	4	2295	204	49.89	6
†W W Whysall (*Notts*)	30	47	3	2174	248	49.40	8
A Ducat (*Surrey*)	32	48	6	2067	218	49.21	5
W H Ponsford (*Austr*)	24	33	4	1425	220*	49.13	4
G E Tyldesley (*Lancs*)	32	47	8	1904	256*	48.82	7
F R Brown (*CU*)	12	17	3	674	150	48.14	2
E T Killick (*CU*)	12	20	1	903	182	47.52	2
A M Crawley (*OU/Kt*)	11	19	1	843	175	46.83	3
F B Watson (*Lancs*)	32	47	2	2031	135	45.13	3
†F E Woolley (*Kent*)	29	50	5	2023	120	44.95	5
G C Grant (*CU*)	11	17	1	716	100	44.75	1

BOWLING	M	O	M	R	W	Avge
H Verity (*Yorks*)	12	406.1	154	795	64	12.42
C W L Parker (*Gloucs*)	25	1016.3	301	2299	179	12.84
E Dynes (*Army*)	3	92.2	20	266	17	15.64
J E S Walford (*Worcs*)	3	86.4	15	241	15	16.06
†R K Tyldesley (*Lancs*)	31	1052.1	352	2263	140	16.16
D L Russell (*OU/Mx*)	9	97.5	29	163	10	16.30
†H Larwood (*Notts*)	25	621	124	1622	99	16.38
F S Booth (*Lancs*)	6	188.3	47	432	26	16.61
D G Foster (*Warw*)	4	113.4	24	302	18	16.77
A P Freeman (*Kent*)	33	1914.3	472	4632	275	16.84
C V Grimmett (*Austr*)	26	1015.1	262	2427	144	16.85
S J Pegler (*MCC*)	3	117.2	35	306	18	17.00
F B R Browne (*Sussex*)	3	115	38	214	12	17.83
A Young (*Som*)	29	617.3	229	1278	71	18.00
T B Mitchell (*Derbys*)	27	1102.2	311	2526	138	18.30
†I A R Peebles (*CU/Mx*)	22	871.4	143	2453	133	18.44
H J Palmer (*Essex*)	5	124.4	31	336	18	18.66
P M Hornibrook (*Austr*)	26	819.2	240	1802	96	18.77
R C Rought-Rought (*CU*)	9	292.2	72	814	43	18.93
C H Hall (*Yorks*)	4	120.3	23	341	18	18.94

†Played for England but not featured above: A P F Chapman, E H Hendren, M W Tate, G Duckworth, R W V Robins, G O B Allen, G Geary, M S Nichols, J C White, R E S Wyatt and T W J Goddard.

First-class averages: 1931

BATTING	M	I	NO	Runs	HS	Avge	100s
†H Sutcliffe (*Yorks*)	34	42	11	3006	230	96.96	13
Nawab of Pataudi (*OU*)	14	25	4	1454	238*	69.23	6
†D R Jardine (*Surrey*)	19	30	13	1104	106*	64.94	2
J H Parsons (*Warw*)	21	27	7	1202	190	60.10	4
C S Dempster (*NZ*)	23	36	6	1778	212	59.26	7
E H Hendren (*Middx*)	34	54	9	2548	232	56.62	7
J B Hobbs (*Surrey*)	31	49	6	2418	153	56.23	10
†K S Duleepsinhji (*Sussex*)	36	51	2	2684	162	54.77	12
A Sandham (*Surrey*)	32	50	8	2209	175	52.59	9
C B Harris (*Notts*)	13	19	9	502	64	50.20	0
†F E Woolley (*Kent*)	34	51	4	2301	224	48.95	5
C P Mead (*Hants*)	29	46	9	1596	169*	43.13	3
R C Blunt (*NZ*)	29	42	5	1592	225*	43.02	3
†W R Hammond (*Gloucs*)	32	49	7	1781	168*	42.40	6
R E S Wyatt (*Warw*)	34	49	7	1764	161*	42.00	3
T E Cook (*Sussex*)	29	42	7	1444	109	41.25	3
G Gunn (*Notts*)	25	39	5	1329	183	39.08	3
†L E G Ames (*Kent*)	35	50	6	1711	172	38.88	4
G E Tyldesley (*Lancs*)	27	43	4	1516	144	38.87	4
E H Bowley (*Sussex*)	26	41	3	1474	144	38.78	5

BOWLING	M	O	M	R	W	Avge
J C Boucher (*Ireland*)	1	27.4	10	65	11	5.90
†H Larwood (*Notts*)	25	651.3	142	1553	129	12.03
D S Hiddleston (*Scotland*)	2	62.5	4	200	15	13.33
†H Verity (*Yorks*)	35	1137.3	356	2542	188	13.52
C W L Parker (*Gloucs*)	30	1320.4	386	3125	219	14.26
C S Marriott (*Kent*)	12	550	176	1111	76	14.61
H T O Smith (*Essex*)	5	98.2	32	210	14	15.00
†M W Tate (*Sussex*)	33	1253	398	2179	141	15.45
L F Townsend (*Derbys*)	26	522	144	1117	72	15.51
A P Freeman (*Kent*)	33	1618	360	4307	276	15.60
W E Bowes (*Yorks*)	32	949.5	241	2131	136	15.66
G G Macaulay (*Yorks*)	35	921.2	358	1528	97	15.75
J C Clay (*Glam*)	9	224	51	557	35	15.91
R K Tyldesley (*Lancs*)	23	865.3	264	1853	116	15.97
C F Root (*Worcs*)	29	1065	374	2020	126	16.03
A G Slater (*Derbys*)	28	948	297	1756	108	16.25
A S Kennedy (*Hants*)	29	1161.4	388	2268	131	17.31
G Geary (*Leics*)	30	1289.4	425	2287	130	17.59
H C Snary (*Leics*)	30	1117.1	390	1830	101	18.11
T C Lowry (*NZ*)	31	103	26	274	15	18.26

†Played for England but not featured above: G O B Allen, A H Bakewell, J Arnold, R W V Robins, E Paynter, W Voce and F R Brown.

First-class averages: 1932

BATTING	M	I	NO	Runs	HS	Avge	100s
†H Sutcliffe (*Yorks*)	35	52	7	3336	313	74.13	14
G E Tyldesley (*Lancs*)	30	48	7	2420	225*	59.02	8
†L E G Ames (*Kent*)	33	50	7	2482	180	57.72	9
J B Hobbs (*Surrey*)	24	35	4	1764	161*	56.90	5
†W R Hammond (*Gloucs*)	30	49	4	2528	264	56.17	8
B W Hone (*OU*)	10	12	0	646	167	53.83	3
K S Duleepsinhji (*Sussex*)	27	33	2	1633	132	52.67	5
†D R Jardine (*Surrey*)	29	39	11	1464	164	52.28	3
M Leyland (*Yorks*)	32	40	2	1980	189	52.10	6
L G Crawley (*Essex*)	9	17	1	830	155	51.87	2
E H Hendren (*Middx*)	30	47	7	2041	194*	51.02	5
R H J Brooke (*OU*)	11	19	3	800	140	50.00	4
J O'Connor (*Essex*)	21	36	8	1350	119	48.21	4
Nawab of Pataudi (*Worcs*)	10	18	2	748	165	46.62	2
P G V van der Bijl (*OU*)	10	16	4	540	97*	45.00	0
†P Holmes (*Yorks*)	21	31	4	1208	224*	44.74	2
E F Wilson (*Surrey*)	10	16	5	492	72	44.72	0
J W Hearne (*Middx*)	34	52	3	2151	176	43.89	6
R E S Wyatt (*Warw*)	32	49	7	1808	171*	43.04	3
W W Keeton (*Notts*)	32	51	3	2062	242	42.95	7

BOWLING	M	O	M	R	W	Avge
H Larwood (*Notts*)	32	866.4	203	2084	162	12.86
A Minnis (*Army*)	2	71.5	18	152	11	13.81
H Verity (*Yorks*)	35	1117.5	401	2250	162	13.88
H Fisher (*Yorks*)	8	173	66	310	22	14.09
†W E Bowes (*Yorks*)	33	1194.2	271	2877	190	15.14
M W Tate (*Sussex*)	35	1380.1	440	2494	160	15.58
D Ayling (*S Amer*)	6	233	80	530	33	16.06
A P Freeman (*Kent*)	33	1565.5	404	4149	253	16.39
†W Voce (*Notts*)	32	973.4	201	2295	136	16.87
J C White (*Som*)	17	978.5	360	1813	107	16.94
C S Marriott (*Kent*)	11	607	209	1169	68	17.19
C H Hall (*Yorks*)	7	103.2	31	244	14	17.42
Jas Langridge (*Sussex*)	35	940.3	232	2032	115	17.66
J Iddon (*Lancs*)	32	796	291	1418	80	17.72
R C Robertson-Glasgow (*Som*)	2	105.3	31	253	14	18.07
M Nissar (*India*)	18	532	128	1285	71	18.09
F M Sibbles (*Lancs*)	29	1195.4	362	2392	131	18.25
†R W V Robins (*Middx*)	7	215.1	33	585	32	18.28
L F Townsend (*Derbys*)	29	1109.3	321	2159	117	18.45
A D Baxter (*Scotld*)	3	152.1	21	488	26	18.76

†Played for England but not featured above: F E Woolley, E Paynter and F R Brown.

First-class averages: 1933

BATTING	M	I	NO	Runs	HS	Avge	100s
†W R Hammond (*Gloucs*)	34	54	5	3323	264*	67.81	13
C P Mead (*Hants*)	27	44	6	2576	227	67.78	10
G A Headley (*WI*)	23	38	3	2320	224	66.28	7
J B Hobbs (*Surrey*)	12	18	0	1115	221	61.38	6
†R E S Wyatt (*Warw*)	33	50	10	2379	187*	59.47	8
A Mitchell (*Yorks*)	35	51	12	2300	158	58.97	8
†L E G Ames (*Kent*)	36	57	5	3058	295	58.80	9
E H Hendren (*Middx*)	36	65	9	3186	301*	56.89	11
†D R Jardine (*Surrey*)	11	15	0	779	127	51.93	3
C P Johnstone (*Kent*)	6	10	2	412	133	51.50	2
†M Leyland (*Yorks*)	34	50	4	2317	210*	50.36	7
†C F Walters (*Worcs*)	30	52	4	2404	226	50.08	9
Nawab of Pataudi (*Worcs*)	23	41	5	1754	231*	48.72	5
J Iddon (*Lancs*)	29	39	6	1600	204*	48.48	4
T E Cook (*Sussex*)	34	47	5	1983	214	47.21	5
†H Sutcliffe (*Yorks*)	35	52	5	2211	205	47.04	7
J L Hopwood (*Lancs*)	32	46	4	1972	142	46.95	7
†A H Bakewell (*Nrthts*)	27	47	1	2149	257	46.71	7
H T Barling (*Surrey*)	28	44	3	1915	269	46.70	5
F R Santall (*Warw*)	30	46	9	1727	201*	46.67	4

BOWLING	M	O	M	R	W	Avge
H R Morgan (*Ireland*)	1	54	26	81	10	8.10
†G O B Allen (*Middx*)	3	66	20	117	13	9.00
F Edwards (*M Cou*)	1	36	9	110	10	11.00
A D Baxter (*Lancs*)	3	101.4	26	240	19	12.63
H G O Owen-Smith (*OU*)	6	173.3	28	466	35	13.31
†H Verity (*Yorks*)	34	1195.4	428	2553	190	13.43
A P Freeman (*Kent*)	35	2039	651	4549	298	15.26
†G G Macaulay (*Yorks*)	34	1214.2	423	2435	148	16.45
†Jas Langridge (*Sussex*)	34	1228.3	355	2617	158	16.56
T W J Goddard (*Gloucs*)	31	1371.5	414	3187	183	17.41
†E W Clark (*Nrthts*)	20	657.5	143	1714	98	17.48
W E Bowes (*Yorks*)	27	1010.4	226	2828	159	17.78
R R Relf (*M Cou*)	1	84.4	25	179	10	17.90
M W Tate (*Sussex*)	28	989.5	309	1808	99	18.26
K Farnes (*Essex*)	23	735.2	162	2078	113	18.38
†C S Marriott (*Kent*)	10	465	139	996	54	18.44
L F Townsend (*Derbys*)	33	928.1	294	1871	100	18.71
P F Judge (*Middx*)	4	139	40	340	18	18.88
T B Mitchell (*Derbys*)	26	1188.4	341	2742	142	19.30
H E Hammond (*Sussex*)	6	103	22	257	13	19.76

†Played for England but not featured above: M S Nichols, C J Barnett, R W V Robins and M J L Turnbull.

First-class averages: 1934

BATTING	M	I	NO	Runs	HS	Avge	100s
D G Bradman (*Austr*)	22	27	3	2020	304	84.16	7
†Nawab of Pataudi (*Worcs*)	10	15	3	945	214*	78.75	3
W H Ponsford (*Austr*)	22	27	4	1784	281*	77.56	5
†W R Hammond (*Gloucs*)	23	35	4	2366	302*	76.32	8
S J McCabe (*Austr*)	26	37	7	2078	240	69.26	8
G E Tyldesley (*Lancs*)	33	51	8	2487	239	57.83	8
†L E G Ames (*Kent*)	27	43	6	2113	202*	57.10	5
J O'Connor (*Essex*)	30	49	7	2350	248	55.95	9
T E Cook (*Sussex*)	31	45	6	2132	220	54.66	4
J H Human (*C U*)	18	29	3	1399	146*	53.80	5
†M Leyland (*Yorks*)	32	44	4	2142	182	53.55	7
C P Mead (*Hants*)	29	46	8	2011	198	52.92	6
J Iddon (*Lancs*)	33	51	6	2381	200*	52.91	6
W M Woodfull (*Austr*)	22	27	3	1628	228*	52.83	3
L J Todd (*Kent*)	31	52	16	1897	130	52.69	3
H H I Gibbons (*Worcs*)	31	57	6	2654	157	52.03	8
R J Gregory (*Surrey*)	29	49	3	2379	180	51.71	8
F C de Saram (*O U*)	12	23	1	1119	208	50.86	3
†R E S Wyatt (*Warw*)	26	42	7	1776	161*	50.74	5
A F Kippax (*Austr*)	19	23	4	961	250	50.57	1

BOWLING	M	O	M	R	W	Avge
W J O'Reilly (*Austr*)	19	870	320	1858	109	17.04
G A E Paine (*Warw*)	26	1285.5	463	2664	156	17.07
H Larwood (*Notts*)	23	512.2	103	1415	82	17.25
†H Verity (*Yorks*)	32	1282.1	500	2645	150	17.63
J C Clay (*Glam*)	20	863	258	1829	103	17.75
W H Copson (*Derbys*)	22	697.2	169	1648	91	18.10
C I J Smith (*Middx*)	34	1398	346	3248	172	18.88
L O'B Fleetwood-Smith (*Austr*)	20	713.5	150	2036	106	19.20
†T B Mitchell (*Derbys*)	26	986.1	202	3064	159	19.27
†G Geary (*Leics*)	20	682.3	212	1293	67	19.29
†W E Bowes (*Yorks*)	32	1141.4	301	2860	147	19.45
M W Tate (*Sussex*)	31	1475.2	461	2796	142	19.69
C V Grimmett (*Austr*)	21	985.4	308	2159	109	19.80
A V Pope (*Derbys*)	26	486.3	123	1022	51	20.03
J H Mayer (*Warw*)	25	853.3	234	1791	89	20.12
T F Smailes (*Yorks*)	34	825.3	207	2135	105	20.23
†J L Hopwood (*Lancs*)	31	1155.3	402	2297	111	20.69
H S Hargreaves (*Yorks*)	7	216	48	564	27	20.88
I A R Peebles (*Middx*)	8	362.4	63	975	46	21.19
R Pollard (*Lancs*)	12	379.4	104	859	40	21.47

†Played for England but not featured above: H Sutcliffe, C F Walters, E H Hendren, G O B Allen, K Farnes, E W Clark, W W Keeton and F E Woolley

First-class averages: 1935

BATTING	M	I	NO	Runs	HS	Avge	100s
†W R Hammond (*Gloucs*)	35	58	5	2616	252	49.35	7
†H Sutcliffe (*Yorks*)	36	54	3	2494	212	48.90	8
K G Viljoen (*S Afr*)	25	35	4	1454	168	46.90	5
G E Tyldesley (*Lancs*)	11	15	1	654	137	46.71	1
C S Dempster (*Leics*)	6	10	2	369	207*	46.12	1
C Washbrook (*Lancs*)	31	47	9	1724	228	45.36	3
B Mitchell (*S Afr*)	22	35	3	1451	195	45.34	4
E A B Rowan (*S Afr*)	28	46	2	1948	171	44.27	6
†R E S Wyatt (*Warw*)	33	55	9	2019	149	43.89	4
E H Hendren (*Middx*)	30	50	7	1867	195	43.41	5
H W Parks (*Sussex*)	32	49	13	1530	119*	42.50	3
†W Barber (*Yorks*)	36	55	4	2147	255	42.09	4
†E R T Holmes (*Surrey*)	31	51	5	1925	206	41.84	4
F E Woolley (*Kent*)	32	56	0	2339	229	41.76	6
H B Cameron (*S Afr*)	27	38	3	1458	160	41.65	3
A D Nourse (*S Afr*)	30	46	5	1681	160*	41.00	4
A Melville (*Sussex*)	30	50	3	1904	124	40.51	4
†A H Bakewell (*Nrthts*)	26	49	2	1870	143	39.78	3
I J Siedle (*S Afr*)	22	37	3	1346	164*	39.58	3
†D Smith (*Derbys*)	31	61	6	2175	225	39.54	2

BOWLING	M	O	M	R	W	Avge
G O B Allen (*Middx*)	2	39.1	6	74	11	6.72
A D Baxter (*MCC*)	7	200	48	550	42	13.09
†H Verity (*Yorks*)	38	1279.2	453	3032	211	14.36
†J C Clay (*Glam*)	11	455.4	120	1017	67	15.17
G Geary (*Leics*)	23	908.2	258	1977	129	15.32
†W E Bowes (*Yorks*)	36	1286.5	342	2981	193	15.44
W H Copson (*Derbys*)	18	490	113	1174	71	16.53
†M S Nichols (*Essex*)	32	972.3	196	2610	157	16.62
H R W Butterworth (*M Cou*)	3	76.3	10	258	15	17.20
C Oakes (*Sussex*)	6	67.3	11	208	12	17.33
†R W V Robins (*Middx*)	25	503.3	86	1456	80	18.20
C I J Smith (*Middx*)	28	890	115	2058	113	18.21
E W Clark (*Nrthts*)	20	564.3	122	1462	79	18.50
†M W Tate (*Sussex*)	31	1089	333	2141	113	18.94
B Mitchell (*S Afr*)	22	206	14	666	35	19.02
F S Booth (*Lancs*)	19	646.3	123	1709	89	19.20
R Pollard (*Lancs*)	25	844.5	198	1956	100	19.56
J H Parks (*Sussex*)	33	952.3	292	2016	103	19.57
L C Eastman (*Essex*)	28	826.1	237	1939	99	19.58
R J Crisp (*S Afr*)	26	690.5	105	2096	107	19.58

†Played for England but not featured above: M Leyland, A Mitchell, L E G Ames, G Duckworth, W Farrimond, J Iddon, Jas Langridge, T B Mitchell, M S Mitchell-Innes, J M Sims, J Hardstaff and H D Read.

First-class averages: 1936

BATTING	M	I	NO	Runs	HS	Avge	100s
†W R Hammond (*Gloucs*)	25	42	5	2107	317	56.94	5
†L B Fishlock (*Surrey*)	35	53	13	2129	133*	53.22	5
V M Merchant (*India*)	23	40	6	1745	151	51.32	3
E H Hendren (*Middx*)	35	58	2	2654	202	47.39	9
A Melville (*Sussex*)	13	21	0	982	152	46.76	4
†M Leyland (*Yorks*)	34	44	5	1790	263	45.89	7
E Paynter (*Lancs*)	33	54	10	2016	177	45.81	4
N S Mitchell-Innes (*Som/O U*)	20	37	5	1438	207	44.93	3
†J Hardstaff jun (*Notts*)	27	40	4	1615	145	44.86	4
L E G Ames (*Kent*)	9	16	0	717	145	44.81	3
C S Dempster (*Leics*)	24	38	6	1429	164*	44.65	5
R C M Kimpton (*O U*)	12	21	1	884	115	44.20	5
R J O Meyer (*Som*)	7	13	3	434	202*	43.40	1
H W Parks (*Sussex*)	34	51	10	1695	174	41.34	4
†T S Worthington (*Derbys*)	30	45	3	1734	174	41.28	5
R H C Human (*Worcs*)	9	16	2	551	80	39.35	0
†A E Fagg (*Kent*)	31	52	3	1927	257	39.32	4
E R T Holmes (*Surrey*)	35	53	5	1874	172	39.04	3
D R Wilcox (*Essex*)	12	18	1	653	133	38.41	1
†C J Barnett (*Gloucs*)	34	58	3	2098	204*	38.14	6

BOWLING	M	O	M	R	W	Avge
E Ingram (*Ireland*)	2	68.2	24	142	11	12.90
H Larwood (*Notts*)	22	679.1	165	1544	119	12.97
†H Verity (*Yorks*)	36	1289.3	463	2847	216	13.18
W H Copson (*Derbys*)	31	946.4	239	2135	160	13.34
W E Bowes (*Yorks*)	30	874.4	277	1649	123	13.40
J C Boucher (*Ireland*)	3	67.4	9	192	14	13.71
C I J Smith (*Middx*)	31	985.4	254	2006	133	15.08
C G Cole (*Kent*)	3	98.3	26	247	15	15.43
J C Clay (*Glam*)	10	397.4	104	977	62	15.75
T F Smailes (*Yorks*)	32	864.4	207	2281	130	17.54
†A R Gover (*Surrey*)	34	1159.2	185	3547	200	17.73
†G O B Allen (*Middx*)	16	500.3	96	1442	81	17.80
L C Eastman (*Essex*)	24	635.1	222	1340	74	18.10
A V Pope (*Derbys*)	30	918	279	1975	99	18.13
J M Brocklebank (*C U*)	7	207	62	610	33	18.48
G S Boyes (*Hants*)	27	769.2	230	1675	90	18.61
R T D Perks (*Worcs*)	31	943.5	174	2588	139	18.61
†R W V Robins (*Middx*)	24	533.1	106	1553	82	18.93
H Hunt (*Som*)	11	95.2	25	285	15	19.00
G W Robinson (*Notts*)	2	106.4	35	228	12	19.00

†Played for England but not featured above: H Gimblett, M J L Turnbull, G Duckworth, A Mitchell, Jas Langridge, J M Sims, W Voce and R E S Wyatt.

First-class averages: 1937

BATTING	M	I	NO	Runs	HS	Avge	100s
†W R Hammond (*Gloucs*)	33	55	5	3252	217	65.04	13
†J Hardstaff jun (*Notts*)	28	46	2	2540	266	57.72	8
†L Hutton (*Yorks*)	35	58	7	2888	271*	56.62	10
C S Dempster (*Leics*)	17	26	3	1247	154*	54.21	5
†E Paynter (*Lancs*)	34	58	4	2904	322	53.77	5
R E S Wyatt (*Warw*)	32	54	5	2625	232	53.37	9
G L Berry (*Leics*)	28	51	4	2446	184*	52.04	7
†J H Parks (*Sussex*)	35	63	4	3003	168	50.89	11
†L E G Ames (*Kent*)	30	52	4	2347	201*	48.89	7
†D C S Compton (*Middx*)	32	46	4	1980	177	47.14	3
R J Gregory (*Surrey*)	31	50	3	2166	154	46.08	7
W W Keeton (*Notts*)	30	52	8	2004	136	45.54	4
L B Fishlock (*Surrey*)	28	45	4	1850	146	45.12	7
W J Edrich (*Middx*)	34	53	5	2154	175	44.87	3
D R Wilcox (*Essex*)	16	31	0	1390	142	44.83	4
G W Parker (*Gloucs*)	9	15	0	662	210	44.13	3
H Sutcliffe (*Yorks*)	33	54	5	2162	189	44.12	4
G V Gunn (*Notts*)	30	48	8	1763	149*	44.07	3
C B Harris (*Notts*)	29	49	6	1877	113	43.65	2
†C Washbrook (*Lancs*)	25	40	4	1546	145	42.94	4

BOWLING	M	O	M	R	W	Avge
J C Boucher (*Ireland*)	3	75	19	155	26	5.96
†A D G Matthews (*Glam*)	8	253.3	59	680	47	14.46
†H Verity (*Yorks*)	33	1386.2	487	3168	202	15.68
J H Melville (*Scotld*)	3	84.5	12	290	18	16.11
†T W J Goddard (*Gloucs*)	33	1478.1	359	4158	248	16.76
J C Clay (*Glam*)	26	1103.3	229	3052	176	17.34
†C I J Smith (*Middx*)	34	1150.5	278	2604	149	17.47
W H Copson (*Derbys*)	17	495.5	101	1398	76	18.39
M S Nichols (*Essex*)	31	1023.2	239	2742	148	18.52
J M Sims (*Middx*)	31	829.1	150	2442	129	18.93
†A R Gover (*Surrey*)	33	1219.4	191	3816	201	18.98
W E Bowes (*Yorks*)	21	711	194	1606	82	19.58
T P B Smith (*Essex*)	31	995.3	186	3039	155	19.60
I A R Peebles (*Middx*)	6	112.4	20	334	17	19.64
R F H Darwall-Smith (*O U*)	12	394.3	77	1102	56	19.67
G S Boyes (*Hants*)	12	454.1	148	907	46	19.71
J Cowie (*NZ*)	24	860.1	184	2275	114	19.95
†R W V Robins (*Middx*)	29	664.2	96	1980	99	20.00
H S Hargreaves (*Yorks*)	8	172.2	39	445	22	20.22
S H Martin (*Worcs*)	32	883.3	185	2309	114	20.25

†Played for England but not featured above: C J Barnett, F R Brown, A W Wellard and W Voce.

First-class averages: 1938

BATTING	M	I	NO	Runs	HS	Avge	100s
D G Bradman (*Austr*)	20	26	5	2429	278	115.66	13
†W R Hammond (*Gloucs*)	26	42	2	3011	271	75.27	15
†J Hardstaff jun (*Notts*)	22	37	7	1827	169*	60.90	7
†L Hutton (*Yorks*)	25	37	6	1874	364	60.45	6
†E Paynter (*Lancs*)	31	52	6	2691	291	58.50	8
W A Brown (*Austr*)	25	37	5	1854	265*	57.93	5
H T Bartlett (*Sussex*)	21	31	4	1548	175*	57.33	5
A L Hassett (*Austr*)	24	32	3	1589	220*	54.79	5
†W J Edrich (*Middx*)	30	51	6	2378	245	52.84	6
A E Fagg (*Kent*)	29	53	6	2456	244	52.25	9
C S Dempster (*Leics*)	17	26	1	1300	187	52.00	6
J R Thompson (*C U/Warw*)	11	18	1	858	191	50.47	2
P A Gibb (*C U/Yks*)	23	37	3	1658	204	48.76	4
John G Langridge (*Sussex*)	32	54	4	2347	227	46.94	5
C L Badcock (*Austr*)	24	39	4	1604	198	45.82	4
†D C S Compton (*Middx*)	30	47	6	1868	180*	45.56	5
R E S Wyatt (*Warw*)	26	41	7	1549	149	45.55	3
J M Lomas (*O U*)	11	21	1	908	124	45.40	1
F S Lee (*Som*)	29	51	6	2019	162	44.86	7
B H Valentine (*Kent*)	22	37	1	1593	242	44.25	6

BOWLING	M	O	M	R	W	Avge
A D G Matthews (*Glam*)	7	180.5	36	395	30	13.16
†W E Bowes (*Yorks*)	29	932.3	294	1844	121	15.23
†H Verity (*Yorks*)	31	1191.4	424	2476	158	15.67
W J O'Reilly (*Austr*)	20	709.4	215	1726	104	16.59
H J Butler (*Notts*)	10	257.1	55	648	39	16.61
I A R Peebles (*Middx*)	12	234.5	51	649	38	17.07
J C Clay (*Glam*)	21	648	150	1639	94	17.43
W Wooller (*Glam*)	5	143.2	30	374	21	17.80
E A Watts (*Surrey*)	31	777.1	141	2383	129	18.47
†K Farnes (*Essex*)	19	701.2	137	2016	107	18.84
E Ingram (*Middx*)	5	114	39	227	12	18.91
F Ward (*Austr*)	19	526.2	99	1773	92	19.27
J H Mayer (*Warw*)	24	687.4	145	1868	96	19.45
L O'B Fleetwood-Smith (*Austr*)	20	555	98	1719	88	19.53
T B Mitchell (*Derbys*)	28	717	104	2570	131	19.61
†M Leyland (*Yorks*)	35	385.4	99	1237	63	19.63
W H Copson (*Derbys*)	24	742.4	156	1995	101	19.75
M S Nichols (*Essex*)	30	1228.1	264	3408	171	19.92
C I J Smith (*Middx*)	31	1153	283	2672	132	20.24
†A W Wellard (*Som*)	29	1233.4	241	3491	172	20.29

†Played for England but not featured above: L E G Ames, C J Barnett, D V P Wright, W F F Price, R A Sinfield and A Wood.

First-class averages: 1939

BATTING	M	I	NO	Runs	HS	Avge	100s
G A Headley (*W I*)	20	30	6	1745	234*	72.60	6
†W R Hammond (*Gloucs*)	28	46	7	2479	302	63.56	7
†L Hutton (*Yorks*)	33	52	6	2883	280*	62.27	12
†D C S Compton (*Middx*)	31	50	6	2468	214*	56.09	8
†J Hardstaff jun (*Notts*)	30	46	7	2129	159	54.58	5
H Sutcliffe (*Yorks*)	21	29	3	1416	234*	54.46	6
†W W Keeton (*Notts*)	25	39	5	1765	312*	51.91	2
J Iddon (*Lancs*)	31	45	11	1716	217*	50.47	4
W J Edrich (*Middx*)	29	45	1	2186	161	49.68	7
Jas Langridge (*Sussex*)	27	42	8	1652	161	48.58	2
L E G Ames (*Kent*)	25	46	6	1846	201	46.15	5
†N Oldfield (*Lancs*)	33	48	5	1922	147*	44.69	4
†E Paynter (*Lancs*)	31	50	4	1953	222	42.45	4
H E Dollery (*Warw*)	27	41	5	1519	177	42.19	4
A V Avery (*Essex*)	23	36	4	1335	161	41.71	2
John G Langridge (*Sussex*)	31	51	0	2106	202	41.29	6
†A E Fagg (*Kent*)	27	51	6	1851	169*	41.13	5
†H Gimblett (*Som*)	30	50	3	1922	129	40.89	5
J D B Robertson (*Middx*)	28	44	1	1755	154	40.81	4
D E Davies (*Glam*)	28	45	3	1714	287*	40.80	3

BOWLING	M	O	M	R	W	Avge
H Verity (*Yorks*)	33	916.3	270	2509	191	13.13
C W S Lubbock (*O U/Nrthts*)	6	73.4	8	271	19	14.26
†W E Bowes (*Yorks*)	28	712.3	151	1767	122	14.48
†T W J Goddard (*Gloucs*)	29	819	139	2973	200	14.86
†W H Copson (*Derbys*)	31	669.3	92	2238	146	15.36
J C Boucher (*Ireland*)	1	55	11	158	10	15.80
L M Cranfield (*Gloucs*)	3	56.4	5	231	14	16.50
†D V P Wright (*Kent*)	26	571	64	2371	141	16.81
C Lewis (*Kent*)	15	301.5	58	959	56	17.12
L N Constantine (*W I*)	22	488.4	67	1831	103	17.77
A D G Matthews (*Glam*)	11	266.2	33	894	50	17.88
†L Hutton (*Yorks*)	33	220.7	38	822	44	18.68
†M S Nichols (*Essex*)	29	666.5	96	2284	121	18.87
E P Robinson (*Yorks*)	30	659.5	130	2289	120	19.07
K Farnes (*Essex*)	8	179.6	18	726	38	19.10
A E G Rhodes (*Derbys*)	28	123	14	479	25	19.16
†R T D Perks (*Worcs*)	30	828	112	3057	159	19.22
G H Pope (*Derbys*)	31	476.6	69	1640	83	19.75
A V Pope (*Derbys*)	30	567.5	79	1862	94	19.80
S Pether (*O U*)	10	191.4	34	622	31	20.06

†Played for England but not featured above: A Wood.

First-class averages: 1945

BATTING	M	I	NO	Runs	HS	Avge	100s
K R Miller (*AS*)	7	13	3	725	185	72.50	3
W R Hammond (*Eng*)	6	10	0	592	121	59.20	3
C Washbrook (*Lancs*)	8	15	2	637	112	49.00	1
L Hutton (*Yorks*)	9	16	0	782	188	48.87	2
W J Edrich (*Eng*)	9	16	3	602	78	46.30	0
C G Pepper (*AS*)	7	12	1	469	168	42.63	1
D R Cristofani (*AS*)	4	6	1	175	110*	35.00	1
R E S Wyatt (*RAF*)	3	5	1	127	59	31.75	0
L B Fishlock (*Eng*)	5	9	1	243	95	30.37	0
S G Sismey (*AS*)	6	9	0	260	78	28.88	0

BOWLING	M	O	M	R	W	Avge
C F T Price (*AS*)	3	35.4	4	99	7	14.14
A W H Mallett (*U33*)	1	45	8	117	8	14.62
W E Phillipson (*Eng*)	2	74	19	171	10	17.10
D R Cristofani (*AS*)	4	128.4	20	359	19	18.89
E P Robinson (*Yorks*)	2	70	12	136	7	19.42
A E Nutter (*Lancs*)	2	48.3	5	137	7	19.57
R S Ellis (*AS*)	7	247.3	67	498	25	19.92
R S Hodge (*U33*)	1	32	2	109	5	21.80
R Pollard (*Lancs*)	5	218.3	44	679	28	24.25
G H Pope (*Eng*)	4	171.3	46	419	17	24.64

Note: after the war in Europe ended in May, 1945 a very restricted list of first-class fixtures was arranged – 11 matches in all being played.

First-class averages: 1946

BATTING	M	I	NO	Runs	HS	Avge	100s
†W R Hammond (*Gloucs*)	19	26	5	1783	214	84.90	7
V M Merchant (*India*)	26	41	9	2385	242*	74.53	7
†C Washbrook (*Lancs*)	28	43	8	2400	182	68.57	9
†D C S Compton (*Middx*)	30	45	6	2403	235	61.61	10
M P Donnelly (*O U/Mx*)	15	29	2	1425	142	52.77	6
M M Walford (*Som*)	7	10	1	472	141*	52.44	2
D Brookes (*Nrthts*)	28	48	5	2191	200	50.95	7
†L B Fishlock (*Surrey*)	27	46	2	2221	172	50.47	5
H Gimblett (*Som*)	25	41	2	1947	231	49.92	7
V S Hazare (*India*)	25	33	6	1344	244*	49.77	2
†W J Edrich (*Middx*)	29	45	7	1890	222*	49.73	5
H P Crabtree (*Essex*)	11	17	1	793	146	49.56	3
†L Hutton (*Yorks*)	24	38	6	1552	183*	48.50	4
Nawab of Pataudi (*India*)	20	26	5	981	121	46.71	4
L J Todd (*Kent*)	26	44	2	1864	162	44.38	6
W W Keeton (*Notts*)	27	48	2	2021	160	43.93	5
H T Barling (*Surrey*)	32	52	6	2014	233*	43.78	6
H E Dollery (*Warw*)	28	49	4	1944	144	43.20	4
W Place (*Lancs*)	30	51	6	1868	122	41.51	4
D R Wilcox (*Essex*)	10	14	2	484	134	40.33	1

BOWLING	M	O	M	R	W	Avge
A Booth (*Yorks*)	28	917.2	423	1289	111	11.61
J C Clay (*Glam*)	26	812.2	204	1742	130	13.40
A D G Matthews (*Glam*)	23	693.2	215	1329	93	14.29
E P Robinson (*Yorks*)	33	1138.2	354	2498	167	14.95
E Crush (*Kent*)	4	93.3	27	226	15	15.06
†W E Bowes (*Yorks*)	21	596.2	203	987	65	15.18
J F Parker (*Surrey*)	25	384.5	102	873	56	15.58
W E Hollies (*Warw*)	28	1528	433	2871	184	15.60
M Leyland (*Yorks*)	22	86.5	23	250	16	15.62
J A Young (*Middx*)	32	1023.4	321	2036	122	16.68
H L Hazell (*Som*)	23	430.4	124	940	54	17.40
T W J Goddard (*Gloucs*)	29	1310.2	358	3095	177	17.48
T R Armstrong (*Derbys*)	5	187	26	493	28	17.60
G Lester (*Leics*)	18	237	78	556	31	17.93
†D V P Wright (*Kent*)	23	839.1	203	2261	125	18.08
C Gladwin (*Derbys*)	27	866.2	239	2002	109	18.36
L H Gray (*Middx*)	25	841.4	194	1880	102	18.43
C J Knott (*Hants*)	25	841	179	2254	122	18.47
C Cook (*Gloucs*)	30	1123.1	327	2477	133	18.62
A W Wellard (*Som*)	22	983	239	2318	124	18.69

†Played for England but not featured above: J Hardstaff jun, P A Gibb, J T Ikin, A V Bedser, R Pollard, T F Smailes, W Voce, T G Evans, A R Gover, Jas Langridge and T P B Smith.

First-class averages: 1947

BATTING	M	I	NO	Runs	HS	Avge	100s
†D C S Compton (*Middx*)	30	50	8	3816	246	90.85	18
†W J Edrich (*Middx*)	30	52	8	3539	267*	80.43	12
E I Lester (*Yorks*)	7	11	2	657	142	73.00	3
†C Washbrook (*Lancs*)	28	47	8	2662	251*	68.25	11
L E G Ames (*Kent*)	22	42	7	2272	212*	64.91	7
J Hardstaff jun (*Notts*)	28	44	7	2396	221*	64.75	7
†L Hutton (*Yorks*)	26	44	4	2585	270*	64.62	11
W Place (*Lancs*)	31	47	7	2501	266*	62.52	10
M P Donnelly (*O U*)	17	30	6	1488	162*	62.00	5
B Mitchell (*S Afr*)	23	37	4	2014	189*	61.03	8
M M Walford (*Som*)	9	18	2	971	264	60.68	2
†J D B Robertson (*Middx*)	32	57	4	2760	229	52.07	12
K G Viljoen (*S Afr*)	21	33	4	1441	201	49.68	6
L J Todd (*Kent*)	29	55	5	2312	173	46.24	7
T N Pearce (*Essex*)	25	42	7	1597	137*	45.62	2
†N W D Yardley (*Yorks*)	30	46	3	1906	177	44.32	5
G A Edrich (*Lancs*)	29	37	5	1410	132	44.06	2
C H Palmer (*Worcs*)	8	15	1	616	177	44.00	2
A E Fagg (*Kent*)	29	56	5	2203	184	43.19	5
D G W Fletcher (*Surrey*)	27	46	3	1857	194	43.18	3

BOWLING	M	O	M	R	W	Avge
G W Youngson (*Scotld*)	2	58	21	105	13	8.07
J C Clay (*Glam*)	13	495.3	126	1069	65	16.44
T W J Goddard (*Gloucs*)	32	1451.2	344	4119	238	17.30
†J A Young (*Middx*)	33	1291.1	416	2765	159	17.38
W E Bowes (*Yorks*)	25	789.5	270	1277	73	17.49
†R Howorth (*Worcs*)	35	1254	375	2929	164	17.85
J C Laker (*Surrey*)	18	575.5	135	1420	79	17.97
†G H Pope (*Derbys*)	22	786.1	186	2096	114	18.38
†C J Barnett (*Gloucs*)	27	359	102	937	50	18.74
B L Muncer (*Glam*)	28	802.2	206	2018	107	18.85
R Aspinall (*Yorks*)	7	225	37	692	36	19.22
P I Bedford (*Middx*)	4	168.5	35	484	25	19.36
A H Kardar (*O U*)	11	374.1	128	882	45	19.60
T F Smailes (*Yorks*)	22	536	148	1274	65	19.60
†C Gladwin (*Derbys*)	25	917.3	263	2297	117	19.63
J H G Deighton (*CS*)	3	81.1	17	216	11	19.63
R Pollard (*Lancs*)	31	1218.1	322	2855	144	19.82
†C Cook (*Gloucs*)	28	1134.3	352	2927	144	20.32
†D V P Wright (*Kent*)	27	1175.5	252	3739	177	21.12
E P Robinson (*Yorks*)	28	1044	309	2331	108	21.58

†Played for England but not featured above: T G Evans, K Cranston, A V Bedser, W H Copson, H E Dollery, W E Hollies, J W Martin, C J Barnett and H J Butler.

First-class averages: 1948

BATTING	M	I	NO	Runs	HS	Avge	100s
D G Bradman (*Austr*)	23	31	4	2428	187	89.92	11
A L Hassett (*Austr*)	22	27	6	1563	200*	74.42	7
A R Morris (*Austr*)	21	29	2	1922	290	71.18	7
†C Washbrook (*Lancs*)	23	31	4	1900	200	70.37	7
†L Hutton (*Yorks*)	28	48	7	2654	176*	64.73	10
†D C S Compton (*Middx*)	29	47	7	2451	252*	61.27	9
W A Brown (*Austr*)	22	26	1	1448	200	57.92	8
S J E Loxton (*Austr*)	22	22	5	973	159*	57.23	3
A E Fagg (*Kent*)	27	48	3	2423	203	53.84	8
R N Harvey (*Austr*)	22	27	6	1129	126	53.76	4
J D B Robertson (*Middx*)	30	54	7	2366	154	50.34	7
†W J Edrich (*Middx*)	33	55	6	2428	168*	49.55	9
T N Pearce (*Essex*)	29	44	7	1825	211*	49.32	4
†J F Crapp (*Gloucs*)	29	45	6	1872	127	48.00	5
K R Miller (*Austr*)	22	26	3	1088	202*	47.30	2
J T Ikin (*Lancs*)	30	37	5	1493	106	46.65	2
H A Pawson (*O U/Kt*)	17	25	3	1025	128	46.59	2
A V Avery (*Essex*)	26	44	3	1890	214*	46.09	6
L E G Ames (*Kent*)	26	45	2	1943	212	45.18	7
H Gimblett (*Som*)	24	45	1	1857	310	42.20	4

BOWLING	M	O	M	R	W	Avge
J C Boucher (*Ireld*)	2	77	26	159	18	8.83
J C Clay (*Glam*)	9	259.5	61	581	41	14.17
W Nichol (*Scotld*)	2	93.4	30	193	13	14.84
G A R Lock (*CS*)	2	64	12	168	11	15.27
J R Urquhart (*C U*)	4	105.4	34	231	15	15.40
R R Lindwall (*Austr*)	22	573.1	139	1349	86	15.68
P A Whitcombe (*O U/Mx*)	14	391.3	112	749	47	15.93
W A Johnston (*Austr*)	21	850.1	279	1675	102	16.42
C Gladwin (*Derbys*)	26	960.3	266	2174	128	16.98
G H Pope (*Derbys*)	21	699	171	1721	100	17.24
B L Muncer (*Glam*)	31	1289.2	381	2748	159	17.28
A C Shirreff (*CS*)	4	132.2	26	366	21	17.42
K R Miller (*Austr*)	22	429.4	117	985	56	17.58
N G Hever (*Glam*)	25	633.5	150	1493	84	17.77
C L McCool (*Austr*)	17	399.2	97	1016	57	17.82
J Bailey (*Hants*)	29	1118.3	375	2194	121	18.13
†W E Hollies (*Warw*)	27	1270	357	2697	147	18.34
†J A Young (*Middx*)	28	1149.4	432	2165	118	18.34
I W Johnson (*Austr*)	22	667.2	228	1562	85	18.37
E P Robinson (*Yorks*)	19	589.3	222	1148	62	18.51

†Played for England but not featured above: T G Evans, J C Laker, A V Bedser, N W D Yardley, H E Dollery, C J Barnett, A Coxon, K Cranston, J G Dewes, G M Emmett, J Hardstaff jun, R Pollard, A J Watkins and D V P Wright.

First-class averages: 1949

BATTING	M	I	NO	Runs	HS	Avge	100s
J Hardstaff jun (*Notts*)	24	40	9	2251	162*	72.61	8
†L Hutton (*Yorks*)	33	56	6	3429	269*	68.58	12
P B H May (*CS*)	6	12	1	695	175	63.18	1
†R T Simpson (*Notts*)	29	46	6	2525	238	63.12	6
M P Donnelly (*NZ*)	29	45	8	2287	206	61.81	5
J R Thompson (*Warw*)	6	12	2	609	103	60.90	2
John G Langridge (*Sussex*)	28	53	5	2914	234*	60.70	12
B Sutcliffe (*NZ*)	29	49	5	2627	243	59.70	7
W W Keeton (*Notts*)	24	38	1	2049	210	55.37	6
D J Insole (*C U/Ex*)	26	39	9	1640	219*	54.66	4
†C Washbrook (*Lancs*)	18	27	1	1419	141	54.57	5
M M Walford (*Som*)	9	16	2	763	120	54.50	1
N Oldfield (*Nrthts*)	27	47	3	2192	168	49.81	4
W M Wallace (*NZ*)	27	41	6	1722	197	49.20	5
†D C S Compton (*Middx*)	33	56	4	2530	182	48.65	9
H E Dollery (*Warw*)	28	48	4	2084	200	47.36	6
L E G Ames (*Kent*)	25	47	2	2125	160	47.22	7
G H G Doggart (*C U/Sx*)	27	51	6	2063	219*	45.84	5
L B Fishlock (*Surrey*)	32	56	3	2426	210	45.77	7
J F Crapp (*Gloucs*)	27	48	4	2014	140	45.77	7

BOWLING	M	O	M	R	W	Avge
R Aspinall (*Yorks*)	4	133.1	32	289	30	9.63
G O B Allen (*Middx*)	5	81.3	15	216	14	15.42
T W J Goddard (*Gloucs*)	28	1187.2	326	3069	160	19.18
A H Kardar (*O U/War*)	21	922.5	366	1777	92	19.31
R Howorth (*Worcs*)	30	1113.4	386	2278	117	19.47
H L Hazell (*Som*)	25	923.1	303	2065	106	19.48
†J A Young (*Middx*)	32	1453.3	526	2948	150	19.65
†J C Laker (*Surrey*)	28	1191.1	419	2422	122	19.85
†H L Jackson (*Derbys*)	28	1030.1	256	2450	120	20.41
†W E Hollies (*Warw*)	29	1626.4	584	3413	166	20.56
A Coxon (*Yorks*)	26	920.2	238	2100	101	20.79
M H Wrigley (*O U*)	10	314.4	75	792	38	20.84
W K Laidlaw (*Scotld*)	2	54	6	209	10	20.90
R O Jenkins (*Worcs*)	33	1146.1	187	3879	183	21.19
†A V Bedser (*Surrey*)	26	1005.2	244	2344	110	21.30
†C Gladwin (*Derbys*)	28	1045.4	297	2513	117	21.47
M F Tremlett (*Som*)	24	492	116	1324	61	21.70
W B Roberts (*Lancs*)	22	892.4	354	1556	71	21.91
†D V P Wright (*Kent*)	21	755.1	125	2829	129	21.93
G H Chesterton (*O U*)	12	423.2	129	1010	46	21.95

†Played for England but not featured above: T E Bailey, W J Edrich, F G Mann, F R Brown, T G Evans, D B Close, A Wharton, J D B Robertson and A J Watkins.

First-class averages: 1950

BATTING	M	I	NO	Runs	HS	Avge	100s
E de C Weekes (*WI*)	23	33	4	2310	304*	79.65	7
W Watson (*Yorks*)	9	12	2	684	132	68.40	3
F M M Worrell (*WI*)	22	31	5	1775	261	68.26	6
†R T Simpson (*Notts*)	28	47	6	2576	243*	62.82	8
†J G Dewes (*C U/Mx*)	27	45	4	2432	212	59.31	9
†L Hutton (*Yorks*)	25	40	3	2128	202*	57.51	6
M B Hofmeyer (*O U*)	12	21	2	1063	161	55.94	4
C L Walcott (*WI*)	25	36	6	1674	168*	55.80	7
†C Washbrook (*Lancs*)	23	36	3	1807	114	54.75	4
J Hardstaff jun (*Notts*)	19	30	4	1383	149*	53.19	5
D Brookes (*Nrthts*)	29	45	6	2000	171	51.28	5
G Cox (*Sussex*)	33	55	7	2369	165*	49.35	6
L Livingston (*Nrthts*)	31	47	5	1966	123	46.80	2
R J Christiani (*WI*)	24	34	10	1094	131*	45.58	4
†D C S Compton (*Middx*)	14	23	2	957	144	45.57	2
F C Gardner (*Warw*)	31	53	11	1911	215*	45.50	4
†W G A Parkhouse (*Glam*)	29	46	2	1997	162	45.38	7
†D S Sheppard (*C U/Sx*)	26	44	2	1885	227	44.88	5
L B Fishlock (*Surrey*)	33	59	5	2417	147	44.75	6
C B Harris (*Notts*)	25	36	5	1382	239*	44.58	2

BOWLING	M	O	M	R	W	Avge
R Tattersall (*Lancs*)	21	1404.4	502	2623	193	13.59
J C Boucher (*Ireld*)	2	107.5	28	262	18	14.55
A Hamer (*Derbys*)	22	82.3	14	220	15	14.66
S Ramadhin (*WI*)	21	1043.4	398	2009	135	14.88
†J C Laker (*Surrey*)	30	1409.5	522	2544	166	15.32
R Appleyard (*Yorks*)	3	83.4	18	177	11	16.09
D E Davies (*Glam*)	33	413	132	923	57	16.19
J B Statham (*Lancs*)	15	300.5	82	613	37	16.56
†J H Wardle (*Yorks*)	33	1627.5	741	2909	174	16.71
†M J Hilton (*Lancs*)	26	1169.3	484	2267	135	16.79
R T Weeks (*Warw*)	6	146	49	275	16	17.18
C Gladwin (*Derbys*)	19	752.4	223	1682	94	17.89
A L Valentine (*WI*)	21	1185.2	475	2207	123	17.94
A Coxon (*Yorks*)	32	1155.5	299	2437	131	18.60
J D C Goddard (*WI*)	22	295.2	94	618	33	18.72
G W Youngson (*Scotld*)	3	157.1	38	339	18	18.83
†W E Hollies (*Warw*)	28	1329.1	488	2713	144	18.84
A Jessup (*O U*)	2	77.3	21	189	10	18.90
J Lawrence (*Som*)	30	788	158	2174	115	18.90
J W Martin (*Kent*)	6	287	98	536	28	19.14

†Played for England but not featured above: T E Bailey, T G Evans, W J Edrich, G H G Doggart, N W D Yardley, R O Jenkins, A V Bedser, R Berry, F R Brown, H E Dollery, D J Insole, A J W McIntyre, D Shackleton and D V P Wright.

First-class averages: 1951

BATTING	M	I	NO	Runs	HS	Avge	100s
†P B H May (*C U/Sy*)	26	43	9	2339	178*	68.79	9
†D C S Compton (*Middx*)	25	40	6	2193	172	64.50	8
J G Dewes (*Middx*)	7	10	2	515	116*	64.37	2
F Jakeman (*Nrthts*)	27	41	6	1989	258*	56.82	6
J D B Robertson (*Middx*)	35	56	4	2917	201*	56.09	7
†L Hutton (*Yorks*)	31	47	8	2145	194*	55.00	7
D S Sheppard (*C U/Sx*)	23	43	3	2104	183	52.60	7
E A B Rowan (*S Afr*)	26	41	4	1852	236	50.05	5
†J T Ikin (*Lancs*)	22	35	7	1371	192	48.96	4
†T W Graveney (*Gloucs*)	29	50	3	2291	201	48.74	8
J V Wilson (*Yorks*)	35	51	9	2027	223*	48.26	6
L Livingston (*Nrthts*)	25	43	5	1709	210	44.97	5
J D Clay (*Notts*)	14	20	1	851	112	44.78	2
W Place (*Lancs*)	32	44	6	1692	163	44.52	4
†F A Lowson (*Yorks*)	28	41	2	1702	155	43.64	4
G A Edrich (*Lancs*)	31	46	7	1693	155	43.41	7
†R T Simpson (*Notts*)	30	47	3	1899	212	43.15	5
R T Spooner (*Warw*)	27	43	2	1767	158	43.09	4
J Hardstaff jun (*Notts*)	18	28	1	1157	247	42.85	3
J E Cheetham (*S Afr*)	23	33	5	1196	133*	42.71	3

BOWLING	M	O	M	R	W	Avge
S Ramadhin (*Comm*)	2	62	20	90	14	6.42
R Appleyard (*Yorks*)	31	1323.1	391	2829	200	14.14
†J B Statham (*Lancs*)	27	714.2	178	1466	97	15.11
†A V Bedser (*Surrey*)	27	1100	130	2024	130	15.56
J E McConnon (*Glam*)	26	862.3	238	2186	136	16.07
G E Tribe (*Nrthts*)	3	130.4	33	275	17	16.17
E Smith (*Derbys*)	3	50.3	9	167	10	16.70
J J Warr (*C U/Mx*)	16	449.2	119	1011	59	17.13
M F Tremlett (*Som*)	32	179.2	23	192	11	17.45
W E Hollies (*Warw*)	28	1393.2	500	2566	145	17.69
C Gladwin (*Derbys*)	26	1065.1	297	2526	142	17.78
†J C Laker (*Surrey*)	28	1301.3	400	2681	149	17.99
R Howorth (*Worcs*)	28	1066.2	326	2242	124	18.08
†R Tattersall (*Lancs*)	30	1171.5	430	2236	121	18.47
C W Grove (*Warw*)	29	979.4	271	2038	110	18.52
B L Muncer (*Glam*)	32	884.3	290	1914	102	18.76
J A Young (*Middx*)	35	1680.2	741	2976	157	18.95
Jas Langridge (*Sussex*)	32	243.3	68	589	31	19.00
R Berry (*Lancs*)	10	358	168	508	26	19.53
†D Shackleton (*Hants*)	31	1161.2	332	2561	130	19.70

†Played for England but not featured above: T E Bailey, W Watson, J H Wardle, F R Brown, D Brennan, T G Evans and M J Hilton.

First-class averages: 1952

BATTING	M	I	NO	Runs	HS	Avge	100s
†D S Sheppard (*C U/Sx*)	23	39	4	2262	239*	64.62	10
†P B H May (*C U/Sy*)	27	47	7	2498	197	62.45	10
†L Hutton (*Yorks*)	28	45	3	2567	189	61.11	11
E I Lester (*Yorks*)	26	42	6	1786	178	49.61	6
†W Watson (*Yorks*)	29	43	9	1651	114	48.55	3
P R Umrigar (*Ind*)	25	41	6	1688	229*	48.22	5
†T W Graveney (*Gloucs*)	29	50	7	2066	171	48.04	6
D Brookes (*Nrthts*)	30	54	7	2229	204*	47.42	6
J Hardstaff jun (*Notts*)	25	39	5	1597	126	46.97	6
†J T Ikin (*Lancs*)	28	46	4	1912	154	45.52	4
C A Milton (*Gloucs*)	30	55	11	1922	146*	43.68	3
D Kenyon (*Worcs*)	34	60	2	2489	171	42.91	7
W Place (*Lancs*)	26	39	4	1483	133	42.37	1
H E Dollery (*Warw*)	30	51	2	2073	212	42.30	4
†R T Simpson (*Notts*)	31	54	1	2222	216	41.92	5
M Tompkin (*Leics*)	27	46	1	1875	156	41.66	4
G A Edrich (*Lancs*)	33	53	3	2067	162	41.34	4
R Subba Row (*C U*)	14	19	3	661	94	41.31	0
A V Avery (*Essex*)	25	39	4	1441	224	41.17	2
N H Rogers (*Hants*)	33	58	3	2244	164	40.80	3

BOWLING	M	O	M	R	W	Avge
R G Thompson (*Warw*)	3	82.5	14	229	18	12.72
†F S Trueman (*Yorks*)	9	282.4	57	841	61	13.78
W Nichol (*Scotld*)	3	77.2	25	166	11	15.09
G B Shaw (*Glam*)	6	87.2	23	242	15	16.13
†A V Bedser (*Surrey*)	31	1184.4	296	2530	154	16.42
†G A R Lock (*Surrey*)	32	1109.4	416	2237	131	17.07
C W Grove (*Warw*)	28	945.3	238	2022	118	17.13
B L Muncer (*Glam*)	30	862.2	259	1816	105	17.29
A Townsend (*Warw*)	27	508.2	101	1310	74	17.70
R Tattersall (*Lancs*)	30	1165.5	409	2586	146	17.71
†J C Laker (*Surrey*)	30	1072	342	2219	125	17.75
J B Statham (*Lancs*)	28	881.5	186	1989	110	18.08
D Shackleton (*Hants*)	29	1156.1	351	2479	135	18.35
H L Jackson (*Derbys*)	28	907.5	233	2220	119	18.65
R Wood (*Yorks*)	7	234	96	511	27	18.92
C Gladwin (*Derbys*)	30	1258.2	402	2917	152	19.19
J H Wardle (*Yorks*)	36	1857	810	3460	177	19.54
J A Young (*Middx*)	32	1448.1	511	3241	163	19.88
W E Hollies (*Warw*)	28	1148.4	438	2412	118	20.44
J D Bannister (*Warw*)	10	238.5	58	663	32	20.71

†Played for England but not featured above: T G Evans, D C S Compson, R O Jenkins and A J Watkins.

First-class averages: 1953

BATTING	M	I	NO	Runs	HS	Avge	100s
W A Johnston (*Austr*)	16	17	16	102	28*	102.00	0
Jas Langridge (*Sussex*)	7	10	5	358	104*	71.60	1
R N Harvey (*Austr*)	25	35	4	2040	202*	65.80	10
†L Hutton (*Yorks*)	27	44	5	2458	241	63.02	8
L Livingston (*Nrthts*)	24	36	6	1710	140	57.00	7
K R Miller (*Austr*)	24	31	3	1433	262*	51.17	4
†P B H May (*Surrey*)	34	59	9	2554	159	51.08	8
R Subba Row (*C U/Sy*)	30	46	10	1823	146*	50.63	4
D Barrick (*Nrthts*)	26	38	7	1530	166*	49.35	3
†W J Edrich (*Middx*)	32	60	6	2557	211	47.35	5
†R T Simpson (*Notts*)	33	60	5	2505	157	45.54	7
D S Sheppard (*Sussex*)	35	57	7	2270	186*	45.40	7
†W Watson (*Yorks*)	31	48	9	1769	162*	45.35	3
H E Dollery (*Warw*)	30	46	4	1889	173	44.97	3
†D Kenyon (*Worcs*)	32	58	3	2439	238*	44.34	6
A L Hassett (*Austr*)	21	30	2	1236	148	44.14	5
N Oldfield (*Nrthts*)	22	35	6	1280	149*	44.13	3
F A Lowson (*Yorks*)	26	39	2	1622	259*	43.83	4
M C Cowdrey (*O U/Kt*)	28	50	6	1917	154	43.56	4
J S Ord (*Warw*)	10	14	4	420	109	42.00	1

BOWLING	M	O	M	R	W	Avge
J A Bailey (*Essex*)	4	151.4	35	326	25	13.04
C J Knott (*Hants*)	7	223	65	521	38	13.71
H L Jackson (*Derbys*)	24	741.4	229	1574	103	15.28
G A R Lock (Surrey)	19	732.1	282	1590	100	15.90
†J B Statham (*Lancs*)	28	723.5	229	1650	101	16.33
R R Lindwall (*Austr*)	23	639.1	178	1394	85	16.40
B Dooland (*Notts*)	31	1332.3	461	2852	172	16.58
R Carter (*Derbys*)	3	88	35	199	12	16.58
†A V Bedser (*Surrey*)	31	1253	340	2702	162	16.67
R G Archer (*Austr*)	20	395.1	104	955	57	16.75
†T W Graveney (*Gloucs*)	31	94.3	19	324	19	17.05
G Smith (*Kent*)	6	226.5	89	536	31	17.29
†J C Laker (*Surrey*)	31	1165.5	383	2366	135	17.52
†R Tattersall (*Lancs*)	35	1186	345	2974	164	18.13
A V G Wolton (*Warw*)	26	183.2	62	402	22	18.27
P J Loader (*Surrey*)	20	602.2	135	1463	80	18.28
G H McKinna (*O U*)	4	119	32	257	14	18.35
C Gladwin (*Derbys*)	29	1114	369	2430	132	18.40
C W Grove (*Warw*)	20	694.1	174	1536	83	18.50
W E Hollies (*Warw*)	23	912.4	352	1676	90	18.62

†Played for England but not featured above: D C S Compton, T E Bailey, J H Wardle, T G Evans, F R Brown and F S Trueman.

First-class averages: 1954

BATTING	M	I	NO	Runs	HS	Avge	100s
†D C S Compton (*Middx*)	19	28	2	1524	278	58.62	4
†T W Graveney (*Gloucs*)	25	38	4	1950	222	57.35	5
L Livingston (*Nrthts*)	30	48	7	2269	207*	55.34	6
D Kenyon (*Worcs*)	33	58	7	2636	253*	51.68	6
G G Tordoff (*Som*)	6	11	1	512	156*	51.20	2
†P B H May (*Surrey*)	29	41	7	1702	211*	50.05	6
P E Richardson (*Worcs*)	14	23	2	1010	185	48.09	2
†D S Sheppard (*Sussex*)	21	37	4	1398	120	42.36	3
A V Wolton (*Warw*)	31	49	6	1770	165	41.16	3
D J Insole (*Essex*)	32	51	6	1841	172*	40.91	4
K F Barrington (*Surrey*)	19	25	4	848	108*	40.23	3
†W J Edrich (*Middx*)	31	50	5	1783	195	39.62	6
M J K Smith (*O U/Lei*)	24	43	4	1540	201*	39.48	2
Wazir Mohammad (*Pak*)	16	22	6	628	87	39.25	0
J F Pretlove (*C U*)	14	23	3	779	137	38.95	4
F A Lowson (*Yorks*)	32	52	6	1785	165	38.80	6
J V Wilson (*Yorks*)	35	54	5	1870	138	38.16	4
Hanif Mohammad (*Pak*)	28	48	4	1623	142*	36.88	2
D B Close (*Yorks*)	31	43	7	1320	164	36.66	2
†J M Parks (*Sussex*)	31	52	7	1649	135	36.64	2

BOWLING	M	O	M	R	W	Avge
S S J Huey (*Ireld*)	1	52.5	12	97	14	6.92
J H G Deighton (*MCC*)	1	49	13	91	10	9.10
†J B Statham (*Lancs*)	22	615.3	194	1300	92	14.13
†R Appleyard (*Yorks*)	30	1026.3	315	2221	154	14.43
†P J Loader (*Surrey*)	27	699.2	167	1589	109	14.57
H L Jackson (*Derbys*)	29	949.3	296	1851	125	14.80
†A V Bedser (*Surrey*)	30	957.4	299	1828	121	15.10
†J C Laker (*Surrey*)	29	966.2	315	2048	135	15.17
M Heath (*Hants*)	6	128.3	40	262	17	15.41
†J E McConnon (*Glam*)	25	730.2	233	1680	109	15.41
B Dooland (*Notts*)	30	1287.1	408	3035	196	15.48
F S Trueman (*Yorks*)	33	808.2	187	2085	134	15.55
†J H Wardle (*Yorks*)	32	1262	520	2449	155	15.80
A J Watkins (*Glam*)	33	757.3	248	1630	103	15.82
R G Thompson (*Warw*)	7	148.5	36	366	23	15.91
G A R Lock (*Surrey*)	32	1027.1	411	2000	125	16.00
C Gladwin (*Derbys*)	30	1082.1	391	2272	136	16.70
†R Tattersall (*Lancs*)	28	1040.3	359	1967	117	16.81
Fazal Mahmood (*Pak*)	16	665.3	246	1350	77	17.53
A Eato (*Derbys*)	7	133.5	35	299	17	17.58

†Played for England but not featured above: R T Simpson, T E Bailey, T G Evans, L Hutton and F H Tyson.

First-class averages: 1955

BATTING	M	I	NO	Runs	HS	Avge	100s
D J McGlew (*S Afr*)	22	34	2	1871	161	58.46	5
†P B H May (*Surrey*)	25	42	5	1902	125	51.40	5
†M C Cowdrey (*Kent*)	14	25	4	1038	139	49.42	4
J G Dewes (*Middx*)	8	16	2	673	117	48.07	2
†W Watson (*Yorks*)	28	48	14	1623	214*	47.73	4
†T W Graveney (*Gloucs*)	28	51	2	2117	159	43.20	5
†D J Insole (*Essex*)	34	62	5	2427	142	42.57	9
K J Grieves (*Lancs*)	25	35	6	1232	137	42.28	2
J M Parks (*Sussex*)	36	63	8	2314	205*	42.07	5
L Livingston (*Nrthts*)	32	58	5	2172	172*	40.98	5
C Washbrook (*Lancs*)	31	46	3	1743	170	40.53	4
G L Willatt (*Derbys*)	6	11	1	401	133	40.10	1
P E Richardson (*Worcs*)	13	26	3	905	91*	39.34	0
R Subba Row (*Nrthts*)	27	41	5	1384	260*	38.44	4
R A McLean (*S Afr*)	25	41	3	1448	151	38.10	4
D Brookes (*Nrthts*)	32	58	5	2012	177	37.96	3
R E Marshall (*Hants*)	32	60	4	2115	110*	37.76	3
†D Kenyon (*Worcs*)	34	64	3	2296	131	37.63	5
†T E Bailey (*Essex*)	28	50	12	1429	152*	37.60	3
D S Sheppard (*Sussex*)	10	18	1	637	104	37.47	1

BOWLING	M	O	M	R	W	Avge
D F Cox (*Surrey*)	7	76.5	21	169	14	12.07
†R Appleyard (*Yorks*)	16	558.1	185	1106	85	13.01
D Shackleton (*Hants*)	31	1220.2	438	2183	159	13.72
H L Jackson (*Derbys*)	16	469.1	151	914	64	14.28
†G A R Lock (*Surrey*)	33	1407.4	497	3109	216	14.39
†J B Statham (*Lancs*)	22	754.5	216	1573	108	14.56
H R A Kelleher (*Surrey*)	3	74	15	179	12	14.91
R E Marshall (*Hants*)	32	188.4	69	439	28	15.67
H J Tayfield (*S Afr*)	23	1160.5	461	2253	143	15.75
†F S Trueman (*Yorks*)	31	996.5	214	2454	153	16.03
†J H Wardle (*Yorks*)	34	1486.4	572	3149	195	16.14
C Gladwin (*Derbys*)	30	1163.5	435	2383	147	16.21
†F J Titmus (*Middx*)	35	1449.5	522	3117	191	16.31
M Kerrigan (*Scotld*)	2	88.2	27	188	11	17.09
D V P Wright (*Kent*)	28	737.4	193	2185	127	17.20
V H D Cannings (*Hants*)	25	788.1	263	1659	94	17.64
†P J Loader (*Surrey*)	27	718.2	178	1695	96	17.65
E Smith (*Derbys*)	30	885.2	318	1854	105	17.65
W E Hollies (*Warw*)	27	1053.1	400	2035	115	17.69
N W D Yardley (*Yorks*)	32	137.3	58	213	12	17.75

†Played for England but not featured above: D C S Compton, K F Barrington, T G Evans, F H Tyson, A V Bedser, D B Close, J T Ikin, J C Laker, F A Lowson, A J W McIntyre and R T Spooner.

First-class averages: 1956

BATTING	M	I	NO	Runs	HS	Avge	100s
K D Mackay (*Austr*)	20	28	7	1103	163*	52.52	3
†T W Graveney (*Gloucs*)	31	54	6	2397	200	49.93	9
L Livingston (*Nrthts*)	28	47	6	2006	188*	48.92	2
J W Burke (*Austr*)	21	35	7	1339	194	47.82	4
†T E Bailey (*Essex*)	25	38	11	1186	141*	43.92	3
D Brookes (*Nrthts*)	30	52	7	1916	203*	42.57	4
M A Eager (*O U*)	13	21	4	713	125	41.94	1
†D S Sheppard (*Sussex*)	11	17	1	670	113	41.87	1
J M Parks (*Sussex*)	32	51	6	1884	129	41.86	4
†D J Insole (*Essex*)	31	51	3	1988	162	41.41	4
A Wharton (*Lancs*)	30	48	6	1738	137	41.38	4
D Kenyon (*Worcs*)	31	52	3	1994	259	40.69	4
†P E Richardson (*Worcs*)	29	45	2	1718	147	39.95	5
M J K Smith (*O U/Warw*)	17	32	2	1163	126	38.76	3
A C Walton (*O U*)	17	33	2	1200	152	38.70	3
†W Watson (*Yorks*)	33	49	9	1540	149	38.50	4
†M C Cowdrey (*Kent*)	28	45	4	1569	204*	38.26	3
†A S M Oakman (*Sussex*)	32	52	3	1866	178	38.08	5
S E Leary (*Kent*)	10	18	2	609	91	38.06	0
†P B H May (*Surrey*)	30	50	7	1631	128*	37.93	3

BOWLING	M	O	M	R	W	Avge
F Fee (*Ireld*)	1	52	19	100	14	7.14
†G A R Lock (*Surrey*)	26	1058.2	437	1932	155	12.46
R Illingworth (*Yorks*)	34	620.4	206	1348	103	13.08
T Angus (*Middx*)	4	86.3	23	197	15	13.13
F R Brown (*F F*)	1	51.4	11	151	11	13.72
M J Hilton (*Lancs*)	34	1199.5	558	2207	158	13.96
C Cook (*Gloucs*)	29	1195.1	475	2111	149	14.16
R K Platt (*Yorks*)	10	269	78	584	41	14.24
†J C Laker (*Surrey*)	25	959.3	353	1906	132	14.43
R Tattersall (*Lancs*)	26	955.4	387	1722	117	14.71
†J B Statham (*Lancs*)	25	679.3	210	1351	91	14.84
D J Shepherd (*Glam*)	32	1226.5	433	2719	177	15.36
J V C Griffiths (*Gloucs*)	3	71.3	22	171	11	15.54
P J Loader (*Surrey*)	33	893.2	227	1946	124	15.69
†J H Wardle (*Yorks*)	35	1230.2	464	2482	153	16.22
D Shackleton (*Hants*)	31	1273	455	2288	140	16.34
K G Suttle (*Sussex*)	32	203	76	402	24	16.75
T Greenhough (*Lancs*)	19	444.2	141	1044	62	16.83
F W Moore (*Lancs*)	5	113.5	26	291	17	17.11
†R Appleyard (*Yorks*)	26	870.4	260	1932	112	17.25

†Played for England but not featured above: C Washbrook, T G Evans, F S Trueman, D C S Compton, F H Tyson and A E Moss.

First-class averages: 1957

BATTING	M	I	NO	Runs	HS	Avge	100s
†P B H May (Surrey)	29	41	3	2347	285*	61.76	7
F M M Worrell (WI)	20	34	9	1470	191*	55.80	4
†M C Cowdrey (Kent)	27	43	6	1917	165	51.81	5
†T W Graveney (Gloucs)	32	53	5	2361	258	49.18	8
C L Walcott (WI)	21	36	5	1414	131	45.61	3
J M Parks (Sussex)	31	55	6	2171	132*	44.30	4
F A Lowson (Yorks)	13	19	2	752	154	44.23	3
G St A Sobers (WI)	25	44	6	1644	219*	43.26	3
C A Milton (Gloucs)	19	31	9	943	89	42.86	0
†D V Smith (Sussex)	31	54	5	2088	166	42.61	5
O G Smith (WI)	26	45	9	1483	168	41.19	3
D R W Silk (Som)	9	16	3	526	79	40.46	0
W Watson (Yorks)	26	39	2	1462	162	39.51	4
†D J Insole (Essex)	29	49	5	1725	150*	39.20	4
K F Barrington (Surrey)	35	53	11	1642	136	39.09	6
†T E Bailey (Essex)	27	42	8	1322	132	38.88	2
C J Poole (Notts)	24	46	6	1535	110*	38.37	1
D Kenyon (Worcs)	34	62	3	2231	200*	37.81	6
J D B Robertson (Middx)	32	59	2	2155	201*	37.80	4
C D M Melville (O U)	11	21	2	715	142	37.63	2

BOWLING	M	O	M	R	W	Avge
F Fee (Ireld)	1	43	19	60	12	5.00
C J M Kenny (FF)	1	36.5	7	96	10	9.60
†G A R Lock (Surrey)	31	1194.1	449	2550	212	12.02
V Broderick (Nrthts)	5	130.3	52	236	17	13.88
S Ramadhin (WI)	20	938.1	361	1664	119	13.98
†J B Statham (Lancs)	28	896.4	251	1895	126	15.03
†J C Laker (Surrey)	28	1016.5	393	1921	126	15.24
E A Bedser (Surrey)	33	548.5	178	1188	77	15.42
†P J Loader (Surrey)	34	878.2	215	2058	133	15.47
D Gibson (Surrey)	3	102	18	265	17	15.58
D Shackleton (Hants)	29	1217.3	446	2429	155	15.67
C W Leach (Warw)	15	155.2	58	305	19	16.05
G Smith (Kent)	10	389.1	109	923	57	16.19
H L Jackson (Derbys)	30	1014.2	362	2295	141	16.27
M H J Allen (Nrthts)	29	626	246	1277	78	16.37
A V Bedser (Surrey)	34	1031.4	267	2170	131	16.56
†T E Bailey (Essex)	27	738.3	207	1771	104	17.02
†F S Trueman (Yorks)	32	842.2	184	2303	135	17.05
D Pickles (Yorks)	13	239.4	52	651	37	17.59
D Livingstone (Scotld)	5	152.5	43	322	18	17.88

†Played for England but not featured above: P E Richardson, D S Sheppard, T G Evans, D B Close, D W Richardson and J H Wardle.

First-class averages: 1958

BATTING	M	I	NO	Runs	HS	Avge	100s
†P B H May (Surrey)	29	41	6	2231	174	63.74	8
†W Watson (Leics)	25	44	9	1632	141	46.62	3
†R Subba Row (Nrthts)	32	48	9	1810	300	46.41	5
†M J K Smith (Warw)	31	51	3	2126	160	44.29	3
J R Reid (NZ)	28	39	3	1429	161	39.69	3
R E Marshall (Hants)	33	57	3	2118	193	39.22	5
†M C Cowdrey (Kent)	28	41	4	1437	139	38.83	3
P T Marner (Lancs)	32	50	6	1685	110	38.29	1
D M Young (Gloucs)	32	57	5	1914	194	36.80	5
W B Stott (Yorks)	20	30	1	1036	141	35.72	2
†T W Graveney (Gloucs)	28	47	6	1459	156	35.58	2
†E R Dexter (C U/Sx)	26	46	2	1565	114	35.56	3
G H G Doggart (Sussex)	8	11	1	352	162*	35.20	1
A V G Wolton (Warw)	25	42	8	1186	102	34.88	1
G Atkinson (Som)	9	16	1	514	164	34.26	2
K G Suttle (Sussex)	30	50	6	1499	186	34.06	3
J D B Robertson (Middx)	30	50	4	1560	99	33.91	0
A H Phebey (Kent)	22	38	5	1112	157	33.69	3
G Barker (Essex)	27	42	1	1378	157	33.60	1
†P E Richardson (Worcs)	27	46	1	1498	123	33.28	3

BOWLING	M	O	M	R	W	Avge
S S J Huey (Ireld)	2	55	17	102	13	7.84
H L Jackson (Derbys)	26	829	295	1572	143	10.99
†G A R Lock (Surrey)	29	1014.4	382	2055	170	12.08
†J B Statham (Lancs)	29	894.2	275	1648	134	12.29
†F S Trueman (Yorks)	30	637.5	176	1414	106	13.33
J M Allan (Scotld)	3	102	41	176	13	13.53
D M Sayer (O U/Kt)	21	552.2	155	1206	89	13.55
†J C Laker (Surrey)	28	882.5	330	1651	116	14.23
F Ridgway (Kent)	26	649.5	181	1454	98	14.83
J H Wardle (Yorks)	24	715.4	281	1401	91	15.39
D Shackleton (Hants)	29	1320.2	505	2549	165	15.44
B D Wells (Gloucs)	11	276.5	105	572	37	15.45
M J Hilton (Lancs)	26	692.4	292	1518	94	16.14
J A Bailey (O U/Ex)	16	427.3	126	962	59	16.30
C Gladwin (Derbys)	27	867.4	306	2011	123	16.34
M Heath (Hants)	28	910.4	264	2070	126	16.42
N I Thomson (Sussex)	30	985	310	2204	133	16.57
R Appleyard (Yorks)	10	187.3	56	448	27	16.59
K J Aldridge (Worcs)	16	417.1	94	1008	60	16.80
A E Moss (Middx)	29	831.5	227	2120	126	16.82

†Played for England but not featured above: C A Milton, T E Bailey, P J Loader, T G Evans and R Illingworth.

First-class averages: 1959

BATTING	M	I	NO	Runs	HS	Avge	100s
V L Manjrekar (India)	9	14	3	755	204*	68.63	2
†M J K Smith (Warw)	36	67	11	3245	200*	57.94	8
P R Umrigar (India)	22	38	5	1826	252*	55.33	5
W Watson (Leics)	27	50	10	2212	173	55.30	7
†G Pullar (Lancs)	31	55	7	2647	161	55.14	8
†K F Barrington (Surrey)	32	52	6	2499	186	54.32	6
P B Wight (Som)	23	39	3	1930	222*	53.61	6
J H Edrich (Surrey)	24	45	11	1799	126	52.91	7
J M Parks (Sussex)	32	56	11	2313	157*	51.40	6
†M C Cowdrey (Kent)	26	44	4	2008	250	50.20	6
†W G A Parkhouse (Glam)	28	49	3	2243	154	48.76	6
H Horton (Hants)	32	59	8	2428	140*	47.60	4
†P B H May (Surrey)	11	16	2	663	143	47.35	2
T E Bailey (Essex)	33	55	12	2011	146	46.76	6
†R Subba Row (Nrthts)	27	46	5	1917	183*	46.75	6
†R Illingworth (Yorks)	33	50	13	1726	162	46.64	5
†E R Dexter (Sussex)	30	53	8	2055	127	45.66	7
D J Insole (Essex)	28	50	5	2045	180	45.44	5
†M J Horton (Worcs)	32	58	3	2468	212	44.87	4
D B Carr (Derbys)	33	60	8	2292	156*	44.07	5

BOWLING	M	O	M	R	W	Avge
†J B Statham (Lancs)	26	977.4	267	2087	139	15.01
D A Allen (Gloucs)	30	635.5	286	1322	84	15.73
D A D Sydenham (Surrey)	5	174.4	41	399	25	15.96
J J Warr (Middx)	29	804.5	218	1798	109	16.49
H L Jackson (Derbys)	31	1168.5	349	2461	140	17.57
R G Thompson (Warw)	22	789.1	207	1743	97	17.96
J E McConnon (Glam)	30	789.1	202	2059	113	18.22
†J B Mortimore (Gloucs)	32	1091.3	472	2066	113	18.28
C Cook (Gloucs)	30	932.4	404	1850	101	18.31
†A E Moss (Middx)	26	785.5	228	1796	96	18.70
P J Loader (Surrey)	30	829.1	163	2196	115	19.09
†F S Trueman (Yorks)	30	1072.4	269	2730	140	19.50
F H Tyson (Nrthts)	22	702.5	180	1726	88	19.61
K G Suttle (Sussex)	31	81	13	237	12	19.75
C G Borde (India)	26	512.3	118	1485	72	20.62
R E Hitchcock (Warw)	10	153.4	50	374	18	20.77
D J Shepherd (Glam)	30	1084.5	328	2227	107	20.81
D Livingstone (Sctld)	4	137.1	29	354	17	20.82
L J Coldwell (Worcs)	21	705.4	192	1794	86	20.86
M Ryan (Yorks)	7	256.4	78	640	30	21.33

†Played for England but not featured above: R Swetman, T G Evans, K Taylor, C A Milton, T Greenhough, H J Rhodes and D B Close.

First-class averages: 1960

BATTING	M	I	NO	Runs	HS	Avge	100s
†R Subba Row (Nrthts)	18	32	5	1503	147*	55.66	4
Javed Burki (O U)	13	22	4	961	144*	53.38	3
†M J K Smith (Warw)	34	63	7	2551	169*	45.55	4
†E R Dexter (Sussex)	30	53	2	2217	157	43.47	7
H Horton (Hants)	34	59	9	2170	131	43.40	7
D J McGlew (S Afr)	25	39	8	1327	151*	42.80	2
†K F Barrington (Surrey)	31	53	9	1878	126	42.68	2
W J Stewart (Warw)	26	45	3	1764	129	42.00	1
R E Marshall (Hants)	35	62	5	2380	168	41.75	5
P B Wight (Som)	35	62	5	2375	155*	41.66	7
M J Stewart (Surrey)	30	51	6	1866	169*	41.46	5
C J Poole (Notts)	25	48	6	1701	133	40.50	2
S E Leary (Kent)	23	31	3	1129	117	40.32	3
G Atkinson (Som)	29	52	3	1928	190	39.34	5
T E Bailey (Essex)	32	48	6	1639	118	39.02	1
J H Edrich (Surrey)	30	52	3	1887	154	38.51	5
K G Suttle (Sussex)	34	58	7	1944	122	38.11	3
W E Russell (Middx)	34	63	9	2051	182	37.98	2
R A McLean (S Afr)	26	43	3	1516	207	37.90	4
H L Johnson (Derbys)	31	56	6	1872	140	37.44	4

BOWLING	M	O	M	R	W	Avge
†J B Statham (Lancs)	27	844.1	274	1662	135	12.31
M Kerrigan (Sctld)	1	69	26	131	10	13.10
H L Jackson (Derbys)	31	1082.2	310	2179	160	13.61
†A E Moss (Middx)	31	852	223	1866	136	13.72
A C Smith (O U/War)	29	54.5	14	139	10	13.90
†F S Trueman (Yorks)	32	1068.4	274	2447	175	13.98
N A T Adcock (S Afr)	20	738	196	1515	108	14.02
J D F Larter (Nrthts)	16	325.2	108	750	46	16.30
H J Rhodes (Derbys)	25	722.2	184	1550	91	17.03
D J Shepherd (Glam)	33	1130.4	358	2488	142	17.52
†R Illingworth (Yorks)	33	992.4	422	1914	109	17.55
D Gibson (Surrey)	27	636.2	144	1584	90	17.60
D Shackleton (Hants)	30	1271.5	503	2300	130	17.69
R J Hurst (Middx)	5	80.1	31	196	11	17.81
N Gifford (Worcs)	11	272	88	734	41	17.90
H W Tilly (Middx)	9	169	58	359	20	17.95
M H J Allen (Nrthts)	23	699.2	293	1497	83	18.03
N I Thomson (Sussex)	27	998.3	356	2002	106	18.88
†T Greenhough (Lancs)	35	1090.2	385	2289	121	18.91
D W White (Hants)	26	829.5	157	2369	124	19.10

†Played for England but not featured above: G Pullar, M C Cowdrey, P M Walker, J M Parks, D A Allen, D E V Padgett and R W Barber.

First-class averages: 1961

BATTING	M	I	NO	Runs	HS	Avge	100s
W M Lawry (Austr)	23	39	6	2019	165	61.18	9
N C O'Neill (Austr)	24	37	4	1981	162	60.03	7
†K F Barrington (Surrey)	24	42	7	2070	163	59.14	4
W E Alley (Som)	35	64	11	3019	221*	56.96	11
Nawab of Pataudi (O U)	15	24	2	1216	144	55.27	4
P J P Burge (Austr)	24	36	11	1376	181	55.04	4
F W Neate (O U)	11	19	6	712	112	54.76	1
†M C Cowdrey (Kent)	19	34	1	1730	156	52.42	7
R B Simpson (Austr)	26	44	6	1947	160	51.23	6
C C McDonald (Austr)	17	26	7	913	140	48.05	4
R A E Tindall (Surrey)	13	22	5	751	100*	44.17	1
B C Booth (Austr)	23	32	3	1279	127*	44.10	2
R N Harvey (Austr)	24	35	2	1452	140	44.00	5
R E Marshall (Hants)	32	62	2	2607	212	43.45	5
†G Pullar (Lancs)	32	61	7	2344	165*	43.40	5
E J Craig (C U/Lancs)	21	41	5	1528	208*	42.44	5
†M J K Smith (Warw)	35	67	5	2587	145	41.72	5
W Watson (Leics)	20	37	4	1349	217*	40.87	3
†P B H May (Surrey)	22	42	5	1499	153*	40.51	2
N W Hill (Notts)	31	60	4	2239	201*	39.98	6

BOWLING	M	O	M	R	W	Avge
W R Hunter (Ireld)	2	50.3	22	89	10	8.90
R V Webster (Sctld)	1	43	13	100	11	9.09
J T Botten (S Afr F)	3	105.5	24	243	21	11.57
J M Allen (Sctld)	3	104.4	36	188	15	12.53
A B Bainbridge (Yorks)	4	169.4	78	288	19	15.15
G St A Sobers (MCC)	3	78	19	214	13	16.46
P N Broughton (Leics)	3	78.3	24	210	12	17.50
†J A Flavell (Worcs)	34	1245.2	300	3043	171	17.79
B S Boshier (Leics)	26	800	193	1930	108	17.87
†R Illingworth (Yorks)	34	1104.3	437	2292	128	17.90
J S Savage (Leics)	35	1013.3	378	2310	122	18.93
D Shackleton (Hants)	33	1501.5	532	3017	158	19.09
M J Cowan (Yorks)	4	97.5	25	269	14	19.21
L J Coldwell (Worcs)	34	1142.4	295	2696	140	19.25
†F S Trueman (Yorks)	34	1190.1	302	3000	155	19.35
†D A Allen (Gloucs)	31	907.1	315	2410	124	19.43
C T Spencer (Leics)	30	999.4	247	2406	123	19.56
A E Moss (Middx)	28	922	282	2260	115	19.65
N Gifford (Worcs)	35	1145.1	447	2616	133	19.66
†H L Jackson (Derbys)	23	894.1	324	1719	86	19.98

†Played for England but not featured above: R Subba Row, E R Dexter, J T Murray, J B Statham, G A R Lock and D B Close.

First-class averages: 1962

BATTING	M	I	NO	Runs	HS	Avge	100s
R T Simpson (Notts)	11	20	4	867	105	54.18	2
†T W Graveney (Worcs)	29	48	6	2269	164*	54.02	9
†E R Dexter (Sussex)	29	47	7	2148	172	53.70	5
†M C Cowdrey (Kent)	24	38	3	1839	182	52.54	6
P B H May (Surrey)	20	31	5	1352	135	52.00	3
J H Edrich (Surrey)	30	55	7	2482	216	51.70	7
†K F Barrington (Surrey)	29	46	8	1865	146	49.07	6
D C Morgan (Derbys)	32	51	15	1669	124	46.36	3
†P H Parfitt (Middx)	31	51	4	2121	138	45.12	8
†M J Stewart (Surrey)	30	55	9	2045	200*	44.45	5
†D S Sheppard (Sussex)	14	26	3	1017	112	44.21	3
P B Wight (Som)	30	55	9	2030	215	44.13	4
M J K Smith (Warw)	37	64	12	2290	163	44.03	5
P J Watts (Nrthts)	30	50	9	1798	145	43.85	2
W J Stewart (Warw)	35	62	9	2318	182*	43.73	7
C A Milton (Gloucs)	26	47	10	1617	110*	43.70	4
R E Marshall (Hants)	28	52	3	2124	228*	43.34	6
W Watson (Leics)	17	29	2	1139	142	42.18	3
A Lightfoot (Nrthts)	30	51	6	1878	122*	41.73	5
Mushtaq Mohammad (Pak)	26	47	8	1614	176	41.38	3

BOWLING	M	O	M	R	W	Avge
F E Rumsey (Worcs)	2	93.2	29	170	18	9.44
R A Collinge (CS)	2	69.5	18	186	11	16.90
N Ferguson (Ireld)	2	66.5	15	188	11	17.09
C Cook (Gloucs)	19	477.1	209	994	58	17.13
D A D Sydenham (Surrey)	31	985.2	295	2030	115	17.65
†F S Trueman (Yorks)	33	1141.5	273	2717	153	17.75
†L J Coldwell (Worcs)	28	1104	253	2722	152	17.90
P J Loader (Surrey)	28	991.4	236	2426	131	18.51
J C Laker (Essex)	12	379.5	96	962	51	18.86
R V Webster (Warw)	4	148	37	400	21	19.04
†J D F Larter (Nrthts)	24	817.1	212	1924	101	19.04
H L Jackson (Derbys)	28	1018	326	2012	105	19.16
O S Wheatley (Glam)	32	1202.2	355	2628	136	19.32
H J Rhodes (Derbys)	19	654.2	198	1321	68	19.42
†R Illingworth (Yorks)	36	1081.2	426	2276	117	19.45
J A Flavell (Worcs)	20	761	172	1767	89	19.85
T W Cartwright (Warw)	28	923.2	338	2126	106	20.05
D Shackleton (Hants)	34	1717.1	678	3467	172	20.15
K E Palmer (Som)	25	802.3	201	1908	94	20.29
T E Bailey (Essex)	31	1091	297	2574	125	20.59

†Played for England but not featured above: D A Allen, J T Murray, G Pullar, F J Titmus, B R Knight, G Millman, G A R Lock and J B Statham.

First-class averages: 1963

BATTING	M	I	NO	Runs	HS	Avge	100s
Mushtaq Mohammad (*PakEg*)	8	12	1	593	137	53.90	2
G St A Sobers (*WI*)	24	34	6	1333	112	47.60	4
M J K Smith (*Warw*)	26	39	6	1566	144*	47.45	3
G Boycott (*Yorks*)	28	43	7	1628	165*	45.22	3
B F Butcher (*WI*)	22	34	5	1294	133	44.62	2
C C Hunte (*WI*)	21	37	6	1367	182	44.09	3
C C Inman (*Leics*)	31	51	11	1708	120*	42.70	1
†J B Bolus (*Notts*)	31	57	4	2190	202*	41.32	5
†K F Barrington (*Surrey*)	28	45	7	1568	110*	41.26	2
R B Kanhai (*WI*)	21	32	4	1149	119	41.03	1
†J H Edrich (*Surrey*)	31	55	7	1921	125	40.02	2
S E Leary (*Kent*)	21	38	5	1311	158	39.72	2
†P E Richardson (*Kent*)	31	56	2	2110	172	39.07	5
P H Parfitt (*Middx*)	33	53	5	1813	135*	37.77	3
G Atkinson (*Som*)	29	50	2	1797	177	37.43	3
T E Bailey (*Essex*)	33	54	12	1568	122	37.33	1
D B Carr (*Derbys*)	5	10	0	368	136	36.80	1
E D S A McMorris (*WI*)	17	29	5	878	190*	36.58	2
K G Suttle (*Sussex*)	31	57	4	1854	141	34.98	3
T W Graveney (*Worcs*)	28	50	7	1492	100	34.69	1

BOWLING	M	O	M	R	W	Avge
C C Griffith (*WI*)	20	695.5	192	1527	119	12.82
Antao d'Souza (*PakEg*)	5	115.5	38	221	16	13.81
Asif Iqbal (*PakEg*)	5	102.2	22	280	19	14.73
J S Waring (*Yorks*)	5	72.3	20	196	13	15.07
†F S Trueman (*Yorks*)	27	844.3	206	1955	129	15.15
P H Parfitt (*Middx*)	33	105	31	286	18	15.88
Mushtaq Mohammad (*PakEg*)	8	74.3	23	208	13	16.00
K E Palmer (*Som*)	30	1018.5	289	2234	139	16.07
A E Moss (*Middx*)	25	642.5	249	1355	84	16.13
D A D Sydenham (*Surrey*)	29	819.1	239	1753	108	16.23
†J B Statham (*Lancs*)	25	791	168	1874	113	16.58
†D Shackleton (*Hants*)	27	1387.3	583	2446	146	16.75
J D F Larter (*Nrthts*)	25	821.1	226	2028	121	16.76
A G Nicholson (*Yorks*)	23	589	180	1189	69	17.23
A S M Oakman (*Sussex*)	31	408.2	136	953	55	17.32
O S Wheatley (*Glam*)	27	752.1	228	1666	94	17.72
T W Cartwright (*Warw*)	26	888.1	360	1786	100	17.86
R V Webster (*Warw*)	18	571	138	1430	80	17.87
R Illingworth (*Yorks*)	22	483.4	170	1078	60	17.96
D G Doughty (*Som*)	16	214.1	68	635	35	18.14

†Played for England but not featured above: P J Sharpe, E R Dexter, D B Close, M J Stewart, J M Parks, F J Titmus, G A R Lock, M C Cowdrey, D A Allen and K V Andrew.

First-class averages: 1964

BATTING	M	I	NO	Runs	HS	Avge	100s
†K F Barrington (*Surrey*)	22	35	5	1872	256	62.40	4
B L d'Oliveira (*Worcs*)	5	8	2	370	119	61.66	2
R B Simpson (*Austr*)	22	38	8	1714	311	57.13	5
B C Booth (*Austr*)	23	36	8	1551	193*	55.39	3
†M C Cowdrey (*Kent*)	23	37	5	1763	117	55.09	4
T W Graveney (*Worcs*)	30	51	7	2385	164	54.20	5
†G Boycott (*Yorks*)	27	44	4	2110	177	52.75	6
R M Cowper (*Austr*)	20	29	4	1286	113	51.44	3
M J Stewart (*Surrey*)	24	44	5	1980	227*	50.76	6
R C Wilson (*Kent*)	28	49	5	2038	156	46.31	4
W E Russell (*Middx*)	31	56	5	2342	193	45.92	5
M D Willett (*Surrey*)	29	51	12	1789	126	45.87	4
N C O'Neill (*Austr*)	20	34	4	1369	151	45.63	4
J M Brearley (*CU/Mx*)	29	54	5	2178	169	44.44	5
†E R Dexter (*Sussex*)	27	49	5	1948	174	44.27	5
W M Lawry (*Austr*)	24	41	3	1601	121	42.13	5
G Pullar (*Lancs*)	29	53	5	1974	132*	41.12	3
†J H Edrich (*Surrey*)	26	45	3	1727	124	41.11	2
S E Leary (*Kent*)	22	37	7	1190	137*	39.66	1
M J Smith (*Middx*)	20	30	11	743	108*	39.10	1

BOWLING	M	O	M	R	W	Avge
J P Fellowes-Smith (*FF*)	1	35.5	7	95	11	8.63
J A Standen (*Worcs*)	13	422.2	131	832	64	13.00
†L J Coldwell (*Worcs*)	23	736.1	211	1518	98	15.48
A G Nicholson (*Yorks*)	22	581.4	159	1193	76	15.69
†T W Cartwright (*Warw*)	28	1146.2	502	2141	134	15.97
R R Bailey (*Nrthts*)	6	127.1	34	273	17	16.05
N I Thomson (*Sussex*)	29	925.5	293	1891	116	16.30
J C Balderstone (*Yorks*)	11	81.1	37	187	11	17.00
†F J Titmus (*Middx*)	27	1135.3	441	2106	123	17.12
R Illingworth (*Yorks*)	33	1012.1	374	2131	122	17.46
M K Kettle (*Nrthts*)	4	84.5	15	210	12	17.50
C Forbes (*Notts*)	13	442.3	143	950	53	17.92
†J A Flavell (*Worcs*)	24	786.3	170	1934	107	18.07
D A D Sydenham (*Surrey*)	19	626	176	1503	82	18.32
†N Gifford (*Worcs*)	31	978.5	399	2123	114	18.62
T Greenhough (*Lancs*)	7	259.2	68	658	35	18.80
P J Watts (*Nrthts*)	23	517.3	135	1178	62	19.00
D J Brown (*Warw*)	23	700.4	183	1648	86	19.16
M E Scott (*Nrthts*)	30	1037.4	416	2178	113	19.27
J S Pressdee (*Glam*)	32	773	204	2036	105	19.39

†Played for England but not featured above: P J Sharpe, J M Parks, P H Parfitt, F S Trueman, J S E Price, D A Allen, R W Barber, K Taylor, J B Mortimore and F E Rumsey.

First-class averages: 1965

BATTING	M	I	NO	Runs	HS	Avge	100s
†M C Cowdrey (*Kent*)	27	43	10	2093	196*	63.42	5
†J H Edrich (*Surrey*)	28	44	7	2319	310*	62.67	8
R G Pollock (*S Afr*)	14	24	4	1147	203*	57.35	3
†P H Parfitt (*Middx*)	28	44	9	1774	128	50.68	3
T W Graveney (*Worcs*)	28	45	9	1768	126	49.11	4
F J Cameron (*NZ*)	13	14	12	90	29*	45.00	0
B L d'Oliveira (*Worcs*)	31	45	6	1691	163	43.35	6
†E R Dexter (*Sussex*)	11	19	3	676	98	42.25	0
K C Bland (*S Afr*)	17	28	4	969	127	40.37	1
A Bacher (*S Afr*)	16	26	1	1008	121	40.32	2
†W E Russell (*Middx*)	30	54	5	1930	156	39.38	4
W J Stewart (*Warw*)	23	39	8	1187	102	38.29	1
E J Barlow (*S Afr*)	17	30	3	1026	129	38.00	2
†J M Parks (*Sussex*)	25	39	7	1212	106*	37.87	3
†K F Barrington (*Surrey*)	28	41	4	1384	163	37.40	4
J A Ormrod (*Worcs*)	18	26	9	634	66*	37.29	0
A Jones (*Glam*)	33	57	7	1837	142	36.74	5
B W Sinclair (*NZ*)	15	23	1	807	130	36.68	1
B E Congdon (*NZ*)	16	27	2	885	176*	35.40	2
†G Boycott (*Yorks*)	26	44	3	1447	95	35.29	0

BOWLING	M	O	M	R	W	Avge
H J Rhodes (*Derbys*)	24	646.5	187	1314	119	11.04
A B Jackson (*Derbys*)	28	807.5	262	1491	120	12.42
†J B Statham (*Lancs*)	24	771	205	1716	137	12.52
†T W Cartwright (*Warw*)	23	735.1	305	1505	108	13.93
†F S Trueman (*Yorks*)	30	754.4	180	1811	127	14.25
J A Flavell (*Worcs*)	29	910	217	2100	142	14.78
J D F Larter (*Nrthts*)	21	589.2	169	1333	87	15.32
D J Shepherd (*Glam*)	29	1053.2	461	1765	112	15.75
I J Jones (*Glam*)	23	654.3	203	1336	84	15.90
D Shackleton (*Hants*)	30	1246	529	2316	144	16.08
†F E Rumsey (*Som*)	28	823.4	234	1926	119	16.18
L J Coldwell (*Worcs*)	19	590.1	168	1324	80	16.55
†R Illingworth (*Yorks*)	32	854	360	1630	98	16.63
P M Pollock (*S Afr*)	12	371.4	108	851	50	17.02
W D F Dow (*Sctld*)	4	113.3	33	296	17	17.41
V C Brewster (*Warw*)	2	71.3	29	175	10	17.50
D M Sayer (*Kent*)	11	303.5	76	746	42	17.76
G G Arnold (*Surrey*)	24	607.2	149	1378	77	17.89
D R Smith (*Gloucs*)	27	822	223	1794	100	17.94
H Sully (*Nrthts*)	10	284.5	97	757	42	18.02

†Played for England but not featured above: R W Barber, M J K Smith, F J Titmus, J A Snow, J D F Larter, D J Brown and K Higgs.

First-class averages: 1966

BATTING	M	I	NO	Runs	HS	Avge	100s
G St A Sobers (*WI*)	18	25	3	1349	174	61.31	4
†T W Graveney (*Worcs*)	24	40	6	1777	166	52.26	4
†C Milburn (*Nrthts*)	23	44	6	1861	203	48.97	6
B F Butcher (*WI*)	19	25	2	1105	209*	48.04	3
W J Stewart (*Warw*)	9	14	3	505	166	45.90	1
†M J K Smith (*Warw*)	28	50	9	1824	140	44.48	4
S M Nurse (*WI*)	19	26	1	1105	155	44.20	2
†J H Edrich (*Surrey*)	28	49	3	1978	137	43.00	3
A R Lewis (*Glam*)	32	61	8	2190	223	41.32	5
P H Parfitt (*Middx*)	30	57	8	2018	114*	41.18	2
R M Prideaux (*Nrthts*)	29	55	7	1947	153*	40.56	6
†G Boycott (*Yorks*)	28	50	3	1854	164	39.44	6
†B L d'Oliveira (*Worcs*)	28	45	5	1536	126	38.40	2
R B Kanhai (*WI*)	19	28	1	1028	192*	38.07	3
D A J Holford (*WI*)	19	26	6	759	107*	37.95	2
†D L Amiss (*Warw*)	29	52	5	1765	160*	37.55	2
†J T Murray (*Middx*)	19	28	7	784	114	37.33	3
G Pullar (*Lancs*)	23	38	6	1184	167*	37.00	2
†K F Barrington (*Surrey*)	20	33	6	987	117*	36.55	3
R E Marshall (*Hants*)	29	54	2	1882	133	36.19	3

BOWLING	M	O	M	R	W	Avge
J A Bailey (*MCC*)	1	51.3	29	57	13	4.38
K D Boyce (*Essex*)	2	55.5	7	172	14	12.28
†D L Underwood (*Kent*)	29	1104.5	475	2167	157	13.80
A J O'Riordan (*Ireld*)	2	84	24	196	14	14.00
J A Flavell (*Worcs*)	26	822.3	199	1891	135	14.00
J B Statham (*Lancs*)	25	624.4	135	1479	102	14.50
A G Nicholson (*Yorks*)	29	879.3	297	1752	113	15.50
O S Wheatley (*Glam*)	29	865.3	269	1642	103	15.94
N Gifford (*Worcs*)	29	806.5	366	1458	91	16.02
J G Saunders (*OU*)	2	98.3	47	163	10	16.30
D J Shepherd (*Glam*)	28	1025.1	427	1844	111	16.61
D R Smith (*Gloucs*)	14	358.1	73	947	57	16.61
†R Illingworth (*Yorks*)	27	830.1	316	1680	100	16.80
Mushtaq Mohammad (*Nrthts*)	31	403	113	976	57	17.12
D S Steele (*Nrthts*)	30	235	82	505	29	17.41
D Wilson (*Yorks*)	31	861	341	1753	100	17.53
B A Langford (*Som*)	29	1026.4	438	1971	112	17.59
D Shackleton (*Hants*)	27	1306.2	574	2088	117	17.84
T W Cartwright (*Warw*)	25	842.5	304	1795	100	17.95
K E Palmer (*Som*)	31	729.1	149	1967	109	18.04

†Played for England but not featured above: R W Barber, M C Cowdrey, J M Parks, J A Snow, K Higgs, W E Russell, F J Titmus, I J Jones, D A Allen, D J Brown, B R Knight and D B Close.

First-class averages: 1967

BATTING	M	I	NO	Runs	HS	Avge	100s
†K F Barrington (*Surrey*)	28	40	10	2059	158*	68.63	6
†D L Amiss (*Warw*)	26	43	9	1850	176*	54.41	5
†G Boycott (*Yorks*)	24	40	4	1910	246*	53.05	4
†J H Edrich (*Surrey*)	31	47	5	2077	226*	49.45	5
R M Prideaux (*Nrthts*)	26	41	6	1637	125	46.77	3
C A Milton (*Gloucs*)	29	49	4	2089	145	46.42	7
Hanif Mohammad (*Pak*)	14	24	5	855	187*	45.00	3
†B L d'Oliveira (*Worcs*)	28	44	8	1618	174*	44.94	6
†W E Russell (*Middx*)	29	47	5	1885	167	44.88	4
†T W Graveney (*Worcs*)	26	42	4	1668	151	43.89	4
Majid Khan (*Pak*)	14	26	3	973	147*	42.30	4
M J Stewart (*Surrey*)	23	31	3	1184	112	42.28	2
M J Harris (*Middx*)	29	47	6	1715	160	41.82	4
M J K Smith (*Warw*)	28	46	6	1656	173*	41.40	3
N J Cosh (*CU*)	9	18	1	664	138	39.05	2
J B Bolus (*Notts*)	31	52	3	1911	149	39.00	4
†M C Cowdrey (*Kent*)	27	38	5	1281	150	38.81	3
P H Parfitt (*Middx*)	35	57	10	1819	162*	38.70	3
J M Parks (*Sussex*)	29	46	5	1571	150	38.31	2
B W Luckhurst (*Kent*)	23	33	4	1111	126*	38.31	3

BOWLING	M	O	M	R	W	Avge
M J Smithyman (*SAU*)	2	50.4	17	113	10	11.30
†D L Underwood (*Kent*)	27	979.1	459	1686	136	12.39
G A Cope (*Yorks*)	11	277.4	129	553	40	13.82
J N Graham (*Kent*)	24	906.2	353	1446	104	13.90
B R Knight (*Leics*)	5	146.4	35	357	23	15.52
T W Cartwright (*Warw*)	30	1194	495	2282	147	15.52
H J Rhodes (*Derbys*)	29	820.1	263	1585	102	15.53
A S M Oakman (*Sussex*)	18	159.4	61	271	17	15.94
†R Illingworth (*Yorks*)	27	881.3	365	1613	101	15.97
D R Cook (*Warw*)	5	160.5	45	330	20	16.50
J B Statham (*Lancs*)	24	635.2	156	1530	92	16.63
D Shackleton (*Hants*)	28	1157.1	529	1920	114	16.84
†K Higgs (*Lancs*)	23	743.5	203	1608	95	16.92
A G Nicholson (*Yorks*)	25	740.3	202	1725	101	17.07
G St A Sobers (*RofW*)	2	75.5	16	195	11	17.72
J A Flavell (*Worcs*)	16	496	110	1214	68	17.85
A B Jackson (*Derbys*)	26	617.4	211	1168	65	17.96
D Wilson (*Yorks*)	29	707.5	293	1368	76	18.00
G A R Lock (*Leics*)	28	1154.1	431	2319	128	18.11
Intikhab Alam (*Pak*)	7	241.4	47	637	35	18.20

†Played for England but not featured above: D B Close, C Milburn, J T Murray, D J Brown, J A Snow, R N S Hobbs, F J Titmus, G G Arnold and A P E Knott.

First-class averages: 1968

BATTING	M	I	NO	Runs	HS	Avge	100s
†G Boycott (*Yorks*)	20	30	7	1487	180*	64.65	7
I M Chappell (*Austr*)	20	30	4	1261	202*	48.50	3
B A Richards (*Hants*)	33	55	5	2395	206	47.90	5
R B Kanhai (*Warw*)	29	42	3	1819	253	46.64	6
†J H Edrich (*Surrey*)	27	50	5	2009	164	44.64	5
W M Lawry (*Austr*)	18	25	3	970	135	44.09	2
I R Redpath (*Austr*)	22	37	3	1474	135	43.35	4
G St A Sobers (*Notts*)	27	44	7	1590	105*	42.97	2
†M C Cowdrey (*Kent*)	20	28	2	1093	129	42.03	5
†R M Prideaux (*Nrthts*)	29	53	5	1993	108*	41.52	2
†K W R Fletcher (*Essex*)	30	54	8	1890	228*	41.08	4
F S Goldstein (*OU*)	14	25	1	980	155	40.83	1
D M Green (*Gloucs*)	30	54	1	2137	233	40.32	4
J B Bolus (*Notts*)	29	52	6	1827	140	39.71	4
D C Morgan (*Derbys*)	23	37	10	1057	103*	39.14	1
W J Stewart (*Warw*)	25	35	6	1131	143*	39.00	4
A Jones (*Glam*)	30	53	4	1862	110	38.00	2
A G E Ealham (*Kent*)	12	16	4	452	94*	37.66	0
†T W Graveney (*Worcs*)	21	34	4	1130	107*	37.66	1
C C Inman (*Leics*)	31	47	0	1735	108	36.91	1

BOWLING	M	O	M	R	W	Avge
J D Piachaud (*MCC*)	2	71.3	41	93	12	7.75
G Goonesena (*FF*)	1	44.5	13	87	10	8.70
G F Cross (*Leics*)	2	54.5	14	141	11	12.81
O S Wheatley (*Glam*)	16	549	222	1062	82	12.95
A Ward (*Derbys*)	5	147.5	41	399	30	13.30
D Wilson (*Yorks*)	30	815.5	335	1521	109	13.95
G A Cope (*Yorks*)	5	114.3	36	284	20	14.20
†R Illingworth (*Yorks*)	31	957.2	360	1882	131	14.36
†D L Underwood (*Kent*)	29	957.4	435	1821	123	14.80
†K Higgs (*Lancs*)	27	778.2	223	1637	108	15.15
J C J Dye (*Kent*)	14	254.2	65	535	35	15.28
T W Cartwright (*Warw*)	18	608.4	258	1145	71	16.12
†B L d'Oliveira (*Worcs*)	28	467.3	145	990	61	16.22
A G Nicholson (*Yorks*)	26	680	225	1430	87	16.43
J S E Price (*Middx*)	25	588.5	141	1470	89	16.51
N Gifford (*Worcs*)	29	760.3	327	1428	85	16.80
B Wood (*Lancs*)	26	210.3	68	504	30	16.80
J B Statham (*Lancs*)	20	488.5	124	1179	69	17.08
H J Rhodes (*Derbys*)	28	770.1	215	1700	99	17.17
D Shackleton (*Hants*)	28	1086.5	452	1888	109	17.32

†Played for England but not featured above: K F Barrington, C Milburn, E R Dexter, B R Knight, A P E Knott, J A Snow, D J Brown, D L Amiss, R W Barber and P I Pocock.

First-class averages: 1969

BATTING	M	I	NO	Runs	HS	Avge	100s
†J H Edrich (*Surrey*)	22	39	7	2238	181	69.93	8
B F Butcher (*WI*)	15	20	4	984	151	61.50	3
E J O Hemsley (*Worcs*)	10	16	5	676	138*	61.45	1
Mushtaq Mohammad (*Nrthts*)	24	40	9	1831	156*	59.06	6
B A Richards (*Hants*)	20	31	6	1440	155	57.60	5
B W Yuile (*NZ*)	11	13	5	400	81	50.00	0
C H Lloyd (*La/WI*)	26	36	6	1458	201*	48.60	2
B W Luckhurst (*Kent*)	27	44	4	1914	169	47.85	4
Younis Ahmed (*Surrey*)	28	46	9	1760	127*	47.56	5
M C Carew (*WI*)	12	18	3	677	172*	45.13	3
R C Fredericks (*WI*)	19	31	4	1215	168*	45.00	3
M J Stewart (*Surrey*)	23	37	7	1317	105	43.90	2
G St A Sobers (*Nt/WI*)	20	26	2	1023	104	42.62	2
C A Davis (*WI*)	16	25	5	848	106*	42.40	2
J B Bolus (*Notts*)	28	43	5	1603	147	42.18	4
R B Kanhai (*Warw*)	17	29	4	1044	173	41.76	1
B A G Murray (*NZ*)	12	21	1	800	123	40.00	1
M H Page (*Derbys*)	20	30	4	1037	162	39.88	2
Majid Khan (*Glam*)	28	38	3	1386	156	39.66	3
R M C Gilliat (*Hants*)	24	38	3	1386	223*	39.60	6

BOWLING	M	O	M	R	W	Avge
K Griffith (*Worcs*)	9	40.4	11	154	12	12.83
†A Ward (*Derbys*)	20	482.5	135	1023	69	14.82
M J Procter (*Gloucs*)	25	639.3	160	1623	108	15.02
†D L Underwood (*Kent*)	24	808.3	355	1561	101	15.45
T W Cartwright (*Warw*)	26	880.5	373	1748	108	16.18
R G D Willis (*Surrey*)	6	151	29	379	22	17.22
D Wilson (*Yorks*)	28	964.1	384	1772	102	17.37
D N F Slade (*Worcs*)	27	393.1	156	734	42	17.47
H J Rhodes (*Derbys*)	20	508.1	143	1167	64	18.23
J N Graham (*Kent*)	20	726	218	1460	79	18.48
G C Shillingford (*WI*)	11	221.2	41	669	36	18.58
C M Old (*Yorks*)	22	433	97	1061	57	18.61
†R Illingworth (*Yorks*)	25	599.1	206	1186	62	19.17
D W White (*Hants*)	22	695.3	156	1775	92	19.29
S Turner (*Essex*)	14	201.1	52	428	22	19.45
M A Nash (*Glam*)	25	659.1	191	1560	80	19.50
H J Howarth (*NZ*)	12	556.5	220	1126	57	19.75
Majid Khan (*Glam*)	28	154	40	298	15	19.86
†J A Snow (*Sussex*)	23	680.1	164	1740	87	20.00
N M McVicker (*Warw*)	23	518	124	1484	74	20.05

†Played for England but not featured above: G Boycott, J H Hampshire, B L d'Oliveira, A P E Knott, P J Sharpe, B R Knight, D J Brown, P H Parfitt, T W Graveney, K W R Fletcher, M H Denness and G G Arnold.

First-class averages: 1970

BATTING	M	I	NO	Runs	HS	Avge	100s
G St A Sobers (*Notts*)	19	32	9	1742	183	75.73	7
T W Graveney (*Worcs*)	21	34	13	1316	114	62.66	2
G M Turner (*Worcs*)	25	46	7	2379	154*	61.00	10
R B Kanhai (*Warw*)	21	37	4	1894	187*	57.39	7
†G Boycott (*Yorks*)	25	42	5	2051	260*	55.43	4
B A Richards (*Hants*)	20	33	2	1667	153	53.77	3
D W White (*Hants*)	14	12	9	150	57	50.00	0
J B Bolus (*Notts*)	27	53	9	2143	147*	48.70	2
†B W Luckhurst (*Kent*)	23	38	4	1633	203*	48.02	4
R T Virgin (*Som*)	24	47	0	2223	178	47.29	7
C H Lloyd (*Lancs*)	23	37	3	1603	163	47.14	5
†J H Edrich (*Surrey*)	21	37	3	1586	143	46.64	5
Majid Khan (*CU/Glam*)	22	42	2	1862	200	46.55	7
†D L Amiss (*Warw*)	27	48	10	1757	110	46.23	2
†K W R Fletcher (*Essex*)	25	44	6	1732	169*	45.57	4
W E Russell (*Middx*)	22	37	2	1580	128*	45.14	3
†B L d'Oliveira (*Worcs*)	19	31	3	1242	111	44.35	4
†M C Cowdrey (*Kent*)	21	35	6	1254	126	43.24	3
M J Harris (*Notts*)	25	49	4	1914	120	42.53	3
J M Parks (*Sussex*)	21	38	7	1300	166*	41.93	2

BOWLING	M	O	M	R	W	Avge
O Miles (*Jam*)	4	98.5	14	320	20	16.00
K J Wheatley (*Hants*)	14	106.5	31	253	15	16.86
Majid Khan (*CU/Glam*)	22	93	28	207	11	18.81
C Folkes (*Jam*)	4	90.3	24	190	10	19.00
D J Shepherd (*Glam*)	27	1123.3	420	2031	106	19.16
B Wood (*Lancs*)	26	287	80	601	31	19.38
E J Barlow (*RofW*)	5	152	33	396	20	19.80
N Gifford (*Worcs*)	25	965.5	331	2092	105	19.92
G D McKenzie (*Leics*)	22	736.4	186	1860	91	20.43
V A Holder (*Worcs*)	23	707.3	141	1773	84	21.10
J Sullivan (*Lancs*)	21	183.2	51	470	22	21.36
†P Lever (*Lancs*)	22	690.2	175	1774	83	21.37
R N S Hobbs (*Essex*)	27	736	178	2183	102	21.40
M J Procter (*Gloucs*)	20	647	181	1398	65	21.50
R A Hutton (*Yorks*)	26	619.1	152	1597	74	21.58
T W Cartwright (*Som*)	24	851.4	318	1891	86	21.98
I R Buxton (*Derbys*)	25	422.2	142	1018	46	22.13
P Carrick (*Yorks*)	3	84.3	14	312	14	22.28
M A Nash (*Glam*)	26	705.2	202	1761	79	22.29
†C M Old (*Yorks*)	24	629.4	138	1674	74	22.62

†Played for England but not featured above: R Illingworth, A P E Knott, A W Greig, J A Snow, D J Brown, D L Underwood, D Wilson, M H Denness, A Jones, K Shuttleworth and P J Sharpe (not official Tests).

First-class averages: 1971

BATTING	M	I	NO	Runs	HS	Avge	100s
†G Boycott (*Yorks*)	21	30	5	2503	233	100.12	13
Zaheer Abbas (*Pak*)	19	31	4	1508	274	55.85	4
†K W R Fletcher (*Essex*)	24	41	12	1490	164*	51.37	3
M J Harris (*Notts*)	26	45	1	2238	177	50.86	9
M J K Smith (*Warw*)	28	48	9	1951	127	50.02	6
†B W Luckhurst (*Kent*)	23	41	3	1861	155*	48.97	6
R B Kanhai (*Warw*)	24	41	9	1529	135*	47.78	3
B A Richards (*Hants*)	24	45	4	1938	141*	47.26	2
†J H Edrich (*Surrey*)	24	44	1	2031	195*	47.23	6
G St A Sobers (*Notts*)	23	38	6	1485	151*	46.40	3
Asif Iqbal (*Kt/Pak*)	23	34	6	1294	120	46.21	3
Aftab Gul (*Pak*)	16	27	2	1154	106	46.16	2
R C Fredericks (*Glam*)	18	33	3	1377	145*	45.90	2
M J Procter (*Gloucs*)	24	43	4	1786	167	45.79	7
R G A Headley (*Worcs*)	23	42	2	1805	187	45.12	4
E D Solkar (*India*)	16	24	6	802	113	44.55	1
G R J Roope (*Surrey*)	27	46	9	1641	171	44.35	5
S M Gavaskar (*India*)	15	27	1	1141	194	43.88	3
†M C Cowdrey (*Kent*)	10	16	1	655	132	43.66	1
D B Close (*Som*)	26	42	10	1389	116*	43.40	5

BOWLING	M	O	M	R	W	Avge
J M Allan (*Sctld*)	2	68	23	129	11	11.72
F Robertson (*Sctld*)	2	54.2	5	140	10	14.00
G G Arnold (*Surrey*)	21	632	171	1421	83	17.12
P J Sainsbury (*Hants*)	25	845.5	332	1874	107	17.51
T W Cartwright (*Som*)	25	976.4	407	1852	104	17.80
D Wilson (*Yorks*)	19	527.2	210	1095	60	18.25
N G Featherstone (*Middx*)	23	128.3	33	329	18	18.27
L R Gibbs (*Warw*)	26	1024.1	295	2475	131	18.89
M J Procter (*Gloucs*)	24	535	149	1232	65	18.95
†D L Underwood (*Kent*)	25	945.5	368	1986	102	19.47
J C Balderstone (*Leics*)	10	162.5	59	354	18	19.66
Mohammad Nazir (*Pak*)	6	164.1	52	396	20	19.80
†R Illingworth (*Leics*)	22	633	230	1269	64	19.82
D S Steele (*Nrthts*)	26	301.5	100	813	40	20.32
G D McKenzie (*Leics*)	26	716.4	196	1667	82	20.32
†R A Hutton (*Yorks*)	29	720.3	182	1628	80	20.35
†P Lever (*Lancs*)	18	453	122	1142	56	20.39
J N Graham (*Kent*)	21	638.4	176	1648	78	21.12
M J Llewellyn (*Glam*)	7	117	39	275	13	21.15
C E Waller (*Surrey*)	16	377.4	126	914	43	21.25

†Played for England but not featured above: B L d'Oliveira, A P E Knott, D L Amiss, N Gifford, R N S Hobbs, K Shuttleworth, A Ward, J S E Price, J A Jameson and J A Snow.

First-class averages: 1972

BATTING	M	I	NO	Runs	HS	Avge	100s
†G Boycott (*Yorks*)	13	22	5	1230	204*	72.35	6
G S Chappell (*Austr*)	18	28	10	1260	181	70.00	4
R B Kanhai (*Warw*)	21	30	5	1607	199	64.28	8
Majid Khan (*CU/Glam*)	21	38	4	2074	204	61.00	8
Mushtaq Mohammad (*Nrthts*)	23	40	7	1949	137*	59.06	6
†K W R Fletcher (*Essex*)	22	36	6	1763	181*	58.76	5
D L Amiss (*Warw*)	18	29	7	1219	192	55.40	5
†B W Luckhurst (*Kent*)	20	37	6	1706	184*	55.03	3
D S Steele (*Nrthts*)	22	39	8	1618	131	52.19	5
G M Turner (*Worcs*)	21	38	4	1764	170	51.88	7
D B Close (*Som*)	20	33	6	1396	135	51.70	3
R M Prideaux (*Sussex*)	22	39	6	1596	169*	48.36	4
D Lloyd (*Lancs*)	22	37	5	1510	177	47.18	6
E J O Hemsley (*Worcs*)	9	15	3	565	92	47.08	0
†B Wood (*Lancs*)	21	34	5	1341	186	46.24	2
H Pilling (*Lancs*)	17	30	5	1137	118	45.48	2
†A W Greig (*Sussex*)	16	27	4	1031	112	44.82	1
†M J K Smith (*Warw*)	22	34	6	1247	119	44.53	2
B A Richards (*Hants*)	19	33	1	1425	118	44.53	4
K R Stackpole (*Austr*)	21	35	5	1309	154*	43.63	3

BOWLING	M	O	M	R	W	Avge
G F Goddard (*Sctld*)	1	35	17	77	11	7.00
I M Chappell (*Austr*)	20	43.5	14	106	10	10.60
A Ward (*Derbys*)	8	164.5	35	506	31	16.32
M J Procter (*Gloucs*)	19	426.1	107	960	58	16.55
R A L Massie (*Austr*)	12	381.4	115	851	50	17.02
C M Old (*Yorks*)	15	378.5	101	931	54	17.24
C T Spencer (*Leics*)	12	164	46	333	19	17.52
G A Cope (*Yorks*)	9	221.5	97	407	23	17.69
J C J Dye (*Nrthts*)	21	530.1	132	1427	79	18.06
R M H Cottam (*Nrthts*)	15	364.3	109	918	50	18.36
T W Cartwright (*Som*)	21	863	373	1827	98	18.64
†N Gifford (*Worcs*)	21	580	157	1395	74	18.85
A G Nicholson (*Yorks*)	18	547.3	152	1203	62	19.40
A S Brown (*Gloucs*)	20	387.2	109	955	49	19.48
Mushtaq Mohammad (*Nrthts*)	23	408.2	135	1130	57	19.82
†R Illingworth (*Yorks*)	17	376.3	105	778	39	19.94
K D Boyce (*Essex*)	22	617.1	131	1657	82	20.20
T J Mottram (*Hants*)	4	129.2	30	405	20	20.25
B Stead (*Notts*)	22	747	173	1998	98	20.38
Sadiq Mohammad (*Gloucs*)	21	197.4	31	673	33	20.39

†Played for England but not featured above: B L d'Oliveira, A P E Knott, P H Parfitt, J H Edrich, J A Snow, G G Arnold, D L Underwood, J H Hampshire, J S E Price and P Lever.

First-class averages: 1973

BATTING	M	I	NO	Runs	HS	Avge	100s
G M Turner (*NZ/Wor*)	26	44	8	2416	153*	67.11	9
M L C Foster (*WI*)	15	20	7	828	127	63.69	1
†G Boycott (*Yorks*)	18	30	6	1527	141*	63.62	5
R B Kanhai (*WI/War*)	17	22	4	1129	230*	62.72	4
M J Procter (*Gloucs*)	18	29	5	1475	152	61.45	6
B E Congdon (*NZ*)	16	22	4	1081	176	60.05	3
†D L Amiss (*Warw*)	23	39	9	1634	146*	54.46	3
Younis Ahmed (*Surrey*)	24	38	7	1620	155*	52.25	4
B A Richards (*Hants*)	18	30	2	1452	240	51.85	5
B D Julien (*WI/Kt*)	16	17	2	772	127	51.46	2
G St A Sobers (*WI/Nt*)	18	29	5	1215	150*	50.62	3
†K W R Fletcher (*Essex*)	19	31	6	1259	178	50.36	2
C H Lloyd (*WI/La*)	21	33	5	1399	174	49.96	3
B F Davison (*Leics*)	18	28	3	1235	105	49.40	3
M G Burgess (*NZ*)	16	20	3	836	141	49.17	3
C G Greenidge (*Hants*)	22	38	4	1656	196*	48.70	5
J A Jameson (*Warw*)	25	43	3	1948	168	48.70	5
V Pollard (*NZ*)	15	18	5	629	116	48.38	2
M C Cowdrey (*Kent*)	21	33	8	1183	123*	47.32	2
Sadiq Mohammad (*Gloucs*)	22	37	3	1582	184*	46.52	4

BOWLING	M	O	M	R	W	Avge
J D Monteith (*Ireld*)	1	66	31	95	12	7.91
T W Cartwright (*Som*)	20	810.4	349	1410	89	15.84
P J Sainsbury (*Hants*)	22	549.1	253	945	53	17.83
J S E Price (*Middx*)	8	185.1	43	466	26	17.92
B S Bedi (*Nrthts*)	23	864.2	309	1884	105	17.94
G Edwards (*Notts*)	9	86.4	27	224	12	18.66
P G Lee (*Lancs*)	21	740.3	181	1901	101	18.82
A G Nicholson (*Yorks*)	18	553.5	165	1232	65	18.95
B M Brain (*Worcs*)	20	577.3	117	1621	84	19.29
P Lever (*Lancs*)	17	409.5	117	1011	52	19.44
†R G D Willis (*Warw*)	19	470.1	133	1164	58	20.06
R M H Cottam (*Nrthts*)	24	622.5	166	1541	76	20.27
A S Brown (*Gloucs*)	22	450	103	1250	61	20.49
R D Jackman (*Surrey*)	24	652	141	1888	92	20.52
M Hendrick (*Derbys*)	21	547	147	1355	66	20.53
D R O'Sullivan (*Hants*)	14	523.1	213	992	47	21.10
†C M Old (*Yorks*)	16	414.4	99	1060	50	21.20
M J Procter (*Gloucs*)	18	269.2	82	684	32	21.37
A C Smith (*Warw*)	17	335.3	92	855	40	21.37
M N S Taylor (*Hants*)	22	572.3	148	1390	64	21.71

†Played for England but not featured above: A W Greig, N Gifford, G G Arnold, G R J Roope, R Illingworth, A P E Knott, J A Snow, A R Lewis, D L Underwood, F C Hayes and B W Luckhurst.

First-class averages: 1974

BATTING	M	I	NO	Runs	HS	Avge	100s
C H Lloyd (*Lancs*)	20	31	8	1458	178*	63.39	4
B A Richards (*Hants*)	19	27	4	1406	225*	61.13	4
G M Turner (*Worcs*)	20	31	9	1332	202*	60.54	3
†G Boycott (*Yorks*)	21	36	6	1783	160*	59.43	6
R T Virgin (*Nrthts*)	23	39	5	1936	144*	56.94	7
Wasim Raja (*Pak*)	11	15	6	486	139*	54.00	1
†D L Amiss (*Warw*)	18	31	3	1510	195	53.92	5
†J H Edrich (*Surrey*)	16	23	2	1126	152*	53.61	3
J H Hampshire (*Yorks*)	14	23	6	901	158	53.00	2
R B Kanhai (*Warw*)	14	22	4	936	213*	52.00	3
Shafiq Ahmed (*Pak*)	7	12	3	451	100*	50.11	1
J A Jameson (*Warw*)	24	42	2	1932	240*	48.30	6
G St A Sobers (*Notts*)	15	27	4	1110	132*	48.26	4
S M H Kirmani (*India*)	9	10	7	144	46*	48.00	0
†D Lloyd (*Lancs*)	15	22	2	958	214*	47.90	3
B F Davison (*Leics*)	24	39	3	1670	142	46.38	4
Zaheer Abbas (*Pak/Glo*)	21	30	4	1182	240	45.46	5
Majid Khan (*Pak/Gla*)	20	35	3	1451	164	45.34	5
B L d'Oliveira (*Worcs*)	14	26	3	1026	227	44.60	2
M J Harris (*Notts*)	23	41	3	1690	133	44.47	6

BOWLING	M	O	M	R	W	Avge
A M E Roberts (*Hants*)	21	727.4	198	1621	119	13.62
†G G Arnold (*Surrey*)	14	487	139	1069	75	14.25
V A Holder (*Worcs*)	21	659	146	1493	94	15.88
M J Procter (*Gloucs*)	19	311.3	80	776	47	16.51
B L d'Oliveira (*Worcs*)	18	345.3	105	697	40	17.42
M N S Taylor (*Hants*)	21	541	147	1259	72	17.48
H R Moseley (*Som*)	20	661.5	198	1420	81	17.53
R Illingworth (*Leics*)	21	535.1	204	1014	57	17.78
P Carrick (*Yorks*)	21	405.4	167	840	47	17.87
S J Rouse (*Warw*)	9	164.5	34	489	27	18.11
S Turner (*Essex*)	22	618.5	166	1323	73	18.12
†D L Underwood (*Kent*)	16	563	229	1181	65	18.16
J C Balderstone (*Leics*)	14	134.4	33	351	19	18.47
R P Baker (*Surrey*)	9	207.1	48	511	27	18.92
G D McKenzie (*Leics*)	21	531.3	131	1345	71	18.94
†C M Old (*Yorks*)	18	526.3	132	1366	72	18.97
R A Woolmer (*Kent*)	23	467.4	138	1065	56	19.01
N Gifford (*Worcs*)	22	617	197	1333	69	19.31
R S Herman (*Hants*)	21	657.4	202	1426	73	19.51
R M H Cottam (*Nrthts*)	14	454	113	1101	56	19.66

†Played for England but not featured above: K W R Fletcher, M H Denness, A W Greig, A P E Knott, M Hendrick and R G D Willis.

First-class averages: 1975

BATTING	M	I	NO	Runs	HS	Avge	100s
R B Kanhai (*Warw*)	13	22	9	1073	178*	82.53	3
G Boycott (*Yorks*)	19	34	8	1915	201*	73.65	6
C H Lloyd (*Lancs*)	18	27	4	1423	167*	61.86	6
K D Walters (*Austr*)	12	18	5	784	103*	60.30	3
B A Richards (*Hants*)	19	32	5	1621	135*	60.03	3
R B McCosker (*Austr*)	11	20	2	1078	127	59.88	4
G M Turner (*Worcs*)	17	29	5	1362	214*	56.75	3
I M Chappell (*Austr*)	11	19	0	1022	192	53.78	4
B F Davison (*Leics*)	20	34	6	1498	189	53.50	3
J M Brearley (*Middx*)	20	39	8	1656	150	53.41	4
†D S Steele (*Nrthts*)	21	39	3	1756	126*	48.77	3
Asif Iqbal (*Kent*)	16	30	4	1262	140	48.53	4
†J H Edrich (*Surrey*)	20	38	5	1569	175	47.54	4
Zaheer Abbas (*Gloucs*)	16	31	1	1426	123	47.53	2
†A W Greig (*Sussex*)	20	37	1	1699	226	47.19	5
R W Tolchard (*Leics*)	21	31	10	973	106	46.33	2
R Illingworth (*Leics*)	21	33	11	997	88	45.31	0
G S Chappell (*Austr*)	12	20	3	762	144	44.82	2
†D L Amiss (*Warw*)	19	37	2	1564	158*	44.68	4
B L d'Oliveira (*Worcs*)	20	34	6	1225	97*	43.75	0

BOWLING	M	O	M	R	W	Avge
D S Steele (*Nrthts*)	21	75.3	34	148	11	13.45
A M E Roberts (*Hants*)	13	418.3	141	901	57	15.80
M Hendrick (*Derbys*)	18	493.1	148	1077	68	15.83
B D Julien (*Kent*)	13	270	76	707	40	17.67
†P Lever (*Lancs*)	16	419.1	116	1098	61	18.00
†D L Underwood (*Kent*)	17	576.1	233	1210	67	18.05
K D Boyce (*Essex*)	15	471	92	1309	72	18.18
P G Lee (*Lancs*)	21	799.5	199	2067	112	18.45
†B Wood (*Lancs*)	13	127	47	244	13	18.76
R G D Willis (*Warw*)	4	129.5	33	338	18	18.77
J E Emburey (*Middx*)	4	111.4	29	286	15	19.06
T E Jesty (*Hants*)	17	383.5	108	960	50	19.20
K Shuttleworth (*Lancs*)	13	304.5	86	717	37	19.37
A G Nicholson (*Yorks*)	6	106.5	31	253	13	19.46
J W Solanky (*Glam*)	19	436.3	107	1154	59	19.55
Asif Iqbal (*Kent*)	16	77	13	282	14	20.14
P Willey (*Nrthts*)	21	292	73	791	39	20.28
Sarfraz Nawaz (*Nrthts*)	22	728.3	175	2051	101	20.30
R Illingworth (*Leics*)	21	459.1	158	1068	51	20.94
P Carrick (*Yorks*)	21	641	223	1673	79	21.17

†Played for England but not featured above: R A Woolmer, A P E Knott, K W R Fletcher, C M Old, J A Snow, P H Edmonds, G A Gooch, G R J Roope, J H Hampshire, G G Arnold and M H Denness.

First-class averages: 1976

BATTING	M	I	NO	Runs	HS	Avge	100s
Zaheer Abbas (*Gloucs*)	21	39	5	2554	230*	75.11	11
I V A Richards (*WI*)	16	25	1	1724	291	71.83	6
G Boycott (*Yorks*)	12	24	5	1288	207*	67.78	5
†D L Amiss (*Warw*)	21	38	6	2110	203	65.93	8
C H Lloyd (*WI*)	19	26	4	1363	201*	61.95	3
Javed Miandad (*Sussex*)	5	10	1	523	162	58.11	2
B F Davison (*Leics*)	22	41	9	1818	132	56.81	6
C G Greenidge (*WI*)	20	38	3	1952	134	55.77	8
C L King (*WI*)	21	34	10	1320	163	55.00	6
K W R Fletcher (*Essex*)	22	36	7	1588	128*	54.75	4
H Pilling (*Lancs*)	20	35	5	1569	149*	52.30	3
Mushtaq Mohammad (*Nrthts*)	21	36	4	1620	204*	50.62	4
G M Turner (*Worcs*)	20	37	2	1752	169	50.05	4
G D Barlow (*Middx*)	21	37	7	1478	160*	49.26	3
K S McEwan (*Essex*)	22	38	1	1821	156	49.21	6
B A Richards (*Hants*)	18	34	2	1572	179	49.12	7
H A Gomes (*Mx/WI*)	22	37	7	1435	190	47.83	5
Sadiq Mohammad (*Gloucs*)	21	39	2	1759	163*	47.54	8
†R A Woolmer (*Kent*)	21	39	2	1749	143	47.27	3
E J O Hemsley (*Worcs*)	9	14	5	421	157	46.77	1

BOWLING	M	O	M	R	W	Avge
M A Holding (*WI*)	12	339.3	111	791	55	14.38
N G Featherstone (*Middx*)	21	232	64	569	36	15.80
R M H Cottam (*Nrthts*)	8	213.5	54	584	36	16.22
Asif Iqbal (*Kent*)	16	69.4	12	214	13	16.46
P J Sainsbury (*Hants*)	16	572.3	228	1236	66	18.72
V A Holder (*WI*)	13	387.1	109	1004	52	19.38
E J Barlow (*Derbys*)	23	308.5	60	897	46	19.50
P B Clift (*Leics*)	23	572.5	128	1493	74	20.17
W Larkins (*Nrthts*)	21	67.2	9	245	12	20.41
R D Jackman (*Surrey*)	17	563.4	120	1760	85	20.70
†M W W Selvey (*Middx*)	21	644.3	130	1913	90	21.25
W W Daniel (*WI*)	15	371.3	88	1106	52	21.26
K Higgs (*Leics*)	19	473.4	114	1175	55	21.36
R Illingworth (*Leics*)	23	389.2	143	772	36	21.44
†G Miller (*Derbys*)	22	565.2	147	1660	77	21.55
F J Titmus (*Middx*)	19	640.4	187	1553	72	21.56
S P Perryman (*Warw*)	14	392	114	892	41	21.75
J R T Barclay (*Sussex*)	21	240.1	63	660	30	22.00
R Arrowsmith (*Lancs*)	5	182.5	74	399	18	22.16
Sarfraz Nawaz (*Nrthts*)	19	639.2	143	1867	82	22.76

†Played for England but not featured above: J H Edrich, D B Close, D S Steele, A W Greig, A P E Knott, P Willey, C M Old, J A Snow, J M Brearley, F C Hayes, D I Underwood, P I Pocock, M Hendrick, R G D Willis, A Ward, J C Balderstone and B Wood.

First-class averages: 1977

BATTING	M	I	NO	Runs	HS	Avge	100s
R P Baker (*Surrey*)	12	12	9	215	77*	71.66	0
†G Boycott (*Yorks*)	20	30	5	1701	191	68.04	7
I V A Richards (*Som*)	20	35	2	2161	241*	65.48	7
C G Greenidge (*Hants*)	19	32	3	1771	208	61.06	6
G S Chappell (*Austr*)	16	25	5	1182	161*	59.10	5
†G R J Roope (*Surrey*)	20	31	5	1431	115	55.03	5
Zaheer Abbas (*Gloucs*)	20	36	6	1584	205*	52.80	5
†D L Amiss (*Warw*)	19	34	5	1513	162*	52.17	6
K S McEwan (*Essex*)	23	37	4	1702	218	51.57	8
B Wood (*Lancs*)	23	34	6	1439	155*	51.39	3
K J O'Keeffe (*Austr*)	13	19	12	355	48*	50.71	0
F C Hayes (*Lancs*)	20	26	3	1152	157*	50.08	3
†R A Woolmer (*Kent*)	20	30	4	1238	137	47.61	6
J H Edrich (*Surrey*)	15	26	4	1044	140	47.45	3
K C Wessels (*Sussex*)	11	17	3	663	138*	47.35	2
†J M Brearley (*Middx*)	20	31	4	1251	152	46.33	3
Mushtaq Mohammad (*Nrthts*)	21	37	5	1469	147	45.90	5
B L d'Oliveira (*Worcs*)	22	36	7	1257	156*	43.34	1
J H Hampshire (*Yorks*)	18	23	5	779	100*	43.27	1
J C Balderstone (*Leics*)	25	38	8	1297	178*	43.23	2

BOWLING	M	O	M	R	W	Avge
†R A Woolmer (*Kent*)	20	134.1	50	289	19	15.21
†M Hendrick (*Derbys*)	21	562.3	189	1068	67	15.94
W W Daniel (*Middx*)	23	516.1	142	1233	75	16.44
Sarfraz Nawaz (*Nrthts*)	18	486.4	130	1246	73	17.06
R W Hills (*Kent*)	17	215.3	60	566	33	17.15
†G Miller (*Derbys*)	21	655.4	224	1551	87	17.82
M J Procter (*Gloucs*)	21	777.3	226	1967	109	18.04
J E Emburey (*Middx*)	18	686.1	205	1488	81	18.37
†D L Underwood (*Kent*)	17	436.2	164	896	46	19.47
M W W Selvey (*Middx*)	24	629.1	158	1540	78	19.74
P Booth (*Leics*)	11	179	37	494	25	19.76
A M E Roberts (*Hants*)	14	349.2	109	793	40	19.82
J N Shepherd (*Kent*)	20	738.4	216	1734	87	19.93
J Garner (*Som*)	5	215.1	60	539	27	19.96
A A Jones (*Middx*)	9	139.4	32	421	21	20.04
R E East (*Essex*)	22	658.4	197	1477	73	20.23
R J Bright (*Austr*)	14	333.5	114	794	39	20.35
†R G D Willis (*Warw*)	16	399	94	1183	58	20.39
B Wood (*Lancs*)	23	120.3	40	306	15	20.40
K Shuttleworth (*Leics*)	13	293.4	57	825	40	20.62

†Played for England but not featured above: A P E Knott, D W Randall, A W Greig, C M Old, I T Botham, J K Lever and G D Barlow.

First-class averages: 1978

BATTING	M	I	NO	Runs	HS	Avge	100s
C E B Rice (*Notts*)	23	37	9	1871	213*	66.82	5
G M Turner (*Worcs*)	22	38	7	1711	202*	55.19	6
C G Greenidge (*Hants*)	19	34	1	1771	211	53.66	5
D L Amiss (*Warw*)	23	41	3	2030	162	53.42	7
J H Hampshire (*Yorks*)	22	36	6	1596	132	53.20	3
†G Boycott (*Yorks*)	16	25	1	1233	131	51.37	6
B F Davison (*Leics*)	23	35	3	1644	180*	51.37	4
M J Procter (*Gloucs*)	21	36	3	1655	203	50.15	3
K S McEwan (*Essex*)	24	37	3	1682	186	49.47	5
Asif Iqbal (*Kent*)	18	25	6	934	171	49.15	3
A J Lamb (*Nrthts*)	17	27	8	883	106*	46.47	2
D W Randall (*Notts*)	24	40	7	1525	157*	46.21	2
I V A Richards (*Som*)	21	38	4	1558	118	45.82	2
J A Ormrod (*Worcs*)	24	41	7	1535	173	45.14	5
Zaheer Abbas (*Gloucs*)	22	35	1	1535	213	45.14	6
C J Tavaré (*Kent*)	25	39	5	1534	105	45.11	2
R W Tolchard (*Leics*)	24	35	16	841	103*	44.26	1
A I Kallicharran (*Warw*)	16	29	5	1041	129	43.37	3
B L d'Oliveira (*Worcs*)	17	22	5	728	146*	42.82	1
Imran Khan (*Sussex*)	22	37	5	1339	167	41.84	3

BOWLING	M	O	M	R	W	Avge
A J Mack (*Glam*)	5	77.3	26	195	16	12.18
D L Underwood (*Kent*)	22	815.1	359	1594	110	14.49
R A Woolmer (*Kent*)	21	135.4	46	292	20	14.60
W W Daniel (*Middx*)	21	453.3	113	1114	76	14.65
†M Hendrick (*Derbys*)	17	473.5	167	895	59	15.16
J K Lever (*Essex*)	22	681.1	160	1610	106	15.18
†P H Edmonds (*Middx*)	18	503	174	912	60	15.20
M W Gatting (*Middx*)	26	168.3	36	411	26	15.80
J Garner (*Som*)	4	170.1	61	351	22	15.95
R J Hadlee (*NZ/Nt*)	17	497.1	120	1269	78	16.26
R E East (*Essex*)	23	700.2	226	1506	92	16.36
†I T Botham (*Som*)	17	605.2	143	1640	100	16.40
†C M Old (*Yorks*)	14	520.1	166	1108	64	17.31
†R G D Willis (*Warw*)	18	474.2	116	1197	65	18.41
G G Arnold (*Sussex*)	17	401	102	910	49	18.57
C E Waller (*Sussex*)	13	371	125	861	46	18.71
M W W Selvey (*Middx*)	24	743.5	199	1929	101	19.09
G W Johnson (*Kent*)	24	510.4	173	1084	56	19.35
H R Moseley (*Som*)	14	348.1	103	813	41	19.82
P E Russell (*Derbys*)	15	235.4	88	423	21	20.14

†Played for England but not featured above: D I Gower, C T Radley, G R J Roope, G A Gooch, G Miller, J M Brearley, R W Taylor and B Wood.

First-class averages: 1979

BATTING	M	I	NO	Runs	HS	Avge	100s
†G Boycott (*Yorks*)	15	20	5	1538	175*	102.53	6
Younis Ahmed (*Worcs*)	22	30	8	1539	221*	69.95	4
A J Lamb (*Nrthts*)	21	34	8	1747	178	67.19	4
Yashpal Sharma (*India*)	12	21	6	884	111	58.93	3
G M Turner (*Worcs*)	18	31	2	1669	150*	57.55	8
Sadiq Mohammad (*Gloucs*)	17	30	2	1595	171	56.96	8
S M Gavaskar (*India*)	13	20	1	1062	221	55.89	3
K C Wessels (*Sussex*)	21	36	2	1800	187	52.94	6
A I Kallicharran (*Warw*)	17	26	5	1098	170*	52.28	4
G R Viswanath (*India*)	13	17	2	757	113	50.46	3
C G Greenidge (*Hants*)	17	30	2	1404	145	50.14	3
D L Amiss (*Warw*)	22	37	3	1672	232*	49.17	6
C H Lloyd (*Lancs*)	17	22	4	880	104*	48.88	3
G P Howarth (*Surrey*)	19	30	4	1238	183	47.61	4
†D W Randall (*Notts*)	14	25	1	1138	209	47.41	3
P M Roebuck (*Som*)	23	37	10	1273	89	47.14	0
Zaheer Abbas (*Gloucs*)	17	30	2	1304	151*	46.57	3
M Amarnath (*India*)	11	16	3	592	123	45.53	1
†P H Edmonds (*Middx*)	15	17	6	490	141*	44.54	1
R G Lumb (*Yorks*)	22	35	2	1465	159	44.39	5

BOWLING	M	O	M	R	W	Avge
M F Malone (*Lancs*)	3	102.3	32	230	19	12.10
C M Wells (*Sussex*)	5	73.1	30	137	10	13.70
J Garner (*Som*)	14	393.1	127	761	55	13.83
D L Underwood (*Kent*)	23	799.2	335	1575	106	14.85
D Lloyd (*Lancs*)	22	59.3	19	164	11	14.90
Imran Khan (*Sussex*)	16	415.4	106	1091	73	14.94
H R Moseley (*Som*)	8	196.4	50	495	31	15.96
R J Hadlee (*Notts*)	12	317	103	753	47	16.02
R D Jackman (*Surrey*)	21	628.1	173	1595	93	17.15
†J K Lever (*Essex*)	21	700	166	1834	106	17.30
S T Clarke (*Surrey*)	11	320.1	106	757	43	17.60
G G Arnold (*Sussex*)	18	435.5	147	950	52	18.26
K Higgs (*Leics*)	19	404.5	133	872	47	18.55
M J Procter (*Gloucs*)	21	574.5	140	1532	81	18.91
J D Monteith (*Ireld*)	2	86	28	194	10	19.40
C E B Rice (*Notts*)	21	448	134	1159	58	19.63
Sarfraz Nawaz (*Nrthts*)	13	408.5	130	913	45	20.28
P I Pocock (*Surrey*)	22	595.5	189	1435	70	20.50
S Turner (*Essex*)	23	576.3	164	1285	61	21.06
†M Hendrick (*Derbys*)	15	456	150	885	42	21.07

†Played for England but not featured above: G Miller, D I Gower, I T Botham, G A Gooch, J M Brearley, R W Taylor, R G D Willis, D L Bairstow, A R Butcher and P Willey.

First-class averages: 1980

BATTING	M	I	NO	Runs	HS	Avge	100s
A J Lamb (*Nrthts*)	23	39	12	1797	152	66.55	5
J Whitehouse (*Warw*)	10	19	8	725	197	65.90	1
K C Wessels (*Sussex*)	15	29	5	1562	254	65.08	2
P N Kirsten (*Derbys*)	21	36	6	1895	213*	63.16	6
G M Turner (*Worcs*)	21	35	4	1817	228*	58.61	7
C T Radley (*Middx*)	24	34	8	1491	136*	57.34	5
Javed Miandad (*Glam*)	20	32	5	1460	181	54.07	3
C E B Rice (*Notts*)	23	36	9	1448	131*	53.62	5
†G Boycott (*Yorks*)	17	28	4	1264	154*	52.66	3
J H Hampshire (*Yorks*)	18	27	8	987	124	51.94	2
I V A Richards (*WI/Som*)	17	25	1	1217	170	50.70	5
†B C Rose (*Som*)	17	26	4	1084	150*	49.27	2
J G Wright (*Derbys*)	20	36	5	1504	166*	48.51	3
†G A Gooch (*Essex*)	19	35	5	1437	205	47.90	6
C H Lloyd (*WI/La*)	14	15	2	621	116	47.76	4
J M Brearley (*Middx*)	23	33	5	1335	134*	47.67	5
G R J Roope (*Surrey*)	23	30	9	996	101	47.42	1
N Russom (*CU/Som*)	10	13	8	235	79*	47.00	0
B F Davison (*Leics*)	21	32	4	1310	151	46.78	2
J A Ormrod (*Worcs*)	22	35	3	1495	131*	46.71	5

BOWLING	M	O	M	R	W	Avge
R A White (*Notts*)	2	48	16	85	11	7.72
J Garner (*WI*)	11	351	123	683	49	13.93
R J Hadlee (*Notts*)	8	222.1	82	410	29	14.13
V A P van der Bijl (*Middx*)	20	642.3	213	1252	85	14.72
R D Jackman (*Surrey*)	23	745.2	220	1864	121	15.40
J F Steele (*Leics*)	22	347.5	139	704	40	17.60
M D Marshall (*WI/Hts*)	17	477.3	128	1170	66	17.72
†M Hendrick (*Derbys*)	15	444.5	128	980	55	17.81
Imran Khan (*Sussex*)	17	402.5	109	967	54	17.90
M J Procter (*Gloucs*)	19	372.1	102	931	51	18.25
D K Lillee (*Austr*)	4	116.2	25	391	20	19.55
S P Hughes (*Middx*)	5	110.4	25	352	18	19.55
D R Parry (*WI*)	11	303.1	93	800	40	20.00
W G Merry (*Middx*)	5	96	21	300	15	20.00
†J E Emburey (*Middx*)	21	735.2	243	1518	75	20.24
P J W Allott (*Lancs*)	11	183	47	473	23	20.56
P J Hacker (*Notts*)	17	379.2	99	1092	52	21.00
†C M Old (*Yorks*)	18	503	160	1159	55	21.07
S T Clarke (*Surrey*)	21	605.3	139	1700	79	21.51
W W Daniel (*Middx*)	19	492.5	112	1454	67	21.70

†Played for England but not featured above: P Willey, R A Woolmer, M W Gatting, R G D Willis, I T Botham, C J Tavaré, A P E Knott, G R Dilley, D L Bairstow, D I Gower, J K Lever, D L Underwood and C W J Athey.

First-class averages: 1981

BATTING	M	I	NO	Runs	HS	Avge	100s
Zaheer Abbas (Gloucs)	21	36	10	2306	215*	88.69	10
Javed Miandad (Glam)	22	37	7	2083	200*	69.43	8
A J Lamb (Nrthts)	24	43	9	2049	162	60.26	5
I V A Richards (Som)	20	33	3	1718	196	57.26	7
C E B Rice (Notts)	21	30	4	1462	172	56.23	6
P N Kirsten (Derbys)	21	35	6	1605	228	55.34	4
G M Turner (Worcs)	24	42	4	2101	168	55.28	9
†M W Gatting (Middx)	19	33	6	1492	186*	55.25	4
D M Wellham (Austr)	9	13	4	497	135*	55.22	2
A I Kallicharran (Warw)	13	23	6	923	135	54.29	3
†C J Tavare (Kent)	22	40	7	1770	156	53.63	4
Younis Ahmed (Worcs)	22	39	8	1637	116	52.80	3
A R Border (Austr)	13	21	5	807	123*	50.43	3
P R Oliver (Warw)	8	14	3	554	171*	50.36	2
G W Humpage (Warw)	22	39	5	1701	146	50.02	6
C G Greenidge (Hants)	19	30	1	1442	140	49.72	4
†D I Gower (Leics)	19	33	4	1418	156*	48.89	5
R M Ellison (Kent)	7	11	6	237	61*	47.40	0
W N Slack (Middx)	18	32	3	1372	248*	47.31	3
K W R Fletcher (Essex)	18	29	4	1180	165*	47.20	4

BOWLING	M	O	M	R	W	Avge
R J Hadlee (Notts)	21	708.4	231	1564	105	14.89
S T Clarke (Surrey)	10	339.4	98	734	49	14.97
J Garner (Som)	18	605.4	182	1349	88	15.32
A N Jones (Sussex)	5	83	11	283	17	16.64
M A Holding (Lancs)	7	271.1	75	715	40	17.87
E A Moseley (Glam)	15	355.4	87	942	52	18.11
A Sidebottom (Yorks)	15	305.5	88	899	47	19.12
C E B Rice (Notts)	21	494.5	142	1248	65	19.20
I A Greig (Sussex)	23	477	100	1469	76	19.32
M D Marshall (Hants)	17	531.3	166	1321	68	19.42
P J Hacker (Notts)	7	175.5	53	446	23	19.39
G S le Roux (Sussex)	19	559.1	133	1582	81	19.53
T E Jesty (Hants)	21	437.4	136	1033	52	19.86
E E Hemmings (Notts)	22	804.2	262	1857	90	20.63
T M Alderman (Austr)	12	402.5	100	1064	51	20.86
L B Taylor (Leics)	21	547.1	131	1628	75	21.70
D K Lillee (Austr)	8	377.4	102	1028	47	21.87
D S Steele (Derbys)	21	403	141	1019	46	22.15
Imran Khan (Sussex)	18	565.1	137	1464	66	22.18
W W Daniel (Middx)	21	514.2	103	1494	67	22.29

†Played for England but not featured above: A P E Knott, G R Dilley, I T Botham, G Boycott, J E Emburey, P Willey, C M Old, J M Brearley, G A Gooch, R A Woolmer, R G D Willis, R W Taylor, M Hendrick, P J W Allott, P R Downton, W Larkins and P W G Parker.

First-class averages: 1982

BATTING	M	I	NO	Runs	HS	Avge	100s
G M Turner (Worcs)	9	16	3	1171	311*	90.07	5
Mudassar Nazar (Pak)	11	16	6	825	211*	82.50	4
Mohsin Khan (Pak)	13	20	3	1248	203*	73.41	4
Zaheer Abbas (Glo/Pak)	16	25	4	1475	162*	70.23	5
A I Kallicharran (Warw)	22	37	5	2120	235	66.25	8
P N Kirsten (Derbys)	21	37	7	1941	164*	64.70	8
G R Viswanath (India)	9	12	3	561	106*	62.33	2
Madan Lal (India)	9	15	10	309	58*	61.80	0
G Boycott (Yorks)	21	37	6	1913	159	61.70	6
M W Gatting (Middx)	23	34	6	1651	192	58.96	6
T E Jesty (Hants)	22	36	8	1645	164*	58.75	8
J G Wright (Derbys)	21	39	6	1830	190	55.45	7
D B Vengsarkar (India)	9	13	2	610	157	55.45	1
B F Davison (Leics)	22	37	4	1800	172	54.54	7
Younis Ahmed (Worcs)	18	29	6	1247	122	54.21	4
J Simmons (Lancs)	18	21	12	487	79*	54.11	0
P Willey (Nrthts)	23	41	6	1783	145	50.94	5
D M Smith (Surrey)	14	25	4	1065	160	50.71	3
Javed Miandad (Glam/Pak)	18	29	8	1051	105*	50.04	1
D P Hughes (Lancs)	23	36	9	1303	126*	48.25	3

BOWLING	M	O	M	R	W	Avge
R J Hadlee (Notts)	18	403.5	122	889	61	14.57
M D Marshall (Hants)	22	822	225	2108	134	15.73
K R Pont (Essex)	16	62	11	158	10	15.80
†M W Gatting (Middx)	23	135	40	343	21	16.33
Imran Khan (Sx/Pak)	16	484.4	134	1079	64	16.85
Mudassar Nazar (Pak)	11	139	35	368	21	17.52
W W Daniel (Middx)	19	469.4	107	1245	71	17.53
J Garner (Som)	10	259.1	76	583	33	17.66
M Hendrick (Notts)	10	244.2	86	473	26	18.19
G S le Roux (Sussex)	20	467	116	1210	65	18.61
A M E Roberts (Leics)	13	428.2	114	1081	55	19.65
F D Stephenson (Gloucs)	8	197.3	40	632	32	19.75
S T Clarke (Surrey)	22	659.3	162	1696	85	19.95
J F Steele (Leics)	20	470.2	134	1075	52	20.67
Abdul Qadir (Pak)	12	542.4	123	1187	57	20.82
T E Jesty (Hants)	22	288.1	89	750	35	21.42
K Saxelby (Notts)	14	291.4	68	799	37	21.59
M K Bore (Notts)	8	279.1	104	609	28	21.75
N G Cowans (Middx)	11	222.3	50	721	33	21.84
L B Taylor (Leics)	20	582.1	153	1465	67	21.86

†Played for England, but not featured above: G Cook, C J Tavaré, A J Lamb, D I Gower, P H Edmunds, R W Taylor, P J W Allott, R G D Willis, G Miller, E E Hemmings, R D Jackman, I A Greig, G Fowler and V J Marks.

Bs

For a period of some 30 years a substantial percentage of the greatest cricketers in England had surnames beginning with the letter B. So pronounced was the strength of the 'Bs' that several times they challenged and beat the Rest of England, notably in 1817 by 114 runs, in 1822 by 7 wickets, in 1823 by an innings and 14 runs and in 1824 by 183 runs. In all there were 12 matches between 1805 and 1837 in which the Bs took part. The Bs match against England at Lord's on June 12, 13 and 14, 1810 was the most remarkable of all, since the Bs were dismissed for 6 in their second innings, easily the lowest total ever recorded in an important match. The Bs scored 137 in their first innings and by bowling out England for 100 obtained a lead of 37, which makes their collapse even more inexplicable.

Bails

In any match the longest recorded distance travelled by a bail after a batsman has been bowled is 83yds 1ft and 9ins. The match was New Town v North West Hobart on the New Town Ground, Hobart, November 21, 1925, the bowler being A O Burrows.

R D Burrows of Worcestershire who sent a bail over 67 yards when bowling W Huddleston at Old Trafford, a first-class record.

The English record took place at Wardown Park, Luton on August 11, 1908. A F Morcom, in bowling F H Mustard during the Bedfordshire v Suffolk match, sent the bail 70yds 1ft and 6ins.

In first-class cricket the record was achieved by R D Burrows, playing for Worcestershire v Lancashire at Old Trafford on June 29, 1911, who sent a bail 67yds and 6ins when bowling W Huddleston.

Bassetlaw League

Championship Winners

1904	Worksop	1945	Whitwell
1905	Gainsborough	1946	Harworth
1906	Shirebrook	1947	Warsop
1907	Worksop	1948	Warsop
1908	Worksop	1949	Retford
1909	Gainsborough	1950	Gainsborough
1910	Shirebrook	1951	Ruston Hornsby, Worksop
1911	Worksop	1952	Ruston Hornsby
1912	Gainsborough	1953	Ruston Hornsby
1913	Creswell	1954	Steetley
1914	Worksop	1955	Steetley
1919	Langwith	1956	Steetley
1920	Mansfield Coll	1957	Steetley
1921	Dinnington	1958	Worksop
1922	Manton	1959	Worksop
1923	Dinnington	1960	Steetley
1924	Whitwell	1961	Steetley
1925	Whitwell	1962	Gainsborough, Steetley
1926	Kiveton Park	1963	Steetley
1927	Whitwell	1964	Steetley
1928	Warsop	1965	Steetley
1929	Langwith	1966	Clipstone
1930	Dinnington	1967	Grassmoor
1931	Whitwell	1968	Retford
1932	Dinnington	1969	Retford
1933	Dinnington	1970	Steetley
1934	Bolsover	1971	Steetley
1935	Gainsborough	1972	Steetley
1936	Dinnington	1973	Steetley
1937	Glapwell	1974	Steetley
1938	Dinnington	1975	Worksop
1939	Glapwell, Ollerton	1976	Retford
1940	Shireoaks	1977	Retford
1941	Thurcroft	1978	Retford
1942	Warsop	1979	Notts Colts
1943	Shireoaks	1980	Bridon
1944	Shireoaks	1981	Bridon
		1982	Bridon

The League records are

Highest team total 347–4 Dinnington v Retford 1919
Lowest team total 1 Shireoaks v Harthill 1909
Highest individual innings 195 A Davis Thurcroft v Rose Bros 1934
Best bowling 10 for 2 P Coxon Wales v Bilsthorpe 1960
Most runs in season 1089 M J Smedley (*Kiveton Park*) 1960
Most wickets in season 106 M Farooq (*Gainsborough*) 1964

Batting

Highest individual innings The first recorded score of three figures was hit by John Minshull for Duke of Dorset's XI v Wrotham on August 31, 1769. He made 107.

This record was broken by J Small, who scored 136 on Broadhalfpenny Down for Hampshire v Surrey, July 13, 1775.

In 1777, J Aylward hit 167 for Hampshire v England on the Vine at Sevenoaks – he started batting at 5 pm on June 18 and his innings ended at 3 pm on June 20.

The first double century was hit by W Ward, who made 278 for MCC v Norfolk at Lord's, July 24, 1820. Alfred Adams then scored 279 for

A E J Collins, who wrote his name in cricket records over four afternoons in 1899, when he scored 628 not out, the highest recorded innings in cricket.

Saffron Walden v Bishop Stortford on July 11, 1837.

In May 1868 E F S Tylecote, batting over 8 afternoons (playing time 3.00 to 5.30) hit 404 not out for Classical v Modern at Clifton College.

W N Roe created a new record of 415* for Emmanuel College L V C v Caius College L V C at Cambridge on July 12, 1881; this was broken by J S Carrick with 419* for West of Scotland v Priory Park, Chichester, July 13, 1885; then A E Stoddart hit 485 for Hampstead v Stoics at Hampstead on August 4, 1886.

The present record was obtained by A E J Collins in 1899 with 628, the details of the innings in which he made his record score being:

CLARK'S HOUSE

1.	Collins	*not out*	628
2.	Champion	*c* Monteath *b* Rendall	27
3.	Gilbert	*b* Crew	9
4.	Studdy	*c* Davis *b* Sainsbury	8
5.	Sheriff	*b* Crew	6
6.	Galway	*b* Crew	11
7.	Whitty	*c* and *b* Monteath	42
8.	Spooner	*b* Monteath	0
9.	Leake	*b* Monteath	32
10.	Raine	*b* Monteath	14
11.	Redfern	*c* Fuller-Eberle *b* Crew	13
		Extras	46
		TOTAL	836

Collins' innings was spread over 4 afternoons lasted 6 hours and 50 minutes; he hit a six, 4 fives and 31 fours. The match was a Junior House game between Clark's and North Town at Clifton College.

First-class highest individual innings The present record is held by Hanif Mohammad who scored 499 for Karachi v Bahawalpur in Karachi on January 9 and 11, 1959. Details of the innings are:

KARACHI

1.	Hanif Mohammad	run out	499
2.	Alimuddin	*c* Zulfiqar *b* Aziz	32
3.	Waqar Hassan	*c* Tanveer *b* Iqbal	37
4.	Wazir Mohammad	*st* Tanver *b* Jamil	31
5.	Wallis Mathias	run out	103
6.	Mushtaq Mohammad	lbw *b* Aziz	21
7.	Mohammad Munaf	*b* Iqbal	18
8.	Abdul Aziz	not out	9
		Extras	22
		TOTAL (for 7 wkts dec)	772

Hanif batted 10 hours and 40 minutes, hitting 64 fours. He was run out trying to take a second run in order to reach 500. The side declared as soon as Hanif was dismissed.

For highest individual scores in various countries and competitions, see under appropriate heading.

Longest individual innings During the West Indies *v* Pakistan Test at Bridgetown on January 17 to 23, 1958, the West Indies batted first scoring 579 for 9 declared. Pakistan were dismissed for 106 and followed on 473 runs behind. Hanif Mohammad opened the second innings and occupied the crease for 16 hours and 10 minutes, making 337. His stay lasted nearly three hours longer than the previous record of 13 hours and 17 minutes, set up by L Hutton for England *v* Australia at the Oval in August 1938. The latter remains the record for matches in England.

Most runs in a match by one batsman A E J Collins and Hanif Mohammad's scores in a single innings have not been exceeded by any batsman in two innings of a match.

For most runs on first-class debut, see Debut.

Most runs in only first-class match Playing for New South Wales *v* Queensland on February 18 and 20, 1915 at Sydney Cricket Ground, N F Callaway hit 207 in 206 minutes, this being his only innings in first-class cricket.

Benefit Matches

When A Watson received £1,101 11s 1d from the net proceeds of the match between North and South at Old Trafford on July 9, 10 and 11, 1885, it was stated to be the largest sum up to that time collected for a cricketer's benefit.

Due to the fall in the value of the pound it is difficult to compare the sums received from benefit matches in different decades. The highest amounts received since the 1880s are, it is believed, as follows:

1890–99	£2,000	R Peel	Yorks v Lancs (*Bradford*)	1894
1900–09	£3,703	G H Hirst	Yorks v Lancs (*Headingley*)	1904
1910–14	£2,202	W Rhodes	Yorks v Lancs (*Bramall Lane*)	1911
1920–29	£4,016	R Kilner	Yorks v Middx (*Headingley*)	1925
1930–39	£3,648	M Leyland	Yorks v Notts (*Headingley*)	1934
1946–49	£14,000	C Washbrook	Lancs v Austr (*Old Trafford*)	1948
1950–59	£12,866	A V Bedser	Surrey v Yorks (*Oval*)	1953
1960–69	£13,047	J B Statham	Lancs v Austr (*Old Trafford*)	1961
1970–79	£62,429	B Wood	Lancs – Testimonial	1979

At the present time the record benefit is £128,000 received by J Simmons for Lancashire in 1980.

Benson and Hedges Cup

A single-innings-per-side competition limited to 55 overs each, this Cup was inaugurated in 1972. Twenty teams take part with five teams in each of four leagues. The top two teams in each league go through to a knockout section. The teams involved in the league are the 17 first-class counties and 3 other sides – originally Minor Counties (North), Minor Counties (South) and Cambridge University, but in 1982 a Minor Counties XI, Scotland and Combined Oxford and Cambridge Universities.

The principal records in the competition are:

Highest team total 350–3 Essex v Oxf and Camb (*Chelmsford*) 1979
Lowest team total 56 Leics v Minor Counties (*Wellington*) 1982
Highest individual innings 198* G A Gooch Essex v Sussex (*Hove*) (*Hove*) 1982
Best bowling 7–12 W W Daniel Middx v Minor Counties (East) (*Ipswich*) 1978

Jack Simmons of Lancashire holds the record for the largest benefit received by a player: £128,000 in 1980.

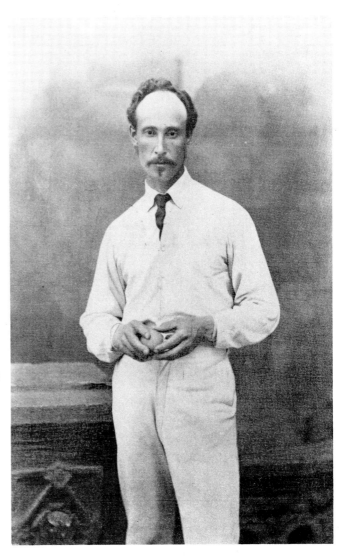

A Watson, whose £1,011 11s 1d was the highest benefit to 1885. It was the proceeds of the North v South match at Old Trafford.

Wicket partnerships

1st 241 S M Gavaskar, B C Rose. Somerset v Kent
    (*Canterbury*) 1980
2nd 285*C G Greenidge, D R Turner. Hants v Minor Counties
    (South)
3rd 268*G A Gooch, K W R Fletcher. Essex v Sussex
    (*Hove*) 1982
4th 184*D Lloyd, B W Reidy. Lancs v Derbys
    (*Chesterfield*) 1980
5th 134 M Maslin, D N F Slade. Minor Counties (East) v Notts
    (*Trent Bridge*) 1976
6th 114 M J Khan, G P Ellis. Glamorgan v Gloucs
    (*Bristol*) 1975
7th 149*J D Love, C M Old. Yorkshire v Scotland
    (*Bradford*) 1981
8th 109 R E East, N Smith. Essex v Northants
    (*Chelmsford*) 1977
9th 81 J N Shepherd, D L Underwood. Kent v Middx
    (*Lord's*) 1975
10th 80*D L Bairstow, M Johnson. Yorkshire v Derbys
    (*Derby*) 1981
(*also see under individual counties*)

Benson and Hedges Cup Results

1972

Quarter Finals
Glamorgan 104–9 lost to Warwickshire 108–5 by 5 wkts
Lancashire 135 lost to Leicestershire 138–3 (B Dudleston 65*) by
  7 wkts
Gloucestershire 238–9 (R D V Knight 92, M J Procter 56, M W W
  Selvey 5–39) beat Middlesex 176 (C T Radley 63, A S Brown
  4–43) by 62 runs
Sussex 85 lost to Yorkshire 89–5 by 5 wkts

Semi Finals
Gloucestershire 131 lost to Yorkshire 134–3 (G Boycott 75*) by 7
  wkts
Warwickshire 96 lost to Leicestershire 98–3 by 7 wkts

Final
Yorkshire 136–6 lost to Leicestershire 140–5 by 5 wkts
(*Lord's 22.7.1972*)
Leicestershire: B Dudleston, M E J C Norman, R W Tolchard, B F
  Davison, J C Balderstone, R Illingworth (Cpt), P R Haywood, J
  F Steele, G D McKenzie, C T Spencer, K Higgs.
Yorkshire: P J Sharpe (Cpt), R G Lumb, B Leadbeater, J H
  Hampshire, R A Hutton, J D Woodford, C Johnson, C M Old,
  D L Bairstow, H P Cooper, A G Nicholson.

1973

Quarter Finals
Leicestershire 177–8 (J C Balderstone 58, B E A Edmeades 5–22)
  lost to Essex 180–4 (B E A Edmeades 50, R M O Cooke 50) by 6
  wkts
Kent 206 (Asif Iqbal 54) beat Hampshire 195 (R M C Gilliat 55) by
  11 runs
Lancashire 227–5 (H Pilling 109*, J Sullivan 50) beat Glamorgan
  68 by 159 runs
Worcestershire 234–8 (R G A Headley 84, J A Ormrod 54) beat
  Nottinghamshire 145–8 (R A White 52*)

Semi Finals
Kent 169–9 (R E East 4–26) beat Essex 123 by 46 runs
Lancashire 159 (N Gifford 5–42) lost to Worcestershire 159–9 (P G
  Lee 4–32) losing more wickets with scores tied

Final
Kent 225–7 (B W Luckhurst 79, Asif Iqbal 59) beat Worcestershire
  186 (Asif Iqbal 4–43) by 39 runs
(*Lord's 21.7.1973*)
Kent: B W Luckhurst, G W Johnson, M H Denness (Cpt), Asif
  Iqbal, A G E Ealham, J N Shepherd, M C Cowdrey, A P E

Knott, R A Woolmer, D L Underwood, J N Graham.
Worcestershire: R G A Headley, G M Turner, E J O Hemsley, G
  R Cass, J A Ormrod, N Gifford (Cpt), B L d'Oliveira, T J
  Yardley, I N Johnson, B M Brain, J Cumbes.

1974

Quarter Finals
Leicestershire 238–8 (B Dudleston 79, B F Davison 65) beat Kent
  230–9 (B W Luckhurst 111, G D McKenzie 5–34) by 8 runs
Hampshire 182 (T E Jesty 79) lost to Somerset 184–9 (T E Jesty
  4–28) by 1 wkt
Surrey 225–7 (G P Howarth 80) beat Yorkshire 201 (B Leadbeater
  62, P J Sharpe 50, R D Jackman 4–35) by 24 runs
Lancashire 204–7 (B Wood 67) beat Worcestershire 168 by 36 runs

Semi Finals
Surrey 193–8 (J H Edrich 62) beat Lancashire 130 (C H Lloyd 50)
  by 63 runs
Leicestershire 270–8 (J F Steele 91, B F Davison 73, B Dudleston
  54) beat Somerset 130 (R Illingworth 5–20) by 140 runs

Final
Surrey 170 (K Higgs 4–10) beat Leicestershire 143 by 27 runs.
(*Lord's 20.7.1974*)
Surrey: J H Edrich, L E Skinner, G P Howarth, Younis Ahmed,
  G R J Roope, S J Storey, R D Jackman, A R Butcher,
  P I Pocock, A Long, G G Arnold.
Leicestershire: B Dudleston, J F Steele, M E J C Norman,
  B F Davison, R W Tolchard, J C Balderstone, R Illingworth (Cpt),
  N M McVicker, G D McKenzie, P Booth, K Higgs.

1975

Quarter Finals
Hampshire 223 beat Somerset 173 (I V A Richards 62*) by 50 runs
Lancashire 180–8 (F C Hayes 67) lost to Leicestershire 183–8 (R W
  Tolchard 57*) by 2 wkts

Opposite above
*Members of the Surrey
team celebrating the
Benson and Hedges Cup
victory in 1974. From
left: J H Edrich, G G
Arnold, A Long, S J
Storey, P I Pocock and
G P Howarth.*

Above *Wayne Daniel
of Middlesex, whose
figures of 7 wickets for
12 against Minor
Counties (East) in 1982
is the best Benson and
Hedges Cup bowling
analysis.*

Right *The highest
individual innings in
Benson and Hedges
Cup matches is 198 not
out, scored by Graham
Gooch for Essex against
Sussex in 1982.*

Yorkshire 182 (G Boycott 58, T M Lamb 5–44) lost to Middlesex
183–6 by 4 wkts

Essex 153 (B E A Edmeades 85, S J Rouse 4–22) lost to
Warwickshire 154–3 (A I Kallicharran 71*) by 7 wkts

Semi Finals

Hampshire 216 (C G Greenidge 111) lost to Leicestershire 217–5
(J C Balderstone 101*) by 5 wkts

Middlesex 247–8 (C T Radley 103, H A Gomes 78) beat
Warwickshire 244–9 (J A Jameson 65, A I Kallicharran 53) by 3
runs

Final

Middlesex 146 (M J Smith 83, N M McVicker 4–20) lost to
Leicestershire 150–5 by 5 wkts

(*Lord's 19.7.1975*)

Leicestershire: B Dudleston, J F Steele, J C Balderstone, B F
Davison, R W Tolchard, G F Cross, R Illingworth (Cpt), N M
McVicker, P Booth, G D McKenzie, K Higgs.

Middlesex: M J Smith, P H Edmonds, C T Radley, J M Brearley
(Cpt), N G Featherstone, H A Gomes, G D Barlow, J T
Murray, F J Titmus, M W W Selvey, J S E Price.

1976

Quarter Finals

Kent 196 (M H Denness 50, B Stead 4–24) beat Nottinghamshire
166 (M J Harris 54, K B S Jarvis 4–54) by 30 runs

Essex 220–9 (G A Gooch 89) lost to Surrey 221–7 (J H Edrich 57*)
by 3 wkts

Lancashire 206–9 (F C Hayes 70, R G D Willis 5–27) lost to
Warwickshire 209–6 (J Whitehouse 71*) by 4 wkts

Leicestershire 268–5 (R W Tolchard 92*, P B Clift 58) lost to
Worcestershire 272–4 (J A Ormrod 95, B L d'Oliveira 63, Imran
Khan 56*) by 6 wkts

Semi Finals

Kent 280–3 (M H Denness 104, G W Johnson 59, Asif Iqbal 56*)
beat Surrey 264 (C J Aworth 67, D L Underwood 5–35) by 16
runs

Worcestershire 281–4 (G M Turner 143*, Imran Khan 72) beat
Warwickshire 269–9 by 12 runs

Final

Kent 236–7 (G W Johnson 78, R A Woolmer 61) beat
Worcestershire 193 (B L d'Oliveira 50, K B S Jarvis 4–34) by 43
runs

(*Lord's 17.7.1976*)

Kent: G W Johnson, R A Woolmer, M H Denness (Cpt), Asif
Iqbal, A G E Ealham, J N Shepherd, A P E Knott, C J C Rowe,
R W Hills, D L Underwood, K B S Jarvis.

Worcestershire: J A Ormrod, G M Turner, P A Neale, Imran
Khan, E J O Hemsley, B L d'Oliveira, C N Boyns, H G
Wilcock, N Gifford (Cpt), J D Inchmore, A P Pridgeon.

1977

Quarter Finals

Glamorgan 209–8 (M J Llewellyn 54) lost to Hampshire 210–4
(T E Jesty 105*) by 6 wkts

Gloucestershire 194–7 (Zaheer Abbas 64, D R Shepherd 60*) beat
Middlesex 176 by 18 runs

Sussex 264–5 (R D V Knight 91, Javed Miandad 56*, K C Wessels
64) lost to Kent 268–4 (C S Cowdrey 114, A G E Ealham 94*)
by 6 wkts

Northants 196 (D S Steele 60) beat Warwickshire 179–9 (B J
Griffiths 4–36) by 17 runs

Semi Finals

Kent 211–6 (Asif Iqbal 65*, R A Woolmer 51) beat Northants
206–7 (D S Steele 64) by 5 runs

Gloucestershire 180 (Sadiq Mohammad 76) beat Hampshire 173
(N G Cowley 59, M J Procter 6–13) by 7 runs

Final

Gloucestershire 237–6 (A W Stovold 71, Zaheer Abbas 70) beat

Kent 173 (R A Woolmer 64, J N Shepherd 55)

(*Lord's 16.7.1977*)

Gloucestershire: Sadiq Mohammad, A W Stovold, Zaheer Abbas,
M J Procter (Cpt), J C Foat, D R Shepherd, D A Graveney,
M J Vernon, M D Partridge, J H Shackleton, B M Brain.

Kent: R A Woolmer, G S Clinton, C J C Rowe, Asif Iqbal, A G E
Ealham, B D Julien, J N Shepherd A P E Knott, R W Hills,
D L Underwood, K B S Jarvis.

1978

Quarter Finals

Derbyshire 154 (A Hill 69) beat Middlesex 125 (M W Gatting 50)
by 29 runs

Nottinghamshire 209–7 (D W Randall 51) lost to Kent 219–3
(A G E Ealham 60*, Asif Iqbal 50*) by 7 wkts

Somerset 218–9 (I T Botham 54) beat Sussex 116 by 102 runs

Warwickshire 205–6 (J Whitehouse 70) beat Glamorgan 159 by 46
runs

Semi Finals

Derbyshire 203–9 (A J Borrington 77) beat Warwickshire 162 (G W
Humpage 78) by 41 runs

Kent 204–8 (C J Tavare 56) beat Somerset 163 by 41 runs

Final

Derbyshire 147 (J N Shepherd 4–25) lost to Kent 151–4 (R A
Woolmer 79) by 6 wkts

(*Lord's 22.7.1978*)

Kent: R A Woolmer, G W Johnson, C J Tavare, Asif Iqbal, A G E
Ealham (Cpt), J N Shepherd, C J C Rowe, C S Cowdrey, D L
Underwood, P R Downton, K B S Jarvis.

Derbyshire: A Hill, A J Borrington, P N Kirsten, E J Barlow (Cpt),
G Miller, H Cartwright, A J Harvey-Walker, R W Taylor,
P E Russell, R C Wincer, M Hendrick.

1979

Quarter Finals

Essex 271–5 (G A Gooch 138, K S McEwan 50) beat Warwickshire
227 (K D Smith 61) by 44 runs

Glamorgan 197–5 (P D Swart 75) lost to Derbyshire 199–4 (J G
Wright 101) by 6 wkts

Middlesex 107 (H P Cooper 4–28) lost to Yorkshire 108–6 by 4
wkts

Worcestershire 199–7 (Younis Ahmed 107) lost to Surrey 201–3
(M A Lynch 67, G P Howarth 51) by 7 wkts

Semi Finals

Surrey 166–8 beat Derbyshire 160 (P N Kirsten 70) by 6 runs

Yorkshire 173–9 (R G Lumb 75, J H Hampshire 53) lost to Essex
174–7 by 3 wkts

Final

Essex 290–6 (G A Gooch 120, K S McEwan 72, P H L Wilson
4–56) beat Surrey 255 (G P Howarth 74, R D V Knight 52) by
35 runs

(*Lord's 21.7.1979*)

Essex: M H Denness, G A Gooch, K S McEwan, K W R Fletcher
(Cpt), B R Hardie, K R Pont, N Phillip, S Turner, N Smith,
R E East, J K Lever.

Surrey: A R Butcher, M A Lynch, G P Howarth, R D V Knight
(Cpt), D M Smith, G R J Roope, Intikhab Alam, R D Jackman,
C J Richards, P I Pocock, P H L Wilson.

1980

Quarter Finals

Essex 270–5 (K S McEwan 95) beat Surrey 184 by 86 runs

Worcestershire 314–5 (P A Neale 128, G M Turner 122) beat
Lancashire 269 (I Cockbain 53, J Simmons 53) by 45 runs

Middlesex 195 (C M Wells 4–21) beat Sussex 166 (P W G Parker
59) by 29 runs

Nottinghamshire 143 (T M Lamb 4–11) lost to Northants 145–3 (G
Cook 66, R G Williams 59) by 7 wkts

Northants 206–8 (R G Williams 73*, W Larkins 62) beat Middlesex 195 (M W Gatting 91, Sarfraz Nawaz 5–21) by 11 runs

Worcestershire 236–9 (J A Ormrod 70) lost to Essex 240–2 (G A Gooch 81, M H Denness 66, K S McEwan 65*) by 8 wkts

Final

Northants 209 (A J Lamb 72, K R Pont 4–60) beat Essex 203–8 (G A Gooch 60) by 6 runs

(*Lord's 19, 21.7.1980*)

Northants: G Cook, W Larkins, R G Williams, A J Lamb, P Willey, T J Yardley, G Sharp, P J Watts (Cpt), Sarfraz Nawaz, T M Lamb, B J Griffiths.

Essex: M H Denness, G A Gooch, K S McEwan, K W R Fletcher (Cpt), B R Hardie, K R Pont, S Turner, N Phillip, N Smith, R E East, J K Lever.

1981

Quarter Finals

Surrey 226–7 (R D V Knight 70) beat Nottinghamshire 179 (D W Randall 62, R D Jackman 4–24) by 47 runs

Yorkshire 221–9 (C W J Athey 58, J H Hampshire 58) lost to Somerset 223–7 (B C Rose 68, P W Denning 66) by 3 wkts

Sussex 196–9 (C P Phillipson 59) lost to Leicestershire 199–6 (J C Balderstone 67) by 4 wkts

Kent 193–8 (C J Tavare 76) beat Warwickshire 179 (T A Lloyd 60) by 14 runs

Semi Finals

Surrey 191–9 (G R J Roope 55*) beat Leicestershire 188 by 3 runs

Kent 154 lost to Somerset 157–5 (P M Roebuck 51*) by 5 wkts

Final

Surrey 194–8 (R D V Knight 92, J Garner 5–14) lost to Somerset 197–3 (I V A Richards 132*) by 7 wkts

(*Lord's 25.7.1981*)

Somerset: B C Rose (Cpt), P W Denning, I V A Richards, P M Roebuck, I T Botham, V J Marks, N F M Popplewell, D Breakwell, D J S Taylor, J Garner, C H Dredge.

Surrey: G S Clinton, C J Richards, R D V Knight (Cpt), G P Howarth, M A Lynch, D M Smith, S T Clarke, G R J Roope, D J Thomas, R D Jackman, P I Pocock.

1982

Quarter Finals

Derbyshire 190 (P N Kirsten 60) lost to Sussex 194–6 (P W G Parker 72) by 4 wkts

Kent 207 (N R Taylor 121, I T Botham 4–52) lost to Somerset 208–7 (B C Rose 52, P M Roebuck 50) by 3 wkts

Lancashire 191–9 (C H Lloyd 66) beat Middlesex 139 (C T Radley 66, I Folley 4–18) by 52 runs

Nottinghamshire 156 beat Leicestershire 154–9 by 2 runs

Semi Finals

Lancashire 182 (C Maynard 60) lost to Nottinghamshire 184–6 (R J Hadlee 55*) by 4 wkts

Sussex 110 (J Garner 4–24) lost to Somerset 112–2 (P W Denning 68*) by 8 wkts

Final

Nottinghamshire 130 lost to Somerset 132–1 (P M Roebuck 53*, I V A Richards 51*) by 9 wkts

(*Lord's 24.7.1982*)

Somerset: P M Roebuck, P W Denning, I V A Richards, B C Rose (Cpt), I T Botham, V J Marks, N F M Popplewell, D J S Taylor, J Garner, C H Dredge, H R Moseley.

Nottinghamshire: P A Todd, R T Robinson, D W Randall, C E B Rice, J D Birch, B Hassan, R J Hadlee, B N French, E E Hemmings, K E Cooper, M Hendrick.

V F S Crawford of Surrey made the longest hit in a first-class match at Bristol in 1900, hitting a ball from Gloucestershire's A J Paish 160 yards before pitching.

Big Hits

For many years Wisden's Cricketers' Almanack recorded the longest hit from strike to pitch to be 175 yards by W Fellows whilst practising on the Christ Church Ground at Oxford in 1856. The bowler, C Rogers, was pitching the ball in order that the batsman might hit it as far as possible, the object being to try out the powers of a new bat. It is not certain that 175 yards was the actual distance between hit and pitch; it was more probably the total distance travelled by the ball.

A more authentic measurement was taken by the Rev James Pycroft at Hove on August 25, 1876, when C I Thornton, whilst practising, hit a ball 168 yards and 2 feet.

The record hit made in a first-class match occurred at Bristol on August 25, 1900 when V F S Crawford hit a delivery from A J Paish out of the ground during the Surrey v Gloucestershire match. It was measured at 160 yards from hit to pitch.

Boundaries

The first mention of a boundary occurred in 1733, when a line was marked round the ground. In 1736 a rope was substituted for the line. The reason for the boundary demarcation was not to give the batsman a four or six without the need to run, but to keep spectators off the playing area. All hits at this time were run out.

When the practice of erecting booths or tents near the playing area became common, a ball stopped by a booth became dead and a given number of runs awarded.

The first known example of a ground using a boundary line in the manner it is used today was at Town Malling in Kent in 1841.

Apart from the use of boundaries when a large crowd attended a match – for example Eton v Harrow or the University matches at Lord's – the general use of a boundary line with hits over it counting either three or four did not appear until the 1880s. It was necessary to

V J S CRAWFORD.

8598

P A Perrin of Essex hit 68 fours in an innings for Essex against Derbyshire in 1904 – a first-class record.

hit the ball right out of the ground for a six until 1910, when the present method of awarding a six was introduced.

Most boundaries in an innings   The most boundaries hit in a single innings were scored by G T S Stevens in an inter-school match in Neasden in 1919. He hit 64 fours and 24 sixes.

In first-class cricket, P A Perrin hit 68 fours for Essex v Derbyshire at Chesterfield on July 18 and 19, 1904 during his innings of 343* – 'the ball travelling over the dry grass so rapidly to the short boundary that the fieldsmen had very little chance of getting to it.'

Innings composed of only boundaries   The highest completed innings by a batsman containing only boundary strokes is 44, which was hit by P T Marner for Lancashire v Notts at Southport on August 22, 1960 – he hit 4 sixes and 5 fours. This was equalled by M J Harris with 11 fours for Notts v Yorkshire at Bradford, August 10, 1976.

Largest innings without a boundary   Since the 1880s the largest first-class innings without a boundary is 103 by A Hill for Orange Free State v Griqualand West at Bloemfontein, March 11 and 12, 1977.

Bowlers

Bowlers unchanged through both innings   Though rarely occurring in first-class matches at the present time, it was fairly common for two bowlers to bowl unchanged through a match until the First World War. The higher the run-getting the less likely it is that no bowling change will take place and the match in which most runs (249) were scored by one side whilst only two bowlers were used in both innings was Australians v Liverpool and District at Liverpool, July 31, August 1 and 2, 1882. G E Palmer and H F Boyle (Australians) were the bowlers, their analyses being:

Palmer   39.2-13-60-5 and 34-11-73-4
Boyle   39-14-51-5 and 33.1-8-56-6

Most bowlers used during a single innings   During the match between Notts and Twenty-Two Colts at Trent Bridge on April 10 and 11, 1871, no less than 19 of the 22 Colts bowled during the only innings of the Notts XI. This is believed to be a record.

Most bowlers used in a first-class match   All twenty-two players

*Yours sincerely
Don Bradman*

bowled in the match between A E R Gilligan's XI and the Australians at Hastings, September 2, 3 and 4, 1964. The report of the game noted: 'The cricket was too lighthearted at times to be treated seriously, but the crowd enjoyed plenty of entertainment.'
(see also Overs)

Bradford League

Championship winners

1903	Shelf	1943	Saltaire
1904	Great Horton	1944	Spen Victoria
1905	Clayton	1945	Undercliffe
1906	Great Horton	1946	Keighley
1907	Undercliffe	1947	Salts
1908	Great Horton	1948	Windhill
1909	Great Horton	1949	Salts
1910	Idle	1950	Baildon
1911	Windhill	1951	Baildon
1912	Bingley	1952	Baildon
1913	Laisterdyke	1953	Salts
1914	Bradford	1954	Salts
1915	Bowling Old Lane	1955	Bradford
1916	Idle	1956	Pudsey St Lawrence
1917	Saltaire	1957	Lidget Green
1918	Saltaire	1958	Bradford
1919	Keighley	1959	Bingley
1920	Saltaire	1960	Brighouse
1921	Bingley	1961	Salts
1922	Saltaire	1962	Farsley
1923	Bowling Old Lane	1963	Undercliffe
1924	Bowling Old Lane	1964	Lidget Green
1925	Undercliffe	1965	Idle
1926	Saltaire	1966	Idle
1927	Bradford	1967	Idle
1928	Bradford	1968	Bradford
1929	Bradford	1969	Bingley
1930	Brighouse	1970	Undercliffe
1931	Brighouse	1971	Undercliffe
1932	Brighouse	1972	Bankfoot
1933	Bradford	1973	Bingley
1934	Bradford	1974	Idle
1935	Undercliffe	1975	Pudsey St Lawrence
1936	Bradford	1976	Pudsey St Lawrence
1937	Windhill	1977	Idle
1938	Windhill	1978	Bowling Old Lane
1939	Windhill	1979	Pudsey St Lawrence
1940	Windhill	1980	Yorkshire Bank
1941	Windhill	1981	East Bierley
1942	Lidget Green	1982	Bingley

The league records are:

Highest team total 488 Saltaire 1930
Lowest team total 14 Greengates 1907
Highest individual innings 230 C H Grimshaw (*Bowling O B*) 1915
Best bowling 10–11 P E Watson (*Spen Victoria*) 1962
Most runs in season 1251 R V Mankad (*Cleckheaton*) 1978
Most wickets in season 122 S F Barnes (*Saltaire*) 1922

Bradman, Sir Donald George

In terms of first-class records, D G Bradman (born August 27, 1908) has no rival as a batsman. His first-class career record and his Test record are without parallel in the history of the game:

	I	NO	R	HS	Avge
First-class matches					
1927–28 to 1948–49	338	43	28067	452*	95.14
Test matches					
1928–29 to 1948	80	10	6996	334	99.94

In 1929–30 he scored 452* for N S W v Queensland at Sydney, which was a new first-class record for an individual batsman, and a few months later at Headingley he hit 334 for Australia v England, which created a new Test record.

He toured England with the Australian team in four seasons and hit over 2,000 runs in each of those seasons: 1930 (2,960 runs), 1934 (2,020 runs), 1938 (2,429 runs) and 1948 (2,428 runs). No other tourist can claim such success.

During the 1938 tour, Bradman averaged 115.66 in first-class matches, the highest ever attained in an English season.

Only seven batsmen have scored 1,000 first-class runs before the end of May. Bradman has performed this feat twice, the only batsman to do this.

Bradman hit 117 centuries in 338 first-class innings – no other batsman with a career of any great length has approached this proportion of 100s to innings.

Brazil

The first known cricket club in Brazil was formed in Rio de Janeiro by December 1840, but it was not until the 1870s that cricket was firmly established in the country.

The first international match played by Brazil was against Argentina in 1921–22. Apart from matches against English touring sides, Argentina remains the only country to oppose Brazil.

Rowland Bowen ranked Brazil as first-class in matches against Argentina between 1921–22 and 1929–30 – Brazil did not play an international match between 1930 and 1953.

The highest team total by Brazil is 534 v Argentina (*Hurlingham*) 1927–28 and the highest individual innings is 163 by H C Morrisy v Argentina (*Hurlingham*), 1927–28.

Best bowling in an innings is 7–46 by C Chatwin v Argentina (*Niteroi*), 1966–67.

Brazil did not take part in the 1979 or 1982 ICC Trophy.

Brothers

In first-class English cricket it is believed that only three families have provided seven brothers, all of whom were first-class cricketers. The first example is the Walker brothers of Southgate and Middlesex: A (1846–60), A H (1855–62), F (1849–60), I D (1882–84), J (1846–68), R D (1861–78) and V E (1856–77). Only four ever appeared in the same first-class team in one match. The dates are the extent of each brother's first-class career.

The second set of seven is the Foster brothers of Worcestershire: B S (1902–12), G N (1903–31), H K (1894–25), M K (1908–36), N J A (1923), R E (1899–12), W L (1899–11), but again they never all appeared together in first-class matches.

The third set of seven are the Studds of Middlesex and Hampshire: E J C (1878–85), A H (1887–88), C T (1879–03), G B (1879–86),

Left Don Bradman, on record the greatest of all batsmen.

Right Four of the seven Foster brothers of Worcestershire: from left H K, W L, R E, G N.

The wicketkeepers with the worst and best records regarding byes in an innings. Above C W Wright, one of the two Cambridge University wicketkeepers to concede 57 byes to Yorkshire in 1884 and above right the Rev A P Wickham, of Somerset, who conceded no byes in Hampshire's 672 for 7 dec in 1899.

H W (1890–98), J E K (1878–85), R A (1895). The first mentioned was in fact the half-brother of the other six.

In Test matches three brothers have appeared on one side on two separate occasions. W G, E M and G F Grace all represented England *v* Australia at the Oval in 1880; and in 1969–70 Hanif, Mushtaq and Sadiq Mohammad all represented Pakistan at Karachi *v* New Zealand.

In South Africa in 1891–92, the brothers A, G G and F Hearne all appeared in the same match, the first two for England and the other for South Africa.

Byes

Most in innings Cambridge University gave away 57 byes in the course of an innings of 539 by Yorkshire at Fenner's, May 26 and 27, 1884. The erring wicket-keepers (Cambridge used two) were C W Wright and Hon C M Knatchbull-Hugessen. This is a world record for first-class matches.

Highest innings without a bye On July 20 and 21, 1899 Hampshire scored 672 for 7 wkts dec against Somerset at Taunton. Somerset did not concede a single bye, their wicket-keeper being Rev A P Wickham.

Cahn, Sir Julien

During the 1920s and 1930s, Sir Julien Cahn (1882–1944) ran his own cricket team, the standard of which was the equal of some of the English first-class county teams of the period, and his team was usually recognised as first-class when opposed to other established first-class sides in three-day matches. The team went on six tours overseas and on four of these tours played first-class matches – in Jamaica 1929, Argentina 1930, Ceylon 1937 and New Zealand 1939.

The records for the team in first-class matches are:

Highest team total   567 *v* Leics (*Nottingham*)   1935
Lowest team total   69 *v* Glamorgan (*Newport*)   1938
Highest individual innings   268 C R N Maxwell *v* Leics (*Nottm*) 1935
Best bowling in innings   9–101 J E Walsh *v* Glam (*Newport*)   1938

K S Duleepsinhji, whose 254 not out against Middlesex in 1927 is a Cambridge University record.

Sir Julien Cahn, with moustache, at Liverpool Street station, London, seeing off members of his team to New Zealand in 1939.

David Sheppard's 1,581 runs in the 1952 season was a record aggregate for Cambridge University.

Cambridgeshire

One of the leading counties in the 1850s and 1860s, Cambridgeshire collapsed as a force in county cricket due to the lack of a strong county club. In T Hayward and R Carpenter the county possessed two of the best professional batsmen of the 1860s and in G F Tarrant one of the best bowlers, but this formidable trio rarely pulled together.

The first first-class inter-county match by Cambridgeshire was against Surrey at Fenner's on May 18 and 19, 1857 and the last one also against Surrey on June 22, 23 and 24, 1871 at the Oval.

The records for the county in first-class matches are:

Highest team total   361 *v* Cambridge Univ (*Fenner's*)   1865
Lowest team total   30 *v* Yorkshire (*Stockton*)   1861
Highest individual innings   112 T Hayward *v* Surrey (*Fenner's*) 1861
Best bowling in innings   8–16 G F Tarrant *v* Kent (*Chatham*)   1862
Highest wicket partnership   3rd Wkt 212 R Carpenter, T Hayward *v* Surrey (*Oval*)   1861
(*See also Minor County Records*)

Cambridge University

The first reference to cricket at the University occurred in 1710 and the annual match between the University and Cambridge Town is first known to have taken place in 1819. It is believed that the match series against Oxford University commenced at Lord's on June 4, 1827.

Cambridge can be regarded as 'first-class' since 1819, though until the 1860s the standard of cricket was not equal to that of the major counties and the relative strengths before 1860 are possibly the same as at the present time.

The records for the University in first-class cricket are:

Highest team total   703–9d *v* Sussex (*Hove*)   1890
Lowest team total   28 *v* MCC (*Lord's*)   1845
Highest individual innings   254* K S Duleepsinhji *v* Middx (*Fenner's*)   1927
Best bowling in innings   10–69 S M J Woods *v* C I Thornton's XI (*Fenner's*)   1890
Best bowling in match   15–88 as above
(J H Kirwan also took 15 wkts – *v* Cambridge Town in 1836, but no analysis has yet been found)
Most runs in season   1581 (*avge* 79.05) D S Sheppard   1952
Most runs in career   4310 (*avge* 38.48) J M Brearley   1961–68
Most wickets in season   80 (*avge* 17.63) O S Wheatley   1958
Most wickets in career   208 (*avge* 21.82) G Goonesena   1954–57

Wicket partnerships

1st 349 J G Dewes, D S Sheppard v Sussex (*Hove*) 1950
2nd 429* J G Dewes, G H G Doggart. v Essex (*Fenner's*) 1949
3rd 284 E T Killick, G C Grant. v Essex (*Fenner's*) 1929
4th 275 R de W K Winlaw, J H Human. v Essex (*Fenner's*) 1934
5th 220 R Subba Row, F C M Alexander. v Notts (*Trent Bridge*) 1953
6th 245 J L Bryan, C T Ashton. v Surrey (*Oval*) 1921
7th 289 G Goonesena, G W Cook. v Oxford U (*Lord's*) 1957
8th 145 H Ashton, A E R Gilligan. v Free Foresters (*Fenner's*) 1920
9th 200 G W Cook, C S Smith. v Lancs (*Liverpool*) 1957
10th 177 J H Naumann, A E R Gilligan. v Sussex (*Hove*) 1919
(*See also University Match*)

Canada

There is a report of Canadians playing cricket in Montreal as early as 1785, but the game appears to have been established on an organised basis in 1834 when a cricket club was formed in Toronto and matches also reported in Hamilton and Guelph.

The first game by 'Canada' was played against the United States on September 24 and 25, 1844, though New York had played Toronto in 1840 and the sides were in fact of similar strength to those which took part in the 'international' of 1844.

Canada took part in the 1979 ICC Trophy and beat Bermuda by 4 wickets in the semi-final, but lost to Sri Lanka in the final by 60 runs. They qualified for the Prudential Cup, but were beaten in all their matches. In the 1982 ICC Trophy, Canada won three matches and obtained third place in their group.

The highest individual innings made in Canada is 260* by D G Bradman for the Australians v XVIII of Western Ontario on July 4, 1932.

(*See under United States for details of matches v United States*)

Cancelled

The only Test match to be cancelled just days prior to its scheduled starting date, due to political reasons, should have taken place at Georgetown, Guyana on February 28, March 1, 2, 4 and 5, 1981. The reason for the cancellation was that the Guyana Government withdrew R D Jackman's visitor's permit, thus preventing the English selectors from picking Jackman for the Test. Jackman's connections with South African cricket were the reason for the permit's withdrawal. Guyana had some years before cancelled their Shell Shield match with Barbados because the latter included G A Greenidge who had played in South Africa.

The last time a tour from England involving Test matches was cancelled after the team had been chosen was for the 1968–69 tour to South Africa, when B L d'Oliveira was selected as a replacement at the last minute for T W Cartwright, who was unfit, and the South African Prime Minister then said that South Africa was not prepared to receive the team which included d'Oliveira.

In 1939–40, after the English team to tour India had been chosen, war was declared and the tour cancelled.

The only post-war tour involving Test matches and coming to England which was cancelled at the last moment was the 1970 South African visit. In this case the British Government instructed the Cricket Council to cancel the tour.

Captains

Most successful in county championship W S Surridge captained Surrey for five seasons, 1952 to 1956, and won the County Championship in each of those seasons. In those seasons he missed 10 championship games and the complete record for Surrey in matches with Surridge as leader reads:

Played 129, Won 89, Lost 19, Drawn 31

Most successful in Test cricket Of those captains who have led their country in 10 or more Tests, only one has remained undefeated. W

Mike Brearley scored most runs for Cambridge University in a career, making 4,310 between 1961 and 1968. He later became a successful captain of England.

W Armstrong captained Australia in 10 matches, all against England, and won 8 times, the other two games being drawn. The two series were 1920–21 in Australia and 1921 in England.

Longest serving county captain W G Grace (Gloucestershire 1871–1898) and Lord Hawke (Yorkshire 1883–1910) have the joint record, both leading their counties for 28 seasons.

Successful tours to England The only captain to lead an Australian team to England and return home undefeated was D G Bradman in 1948. Intikhab Alam achieved a similar feat for Pakistan in England in 1974.

Career Records

Batting J B Hobbs holds the first-class record for both runs and centuries. His complete figures read:

834 matches, 1325 inns, 106 no, 61760 runs, 316* hs, 50.66 av and 199 centuries. His career ran from 1905 to 1934

(These figures include 9 matches played in India and Ceylon in 1930–31, which are not always regarded as first-class – Hobbs scored 2 centuries – but exclude MCC v Reef, 1909–10.)

Bowling W Rhodes is the only bowler to exceed 4,000 wickets in his career, which ran from 1898 to 1930. His bowling record reads:

70322 runs, 4204 wkts, 16.72 av

Fielding Only F E Woolley has held more than 1,000 catches, his total being 1,020. His career lasted from 1906 to 1938.

Longest break in first-class career R H Moss made his final first-class appearance for Worcestershire v Gloucestershire on May 23, 25 and 26, 1925, his previous first-class match being Liverpool and District v Australians, August 10 and 11, 1893.

Wicket keeping Most dismissals in a first-class career are: ct 1,270, st 257 by J T Murray, 1952 to 1975.

Longest career in England John Sherman appeared in an important match at Lord's on September 20, 21 and 22, 1809 and his last

Robin Jackman leaves Guyana in 1981 after the cancellation of the Test match because of his connections with South Africa.

Basil d'Oliveira, whose selection for the England tour to South Africa in 1968–69 caused the cancellation of the tour.

Warwick Armstrong, of Australia, the most successful Test match captain, unbeaten in ten Tests against England.

Jack Hobbs, on the left, seen going out to bat with Herbert Sutcliffe, scored more first-class runs and centuries than any other player.

Frank Woolley catches Bardsley in the England–Australia Test match at Leeds, July 1921. Woolley was the only player to make over 1,000 catches.

important match was Manchester *v* Sheffield on July 26 and 27, 1852, his career spanning 44 seasons. This feat was equalled by W G Grace: June 22, 1865 to April 22, 1908.

Carrying bat through an innings

Largest innings The most runs scored by a batsman who opened the innings and saw all ten wickets fall are 357* by R Abel for Surrey *v* Somerset at the Oval on May 29 and 30, 1899. The Surrey total of 811 is the largest team total through which a batsman has carried his bat. Abel batted 510 minutes and gave only two chances, both stumpings. A collection on the ground realised £33 3s for his feat.

Most occasions W G Grace carried his bat through the innings on no less than 17 occasions in first-class cricket, a feat subsequently equalled only by C J B Wood.

In both innings of the same match This feat has been accomplished four times in first-class matches as follows:

H Jupp 43* and 109* Surrey *v* Yorks (*Oval*) 1874
S Kinneir 70* and 69* Warwicks *v* Leics (*Leicester*) 1907
C J B Wood 107* and 117* Leics *v* Yorks (*Bradford*) 1911
V M Merchant 135* and 77* Indians *v* Lancs (*Liverpool*) 1946

Catches (*excluding wicket keepers*)

Most in an innings In first-class cricket two fieldsmen have taken a record 7 catches in an innings, namely:

A S Brown, for Gloucs in 2nd inns of Notts *v* Gloucs (*Trent Bridge*) 1966
M J Stewart, for Surrey in 2nd inns of Northants *v* Surrey (*Northampton*) 1957

According to the historian G B Buckley a cricketer playing for Islington Albion took ten catches in an innings, but the details have been lost. This remarkable feat was equalled by a player called Barker who caught all ten for London Schools *v* Southend Schools at Lord's in 1904.

Most in a match Only one cricketer has taken ten catches in a first-class match: W R Hammond for Gloucestershire *v* Surrey at Cheltenham on August 15, 16 and 17, 1928. Hammond also performed the feat of hitting a century in both innings of the same game.

In an odds game, the All England Eleven *v* XXII of Birmingham at Birmingham on August 31, September 1 and 2, 1854, R C Tinley caught out 12 Birmingham players.

Most in a season The record number of catches in a first-class season is 78 by W R Hammond, chiefly for Gloucestershire, in 1928. Hammond played in 35 matches.
(*See also under 'wicket-keeping'*)

Ten catches by ten different fielders in one innings During the innings of Northants at Leicester on August 31, 1967, ten Leicestershire fielders each held a catch.

Central Lancashire League

Championship winners

1892	Littleborough	1937	Radcliffe
1893	Rochdale	1938	Middleton
1894	Rochdale	1939	Werneth
1895	Rochdale	1940	Ashton
1896	Todmorden	1941	Stockport
1897	Rochdale	1942	Stockport
1898	Middleton	1943	Castleton Moor
1899	Middleton	1944	Radcliffe
1900	Rochdale	1945	Heywood
1901	Glossop	1946	Radcliffe
1902	Crompton	1947	Milnrow
1903	Glossop	1948	Rochdale
1904	Heywood	1949	Stockport, Milnrow
1905	Rochdale	1950	Rochdale
1906	Rochdale	1951	Rochdale
1907	Moorside	1952	Rochdale
1908	Glossop	1953	Rochdale
1909	Oldham	1954	Crompton
1910	Milnrow	1955	Rochdale
1911	Littleborough	1956	Rochdale
1912	Littleborough	1957	Oldham
1913	Glossop	1958	Middleton
1914	Royton	1959	Middleton
1915	Moorside	1960	Heywood
1916	Oldham	1961	Radcliffe
1917	Littleborough	1962	Walsden, Stockport
1918	Crompton	1963	Heywood
1919	Littleborough	1964	Walsden
1920	Middleton	1965	Crompton, Stockport
1921	Littleborough	1966	Stockport
1922	Rochdale	1967	Heywood
1923	Rochdale	1968	Heywood
1924	Rochdale	1969	Radcliffe
1925	Rochdale	1970	Middleton
1926	Castleton Moor	1971	Radcliffe
1927	Rochdale	1972	Milnrow
1928	Castleton Moor	1973	Middleton
1929	Heywood	1974	Heywood
1930	Middleton	1975	Milnrow
1931	Heywood	1976	Heywood
1932	Littleborough	1977	Littleborough
1933	Ashton	1978	Littleborough
1934	Littleborough	1979	Oldham
1935		1980	Royton
1936	Littleborough	1981	Hyde

The league records are:

Highest individual innings 205 H Smith, Walsden *v* Moorside
1915
Highest team total 419 Castleton Moor *v* Rochdale 1949
Lowest team total 8 Heywood *v* Stockport 1944
Best bowling 10–4 E Price, Middleton *v* Littleborough 1952
Best wkt partnership 303 F M M Worrell, W Greenhalgh,
Radcliffe *v* Middleton 1952

Centuries

Most in successive innings In first-class matches three batsmen have hit six centuries in successive innings. The details are:

C B Fry

106	Sussex *v* Hants (*Portsmouth*)	Aug 15–17, 1901
209	Sussex *v* Yorkshire (*Hove*)	Aug 19–21, 1901
149	Sussex *v* Middlesex (*Hove*)	Aug 22–24, 1901
105	Sussex *v* Surrey (*Oval*)	Aug 26–28, 1901
140	Sussex *v* Kent (*Hove*)	Aug 29–31, 1901
105	Rest *v* Yorkshire (*Lord's*)	Sept 12–14, 1901

H Jupp, left, *and V M Merchant*, right, *two of only four players to carry their bats through both innings of a match.*

Alan Brown, left, *of Gloucestershire, and Mickey Stewart*, right, *of Surrey, are the only two fieldsmen to take seven catches in an innings.*

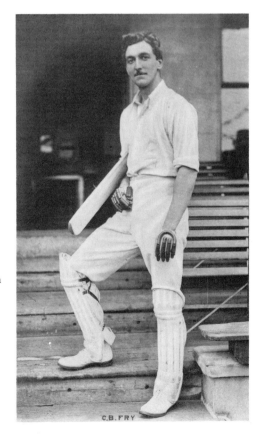

C B Fry, in 1901 the first player to score six centuries in successive innings.

D G Bradman

118	D G Bradman's XI v K E Rigg's XI (*Melbourne*) Dec 9–13, 1938
143	S Australia v N S W (*Adelaide*) Dec 16–20, 1938
225	S Australia v Queensland (*Adelaide*) Dec 24–28, 1938
107	S Australia v Victoria (*Melbourne*) Dec 30–Jan 3, 1938–39
186	S Australia v Queensland (*Brisbane*) Jan 7–11, 1939
135*	S Australia v N S W (*Sydney*) Jan 14–18, 1939

M J Procter

119	Rhodesia v Natal B (*Bulawayo*) Nov 21–23, 1970
129	Rhodesia v Transvaal B (*Salisbury*) Nov 28–30, 1970
107	Rhodesia v OFS (*Bloemfontein*) Dec 28–29, 1970
174	Rhodesia v N E Transvaal (*Pretoria*) Jan 1–4, 1971
106	Rhodesia v Griqualand West (*Kimberley*) Jan 7–8, 1971
254	Rhodesia v W Province (*Salisbury*) Mar 5–7, 1971

The remarkable point of coincidence between the three sets of hundreds is that none of the batsmen scored two hundreds in a single match.
In each innings of the same match   Only two batsmen have scored a century in each innings of a first-class match on seven occasions, namely:

W R Hammond

108	128	Gloucestershire v Surrey (*Oval*) 1927
139	143	Gloucestershire v Surrey (*Cheltenham*) 1928
119*	177	England v Australia (*Adelaide*) 1928–29
122	111*	Gloucestershire v Worcestershire (*Worcester*) 1933
104	136	MCC v South Australia (*Adelaide*) 1936–37
110	123	Gloucestershire v Derbyshire (*Burton-on-Trent*) 1938
121	102	England v Dominions (*Lord's*) 1945

Zaheer Abbas

216*	156*	Gloucestershire v Surrey (*Oval*) 1976
230*	104*	Gloucestershire v Kent (*Canterbury*) 1976
205*	108*	Gloucestershire v Sussex (*Cheltenham*) 1977
100*	100*	PIA v Railways (*Lahore*) 1980–81
215*	150*	Gloucestershire v Somerset (*Bath*) 1981
135*	128	Gloucestershire v Nrthts (*Northampton*) 1981
162*	107	Gloucestershire v Lancashire (*Gloucester*) 1982

Most centuries in a season   D C S Compton hit a record 18 centuries during the 1947 season; 13 of these were for Middlesex, 4 for England and one for the South. The most centuries in an Australian first-class season is 8 in 1947–48 by D G Bradman, and the same number is the record in South Africa by three batsmen: D C S Compton (1948–49), R N Harvey and A R Morris, both in 1949–50.

In the 1978–79 season on the Indian sub-continent S M Gavaskar hit 10 centuries.

Chile

Cricket was first played in Chile in 1818, but was not firmly established until the 1870s, the chief centres being Valparaiso and Santiago. The first international match by Chile took place in December 1920 against Argentina.

The following are the records by Chile in international matches:
Highest team total   387–8d v Argentina (*Santiago*) 1955–56
Highest individual innings   164 B Neary v Argentina (*Santiago*) 1955–56
Best bowling in innings   7–49 D S Marshall v Argentina (*Santiago*) 1955–56

There have been 20 matches between Chile and Argentina of which 12 have been won by Argentina and 5 by Chile. The only other South American country to play Chile is Peru – a single match in 1957–58.

Chile did not take part in the ICC Trophy of 1979 or 1982.

The highest individual score made in the County Championship is 424 by Archie MacLaren of Lancashire, scored against Somerset in 1895.

Mike Procter, in 1970–71, was the last batsman to score a century in six successive innings.

The only two players to make a century in each innings of a match seven times both played for Gloucestershire, Walter Hammond and Zaheer Abbas (above).

Among the records of Denis Compton is that for the most centuries in a season – 18 in 1947, when he also scored a record aggregate of runs.

County Championship

The records

TEAM

Highest team total   887 Yorkshire *v* Warwickshire (*Edgbaston*) 1896

Lowest team total   12 Northants *v* Gloucestershire (*Gloucester*) 1907

Largest victory   Inns and 485 runs by Surrey *v* Sussex (*Oval*) 1888

Shortest completed match   185 mins Middx *v* Somerset (*Lord's*) 1899

Fewest runs in a full day   134–3 by Glamorgan *v* Hants (*Portsmouth*) 1964

Most runs in a day by one side   645–4 by Surrey *v* Hants (*Oval*) 1909

Most extras in innings   73 by Northants *v* Kent (*Northampton*) 1955

BATTING

Highest individual innings   424 A C MacLaren, Lancs *v* Somerset (*Taunton*) 1895

Most double centuries   22 W R Hammond for Gloucestershire 1925–46

Most centuries   132 C P Mead for Hampshire 1906–36

Highest innings on debut   195* J Ricketts, Lancs *v* Surrey (*Oval*) 1867

Fastest fifty   8 mins C C Inman, Leics *v* Notts (*Trent Bridge*) 1965

Fastest century   35 mins P G H Fender, Surrey *v* Nrthts (*Northampton*) 1920

Fastest double century   120 mins G L Jessop, Gloucs *v* Sussex (*Hove*) 1903

Most sixes in innings   13 C G Greenidge, Hants *v* Sussex (*Southampton*) 1975

Most fours in innings   68 P A Perrin, Essex *v* Derbys (*Chesterfield*) 1904

Slowest century   420 mins W H Denton, Northants *v* Derbys (*Derby*) 1914

Longest innings   615 mins A Shrewsbury, Notts *v* Middx (*Trent Bridge*) 1887

Most runs in season   2843 C P Mead, Hampshire   1928

Most runs in career   46268 C P Mead, Hampshire   1906–36

WICKET PARTNERSHIPS

1st	555	P Holmes, H Sutcliffe. Yorks *v* Essex (*Leyton*) 1932
2nd	465*	J A Jameson, R B Kanhai. Warwicks *v* Gloucs (*Edgbaston*) 1974
3rd	424*	W J Edrich, D C S Compton. Middx *v* Somerset (*Lord's*) 1948
4th	470	A I Kallicharran, G W Humpage. Warwicks *v* Lancs (*Southport*) 1982
5th	393	E G Arnold, W B Burns. Worcs *v* Warwicks (*Edgbaston*) 1909
6th	411	R M Poore, E G Wynyard. Hants *v* Somerset (*Taunton*) 1899
7th	344	K S Ranjitsinhji, W Newham. Sussex *v* Essex (*Leyton*) 1902
8th	292	R Peel, Lord Hawke. Yorks *v* Warwicks (*Edgbaston*) 1896
9th	283	A Warren, J Chapman. Derbys *v* Warwicks (*Blackwell*) 1910
10th	235	F E Woolley, A Fielder. Kent *v* Worcs (*Stourbridge*) 1909

Gilbert Jessop shares the record for the fastest double-century in the County Championship, scored in only 120 minutes in 1903.

The man who has scored most runs in the County Championship is C P Mead of Hampshire, who made 46,268 in his career.

BOWLING

Best innings analysis 19.4-16-10-10 H Verity, Yorks v Notts (*Headingley*) 1932

Best match analysis 31.1-14-48-17 C Blythe, Kent v Northants (*Northampton*) 1907

Most runs conceded in innings 231-6 C W L Parker, Gloucs v Somerset (*Bristol*) 1923

Most balls bowled in innings 501 A Shaw, Sussex v Notts (*Trent Bridge*) 1895

Most balls bowled in match 630 J Briggs, Lancs v Sussex (*Old Trafford*) 1897

Most hat-tricks 6 D V P Wright, Kent 1937–49

Most maiden overs in succession

4-ball 18 W Flowers, Nottd v Sussex (*Hove*) 1885

5-ball 10 E Robson, Somerset v Sussex (*Hove*) 1897

6-ball 17 H L Hazell, Somerset v Gloucs (*Taunton*) 1949

Best innings bowling on debut 8–70 G A Wilson, Worcs v Yorks (*Worcester*) 1899

Best match bowling on debut 14–171 F G Roberts, Gloucs v Yorks (*Dewsbury*) 1887

Most wickets in season 252 A P Freeman, Kent 1933

Most wickets in career 3151 A P Freeman, Kent 1914–36

General Only two players have appeared in over 700 county championship matches: W Rhodes (*Yorkshire*) in 763 and F E Woolley (*Kent*) in 707. The most seasons in which a player has appeared is 33 by A N Hornby for Lancashire.

History Sussex were publicly acknowledged as the best county in 1827, when the question of which county was champion was resolved in the same manner as in boxing: the reigning champion being challenged by any aspiring contender. With three or four southern counties so much more skilled at cricket than the remainder, this informal challenge

system was fairly satisfactory, but by the mid-1860s there were eight or nine contending counties and the press increasingly began to advocate the idea of some sort of 'league system'.

Arguments as to the best method to be used in a county league went on through the 1870s and 1880s and with increasing confusion – each journalist pushing his own pet ideas. On December 10, 1889 a meeting of the secretaries of the major county cricket clubs decided on a method to be used in compiling the Championship table for 1890 and an official Championship table operated therefore only from the 1890 season.

The early champions The counties who were acclaimed as 'Champions' by the press in the period between 1827 and 1863 are as follows:

1827	Sussex	1847	Kent
1828	Kent	1848	Sussex
1830	Surrey	1849	Kent
1831	Surrey	1850	Surrey
1833	Sussex	1851	Surrey
1837	Kent	1853	Notts
1838	Kent	1854	Surrey
1839	Kent	1855	Sussex
1841	Kent	1856	Surrey
1842	Kent	1857	Surrey
1843	Kent	1858	Surrey
1845	Sussex	1862	Notts

Transitional period From 1864 to 1889, periodicals printed tables of inter-county results and pronounced a county champion for each season, but there was no universally recognised method of positioning the counties in a table. Some cricket annuals simply printed a table of results in alphabetical order and this would seem the fairest way of setting out the county results. In the tables which follow the county designated 'Champion' is denoted by an asterisk.

Tables of Results 1864 to 1889

1864

	P	W	L	D
Cambridgeshire	3	3	0	0
Hampshire	4	0	4	0
Kent	7	0	7	0
Middlesex	4	3	1	0
Nottinghamshire	7	3	4	0
*Surrey	8	6	0	2
Sussex	8	5	2	1
Yorkshire	7	3	3	1

(Surrey also beat England by 9 wickets)

1865

	P	W	L	D
Cambridgeshire	3	1	1	1
Hampshire	3	1	2	0
Kent	7	2	3	2
Lancashire	2	1	1	0
Middlesex	5	3	1	1
*Nottinghamshire	7	6	1	0
Surrey	12	7	3	2
Sussex	7	1	4	2
Yorkshire	8	0	6	2

(Lancashire's first year in the Championship)

1866

	P	W	L	D
Cambridgeshire	5	2	2	1
Hampshire	2	1	1	0
Kent	5	1	1	3
Lancashire	4	0	3	1
*Middlesex	8	6	1	1
Nottinghamshire	6	2	1	3
Surrey	10	4	5	1
Sussex	5	1	1	3
Yorkshire	3	0	2	1

1867

	P	W	L	D
Cambridgeshire	4	1	3	0
Hampshire	3	0	2	1
Kent	8	4	2	2
Lancashire	5	0	3	2
Middlesex	4	0	3	1
Nottinghamshire	4	3	1	0
Surrey	10	2	4	4
Sussex	5	3	2	0
*Yorkshire	7	7	0	0

1868

	P	W	L	D
Cambridgeshire	2	1	1	0
Kent	8	5	3	0
Lancashire	5	1	4	0
Middlesex	8	4	3	0
				(1 tie)
*Nottinghamshire	6	4	2	0
Surrey	12	5	6	0
				(1 tie)
Sussex	6	2	4	0
Yorkshire	7	4	3	0

(Hampshire did not play another major county this season or the following one)
Not a single drawn match – unique event

1869

	P	W	L	D
Cambridgeshire	1	0	1	0
Kent	7	4	2	1
Lancashire	4	2	2	0
Middlesex	2	1	1	0
*Nottinghamshire	6	5	1	0
Surrey	12	3	7	2
Sussex	7	1	5	1
*Yorkshire	5	4	1	0

(Notts and Yorks were joint-champions, having beaten each other once and not being otherwise defeated)

1870

	P	W	L	D
Gloucestershire	2	2	0	0
Hampshire	2	0	2	0
Kent	8	2	6	0
Lancashire	4	3	1	0
Middlesex	2	1	1	0
Nottinghamshire	6	3	2	1
Surrey	14	5	9	0
Sussex	4	2	2	0
*Yorkshire	6	5	0	1

(Cambridgeshire played no inter-county matches; Gloucestershire's first year in the Championship)

1871

	P	W	L	D
Cambridgeshire	1	0	0	1
Derbyshire	2	1	1	0
Gloucestershire	4	2	1	1
Kent	6	2	3	1
Lancashire	6	4	2	0
Middlesex	2	1	0	1
*Nottinghamshire	6	4	1	1
Surrey	13	0	9	4
Sussex	4	4	0	0
Yorkshire	6	2	3	1

(Hampshire played no inter-county matches; Derbyshire's first year in the Championship; owing to internal dissent, Cambridgeshire ceased to play first-class matches after 1871)

1872

	P	W	L	D
Derbyshire	2	0	2	0
Gloucestershire	7	3	1	3
Kent	4	0	4	0
Lancashire	4	4	0	0
Middlesex	3	0	3	0
*Nottinghamshire	7	2	0	5
Surrey	12	7	3	2
Sussex	6	3	2	2
Yorkshire	9	2	6	1

(Notts and Yorks met three times, the extra game taking place at Prince's Ground, London on July 18, 19, 20)

1873

	P	W	L	D
Derbyshire	2	0	2	0
*Gloucestershire	6	4	0	2
Kent	5	3	2	0
Lancashire	7	4	3	0
Middlesex	3	2	1	0
*Nottinghamshire	7	5	1	1
Surrey	14	2	10	2
Sussex	10	2	6	2
Yorkshire	12	7	4	1

(Includes the County Cup match at Lord's between Kent and Sussex, also the third Notts v Yorks match organised privately by R Daft, the Notts captain – Notts lost)

1874

	P	W	L	D
Derbyshire	4	3	0	1
*Gloucestershire	6	4	1	1
Kent	4	1	2	1
Lancashire	6	1	3	2
Middlesex	6	1	4	1
Nottinghamshire	8	5	3	0
Surrey	10	3	6	1
Sussex	8	1	5	2
Yorkshire	12	8	3	1

(Derbyshire's record was not considered as good as Gloucestershire's, since the former only played Lancashire and Kent)

1875

	P	W	L	D
Derbyshire	6	2	3	1
Gloucestershire	8	3	4	1
Hampshire	4	1	3	0
Kent	8	2	6	0
Lancashire	6	4	1	1
Middlesex	6	0	4	2
*Nottinghamshire	10	6	1	3
Surrey	10	3	5	2
Sussex	8	5	2	1
Yorkshire	10	6	3	1

(Hampshire returned after four seasons absence)

1876

	P	W	L	D
Derbyshire	6	2	4	0
*Gloucestershire	8	5	0	3
Hampshire	4	3	1	0
Kent	10	4	6	0
Lancashire	10	5	5	0
Middlesex	6	1	1	3
				(1 tie)
Nottinghamshire	10	4	3	3
Surrey	12	2	8	1
				(1 tie)
Sussex	8	3	4	1
Yorkshire	10	5	2	3

1877

	P	W	L	D
Derbyshire	8	5	2	1
*Gloucestershire	8	7	0	1
Hampshire	4	0	4	0
Kent	12	7	4	1
Lancashire	10	6	4	0
Middlesex	6	0	4	2
Nottinghamshire	12	5	5	2
Surrey	12	6	3	3
Sussex	8	0	7	1
Yorkshire	12	2	5	5

(Gloucs also beat England by 5 wickets)

1878

	P	W	L	D
Derbyshire	10	3	6	1
Gloucestershire	10	4	2	4
Hampshire	4	0	3	1
Kent	12	6	4	2
Lancashire	10	5	3	2
Middlesex	6	3	0	3
Nottinghamshire	14	7	3	4
Surrey	12	3	6	3
Sussex	8	1	7	0
Yorkshire	14	7	5	2

(Middx, Notts and Yorks all had some claim to the Championship, but the general consensus among contemporary journals was that no county could really claim superiority over all others)

1879

	P	W	L	D
Derbyshire	6	2	4	0
Gloucestershire	10	1	3	6
Kent	10	2	7	1
*Lancashire	10	5	1	4
Middlesex	8	2	2	4
*Nottinghamshire	12	5	1	6
Surrey	10	3	4	3
Sussex	4	1	2	1
Yorkshire	14	7	4	3

(Hampshire played no inter-county matches)

1880

	P	W	L	D
Derbyshire	8	2	5	1
Gloucestershire	10	4	1	5
Hampshire	2	0	2	0
Kent	8	5	3	2
Lancashire	12	6	3	3
Middlesex	8	2	4	2
*Nottinghamshire	10	6	1	3
Surrey	14	2	7	5
Sussex	8	2	4	2
Yorkshire	14	5	4	5

1881

	P	W	L	D
Derbyshire	8	2	5	1
Gloucestershire	10	4	2	4
Hampshire	2	0	2	0
Kent	10	3	7	0
*Lancashire	13	10	0	3
Middlesex	9	3	3	3
Nottinghamshire	12	4	4	4
Surrey	14	4	9	1
Sussex	12	3	8	1
Yorkshire	16	10	3	3

(*The return match at Lord's between Middx and Lancs was cancelled because Harrow Wanderers had booked the ground on the same days*)

1882

	P	W	L	D
Derbyshire	6	1	5	0
Gloucestershire	11	3	6	2
Hampshire	4	2	2	0
Kent	9	2	6	1
*Lancashire	16	12	1	3
Middlesex	11	5	5	1
*Nottinghamshire	12	8	1	3
Somersetshire	5	1	4	0
Surrey	14	4	7	3
Sussex	12	3	8	1
Yorkshire	16	9	5	2

(*Somerset joined the first-class counties*)

1883

	P	W	L	D
Derbyshire	8	2	5	1
Gloucestershire	12	3	6	3
Hampshire	6	2	3	1
Kent	10	2	6	2
Lancashire	12	6	5	1
Middlesex	10	4	2	4
*Nottinghamshire	12	4	1	7
Somersetshire	6	1	5	0
Surrey	20	10	5	5
Sussex	12	4	7	1
Yorkshire	16	9	2	5

(*Notts refused to play Lancs for two seasons after 1883, due to a dispute over the qualification of J Crossland, who was born in Notts*)

1884

	P	W	L	D
Derbyshire	10	0	10	0
Gloucestershire	12	1	8	3
Hampshire	8	2	6	0
Kent	16	7	7	2
Lancashire	12	7	4	1
Middlesex	10	4	3	3
*Nottinghamshire	10	9	0	1
Somersetshire	6	1	5	0
Surrey	18	9	4	5
Sussex	14	8	5	1
Yorkshire	16	8	4	4

(*The match between Lancs and Gloucs at Old Trafford was ended immediately the telegram arrived announcing the death of Mrs Grace, mother of W G and E M Grace; in the table above it is shown as a draw*)

1885

	P	W	L	D
Derbyshire	10	3	5	2
Gloucestershire	14	6	7	1
Hampshire	10	2	8	0
Kent	11	6	3	2
Lancashire	11	6	3	2
Middlesex	10	2	7	1
*Nottinghamshire	12	6	1	5
Somersetshire	6	1	5	0
Surrey	20	12	4	4
Sussex	14	3	9	2
Yorkshire	16	7	2	7

(*The return match between Kent and Lancs, fixed for Tonbridge, was not played due to the objection of the Kent captain, Lord Harris, to the 'unfair' bowling of two Lancashire players*)

1886

	P	W	L	D
Derbyshire	9	0	8	1
Gloucestershire	13	3	6	4
Kent	14	5	6	3
Lancashire	14	5	5	4
Middlesex	10	3	4	3
*Nottinghamshire	14	7	0	7
Surrey	16	12	3	1
Sussex	12	4	6	2
Yorkshire	16	4	5	7

(*Hampshire, although playing Sussex and Surrey, were excluded from the list of first-class counties by all contemporary annuals; Somerset played none of the major counties*)

1887

	P	W	L	D
Derbyshire	6	0	6	0
Gloucestershire	14	1	9	4
Kent	14	1	8	5
Lancashire	14	10	3	1
Middlesex	10	4	2	4
Nottinghamshire	14	8	3	3
*Surrey	16	12	2	2
Sussex	12	2	8	2
Yorkshire	16	6	3	7

1888

	P	W	L	D
Gloucestershire	14	5	5	4
Kent	14	7	5	2
Lancashire	14	4	5	5
Middlesex	12	4	7	1
Nottinghamshire	14	3	6	5
*Surrey	14	12	1	1
Sussex	12	1	9	2
Yorkshire	14	6	4	4
(Derbyshire	7	1	6	0)

(*Derbyshire were 'demoted' from first-class status midway through the season - it would appear that the move was made by the Cricket Reporting Agency, who were anxious to draw a definitive line between the 'first-class' and 'second-class' counties*)

1889

	P	W	L	D
Gloucestershire	14	3	7	4
Kent	13	7	5	1
*Lancashire	14	10	3	1
Middlesex	11	3	5	3
*Nottinghamshire	14	9	2	3
*Surrey	14	10	3	1
Sussex	12	1	10	1
Yorkshire	14	2	10	2

(*The match between Middx and Kent at Lord's was completely washed out*)

During the previous two seasons, the Cricket Reporting Agency had been pushing the idea of a points system for deciding the Champion County – the system being one point for a win, ½ for a draw. In 1889 this system produced a triple tie, Notts, Lancs and Surrey all getting 10½ points. This ridiculous situation forced the county secretaries to establish an 'official' method for 1890

Championship Tables 1890 to date

The method agreed upon for the first official Championship was to deduct wins from losses and to ignore drawn matches.

1890

		P	W	L	D	Pts
1	Surrey	14	9	3	2	6
2	Lancashire	14	7	3	4	4
3	Kent	14	6	3	5	3
	Yorkshire	14	6	3	5	3
5	Nottinghamshire	14	5	5	4	0
6	Gloucestershire	14	5	6	3	−1
7	Middlesex	12	3	8	1	−10
8	Sussex	12	1	11	0	−10

1891

		P	W	L	D	Pts
1	Surrey	16	12	2	2	10
2	Lancashire	15	8	4	3	4
3	Middlesex	16	8	5	3	3
4	Nottinghamshire	14	5	4	5	1
5	Kent	15	4	5	6	−1
	Somersetshire	12	5	6	1	−1
7	Sussex	14	4	7	3	−3
8	Yorkshire	16	5	10	1	−5
9	Gloucestershire	16	2	10	4	−8

(*The Lancs v Kent match at Liverpool was abandoned without a ball being bowled and is not included above*)

Somersetshire arranged home and away fixtures with six of the 1890 first-class counties, thereby forcing the County back into the Championship table

1892

		P	W	L	D	Pts
1	Surrey	16	13	2	1	11
2	Nottinghamshire	16	10	2	4	8
3	Somersetshire	16	8	5	3	3
4	Lancashire	16	7	5	4	2
5	Middlesex	16	7	6	3	1
6	Yorkshire	16	5	5	6	0
7	Gloucestershire	16	1	8	7	−7
	Kent	16	2	9	5	−7
9	Sussex	16	1	12	3	−11

1893

		P	W	L	D	Pts
1	Yorkshire	16	12	3	1	9
2	Lancashire	16	9	5	2	4
3	Middlesex	16	9	6	1	3
4	Kent	16	6	4	6	2
5	Surrey	16	7	8	1	−1
6	Nottinghamshire	16	5	7	4	−2
7	Sussex	16	4	7	5	−3
8	Somersetshire	16	4	8	4	−4
9	Gloucestershire	16	3	11	2	−8

1894

		P	W	L	D	Tie	Pts
1	Surrey	16	13	2	0	1	11
2	Yorkshire	15	12	2	1	0	10
3	Middlesex	16	8	5	3	0	3
4	Kent	15	6	6	3	0	0
	Lancashire	16	7	7	1	1	0
6	Somersetshire	16	6	7	3	0	−1
7	Nottinghamshire	16	4	8	4	0	−4
8	Sussex	16	3	11	2	0	−8
9	Gloucestershire	16	2	13	1	0	−11

(*The Yorks v Kent match at Bradford was abandoned without a ball being bowled and is not included above*)

1895

During 1894 the MCC prepared a scheme for the future regulation of the County Championship. This scheme was approved by the various counties and came into operation for the 1895 season. In addition to the nine counties who competed in 1894, Derbyshire, Essex, Hampshire, Leicestershire and Warwickshire were added to the competition. Each county had to play a minimum of eight other counties, home and away. The points system remained the same, but as counties played differing numbers of matches, 'the county which, during the season, shall have, in finished matches, obtained the greatest proportionate number of points, shall be reckoned Champion County.'

		P	W	L	D	Pts	Finished Games
1	Surrey	26	17	4	5	13	21
2	Lancashire	21	14	4	3	10	18
3	Yorkshire	26	14	7	5	7	21
4	Gloucestershire	18	8	6	4	2	14
5	Derbyshire	16	5	4	7	1	9
6	Middlesex	18	6	6	6	0	12
	Warwickshire	18	6	6	6	0	12
8	Somersetshire	17	6	8	3	−2	14
9	Essex	16	5	7	4	−2	12
10	Hampshire	16	6	9	1	−3	15
11	Sussex	18	5	9	4	−4	14
12	Leicestershire	16	3	10	3	−7	13
	Nottinghamshire	18	3	10	5	−7	13
14	Kent	18	3	11	4	−8	14

(*The Lancs v Somerset match at Old Trafford was abandoned without a ball being bowled and is not included above*)

1896

		P	W	L	D	Pts	Finished Games	%
1	Yorkshire	26	16	3	7	13	19	68
2	Lancashire	22	11	4	7	7	15	46
3	Middlesex	16	8	3	5	5	11	45
4	Surrey	26	17	7	2	10	24	41
5	Essex	12	5	4	3	1	9	11
6	Nottinghamshire	16	5	5	6	0	10	—
7	Derbyshire	16	4	6	6	−2	10	−20
8	Hampshire	16	5	8	3	−3	13	−23
9	Kent	18	5	9	4	−4	14	−28
10	Gloucestershire	18	5	10	3	−5	15	−33
11	Somersetshire	16	3	7	6	−4	10	−40
12	Warwickshire	18	3	8	7	−5	11	−45
13	Leicestershire	14	2	8	4	−6	10	−60
14	Sussex	18	2	9	7	−7	11	−63

(*Owing to the visit of the Australian touring team, two counties were unable to arrange the minimum number of matches to qualify for the Championship. In these circumstances the MCC reduced the minimum from 16 to 12*)

For the first time a percentage column was added to the table

1897

		P	W	L	D	Pts	Finished Games	%
1	Lancashire	26	16	3	7	13	19	68.42
2	Surrey	26	17	4	5	13	21	61.90
3	Essex	16	7	2	7	5	9	55.55
4	Yorkshire	26	13	5	8	8	18	44.44
5	Gloucestershire	18	7	5	6	2	12	16.66
6	Sussex	20	5	6	9	−1	11	−9.09
7	Earwickshire	18	3	4	11	−1	7	−14.28
	Middlesex	16	3	4	9	−1	7	−14.28
9	Hampshire	18	4	7	7	−3	11	−27.27
10	Nottinghamshire	16	2	5	9	−3	7	−42.85
11	Somersetshire	16	3	9	4	−6	12	−50.00
12	Kent	18	2	10	6	−8	12	−66.66
13	Leicestershire	14	1	10	3	−9	11	−81.81
14	Derbyshire	16	0	9	7	−9	9	−100.00

(*Leicestershire were unable to arrange the minimum 16 matches and after consideration it was agreed to reduce the minimum required to qualify to 14*)

1898

		P	W	L	D	Pts	%
1	Yorkshire	26	16	3	7	13	68.42
2	Middlesex	18	10	3	5	7	53.84
3	Gloucestershire	20	9	3	8	6	50.00
4	Surrey	24	11	4	9	7	46.66
5	Essex	20	10	6	4	4	25.00
6	Lancashire	26	9	6	11	3	20.00
7	Kent	20	5	6	9	−1	−9.09
8	Nottinghamshire	16	1	2	13	−1	−33.33
9	Warwickshire	17	2	6	9	−4	−50.00
	Derbyshire	15	2	6	7	−4	−50.00
	Sussex	20	3	9	8	−6	−50.00
12	Hampshire	18	2	8	8	−6	−60.00
13	Leicestershire	16	1	10	5	−9	−81.81
	Somersetshire	16	1	10	5	−9	−81.81

(*The Surrey v Derbyshire and Warwickshire v Surrey matches were abandoned without a ball being bowled and are not included above*)

1899

		P	W	L	D	Pts	%
1	Surrey	26	10	2	14	8	66.66
2	Middlesex	18	11	3	4	8	57.14
3	Yorkshire	28	14	4	10	10	55.55
4	Lancashire	25	12	6	7	6	33.33
5	Sussex	22	7	5	10	2	16.66
6	Essex	20	6	6	8	0	0.00
7	Warwickshire	20	4	5	11	−1	−11.11
8	Kent	19	6	8	5	2	−14.28
9	Gloucestershire	20	5	8	7	−3	−23.76
10	Hampshire	20	4	8	8	−4	−33.33
	Nottinghamshire	16	2	4	10	−2	−33.33
12	Worcestershire	12	2	5	5	−3	−42.85
13	Leicestershire	18	2	8	8	−6	−60.00
	Somersetshire	16	2	8	6	−6	−60.00
15	Derbyshire	18	2	9	7	−7	−63.63

(*The Lancs v Kent match at Old Trafford was abandoned without a ball being bowled and is not included above*)

Worcestershire were admitted to the Championship and the number of matches required to qualify was reduced from 14 to 12

1900

		P	W	L	D	Pts	%
1	Yorkshire	28	16	0	12	16	100.00
2	Lancashire	28	15	2	11	13	76.47
3	Kent	22	8	4	10	4	33.33
	Sussex	24	4	2	18	2	33.33
5	Nottinghamshire	18	7	4	7	3	27.27
6	Warwickshire	18	3	2	13	1	20.00
7	Middlesex	22	9	7	6	2	12.50
	Gloucestershire	22	9	7	6	2	12.50
	Surrey	28	9	7	12	2	12.50
10	Essex	22	4	6	12	−2	−20.00
11	Somerset	16	4	11	1	−7	−46.66
12	Worcestershire	22	3	10	9	−7	−53.84
13	Derbyshire	18	2	7	9	−5	−55.55
14	Leicestershire	22	3	11	8	−8	−57.14
15	Hampshire	22	0	16	6	−16	−100.00

1901

		P	W	L	D	Pts	%
1	Yorkshire	27	20	1	6	19	90.47
2	Middlesex	18	6	2	10	4	50.00
3	Lancashire	28	11	5	12	6	37.50
4	Sussex	24	8	4	12	4	33.33
5	Warwickshire	16	7	4	5	3	27.27
6	Surrey	27	7	6	14	1	7.69
7	Kent	21	7	7	7	0	0.00
	Hampshire	18	6	6	6	0	0.00
9	Nottinghamshire	19	5	6	8	−1	−9.09
10	Essex	21	4	5	12	−1	−11.11
11	Worcestershire	21	7	10	4	−3	−17.64
12	Leicestershire	19	4	10	5	−6	−42.85
	Somerset	17	4	10	3	−6	−42.85

1901 continued	P	W	L	D	Pts	%
14 Gloucestershire	24	3	10	11	−7	−53.84
15 Derbyshire	20	0	13	7	−13	−100.00

(*The Surrey v Yorks, Essex v Leics, Notts v Kent and Worcs v Somerset matches were abandoned without a ball being bowled and are not included above. Surrey in fact re-arranged the first mentioned match v Yorks and it was played on Sept 16, 17 and 18, but was excluded from the Championship*)

1902	P	W	L	D	Pts	%
1 Yorkshire	25	13	1	11	12	85.71
2 Sussex	24	7	3	14	4	40.00
3 Nottinghamshire	20	6	3	11	3	33.33
4 Surrey	28	8	5	15	3	23.07
5 Lancashire	23	7	5	11	2	16.16
6 Warwickshire	18	6	5	7	1	9.09
7 Kent	22	8	8	6	0	0.00
Somerset	18	7	7	4	0	0.00
9 Worcestershire	22	5	6	11	−1	−9.09
10 Derbyshire	16	4	5	7	−1	−11.11
11 Leicestershire	19	2	4	13	−2	−33.33
12 Middlesex	17	3	7	7	−4	−40.00
13 Essex	20	2	5	13	−3	−42.85
14 Gloucestershire	20	3	9	8	−6	−50.00
15 Hampshire	16	2	10	4	−8	−66.66

(*The matches Leics v Yorks and Middx v Lancs were abandoned without a ball being bowled and are not included above*)

1903	P	W	L	D	Pts	%
1 Middlesex	16	8	1	7	7	77.77
2 Sussex	23	7	2	14	5	55.55
3 Yorkshire	26	13	5	8	8	44.44
4 Lancashire	26	10	5	11	5	33.33
5 Nottinghamshire	20	6	4	10	2	20.00
6 Worcestershire	20	8	6	6	2	14.28
7 Warwickshire	18	5	4	9	1	11.11
8 Kent	20	7	6	7	1	7.69
Essex	20	7	6	7	1	7.69
10 Somerset	17	6	6	5	0	0.00
11 Surrey	27	7	11	9	−4	−22.22
12 Derbyshire	16	4	7	5	−3	−27.27
13 Gloucestershire	20	3	10	7	−7	−53.84
14 Leicestershire	20	1	10	9	−9	−81.81
Hampshire	15	1	10	4	−9	−81.81

(*The matches Surrey v Hants, Middx v Essex, Somerset v Hants, Kent v Sussex, Essex v Hants, Middx v Kent were all abandoned without a ball being bowled and are not included above*)

1904	P	W	L	D	Pts	%
1 Lancashire	26	16	0	10	16	100.00
2 Yorkshire	27	9	2	16	7	63.63
3 Kent	21	10	4	7	6	42.85
4 Middlesex	18	9	4	5	5	38.46
5 Nottinghamshire	20	7	4	9	3	27.27
6 Sussex	24	5	4	15	1	11.11
7 Leicestershire	20	6	6	8	0	0.00
Warwickshire	16	5	5	6	0	0.00
9 Gloucestershire	18	5	6	7	−1	−9.09
10 Derbyshire	18	5	8	5	−3	−23.07
11 Surrey	28	6	12	10	−1	−33.33
12 Somerset	18	5	11	2	−6	−37.50
13 Worcestershire	18	3	8	7	−5	−45.45
14 Essex	20	3	10	7	−7	−53.84
15 Hampshire	18	2	12	4	1−10	−71.42

(*The match between Yorks and Kent at Harrogate on July 7 and 8 was abandoned on the second day when it was discovered that the pitch had been tampered with. It is not included above*)

1905	P	W	L	Tie	D	Pts	%
1 Yorkshire	28	18	3	0	7	15	71.42
2 Lancashire	25	12	3	0	10	9	60.00
3 Sussex	28	13	4	0	11	9	52.94

1905 continued	P	W	L	Tie	D	Pts	%
4 Surrey	27	14	6	1	6	8	40.00
5 Leicestershire	22	8	5	0	9	3	23.07
6 Kent	22	10	7	1	4	3	17.64
7 Warwickshire	22	5	4	0	13	1	11.11
8 Worcestershire	18	5	5	0	8	0	0.00
Gloucestershire	18	8	8	0	2	0	0.00
10 Nottinghamshire	20	6	7	0	7	−1	−7.69
11 Middlesex	18	4	7	0	7	−3	−27.27
12 Essex	20	3	10	0	7	−7	−53.84
13 Northamptonshire	12	2	8	0	2	−6	−60.00
14 Derbyshire	20	3	14	0	3	−11	−64.70
15 Somerset	18	1	10	0	7	−9	−81.81
16 Hampshire	20	1	12	0	7	−11	−84.61

(*The match Surrey v Lancs was abandoned without a ball being bowled and is not included above*)

Northamptonshire were admitted to the Championship

1906	P	W	L	D	Pts	%
1 Kent	22	16	2	4	14	77.77
2 Yorkshire	28	17	3	8	14	70.00
3 Surrey	28	18	4	6	14	63.63
4 Lancashire	26	15	6	5	9	42.85
5 Nottinghamshire	20	9	4	7	5	38.46
6 Warwickshire	20	7	4	9	3	27.27
7 Essex	22	9	6	7	3	23.00
8 Hampshire	20	7	9	4	−2	−12.50
9 Gloucestershire	20	6	10	4	−4	−20.00
10 Sussex	24	6	12	6	−6	−33.33
11 Somerset	18	4	10	4	−6	−42.85
Middlesex	18	4	10	4	−6	−42.85
Northamptonshire	16	4	10	2	−6	−42.85
14 Worcestershire	20	2	8	10	−6	−60.00
15 Leicestershire	22	3	14	5	−11	−64.70
16 Derbyshire	20	2	17	1	−15	−78.94

1907	P	W	L	D	Pts	%
1 Nottinghamshire	19	15	0	4	15	100.00
2 Worcestershire	18	8	2	8	6	60.00
Yorkshire	26	12	3	11	9	60.00
4 Surrey	28	12	4	12	8	50.00
5 Middlesex	20	8	4	8	4	33.33
6 Lancashire	26	11	7	8	4	22.22
7 Essex	22	10	7	5	3	17.64
8 Kent	26	12	9	5	3	14.28
9 Warwickshire	19	6	5	8	1	9.09
10 Gloucestershire	22	8	12	2	−4	−20.00
11 Leicestershire	20	6	10	4	−4	−25.00
12 Hampshire	24	6	11	7	−5	−29.41
13 Sussex	26	7	13	6	−6	−30.00
14 Somerset	18	3	12	3	−9	−60.00
15 Northamptonshire	20	2	12	6	−10	−71.42
16 Derbyshire	20	2	17	1	−15	−78.94

(*The matches Yorks v Derbys, Derbys v Warwicks, Yorks v Notts were abandoned without a ball being bowled and are not included above. The match between Middx and Lancs at Lord's on July 22 is included above as 'drawn'; the Lancs captain refused to continue after spectators had damaged the pitch*)

1908	P	W	L	D	Pts	%
1 Yorkshire	28	16	0	12	16	100.00
2 Kent	25	17	3	5	14	70.00
3 Surrey	29	13	4	12	9	52.94
4 Middlesex	19	6	3	10	3	33.33
5 Sussex	28	6	4	18	2	20.00
6 Worcestershire	18	6	5	7	1	9.09
7 Lancashire	25	10	9	6	1	5.26
8 Nottinghamshire	20	6	7	7	−1	−7.69
9 Hampshire	22	7	9	6	−2	−12.50
10 Gloucestershire	24	8	11	5	−3	−15.78
11 Essex	22	5	7	10	−2	−16.66
12 Warwickshire	21	5	9	7	−4	−28.57

1908 continued	P	W	L	D	Pts	%
13 Leicestershire	21	4	8	9	−4	−33.33
14 Derbyshire	22	5	13	4	−8	−44.44
15 Northamptonshire	22	3	14	5	−11	−64.70
16 Somerset	20	2	13	5	−11	−73.33

(The matches Surrey v Lancs, Kent v Middx and Warwicks v Leics were abandoned without a ball being bowled and are not included above)

1909	P	W	L	D	Pts	%
1 Kent	26	16	2	8	14	77.77
2 Lancashire	24	14	4	6	10	55.55
3 Yorkshire	26	12	4	10	8	50.00
4 Sussex	26	7	3	16	4	40.00
5 Surrey	30	16	7	7	9	39.13
6 Middlesex	21	6	5	10	1	9.09
7 Northamptonshire	18	9	8	1	1	5.88
8 Hampshire	22	7	7	8	0	0.00
Worcestershire	20	8	8	4	0	0.00
10 Nottinghamshire	19	6	8	5	−2	−14.28
11 Somerset	16	4	7	5	−3	−27.27
12 Warwickshire	20	3	8	9	−5	−45.45
13 Leicestershire	21	3	10	8	−7	−53.84
14 Essex	18	2	7	9	−5	−55.55
15 Derbyshire	21	2	15	4	−13	−76.47
16 Gloucestershire	22	1	13	8	−12	−85.71

(The matches Essex v Leics, Essex v Middx and Derbys v Notts were abandoned without a ball being bowled and are not included above)

1910	P	W	L	D	%
1 Kent	25	19	3	3	76.00
2 Surrey	28	16	7	5	57.14
3 Middlesex	22	11	5	6	50.00
4 Lancashire	29	14	5	10	48.27
5 Nottinghamshire	20	9	4	7	45.00
6 Hampshire	24	10	10	4	41.66
7 Sussex	25	10	9	6	40.00
8 Yorkshire	27	10	7	10	37.03
9 Northamptonshire	19	7	8	4	36.84
10 Leicestershire	17	6	11	0	35.29
11 Essex	17	5	8	4	29.41
12 Gloucestershire	20	5	11	4	25.00
13 Worcestershire	22	5	8	9	22.72
14 Warwickshire	19	4	8	7	21.05
15 Derbyshire	20	2	14	4	10.00
16 Somerset	18	0	15	3	0.00

(The match between Surrey and Derbyshire was abandoned owing to the death of King Edward and, together with the games Surrey v Essex, Lancs v Kent, Leics v Yorks, Warw v Northants and Sussex v Derbys, which were limited to two days on account of the funeral of His Majesty, was not reckoned in the above)

The method of compiling the table was altered in 1910 on an experimental basis for one year – the order being determined by a percentage of matches played to matches won

1911				1st inns		Points		
	P	W	L	W	L	Poss	Obtd	%
1 Warwickshire	20	13	4	3	0	100	74	74.00
2 Kent	26	17	4	3	2	130	96	73.84
3 Middlesex	22	14	5	3	0	110	79	71.81
4 Lancashire	30	15	7	5	3	150	93	62.00
5 Surrey	30	15	7	4	4	150	91	60.66
6 Essex	18	8	5	4	1	90	53	58.88
7 Yorkshire	27	14	8	1	4	135	77	57.03
8 Nottinghamshire	20	9	5	3	3	100	57	57.00
9 Worcestershire	24	12	11	0	1	120	61	50.83
10 Northamptonshire	17	8	9	0	0	85	40	47.05
11 Hampshire	24	7	10	4	3	120	50	41.66
12 Gloucestershire	20	5	12	0	3	100	28	28.00
13 Sussex	24	4	16	2	2	120	28	23.33
14 Derbyshire	18	2	13	0	3	90	13	14.44
15 Leicestershire	22	1	16	2	1	110	14	12.72
16 Somerset	16	1	13	0	2	80	7	8.75

Another new method was introduced: A win counted 5 pts and in drawn games the side leading on 1st inns scored 3 pts and the other side 1 pt. The match Yorks v Northants is not included above, as no decision was reached on 1st innings

1912				Drawn			Points		
	P	W	L	W	L	NR	Poss	Obtd	%
1 Yorkshire	28	13	1	7	4	3	125	90	72.00
2 Northamptonshire	18	10	1	2	4	1	85	60	70.58
3 Kent	26	14	5	3	3	1	125	82	65.60
4 Lancashire	22	8	2	4	3	5	85	55	64.70
5 Middlesex	20	7	4	5	2	2	90	52	57.77
6 Hampshire	24	7	3	4	4	6	90	51	56.66
7 Surrey	26	7	5	6	5	3	115	58	50.43
8 Nottinghamshire	18	5	5	5	2	1	85	42	49.41
9 Warwickshire	22	6	5	3	4	4	90	43	47.77
10 Sussex	28	6	10	6	4	2	130	52	40.00
11 Gloucestershire	18	3	8	1	1	5	65	19	29.23
12 Derbyshire	18	2	7	2	3	4	70	19	27.14
13 Leicestershire	22	3	13	2	2	2	100	23	23.00
14 Somerset	16	2	8	1	3	2	70	16	22.85
15 Essex	18	1	8	2	3	4	70	14	20.00
16 Worcestershire	20	1	10	0	6	3	85	11	12.94

A No Result (NR) column is introduced for the first time which includes all matches in which no decision was reached on first innings; these games are not used when calculating maximum possible points. Five matches were abandoned without a ball being bowled and are included in the No Result column

1913				Drawn			Points		
	P	W	L	W	L	NR	Poss	Obtd	%
1 Kent	28	20	3	3	1	1	135	110	81.48
2 Yorkshire	28	16	4	4	3	1	135	95	70.37
3 Surrey	26	13	5	4	4	0	130	81	62.30
4 Northamptonshire	22	12	4	1	5	0	110	68	61.81
5 Nottinghamshire	20	8	5	3	4	0	100	53	53.00
6 Middlesex	20	7	6	4	3	0	100	50	50.00
7 Sussex	28	10	10	4	3	1	135	65	48.14
8 Lancashire	26	7	11	7	0	1	125	56	44.80
9 Gloucestershire	22	8	11	1	2	0	110	45	40.90
10 Hampshire	26	7	11	4	4	0	130	51	39.23
11 Warwickshire	24	7	11	3	3	0	120	47	39.16
12 Worcestershire	20	6	9	1	3	1	95	36	37.89
13 Derbyshire	18	4	10	2	2	0	90	28	31.11
14 Leicestershire	22	4	13	1	4	0	110	27	24.54
15 Essex	18	2	9	2	4	1	85	20	23.52
16 Somerset	16	2	11	1	2	0	80	17	21.25

1914				Drawn			Points		
	P	W	L	W	L	NR	Poss	Obtd	%
1 Surrey	26	15	2	5	3	1	125	93	74.40
2 Middlesex	20	11	2	4	3	0	100	70	70.00
3 Kent	28	16	7	1	4	0	140	87	62.14
4 Yorkshire	28	14	4	3	7	0	140	86	61.42
5 Hampshire	28	13	4	3	8	0	140	82	58.57
6 Sussex	27	10	6	4	6	1	130	68	52.30
7 Warwickshire	24	9	7	4	4	0	120	61	50.83
8 Essex	24	9	9	4	2	0	120	59	49.16
9 Northamptonshire	21	7	6	4	4	0	105	51	48.57
10 Nottinghamshire	20	5	5	6	3	1	95	46	48.42
11 Lancashire	26	6	9	5	6	0	130	51	39.23
12 Derbyshire	20	5	12	3	0	0	100	34	34.00
13 Leicestershire	23	4	11	5	3	0	115	38	33.04
14 Worcestershire	22	2	13	3	3	1	105	22	20.95
15 Somerset	19	3	16	0	0	0	95	15	15.78
16 Gloucestershire	22	1	17	3	1	0	110	15	13.63

Owing to the declaration of war, the matches Somerset v Northants, Sussex v Surrey and Surrey v Leics were not played and are not included above. In view of the fact that two of these games involved Surrey, the leading county, it was suggested that the Championship title should not be awarded, but Middlesex, as runners-up, did not agree with this view and Surrey were acclaimed champions

1919

	P	W	L	D	%
1 Yorkshire	26	12	3	11	46.15
2 Kent	14	6	1	7	42.85
3 Nottinghamshire	14	5	1	8	35.71
4 Surrey	20	7	3	10	35.00
5 Somerset	12	4	3	5	33.33
Lancashire	24	8	4	12	33.33
7 Hampshire	16	5	4	7	31.25
8 Gloucestershire	16	4	7	5	25.00
9 Leicestershire	14	3	4	7	21.42
Derbyshire	14	3	9	2	21.42
11 Sussex	20	4	11	5	20.00
12 Northamptonshire	12	2	4	6	16.66
13 Middlesex	14	2	3	9	14.28
14 Essex	18	2	4	12	11.76
15 Warwickshire	14	1	7	6	7.14

The method used in reckoning the positions was a percentage of wins to matches played. The match Somerset v Sussex at Taunton ended in a tie, but as there were no provisions in the rules to deal with a tie, the match was included under 'draws' and therefore ignored

Worcestershire did not compete in the Competition, but returned in 1920

1920

	P	W	L	Drawn			Points		
				W	L	NR	Poss	Obtd	%
1 Middlesex	20	15	2	1	2	0	100	77	77.00
2 Lancashire	28	19	5	1	1	2	130	97	74.61
3 Surrey	24	15	6	2	0	1	115	79	68.69
4 Yorkshire	28	15	6	3	0	4	120	81	67.50
5 Kent	26	16	6	1	2	1	125	82	65.50
6 Sussex	30	18	8	0	2	2	140	90	64.28
7 Nottinghamshire	20	10	6	2	0	2	90	54	60.00
8 Gloucestershire	20	8	9	0	0	3	85	40	47.05
9 Essex	24	9	9	0	4	2	110	45	40.90
10 Somerset	20	7	10	2	1	0	100	39	39.00
11 Hampshire	26	7	14	3	1	1	125	41	32.80
12 Warwickshire	26	7	13	2	2	2	120	39	32.50
13 Leicestershire	24	7	14	0	1	2	110	35	31.81
14 Northamptonshire	20	3	16	0	1	0	100	15	15.00
15 Worcestershire	18	5	16	0	0	1	85	5	5.88
16 Derbyshire	18	0	17	0	0	1	85	0	0.00

The method used in the table reverted to that of 1914 except that in drawn matches, 2 pts were awarded to 1st innings winners and none to the 1st innings losers. The match Derbyshire v Notts was abandoned without a ball being bowled and is included in the No Result column

1921

	P	W	L	Drawn			Points		
				W	L	NR	Poss	Obtd	%
1 Middlesex	20	15	2	0	2	1	95	75	78.94
2 Surrey	24	15	2	3	3	1	115	81	70.43
3 Yorkshire	26	16	3	4	2	1	125	88	70.40
4 Kent	26	16	7	2	1	0	130	84	64.61
5 Lancashire	28	15	4	4	3	2	130	83	63.84
6 Hampshire	28	14	9	4	1	0	140	78	55.71
7 Gloucestershire	24	12	12	0	0	0	120	60	50.00
8 Nottinghamshire	24	10	8	3	2	1	115	56	48.69
9 Sussex	28	13	12	1	2	0	140	67	47.85
10 Somerset	22	8	11	2	1	0	110	44	40.00
11 Leicestershire	26	10	14	0	2	0	130	50	38.46
12 Derbyshire	20	5	12	3	0	0	100	31	31.00
13 Northamptonshire	24	5	15	1	2	1	115	27	23.47
14 Worcestershire	22	5	15	0	2	0	110	25	22.72
15 Essex	26	5	13	2	6	0	130	29	22.30
16 Warwickshire	26	5	18	1	2	0	130	27	20.76
17 Glamorgan	18	2	14	1	0	1	85	12	14.11

Glamorgan were admitted to the Championship

1922

	P	W	L	Drawn			Points		
				W	L	NR	Poss	Obtd	%
1 Yorkshire	30	19	2	6	2	1	145	107	73.79
2 Nottinghamshire	28	17	5	4	0	2	130	93	71.53
3 Surrey	24	13	1	6	3	1	115	77	66.95

1922 continued

	P	W	L	W	L	NR	Poss	Obtd	%
4 Kent	28	16	3	3	5	1	135	86	63.70
5 Lancashire	30	15	7	2	4	2	140	79	56.42
6 Hampshire	28	13	6	3	4	2	130	71	54.61
7 Middlesex	22	10	6	3	3	0	110	56	50.90
8 Essex	26	7	4	6	5	4	110	47	42.72
9 Sussex	30	11	16	1	2	0	150	57	38.00
10 Somerset	24	6	11	6	1	0	120	42	35.00
11 Derbyshire	22	6	10	2	2	2	100	34	34.00
12 Warwickshire	28	8	15	0	2	3	125	40	32.00
13 Gloucestershire	28	8	17	1	1	1	135	42	31.11
14 Leicestershire	26	6	11	4	4	1	125	38	30.40
15 Northamptonshire	22	5	14	0	2	1	105	25	23.80
16 Glamorgan	22	1	18	1	1	1	105	7	6.66
17 Worcestershire	26	1	16	1	8	0	130	7	5.38

The minimum number of matches needed to qualify for inclusion in the Championship was increased this season to 11 home and away

1923

	P	W	L	Drawn			Points		
				W	L	NR	Poss	Obtd	%
1 Yorkshire	32	25	1	4	1	1	155	133	85.80
2 Nottinghamshire	26	15	3	5	2	1	125	85	68.00
3 Lancashire	30	15	2	6	6	1	145	87	60.00
4 Surrey	26	11	2	6	4	3	115	67	58.26
5 Kent	28	15	9	0	3	1	135	75	55.55
6 Sussex	30	15	8	2	5	0	150	79	52.66
7 Hampshire	28	10	8	6	3	1	135	62	45.92
8 Middlesex	22	7	7	5	3	0	110	45	40.90
9 Somerset	24	9	11	1	3	0	120	47	39.16
10 Derbyshire	22	4	7	6	4	1	105	32	30.47
11 Gloucestershire	28	7	16	3	2	0	140	41	29.29
12 Warwickshire	26	6	12	3	4	1	125	36	28.80
13 Essex	26	6	11	3	6	0	130	36	27.69
14 Leicestershire	24	5	13	4	2	0	120	33	27.50
15 Worcestershire	26	5	16	1	4	0	130	27	20.76
16 Glamorgan	24	2	17	2	3	0	120	14	11.66
17 Northamptonshire	22	2	16	1	3	0	110	12	10.90

1924

	P	W	L	Drawn				Points		
				W	L	Tie	NR	Poss	Obtd	%
1 Yorkshire	30	16	3	2	2	0	7	115	88	76.52
2 Middlesex	22	11	3	4	2	0	2	100	69	69.00
3 Surrey	24	9	1	6	4	0	4	100	67	67.00
4 Lancashire	30	11	2	6	6	0	5	125	79	63.20
5 Kent	28	12	4	5	4	1	2	130	81	62.30
6 Gloucestershire	26	9	7	6	1	0	3	115	64	55.65
Nottinghamshire	27	9	3	4	7	0	4	115	64	55.65
8 Somerset	22	9	7	1	2	1	2	100	52	52.00
9 Warwickshire	25	7	6	2	5	0	5	100	46	46.00
10 Sussex	26	7	12	5	1	0	1	125	51	40.80
11 Leicestershire	25	7	12	4	2	0	0	125	49	39.20
12 Hampshire	28	5	9	4	6	0	4	120	43	35.83
13 Glamorgan	21	5	11	3	1	0	1	100	35	35.00
14 Worcestershire	24	4	11	3	5	0	1	115	34	29.56
15 Essex	26	2	12	4	5	0	3	115	27	23.47
16 Northamptonshire	22	2	9	0	6	0	5	85	16	18.82
17 Derbyshire	24	0	13	4	4	0	3	105	16	15.23

The matches Warwicks v Notts, Surrey v Essex, Leics v Surrey, Somerset v Essex and Glamorgan v Somerset were abandoned without a ball being bowled and are not included above

The points for a win on first innings in drawn matches returned to 3 and in a match lost to 1

1925

	P	W	L	Drawn			Points		
				W	L	NR	Poss	Obtd	%
1 Yorkshire	32	21	0	3	3	5	135	117	86.66
2 Surrey	26	14	2	4	2	4	110	84	76.36
3 Lancashire	32	19	4	7	1	1	155	117	75.48
4 Nottinghamshire	26	15	3	1	6	1	125	84	67.20
5 Kent	28	15	7	1	1	4	120	79	65.83
6 Middlesex	24	12	3	2	5	2	110	71	64.54

	P	W	L	W	L	NR	Poss	Obtd	%
7 Essex	28	9	7	5	5	2	130	65	50.00
8 Warwickshire	26	8	11	4	2	1	125	54	43.20
9 Hampshire	28	6	11	6	0	5	115	48	41.73
10 Gloucestershire	28	9	13	3	3	0	140	57	40.71
11 Northamptonshire	24	9	12	0	3	0	120	48	40.00
12 Leicestershire	26	7	13	3	2	1	125	46	36.80
13 Sussex	30	9	16	1	3	1	145	51	35.17
14 Derbyshire	24	5	12	2	4	1	115	35	30.43
15 Somerset	26	3	15	4	2	2	120	29	24.16
16 Worcestershire	26	5	18	0	3	0	130	28	21.53
17 Glamorgan	26	1	20	1	2	2	120	10	8.33

The minimum number of matches needed to qualify for inclusion in the Championship was increased to 12 home and away, but only in non-Test match seasons

1926	P	W	L	Drawn W	L	Tie	NR	Points Poss	Obtd	%
1 Lancashire	32	17	2	6	3	0	4	140	106	75.71
2 Yorkshire	31	14	0	10	4	0	3	140	104	74.28
3 Kent	28	15	2	3	8	0	0	140	92	65.71
4 Nottinghamshire	29	13	7	4	5	0	0	145	82	56.55
5 Surrey	26	7	4	8	3	0	4	110	62	56.36
6 Middlesex	24	9	4	0	6	0	5	95	51	53.68
7 Hampshire	28	10	5	4	8	0	1	135	70	51.85
8 Glamorgan	24	9	9	1	0	0	5	95	48	50.52
9 Essex	30	6	9	9	3	1	2	140	62½	44.64
10 Sussex	27	6	10	6	5	0	0	135	53	39.25
11 Derbyshire	23	5	7	4	6	0	1	110	43	39.09
12 Warwickshire	28	2	9	8	5	0	4	120	39	32.50
13 Leicestershire	27	5	12	3	4	0	3	120	38	31.66
14 Somerset	26	3	9	3	6	1	4	110	32½	29.54
15 Gloucestershire	30	5	17	3	4	0	1	145	38	26.20
16 Northamptonshire	25	3	13	4	5	0	0	125	32	25.60
17 Worcestershire	28	3	13	3	4	0	5	115	28	24.34

The matches Yorks v Notts, Derbys v Leics, Northants v Sussex were abandoned without a ball being bowled and are not included above. Essex and Somerset were awarded 2½ pts each for a tied match – the scorers were level, but Essex still had one wicket to fall when play ended

1927

In March 1927 the MCC revised the method of deciding the Championship. Eight points were awarded for each win and in drawn matches the side which gained a lead on first innings received five points and the opposing side three points. In the event of a tie, either in the whole match, or on first innings in a drawn match, each side shall be awarded four points. If there is no result on first innings but more than 6 hours playing time, each side receives 4 points. If the weather reduces a match to less than 6 hours playing time and there has not, in that time, been a result on first innings, then the match shall not be included in the Championship. The final positioning of the counties shall be decided on the percentage of points obtained to points obtainable. This revised method was first used in the 1927 season.

	P	W	L	Drawn W	L	NR	Points Poss	Obtd	%
1 Lancashire	28	10	1	11	5	1	224	154	68.75
2 Nottinghamshire	28	12	3	8	4	1	224	152	67.85
3 Yorkshire	27	10	3	5	6	3	216	135	62.54
4 Kent	26	12	6	4	3	1*	208	129	62.01
5 Derbyshire	20	8	3	2	3	4	160	99	61.87
6 Surrey	22	8	3	4	5	2*	176	107	60.79
7 Leicestershire	22	7	3	5	5	2*	176	104	59.09
8 Essex	26	8	8	5	3	2	208	106	50.96
9 Middlesex	20	5	5	5	4	1	160	81	50.62
10 Sussex	28	7	9	6	2	4*	224	108	48.92
11 Warwickshire	23	3	4	7	7	2	184	88	47.82
12 Gloucestershire	26	6	7	1	9	3	208	92	44.23
13 Hampshire	23	5	9	5	3	1	184	78	42.39
14 Somerset	23	3	9	4	7	0	184	65	35.32
15 Glamorgan	21	1	8	7	4	1	168	59	35.11
16 Northamptonshire	24	4	12	1	6	1	192	59	30.72
17 Worcestershire	27	1	17	2	6	1	216	40	18.51

Including a tie on first innings

The matches Yorks v Kent, Glamorgan v Northants, Lancs v Glamorgan, Worcs v Hants and Gloucs v Kent were abandoned without a ball being bowled and are not included above

In addition counties were involved in matches with less than six hours' play as follows: Derbys 4, Essex 4, Glamorgan 3, Gloucs 3, Hants 4, Kent 2, Lancs 3, Leics 6, Middx 4, Northts 1, Notts 2, Somerset 3, Surrey 4, Sussex 2, Warwicks 5, Worcs 2, Yorks 4; these matches are also not included

1928	P	W	L	Drawn W	L	NR	Points Poss	Obtd	%
1 Lancashire	30	15	0	9	3	3	240	186	77.50
2 Kent	30	15	5	8	1	1	240	167	69.58
3 Nottinghamshire	31	13	3	9	5	1	248	168	67.96
4 Yorkshire	26	8	0	8	7	3	208	137	65.86
5 Gloucestershire	28	9	6	9	0	4	224	133	59.37
6 Surrey	25	5	3	10	6	1	200	112	56.00
7 Sussex	30	12	8	4	6	0	240	134	55.83
8 Middlesex	24	6	5	7	5	1	192	102	53.17
9 Leicestershire	28	6	4	6	11	1	224	115	51.33
10 Derbyshire	25	6	6	4	7	2	200	97	48.50
11 Warwickshire	28	3	6	10	7	2	224	103	45.98
12 Hampshire	28	5	7	5	11	0	224	98	43.75
13 Northamptonshire	28	7	13	3	5	0	224	86	38.37
14 Somerset	23	4	11	3	5	0	184	62	33.69
15 Glamorgan	24	2	9	1	10	2	192	59	30.72
16 Essex	28	2	13	5	6	2	224	67	29.91
17 Worcestershire	30	0	19	2	8	1	240	38	15.83

In the following matches less than six hours play took place and there was no result on first innings: Surrey v Glamorgan, Surrey v Essex, Derbyshire v Som, Yorks v Sussex, Surrey v Sussex, Essex v Notts, Yorks v Glamorgan. These matches are not included above

1929	P	W	L	Drawn W	L	NR	Pts
1 Nottinghamshire	28	14	2	4	6	2	158
2 Lancashire	28	12	3	6	6	1	148
Yorkshire	28	10	2	9	5	2	148
4 Gloucestershire	28	15	6	1	4	2	145
Sussex	28	13	6	7	2	0	145
6 Middlesex	28	12	7	6	3	0	135
7 Derbyshire	28	10	6	8	3	1	133
8 Kent	28	12	8	6	2	0	132
9 Leicestershire	28	9	6	9	4	0	129
10 Surrey	28	8	7	5	6	2	115
11 Hampshire	28	8	10	0	8	2	96
12 Essex	28	6	9	3	9	1	94
13 Northamptonshire	28	7	13	2	6	0	84
14 Warwickshire	28	5	13	4	5	1	79
15 Somerset	28	3	17	5	3	0	58
16 Worcestershire	28	2	15	3	6	2	57
17 Glamorgan	28	3	19	3	3	0	48

A new method of deciding the Championship was introduced in 1929. All counties had to play 28 matches. A win counted 8 points and in drawn matches 5 pts went to the side ahead on first innings and 3 pts to the other side. If the match ended in a tie, or if it was a draw and tied on first innings, or if there was no result on first innings, each side received 4 pts

1930	P	W	L	Drawn W	L	NR	Pts
1 Lancashire	28	10	0	8	5	5	155
2 Gloucestershire	28	15	4	2	6	1	152
3 Yorkshire	28	11	2	6	4	5	150
4 Nottinghamshire	28	9	1	10	5	3	149
5 Kent	28	12	7	5	4	0	133
6 Essex	28	7	5	7	6	3	121
7 Sussex	28	7	5	6	8	2	118
8 Surrey	28	3	4	13	5	3	116
9 Derbyshire	28	7	8	4	6	3	106
10 Worcestershire	28	5	9	8	5	1	99
11 Glamorgan	28	5	9	6	4	4	98

59

1930 continued

		P	W	L	W	L	NR	Pts
12	Leicestershire	28	4	10	6	5	3	89
13	Hampshire	28	5	8	1	14	0	87
	Somerset	28	4	11	7	4	2	87
15	Warwickshire	28	2	9	8	7	2	85
16	Middlesex	28	3	9	3	10	3	81
17	Northamptonshire	28	4	12	3	5	4	78

1931

					Drawn			
		P	W	L	W	L	NR	Pts
1	Yorkshire	28	16	1	4	1	6	287
2	Gloucestershire	28	11	4	7	5	1	219
3	Kent	28	12	7	3	3	3	216
4	Sussex	28	10	6	8	1	3	205
5	Nottinghamshire	28	9	3	9	6	1	202
6	Lancashire	28	7	4	7	6	4	174
7	Derbyshire	28	7	6	8	3	4	170
8	Surrey	28	6	4	7	7	4	162
9	Warwickshire	28	6	5	5	7	5*	156
10	Essex	28	7	11	5	4	1	146
11	Middlesex	28	5	8	9	2	4	142
12	Hampshire	28	5	9	4	6	4	129
13	Somerset	28	6	11	2	8	1	128
14	Worcestershire	28	5	10	4	7	2	124
15	Glamorgan	28	4	11	1	8	4	105
16	Leicestershire	28	2	7	7	10	2*	103
17	Northamptonshire	28	2	13	3	9	1	76

*The method of scoring was again changed. The side winning the match received 15 pts. Both sides received 7½ pts in a tied match. In a drawn match the side winning on first innings received 5 pts and the side losing 3 pts. In a match with no result on first innings each side received 4 pts *Including one tie on first innings*

1932

					Drawn			
		P	W	L	W	L	NR	Pts
1	Yorkshire	28	19	2	3	1	3	315
2	Sussex	28	14	1	4	4	5	262
3	Kent	28	14	3	1	7	3	248
4	Nottinghamshire	28	13	4	6	4	1	241
5	Surrey	28	9	2	10	3	4	210
6	Lancashire	28	8	6	7	4	3	179
7	Somerset	28	8	7	3	7	3	168
8	Hampshire	28	8	10	3	6	1	157
9	Warwickshire	28	5	5	8	8	2	147
10	Derbyshire	28	6	6	5	6	3	145
	Middlesex	28	6	9	8	5	0	145
12	Leicestershire	28	6	11	7	3	1	138
13	Gloucestershire	28	6	12	6	1	3	135
14	Essex	28	4	14	2	6	2	96
15	Glamorgan	28	3	12	2	9	2	90
16	Northamptonshire	28	3	15	3	5	2	83
17	Worcestershire	28	1	12	6	5	4	76

1933

					Drawn			Points		
		P	W	L	W	L	NR	Poss	Obtd	%
1	Yorkshire	30	19	3	3	5	0	450	315	70.00
2	Sussex	32	18	5	7	2	0	480	311	64.79
3	Kent	30	15	8	3	3	1	450	253	56.22
4	Essex	28	13	8	4	3	0	420	224	53.33
5	Lancashire	28	9	1	10	7	1	420	210	50.00
6	Derbyshire	28	11	11	3	3	0	420	189	45.00
7	Warwickshire	28	9	5	5	8	1	420	188	44.76
8	Nottinghamshire	28	7	3	7	8	3	420	176	41.90
9	Surrey	26	6	5	12	3	0	390	159	40.76
10	Gloucestershire	30	10	13	5	2	0	450	181	40.22
11	Somerset	26	6	10	2	5	3	390	127	32.56
12	Middlesex	26	7	14	2	2	1	390	125	32.05
13	Northamptonshire	24	5	11	5	3	0	360	109	30.27
14	Hampshire	28	2	9	4	11	2	420	91	21.66
15	Worcestershire	30	2	13	7	6	2	450	91	20.22
16	Glamorgan	24	1	9	5	7	2	360	69	19.16
17	Leicestershire	26	3	15	1	7	0	390	71	18.20

The method of deciding the championship was changed for 1933. Counties could play a minimum of 24 matches and, with the points for wins and draws remaining unaltered, the positions of the counties were decided by a percentage of points obtained to maximum possible points – all matches to count no matter how little play took place. There was however a new provision for matches in which the first two days were entirely washed out; these would then be played as 'one-day' matches and decided on first innings, with 10 pts for the winner and 3 pts for the loser

1934

					Drawn			Points		
		P	W	L	W	L	NR	Poss	Obtd	%
1	Lancashire	30	13	3	10	4	0	450	257	57.11
2	Sussex	30	12	2	7	8	1	450	243	54.00
3	Derbyshire	28	12	6	6	3	1	420	223	53.09
4	Warwickshire	24	10	4	4	4	2	360	190	52.77
5	Kent	30	12	7	6	5	0	450	225	50.00
	Yorkshire	30	12	7	5	4	2	450	225	50.00
7	Gloucestershire	30	12	10	2	4	2	450	210	46.66
8	Essex	28	9	4	5	9	1	420	191	45.47
9	Nottinghamshire	28	8	7	7	6	0	420	173	41.19
10	Middlesex	28	9	9	7	2	2	420	169	40.23
11	Surrey	26	6	9	9	3	0	390	144	36.92
12	Leicestershire	24	6	9	3	6	0	360	123	34.16
13	Glamorgan	24	3	8	5	5	3	360	97	26.94
14	Hampshire	28	3	11	8	5	1	420	104	24.76
15	Somerset	24	3	10	0	11	0	360	78	21.66
	Worcestershire	28	3	12	3	9	1	420	91	21.66
17	Northamptonshire	24	2	17	3	2	0	360	51	14.16

1935

					Drawn			Points		
		P	W	L	W	L	NR	Poss	Obtd	%
1	Yorkshire	30	19	1	3	7	0	450	321	71.33
2	Derbyshire	28	16	6	4	2	0	420	266	63.33
3	Middlesex	24	11	5	6	1	1	360	202	56.11
4	Lancashire	28	12	6	8	1	1	420	227	54.04
5	Nottinghamshire	28	10	3	8	5	2	420	213	50.71
6	Leicestershire	24	11	9	2	2	0	360	181	50.27
7	Sussex	32	13	10	3	2	4*	480	232	48.33
8	Warwickshire	24	9	6	3	6	0	360	168	46.66
9	Essex	28	11	12	3	2	0	420	186	44.28
10	Kent	30	10	12	5	2	1	450	185	41.11
11	Surrey	26	7	5	5	7	2	390	159	40.76
12	Worcestershire	30	9	16	0	4	1	450	151	33.55
13	Glamorgan	26	6	11	5	2	2	390	129	33.07
14	Somerset	26	5	11	4	6	0	390	113	28.97
15	Gloucestershire	30	6	16	2	6	0	450	118	26.22
16	Hampshire	30	5	16	1	8	0	450	104	23.11
17	Northamptonshire	24	1	16	3	2	2*	360	44	12.22

*The match between Sussex and Northants was tied on first innings

1936

					Drawn			Points		
		P	W	L	W	L	NR	Poss	Obtd	%
1	Derbyshire	28	13	4	5	5	1	420	239	56.90
2	Middlesex	26	10	4	8	3	1	390	203	52.05
3	Yorkshire	30	10	2	12	4	2	450	230	51.11
4	Gloucestershire	30	10	7	4*	8	1	450	203	45.11
5	Nottinghamshire	28	8	3	9	8	0	420	189	45.00
6	Surrey	30	9	7	6	6	2	450	191	42.44
7	Somerset	26	9	10	2	3	2	390	162	41.53
8	Kent	28	9	9	4	5	1	420	174	41.42
9	Essex	26	8	8	5	5	0	390	160	41.02
10	Hampshire	30	7	5	9	9	0	450	177	39.33
11	Lancashire	30	7	6	7	5	5	450	175	38.88
12	Worcestershire	28	7	9	4	7	1	420	150	35.71
13	Warwickshire	24	4	8	2	7	3	360	103	28.61
14	Sussex	30	4	10	7	6	3	450	125	27.77
15	Leicestershire	24	2	5	8	8	1	360	98	27.22
16	Glamorgan	26	1	12	6	5	2	390	68	17.43
17	Northamptonshire	24	0	9	5*	9	1	360	61	16.94

*Northants beat Sussex under 'one-day' rules and Gloucs beat Warwicks

1937

	P	W	L	Drawn W	Drawn L	NR	Points Poss	Points Obtd	%
1 Yorkshire	28	18	2	4	4	0	420	302	71.90
2 Middlesex	24	15	4	3	2	0	360	246	68.33
3 Derbyshire	28	14	6	2	4	2	420	240	57.14
4 Gloucestershire	30	15	10	2	3	0	450	244	54.22
5 Sussex	32	13	7	8	4	0	480	247	51.45
6 Essex	28	13	11	2	1	1	420	212	50.47
7 Glamorgan	28	11	7	4	6	0	420	203	48.33
8 Surrey	26	8	5	7	4	2	390	175	44.87
9 Lancashire	32	9	5	12	6	0	480	213	44.37
10 Nottinghamshire	28	6	4	8	8	2	420	162	38.57
11 Warwickshire	24	6	8	6	4	0	360	132	36.66
12 Kent	28	8	16	2	2	0	420	136	32.38
13 Somerset	28	7	14	2	5	0	420	130	30.95
14 Hampshire	28	7	16	4	1	0	420	128	30.47
15 Worcestershire	30	8	17	0	5	0	450	135	30.00
16 Leicestershire	26	1	11	3	11	0	390	63	16.15
17 Northamptonshire	24	0	16	4	3	1	360	33	9.16

1938

	P	W	L	D	1st Inns L	1st Inns D	Pts	Avge
1 Yorkshire	28	20	2	6	0	4	256	9.14
2 Middlesex	22	15	5	2	0	1	184	8.36
3 Surrey	25	12	6	7	2	5	172	6.88
4 Lancashire	28	14	6	8	0	6	192	6.85
5 Derbyshire	25	11	8	6	3	4	160	6.40
6 Essex	26	12	11	3	3	2	164	6.30
7 Somerset	25	10	9	6	1	5	144	5.76
8 Sussex	29	11	9	9	3	3	156	5.37
9 Kent	27	8	14	5	2	4	120	4.44
10 Gloucestershire	28	8	13	7	2	4	122*	4.35
11 Worcestershire	30	9	11	10	2	3	128	4.26
12 Nottinghamshire	25	7	10	8	2	3	106*	4.24
13 Warwickshire	22	7	7	8	0	2	92	4.18
14 Hampshire	30	9	16	5	4	0	124	4.13
15 Leicestershire	22	4	9	9	1	7	80	3.63
16 Glamorgan	22	5	9	8	1	3	76	3.45
17 Northamptonshire	24	0	17	7	3	1	16	0.66

*Includes 2 pts for a tie on first innings of match lost

The points system was altered for 1938 as follows: 12 pts for a win; 6 pts for a tie; 4 pts for first innings lead in a match either drawn or lost; 8 pts for a win in a match under One-day rules. Matches in which there was no result in the first innings are not included in the table – there were 19 such matches in 1938

1939

	P	W	L	D	T	1st Inns L	1st Inns D	Pts	Avge
1 Yorkshire	28	20	4	4	0	2	3	260	9.28
2 Middlesex	22	14	6	2	0	3	1	180	8.18
3 Gloucestershire	26	15	7	4	0	1	3	196	7.53
4 Essex	24	12	10	2	0	4	2	170*	7.08
5 Kent	26	14	9	3	0	2	1	180	6.92
6 Lancashire	21	10	6	5	0	3	2	140	6.66
7 Worcestershire	27	11	10	5	1	2	4	162	6.00
8 Surrey	24	11	7	6	0	0	2	140	5.83
9 Derbyshire	25	10	8	7	0	1	5	144	5.76
10 Sussex	29	10	12	7	0	1	4	140	4.82
11 Warwickshire	22	7	8	7	0	1	2	98*	4.45
12 Nottinghamshire	23	6	8	9	0	2	5	100	4.34
13 Glamorgan	24	6	8	10	0	1	5	96	4.00
14 Somerset	27	6	11	9	1	2	4	102	3.77
15 Hampshire	26	3	17	6	0	8	4	84	3.23
16 Northamptonshire	22	1	12	9	0	3	3	36	1.63
17 Leicestershire	20	1	14	5	0	1	0	16	0.80

*Includes 2 pts for a tie on first innings in match lost

Middlesex's win total includes 8 pts for a win under One-day rules (v Northants). 26 matches are not included above as a result was not reached on 1st innings; in addition three matches were not played due to the war – Middx v Kent, Gloucs v Notts and Lancs v Leics – also Lancs v Surrey was abandoned on the third day due to war; none of these games are included above

1946

	P	W	L	D	ND	1st Inns L	1st Inns D	Pts
1 Yorks	26	17	1	5	3	0	4	216
2 Middlesex	26	16	5	5	0	1	2	204
3 Lancashire	26	15	4	5	2	1	4	200
4 Somerset	26	12	6	7	1	2	3	166
5 Gloucestershire	26	12	6	4	4	1	3	160
6 Glamorgan	26	10	8	6	2	3	3	144
Kent	26	11	8	7	0	0	3	144
8 Essex	26	8	9	8	1	2	4	120
Worcestershire	26	9	12	2	3	3	0	120
10 Hampshire	26	8	15	3	0	2	2	112
11 Leicestershire	26	7	13	4	2	2	2	100
Surrey	26	6	11	7	2	3	4	100
13 Nottinghamshire	26	6	8	11	1	1	5	96
14 Warwickshire	26	7	15	3	1	1	1	92
15 Derbyshire	26	5	12	8	1	3	4	88
16 Northamptonshire	26	2	11	11	2	2	8	64
17 Sussex	26	4	11	10	1	2	1	60

*Includes 2 pts for tie on first innings in match lost

Yorkshire's win total includes 8 pts for a win under One-day rules (v Warwicks)

The points system was the same as 1939, except each county played 26 matches

1947

	P	W	L	D	T	ND	1st Inns L	1st Inns D	Pts
1 Middlesex	26	19	5	2	0	0	1	1	236
2 Gloucestershire	26	17	4	5	0	0	1	2	216
3 Lancashire	26	13	1	10	1	1	0	6	186
4 Kent	26	12	8	6	0	0	2	5	172
5 Derbyshire	26	11	9	5	0	1	3	4	160
6 Surrey	26	10	7	8	0	1	0	5	140
7 Worcestershire	26	7	11	8	0	0	4	5	120
Yorkshire	26	8	7	10	0	1	1	5	120
9 Glamorgan	26	8	8	8	0	2	3	2	116
Sussex	26	9	12	5	0	0	1	1	116
11 Essex	26	6	9	10	1	0	1	4	100
Nottinghamshire	26	6	13	6	0	1	1	6	100
Somerset	26	8	12	6	0	0	0	1	100
14 Leicestershire	26	6	14	5	0	1	2	3	92
15 Warwickshire	26	6	12	7	0	1	2	1	84
16 Hampshire	26	4	11	8	1	2	0	6	78
17 Northamptonshire	26	2	16	6	1	1	2	4	54

*Includes 2 pts for tie on first innings in match lost

1948

	P	W	L	D	ND	Drawn L	Drawn D	Pts
1 Glamorgan	26	13	5	6	2	1	3	172
2 Surrey	26	13	9	4	0	1	3	168
3 Middlesex	26	13	4	8	1	0	1	160
4 Yorkshire	26	11	4	10	1	3	3	156
5 Lancashire	26	8	2	15	1	0	14	152
6 Derbyshire	26	11	6	7	2	0	4	148
7 Warwickshire	26	9	7	8	2	1	5	132
8 Gloucestershire	26	9	7	9	1	1	4	128
9 Hampshire	26	9	8	8	1	2	1	120
10 Worcestershire	26	6	8	11	1	1	7	104
11 Leicestershire	26	6	11	8	1	1	6	96
12 Somerset	26	5	14	6	1	4	4	90
13 Essex	26	5	8	11*	2	2	4	90
14 Nottinghamshire	26	5	10	9*	2	1	3	82
15 Kent	26	4	11	10	1	0	7	76
16 Sussex	26	4	11	10	1	1	5	72
17 Northamptonshire	26	3	9	14	0	1	3	52

*Essex and Notts, whose aggregate scores were equal, each gained 6 pts in a drawn match. Surrey's win total includes 8 pts for a win under One-day rules (v Gloucs)

1949

	P	W	L	D	ND	1st Inns L	1st Inns D	Pts
1 Middlesex	26	14	3	9	0	1	5	192
Yorkshire	26	14	2	10	0	0	6	192
3 Worcestershire	26	12	7	7	0	2	5	172

1949 *continued*

	County	P	W	L	D	ND	1st Inns L	1st Inns D	Pts
4	Warwickshire	26	12	5	8	1	0	6	168
5	Surrey	26	11	8	6	1	2	4	156
6	Northamptonshire	26	10	7	9	0	2	3	140
7	Gloucestershire	26	10	7	7	2	0	3	132
8	Glamorgan	26	7	6	12	1	2	7	120
9	Essex	26	7	9	10	0	0	6	108
	Somerset	26	8	15	3	0	2	1	108
11	Lancashire	26	6	7	13	0	0	7	100
	Nottinghamshire	26	6	5	13	2	0	7	100
13	Kent	26	7	15	4	0	1	2	96
	Sussex	26	7	10	7	2	1	2	96
15	Derbyshire	26	6	13	6	1	2	2	88
16	Hampshire	26	6	13	6	1	2	1	84
17	Leicestershire	26	3	14	8	1	3	2	56

The number of points awarded for a tie or a drawn match where scores are level was altered to 8 for the side with first innings lead and 4 for the other side

1950

	County	P	W	L	D	T	ND	1st Inns L	1st Inns D	Pts
1	Lancashire	28	16	2	10	0	0	1	6	220
	Surrey	28	17	4	6	0	1	0	4	220
3	Yorkshire	28	14	2	10	0	2	0	8	200
4	Warwickshire	28	8	6	13	0	1	1	8	132
5	Derbyshire	28	8	9	9	0	2	3	4	124
6	Worcestershire	28	7	9	9	0	3	0	7	114
7	Gloucestershire	28	6	6	16	0	0	2	9	112
	Somerset	28	8	8	10	0	2	1	3	112
9	Kent	28	6	12	8	1	1	3	5	108
10	Northamptonshire	28	6	4	15	0	3	2	6	104
11	Glamorgan	28	6	4	9	0	9	0	7	100
12	Hampshire	28	7	9	9	1	2	0	2	96
13	Sussex	28	5	11	11	0	1	6	2	92
14	Middlesex	28	5	12	8	0	3	2	4	84
15	Nottinghamshire	28	3	6	17	0	2	0	8	68
16	Leicestershire	28	3	13	11	0	1	2	5	64
17	Essex	28	4	12	11	0	1	0	3	60

The Hampshire (v Middx) and Gloucs (v Sussex) win totals include 8 pts for a win under One-day rules. Hampshire also received 8 pts for tie, where the county obtained a lead on 1st innings – the opposition, Kent, received 4 pts. Worcs received 2 pts for a tie on 1st innings in a match lost

1951

	County	P	W	L	D	ND	1st Inns L	1st Inns D	Pts
1	Warwickshire	28	16	2	10	0	0	6	216
2	Yorkshire	28	12	3	11	2	0	10	184
3	Lancashire	28	8	2	14	4	1	9	136
4	Worcestershire	28	9	7	10	2	2	4	132
5	Glamorgan	28	8	4	13	3	1	7	128
6	Surrey	28	7	6	13	2	0	9	120
7	Middlesex	28	7	6	13	2	1	7	116
8	Essex	28	6	2	18	2	0	9	110
9	Hampshire	28	5	7	13	3	1	9	100
10	Sussex	28	6	6	15	1	0	5	94
11	Derbyshire	28	5	6	16	1	2	6	92
12	Gloucestershire	28	5	9	12	2	1	6	88
13	Northamptonshire	28	4	4	17	3	1	7	80
14	Somerset	28	5	15	6	2	3	1	76
15	Leicestershire	28	4	7	16	1	0	4	64
16	Kent	28	4	15	8	1	1	2	60
17	Nottinghamshire	28	1	11	13	3	0	7	40

The records of Essex and Sussex include 2 pts for a tie on 1st innings in a drawn match

1952

	County	P	W	L	D	T	ND	1st Inns L	1st Inns D	Pts
1	Surrey	28	20	3	5	0	0	0	4	256
2	Yorkshire	28	17	2	8	0	1	0	5	224
3	Lancashire	28	12	3	11	1	1	1	8	188
4	Derbyshire	28	11	8	9	0	0	2	6	164
5	Middlesex	28	11	12	4	0	1	0	1	136
6	Leicestershire	28	9	9	9	0	1	1	5	132

1952 *continued*

	County	P	W	L	D	T	ND	1st Inns L	1st Inns D	Pts
7	Glamorgan	28	8	7	13	0	0	2	6	130
8	Northamptonshire	28	7	8	12	0	1	3	8	128
9	Gloucestershire	28	7	10	11	0	0	4	6	124
10	Essex	28	8	4	13	1	2	1	4	120
	Warwickshire	28	8	10	8	1	0		4	120
12	Hampshire	28	7	11	9	0	1	4	3	112
13	Sussex	28	7	12	6	1	2	0	2	96
14	Worcestershire	28	6	11	10	0	1	1	3	90
15	Kent	28	5	15	8	0	0	2	4	84
16	Nottinghamshire	28	3	11	13	0	1	2	7	72
17	Somerset	28	2	12	13	0	1	1	4	44

Warwickshire and Lancashire records include 8 pts for first innings lead in a match tied and Sussex and Essex 4 pts, being the opposition in these matches. Glamorgan and Worcestershire obtained 2 pts each for a tie on first innings in a drawn match

1953

	County	P	W	L	D	T	ND	1st Inns L	1st Inns D	Pts
1	Surrey	28	13	4	10	0	1	0	7	184
2	Sussex	28	11	3	13	0	1	1	8	168
3	Lancashire	28	10	4	10	0	4	1	8	156
	Leicestershire	28	10	7	11	0	0	3	6	156
5	Middlesex	28	10	5	11	1	1	1	5	150
6	Derbyshire	28	9	7	9	0	3	2	5	136
	Gloucestershire	28	9	7	10	0	2	2	5	136
8	Nottinghamshire	28	9	10	8	0	1	4	1	128
9	Warwickshire	28	6	7	14	0	1	2	11	124
10	Glamorgan	28	8	4	14	0	2	0	6	120
11	Northamptonshire	28	6	3	15	1	3	2	7	114
12	Essex	28	6	7	13	0	2	1	6	100
	Yorkshire	28	6	6	13	0	3	1	6	100
14	Hampshire	28	6	11	11	0	0	2	4	96
15	Worcestershire	28	5	12	10	0	1	1	2	72
16	Kent	28	4	14	8	0	2	1	3	64
17	Somerset	28	2	19	6	0	1	0	3	36

The number of points awarded for a tie was altered to 6 for each side – previously it was 8 for the side with 1st innings lead and 4 for the other side. If the scores were level in a drawn match the side batting second received 6 points (irrespective of first innings lead)

1954

	County	P	W	L	D	T	ND	1st Inns L	1st Inns D	Pts
1	Surrey	28	15	3	8	0	2	1	6	208
2	Yorkshire	28	13	3	8	1	3	0	5	186
3	Derbyshire	28	11	6	9	0	2	3	6	168
4	Glamorgan	28	11	5	10	0	2	0	4	148
5	Nottinghamshire	28	10	6	8	0	4	2	4	144
6	Warwickshire	28	10	5	10	0	3	1	4	140
7	Middlesex	28	10	5	10	0	3	1	3	136
	Northamptonshire	28	9	9	9	0	1	3	4	136
9	Sussex	28	8	7	12	0	1	1	5	120
10	Lancashire	28	6	3	12	0	7	1	8	108
11	Kent	28	5	7	15	0	1	3	7	100
	Worcestershire	28	5	12	9	0	2	2	7	100
13	Gloucestershire	28	5	11	10	0	2	4	5	96
14	Hampshire	28	4	10	13	0	1	1	7	80
15	Essex	28	3	11	12	0	2	2	5	64
16	Leicestershire	28	3	9	11	1	4	0	5	62
17	Somerset	28	2	18	8	0	0	2	2	40

Yorkshire (v Somerset) and Worcestershire (v Northants) obtained 8 pts each for a win under One-day rules – included as draws

1955

	County	P	W	L	D	T	ND	1st Inns L	1st Inns D	Pts
1	Surrey	28	23	5	0	0	0	2	0	284
2	Yorkshire	28	21	5	2	0	0	2	2	268
3	Hampshire	28	16	5	6	1	0	1	3	210
4	Sussex	28	13	8	6	1	0	3	5	196
5	Middlesex	28	14	12	2	0	0	6	0	192
6	Leicestershire	28	11	10	7	0	0	3	2	154
7	Northamptonshire	28	9	10	9	0	0	3	7	148

1955 *continued*	P	W	L	D	T	ND	L	D	Pts
8 Derbyshire	28	9	10	9	0	0	2	7	146
9 Lancashire	28	10	9	8	0	1	2	3	140
Warwickshire	28	10	9	9	0	0	2	3	140
11 Nottinghamshire	28	10	11	7	0	0	1	2	132
12 Gloucestershire	28	9	13	6	0	0	2	3	128
13 Kent	28	8	13	7	0	0	0	2	104
14 Essex	28	6	15	7	0	0	3	4	100
15 Worcestershire	28	5	17	6	0	0	2	4	84
16 Glamorgan	28	5	14	8	0	1	2	3	80
17 Somerset	28	4	17	7	0	0	2	2	64

Derbyshire and Leics obtained 2 pts for a tie on 1st innings in a drawn match and Sussex 2 pts for a tie on 1st innings in a match lost

							1st Inns		
1956	P	W	L	D	ND	L	D	Pts	
1 Surrey	28	15	5	6	2	1	4	200	
2 Lancashire	28	12	2	12	2	0	9	180	
3 Gloucestershire	28	14	7	5	2	1	1	176	
4 Northamptonshire	28	8	5	15	0	2	11	148	
5 Middlesex	28	11	9	7	1	1	2	144	
6 Hampshire	28	9	6	10	3	1	7	140	
7 Yorkshire	28	8	7	10	3	4	6	136	
8 Nottinghamshire	28	7	4	15	2	1	9	128	
9 Sussex	28	7	10	9	2	2	5	112	
Worcestershire	28	8	4	14	2	0	4	112	
11 Essex	28	6	10	9	3	5	4	110	
12 Derbyshire	28	7	6	11	4	0	4	102	
13 Glamorgan	28	6	9	9	4	2	5	100	
14 Warwickshire	28	5	11	9	3	3	2	80	
15 Somerset	28	4	15	8	1	3	4	76	
16 Kent	28	4	12	10	2	1	2	60	
17 Leicestershire	28	3	12	9	4	1	4	56	

Notts (v Lancs) obtained 8 pts for a win under One-day rules – included in draws. Essex and Derbys obtained 2 pts each for a tie on 1st innings in a drawn match

						1st Inns	Bonus		
1957	P	W	L	D	ND	L	D	Pts	Pts
1 Surrey	28	21	3	3	1	3	3	48	312
2 Northamptonshire	28	15	2	10	1	0	8	22	218
3 Yorkshire	28	13	4	11	0	0	5	24	190
4 Derbyshire	28	10	8	9	1	2	4	30	162
5 Essex	28	11	6	10	1	0	5	16	158
6 Lancashire	28	10	8	8	2	2	4	24	156
7 Middlesex	28	10	12	3	3	2	1	22	148
8 Somerset	28	9	14	5	0	3	2	20	138
9 Glamorgan	28	10	9	8	1	0	2	12	136
Sussex	28	8	9	9	2	2	6	24	136
11 Warwickshire	28	9	7	11	1	0	5	16	134
12 Gloucestershire	28	8	13	6	1	1	5	24	132
13 Hampshire	28	7	12	8	1	1	5	20	116
14 Kent	28	6	13	9	0	2	3	8	90
15 Nottinghamshire	28	5	13	9	1	3	4	14	88
16 Worcestershire	28	4	9	14	1	1	4	8	72
17 Leicestershire	28	2	16	9	1	2	5	4	40

The points system was changed, in that the side gaining a lead on 1st innings in a match drawn or lost was awarded 2 pts instead of 4, but received 2 bonus points if it scored faster, in runs per over, than the opponents and a side winning a match also received 2 bonus pts if it scored faster than its opponents in the first innings. The One-day rule now applied to matches restricted to the last third of the playing time, not necessarily the last day

						1st Inns	Bonus		
1958	P	W	L	D	ND	L	D	Pts	Pts
1 Surrey	28	14	5	8	1	0	6	32	212
2 Hampshire	28	12	6	10	0	3	4	28	186
3 Somerset	28	12	9	7	0	2	3	20	174
4 Northamptonshire	28	11	6	6	5	0	5	18	160
5 Derbyshire	28	9	9	8	2	4	5	24	151
6 Essex	28	9	7	7	5	4	3	24	146
7 Lancashire	28	9	7	8	4	3	5	18	142

1958 *continued*	P	W	L	D	ND	L	D	Pts	Pts
8 Kent	28	9	10	7	2	1	4	20	139
9 Worcestershire	28	9	7	8	4	1	2	20	134
10 Middlesex	28	7	4	16	1	1	10	18	130
11 Yorkshire	28	7	5	10	6	2	6	14	126
12 Leicestershire	28	7	13	6	2	3	1	12	104
13 Sussex	28	6	7	11	4	2	4	18	102
14 Gloucestershire	28	5	9	11	3	3	4	14	89
15 Glamorgan	28	5	11	11	1	1	5	10	82
16 Warwickshire	28	3	7	14	4	2	6	16	68
17 Nottinghamshire	28	3	15	8	2	1	4	4	50

Yorkshire (v Hants and Notts) obtained 16 pts from 2 matches, both restricted to the last third, Middlesex obtained 8 pts from a similar match. Derbys, Kent and Gloucs all obtained 1 pt for a tie on 1st innings

							1st Inns	Bonus		
1959	P	W	L	D	T	ND	L	D	Pts	Pts
1 Yorkshire	28	14	7	7	0	0	0	5	26	204
2 Gloucestershire	28	12	11	4	1	0	1	3	28	186
Surrey	28	12	5	11	0	0	0	8	26	186
4 Warwickshire	28	13	10	5	0	0	2	1	22	184
Lancashire	28	12	7	9	0	0	1	5	28	184
6 Glamorgan	28	12	8	7	0	1	3	4	20	178
7 Derbyshire	28	12	6	10	0	0	3	2	20	174
8 Hampshire	28	11	10	7	0	0	1	4	26	168
Essex	28	11	7	9	1	0	0	4	22	168
10 Middlesex	28	10	9	9	0	0	3	3	24	157
11 Northamptonshire	28	8	10	10	0	0	4	9	24	146
12 Somerset	28	8	13	7	0	0	4	3	20	130
13 Kent	28	8	12	8	0	0	2	5	18	128
14 Worcestershire	28	6	8	13	0	1	1	7	18	106
15 Sussex	28	6	11	10	0	1	3	3	18	102
16 Leicestershire	28	5	16	7	0	0	0	2	8	72
17 Nottinghamshire	28	4	14	9	0	1	1	3	6	62

Middlesex obtained 1 pt for a tie on 1st innings in a match lost

						1st Inns	Bonus			
1960	P	W	L	D	ND	L	D	Pts	Pts	Avge
1 Yorkshire	32	17	6	6	3	2	2	34	246	7.68
2 Lancashire	32	13	8	10	1	3	9	34	214	6.68
3 Middlesex	28	12	4	12	0	0	7	28	186	6.64
4 Sussex	32	12	6	12	2	2	6	28	188	5.87
5 Derbyshire	28	10	7	10	1	1	5	20	152	5.42
Essex	28	9	3	14	2	1	7	28	152	5.42
7 Surrey	28	9	6	10	3	2	3	20	138	4.92
8 Gloucestershire	28	9	7	12	0	0	3	16	130	4.64
9 Northamptonshire	28	8	6	13	1	1	6	16	126	4.50
10 Kent	28	7	7	12	2	1	6	20	118	4.21
11 Glamorgan	32	9	14	7	2	0	4	16	133	4.15
12 Hampshire	32	8	8	14	2	1	6	22	132	4.12
13 Worcestershire	32	8	12	10	2	1	6	20	130	4.06
14 Somerset	32	5	11	15	1	2	10	22	106	3.31
15 Warwickshire	32	4	12	16	0	2	9	26	96	3.00
16 Nottinghamshire	28	4	16	7	1	4	2	12	72	2.57
17 Leicestershire	28	2	13	12	1	5	2	12	46	1.64

Glamorgan obtained 1 pt for a tie on 1st innings in a match lost

The method of obtaining points remained unchanged, but counties could play either 28 or 32 matches and the final average was obtained by dividing the total points by the matches played

If scores were level in a match under One-day rules, the side batting second received 4 pts and the other side none

						1st Inns	Bonus			
1961	P	W	L	D	ND	L	D	Pts	Pts	Avge
1 Hampshire	32	19	7	6	0	1	3	32	268	8.37
2 Yorkshire	32	17	5	10	0	1	5	34	250	7.81
3 Middlesex	28	15	6	6	1	3	1	26	214	7.64
4 Worcestershire	32	16	9	7	0	2	3	24	226	7.06
5 Gloucestershire	28	11	11	5	1	2	2	18	158	5.64
6 Essex	28	10	8	10	0	2	4	26	158	5.64

1961 *continued*

		P	W	L	D	ND	L	D	Pts	Pts	Avge
7	Derbyshire	28	10	9	9	0	3	3	22	154	5.50
8	Sussex	32	11	10	11	0	1	8	20	170	5.31
9	Leicestershire	28	9	13	5	1	2	4	26	146	5.21
10	Somerset	32	10	15	7	0	6	3	24	162	5.06
11	Kent	28	8	8	12	0	1	7	20	132	4.71
12	Warwickshire	32	9	10	13	0	1	7	26	150	4.68
13	Lancashire	32	9	7	15	1	1	7	18	142	4.43
14	Glamorgan	32	9	12	11	0	1	4	10	128	4.00
15	Surrey	28	4	13	11	0	6	8	24	100	3.57
16	Northamptonshire	28	5	13	10	0	1	5	10	82	2.92
17	Nottinghamshire	28	4	20	4	0	6	2	12	76	2.71

The follow-on was abolished when play was possible on the first day, but a team could forfeit its second innings

1962

		P	W	L	D	ND	1st Inns Bonus L	D	Pts	Pts	Avge
1	Yorkshire	32	14	4	14	0	1	9	36	224	7.00
2	Worcestershire	32	14	3	14	1	1	8	34	220	6.87
3	Warwickshire	32	12	5	15	0	2	11	32	202	6.31
4	Gloucestershire	28	11	11	6	0	5	4	24	174	6.21
5	Surrey	28	10	3	14	1	2	9	32	174	6.21
6	Somerset	32	12	7	13	0	1	7	30	190	5.93
7	Derbyshire	28	8	6	13	1	2	8	28	144	5.14
8	Northamptonshire	28	7	5	16	0	1	10	22	128	4.57
9	Essex	28	8	6	13	1	2	7	12	126	4.50
10	Hampshire	32	7	5	19	1	2	11	30	140	4.37
11	Kent	28	7	9	10	2	2	3	16	110	3.92
12	Sussex	32	7	12	13	0	4	6	18	122	3.81
13	Middlesex	28	6	8	13	1	2	4	18	102	3.64
14	Glamorgan	32	6	13	13	0	1	4	14	96	3.00
15	Nottinghamshire	28	4	12	11	1	0	1	4	54	1.92
16	Lancashire	32	2	16	14	0	6	5	14	60	1.87
17	Leicestershire	28	2	12	13	1	2	5	12	50	1.78

1963

		P	W	L	D	ND	1st Inns L	D	Pts
1	Yorkshire	28	13	3	11	1	1	6	144
2	Glamorgan	28	11	8	8	1	1	6	124
3	Somerset	28	10	6	11	1	2	7	118
4	Sussex	28	10	6	12	0	1	7	116
	Warwickshire	28	10	3	14	1	1	7	116
6	Middlesex	28	9	5	11	3	1	7	106
7	Northamptonshire	28	9	8	11	0	1	5	105
8	Gloucestershire	28	9	7	11	1	2	3	100
9	Nottinghamshire	28	6	8	13	1	4	7	82
10	Hampshire	28	7	8	10	3	1	4	80
11	Surrey	28	5	6	17	0	1	11	74
12	Essex	28	6	4	17	1	0	5	70
13	Kent	28	5	6	17	0	1	8	68
14	Worcestershire	28	4	8	13	3	2	8	60
15	Lancashire	28	4	10	13	1	2	7	58
16	Leicestershire	28	3	13	10	2	2	3	40
17	Derbyshire	28	2	14	9	3	1	3	28

Northants obtained 5 pts instead of 2 in a drawn match, when the scores finished level and they were batting

The method of deciding the championship was altered as follows: 10 pts for a win; 5 pts for a tie; 2 pts for 1st innings lead in a match drawn or lost; 1 pt for a tie on 1st innings in a match drawn or lost; 6 pts for a win under One-day rules, if the first two-thirds of the playing time had been lost through the weather. The follow-on was restored

1964

		P	W	L	D	ND	1st Inns L	D	Pts
1	Worcestershire	28	18	3	6	1	0	5	191
2	Warwickshire	28	14	5	9	0	0	5	150
3	Northamptonshire	28	12	4	11	1	0	5	130
4	Surrey	28	11	3	13	1	0	9	129
5	Yorkshire	28	11	3	14	0	0	8	126
6	Middlesex	28	9	6	12	1	2	9	112
7	Kent	28	9	6	12	1	3	6	108
8	Somerset	28	8	8	8	4	4	4	96

1964 *continued*

		P	W	L	D	ND	L	D	Pts
9	Sussex	28	8	9	10	1	1	3	88
10	Essex	28	7	11	8	2	5	3	86
11	Glamorgan	28	7	7	12	2	1	6	84
12	Derbyshire	28	5	9	12	2	4	5	68
	Hampshire	28	5	8	14	1	1	5	68
14	Lancashire	28	4	10	13	1	4	8	64
15	Nottinghamshire	28	4	13	11	0	3	4	54
16	Leicestershire	28	3	18	5	2	7	0	44
17	Gloucestershire	28	3	15	10	0	2	4	43

Surrey, Worcs and Gloucs obtained 1 pt for a tie on first innings; Hants obtained 5 pts in a drawn match which ended with the scores level and Hants batting

1965

		P	W	L	D	ND	1st Inns L	D	Pts
1	Worcestershire	28	13	4	10	1	1	6	144
2	Northamptonshire	28	13	4	9	2	0	5	140
3	Glamorgan	28	12	6	8	2	2	4	132
4	Yorkshire	28	9	4	14	1	1	11	114
5	Kent	28	8	5	14	1	0	8	96
6	Middlesex	28	8	7	12	1	0	7	94
7	Somerset	28	8	11	8	1	2	4	92
8	Surrey	28	7	4	15	2	1	8	92
9	Derbyshire	28	7	9	11	1	2	6	86
10	Gloucestershire	28	7	8	11	2	1	5	82
11	Warwickshire	28	5	5	18	0	1	9	70
12	Hampshire	28	5	4	17	2	0	8	66
13	Lancashire	28	5	13	9	1	0	5	60
14	Leicestershire	28	5	11	11	1	2	2	58
15	Essex	28	4	7	16	1	0	7	54
16	Sussex	28	4	10	14	0	2	4	52
17	Nottinghamshire	28	3	11	13	1	3	6	48

Surrey obtained 6 pts for a win under One-day rules v Lancs (included as a draw)

1966

		P	W	L	D	ND	1st Inns	Pts
1	Yorkshire	28	15	5	8	0	17	184
2	Worcestershire	28	13	5	9	1	18	166
3	Somerset	28	13	7	7	1	13	156
4	Kent	28	11	8	8	1	17	144
5	Northamptonshire	28	10	9	9	0	15	130
6	Warwickshire	28	8	8	10	2	16	113
7	Surrey	28	8	3	16	1	15	110
8	Leicestershire	28	8	7	12	1	14	108
9	Derbyshire	28	8	12	7	1	8	96
10	Sussex	28	6	11	11	0	16	92
11	Hampshire	28	5	4	18	1	16	87
12	Lancashire	28	6	11	8	3	13	86
	Middlesex	28	6	5	14	3	13	86
14	Glamorgan	28	6	8	13	1	10	85
15	Gloucestershire	28	6	12	9	1	7	75
16	Essex	28	4	10	11	3	10	60
17	Nottinghamshire	28	3	11	12	2	8	46

The method of obtaining points altered in that 2 pts were awarded for 1st innings lead regardless as to whether the match was won, lost or drawn. Warwicks and Gloucs obtained 1 pt for a tie on first innings; Hants and Glamorgan obtained 5 pts in a drawn match with the scores level

1967

		P	W	L	D	T	ND	1st Inns	Pts
1	Yorkshire	28	12	5	9	0	2	18	186
2	Kent	28	11	3	12	0	2	16	176
3	Leicestershire	28	10	3	12	0	3	18	176
4	Surrey	28	8	4	12	0	4	15	148
5	Worcestershire	28	6	6	16	0	0	13	132
6	Derbyshire	28	5	5	17	0	1	14	130
7	Middlesex	28	5	4	14	1	4	14	128
8	Somerset	28	5	7	14	0	2	13	120
9	Northamptonshire	28	7	8	11	0	2	10	118
10	Warwickshire	28	5	4	15	0	4	11	118
11	Lancashire	28	4	3	17	0	4	12	116
12	Hampshire	28	5	6	13	1	3	10	114

1967 continued

		P	W	L	D	T	ND	Inns	Pts
13	Sussex	28	5	9	12	0	2	10	104
14	Glamorgan	28	4	7	15	0	2	9	100
15	Essex	28	3	9	14	0	2	9	88
16	Nottinghamshire	28	0	4	22	0	2	11	88
17	Gloucestershire	28	3	11	9	0	5	11	86

The method of obtaining points was altered as follows: for a win 8pts; for a tie 4 pts; for a drawn match with the scores level, 4 pts to the side batting last; for 1st innings lead 4 pts; for tie on 1st innings 2 pts; for a draw, providing there is a 1st innings result, 2 pts. No 'One-day' rule

Warwicks and Hants obtained 4 pts for a drawn match with scores level; Lancs, Glamorgan, Warwicks and Hants obtained 2 pts for a tie on 1st innings

1968

		P	W	L	D	NR	Bat	Bowl	Pts
1	Yorkshire	28	11	4	13	0	46	114	270
2	Kent	28	12	5	11	0	41	95	256
3	Glamorgan	28	11	6	9	2	42	85	237
4	Nottinghamshire	28	7	3	17	1	53	99	222
5	Hampshire	28	8	5	15	0	43	92	215
6	Lancashire	28	8	6	14	0	24	105	209
7	Worcestershire	28	8	7	13	0	26	97	203
8	Derbyshire	28	6	5	16	1	47	92	199
9	Leicestershire	28	6	10	12	0	52	85	197
10	Middlesex	28	8	6	14	0	21	91	192
11	Warwickshire	28	7	8	12	1	38	82	190
12	Somerset	28	5	11	11	1	36	86	172
13	Northamptonshire	28	5	6	17	0	34	86	170
14	Essex	28	5	6	16	1	31	88	169
15	Surrey	28	4	7	17	0	25	92	157
16	Gloucestershire	28	2	8	17	1	40	93	153
17	Sussex	28	2	12	14	0	43	77	140

The method of obtaining points was altered as follows: 10 pts for a win; 5 pts for a tie; 5 pts for team batting last in a drawn match with the scores level; in the first 85 overs only of the 1st innings 1 bonus pt for every 25 runs over 150 and for every 2 wickets taken

If less than 8 hours remain at the start, the winning side received 10 pts, but no bonus points are awarded

1969

		P	W	L	D	Bat	Bowl	Pts
1	Glamorgan	24	11	0	13	67	73	250
2	Gloucestershire	24	10	6	8	26	93	219
3	Surrey	24	7	1	16	64	76	210
4	Warwickshire	24	7	3	14	41	89	205
5	Hampshire	24	6	7	11	56	87	203
6	Essex	24	6	6	12	44	85	189
7	Sussex	24	5	8	11	46	89	185
8	Nottinghamshire	24	6	2	16	49	75	184
9	Northamptonshire	24	5	7	12	47	66	163
10	Kent	24	4	6	14	35	76	151
11	Middlesex	24	3	7	14	40	76	146
12	Worcestershire	24	5	7	12*	30	62	142
13	Yorkshire	24	3	6	15	30	77	142
14	Leicestershire	24	4	7	13	26	64	130
15	Lancashire	24	2	1	21	39	67	126
16	Derbyshire	24	3	5	16*	22	67	119
17	Somerset	24	1	9	14	17	69	96

*Includes one match abandoned without a ball bowled

Warwicks and Yorks obtained 5 pts in drawn matches with the scores level

1970

		P	W	L	D	Bat	Bowl	Pts
1	Kent	24	9	5	10	70	77	237
2	Glamorgan	24	9	6	9	48	82	220
3	Lancashire	24	6	2	16	78	78	216
4	Yorkshire	24	8	5	11	49	86	215
5	Surrey	24	6	4	14	60	83	203
6	Worcestershire	24	7	1	16	46	84	200
7	Derbyshire	24	7	7	10	51	78	199
	Warwickshire	24	7	6	11	53	71	199

1970 continued

		P	W	L	D	Bat	Bowl	Pts
9	Sussex	24	5	7	12	62	87	199
10	Hampshire	24	4	6	14	69	88	197
11	Nottinghamshire	24	4	8	12	71	73	184
12	Essex	24	4	6	14	64	76	180
13	Somerset	24	5	10	9	40	86	176
14	Northamptonshire	24	4	6	14	60	74	174
15	Leicestershire	24	5	6	13	46	77	173
16	Middlesex	24	5	5	14	47	69	166
17	Gloucestershire	24	3	8	13	56	80	166

Warwicks obtained 5 pts in a drawn match with the scores level

1971

		P	W	L	D	Bat	Bowl	Pts
1	Surrey	24	11	3	10	63	82	255
2	Warwickshire	24	9	9	6	73	92	255
3	Lancashire	24	9	4	11	76	75	241
4	Kent	24	7	6	11	82	82	234
5	Leicestershire	24	6	2	16	76	74	215
6	Middlesex	24	7	6	11	61	81	212
7	Somerset	24	7	4	13	50	89	209
8	Gloucestershire	24	7	3	13	50	81	201
9	Hampshire	24	4	6	14	70	82	192
10	Essex	24	6	5	13	43	84	187
11	Sussex	24	5	9	10	55	77	182
12	Nottinghamshire	24	3	7	14	58	83	171
13	Yorkshire	24	4	8	12	47	75	162
14	Northamptonshire	24	4	8	12	36	83	159
15	Worcestershire	24	3	7	14	46	76	152
16	Glamorgan	24	3	5	15	55	63	148
17	Derbyshire	24	1	4	19	51	81	142

Leics obtained 5 pts in a drawn match with the scores level. The Gloucs v Glamorgan match was abandoned without a ball being bowled

Surrey were awarded the title, having won more matches than Warwicks

1972

		P	W	L	D	Bat	Bowl	Pts
1	Warwickshire	20	9	0	11	68	69	227
2	Kent	20	7	4	9	69	52	191
3	Gloucestershire	20	7	4	9	38	77	185
4	Northamptonshire	20	7	3	10	34	77	181
5	Essex	20	6	4	10	50	63	173
6	Leicestershire	20	6	2	12	43	68	171
7	Worcestershire	20	4	4	12	59	68	167
8	Middlesex	20	5	5	10	48	61	159
9	Hampshire	20	4	6	10	50	64	154
10	Yorkshire	20	4	5	11	39	73	152
11	Somerset	20	4	2	14	34	71	145
12	Surrey	20	3	5	12	49	61	140
13	Glamorgan	20	1	7	12	55	61	126
14	Nottinghamshire	20	1	6	13	38	73	121
15	Lancashire	19	2	3	14	42	56	118
16	Sussex	20	2	8	10	46	49	115
17	Derbyshire	19	1	5	13	27	60	97

The match Derbys v Lancs at Buxton was abandoned without a ball being bowled and is not included above

1973

		P	W	L	D	T	Bat	Bowl	Pts
1	Hampshire	20	10	0	10	0	84	81	265
2	Surrey	20	9	3	8	0	71	73	234
3	Northamptonshire	20	8	4	8	0	53	75	208
4	Kent	20	4	3	13	0	98	59	197
5	Gloucestershire	19	6	4	9	0	63	70	193
6	Worcestershire	20	6	4	10	0	56	75	191
7	Warwickshire	20	5	5	10	0	74	62	186
8	Essex	20	6	5	9	0	46	72	178
9	Leicestershire	19	4	3	12	0	66	60	166
10	Somerset	20	7	2	11	0	29	60	159
11	Glamorgan	20	4	8	8	0	44	68	152
12	Lancashire	20	4	6	10	0	44	67	151

	P	W	L	D	T	Bat	Bowl	Pts
13 Middlesex	20	4	5	10	1	49	54	148
14 Yorkshire	20	3	5	11	1	28	69	132
15 Sussex	20	2	10	8	0	42	67	129
16 Derbyshire	20	2	10	8	0	15	67	102
17 Nottinghamshire	20	1	8	11	0	28	63	101

The match Gloucs v Leics at Bristol was abandoned without a ball being bowled and is not included above. Additional bonus points were awarded for scoring 75 runs within the first 25 overs and 150 runs within the first 50 overs

1974

	P	W	L	D	T	Bat	Bowl	Pts
1 Worcestershire	20	11	3	6	0	45	72	227
2 Hampshire	19	10	3	6	0	55	70	225
3 Northamptonshire	20	9	2	9	0	46	67	203
4 Leicestershire	20	7	7	6	0	47	69	186
5 Somerset	20	6	4	10	0	49	72	181
6 Middlesex	20	7	5	8	0	45	56	171
7 Surrey	20	6	4	10	0	42	69	171
8 Lancashire	20	5	0	15	0	47	66	163
9 Warwickshire	20	5	5	10	0	44	65	159
10 Kent	20	5	8	7	0	33	63	146
11 Yorkshire	19	4	7	8	0	37	69	146
12 Essex	20	4	3	12	1	44	52	141
13 Sussex	20	4	9	6	1	29	63	137
14 Gloucestershire	19	4	9	6	0	29	55	124
15 Nottinghamshire	20	1	9	10	0	42	66	118
16 Glamorgan	19	2	7	10	0	28	56	104
17 Derbyshire	20	1	6	13	0	23	62	95

The matches Hants v Yorks at Bournemouth and Gloucs v Glamorgan at Bristol were abandoned without a ball being bowled and are not included above

The method of obtaining bonus points was altered as follows: batting: 1 pt for scoring 150 to 199, 2 pts for 200 to 249, 3 pts for 250 to 299, 4 pts for over 300; bowling: 1 pt for 3 or 4 wkts, 2 pts for 5 or 6 wkts, 3 pts for 7 or 8 wkts, 4 pts for 9 or 10 wkts. These points can only be obtained during the first 100 overs of each first innings

1975

	P	W	L	D	Bat	Bowl	Pts
1 Leicestershire	20	12	1	7	61	59	240
2 Yorkshire	20	10	1	9	56	68	224
3 Hampshire	20	10	6	4	51	72	223
4 Lancashire	20	9	3	8	57	72	219
5 Kent	20	8	4	8	59	70	209
6 Surrey	20	8	3	9	55	67	202
7 Essex	20	7	6	7	61	67	198
8 Northamptonshire	20	7	9	4	40	72	182
9 Glamorgan	20	7	8	5	45	66	181
10 Worcestershire	20	5	6	9	55	63	168
11 Middlesex	20	6	7	7	45	59	164
12 Somerset	20	4	8	8	51	65	156
13 Nottinghamshire	20	3	9	8	59	67	156
14 Warwickshire	20	4	10	6	48	65	153
15 Derbyshire	20	5	7	8	33	69	152
16 Gloucestershire	20	4	10	6	43	62	145
17 Sussex	20	2	13	5	37	62	119

1976

	P	W	L	D	Bat	Bowl	Pts
1 Middlesex	20	11	5	4	57	67	234
2 Northamptonshire	20	9	3	8	54	74	218
3 Gloucestershire	19	9	5	5	54	66	210
4 Leicestershire	20	9	3	8	51	68	209
5 Warwickshire	20	6	7	7	65	70	195
6 Essex	20	7	4	9	57	62	189
7 Somerset	20	7	5	8	47	63	180
8 Yorkshire	20	6	6	8	49	67	176
9 Surrey	20	6	4	10	54	61	175
10 Sussex	20	5	8	7	49	71	170
11 Worcestershire	19	6	3	10	50	59	169
12 Hampshire	20	4	10	6	52	67	159
13 Nottinghamshire	20	4	7	9	58	60	158

	P	W	L	D	Bat	Bowl	Pts
14 Kent	20	5	7	8	48	57	155
15 Derbyshire	20	4	7	9	39	70	149
16 Lancashire	20	3	7	10	43	75	148
17 Glamorgan	20	3	10	7	37	60	127

The match Gloucs v Worcs at Bristol was abandoned without a ball being bowled and is not included above

1977

	P	W	L	D	Bat	Bowl	Pts
1 Middlesex	22	9	5	8	43	76	227
Kent	21	9	2	10	54	65	227
3 Gloucestershire	20	9	5	6	44	70	222
4 Somerset	21	6	4	11	58	64	194
5 Leicestershire	22	6	4	12	44	73	189
6 Essex	21	7	5	9	38	65	187
7 Derbyshire	21	7	3	11	38	64	186
8 Sussex	22	6	5	11	52	60	184
9 Northamptonshire	20	6	6	8	43	68	183
10 Warwickshire	22	4	8	10	61	72	181
11 Hampshire	22	6	5	11	53	54	179
12 Yorkshire	21	6	5	10	36	63	171
13 Worcestershire	22	5	10	7	29	55	144
14 Glamorgan	21	3	7	11	36	60	132
Surrey	21	3	6	12	42	54	132
16 Lancashire	21	2	4	15	36	57	117
17 Nottinghamshire	22	1	11	10	34	52	98

The matches Gloucs v Northants at Gloucester, Somerset v Derbys at Taunton, Northants v Glamorgan at Northampton, Essex v Kent at Colchester, Gloucs v Yorks at Bristol and Lancs v Surrey at Manchester were all abandoned without a ball being bowled and are not included above. 12 pts were awarded for a win in place of 10 pts, otherwise no change

1978

	P	W	L	D	Bat	Bowl	Pts
1 Kent	22	13	3	6	56	80	292
2 Essex	22	12	1	9	55	74	273
3 Middlesex	21	11	5	5	48	75	255
4 Yorkshire	22	10	3	9	58	55	233
5 Somerset	22	9	4	9	44	76	228
6 Leicestershire	22	4	5	13	57	68	173
7 Nottinghamshire	22	3	7	12	63	67	166
8 Hampshire	21	4	6	11	53	60	161
9 Sussex	22	4	7	11	39	64	151*
10 Gloucestershire	21	4	8	9	42	55	145
11 Warwickshire	22	4	5	13	39	56	143
12 Lancashire	21	4	8	9	28	59	135*
13 Glamorgan	22	3	8	11	43	54	133
14 Derbyshire	22	3	7	12	33	63	132
15 Worcestershire	22	2	5	15	56	51	131
16 Surrey	22	3	7	12	36	58	130
17 Northamptonshire	20	2	6	12	41	56	121

*Six points deducted for breach of regulations

The matches Gloucs v Northants at Bristol, Middx v Hants at Lord's and Lancs v Northants at Manchester were abandoned without a ball being bowled and are not included above

1979

	P	W	L	D	Bat	Bowl	Pts
1 Essex	21	13	4	4	56	69	281
2 Worcestershire	21	7	4	10	58	62	204
3 Surrey	21	6	3	12	50	70	192
4 Sussex	20	6	4	10	47	65	184
5 Kent	22	6	3	13	49	60	181
6 Leicestershire	21	4	5	12	60	68	176
7 Yorkshire	21	5	3	13	52	63	175
8 Somerset	21	5	1	15	56	53	171
9 Nottinghamshire	19	6	4	9	43	54	169
10 Gloucestershire	20	5	4	11	53	54	167
11 Northamptonshire	21	3	6	12	59	58	153
12 Hampshire	21	3	9	9	39	66	141
13 Lancashire	22	4	4	14	37	55	140

1979 *continued*

		P	W	L	D	Bat	Bowl	Pts
	Middlesex	20	3	3	14	44	60	140
15	Warwickshire	21	3	7	11	46	51	133
16	Derbyshire	21	1	6	14	46	60	118
17	Glamorgan	21	0	10	11	35	58	93

The matches Sussex v Gloucs at Hove, Derbys v Notts at Derby, Gloucs v Somerset at Bristol, Middx v Sussex at Lord's, Northants v Glamorgan at Northampton, Surrey v Essex at The Oval, Warwicks v Worcs at Edgbaston, Yorks v Notts at Sheffield, Leics v Hants at Leicester and Middx v Notts at Lord's were all abandoned without a ball being bowled and are not included above

The number of points awarded for a tie and to the side batting last in a drawn match with the scores level was increased from 5 to 6

1980

		P	W	L	D	Bat	Bowl	Pts
						Bonus Pts		
1	Middlesex	22	10	2	10	58	80	258
2	Surrey	22	10	4	8	51	74	245
3	Nottinghamshire	22	6	5	11	42	64	178
4	Sussex	22	4	3	15	60	60	168
5	Somerset	21	3	5	13	56	70	168
6	Yorkshire	22	4	3	15	51	64	163
7	Gloucestershire	21	4	5	12	39	74	161
8	Essex	22	4	3	15	48	64	160
9	Derbyshire	20	4	3	13	47	62	157
	Leicestershire	22	4	2	16	45	58	157
11	Worcestershire	21	3	7	11	54	61	151
12	Northamptonshire	22	5	4	13	41	47	148
13	Glamorgan	21	4	4	13	43	57	148
14	Warwickshire	22	3	4	15	55	54	145
15	Lancashire	20	4	3	13	26	58	132
16	Kent	22	2	8	12	36	59	119
17	Hampshire	22	1	10	11	34	56	102

Leics and Sussex both obtained 6 pts in a drawn match, which ended with the scores level. The matches Glamorgan v Worcs at Swansea, Gloucs v Derbys at Bristol, Somerset v Lancs at Bath and Derbys v Lancs at Buxton were abandoned without a ball being bowled and are not included above

1981

		P	W	L	D	Bat	Bowl	Pts
						Bonus Pts		
1	Nottinghamshire	22	11	4	7	56	72	304
2	Sussex	22	11	3	8	58	68	302
3	Somerset	22	10	2	10	54	65	279
4	Middlesex	22	9	3	10	49	64	257
5	Essex	22	8	4	10	62	64	254
6	Surrey	22	7	5	10	52	72	236
7	Hampshire	22	6	7	9	45	65	206
8	Leicestershire	22	6	6	10	45	58	199
9	Kent	22	5	7	10	51	58	189
10	Yorkshire	22	5	9	8	41	66	187
11	Worcestershire	22	5	9	8	44	52	172
12	Derbyshire	22	4	7	11	51	57	172
13	Gloucestershire	22	4	3	15	51	55	170
14	Glamorgan	22	3	10	9	50	69	167
15	Northamptonshire	22	3	6	13	51	67	166
16	Lancashire	22	4	7	11	47	57	164
17	Warwickshire	22	2	11	9	56	47	135

The number of points awarded for a win increased to 16. Worcestershire and Lancashire win totals include 12 points for win in one-innings match

1982

		P	W	L	D	Bat	Bowl	Pts
						Bonus Pts		
1	Middlesex	22	12	2	8	59	74	325
2	Leicestershire	22	10	4	8	57	69	286
3	Hampshire	22	8	6	8	48	74	250
4	Nottinghamshire	22	7	7	8	44	65	221
5	Surrey	22	6	6	10	56	62	214
6	Somerset	22	6	6	10	51	66	213
7	Essex	22	5	5	12	57	75	212
8	Sussex	22	6	7	9	43	68	207
9	Northamptonshire	22	5	3	14	61	54	195
10	Yorkshire	22	5	1	16	48	51	179

1982 *continued*

		P	W	L	D	Bat	Bowl	Pts
11	Derbyshire	22	4	3	15	45	64	173
12	Lancashire	22	4	3	15	48	55	167
13	Kent	22	3	4	15	55	63	166
14	Worcestershire	22	3	5	14	43	54	141
15	Gloucestershire	22	2	9	11	46	55	133
16	Glamorgan	22	1	8	13	43	60	119
17	Warwickshire	22	0	8	14	58	53	111

Worcestershire total includes 12 pts from a match reduced to one innings

Currie Cup

The South African equivalent of the County Championship has been competed for by the major South African teams since 1889–90. In 1951–52 the Competition was divided into two sections A and B. In 1960–61 it was restored to one section only, but returned to two in 1962–63. For one season only (1978–79) the Section B was divided into two groups, one containing Section A Second Teams and the other the Section B First Teams.

Holders of the Cup are as follows:

1889–90	Transvaal	1950–51	Transvaal
1890–91	Kimberley	1951–52	Natal
1892–93	Western Province	1952–53	Western Province
1893–94	Western Province	1954–55	Natal
1894–95	Transvaal	1955–56	Western Province
1896–97	Western Province	1958–59	Transvaal
1897–98	Western Province	1959–60	Natal
1902–03	Transvaal	1960–61	Natal
1903–04	Transvaal	1962–63	Natal
1904–05	Transvaal	1963–64	Natal
1906–07	Transvaal	1965–66	Natal, Transvaal
1908–09	Western Province	1966–67	Natal
1910–11	Natal	1967–68	Natal
1912–13	Natal	1968–69	Transvaal
1920–21	Western Province	1969–70	Transvaal,
1921–22	Natal, Transvaal,		Western Province
	Western Province	1970–71	Transvaal
1923–24	Transvaal	1971–72	Transvaal
1925–26	Transvaal	1972–73	Transvaal
1926–27	Transvaal	1973–74	Natal
1929–30	Transvaal	1974–75	Western Province
1931–32	Western Province	1975–76	Natal
1933–34	Natal	1976–77	Natal
1934–35	Transvaal	1977–78	Western Province
1936–37	Natal	1978–79	Transvaal
1937–38	Natal, Transvaal	1979–80	Transvaal
1946–47	Natal	1980–81	Natal
1947–48	Natal	1981–82	Western Province

Section B Winners are as follows:

1951–52	Orange Free State	1969–70	Transvaal B
1952–53	Transvaal	1970–71	Rhodesia
1954–55	Eastern Province	1971–72	Northern Transvaal
1955–56	Rhodesia	1972–73	Transvaal B
1958–59	Border	1973–73	Natal B
1959–60	Eastern Province,	1974–75	Transvaal B
	Transvaal B	1975–76	Orange Free State
1962–63	Transvaal B	1976–77	Transvaal B
1963–64	Rhodesia	1977–78	Northern Transvaal
1965–66	NE Transvaal	1978–79	Northern Transvaal
1966–67	NE Transvaal	1979–80	Natal B
1967–68	Rhodesia	1980–81	Western Province B
1968–69	Western Province	1981–82	Boland

Note: The Competition was not usually held in seasons when Test-playing touring teams visited South Africa.

Since 1977–78 Section B has been known as the Castle Bowl.

In 1978–79 Transvaal B won the 'President's Competition' for Section A Second Elevens – the only season it was held.

Debuts

Most runs in first first-class innings W F E Marx scored 240 on his debut in first-class cricket, playing for Transvaal *v* Griqualand West at Johannesburg in 1920–21. The English record is 215* by G H G Doggart for Cambridge U *v* Lancashire at Fenner's, May 3, 1948; he batted nearly 6 hours. The innings of 227 by T Marsden on July 24 and 25, 1826 for Sheffield and Leicester *v* Nottingham at Darnall, Sheffield, should also be noted.

Most wickets in an innings on first-class debut A E Moss is the only bowler to take all ten wickets (in an 11-a-side match) on his first-class debut, for Canterbury *v* Wellington, December 27 and 28, 1889 at Christchurch, New Zealand. His figures were 32.1-10-28-10.

F Hinds also took 10 wickets (for 36) on his debut for A B H Hill's XII *v* Trinidad (Port of Spain) 1900–01 (this was a 12-a-side match).

The best return in English first-class cricket is 35.2-?-29-9 by James Lillywhite jun for Sussex *v* MCC at Lord's, June 16 and 17, 1862. In the whole match Lillywhite took 14 for 57. J H Kirwan also took 9 wkts on his debut for Cambridge U in 1836, but his analysis is not yet known.

Most runs in debut season H Sutcliffe of Yorkshire hit 1,839 runs (av 44.85) in his first season in first-class cricket, which was 1919. There is little doubt, however, that but for the First World War 1914–18, he would have made his debut earlier.

Most wickets in debut season W Rhodes of Yorkshire took 154 wickets (av 14.60) in his first season in first-class cricket, which was 1898. Though this is the record, mention must be made of A G Steel, who played in a single match in 1877 and then the following year took 164 wickets (av 9.40) for Cambridge University and Lancashire.

Declarations

The Laws of Cricket were altered to permit declarations in 1889, and the first match in first-class cricket in which a captain (J Shuter) declared was Surrey *v* Gloucestershire at the Oval, June 6, 7 and 8, 1889. The first declaration in Australian first-class cricket did not occur until November 7, 9, 10 and 11, 1903 when P F Warner declared the MCC innings closed *v* South Australia at Adelaide. In 1931 there was a spate of contrived declarations in order to get the full 15 points awarded for an outright win. The first of these declarations took place at Bramall Lane, Sheffield when the first two days of the match were washed out. On the third morning B H Lyon (Gloucester captain) declared after one ball, then F E Greenwood (Yorkshire captain) followed suit. The two second innings were then played out.

Defeats

The most defeats of a county in a single year in first-class matches are 21 by Warwickshire in 1921. In County Championship matches only, this dubious honour goes jointly to Glamorgan in 1925 and Nottinghamshire in 1961 with 20 defeats.

The worst record in modern times by a first-class team would appear to be held by Jammu and Kashmir, who, between 1959–60 and 1981–82 have played 95 first-class matches, lost 87 and drawn 8, therefore have yet to win – only once have they achieved even a first innings lead!

Denmark

The first reported cricket match took place at Randers in Jutland in 1865, though it is believed that cricket was played in Denmark in a haphazard manner for perhaps 60 years prior to this.

The first international match played by Denmark and recognised by the Danish Cricket Association took place in Copenhagen in 1932 against Sir Julien Cahn's team.

The records in Danish domestic cricket are:

Highest team total 562 Hjorring *v* Viborg. 1936
Highest individual innings 252* Ove Jensen for B.93 *v* Naestved. 1951
Best bowling in innings 10–9 S A Hansen, Kerteminde *v* Kolding. 1957
Best bowling in match 18–102 Herluf Hansen, Horsens *v* Olympia. 1944
Highest wicket partnership 1st wkt 294 K B Rieck, E Knudsen. Zealand *v* Fyn. 1949

G H G Doggart made 215 not out in his first-class debut for Cambridge University against Lancashire in 1948, an English record.

Pelham Warner, the MCC captain, was the first man to declare an innings closed in Australia.

Denmark took part in the 1979 ICC Trophy and were very successful, winning their group with victories in all four matches. They were however beaten by Sri Lanka in the semi-finals.

Derbyshire

In September 1757 Wirksworth played Sheffield at Brampton Moor, near Chesterfield, the first mention of cricket in the county.

Formation of the county club   For many years the principal cricket club in the county was the South Derbyshire Club, which dates from at least 1836; the present County Club was formed on November 4 1870 at a meeting held in the Guildhall, Derby.

First-class status   The first match recognised as first-class by contemporary opinion was played against Lancashire at Old Trafford on May 26 and 27, 1871; at the close of the 1887 season however some leading sports journalists ceased to rank Derbyshire matches as first-class and by the close of 1888 this demotion had been accepted by every authority. Derbyshire resumed as a first-class county at the start of 1894.

Grounds   The County Ground on the Racecourse at Derby has been the principal venue for first-class county matches since 1871, though the exact location of the square on the ground has been altered twice.

Other towns to stage first-class county matches are: Chesterfield (at Saltergate 1874–75; at Queen's Park since 1898); Wirksworth 1874; Long Eaton (Recreation Ground 1887; only JPL matches at Trent College); Glossop 1899–1910; Blackwell 1909–13; Burton-on-Trent (at three different grounds since 1922); Buxton (1923–1976); Ilkeston (1925 to date) and at Abbeydale Park, Dore 1946–47 (now used by Yorkshire).

Honours   The County have won the County Championship once (in 1936), though in some publications they are erroneously credited with winning in 1874 as well. In 1981 they won the NatWest Cup. The best performance in the John Player League is third in 1970 and in the Benson and Hedges Cup they were the beaten finalists in 1978.

The players   D C Morgan, who appeared for the county from 1950 to 1969, has made the most appearances, playing in 540 matches. The longest serving captain is G R Jackson, who led the side for 9 seasons between 1922 and 1930. The youngest cricketer to appear is F W Swarbrook who played against Cambridge University in 1967, when he was 16 yrs and 6 months and the oldest cricketer was H Elliott who was 55 years and 9 months when he played against Warwickshire in 1947.

The cricketer to gain the most England caps whilst being on the County staff is R W Taylor (42 to end of 1982 season).

Team performances   The highest totals both for and against the County occurred in 1898; on August 1 and 2 at Derby, the county hit 645 against Hampshire and at Chesterfield on August 18 and 19, Yorkshire scored 662 off the county attack. In the latter match J T Brown and J Tunnicliffe put on 554 for the first Yorkshire wicket, creating a new world first-class record.

The lowest total for the County is 16 on July 10 and 11, 1879 against Notts at Trent Bridge; the innings lasted 50 minutes. The lowest against the county is 23 by Hampshire at Burton-on-Trent on August 14, 1958; Hampshire were all out for 55 in their second innings. Derbyshire dismissed Notts for 14 at Wirksworth in 1873, but this was an odds match, Derbyshire having 16 players against Notts' eleven.

Individual performances   G Davidson's innings of 274 against Lancashire at Old Trafford on August 10 and 11, 1896, is the highest for the county, whilst the highest against is 343 not out by P A Perrin of Essex at Chesterfield on July 18, 1904. Perrin batted 345 minutes and hit 68 fours.

Ten wickets in an innings has been achieved twice for Derbyshire, by W Bestwick at a cost of 40 runs v Glamorgan at Cardiff Arms Park on June 20, 1921 and by T B Mitchell, at a cost of 64 runs v Leicestershire at Aylestone Rd, Leicester on June 15 and 17, 1935.

Only T F Smailes of Yorkshire has achieved this feat against Derbyshire – 10 for 74 at Bramall Lane, Sheffield on June 27, 1939.

Best bowling performance in a match is 17 wkts for 103 runs by W Mycroft against Hampshire on July 24 and 25, 1876 at the Antelope Ground, Southampton; G Giffen took 16 for 101 for the Australians at Derby on June 7 and 8, 1886.

Only D B Carr has hit over 2,000 runs in a season for the county – he totalled 2,165 in 1959. D Smith scored 1,000 runs in a season on 12 occasions between 1931 and 1950.

Above   *The County Ground at Queen's Park, Chesterfield, with the well-known crooked spire behind the trees.*

Left   *D C Morgan's 540 appearances from 1950 to 1969 is the most for Derbyshire.*

The most wickets in a season for Derbyshire is 168 by T B Mitchell in 1935; other bowlers to take 150 are W H Copson (153, 1936), C Gladwin (151, 1952) and H L Jackson (150, 1960). Gladwin took 100 wickets in a season on 12 occasions between 1946 and 1958.

D Smith with 20,516 runs (average 31.41) is the only player to top 20,000 runs in his career, but two bowlers have taken over 1,500 wickets, H L Jackson with 1,670 (average 17.11) and C Gladwin 1,536 (average 17.67).

Wicket partnerships   The highest stands in first-class matches for the county are:

1st	322	H Storer, J Bowden v Essex (*Derby*)	1929
2nd	349	C S Elliott, J D Eggar v Notts (*Trent Bridge*)	1947
3rd	291	P N Kirsten, D S Steele v Somerset (*Taunton*)	1981
4th	328	P Vaulkhard, D Smith v Notts (*Trent Bridge*)	1946
5th	203	C P Wilkins, I R Buxton v Lancs (*Old Trafford*)	1971
6th	212	G M Lee, T S Worthington v Essex (*Chesterfield*)	1932
7th	241	G H Pope, A E G Rhodes v Hants (*Portsmouth*)	1948
8th	182	W Carter, A H M Jackson v Leics (*Aylestone Rd, Leics*) 1922	
9th	283	J Chapman, A Warren v Warwicks (*Blackwell*)	1910
10th	93	J Humphries, J Horsley v Lancs (*Derby*)	1914

The 283 by Chapman and Warren created a new world first-class record, which still stands. Derbyshire had followed on, no less than 242 behind on the first innings, and when Chapman came in at no. 10, Derbyshire were 131 for 8, still needing 111 to avoid an innings defeat. The pair batted just 175 minutes to establish the record – Warren hit 123, his only first-class hundred, and Chapman 165. Owing to lameness, Warren could not take quick singles.

Limited Overs Cricket Records

GILLETTE/NATWEST CUP
Highest team total   250–9 v Hampshire (*Bournemouth*)   1963
Lowest team total   79 v Surrey (*Oval*)   1967
Highest innings   110* P N Kirsten v Hants (*Southampton*)   1982
Best bowling   6–18 T J P Eyre v Sussex (*Chesterfield*)   1969
JOHN PLAYER LEAGUE
Highest team total   260–6 v Gloucs (*Derby*)   1972
Lowest team total   70 v Surrey (*Derby*)   1972
Highest innings   120 A Hill v Northants (*Buxton*)   1976
Best bowling   6–7 M Hendrick v Notts (*Trent Bridge*)   1972
BENSON AND HEDGES CUP
Highest team total   284 v Worcestershire (*Worcester*)   1982
Lowest team total   102 v Yorks (*Bradford*)   1975
Highest innings   111* P J Sharpe v Glam (*Chesterfield*)   1976
Best bowling   6–33 E J Barlow v Gloucs (*Bristol*)   1978

In 1938 Arthur Fagg of Kent scored a double century in each innings against Essex – the only occasion this feat has been performed.

The Double
The feat of scoring 1,000 runs and taking 100 wickets in first-class cricket in an English season has not been performed since 1967 due to the reduction in the number of first-class matches.

The Middlesex all-rounder F J Titmus was the last to accomplish the feat.

(*See also All-round Records*)

Double Centuries
The first recorded instance of a batsman making 200 runs in a single innings took place at Lord's on July 24, 1820 when W Ward hit 278 for MCC v Norfolk.

Most double centuries in first-class matches in one season are 6 by D G Bradman during 1930. Bradman also holds the record for the most in a first-class career with 37, though he is closely followed by W R Hammond with 36 – no other batsman can claim even 25.

A E Fagg scored 244 and 202* for Kent v Essex at Colchester in 1938 – the only instance of a batsman hitting two double centuries in one match.

Draws
The record number of draws in a single season in first-class matches was 26 by Nottinghamshire in 1967 and in the same year Notts also broke the record for the most draws in County Championship matches. The last time a County went through its first-class programme without a single drawn game was in 1955, when Surrey played 34 matches, won 27 and lost 7 – Surrey played 28 Championship matches.

Dublin University
Dublin University sent a team to England in 1895 and played Leicestershire and Cambridge University. The latter sent a team to Dublin for a return match later in the season, as did the MCC, and these four games were regarded as first-class. In the 1920s, Dublin University played five more first-class matches, the last taking place in 1926.

The University had opposed first-class counties since 1889, when Lancashire were met and the reasoning behind the granting of first-class status to some Dublin University matches, but not others is, to say the least, muddled.

The first-class records for the University are:
Highest team total   274 v Leics (*Leicester*)   1895
Lowest team total   58 v Northants (*Northampton*)   1926
Highest individual innings   153* L H Gwynn v Leics (*Leicester*) 1895
Best bowling in innings   6–42 T H Dixon v Jupp's XI (*Dublin*) 1926

Duleep Trophy

The Trophy was instituted in 1961–62 and is competed for by the five Indian Zones – North, South, East, West and Central – on a knock-out basis. The Trophy is named after K S Duleepsinhji, the Sussex and England batsman.

Holders of the Trophy

1961–62	West	1968–69	West	1975–76	South
1962–63	West	1969–70	West	1976–77	West
1963–64	West	1970–71	South	1977–78	West
1964–65	West	1971–72	Central	1978–79	North
1965–66	South	1972–73	West	1979–80	North
1966–67	South	1973–74	North	1980–81	West
1967–68	South	1974–75	South	1981–82	West

The leading records in the Trophy are:

Highest team total 555 West v Central (*Bombay*) 1964–65
Lowest team total 48 North v South (*Madras*) 1961–62; and 48 East v South (*Calcutta*) 1968–69
Highest individual innings 229 A L Wadekar West v East (*Calcutta*) 1964–65
Best bowling in innings 9–55 B P Gupte West v South (*Calcutta*) 1962–3

England

First reference to cricket The first mention of cricket in England was in 1300 in Kent and the first definite mention of a match in England was in the same county in 1646 (see under 'Kent' for details).

First match by England The first match in which a team styled 'England' took part was against Kent on July 9, 1739 on Bromley Common, a return game being played on the Artillery Ground, London on July 23.

The team called 'England' was of necessity actually 'The Rest of England'.

The first match by a team representing England outside the British Isles took place on September 24 and 26, 1859 at Montreal, Canada, against XXII of Lower Canada. England won by 8 wickets.

The first eleven-a-side match between an England side and an overseas team took place on January 15 and 16, 1877 on the Albert Ground, Sydney against New South Wales and the first international match eleven-a-side against an overseas team was played on the Melbourne Cricket Ground on March 15, 16, 17 and 19, 1877 when England opposed Australia in what is now called the 'First Test Match'.

The first international match in England against an overseas country took place at the Oval on September 6, 7 and 8, 1880 against Australia.

First first-class match in England Throughout this book, the game between England and Surrey played at Lord's on June 24 and 25, 1801 has been taken as the first first-class match for the purpose of compiling 'first-class' records, but other compilers have argued that other dates have an equal claim. Detailed discussion on the status of matches in the British Isles can be found in 'The Guides to Important and First-class Matches' published by the Association of Cricket Statisticians.

Records in England

(where a non-first-class feat holds the record, the first-class record is given immediately below)
Highest team total 920 Orleans Club v Rickling Green (*Rickling Green*) 1882
903–7d England v Australia (*Oval*) 1938
Lowest team total 0 There are a number of instances of sides being dismissed for 0; the first known occurred in Norfolk in 1815
6 Bs v England (*Lord's*) 1810
Highest individual innings 628* A E J Collins, Clark's House v North Town (*Clifton*) 1899
424 A C MacLaren, Lancs v Somerset (*Taunton*) 1895
Best bowling in innings 10–0 First Instance: A Dartnell, Broad Green v Thornton Heath (*Norbury*) 1867
10–10 H Verity, Yorks v Notts (*Headingley*) 1932
Best bowling in innings (with more than eleven players) All 17 (for 58) against XVIII of Hallam (*Hallam*) by R C Tinley 1860

Dublin University played first-class cricket until 1926. L H Gwynn, with 153 not out against Leicestershire in 1895, played their highest innings.

Best bowling in match 20–37 W White, Hughenden v Woodcroft (*Bristol*) 1921
19–90 J C Laker, England v Australia (*Old Trafford*) 1956

Wicket Partnerships

1st 555 P Holmes, H Sutcliffe. Yorks v Essex (*Leyton*) 1932
2nd 605 A H Trevor, G F Vernon. Orleans v Rickling Green (*Rickling Green*) 1882
465* J A Jameson, R B Kanhai. Warwicks v Gloucs (*Edgbaston*) 1974
3rd 454 W Barnes, W E Midwinter. MCC v Leics (*Lord's*) 1882
424* W J Edrich, D C S Compton. Middx v Somerset (*Lord's*) 1948
4th 470 A I Kallicharran, G W Humpage. Warwickshire v Lancashire (*Southport*) 1982
5th 393 E G Arnold, W B Burns. Worcs v Warwicks (*Edgbaston*) 1909
6th 428 W W Armstrong, M A Noble. Australians v Sussex (*Hove*) 1902
7th 344 K S Ranjitsinhji, W Newham. Sussex v Essex (*Leyton*) 1902

8th 292 R Peel, Lord Hawke. Yorks v Warwicks (*Edgbaston*) 1896

9th 293 E A C Druce, V P Johnstone. Trinity Wand v Eastbourne (*Eastbourne*) 1900

283 J Chapman, A Warren. Derbys v Warwicks (*Blackwell*) 1910

10th 249 C T Sarwate, S N Banerjee. Indians v Surrey (*Oval*) 1946

Epsom

From 1814 to 1819 when there was no organised Surrey Eleven, the Epsom Club played matches against Sussex and Hampshire which were regarded as among the most important contests of the time. In a five-day match at Lord's in 1816, Epsom beat Sussex in spite of the fact that Sussex were reinforced by two given men in G Osbaldeston and W Lambert, the best cricketers of the day. In the same fixture the following year over 1,000 runs were scored in all, which created a new record (1,047) and in the same match W Lambert scored a century in each innings, the first time this feat had been performed in an important match.

Essex

On Thursday July 6, 1732 on Epping Forest, London played a combined Essex and Hertfordshire team, the first reference to a match in the county.

Formation of the County Club The first reference to an Essex County Club is a handbill dated 1790, which gives a list of members and the days of meeting of 'Essex Cricket Club'; the headquarters are named as the Green Man, Navestock. In the late 18th century however there was a very powerful club based at Hornchurch. This side played MCC, Kent and Middlesex and is described usually as Hornchurch, but occasionally as Essex. There are several other references to 'Essex' before the formation of the present County Club, which took place at the Shire Hall, Chelmsford on January 14, 1876.

First-class status Essex were members of the Second Class Counties Competition from 1888 to 1893 and the county's first match in first-class cricket took place at Leyton on May 14, 15 and 16, 1894 against Leicestershire.

Grounds The original County ground in 1876 was at Brentwood, but in 1885, the County headquarters moved to the Lyttelton Ground in Leyton. The present County Ground however is at New Writtle St, Chelmsford, which staged its first first-class match in 1925.

Other grounds used at present by the county are: Castle Park, Colchester (since 1914); Valentine's Park, Ilford (since 1923); Southchurch Park, Southend (since 1906).

Grounds that have staged first-class matches are: Old County Ground, Brentwood (1922–69); RHP Ground, Chelmsford (1959–61); Vista Road Ground, Clacton-on-Sea (1931–66); Garrison Ground, Colchester (1920–72); Sportscentre, Harlow (1970); Lyttelton Ground, Leyton (1894–1977); Gidea Park, Romford (1950–68); Chalkwell Park, Westcliff-on-Sea (1934–76).

Honours The County have won the County Championship and the Benson and Hedges Cup once each – both in 1979; also the John Player League once – in 1981. They reached the semi-finals of the Gillette/NatWest Cup twice, in 1978 and 1981.

The players Most appearances for the County are 539 by wicket-keeper B Taylor between 1949 and 1973. The longest serving captain is J W H T Douglas, who led the side for 14 seasons from 1911 to 1928 (no matches 1915–18). B Taylor is also the youngest cricketer to appear for the County, being 16 years and 10 months when he played v Cambridge University in 1949. The oldest player is P A Perrin, who was 52 years and 3 months when playing v Sussex in 1928.

The Essex cricketer to win most England caps is T E Bailey, whose Test career ran from 1949 to 1958, with 61 caps.

Team performances The highest total for the County is 692, hit in about 425 minutes, against Somerset at Taunton on July 11 and 12, 1895, and the highest against the County is 803 for 4 wkts declared by Kent at Brentwood on May 30 and 31, 1934.

Essex were all out for 30 against Yorkshire at Leyton on August 15, 1901, which is their lowest score and they were dismissed for 41 in the

W. MEAD

Opposite above   *W Mead twice took 17 wickets in a match – the only Essex player to achieve this.*

Opposite below   *B Taylor, seen batting against Surrey (A McIntyre the wicket-keeper) made most appearances (539) for Essex.*

Above   *Admiring glances for J W H T Douglas, the Essex captain for 14 seasons, as he goes out to bat in a Test match.*

second innings of the same match. On two occasions Essex have dismissed their opponents for 31 – Derbyshire at Derby on August 4, 1914 and Yorkshire at Huddersfield on July 31, 1935. The latter match was a sensation, since Essex went on to beat Yorkshire (the County Champions) by an innings and 204 runs; it was the sole defeat inflicted on Yorkshire that year.

Individual performances   The highest score for the County is 343 not out by P A Perrin v Derbyshire at Chesterfield on July 18, 1904 and the highest against Essex is 332 by W H Ashdown for Kent at Brentwood on May 30 and 31, 1934 (see highest team total above); Ashdown batted 375 minutes and hit a six and 45 fours. Ten wickets in an innings has been achieved twice for Essex – first by H Pickett (for 32 runs) v Leicestershire at Leyton on June 3, 1895 and second by T E Bailey (for 90 runs) v Lancashire at Clacton on August 24, 1949 – oddly Essex lost both matches, the latter by 10 wickets.

Best bowling against Essex is 10 for 40 by E G Dennett for Gloucs at Bristol on August 6, 1906, Dennett bowled unchanged through both innings. Two other cricketers to take 10 Essex wickets in an innings are T Richardson for Surrey in 1894 and A P Freeman for Kent in 1930.

W Mead, the only Essex bowler to take 17 wickets in a match, performed the feat twice – against Hampshire at Southampton on July 25, 26 and 27, 1895, when his figures were 8–67 and 9–52 (Essex were easily beaten however); and in a non-first-class match v Australians at Leyton on August 3, 4 and 5, 1893 with figures of 9–136 and 8–69; this match was arranged at the last moment, when a fixture between the Cambridge Univ, Past and Present and the tourists fell through.

Best bowling in a match against the County is 17–56 by C W L Parker for Gloucestershire on the Wagon Works Ground, Gloucester, July 25 and 28, 1925, though equally remarkable is the analysis of 17–91 by H Verity for Yorkshire at Leyton on July 14, 1933 – Yorkshire hit 340 on the first day of the game, the second day was entirely washed out by rain and on the last day Verity bowled out Essex twice.

Although Essex batsmen have hit 2,000 runs in a season on 8 occasions, only three cricketers are involved: J O'Connor, 4 times; C A G Russell, 3 times and D J Insole once. The record is 2,308 in 1934 by J O'Connor. P A Perrin hit 1,000 runs in a season 17 times between 1898 and 1925 – J O'Connor comes second with 16 times between 1923 and 1939.

Most wickets in a season for Essex are 172 by T P B Smith in 1947. Smith also reached 150 wickets on one other occasion – 152 in 1937. M S Nichols with 160 in 1938 is the other Essex bowler to top 150. Nichols

73

holds the record for the most seasons taking 100 wickets – 11 times between 1926 and 1939.

In a career, the record number of runs is 29,172 by P A Perrin (1896–1928) at an average of 36.19; other cricketers to exceed 20,000 are J O'Connor (27,722); C A G Russell (23,610); K W R Fletcher (24,649); G Barker (21,895); T E Bailey (21,460) and D J Insole (20,113).

The three bowlers to take 1,500 wickets in their Essex career are T P B Smith (1,610; av 26.28) between 1929 and 1951; M S Nichols (1,608; av 21.26) and T E Bailey (1,593; av 21.99).

Wicket partnerships

The highest stands in first-class cricket for the County are:

1st	270	A V Avery, T C Dodds v Surrey (*The Oval*)	1946
2nd	321	G A Gooch, K S McEwan v Northants (*Ilford*)	1978
3rd	343	P A Gibb, R Horsfall v Kent (*Blackheath*)	1951
4th	298	A V Avery, R Horsfall v Worcs (*Clacton*)	1948
5th	287	J O'Connor, C T Ashton v Surrey (*Brentwood*)	1934
6th	206	J W H T Douglas, J O'Connor v Gloucs (*Cheltenham*) 1923	
	206	B R Knight, R A G Luckin v Middlesex (*Brentwood*) 1962	
7th	261	J W H T Douglas, J R Freeman v Lancashire (*Leyton*) 1914	
8th	263	D R Wilcox, R M Taylor v Warwicks (*Southend*)	1946
9th	251	J W H T Douglas, S N Hare v Derbyshire (*Leyton*) 1921	
10th	218	F H Vigar, T P B Smith v Derbyshire (*Chesterfield*) 1947	

(Smith scored 163, the highest innings ever made by a no. 11 batsman; he batted 150 minutes and hit 3 sixes and 22 fours.)

Limited overs cricket records

GILLETTE/NATWEST CUP
Highest team total 316–6 v Staffordshire (*Stone*) 1976
Lowest team total 100 v Derbyshire (*Brentwood*) 1965
Highest innings 119 K S McEwan v Leics (*Leicester*) 1980
Best bowling 5–8 J K Lever v Middx (*Westcliff*) 1972
JOHN PLAYER LEAGUE
Highest team total 299–4 v Warwickshire (*Colchester*) 1982
Lowest team total 69 v Derbyshire (*Chesterfield*) 1974
Highest innings 156* K S McEwan v Warwickshire (*Colchester*) 1982
Best bowling 8–26 K D Boyce v Lancs (*Old Trafford*) 1971
BENSON AND HEDGES CUP
Highest team total 350–3 v Combined Universities (*Chelmsford*) 1979
Lowest team total 123 v Kent (*Canterbury*) 1973
Highest innings 198* G A Gooch v Sussex (*Hove*) 1982
Best bowling 5–16 J K Lever v Middlesex (*Chelmsford*) 1976

Expensive Bowling

The most runs conceded by a bowler in an innings are 362 (for 4 wkts) by A A Mailey for N S W v Victoria at Melbourne, December 24, 27 and 28, 1926. In England the record stands at 298 (for 1 wkt) by L O'B Fleetwood-Smith for Australia v England at the Oval, August 20, 22 and 23, 1938.

Most runs conceded in a match were 428 by C S Nayudu for Holkar v Bombay at Bombay in 1944–45, the record in England being 331 by A P Freeman for Kent v MCC at Folkestone in 1934.

The most expensive hundred wickets in a season were obtained by R Smith for Essex in 1947, his figures reading:

1557 overs   324 mdns   4658 runs   125 wkts   37.26 average

Extras

Most in an innings British Guiana had 74 extras (b 54, lb 16, w 1, nb 3) in an innings of 529 v W Shepherd's XI at Georgetown in 1909–10. The record in England is 73 (b 48, lb 23, w 2) in an innings by Northants v Kent at Northampton in 1955.

Left *L O'B Fleetwood-Smith, who conceded 298 runs in one innings at the Oval in 1938, a record for English cricket.*

Right *P G H Fender of Surrey, the scorer of the fastest recorded century in first-class cricket – 35 minutes in 1920.*

Below *C G Macartney batting in a Test match at Leeds in 1921 – that year he scored a record 345 in a day against Notts.*

Highest innings with no extras Victoria hit 647 without any extras *v* Tasmania at Melbourne in 1951–52; the Tasmanian wicket-keeper was L J Alexander.

Extras as highest proportion of completed innings There were 8 extras in Auckland's score of 13 (61%) against Canterbury at Auckland in 1877–78.

Most in a match by one side Pakistan had 103 extras in a match with West Indies at Bridgetown in 1976–77. In this match the total number of extras was 173, also a record.

Fast Scoring

O H Dean hit 410 in 210 minutes for Sydney Church of England Grammar School *v* Newington College in Australia in 1904–05.

The record for a single day's play in first-class cricket is 345 by C G Macartney for Australians *v* Notts (*Trent Bridge*) 1921; he batted 235 minutes.

The fastest century in first-class cricket was hit by P G H Fender in 35 minutes for Surrey *v* Northants at Northampton on August 26, 1920. The match created a new record in county cricket for the most runs ever scored, the totals being: Northants 306 and 430; Surrey 619–5d and 120–2.

The fastest fifty in first-class cricket was hit by C C Inman in 8 minutes for Leics *v* Notts at Trent Bridge, August 20, 1965. N W Hill, the Notts captain, bowled slow full tosses in order to speed up the Leicester scoring and thus produce a declaration.

The fastest double century in first-class cricket was hit by G L Jessop in 120 minutes for Gloucestershire *v* Sussex at Hove, June 1, 1903. He reached 100 in 70 minutes and his second 100 took 50 minutes, and his whole innings of 286 about 175 minutes. This was equalled by C H Lloyd for West Indians *v* Glamorgan at Swansea in 1976. He reached 100 after 80 minutes and his second hundred took only 40 minutes.

The fastest triple century in first-class cricket was hit by D C S Compton in 181 minutes for MCC *v* NE Transvaal at Benoni, December 3, 1948. Compton reached 100 in 66 minutes, his second 100 took 78 minutes and his third 100 only 37 minutes.

One of the most notable pieces of fast scoring in first-class cricket was by E B Alletson for Notts *v* Sussex at Hove, May 20, 1911. He hit 142 in 40 minutes, having taken 50 minutes to make 47, and his total of 189 thus took 90 minutes.

Fatalities

The only fatal accident to occur in English first-class cricket took place at Lord's on June 15, 1870, when a ball from John Platts struck George Summers in the second innings of Notts against M C C. Summers died on June 19 as a result of the injury.

A Ducat (*Surrey and England*) dropped dead from heart failure whilst batting at Lord's on July 23, 1942. Aged 56 at the time of his decease, Ducat was playing for Surrey Home Guard *v* Sussex Home Guard.

There have been quite a number of deaths to people practising cricket, watching it, or merely passing by, more especially in the 18th and 19th centuries when medical knowledge was rather rudimentary: one descriptive piece will perhaps suffice. In 1731 a Mr Legat was passing the Artillery Cricket Ground in London when he was hit on the nose by a cricket ball: 'When the bleeding stopt outwardly he bled inwardly and when stopt inwardly, he bled outwardly' – he died from loss of blood on July 6, 1731.

Fathers and Sons

There are over 200 examples of fathers and their sons appearing in first-class cricket and in fact there are 23 examples of fathers and their sons appearing in Test cricket. There is not a single instance of a father and son playing in the same Test Match, but on several occasions a father has appeared with his son in a first-class match. Only once however has both father and son hit a century in the same innings in a first-class match. The pair were G Gunn and G V Gunn and the match was Notts *v* Warwickshire at Edgbaston, July 23 and 24, 1931. G Gunn – on his 53rd birthday – hit 183, whilst G V Gunn was 100 not out when the match ended.

E B Alletson, whose innings of 189 for Notts against Sussex at Hove in 1911 included some of the fastest scoring ever seen, and turned apparently certain defeat into victory.

Clive Lloyd, batting for the West Indians against Glamorgan at Swansea in 1976, scored a double century in 120 minutes, equalling Jessop's feat of 1903.

There are eight examples in English first-class cricket of three generations of players – grandfather, father and son. These are:

E V Bligh, L E Bligh and A S Bligh
E C Freeman, E J Freeman and D P Freeman
D Hayward snr, D Hayward jun, T W Hayward
J Hardstaff snr, J Hardstaff jun and J Hardstaff
G M Hoare, C H Hoare and C T Hoare
F W Lillywhite, John Lillywhite and James Lillywhite
J H Parks, J M Parks and R J Parks
G Beet, G H C Beet and G A Beet

In the Derbyshire *v* Warwickshire match at Derby on June 3 and 5, 1922, there occurred an event unique in County Championship cricket, when in Warwickshire's first innings, William Quaife was batting in partnership with his son B W Quaife, whilst W Bestwick was bowling in partnership with his son, R S Bestwick.

Fenner Trophy/ASDA Trophy
Established in 1971 at Scarborough by J H Fenner Ltd, the Hull engineering firm, the Competition consisted of two 50-over matches involving four first-class counties, the winners of the two matches meeting in a Final to decide the outright winner. The competition ended in 1981.

The Gunns of Nottingham are among the best-known families in the world of cricket, and provide the only instance of a father and son scoring centuries in the same innings of a first-class match. G Gunn (above) and G V Gunn (below) were the centurions.

TABLET
IS ERECTED TO THE
MEMORY OF
GEORGE SUMMERS
BY THE
MARY-LE-BONE
CRICKET CLUB,
TO MARK THEIR SENSE OF HIS
QUALITIES AS A CRICKETER,
AND TO TESTIFY THEIR REGRET
AT THE UNTIMELY ACCIDENT ON
LORD'S GROUND WHICH CUT
SHORT A CAREER SO FULL OF
PROMISE,
JUNE 19TH 1870,
IN THE 26TH YEAR OF HIS AGE,

Above *George Summers, the only player to die as a result of injury on the cricket field, and,* left, *the tablet erected to his memory by the Mary-le-bone Cricket club (*see *Fatalities).*

Brian Close, pictured on the Oval balcony with Gary Sobers, was the first captain to forfeit his team's innings – Yorkshire v Lancashire, 1966.

Winners of the Trophy

1971	Kent	1977	Hampshire
1972	Yorkshire	1978	Northants
1973	Kent	1979	Leicestershire
1974	Yorkshire	1980	Abandoned: rain
1975	Hampshire	1981	Yorkshire
1976	Hampshire		

The major records in the competition:

Highest team total 290–8 Hants v Gloucs 1975
Lowest team total 53 Sussex v Leics 1980
Highest individual innings 141 B W Luckhurst, Kent v Lancs 1973
Best bowling 5–23 J P Agnew, Leics v Sussex 1980; 5–23 A G Nicholson, Yorks v Warw 1974

In 1982 the sponsorship of the competition was taken over by Asda Supermarkets, the rules remaining unaltered.
    The winners for 1982 were Derbyshire.
    None of the major records given above were broken.

Fielding
(see Catches, also Wicket-keeping)

Fiji
The first recorded match in Fiji took place in 1874 and cricket there was soon well-established. Due to the influence of J S Udal, a colonial judge and Attorney-General of Fiji, the standard of play reached was such that in 1894–95, a team from Fiji toured New Zealand and played first-class matches. Two other major tours from Fiji to New Zealand took place in 1947–48 and 1953–54; the latter was ruled first-class by the New Zealand Cricket Council, but not the former. In 1907–08 a team from Bau, one of the Fijian Islands, toured Australia and played six matches against State Second Elevens, winning two.

The first-class records for the Fijians in New Zealand:

Highest team total 344 v Canterbury (*Christchurch*) 1954
Lowest team total 87 v Wellington (*Wellington*) 1895
Highest individual innings 128* J C Collins v Hawke's Bay (*Napier*) 1895
Best bowling in innings 5–16 R Caldwell v Hawke's Bay (*Napier*) 1895

The highest individual innings made in Fiji is 246 scored by I L Bula in a club match in 1959.
    Fiji played in the 1979 ICC Trophy, but failed to win a match. In 1982 they again competed and won one match.

First-Class Cricket
There have been several attempts by the ICC to define the term 'First-class Match'. None of these attempts has been entirely satisfactory however and until the ICC includes representatives of every country in the world in which 'important' cricket matches take place, there will always be matches which some statisticians believe first-class, whilst others do not. The Association of Cricket Statisticians has been studying the problem since 1970 and is producing a series of 'Guides' to first-class matches. By the end of 1981, the Guides have covered the British Isles, Australia, New Zealand and South Africa and Guides to first-class matches in other countries in the world are in preparation.
(See under the headings of each country and County for the date of the first first-class match)

W Gunn, of the cricketing family (see pictures on previous page), played for England at both cricket and association football.

L H Gay of Somerset was one of three nineteenth century cricketers to represent his country at both cricket and soccer.

One of the most successful double internationals in cricket and soccer was Willie Watson, who played in 23 Test matches.

Floodlit Cricket

The first important cricket match organised as a floodlit match took place at the V F L Stadium in Melbourne on December 14, 1977, when An Australian XI played A World XI. The match was 40 overs-a-side and commenced at 2.30 in daylight. The floodlights were switched on at 6.30 and a white ball used against a black sightscreen. The match was part of the World Series Cricket run by Kerry Packer's organisation.

In England there was an experimental competition staged at various football grounds under floodlight at the close of the 1980 season and a competition sponsored by Lambert and Butler at the close of the 1981 season, but the latter, although involving the first-class counties, did not attract much public attention.

Follow On

The 'follow-on' law was introduced on May 20, 1835, when it was made compulsory to follow on if a team were 100 runs or more behind on the first innings.

The first team to be affected by the new Law was Left-handed, who made 63 in reply to the Right-handed score of 202 at Lord's on July 13 and 14, 1835.

There have been a number of changes to the 'follow-on' Law, which is now (1982) optional and is graded according to the length of time allotted to a match, being 200 runs for a match of 5 or more days, 150 runs for 3 or 4 days, 100 runs for 2 days and 75 runs for 1 day.

Following on, yet winning Barbados scored 175 in reply to Trinidad's 559 at Bridgetown in January 1927 and were forced to follow on, being 384 runs behind. Barbados then made 726 for 7 dec and dismissed Trinidad for 217, thus winning the match. This is a record in first-class cricket.

The record in English first-class cricket occurred on May 19, 31 and June 1, 1976 when Gloucestershire were asked to follow on 254 runs behind and yet beat Somerset at Taunton by 8 runs.

Forfeiting an Innings

In County Championship matches D B Close was the first captain to forfeit his team's innings – the match was Yorkshire v Lancashire at Old Trafford, July 30, August 1 and 2, 1966. Close's bold move paid off, Yorkshire winning by 12 runs.

Footballing Cricketers

The following cricketers have represented England in a Test match and England in a full soccer international:

	Soccer Caps	Tests	County
J Arnold	1933 (1)	1931 (1)	Hampshire
A Ducat	1910–21 (6)	1921 (1)	Surrey
R E Foster	1900–02 (5)	1903–07 (8)	Worcestershire
C B Fry	1901 (1)	1899–12 (26)	Sussex, Hants
L H Gay	1893–94 (3)	1894–95 (1)	Somerset
W Gunn	1884 (2)	1888–89 (9)	Notts
H T W Hardinge	1910 (1)	1921 (1)	Kent
Hon A Lyttelton	1877 (1)	1880–84 (4)	Middx
J W H Makepeace	1906–12 (4)	1920–21 (4)	Lancs
C A Milton	1952 (1)	1958–59 (6)	Gloucs
J Sharp	1903–05 (2)	1909 (3)	Lancs
W Watson	1950–51 (4)	1953–58 (23)	Yorks, Leics

The County given is the County for which the cricketer played during his Test career.

Fours

The most 'fours' scored in a single innings in first-class cricket are 68 by P A Perrin (343*) for Essex v Derbyshire at Chesterfield, July 18 and 19, 1904.

The most 'fours' scored in any month by a single batsman are 83 by S V Patker in an inter-school match in Bombay in 1953–54. He hit 431*.

Two bowlers who have taken four wickets in four balls in first-class cricket: A E Trott of Middlesex (top), who performed a separate hat-trick in the same innings, and P I Pocock of Surrey (bottom) the last to perform the feat.

Four Wickets in Four Balls

This feat has been achieved 27 times in first-class cricket, 18 of which have occurred in England. The first instance was by J Wells for Kent *v* Sussex on the Brunswick Ground, Brighton, June 26, 1862, the feat being performed with the last ball of one over and the first three deliveries of the next.

A E Trott performed the feat during his benefit match – Middlesex *v* Somerset at Lord's, May 22, 1907 – later in the same innings he performed the hat-trick, the combination of 4 in 4 and a hat-trick in the same innings being unique in first-class cricket.

The most recent example in English first-class cricket is by P I Pocock for Surrey *v* Sussex at Eastbourne in 1972.

Free Foresters

A Wandering Club founded in 1856 and originally confined to cricketers from the Midland counties, the Free Foresters played first-class matches against Oxford University and Cambridge University from 1912 to 1968, the final first-class match being against Oxford University on June 1, 3 and 4, 1968.

Leading first-class records for the Club:

Highest team total   636–7d *v* Cambridge U (*Fenner's*)   1938
Lowest team total   54 *v* Oxford U (*Oxford*)   1949
Highest individual innings   181 G E V Crutchley *v* Cambridge U (*Fenner's*)   1919
Best bowling in innings   8–60 F R Brown *v* Oxford U (*Oxford*)   1956

Apart from matches in England the Free Foresters have sent numerous teams abroad, notably to Holland, but also to Canada and USA, but none of their overseas matches can be regarded as first-class.

Gentlemen

A series of matches was played in England between amateur and professional cricketers under the title 'Gentlemen *v* Players' from 1806 to 1962, after which the distinction between the two types of cricketer was abolished. Until the appearance of W G Grace in the Gentlemen's ranks, the Players were the dominant side, but from the 1860s onwards the match was more evenly balanced, and until Test matches became an annual feature of the fixture list in England, the Gentlemen *v* Players match at Lord's was the game of the season. The contest was played at other centres as well, notably the Oval and Scarborough. The matches are regarded as first-class and the principal records obtained in them are as follows:

For the Gentlemen

Highest team total   578 The Oval   1904
Lowest team total   31 Lord's   1848
Highest individual innings   232* C B Fry (*Lord's*)   1903
Best bowling in innings   9–46 J W A Stephenson (*Lord's*)   1936

For the Players

Highest team total   651–7d The Oval   1934
Lowest team total   24 Lord's   1829
Highest individual innings   266* J B Hobbs (*Scarborough*)   1925
Best bowling in innings   10–37 A S Kennedy (*The Oval*)   1927

A total of 273 matches was played; Gentlemen won 67 and Players 126, there was one tie and the remainder were drawn.

County Gentlemen   Nearly every English county had, at one time or another, two County sides, one being the team raised by the County Club and the other being Gentlemen of the County. The strongest of the latter were Gentlemen of Kent and this side played a regular series of matches against Gentlemen of England, or Gentlemen of MCC, during the Canterbury Festival. This series is regarded as first-class until 1880.

Gentlemen *v* Australians   This match was played on most visits of the Australians to England from 1878 to 1961, a total of 14 matches in all.

The records for the Gentlemen are:
Highest team total   490 Lord's   1888
Lowest team total   66 Lord's   1905
Highest individual innings   165 W G Grace (*Lord's*)   1888
Best bowling in innings   7–35 A G Steel (*Prince's*)   1878

Ghana (Gold Coast)

The first mention of cricket in Ghana occurs in 1888 and the first international match took place at Lagos on May 25, 1904, when the Gold Coast played Lagos. The fixture was played occasionally until 1913, but a break in the series then took place and matches were not resumed until 1926, since when matches have taken place on a fairly regular, though not annual basis.

In 1973 Ghana sent a team outside West Africa for the first time and played in Kenya, Uganda and Tanzania.

Ghana did not compete in the 1979 or 1982 ICC Trophies.

Gillette Cup (NatWest Trophy)

Inaugurated by Gillette in 1963, but sponsored by the National Westminster Bank since 1981, the Competition is run on a knock-out basis. Originally it was of 65 overs per side and confined to the 17 first-class counties, but it is now 60 overs per side and has been extended to include the leading Minor Counties.

The principal records in the competition are:

Highest team total   371–4 Hants v Glamorgan (*Southampton*)   1975
Lowest team total   41 Cambs v Bucks (*Cambridge*)   1972
    Middx v Essex (*Westcliff*)   1972
    Salop v Essex (*Wellington*)   1974

Highest individual innings   177 C G Greenidge, Hants v Glam (*Southampton*)   1975
Best bowling   7–15 A L Dixon, Kent v Surrey (*Oval*)   1967
Fastest hundred   77 mins R E Marshall, Hants v Beds (*Goldington*)   1968

Wicket partnerships

1st	227	R E Marshall, B L Reed. Hants v Bedford (*Goldington*) 1968
2nd	223	M J Smith, C T Radley. Middx v Hants (*Lord's*) 1977
3rd	160	B Wood, F C Hayes. Lancs v Warwicks (*Edgbaston*) 1976
4th	234*	D Lloyd, C H Lloyd. Lancs v Gloucs (*Old Trafford*) 1978
5th	166	M A Lynch, G R J Roope. Surrey v Durham (*Oval*) 1982
6th	105	G St A Sobers, R A White. Notts v Worcs (*Worcester*) 1974
7th	107	D R Shepherd, D A Graveney. Gloucs v Surrey (*Bristol*) 1973
8th	69	S J Rouse, D J Brown. Warwicks v Middx (*Lord's*) 1977
9th	87	M A Nash, A E Cordle. Glamorgan v Lincolns (*Swansea*) 1974
10th	81	S Turner, R E East. Essex v Yorkshire (*Headingley*) 1982

(*For records for each first-class County see under each County*)

The Gentlemen at Lord's in 1898, captained in his 50th year by W G Grace. The Gentlemen played the Players from 1806 to 1962.

Gillette Cup/NatWest Trophy Results

1963

Quarter Finals

Worcestershire 238–8 (T W Graveney 93, R G Broadbent 51) beat Glamorgan 192 (E J Lewis 78, J A Flavell 5–43) by 46 runs

Derbyshire 148 lost to Lancashire 149–5 by 5 wkts

Middlesex 129 (J D F Larter 4–22) lost to Northants 132–4 (C Milburn 84) by 6 wkts

Sussex 292 (J M Parks 90, R J Langridge 56, D B Close 4–60) beat Yorkshire 270 (G Boycott 71) by 22 runs

Semi Finals

Sussex 292 (E R Dexter 115, J M Parks 71, J D F Larter 4–68) beat Northants 187 (R M Prideaux 73, N I Thomson 4–33) by 105 runs

Lancashire 59 (J A Flavell 6–14) lost to Worcestershire 60–1 by 9 wkts

Final

Sussex 168 (J M Parks 57, N Gifford 4–33) beat Worcestershire 154 by 14 runs

(*Lord's 7.9.1963*)

Sussex: R J Langridge, A S M Oakman, K G Suttle, E R Dexter (cpt), J M Parks, L J Lenham, G C Cooper, N I Thomson, A Buss, J A Snow, D L Bates.

Worcs: D Kenyon (cpt), M J Horton, R G A Headley, T W Graveney, D W Richardson, R G Broadbent, R Booth, D N F Slade, N Gifford, J A Flavell, R G M Carter.

1964

Quarter Finals

Glamorgan 220–6 (P M Walker 62*, B Hedges 55) lost to Lancashire 223–4 (G Pullar 77, K J Grieves 62*) by 6 wkts

Warwickshire 300–8 (R W Barber 114, N F Horner 55, P J Watts 4–48) beat Northants 153 (R M Prideaux 58*, K Ibadulla 5–34) by 147 runs

Sussex 141 (G C Cooper 58, F E Rumsey 4–19, G H Hall 5–34) beat Somerset 125 (R T Virgin 54, D L Bates 4–28) by 16 runs

Surrey 236–8 (J H Edrich 70) beat Middlesex 122 (S J Storey 5–35) by 144 runs

Semi Finals

Warwickshire 294–7 (R W Barber 76, M J K Smith 58) beat Lancashire 209–7 (D M Green 69) by 85 runs

Sussex 215–8 (E R Dexter 84) beat Surrey 125 by 90 runs

Final

Warwickshire 127 (N I Thomson 4–23) lost to Sussex 131–2 by 8 wkts

(*Lord's 5.9.1964*)

Sussex: K G Suttle, L J Lenham, E R Dexter (cpt), J M Parks, G C Cooper, R J Langridge, M G Griffith, N I Thomson, A Buss, J A Snow, D L Bates.

Warw: N F Horner, R W Barber, K Ibadulla, M J K Smith (cpt), W J Stewart, J A Jameson, T W Cartwright, R E Hitchcock, A C Smith, J D Bannister, D J Brown.

1965

Quarter Finals

Middlesex 280–8 (R A Gale 74, P H Parfitt 66) beat Sussex 190 (D Bennett 4–42) by 90 runs

Somerset 63 (F S Trueman 6–15) lost to Yorkshire 64–3 by 7 wkts

Surrey 222–8 (R A E Tindall 73, W A Smith 52) beat Northants 97 (S J Storey 4–14) by 125 runs

Warwickshire 203 (K Ibadulla 75, R M H Cottam 4–56) beat Hampshire 129 (K Ibadulla 6–32) by 74 runs

Semi Finals

Middlesex 250–8 (W E Russell 70, J M Brearley 60) lost to Surrey 252–5 (J H Edrich 71, K F Barrington 68*) by 5 wkts

Yorkshire 177 beat Warwickshire 157 by 20 runs

Final

Yorkshire 317–4 (G Boycott 146, D B Close 79) beat Surrey 142 (R A E Tindall 57, R Illingworth 5–29) by 175 runs

(*Lord's 4.9.1965*)

Yorks: G Boycott, K Taylor, D B Close (cpt), F S Trueman, J H Hampshire, D Wilson, D E V Padgett, P J Sharpe, R Illingworth, R A Hutton, J G Binks.

Surrey: M J Stewart (cpt), J H Edrich, W A Smith, K F Barrington, R A E Tindall, S J Storey, M J Edwards, D Gibson, A Long, G G Arnold, D A D Sydenham.

1966

Quarter Finals

Surrey 173 lost to Hampshire 174–3 (R E Marshall 85) by 7 wkts

Lancashire 103 (R Palmer 5–18) lost to Somerset 104–6 by 4 wkts

Gloucestershire 193 lost to Warwickshire 197–4 (R W Barber 113, D L Amiss 62) by 6 wkts

Worcestershire 211 (M J Horton 51, J A Ormrod 50) beat Essex 129 (L J Coldwell 4–42) by 82 runs

Semi Finals

Somerset 189 (G Atkinson 72) lost to Warwickshire 190–5 (D L Amiss 80*) by 5 wkts

Worcestershire 253–4 (M J Horton 114) beat Hampshire 154 (L J Coldwell 4–39) by 99 runs

Final

Worcestershire 155–8 lost to Warwickshire 159–5 (R W Barber 66) by 5 wkts

(*Lord's 3.9.1966*)

Warwickshire: R W Barber, K Ibadulla, D L Amiss, M J K Smith (cpt), J A Jameson, R N Abberley, A C Smith, T W Cartwright, R V Webster, D J Brown, J D Bannister.

Worcestershire: D Kenyon (cpt), M J Horton, J A Ormrod, T W Graveney, B L d'Oliveira, D W Richardson, R Booth, N Gifford, B M Brain, L J Coldwell, J A Flavell.

1967

Quarter Finals

Lancashire 194 (C M Old 4–32) beat Yorkshire 190 (P Lever 4–38) by 4 runs

Somerset 184 beat Northants 148 (F E Rumsey 4–23) by 36 runs

Surrey 74 (A L Dixon 7–15) lost to Kent 75–4 by 6 wkts

Sussex 233–9 (A T Castell 4–52) beat Hampshire 224 (B S V Timms 55) by 9 runs

Semi Finals

Kent 293–5 (B W Luckhurst 78, M C Cowdrey 78, J N Shepherd 77) beat Sussex 175 by 118 runs

Somerset 210–7 beat Lancashire 110 by 100 runs

Final

Kent 193 (B W Luckhurst 54, M H Denness 50) beat Somerset 161 by 32 runs

(*Lord's 2.9.1967*)

Kent: M H Denness, B W Luckhurst, J N Shepherd, M C Cowdrey (cpt), A P E Knott, A L Dixon, S E Leary, A Brown, A G E Ealham, D L Underwood, J N Graham.

Somerset: R T Virgin, P J Robinson, M J Kitchen, T I Barwell, W E Alley, G I Burgess, C R M Atkinson (cpt), G Clayton, K E Palmer, R Palmer, F E Rumsey.

1968

Quarter Finals

Warwickshire 222 (R B Kanhai 92, R M H Cottam 4–38) beat Hampshire 195 (D A Livingstone 50) by 27 runs

Middlesex 231 (P H Parfitt 69) beat Leicestershire 213 (B J Booth 73, R W Stewart 4–41) by 18 runs

Gloucestershire 296–8 (D M Green 90, C A Milton 87, M J Procter 53) beat Nottinghamshire 271 (G St A Sobers 76, M J Smedley 75) by 25 runs

Sussex 255–7 (K G Suttle 100, E R Dexter 69) beat Northants 248 (R M Prideaux 58, M A Buss 4–51) by 7 runs

Semi Finals

Middlesex 162–9 (W Blenkiron 4–32) lost to Warwickshire 165–7 (R B Kanhai 53, R W Hooker 4–20) by 3 wkts

Sussex 219 (E R Dexter 62) beat Gloucestershire 171 (D L Bates 6–30) by 48 runs

Final

Sussex 214–7 (J M Parks 57) lost to Warwickshire 215–6 (W J Stewart 59) by 4 wkts

(*Lord's 7.9.1968*)

Warwickshire: R W Barber, W J Stewart, J A Jameson, R B Kanhai, K Ibadulla, D L Amiss, R N Abberley, A C Smith (cpt), W Blenkiron, D J Brown, L R Gibbs.

Sussex: M A Buss, A S M Oakman, K G Suttle, E R Dexter, A W Greig, J M Parks, G C Cooper, M G Griffith (cpt), J A Snow, A Buss, D L Bates.

1969

Quarter Finals

Glamorgan 117 (A R Lewis 60, H J Rhodes 4–18) lost to Derbyshire 121–1 by 9 wkts

Essex 180 (K W R Fletcher 74) lost to Nottinghamshire 182–8 by 2 wkts

Yorkshire 272 (D B Close 96, G Boycott 92) beat Surrey 134 (D Wilson 4–31) by 138 runs

Sussex 191 (J M Parks 51, P T Marner 4–30) beat Leicestershire 131 (M A Buss 4–24) by 60 runs

Semi Finals

Derbyshire 136 (A Buss 4–27) beat Sussex 49 (T J P Eyre 6–18) by 87 runs

Yorkshire 191 (P J Sharpe 67) beat Nottinghamshire 123 by 68 runs

Final

Yorkshire 219–8 (B Leadbeater 76) beat Derbyshire 150 by 69 runs

(*Lord's 6.9.1969*)

Yorkshire: B Leadbeater, J D Woodford, D B Close (cpt), P J Sharpe, D E V Padgett, J H Hampshire, R A Hutton, J G Binks, D Wilson, C M Old, A G Nicholson.

Derbyshire: P J K Gibbs, D H K Smith, D C Morgan (cpt), A Ward, I R Buxton, J F Harvey, M H Page, R W Taylor, T J P Eyre, F E Rumsey, H J Rhodes.

1970

Quarter Finals

Sussex 199 (G A Greenidge 56, A W Greig 54) beat Kent 152 (A W Greig 5–42) by 47 runs

Hampshire 142 (P Lever 5–30) lost to Lancashire 143 (B Wood 63*) by 5 wkts

Nottinghamshire 232–5 (M J Harris 101, G St A Sobers 96*) lost to Somerset 233–5 (P J Robinson 57, R T Virgin 52) by 5 wkts

Surrey 280–5 (J H Edrich 91, Younis Ahmed 87, M J Edwards 51) beat Middlesex 272–9 (P H Parfitt 52, R G D Willis 6–49) by 8 runs

Semi Finals

Somerset 207 (R T Virgin 65) lost to Lancashire 210–6 (J Sullivan 50) by 4 wkts

Surrey 196 (M J Edwards 50, J A Snow 4–35) lost to Sussex 196–8 by 2 wkts (the side losing least wickets are the winners in a match where the scores are equal)

Final

Sussex 184–9 lost to Lancashire 185–4 (H Pilling 70*) by 6 wkts

(*Lord's 5.9.1970*)

Sussex: M A Buss, G A Greenidge, R J Langridge, J M Parks, A W Greig, P J Graves, K G Suttle, M G Griffith (cpt), A Buss, J A Snow, J Spencer.

Lancashire: B Wood, D Lloyd, H Pilling, C H Lloyd, J Sullivan, F M Engineer, J D Bond (cpt), D P Hughes, J Simmons, K Shuttleworth, P Lever.

1971

Quarter Finals

Lancashire 203–9 (C H Lloyd 109) beat Essex 191 (S Turner 50, K Shuttleworth 4–26) by 12 runs

Gloucestershire 214 (R B Nicholls 77) beat Surrey 199 (M J Stewart 82, R D V Knight 5–39) by 15 runs

Kent 231–8 (M H Denness 85, B W Luckhurst 58) beat Leicestershire 153 (M E J C Norman 50, R A Woolmer 4–37) by 78 runs

Warwickshire 281–6 (J A Jameson 96, R B Kanhai 56) beat Hampshire 186 (B A Richards 69, L R Gibbs 5–38) by 95 runs

Semi Finals

Kent 238 (B W Luckhurst 84, W Blenkiron 4–51) beat Warwickshire 109 by 129 runs

Gloucestershire 229–6 (M J Procter 65, R B Nicholls 53) lost to Lancashire 230–7 (B Wood 50) by 3 wkts

Final

Lancashire 224–7 (C H Lloyd 66) beat Kent 200 (Asif Iqbal 89) by 24 runs

(*Lord's 4.9.1971*)

Lancashire: B Wood, D Lloyd, H Pilling, C H Lloyd, J Sullivan, F M Engineer, J D Bond (cpt), J Simmons, D P Hughes, P Lever, K Shuttleworth.

Kent: B W Luckhurst, D Nicholls, M H Denness (cpt), A G E Ealham, Asif Iqbal, A P E Knott, J N Shepherd, R A Woolmer, B D Julien, D L Underwood, J C J Dye.

1972

Quarter Finals

Warwickshire 214–9 (A I Kallicharran 88) beat Glamorgan 204–9 (A Jones 58, P M Walker 51) by 10 runs

Kent 137 (Asif Iqbal 52) beat Essex 127 (J N Shepherd 4–23) by 10 runs

Hampshire 223 (B A Richards 129) lost to Lancashire 227–6 (B Wood 66) by 4 wkts

Surrey 105 (N Gifford 4–7) lost to Worcestershire 109–4 by 6 wkts

Semi Finals

Lancashire 224–6 (H Pilling 70) beat Kent 217 (M H Denness 65) by 7 runs

Worcestershire 174–9 (T J Yardley 52) lost to Warwickshire 175–2 (D L Amiss 67, R B Kanhai 85*) by 8 wkts

Final

Warwickshire 234–9 (J Whitehouse 68, A I Kallicharran 54) lost to Lancashire 235–6 (C H Lloyd 126) by 4 wkts

(*Lord's 2.9.1972*)

Lancashire: D Lloyd, B Wood, H Pilling, C H Lloyd, F C Hayes, J Sullivan, F M Engineer, D P Hughes, J D Bond (cpt), J Simmons, P G Lee.

Warwickshire: J Whitehouse, D L Amiss, R B Kanhai, M J K Smith (cpt), A I Kallicharran, D L Murray, N M McVicker, D J Brown, S J Rouse, R G D Willis, L R Gibbs.

1973

Quarter Finals

Gloucestershire 236–9 (R D V Knight 60, Sadiq Mohammad 56, B E A Edmeades 4–71) beat Essex 206 (J Davey 4–35)

Lancashire 224–6 (H Pilling 90) lost to Middlesex 225–6 (M J Smith 90) by 4 wkts

Sussex 263–6 (R M Prideaux 79) beat Kent 135 (G W Johnson 65) by 128 runs

Worcestershire 202–9 (B L d'Oliveira 51) beat Leicestershire 146 (B F Davison 61*) by 56 runs

Semi Finals

Sussex 174–8 (A W Greig 61) beat Middlesex 169 (A W Greig 4–27) by 5 runs

Gloucestershire 243–8 (M J Procter 101) beat Worcestershire 238–9 (G M Turner 109, R G A Headley 56) by 5 runs

Final

Gloucestershire 248–8 (M J Procter 94, A S Brown 77*) beat Sussex 208 (G A Greenidge 76, R D V Knight 4–47)

(*Lord's 1.9.1973*)

Gloucestershire: Sadiq Mohammad, R D V Knight, Zaheer Abbas, M J Procter, D R Shepherd, A W Stovold, A S Brown (cpt), J C Foat, D A Graveney, J B Mortimore, J Davey.

Sussex: G A Greenidge, J D Morley, R M Prideaux, P J Graves, A W Greig (cpt), M A Buss, M G Griffith, M J J Faber, J A Snow, J Spencer, R P T Marshall.

1974

Quarter Finals

Kent 295–8 (B W Luckhurst 125, M H Denness 72) beat Leicestershire 229 (B F Davison 82, D L Underwood 4–57) by 66 runs

Surrey 254–7 (J H Edrich 59, Younis Ahmed 53, H R Moseley 4–31) lost to Somerset 257–5 (P W Denning 112) by 5 wkts

Worcestershire 251–9 (K W Wilkinson 95, B Stead 5–44) beat Nottinghamshire 233–9 (G St A Sobers 84, B L d'Oliveira 4–18) by 18 runs

Lancashire 205 (C H Lloyd 90, G B Stevenson 4–57) beat Yorkshire 173 (P Lever 4–17) by 32 runs

Semi Finals

Somerset 154 lost to Kent 155–7 by 3 wkts

Lancashire 236–7 (B Wood 91, D Lloyd 54, B M Brain 4–51) beat Worcestershire 208 (J Simmons 5–49) by 28 runs

Final

Lancashire 118 lost to Kent 122–6 by 4 wkts

(*Lord's 7–9.9.1974; no play first day due to rain*)

Kent: B W Luckhurst, G W Johnson, M C Cowdrey, M H Denness (cpt), A G E Ealham, J N Shepherd, A P E Knott, R A Woolmer, J M H Graham-Brown, D L Underwood, J N Graham.

Lancashire: D Lloyd (cpt), B Wood, H Pilling, C H Lloyd, A Kennedy, F M Engineer, D P Hughes, J Simmons, K Shuttleworth, P Lever, P G Lee.

1975

Quarter Finals

Hampshire 98 (B Wood 4–17, R M Ratcliffe 4–25) lost to Lancashire 101–4 by 6 wkts

Gloucestershire 314–4 (Zaheer Abbas 131*, Sadiq Mohammad 111) beat Leicestershire 282–9 (R W Tolchard 86*, B Dudleston 54) by 32 runs

Nottinghamshire 166 (M Hendrick 4–26) lost to Derbyshire 167–4 by 6 wkts

Worcestershire 257 (J M Parker 107, J A Ormrod 53) lost to Middlesex 258–2 (C T Radley 105*, M J Smith 70, N G Featherstone 72*) by 8 wkts

Semi Finals

Middlesex 207 (N G Featherstone 70, M Hendrick 4–16) beat Derbyshire 183 (R G A Headley 58, P J Sharpe 55) by 24 runs

Gloucestershire 236 (Sadiq Mohammad 122) lost to Lancashire 239–7 (B Wood 63) by 3 wkts

Final

Middlesex 180–8 lost to Lancashire 182–3 (C H Lloyd 73*, A Kennedy 51) by 7 wkts

(*Lord's 6.9.1975*)

Lancashire: B Wood, A Kennedy, F C Hayes, C H Lloyd, D Lloyd (cpt), F M Engineer, D P Hughes, J Simmons, R M Ratcliffe, P Lever, P G Lee.

Middlesex: M J Smith, J M Brearley (cpt), C T Radley, N G Featherstone, H A Gomes, G D Barlow, J T Murray, P H Edmonds, F J Titmus, T M Lamb, M W W Selvey.

1976

Quarter Finals

Hampshire 226 (P J Sainsbury 63, R M C Gilliat 52, M Hendrick 4–35, E J Barlow 4–51) beat Derbyshire 179 (P J Sainsbury 4–49) by 47 runs

Gloucestershire 125 lost to Lancs 128–3 (B Wood 62*) by 7 wkts

Hertfordshire 69 (Sarfraz Nawaz 4–17) lost to Northants 75–1 (P Willey 52*) by 9 wkts

Sussex 194 (Javed Miandad 69, S J Rouse 4–27, D J Brown 4–38) lost to Warwickshire 195–2 (D L Amiss 87, J A Jameson 57) by 8 wkts

Semi Finals

Hampshire 215–7 (D R Turner 86) lost to Northants 218–8 (R T Virgin 82) by 2 wkts

Warwickshire 233 lost to Lancashire 234–4 (B Wood 105, F C Hayes 93) by 6 wkts

Final

Lancashire 195–7 lost to Northants 199–6 (P Willey 65, R T Virgin 53) by 4 wkts

(*Lord's 4.9.1976*)

Northants: R T Virgin, P Willey, Mushtaq Mohammad (cpt), D S Steele, W Larkins, G Cook, G Sharp, Sarfraz Nawaz, A Hodgson, B S Bedi, J C J Dye.

Lancashire: B Wood, F M Engineer, H Pilling, F C Hayes, D Lloyd (cpt), J Abrahams, D P Hughes, J Simmons, R M Ratcliffe, P Lever, P G Lee.

1977

Quarter Finals

Somerset 248–4 (B C Rose 128) beat Derbyshire 189 (J Garner 5–30) by 59 runs

Surrey 199 (J H Edrich 53) lost to Glamorgan 200–6 (C L King 55, A Jones 54) by 4 wkts

Hampshire 247–7 (T E Jesty 54*, D J Rock 50) lost to Middlesex 248–3 (M J Smith 123, C T Radley 94) by 7 wkts

Northants 228–9 (G Cook 95, P Booth 5–33) lost to Leicestershire 231–5 (B F Davison 80, J C Balderstone 54, A Hodgson 4–32) by 5 wkts

Semi Finals

Leicestershire 172–7 lost to Glamorgan 175–5 (J A Hopkins 63) by 5 wkts

Somerset 59 (W W Daniel 4–24) lost to Middlesex 61–4 (J Garner 4–27) by 6 wkts (match reduced to 15 overs per side)

Final

Glamorgan 177–9 (M J Llewellyn 62) lost to Middlesex 178–5 (C T Radley 85*) by 5 wkts

(*Lord's 3.9.1977*)

Middlesex: J M Brearley (cpt), M J Smith, C T Radley, M W Gatting, G D Barlow, N G Featherstone, P H Edmonds, I J Gould, J E Emburey, M W W Selvey, W W Daniel.

Lancashire's Gillette Cup in 1975. Farokh Engineer, Clive Lloyd and captain David Lloyd with the trophy.

Glamorgan: A Jones (cpt), J A Hopkins, C L King, R C Ontong, M J Llewellyn, G Richards, E W Jones, M A Nash, A E Cordle, T W Cartwright, A H Wilkins.

1978

Quarter Finals

Kent 120 (C H Dredge 4–23) lost to Somerset 122–5 by 5 wkts

Lancashire 279–6 (A Kennedy 131, C H Lloyd 68) beat Middlesex 258 (M W Gatting 62, C T Radley 58, D P Hughes 4–69) by 21 runs

Essex 73–2 beat Leicestershire 70–8 (J K Lever 4–27) by 3 runs (no play was possible on first or second day and the match was reduced to 10 overs per side on the third day)

Sussex 68–6 beat Yorkshire 59–8 by 9 runs (match was reduced to 10 overs per side)

Semi Finals

Somerset 287–6 (I V A Richards 116, P M Roebuck 57) beat Essex 287 (G A Gooch 61, K W R Fletcher 67) by losing less wickets with scores tied

Sussex 277–8 (Javed Miandad 75, P W G Parker 69) beat Lancashire 141 by 136 runs

Final

Somerset 207–7 (I T Botham 80) lost to Sussex 211–5 (P W G Parker 62*) by 5 wkts

(*Lord's 2.9.1978*)

Sussex: J R T Barclay, G D Mendis, P W G Parker, Javed Miandad, Imran Khan, C P Phillipson, S J Storey, A Long (cpt), J Spencer, G G Arnold, R G L Cheatle.

Somerset: B C Rose (cpt), P W Denning, I V A Richards, P M Roebuck, I T Botham, V J Marks, G I Burgess, D J S Taylor, J Garner, K F Jennings, C H Dredge.

1979

Quarter Finals

Middlesex 216 (J M Brearley 76, H P Cooper 4–29) beat Yorkshire 146 by 70 runs

Leicestershire 180 (B Dudleston 59) lost to Northants 184–2 (W Larkins 92*) by 8 wkts

Somerset 190 (G I Burgess 50*, R A Woolmer 4–28) beat Kent 60 (J Garner 5–11) by 130 runs

Nottinghamshire 200 (D W Randall 75, B Hassan 53) lost to Sussex 201–4 (G D Mendis 55) by 6 wkts

Semi Finals

Middlesex 185 (P H Edmonds 63, J Garner 4–24) lost to Somerset 190–3 (P W Denning 90*) by 7 wkts

Northants 255–7 (A J Lamb 101, P Willey 89) beat Sussex 218 (G D Mendis 69, T M Lamb 4–52) by 37 runs

Final

Somerset 269–8 (I V A Richards 117) beat Northants 224 (A J Lamb 78, J Garner 6–29) by 45 runs

(*Lord's 8.9.1979*)

Somerset: B C Rose (cpt), P W Denning, I V A Richards, P M Roebuck, I T Botham, V J Marks, G I Burgess, D Breakwell, J Garner, D J S Taylor, K F Jennings.

Northants: G Cook, W Larkins, R G Williams, A J Lamb, P Willey, T J Yardley, G Sharp, Sarfraz Nawaz, T M Lamb, B J Griffiths, P J Watts (cpt).

1980

Quarter Finals

Surrey 195–7 (G S Clinton 58) beat Essex 195 (B R Hardie 70, R D Jackman 5–22) by losing less wickets with scores tied

Hampshire 196 (D R Turner 53) lost to Yorkshire 197–3 (C W J Athey 93*, J D Love 61*) by 7 wkts

Warwickshire 210–8 (K D Smith 64) lost to Sussex 214–1 (G D Mendis 141*) by 9 wkts

Worcestershire 126 lost to Middlesex 127–0 (C T Radley 64*) by 10 wkts

Semi Finals

Yorkshire 135 (S T Clarke 4–38) lost to Surrey 136–6 by 4 wkts

Middlesex 179 beat Sussex 115 (W W Daniel 6–15) by 64 runs

Final

Surrey 201 (D M Smith 50) lost to Middlesex 202–3 (J M Brearley 96*, R O Butcher 50*) by 7 wkts

(*Lord's 6.9.1980*)

Middlesex: J M Brearley (cpt), P R Downton, C T Radley, M W Gatting, R O Butcher, G D Barlow, S P Hughes, J E Emburey, V A P van der Bijl, M W W Selvey, W W Daniel.

Surrey: A R Butcher, G S Clinton, R D V Knight (cpt), D M Smith, G R J Roope, M A Lynch, Intikhab Alam, D J Thomas, R D Jackman, S T Clarke, C J Richards.

1981

Quarter Finals

Derbyshire 164 beat Nottinghamshire 141 (P A Todd 62) by 23 runs

Hampshire 167–9 lost to Lancashire 169–7 (C H Lloyd 82*) by 3 wkts

Essex 195–9 (G S le Roux 5–35) beat Sussex 170 by 25 runs

Leicestershire 227 (R W Tolchard 70, B F Davison 67) lost to Northants 207–4 (W Larkins 81*, G Cook 63) on scoring rate – rain prevented the match continuing on the second and third day

Semi Finals

Lancashire 186–9 (G Fowler 57, D Lloyd 52) lost to Northants 187–9 by 1 wkt

Essex 149 lost to Derbyshire 149–8 (K J Barnett 59) losing more wickets with the scores tied

Final

Northants 235–9 (G Cook 111, W Larkins 52) lost to Derbyshire 235–6 (J G Wright 76, P N Kirsten 63) losing more wickets with the scores tied

(*Lord's 5.9.1981*)

Derbyshire: A Hill, J G Wright, P N Kirsten, B Wood (cpt), K J Barnett, D S Steele, G Miller, C J Tunnicliffe, R W Taylor, P G Newman, M Hendrick.

Northants: G Cook (cpt), W Larkins, A J Lamb, R G Williams, P Willey, T J Yardley, G Sharp, Sarfraz Nawaz, N A Mallender, T M Lamb, B J Griffiths.

1982

Quarter Finals

Middlesex 215–9 beat Gloucestershire 212–8 (B C Broad 98) by 3 runs

Hampshire 119 (D R Turner 51, R D Jackman 6–22) lost to Surrey 120–2 (D M Smith 62*) by 8 wkts

Essex 132 (S Turner 50*) lost to Yorkshire 133–1 (M D Moxon 78*) by 9 wkts

Somerset 259–9 (I T Botham 85, V J Marks 55, A M Ferreira 4–53) lost to Warwickshire 261–5 (A I Kallicharran 141*, D L Amiss 59) by 5 wkts

Semi Finals

Yorkshire 216–9 (G Boycott 51) lost to Warwickshire 219–3 (K D Smith 113, T A Lloyd 66) by 7 wkts

Surrey 205–9 (A R Butcher 53, W W Daniel 4–24) beat Middlesex 80 (S T Clarke 4–10) by 125 runs

Final

Warwickshire 158 lost to Surrey 159–1 (A R Butcher 86*) by 9 wkts

(*Lord's 4.9.1982*)

Surrey: A R Butcher, G P Howarth, D M Smith, R D V Knight (cpt), M A Lynch, C J Richards, D J Thomas, G Monkhouse, S T Clarke, R D Jackman, K S Mackintosh.

Warwickshire: K D Smith, T A Lloyd, A I Kallicharran, D L Amiss, G W Humpage, P R Oliver, Asif Din, A M Ferreira, C Lethbridge, G C Small, R G D Willis (cpt).

Glamorgan

There is a record of a game played at Swansea in 1780, the first mention of cricket in the county.

Formation of the County Club The first County match is believed to be Glamorgan *v* Carmarthenshire at Neath on August 5, 1861, but nothing definite is known about a County Club at that time. The present County Club was formed at the Angel Hotel, Cardiff on July 5, 1888 and the first inter-county game by the new club was against Warwickshire at St Helen's, Swansea, in the same year.

First-class status The County joined the Minor Counties Competition in 1897 and in 1910 applied to the MCC for first-class status. The MCC's reply was that Glamorgan's request would be considered if the County could arrange fixtures with eight existing first-class counties. This proved impossible at that time, but in the winter of 1920, the county managed to arrange the necessary fixtures and they were granted first-class status for the season of 1921. Glamorgan's first first-class match took place at Cardiff Arms Park *v* Sussex on May 18, 19 and 20, 1921 and resulted in a win for the debutants.

Grounds The principal County ground from 1921 until 1966 was Cardiff Arms Park – adjacent to the international rugby ground – but for the 1967 season Glamorgan moved to Sophia Gardens, playing their first game there *v* Northants on June 7, 8 and 9. The only other ground to be used for first-class matches in 1982 was St Helen's, Swansea, which has been a venue for first-class county matches since 1921.

Other grounds on which Glamorgan have played first-class matches are: Ynysangharad Park, Pontypridd (1926–61); Cowbridge (1931–32); Llanelly (1933–65); The Knoll, Neath (1934–73); Ebbw Vale (1946–68); Port Talbot (1953–63); Colwyn Bay (1966–74); Llandarcy (1971); Newport, Mon (1935–65).

Honours Glamorgan won the County Championship in 1948 and 1969: the County reached the final of the Gillette Cup in 1977; best position in the John Player League is 8th in 1977 and in the Benson and Hedges Cup Glamorgan have never passed the quarter finals.

The players D J Shepherd has made most appearances for the County with 647 between 1950 and 1972; D E Davies also exceeded 600 matches – 612 between 1924 and 1954. The longest serving captain is W Wooller with 14 seasons (1947–60). J S Pressdee, who was 16 years and 2 months when he played *v* Notts in 1949, is the youngest player; the oldest is J C Clay who was 51 years and 5 months on his last appearance *v* Yorkshire in 1949 – Clay was the only survivor of the 1921 side when Glamorgan won the Championship in 1948.

Most England caps by a Glamorgan player are 15, by A J Watkins (1948–52) and I J Jones (1964–68).

Team performances The highest total for the County is 587 for 8 wkts dec on June 2 and 4, 1951 at Cardiff Arms Park against Derbyshire – W Wooller declared after the County had beaten the previous record by one run. Gloucestershire are the only side to score over 600 against Glamorgan, a feat they have performed twice; the record is 653 for 6 wkts dec scored on the County Ground, Bristol on June 30 and July 2, 1928; the feature of the innings was a partnership of 145 in 60 minutes by W R Hammond and C J Barnett.

Thirty-three is the lowest total against the County, scored by Leicestershire at Ebbw Vale on July 30, 1965; D J Shepherd returned the unusual analysis of 10-8-2-5 in this innings.

Three times Glamorgan have been dismissed for under 30, the lowest score being 22 against Lancashire at Liverpool on May 15, 1924 – Glamorgan had dismissed Lancashire for 49 just prior to their own collapse.

Individual performances The match at Newport on May 31, June 1 and 2, 1939 was the scene not only of the highest innings for the County, but against it as well. D E Davies hit 287* batting 7½ hours, whilst W R Hammond hit 302 for the opponents, Gloucestershire. Hammond however just equalled the record against Glamorgan, for in the same fixture in 1934, Hammond had scored 302 not out at the County Ground, Bristol.

J Mercer is the only bowler to take ten wickets in an innings for Glamorgan: 10 for 51 *v* Worcestershire at Worcester on July 29, 1936. The outstanding performance in an innings against Glamorgan is 10 for 18 by G Geary for Leicestershire at Pontypridd on August 15, 1929; as Geary had already taken 6 wickets in the first innings, he had a total in

Only twice have Glamorgan won a competition: the County Championships of 1948 and 1969. This is the victorious 1969 side.

A well-known character of Glamorgan cricket is Wilfred Wooller, the longest-serving captain.

Left *Glamorgan playing at the Sophia Gardens ground, Swansea, in 1979.*

Below *The Gloucestershire County Ground at Ashley Down, Bristol.*

the match of 16 for 96 – a record in a match *v* Glamorgan. The record for Glamorgan in a match is 17 for 212 by J C Clay against Worcestershire at Swansea on June 23, 24 and 25, 1937. No one else has captured 17 wickets for the county.

W G A Parkhouse, A R Lewis and B Hedges have scored over 2,000 runs in a season for the county. The first named holds the record of 2,071 (av 49.31) in 1959. Alan Jones has scored 1,000 runs in every season since 1961 – a total of 22 seasons, which is the county record.

J C Clay's total of 176 wickets in 1937 is the county's record; the other two bowlers to exceed 150 wickets are D J Shepherd (168 in 1956) and B L Muncer (156 in 1948). Shepherd has taken 100 or more wickets in 12 seasons, easily the county record.

Career records are held by A Jones with 32,997 runs between 1957 and 1982 and D J Shepherd with 2,174 wickets between 1950 and 1972; Jones is the only batsman to score more than 30,000 runs and Shepherd the only bowler to take more than 2,000 wickets. Two other cricketers have more than 20,000 runs: D E Davies 26,102 and W G Parkhouse 22,619.

Wicket partnerships

The highest stands in first-class cricket for the County are:

1st	330	R C Fredericks, A Jones *v* Northants (*Swansea*)	1972
2nd	238	A Jones, A R Lewis *v* Sussex (*Hastings*)	1962
3rd	313	D E Davies, W E Jones *v* Essex (*Brentwood*)	1948
4th	263	G Lavis, C C Smart *v* Worcestershire (*Cardiff Arms Park*)	1934
5th	264	M Robinson, S W Montgomery *v* Hampshire (*Bournemouth*)	1949
6th	230	W E Jones, B L Muncer *v* Worcestershire (*Worcester*)	1953
7th	195*	W Wooller, W E Jones *v* Lancashire (*Liverpool*)	1947
8th	202	D Davies, J J Hills *v* Sussex (*Eastbourne*)	1928
9th	203*	J J Hills, J C Clay *v* Worcestershire (*Swansea*)	1929
10th	143	T Davies, S A B Daniels *v* Gloucestershire (*Swansea*)	1982

Limited Overs Cricket Records

GILLETTE/NATWEST CUP
Highest team total 283–3 *v* Warwickshire (*Edgbaston*) 1976
Lowest team total 76 *v* Northants (*Northampton*) 1968
Highest innings 124* A Jones *v* Warwicks (*Edgbaston*) 1976
Best bowling 5–21 P M Walker *v* Cornwall (*Truro*) 1970

JOHN PLAYER LEAGUE
Highest team total 266–6 *v* Northants (*Wellingborough*) 1975
Lowest team total 42 *v* Derbyshire (*Swansea*) 1979
Highest innings 110* A Jones *v* Gloucs (*Cardiff Sophia Gardens*) 1978
Best bowling 6–29 M A Nash *v* Worcs (*Worcester*) 1975

BENSON AND HEDGES CUP
Highest team total 245–7 *v* Hampshire (*Swansea*) 1976
Lowest team total 68 *v* Lancashire (*Old Trafford*) 1973
Highest innings 103* M A Nash *v* Hants (*Swansea*) 1976
J A Hopkins *v* Minor Counties (*Swansea*) 1980
Best bowling 5–17 A H Wilkins *v* Worcs (*Worcester*) 1978

Gloucestershire

The first mention of cricket in the county states: 'Gloucester, Sept 15, 1729: On Monday, the 22nd inst will be play'd in the Town Ham of this city, by eleven men of a side a game of cricket, for upwards of 20 guineas.'

Formation of the County Club The first known match by 'Gloucestershire' took place on August 9 and 10, 1839.

A County Club was based at Cheltenham from 1863 to 1871 and in the latter year the present County Club seems to have been formed, but no exact date of formation has yet been unearthed.

First-class status Contemporary opinion ranks the match against Surrey on Durdham Downs near Bristol, June 2, 3 and 4, 1870 as the first first-class match staged by the County.

Grounds The original ground at Durdham Down was in fact only used once by the county – in the match noted above. The present County Ground on Ashley Down, Bristol was opened in 1889; other grounds in current use are: College Ground, Cheltenham (since 1872); Wagon Works Ground, Gloucester (since 1923); Moreton-in-Marsh (since 1884).

Grounds that have been used by the County are: Clifton College (1871–1932); Greenbank, Bristol (1922–28); East Gloucs Ground, Cheltenham (1888–1903); Victoria Park, Cheltenham (1923–37); Cirencester (1879); The Spa Ground, Gloucester (1883–1923); Lydney (1963–69); Erinoid Ground, Stroud (1956–63); The Swilgate, Tewkesbury (1972–73). Gloucestershire have also played one John Player match on the Wiltshire County Ground at Swindon.

Honours Gloucestershire were joint-County Champions with Notts in 1873 and then won the Championship outright in 1874, 1876 and 1877. The County won the Gillette Cup in 1973 and the Benson and Hedges Cup in 1977. The best position they have obtained in the John Player League is 6th – in 1969, 1973 and 1977.

The players C W L Parker has made the most appearances for the County – 602 between 1903 and 1935. Four other cricketers have exceeded 500 matches: J B Mortimore (594), C A Milton (585), T W J Goddard (558), R B Nicholls (534).

The longest serving captain is Dr W G Grace, who led the County in the first first-class match in 1870 and was in his 30th season as captain when he left midway through 1899 due to a difference of opinion.

The youngest player to represent the County is W W F Pullen, who was 15 years and 11 months when he played against Middlesex in 1882. Dr E M Grace was the oldest player, being 54 years and 7 months in his last game v Warwickshire in 1896.

W R Hammond with 85 Test Matches to his name is the Gloucestershire cricketer capped most times for England.

Team performances The highest total for the County is 653 for 6 wkts dec against Glamorgan at Bristol on June 30 and July 2, 1928 and the highest against the County was hit by the Australians at Bristol on July 3 and 5, 1948, when the total was 774 for 7 wkts dec. The leading scorer was A R Morris, who began with a hundred before lunch on the first morning, hit a second hundred between lunch and tea and ended with 290 in 300 minutes with 42 fours and a six.

The Australians also inflicted the lowest total on the County, dismissing them for 17 at Cheltenham on August 22, 1896 – the wicket, drying after rain, was very awkward; Dr W G Grace with 9 made the best score and H Trumble returned figures of 10-6-8-6. In 1907, however, Gloucestershire created a County Championship record by dismissing Northants for 12 on the Spa Ground, Gloucester on June 11; in a match ruined by rain the scores were Gloucs 60 and 88; Northants 12 and 40 for 7 – no play was possible on the last day.

Individual performances Dr W G Grace hit 318 not out against Yorkshire on the College Ground at Cheltenham on August 17 and 18, 1876. He carried his bat through the completed Gloucestershire innings, being at the crease over 8 hours. This remains the highest innings for the County. The highest against the County is 296 by A O Jones for Notts at Trent Bridge on July 23 and 24, 1903; he batted 6 hours.

Best bowling in an innings for Gloucestershire is 10-40 by E G Dennett against Essex at Bristol on August 6, 1906. Three other bowlers have taken 10 wickets in an innings for the County: J K R Graveney, 10-66 v Derbyshire at Chesterfield, 1949; C W L Parker, 10-79 v Somerset at Bristol, 1921; T W J Goddard, 10-113 v Worcs at Cheltenham, 1937.

Two bowlers have returned identical figures against Gloucestershire: 10-66 was achieved by A A Mailey for the Australians at Cheltenham on August 22 and 23, 1921, and by K Smales for Notts on the Erinoid Ground at Stroud on June 9 and 11, 1956.

Left *W R Hammond, Gloucestershire's most-capped player and most prolific run-getter.*

Opposite *W G Grace, the champion, the most famous of all cricketers, and still the holder of the highest individual score for Gloucestershire.*

The best bowling in a match for the county is 17-56, this being accomplished by C W L Parker against Essex on the Wagon Works Ground at Gloucester on July 25 and 28, 1925 (rain prevented play on Monday 27). No one has achieved similar figures against Gloucestershire, the best being 15-87 by A J Conway for Worcestershire at Moreton-in-Marsh on June 22 and 23, 1914 – Wisden makes the following comment: 'The fielding throughout the game was of a deplorable description, no fewer than fifteen palpable chances being missed.'

On five occasions batsmen have topped 2,500 runs for the county in a season – the leading four instances are by W R Hammond; Zaheer Abbas in 1976 being the other batsman. The record is 2,860 (av 69.75) by Hammond in 1933. Hammond also holds the record for hitting 1,000 runs in a season most times, 17 between 1923 and 1946, but he is closely followed by C A Milton with 16 between 1951 and 1969.

The record for the most wickets in a season is unusual, in that T W J Goddard took 222 wickets in two separate seasons precisely a decade apart – in 1937 and in 1947. On the second occasion he was a veteran of 46. His average in the first year was 16.80 and in the second 16.37. Goddard also reached 200 wickets in 1935. The only other Gloucestershire bowler to attain this figure also achieved it three times: C W L Parker in 1925, 1926 and 1931.

This pair of bowlers also head the table of most wickets in a career – Parker took 3,170 (av 19.43) and Goddard 2,862 (av 19.58); the third player to reach 2,000 is E G Dennett with 2,082 (av 19.88).

The career batting record is held by W R Hammond: 33,664 runs (av 57.06); C A Milton comes second with 30,218 runs (av 33.65). The seven batsmen who hit between 20,000 and 30,000 runs are A E Dipper, R B Nicholls, D M Young, Dr W G Grace, G M Emmett, J F Crapp and C J Barnett.

Wicket partnerships

The highest stands in first-class cricket for the County are:

1st	395	D M Young, R B Nicholls v Oxford Univ (*Oxford*)	1962
2nd	256	C T M Pugh, T W Graveney v Derbys (*Chesterfield*) 1960	
3rd	336	W R Hammond, B H Lyon v Leics (*Aylestone Rd, Leicester*) 1933	
4th	321	W R Hammond, W L Neale v Leics (*Wagon Works, Gloucester*) 1937	
5th	261	Dr W G Grace, W O Moberly v Yorkshire (*Cheltenham*) 1876	
6th	320	G L Jessop, J H Board v Sussex (*Hove*)	1903
7th	248	Dr W G Grace, E L Thomas v Sussex (*Hove*)	1896
8th	239	W R Hammond, A E Wilson v Lancashire (*Bristol*) 1938	
9th	193	Dr W G Grace, S A P Kitcat v Sussex (*Bristol*)	1896
10th	131	W R Gouldsworthy, J Bessant v Somerset (*Bristol*) 1923	

The record for the 6th wicket – made on Whit Monday 1903 – was mainly the work of G L Jessop. He hit his first fifty in 30 minutes, reached 100 in 70 minutes and 200 in 120 minutes and his completed innings of 286 in 175 minutes – the partnership of 320 took about 165 minutes.

Limited overs cricket records

GILLETTE/NATWEST CUP
Highest team total   327–7 v Berkshire (*Reading*)   1966
Lowest team total   86 v Sussex (*Hove*)   1969
Highest innings   131* Zaheer Abbas v Leics (*Grace Rd, Leicester*)   1975
Best bowling   5–11 D A Graveney v Ireland (*Dublin*)   1981

JOHN PLAYER LEAGUE
Highest team total   255 v Somerset (*Imperial Grd, Bristol*)   1975
Lowest team total   49 v Middlesex (*County Grd, Bristol*)   1978
Highest innings   131 Sadiq Mohammad v Somerset (*Imperial Grd, Bristol*)   1975
Best bowling   5–8 M J Procter v Middx (*Wagon Works, Gloucester*)   1977

BENSON AND HEDGES CUP
Highest team total   300–4 v Combined Univs (*Oxford*)   1982
Lowest team total   62 v Hampshire (*County Grd, Bristol*)   1975
Highest innings   154* M J Procter v Somerset (*Taunton*)   1972
Best bowling   6–13 M J Procter v Hampshire (*Southampton*)   1977

Godalming
In the period when there was no Surrey County Club, Godalming succeeded Epsom as the leading Club in the County and from 1821 to 1825 played several matches against Sussex, Hampshire and MCC which ranked as 'important' matches of their time.

Grace, Dr William Gilbert (1848–1915)
Even now, 67 years after his death, W G Grace is probably the most easily recognisable sportsman in England and certainly he towers over all his contemporaries in cricket or indeed in any other sport. Undoubtedly he is the greatest of cricketers. A selection of the records he held in first-class cricket are:

Highest individual innings: 344 MCC v Kent (*Canterbury*)   1876
Most runs in a season: 2,739 in 1871
Highest batting average in a season: 78.25 in 1871
First batsman to score 10 centuries in a season: 1871
First player to perform the 'Double': 1,664 runs and 140 wkts in 1874
First player to score 1,000 runs in a month: 1,024 in August 1871
First player to score 1,000 runs in May: 1,016 in 1895
First player to score 20,000, 30,000, 40,000 and 50,000 runs in a career
First player to hit 100 centuries in a career

Grounds
On the following occasions County Championship matches have been staged on neutral grounds:

Cambridgeshire v Nottinghamshire at Old Trafford in 1864.
Cambridgeshire v Yorkshire at Ashton-under-Lyne in 1865.
Surrey v Kent and v Yorkshire at Lord's in 1914 – the military authorities had taken over the Oval.
Middlesex v Nottinghamshire at the Oval in 1939 – Lord's was required for the Eton v Harrow match.

(See under individual Counties for details of seasons in which each county ground has been used.)

Hambledon

The Hambledon Club organised many of the major cricket matches played in England for some 30 years from the middle 1760s onwards. The Club promoted the Hampshire Eleven of that period and was in some ways the predecessor of the MCC. Home matches organised by the Club were played on Broadhalfpenny Down and later Windmill Down near the village of Hambledon in Hampshire.

Hampshire

As early as 1647 there is a probable reference in a Latin poem to cricket being played at Winchester College, but the first reference to an actual match is Portsmouth Common against Farnham and Titchfield on August 29, 1749.

Formation of the County Club   The first County match seems to be against Sussex in June 1766 – several authorities give August 8, 1750 *v* London, but the team was Hampton and not Hampshire and there are a number of later confusions between Hampshire and Hampton. The Hambleton Club (see under) organised Hampshire matches for many years. According to G B Buckley a Hampshire County Club was formed on April 3, 1849; there are references to at least two prior to this, but the first – at Winchester in 1795 – was not a Cricket club, but a social one and the second – in 1839 – is most probably 'South Hampshire'.

The present County Club was formed on August 12, 1863.

First-class status   In so far as modern County cricket is concerned, Hampshire's initial first class match is *v* MCC at Lord's on July 29 and 30, 1861. Contemporary opinion demoted Hampshire after the 1885 season and the County was restored to first-class status with their match *v* Somerset at Taunton, May 30, 31 and June 1, 1895. The problem of the status of Hampshire matches before 1861 is complex. Further details can be found in the 'Guides to First-class Matches' published by the Association of Cricket Statisticians.

Grounds   The headquarters of the present County Club was originally the Antelope Ground in Southampton, but the County moved to the County Ground, which is in use today, in 1885. The other grounds currently used for first-class matches are: Dean Park, Bournemouth (since 1897); May's Bounty, Basingstoke (since 1906) and the United Services, Portsmouth (since 1882). Other towns to stage first-class county games include Winchester (1875), Alton (1904), Aldershot (1905–48), Newport, IOW (1938–39), Cowes, IOW (1956–62).

Honours   The County Championship has been won twice – in 1961 and 1973; the John Player League twice – in 1975 and 1978. The County has reached the semi-finals of the Gillette Cup twice – in 1966 and 1976 and also the Benson and Hedges Cup semi-finals twice – in 1975 and 1977.

The players   C P Mead has made the most appearances for the County; his total of 700 matches is over a hundred more than any other player. His career spanned from 1905 to 1936.

Longest serving captain is Hon L H Tennyson, who led the County for 15 seasons (1919–33).

The youngest cricketer is C R Young who was 15 years and 131 days when he appeared *v* Kent in 1867; the oldest, aged 52 years and 5 months, was H B Bethune, whose final appearance came *v* Lancashire in 1897 – he was in fact already over 40 when he made his debut in 1885.

C P Mead is the Hampshire cricketer with most England caps – 17 between 1911 and 1923.

Team performances   The highest total for the County is 672 for 7 wkts dec made against Somerset at Taunton on July 21 and 22, 1899 – the size of the score was completely unexpected when at close of play on the second day, Hampshire were struggling at 63 for 4; the fifth wicket then added 196 and the sixth wicket 411 (see under wicket partnerships).

Two sides have exceeded 700 against Hampshire; the Australians hit 708 for 7 wkts dec at Southampton in 1921, but the record was set by Surrey who scored 742 at the Oval on May 6 and 7, 1909. Surrey batted 380 minutes and went on to win the game by an innings and 468 runs – the second largest win recorded in County Championship cricket.

The lowest total by Hampshire is 15 scored in the famous match against Warwickshire at Edgbaston on June 14, 1922. Following on Hampshire hit 521 and eventually won the game by 155 runs. There were no less than 8 ducks in Hampshire's low score. The worst total

Above   *Broadhalfpenny Down, where matches organised by the Hambledon Club were played.*

Opposite above   *The County Ground in Southampton, which will celebrate 100 years of county cricket in 1985.*

Left   *The Hon H L Tennyson, Hampshire's longest serving captain, who also captained England.*

Opposite below   *A match taking place at Hambledon in 1777.*

against Hampshire is 23 by Yorkshire at Middlesbrough on May 19 and 20, 1965 – the most notable innings in the whole of this game was 55 in 29 minutes by F S Trueman.

Individual performances   Two batsmen have hit a triple hundred for Hampshire, Major R M Poore made 304 v Somerset at Taunton in 1899, and this record was beaten by R H Moore, who hit 316 v Warwickshire at Bournemouth on July 28 and 29, 1937. He was at the crease 380 minutes and hit 3 sixes and 43 fours. P Holmes for Yorkshire hit the highest against Hampshire – 302* at Portsmouth on August 28 and 30, 1920; Holmes batted 435 minutes and the Yorkshire first wicket added 347, Holmes being partnered by H Sutcliffe. No one has captured all ten wickets in an innings for the County, though on 11 occasions nine have been taken – no less than four times by D Shackleton. The best analysis however is 9 for 25 by R M H Cottam v Lancashire at Old Trafford on June 9 and 10, 1965 – this was in the first innings; although Lancashire lost all ten wickets in their second innings, Cottam failed to take a single one. The best bowling performance against Hampshire in an innings is 9 for 21 by T L Richmond for Notts at Trent Bridge on September 1, 1922 – the match is however more memorable for the fact that Hon L H Tennyson, the Hampshire captain, ordered J A Newman off the field for refusing to bowl; Newman then kicked over the stumps. J A Newman, in fact, holds the record for the best bowling for the County in a match, taking 16 for 88 against Somerset at Weston-super-Mare on August 3, 4 and 5, 1927; no one else has taken 16 wickets in a match for Hampshire. The best against is 17–119 by W Mead of Essex on July 25, 26 and 27, 1895.

2,000 runs in a season have been reached 23 times for the County, but on no less than ten of those occasions, the batsman was C P Mead – of the leading ten instances, seven are by him. The record total is 2,854 (av 79.27) set by Mead in 1928. He reached 1,000 runs in a season 27 times between 1906 and 1936, easily the leading record.

Most wickets in a season are 190 by A S Kennedy in 1922 and he achieved 100 wickets in a season on 12 occasions; this however is beaten by D Shackleton who performed the feat 19 times between 1949 and 1968 (1954 was the only year he missed 100).

As might be expected, C P Mead holds the career batting record by a huge margin – 48,892 runs (av 48.84). R E Marshall lies second with 30,303 (av 36.03) and there is a gap of over 7,000 runs between Marshall and the third on the list, G Brown with 22,959.

The career bowling record is not so clear cut, two bowlers exceeding 2,500. D Shackleton has 2,669 (av 18.23) and A S Kennedy 2,549 (av 21.16). Shackleton's career spanned 1948 to 1969 and Kennedy's 1907 to 1936.

Wicket partnerships

The highest stands in first-class cricket for the County are:

1st	249	R E Marshall, J R Gray v Middlesex (*Portsmouth*) 1960	
2nd	321	G Brown, E I M Barrett v Gloucestershire (*Southampton*) 1920	
3rd	344	C P Mead, G Brown v Yorkshire (*Portsmouth*) 1927	
4th	263	R E Marshall, D A Livingstone v Middlesex (*Lord's*) 1970	
5th	235	G Hill, D F Walker v Sussex (*Portsmouth*) 1937	
6th	411	R M Poore, E G Wynyard v Somerset (*Taunton*) 1899	
7th	325	G Brown, C H Abercrombie v Essex (*Leyton*) 1913	
8th	178	C P Mead, C P Brutton v Worcs (*Bournemouth*) 1925	
9th	230	D A Livingstone, A T Castell v Surrey (*Southampton*) 1962	
10th	192	H A W Bowell, W H Livsey v Worcs (*Bournemouth*) 1921	

Limited overs cricket records

GILLETTE/NATWEST CUP

Highest team total   371–4 v Glamorgan (*Southampton*) 1975
Lowest team total   98 v Lancashire (*Old Trafford*) 1975
Highest innings   177 C G Greenidge v Glam (*Southampton*) 1975
Best bowling   7–30 P J Sainsbury v Norfolk (*Southampton*) 1965

Gordon Greenidge, who has played Hampshire's highest innings in all three limited-overs competitions, scoring over 150 in each.

JOHN PLAYER LEAGUE

Highest team total   288–5 v Somerset (*Weston-super-Mare*) 1975
Lowest team total   43 v Essex (*Basingstoke*) 1972
Highest innings   163* C G Greenidge v Warwicks (*Edgbaston*) 1979
Best bowling   6–20 T E Jesty v Glamorgan (*Cardiff, Sophia Gdns*) 1975

BENSON AND HEDGES CUP

Highest team total   321–1 v Minor Counties (South) (*Amersham*) 1973
Lowest team total   94 v Glamorgan (*Swansea*) 1973
Highest innings   173* C G Greenidge v Minor Counties (South) (*Amersham*) 1973
Best bowling   5–24 R S Herman v Gloucestershire (*Bristol*) 1975
5–24 K St J D Emery v Essex (*Chelmsford*) 1982

The remarkable feature of these records is that C G Greenidge has achieved the unique feat of hitting over 150 in an innings in all three limited overs competitions.

Handled Ball

The first mention of a batsman being dismissed 'handling ball in play' occurred in 1797.

The only instance of a batsman being dismissed 'handled ball' in a Test occurred in 1978–79 in Australia:

A M J Hilditch   Australia v Pakistan (*Perth*)   1978–79

There are only five instances in English first-class cricket:

J Grundy   MCC v Kent (*Lords*)   1857
G Bennett   Kent v Sussex (*Hove*)   1872
C W Wright   Nottinghamshire v Gloucestershire (*Bristol*)   1893
A W Nourse   South Africans v Sussex (*Hove*)   1907
A Rees   Glamorgan v Middlesex (*Lord's*)   1965

The most recent examples in other countries are:

South Africa   D K Pearse, Natal v Western Province (*Cape Town*)   1978–79
Pakistan   Musleh-ud-Din, Railways v Lahore (*Lahore*)   1979–80
New Zealand   A W Gilbertson, Otago v Auckland (*Auckland*)   1952–53

There are no instances in India or West Indies.

A painting dated 1792 by Francois Jean Sable of Tom Hope of the Amsterdam family of merchants of the eighteenth century, painted in Rome, but an early indication of cricket in Holland.

Hat Trick

Although the first published reference to a player being presented with a hat for taking three wickets with successive deliveries occurs in 1858, the custom was probably established much earlier. The record number of hat-tricks in a first-class career is 7 by D V P Wright; 6 of these were for Kent and the other one for MCC in South Africa.

Two cricketers have performed the hat-trick twice in the same innings, A E Trott for Middlesex v Somerset at Lord's in 1907 – one of his hat-tricks was in fact 4 for 4 – and J S Rao for Services v Northern Punjab at Amritsar in 1963–64.

Hat tricks in which all three batsmen were dismissed in a similar manner are:

All LBW
H Fisher   Yorkshire v Somerset (*Bramall Lane*)   1932
J A Flavell   Worcestershire v Lancashire (*Old Trafford*)   1963
M J Procter   Gloucs v Essex (*Westcliff*)   1972
B J Ikin   Griqualand West v OFS (*Kimberley*)   1973–74
M J Procter   Gloucs v Yorkshire (*Cheltenham*)   1979

The record number of first-class hat-tricks by one player is seven, performed by D V P Wright of Kent.

All caught
S G Smith   c G J Thompson, Northants v Warwicks (*Edgbaston*)
   1914
R Beesly   c C White, Border v Griqualand West (*Queenstown*)
   1946–47
H L Jackson   c G O Dawkes, Derbyshire v Worcs (*Kidderminster*)
   1958

All stumped
C L Townsend   st W H Brain, Gloucs v Somerset (*Cheltenham*)
   1893

Highest Individual Innings
(*See under 'Batting'*)

Highest Team Totals
The highest team total in any class of cricket is 1,107 for Victoria v New South Wales, December 24, 27 and 28, 1926, on Melbourne Cricket Ground. The details are:

New South Wales   221 and 230

VICTORIA

1	W M Woodfull	*c* Ratcliffe *b* Andrews	133
2	W H Ponsford	*b* Morgan	352
3	H S T L Hendry	*c* Morgan *b* Mailey	100
4	J Ryder	*c* Kippax *b* Andrews	295
5	H S B Love	*st* Ratcliffe *b* Mailey	6
6	S P King	*st* Ratcliffe *b* Mailey	7
7	A E V Hartkopf	*c* McGuirk *b* Mailey	61
8	A E Liddicut	*b* McGuirk	36
9	J L Ellis	*run out*	63
10	F L Morton	*run out*	0
11	D D J Blackie	*not out*	27
	Extras		27
	TOTAL		1107

Fall of wkts: 375, 594, 614, 631, 657, 834, 915, 1,043, 1,046, 1,107.

The first recorded instances of team totals of 300, 400, 500 etc. are:

300:   307   Hampshire v England (*Chertsey*)   1774
400:   403   Hampshire v England (*Sevenoaks*)   1777
500:   546–7   Oxford v Purton (*Purton*)   1859
600:   630   Classical v Modern (*Clifton College*)   1868
700:   724   Royal Engineers v I Zingari (*Chatham*)   1875
800 and 900:   920   Orleans Club v Rickling Green (*Rickling Green*)   1882
1000:   1094   Melbourne University v Essenden (*University Grd*)   1897–98
1100:   1107   Victoria v New South Wales (*Melbourne*)   1926–27

(*For individual countries and teams see under appropriate headings*)

Hit Ball Twice
The following instances of a batsman being given out 'hit the ball twice' have occurred in first-class cricket:

G Rawlins   Sheffield v Nottingham (*Nottingham*)   1827
H E Bull   MCC v Oxford University (*Lord's*)   1864
H R J Charlwood   Sussex v Surrey (*Hove*)   1872
R G Barlow   North v South (*Lord's*)   1878
P S Wimble   Transvaal v Griqualand West (*Kimberley*)   1892–93
G B Nichols   Somerset v Gloucestershire (*Bristol*)   1896
A F A Lilley   Warwickshire v Yorkshire (*Edgbaston*)   1897
J H King   Leicestershire v Surrey (*Oval*)   1906
A P Binns   Jamaica v British Guiana (*Georgetown*)   1956–57
K Bavanna   Andhra v Mysore (*Guntur*)   1963–64
Zaheer Abbas   P I A v Karachi Blues (*Karachi*)   1969–70

Holland
The first reference to the game in Holland is at Noorthey in 1845. The Dutch Cricket League was started in 1891 and in the same year a representative Dutch Eleven took the field, when it opposed a team from

England called the Rambling Britons, which included Sir Arthur Conan Doyle in its side.

THE RECORDS IN HOLLAND ARE:
Highest team total   580–8 HCC v Hilversum   1913
Highest individual innings   240* J Offerman Hermes-DVS   1935
Best bowling in innings   All 10 wkts have been taken on at least 10 occasions
Most runs in a season   1270 H W Glerum   1935
Most runs in a career   13573 H van Manen
Most wickets in a career   2338 C J Posthuma

The most famous match so far played by Holland took place at The Hague on August 29, 1964 when Holland beat the Australian Team which was touring England that summer, in a one-day game.

Holland took part in the 1979 ICC Trophy and obtained one win – at the expense of Israel – and also competed in 1982.

ICC Trophy

This International Competition competed for by Associate members of the ICC has been staged twice. The Countries participating were divided into three leagues in 1979, with the best four sides in the leagues then competing between themselves on a knock-out basis. In 1982, there were two leagues instead of three. The matches are 60 overs per side.

1979 Competition

Group One	P	W	D	L	A	Pts
Bermuda	3	3	0	0	1	14
East Africa	4	2	1	1	0	10
Papua-New Guinea	4	1	2	1	0	8
Singapore	3	1	0	2	1	6
Argentina	4	0	1	3	0	2

Group Two	P	W	D	L	A	Pts
Denmark	4	4	0	0	0	16
Canada	4	3	0	1	0	12
Bangladesh	4	2	0	2	0	8
Fiji	3	0	0	3	1	2
Malaysia	3	0	0	3	1	2

Group Three	P	W	D	L	A	Pts
Sri Lanka	3	2	0	1	1	10
USA	3	2	0	1	1	10
Wales	3	2	0	1	1	10
Holland	3	1	0	2	1	6
Israel	4	1	0	3	0	4

(*Sri Lanka won on faster run rate; Wales played in place of Gibraltar who withdrew at the last moment*)

Semi Finals
Sri Lanka 318–8 (R L Dias 88, L R D Mendis 68) beat Denmark 110 by 208 runs
Bermuda 181 lost to Canada 186–6 (B M Mauricette 72) by 4 wkts

Final
Sri Lanka 324–8 (L R D Mendis 66, S A Jayasinghe 64) beat Canada 264–5 (J C B Vaughan 80, C A Marshall 55) by 60 runs

1982 Competition

Group One	P	W	L	NR	Pts
Zimbabwe	7	5	0	2	24
Papua-New Guinea	7	4	2	1	18
Canada	7	3	1	3	18
Kenya	7	3	2	2	16
USA	7	1	2	4	12
Hong Kong	7	2	3	2	12
Gibraltar	7	0	3	4	8
Israel	7	0	5	2	4

Group Two	P	W	L	NR	Pts
Bermuda	7	6	0	1	26
Bangladesh	7	4	1	2	20
Holland	7	3	1	3	18
Singapore	7	1	2	4	12

1982 Competition *continued*	P	W	L	NR	Pts
Fiji	7	1	3	3	10
West Africa	7	0	2	5	10
East Africa	7	1	3	3	10
Malaysia	7	0	4	3	6

Semi Finals
Bangladesh 124 (K M Curran 4–28) lost to Zimbabwe 126–2 (J G Heron 63*) by 8 wkts
Papua-New Guinea 153 (V Pala 72) lost to Bermuda 155–4 (C G Blades 69*) by 6 wkts

Third Place Play-off
Bangladesh 224 (Y Rahman 115, N Shirazi 52, Aukopi 5–14) lost to Papua-New Guinea 225–7 (W Maha 60) by 3 wkts

Final
Bermuda 231–8 lost to Zimbabwe 232–5 (A J Pycroft 82, C A P Hodgson 57*) by 5 wkts

Illness

The only time that an England player travelled to Australia as part of an official MCC touring party but, because of illness, failed to appear in a single match was during the 1928–29 tour. S J Staples (Notts) developed muscular trouble in the back and after spending some time in bed in Melbourne was dispatched home.

In South Africa however the same thing had happened to D C Robinson (Gloucs) who travelled with the 1913–14 MCC team, but was taken ill on arrival and returned home without appearing in a match.

In the fourth Test at Old Trafford, July 24 to 27, 1926, the English captain, A W Carr led the team on to the field on the first day, but after 10 balls had been bowled rain stopped play for the day. Carr was taken ill with tonsillitis and took no further part in the match, J B Hobbs taking on the role as captain.

India

The first mention of cricket in India was in 1721 at Cambay – about 30 miles West of Baroda – the game being played by English sailors.

The first known cricket club was formed in Calcutta and was in existence in 1792.

The first major match was possibly Madras v Calcutta in 1864 and the first match involving 'All India' took place on January 26, 27 and 28, 1893 against the English Touring Team under Lord Hawke.

Records in India in first-class cricket
Highest team total   912–8d Holkar v Mysore (*Indore*)   1945–46
Lowest team total   21 Muslims v Europeans (*Poona*)   1914–15
Highest individual innings   515 D R Havewala, Railway v St Xavier's Coll (*Bombay*)   1933–34
443* B B Nimbalkar, Maharashtra v Kathiawar (*Poona*) 1948–49
Best bowling in innings   10–20 P M Chatterjee, Bengal v Assam (*Jorhat*)   1956–57
Best bowling in match   16–69 F A Tarrant, England v India (*Bombay*)   1915–16

Wicket partnerships
1st   451* S Desai, R M H Binny. Karnataka v Kerala (*Chickmagalur*) 1977–78
2nd   455 K V Bhandarkar, B B Nimbalkar. Maharashtra v Kathiawar (*Poona*) 1948–49
3rd   410 R S Modi, N B Amarnath. India in England v Rest (*Calcutta*) 1946–47
4th   577 Gul Mahomed, V S Hazare. Baroda v Holkar (*Baroda*) 1946–47
5th   360 U M Merchant, M N Raiji. Bombay v Hyderabad (*Bombay*) 1947–48
6th   371 V M Merchant, R S Modi. Bombay v Maharashtra (*Bombay*) 1943–44
7th   274 K C Ibrahim, K M Rangnekar. Bijapur XI v Bengal XI (*Bombay*) 1942–43
8th   236 C T Sarwate, R P Singh. Holkar v Delhi (*Delhi*) 1949–50

Three Indian batsmen who added 415 for the third wicket for India against England at Madras in 1979: (above left) *D Vengsarkar,* (above) *G Vishwanath,* (left) *Y Sharma.*

9th   245   V S Hazare, N D Nagarwalla. Maharashtra v Baroda
          (*Poona*) 1939–40
10th   138   Yadvendrasinhji, S Mubarak Ali. Nawanagar v Bengal
          (*Bombay*) 1936–37
(**Note:** 415 was added for the 3rd wkt by three batsmen: D B
Vengsarkar, G R Viswanath and Yashpal Sharma for India v England
(*Madras*) 1981–82.

   Also A Salaam and Ahsan-al-Haq added about 150 for the 10th wkt
for Muslims v Sikhs (*Lahore*) 1923–24.)

International Cricket Conference

Founded (as the Imperial Cricket Conference) on June 15, 1909 at a
meeting at Lord's, the original function of the ICC was to draw up a set
of rules to govern Test Matches, but its powers are now wider.

   A list of Countries and when they joined is as follows:

England	1909	
Australia	1909	
South Africa	1909	(left 1961)
India	1926	
New Zealand	1926	
West Indies	1926	
Pakistan	1952	
Ceylon* (Sri Lanka)	1965	(Full member 1981)
Fiji*	1965	
USA*	1965	
Bermuda*	1966	
Denmark*	1966	
East Africa*	1966	
Holland*	1966	
Malaysia*	1967	
Canada*	1968	
Hong Kong*	1969	
Gibraltar*	1969	
Papua-New Guinea*	1973	
Argentina*	1974	
Israel*	1974	
Singapore*	1974	
West Africa*	1976	
Bangladesh*	1977	
Zimbabwe*	1981	
Kenya*	1981	*Denotes Associate member*

Ireland

The first recorded cricket match in Ireland took place in 1792 when the
Dublin Garrison beat All Ireland. The match between Ireland and
Scotland was first played in 1888.

   The question of the status of matches played by Ireland has been the
subject of debate for many years and will probably remain so, since the
Irish Cricket Union does not agree with the rulings made by the MCC,
the former being more liberal, whilst the rulings of the latter sometimes
defy logic.

   In this work, the rulings of MCC are adhered to, and the first first-
class match involving Ireland therefore was v London County in 1902.

   Dublin University however had their matches against first-class
opposition ruled first-class in 1895.

I Zingari

Founded as a wandering cricket club (its name means 'The Gypsies') in
1845, I Zingari played 17 first-class matches between 1866 and 1904.
The initial match was played during the Canterbury Festival of 1866,
but all the remaining matches took place at Scarborough. The Club has
sent teams abroad and plays between 20 and 30 matches each season.

The first-class records for the Club are:

Highest team total   412–4 v Gentlemen (*Lord's*) 1904
Lowest team total   78 v Gents of South (*Canterbury*) 1866
Highest individual innings   147 E G Wynyard v Gentlemen
   (*Lord's*) 1904
Best bowling in innings   7–12 R Henderson v Yorkshire
   (*Scarborough*) 1877

*Despite three successive ducks, Len Hutton scored 1,294 runs in June
1949, a record for the month.*

*M J K Smith, of Warwickshire, here batting against Kent in 1971,
holds the record for most runs in July: 1,209 in 1959.*

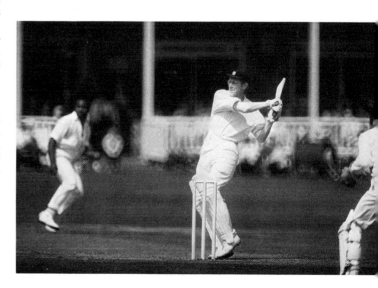

June

Most runs scored in first-class matches in June are 1,294 by L Hutton in 1949, his full details being:

M	I	NO	Runs	HS	Avge	100s
9	16	2	1294	201	92.42	7

Seven of the matches were for Yorkshire and two for England. In the middle of the month Hutton actually suffered three successive ducks!

In June 1981 Zaheer Abbas (*Gloucestershire*) scored 1,016 runs (av 112.88) having had not a single first-class innings in May due to bad weather washing out Gloucestershire's matches.

Most wickets in first-class matches in June are 91 by A P Freeman in 1930.

July

Most runs scored in first-class matches in July are 1,209 by M J K Smith in 1959, his full details being:

M	I	NO	Runs	HS	Avge	100s
9	15	2	1209	200*	93.00	5

Seven of his matches were for Warwickshire, one for England and one for the Gentlemen.

Most wickets in July in first-class matches are 91 by A P Freeman in 1929.

Kent

'Domino Johanni de Leek capellano Domini Edwardi fil' Regis pro den' per ipsum liberat' eidem Domino suo ad ludendum as Creag' at alios ludos per vices per manus proprias apud Westm' 10 die Martii 100s. Et per manus Hugonis camerarii sui apud Newenton mense Martii 20s. – Summa 6.0.0.'

This Latin extract is from the Wardrobe accounts of Edward I, for the year 1299–1300. It refers to the town of 'Newenton' (now Newenden) on the Kent-Sussex border, about 7 miles from Rye and to 'Creag' and other games. All authorities seem to agree that 'Creag' is cricket and this being the case this is the earliest known reference to the game. The exact date is March 10, 1300.

The first match ever recorded also took place in Kent – at Coxheath on May 29, 1646 and the evidence for this comes from the report of a court case which was brought as the result of the non-payment of a debt incurred from a wager at the match.

Formation of the County Club Kent as a cricket team is first recorded in the match Kent v Surrey at Dartford Brent on June 29, 1709 – these were probably little more than village sides with grandiose titles, but the whole of the history of eighteenth century cricket is intertwined with teams playing under the title of Kent. The first major extant cricket score is of the match between Kent and All England on the Artillery Ground in London on June 18, 1744. These Kent sides were organised by various wealthy patrons. In the 1830s, the Town Malling Club undertook the arranging of Kent County matches and it was not until August 6, 1842 that the Kent County Cricket Club was formed in Canterbury – this club is the direct ancestor of the present County Club.

First-class status Since the staging of the Kent v All England match of 1744, Kent has always been one of the 'great' cricketing counties and was automatically included as 'first-class' when that term came into use in the mid-19th century.

Grounds The present headquarters of the County Club is the St Lawrence Ground, Canterbury, used since 1847. Other grounds in current use are: Hesketh Park, Dartford (since 1956); Municipal Sports Ground, Folkestone (since 1926); Mote Park, Maidstone (since 1859); Nevill Ground, Tunbridge Wells (since 1901). Grounds used for first-class County matches since 1842 are: Foxgrove Grd, Beckenham (1886–1905); Hemsted Park, Benenden (1843); Rectory Field, Blackheath (1887–1971); White Hart Field, Bromley (1842); Beverley Grd, Canterbury (1842–46); Private Banks Grd, Catford (1875–1921); Nore Grd, Chatham (1926–27); School Field, Cranbrook (1850–51); Swifts Park, Cranbrook (1862–63); Crystal Palace (1864–70); Crabble Athletic Grd, Dover (1907–76); Mount Field, Faversham (1876); Garrison Grd, Gillingham (1862–1972); Bat and Ball Grd, Gravesend (1849–1971); Margate (1864); New Beckenham (1954); Preston Hall (1846–47);

Most appearances for Kent were made by Frank Woolley, 764 between 1906 and 1938 – over 150 more than any other player.

Sandgate (1862–63); Southborough (1867); Angel Grd, Tonbridge (1869–1939); Town Malling (1878–1890); Common, Tunbridge Wells (1845–84).

A detailed article by Howard Milton on Kent Cricket Grounds appears in *The Cricket Statistician*, December 1979.

Honours The County has won the Championship seven times since 1864 – 1906, 1909, 1910, 1913, 1970, 1977 and 1978. It can also claim the title nine times before 1864. Kent won the Gillette Cup in 1967 and 1974; the John Player League in 1972, 1973 and 1976; the Benson and Hedges Cup in 1973, 1976 and 1978.

The players F E Woolley appeared in 764 matches for the County between 1906 and 1938; the other cricketer to exceed 600 matches is H T W Hardinge with 607 between 1902 and 1933. The longest serving captain is Lord Harris, who led the County for 15 seasons from 1875 to 1889 and probably for the four preceding seasons of 1871 to 1874; M C Cowdrey was captain for 15 seasons from 1957 to 1971.

The youngest player to represent Kent is H T W Hardinge, who was 16 years and 4 months, when he played v Lancashire in 1902; the oldest player is Lord Harris, whose last match was v Indians in 1911, when he was 60 years and 4 months.

M C Cowdrey is the Kent cricketer with most England caps – 114 between 1954 and 1975.

Colin Cowdrey captained Kent from 1957 to 1971, but missed many games because of Test matches.

Lord Harris is Kent's longest-serving captain. He was also captain of MCC and an influential voice in cricket at the end of the 19th century.

Team performances The highest team total for the County is 803 for 4 wkts dec *v* Essex at Brentwood on May 30 and 31, 1934. Kent batted only 420 minutes – just 6 of the 146 overs were maidens. The Australian total of 676 scored at Canterbury on August 10 and 11, 1921 is the record against the County – the tourists used the match as batting practice before the final Test and made no attempt to win; the Kent captain retaliated by scarcely using Woolley, his best bowler.

Eighteen is the lowest total recorded by the County and was made at Gravesend against Sussex on June 7, 1867 (one Kent player, G M Kelson could not bat due to injury). The lowest score against the County was 16 made by Warwickshire at Tonbridge on June 21, 1913; this was a great day for F E Woolley, who bowled unchanged with an analysis of 5.2-1-8-5 to help dismiss Warwickshire in 45 minutes, then hit 76 not out on an 'unplayable' wicket to win the match for his county with 6 wickets in hand – his 76 took 80 minutes.

Individual performances The highest innings for Kent is 332 by W H Ashdown scored in the match noted above *v* Essex at Brentwood in 1934. The highest innings against the County was hit by Dr W G Grace for Gentlemen of MCC at Canterbury on August 11 and 12, 1876. He made 344 in 375 minutes – MCC were 329 behind on the first innings and Grace saved the side from defeat, only one other batsman reaching fifty.

Three bowlers have taken all ten wickets in an innings for the County, A P Freeman performing the feat three times. The bowler with the best analysis, however, is C Blythe whose wickets cost 30 runs, the match being against Northamptonshire at Northampton on May 30, 31 and June 1, 1907. Blythe went on to take 17 for 48 in the match, which is another Kent record.

G A R Lock (in 1956), Dr W G Grace (in 1873), V W C Jupp (in 1932) and C H G Bland (in 1899) have achieved the feat against Kent. The last named has the best figures, 10–48 for Sussex at Tonbridge on June 7 – Kent were set 227 in 170 minutes, but Bland ran right through the side, except for Alec Hearne, who carried his bat for 55 not out.

The best bowling in a match against Kent is 17–106 by T W J Goddard for Gloucestershire at Bristol on July 3, 1939. In this game Gloucestershire batted on Saturday and scored 284, then on Monday, Goddard bowled Kent out twice for 120 and 124. As he had taken 13 wickets in the previous game, Goddard ended with 30 wickets for 205 in the space of 6 days.

2,000 runs in a season have been scored on 26 occasions for Kent. F E Woolley is the only batsman to exceed 2,500, which he did twice, the record being 2,894 (av 59.06) in 1928. Woolley also holds the record for exceeding 1,000 runs in a season most times, his total of 27 between 1907 and 1938, being ten more than the next player – H T W Hardinge.

200 wickets have been taken in a season for the county seven times – all by the same bowler, A P Freeman; his best season was 1933 with 262 (av 14.74). To Freeman also belongs the record for passing 100 wickets most times. Between 1920 and 1936 he did not miss a single season, making 17 in all.

The career records for batting and bowling naturally belong to Woolley and Freeman. The former hit 47,868 runs (av 41.77) between 1906 and 1938, whilst the latter captured 3,340 wickets (av 17.64) between 1914 and 1936; no one else exceeded 40,000 runs or 3,000 wickets.

Wicket partnerships

The highest stands in first-class cricket for the County are:

1st	283	A E Fagg, P R Sunnucks *v* Essex (*Colchester*)	1938
2nd	352	W H Ashdown, F E Woolley *v* Essex (*Brentwood*)	1934
3rd	321*	A Hearne, J R Mason *v* Notts (*Trent Bridge*)	1899
4th	297	H T W Hardinge, A P F Chapman *v* Hants (*Southampton*) 1926	
5th	277	F E Woolley, L E G Ames *v* New Zealanders (*Canterbury*) 1931	
6th	284	A P F Chapman, G B Legge *v* Lancashire (*Maidstone*)	1927
7th	248	A P Day, E Humphreys *v* Somerset (*Taunton*)	1908
8th	157	A L Hilder, A C Wright *v* Essex (*Gravesend*)	1924
9th	161	B R Edrich, F Ridgway *v* Sussex (*Tunbridge Wells*) 1949	
10th	235	F E Woolley, A Fielder *v* Worcs (*Stourbridge*)	1909

A. P. Freeman. Kent.

PHOTO
Flemons Tonbridge.

Above *The Kent ground at Canterbury, showing the famous tree within the boundary.*

Far left *Colin Blythe, slow left-arm bowler, who produced Kent's best match figures of 17–48 against Northamptonshire in 1907.*

Left *'Tich' Freeman, whose 3,340 wickets between 1914 and 1936 is easily a Kent record.*

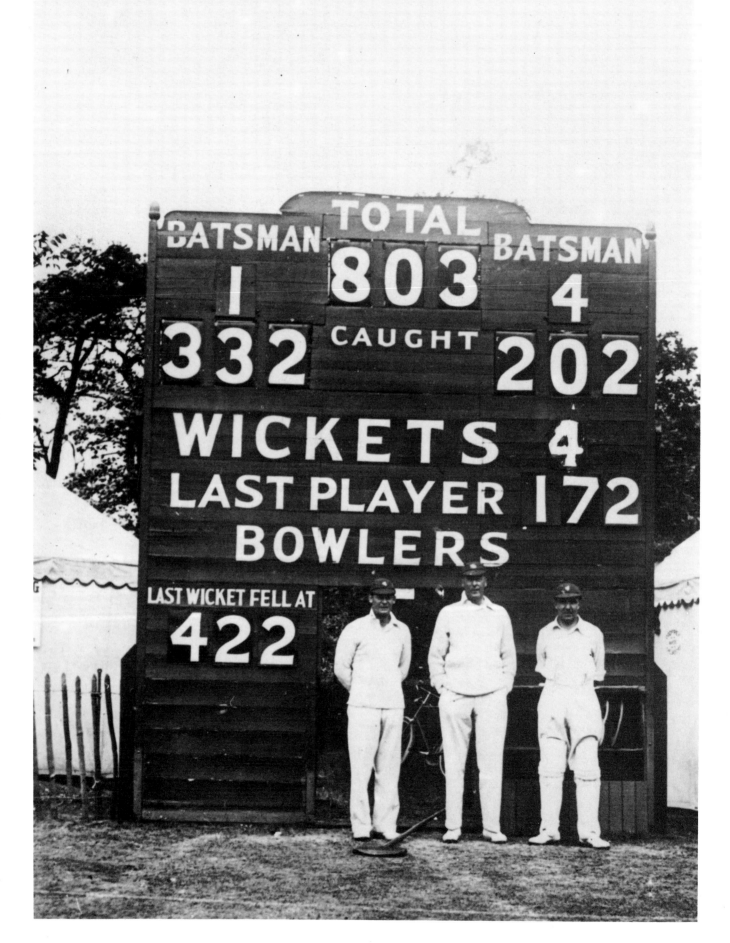

The record for the first wkt was set up in the same match as A E Fagg created a world record by scoring a double century in each innings – 244 and 202*.

Limited overs cricket records

Highest team total 297–3 v Worcestershire (*Canterbury*) 1970
Lowest team total 60 v Somerset (*Taunton*) 1979
Highest innings 129 B W Luckhurst v Durham (*Canterbury*) 1974
Best bowling 7–15 A L Dixon v Surrey (*Oval*) 1967

JOHN PLAYER LEAGUE
Highest team total 278–5 v Gloucestershire (*Maidstone*) 1976
Lowest team total 84 v Gloucestershire (*Folkestone*) 1969
Highest innings 142 B W Luckhurst v Somerset (*Weston-super-Mare*) 1970
Best bowling 6–9 R A Woolmer v Derbyshire (*Chesterfield*) 1979

BENSON AND HEDGES CUP
Highest team total 280–3 v Surrey (*Oval*) 1976
Lowest team total 73 v Middlesex (*Canterbury*) 1979
Highest innings 121 N R Taylor v Sussex (*Hove*) 1982
    121 N R Taylor v Somerset (*Canterbury*) 1982
Best bowling 5–21 B D Julien v Surrey (*Oval*) 1973

Kenya

The first match of any note in Kenya was played in Mombasa in December 1899 when the East African Protectorate opposed 'The Rest of the World'. The first team from Kenya to another country played at Entebbe in 1914 and defeated Uganda by 5 wickets.

The principal series of matches in Kenya have been Officials v Settlers, which ran from 1910 to 1964, and Europeans v Asians, which began in 1933. Kenya first played Tanganyika in 1951 and Uganda in 1952. These matches are not generally regarded as first-class, but representative matches by 'East Africa' against touring sides are usually first-class – these matches have been played at Nairobi.

The records in important matches are:
Highest team total 494–7d Gujerat v Coast XI (*Mombasa*) 1960
Lowest team total 39 Asians v Europeans (*Nairobi*) 1948–49
Highest individual innings 200 P R Umrigar, Gujerat v Coast (*Mombasa*) 1960
Best bowling in innings 9–96 E P Nowrojee, Asians v Europeans (*Nairobi*) 1935–36

In the ICC Trophy of 1979 Kenya formed part of East Africa, but in 1982 they competed as a separate entity and won three matches, finishing third in their Group.

Lancashire

The first-known match in Lancashire was played in August 1781 when a team from Haughton played a team of printers on Brinnington Moor.
Formation of the County Club The first match by Lancashire took place on the Hyde Park Ground at Sheffield against Yorkshire on July 23, 24 and 25, 1849. The County Club however was not formed until January 12, 1864 in Manchester. Between 1880 and 1957 the official name of the County Club was the Lancashire County and Manchester Cricket Club, but this was altered to Lancashire County Cricket Club on January 9, 1957.
First-class status After the formation of the County Club, the first first-class match played by the County took place on July 20, 21 and 22, 1865 at Old Trafford against Middlesex. Before 1864 Manchester or Lancashire – the titles are almost interchangeable – played a few matches which can be regarded as 'important' against Sheffield/Yorkshire, Surrey, Sussex and MCC – for a detailed list see ACS 'Guides'.

Opposite Not the true scoreboard of the Kent innings against Essex at Brentwood in 1934 but one showing the true score, 803 for 4 declared, and the scores of the three batsmen posing: 332 by W H Ashdown (left), 202 not out by L E G Ames (right) and 172 by F E Woolley (centre).

Cyril Washbrook, who played exactly 500 times for Lancashire from 1933 to 1959, and whose benefit in 1948 produced record receipts unequalled for over two decades.

Grounds Since 1864 the principal ground of the County Club has been at Old Trafford. Other grounds now used for first-class County matches are: Aigburth, Liverpool (since 1881); Southport and Birkdale CC, Southport (since 1959); Stanley Park, Blackpool (since 1905). Grounds that have been used in the past are: Edgehill, Liverpool (1866); Whalley (1867); Blackburn (1932–35); Ashton-under-Lyne (1865); Lancaster (1914); Nelson (1925–38); Preston (1936–52); Rochdale (1876).
Honours The County has won the Championship in 1881, 1897, 1904, 1926, 1927, 1928, 1930 and 1934; they tied for the title in 1879, 1882, 1889 and 1950. The Gillette Cup has been won in 1970, 1971, 1972 and 1975 and the John Player League in 1969 and 1970. The best seasons in the Benson and Hedges Cup are 1973, 1974 and 1982, when Lancashire were in the semi-finals.
The players Three cricketers have appeared for the County more than 500 times: G E Tyldesley played in 573 matches between 1909 and 1936; J Sharp in 518 matches (1899–1925); J T Tyldesley 507 (1895–1923); whilst C Washbrook appeared exactly 500 times (1933–59).

A N Hornby led the County side in 14 seasons (1880–91 and 1897–98) and shared the captaincy in two other years (1892 and 1893).

The youngest cricketer to appear for Lancashire is P T Marner, who was 16 years and 5 months when he played v Sussex in 1952. The oldest cricketer is A N Hornby; he was 52 years and 5 months on his final appearance v Leics in 1899.

J B Statham is the Lancashire cricketer with most England caps: 70 between 1951 and 1965.
Team performances The highest total for the County – the only one to exceed 700 – is 801 v Somerset at Taunton on July 15 and 16, 1895. The innings lasted 480 minutes and Lancashire won by an innings and 452 runs. The innings was at the time the highest ever in English first-class cricket.

No side has approached that record against Lancashire and there are only two totals above 600, the best being 634 by Surrey at The Oval on August 18 and 19, 1898 – the first four wickets went down for 133, but T W Hayward came in at No. 5 and carried out his bat for 315.

Lancashire's lowest score is 25 made against Derbyshire on May 26, 1871 at Old Trafford – it was the first important match ever played by the latter county. Glamorgan made the lowest score against Lancashire, being all out for 22 on the Aigburth Ground, Liverpool, on May 15, 1924. The wicket was so difficult that in 2 hours 20 minutes, both sides were in and out, Lancashire making 49. Best bowling figures were by C H Parkin with 8-5-6-6.

Above *The pavilion at Old Trafford, one of England's Test match grounds and the headquarters of Lancashire CCC since 1864.*

Left *Fast bowler Brian Statham, the most-capped Lancashire player with 70 appearances between 1951 and 1965.*

Individual performances The highest innings was made in the Somerset match noted above in 1895: A C MacLaren hit 424 (see under Batting Records in England). Two other players have reached 300 for the County: E Paynter with 322 v Sussex at Hove in 1937 and F B Watson with 300* v Surrey at Old Trafford in 1928. The only triple hundred against Lancashire was made by T W Hayward in 1898 (see previous paragraph).

All ten wickets in an innings has been attained twice for the County – on both occasions against Worcestershire. The first was 10–55 by J Briggs at Old Trafford on May 24, 1900 and the second 10–102 by R Berry at Blackpool on July 31, 1953 – Worcester had been set 337 to win and made 318. G O B Allen took 10–40 for Middlesex v Lancashire at Lord's on June 15, 1929.

A special match was arranged between Lancashire and Yorkshire at Liverpool on July 10, 11 and 12, 1913 to mark the visit of King George V to the city. H Dean, appropriately, achieved the best performance ever recorded in a match by a bowler for Lancashire, namely 17 for 91. One other bowler has taken 17 wickets in a match for the County: W Brearley, 17–137 v Somerset at Old Trafford in 1905. The best bowling in a match against Lancashire is by G Giffen who took 16–65 for the Australians at Old Trafford on June 15 and 16, 1886. Giffen bowled unchanged through both innings.

On 25 occasions batsmen have exceeded 2,000 runs in a season for the County. The record is held by J T Tyldesley, who scored 2,633 runs (av 56.02) in 1901, but he is closely followed by E Paynter with 2,626 (av 58.35) in 1937. J T Tyldesley also holds the record for topping 1,000 runs in a season most times: 19 in all between 1897 and 1919, these being in consecutive summers. G E Tyldesley, his brother, reached 1,000 runs in 18 consecutive seasons between 1913 and 1934. In both cases the years 1915 to 1918 are not counted, there being no first-class cricket.

Most wickets in a season were taken by E A McDonald with 198 in 1925, and J Briggs took 100 wickets in a season 11 times from 1887 to 1900, which is the Lancashire record.

The two Tyldesley brothers are the only batsmen to exceed 30,000 runs for the County. G E is top with 34,222 (av 45.20) from 1909 to 1936; J T scored 31,949 (av 41.38) from 1895 to 1923.

Leading bowler is J B Statham with 1,816 wickets (av 15.12) between 1950 and 1968. Two others who topped 1,500 are J Briggs with 1,688 (av 15.60) and A W Mold 1,541 (av 15.13).

Wicket partnerships

The highest stands in first-class cricket for the County are:

1st	368	A C MacLaren, R H Spooner v Gloucestershire (*Liverpool*) 1903
2nd	371	F B Watson, G E Tyldesley v Surrey (*Old Trafford*) 1928
3rd	306	E Paynter, N Oldfield v Hampshire (*Southampton*) 1938
4th	324	A C MacLaren, J T Tyldesley v Notts (*Trent Bridge*) 1904
5th	249	B Wood, A Kennedy v Warwickshire (*Edgbaston*) 1975
6th	278	J Iddon, H R W Butterworth v Sussex (*Old Trafford*) 1932
7th	245	A H Hornby, J Sharp v Leicestershire (*Old Trafford*) 1912
8th	158	J Lyon, R M Ratcliffe v Warwickshire (*Old Trafford*) 1979
9th	142	L O S Poidevin, A Kermode v Sussex (*Eastbourne*) 1907
10th	173	J Briggs, R Pilling v Surrey (*Liverpool*) 1885

Limited overs cricket records

GILLETTE/NATWEST CUP
Highest team total 304–9 v Leicestershire (*Old Trafford*) 1963
Lowest team total 59 v Worcestershire (*Worcester*) 1963
Highest innings 131 A Kennedy v Middx (*Old Trafford*) 1978
Best bowling 5–28 J B Statham v Leics (*Old Trafford*) 1963
Three of the four records were created in the first season of the Cup and the highest total was actually made in the first-ever game – on May 1 and 2, 1963.

Ernest Tyldesley (left) scored a record 34,222 runs for Lancashire and Johnny Briggs (right) took 1,588 wickets, second only to Statham.

Eddie Paynter was the last Lancashire batsman to score a triple century: 322 v Sussex at Hove in 1937. In the 1932–33 Test match series in Australia he left a hospital sickbed to play a famous innings.

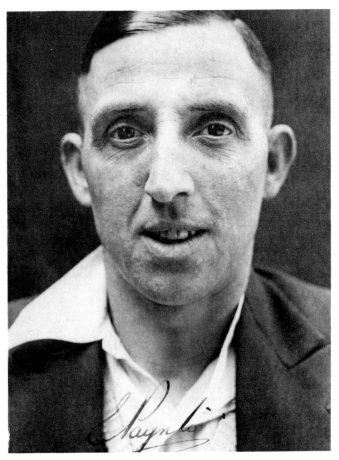

Highest team total 255–5 v Somerset (*Old Trafford*) 1970
Lowest team total 76 v Somerset (*Old Trafford*) 1972
Highest innings 134* C H Lloyd v Somerset (*Old Trafford*) 1970
Best bowling 6–29 D P Hughes v Somerset (*Old Trafford*) 1977
The coincidence in the four records above is quite remarkable.

BENSON AND HEDGES CUP

Highest team total 288–9 v Warwickshire (*Old Trafford*) 1981
Lowest team total 82 v Yorkshire (*Bradford*) 1972
Highest innings 124 C H Lloyd v Warwicks (*Old Trafford*) 1981
Best bowling 6–10 C E H Croft v Scotland (*Old Trafford*) 1982

Lancashire League

Championship winners

1892	Nelson	1938	Todmorden
1893	Burnley	1939	Church
1894	Rawtenstall	1940	Church
1895	Nelson	1941	Church
1896	Nelson	1942	East Lancashire
1897	Burnley	1943	Enfield
1898	Rishton	1944	Rishton
1899	Bacup	1945	Church
1900	Haslingden	1946	Nelson
1901	Burnley	1947	East Lancashire
1902	Colne	1948	Rishton
1903	Nelson	1949	East Lancashire
1904	Rawtenstall	1950	Burnley
1905	Colne	1951	East Lancashire
1906	Burnley	1952	East Lancashire
1907	Burnley	1953	Haslingden
1908	Burnley	1954	Todmorden
1909	Enfield	1955	Rishton
1910	Colne	1956	Burnley
1911	Nelson	1957	Todmorden
1912	Rishton	1958	Bacup
1913	Burnley	1959	Colne
1914	Accrington	1960	Bacup
1915	Accrington	1961	Accrington
1916	Accrington	1962	Church
1919	East Lancashire	1963	East Lancashire
1920	Haslingden	1964	Burnley
1921	Ramsbottom	1965	Nelson
1922	Bacup, Rawtenstall	1966	East Lancashire
1923	Bacup	1967	Nelson
1924	Bacup	1968	Enfield
1925	Ramsbottom	1969	Nelson
1926	Rawtenstall	1970	Burnley
1927	Todmorden	1971	Enfield
1928	Nelson	1972	East Lancashire
1929	Nelson	1973	East Lancashire
1930	Bacup	1974	Ramsbottom
1931	Nelson	1975	Accrington
1932	Nelson	1976	Rawtenstall
1933	Todmorden	1977	Enfield
1934	Nelson	1978	Burnley
1935	Nelson	1979	Burnley
1936	Nelson	1980	East Lancashire
1937	Nelson	1981	Rawtenstall
		1982	Rawtenstall

Leg Before Wicket

The record number of batsmen to be given out lbw in one innings in a first-class match in England is no less than 8 – Oxford University's second innings v Warwickshire at Oxford in 1980.

Leg Byes

The first mention of leg-byes in a match score does not occur until 1848.

The most leg-byes in an innings in a first-class match are 30 for England v West Indies at Old Trafford in 1976, and for Habib Bank v National Bank at Lahore in 1976–77.

Leicestershire

The first known mention of cricket in the County is a notice printed in the *Leicester Journal* of August 17, 1776 announcing a match between Barrow and Mount Sorrel 'to be played on September 9 at Barrow'.

Formation of the County Club It is impossible to differentiate between Leicester and Leicestershire in many of the early matches and indeed Cricket Clubs. The first Leicester match was against Nottingham on September 17 and 18, 1781 at Loughborough. The first known County Club was formed at Loughborough in July 1820; yet another one in September 1830 and a third in September 1835. The last named survived at least until 1860. There were several temporary committees formed to organise Leicestershire matches in the 1870s, but the present County Club was launched on March 25, 1879.

First-class status The first first-class match played by the present County Club took place at Leyton on May 14, 15 and 16, 1894 against Essex. Leicestershire had the satisfaction of winning both this game and their first one at home, which took place on the following two days at Grace Road, Leicester v Yorkshire.

Grounds The present headquarters of the County Club are situated at Grace Road, Leicester. This ground was opened in 1878. At the end of 1900 however, the County Club moved to a new ground at Aylestone Road, Leicester, and the first match was played here on May 13, 14 and 15, 1901. The County returned to Grace Road in 1946 and have remained there since, though a few post-war matches have taken place on the Aylestone Road Ground. The other ground used currently by the County is Leicester Road, Hinckley (since 1981).

Other grounds which have been used for first-class County matches are: Ashby Road, Hinckley (1911–37); Coventry Road, Hinckley (1951–64); three grounds at Loughborough, namely: Park Road Ground (1913–52); College Ground (1928–29) and Brush Sports Ground (1953–65); three grounds at Coalville: Fox and Goose Ground (1913–14); Miners' Welfare Ground (1957–66) and Town Ground

W E Astill, whose 628 appearances between 1906 and 1939 is the most by any Leicestershire player, also took the most wickets.

(1950); Melton Mowbray (1946–48); Oakham (1935–38); Barwell (1946–47); Ashby-de-la-Zouch (1912–64).

Honours The County won the Championship in 1975; the John Player League in 1974 and 1977; the Benson and Hedges Cup in 1972 and 1975. The best year in the Gillette Cup is 1977 when the County were semi-finalists.

The players Two cricketers have appeared in over 600 matches for the County: W E Astill with 628 between 1906 and 1939 heads the list, G L Berry with 605 between 1924 and 1951 is second. Third, and the only other to exceed 500, is J H King with 502 matches between 1894 and 1925.

Longest serving captain is C E de Trafford with 13 seasons (1894–1906).

The youngest player is N E Briers, who was 16 years and 3 months when he played against Cambridge University in 1971. The oldest player is C E de Trafford, who was 56 when playing against Sussex in 1920.

The Leicestershire cricketer with most England caps is D I Gower with 44 (to the end of the 1982 season).

Team performances Leicestershire have once exceeded 700 in an innings, their total being 701 for 4 wkts dec, July 19, 20 and 21, 1906 *v* Worcestershire at Worcester. The scoring throughout the game was high and the total number of runs hit – 1,425 – was the second highest recorded in an inter-county match up to that date. 700 has been scored only once against the County – Nottinghamshire hit 739 for 7 wkts dec at Trent Bridge on May 25 and 26, 1903.

The two lowest totals by the County – 25 and 26 – were made in successive seasons in the same fixture, against Kent at Aylestone Rd, Leicester. In both cases C Blythe was the offending bowler, assisted by F E Woolley. In 1911, Blythe took 6–10 and Woolley 4–16 and the following year Blythe took 7–9 and Woolley 3–15 – the pair bowled unchanged both times.

Leicestershire have only once dismissed a team for under 30 – Glamorgan at Grace Road on August 18 and 19 were all out for 24, and following on were all out for 66. G D McKenzie took 7–8 in the first innings.

Individual performances Leicestershire's batsmen can claim the lowest highest innings of any present first-class County. S Coe holds the record with 252 not out against Northamptonshire at Aylestone Rd on June 1 and 2, 1914. He was at the crease 240 minutes and hit a six, a five and 39 fours.

341 by G H Hirst for Yorkshire at Aylestone Rd on May 19 and 20, 1905 is the only triple hundred against Leicestershire.

G Geary's 10–18 against Glamorgan at Pontypridd on August 15, 1929 is the best analysis in an innings for the County and his record in the whole match of 16–96 is also a County record.

Best bowling in an innings against Leicestershire is 10–32 by H Pickett for Essex at Leyton on June 3, 1895, and in a match 16–102 by C Blythe at Aylestone Rd on May 17, 18 and 19, 1909.

Four batsmen have exceeded 2,000 runs in a season for the County, the record being 2,446 (av 52.04) by G L Berry in 1937; Berry also scored 1,000 runs in a season on most occasions: 18 between 1925 and 1950.

J E Walsh captured most wickets in a season for the County: 170 (av 18.96) in 1948; he took 100 wickets in a season 7 times, but the record is 9 times between 1914 and 1936 by G Geary.

G L Berry holds the career record for most runs and his total of 30,143 (av 30.32) is the only one to exceed 30,000. W E Astill took most wickets in a career, with 2,130 (av 23.19) between 1906 and 1939; second is G Geary with 1,759 (av 19.73) between 1912 and 1938. No one else exceeded 1,500.

The oldest player (56) and the longest-serving Leicestershire captain (1894–1906) is C E de Trafford, pictured in 1895.

G L Berry (who signed his photo L G because he was known as Leslie) is the only Leicestershire batsman to score over 30,000 runs.

The Grace Road ground at Leicester, the headquarters of Leicestershire CCC since 1878.

Wicket partnerships

The highest stands in first-class cricket for the County are:

- 1st 390 B Dudleston, J F Steele v Derbyshire (*Grace Rd, Leicester*) 1979
- 2nd 289* J C Balderstone, D I Gower v Essex (*Grace Rd, Leicester*) 1981
- 3rd 316* W Watson, A Wharton v Somerset (*Taunton*) 1961
- 4th 270 C S Dempster, G S Watson v Yorkshire (*Hull*) 1937
- 5th 233 N E Briers, R W Tolchard v Somerset (*Grace Rd, Leicester*) 1979
- 6th 262 A T Sharp, G H S Fowke v Derbyshire (*Chesterfield*) 1911
- 7th 206 B Dudleston, J Birkenshaw v Kent (*Canterbury*) 1969
- 8th 164 M R Hallam, C T Spencer v Essex (*Grace Rd, Leicester*) 1964
- 9th 160 W W Odell, R T Crawford v Worcestershire (*Aylestone Rd, Leicester*) 1902
- 10th 228 R Illingworth, K Higgs v Northants (*Grace Rd, Leicester*) 1977

The last wicket record stand of 228 is remarkable not only for its size – the second largest in County Championship cricket – but for the fact that Leicester were 45 for 9 when Higgs joined Illingworth. Higgs scored 98 before being run out and Illingworth made 119; none of the other nine batsmen even reached double figures.

Limited overs cricket records

GILLETTE/NATWEST CUP
Highest team total 326-6 v Worcestershire (*Grace Rd, Leicester*) 1979
Lowest team total 56 v Northants (*Grace Rd, Leicester*) 1964
Highest innings 137* B F Davison v Surrey (*Oval*) 1981
Best bowling 6-20 K Higgs v Staffordshire (*Longton*) 1975

JOHN PLAYER LEAGUE
Highest team total 262-6 v Somerset (*Frome*) 1970
Lowest team total 36 v Sussex (*Grace Rd, Leicester*) 1973
Highest innings 152 B Dudleston v Lancs (*Old Trafford*) 1975
Best bowling 6-17 K Higgs v Glam (*Grace Rd, Leicester*) 1973

BENSON AND HEDGES CUP
Highest team total 327-4 v Warwickshire (*Coventry*) 1972
Lowest team total 56 v Minor Counties (*Wellington*) 1982
Highest innings 158* B F Davison v Warwickshire (*Coventry*) 1972
Best bowling 6-35 L B Taylor v Worcestershire (*Worcester*) 1982

Limited Overs Cricket

The first limited overs competition involving the first-class counties was held in 1962 between Leicestershire, Derbyshire, Nottinghamshire and Northamptonshire, under the sponsorship of the first named County. It was a knock-out Competition with overs limited to 65 per innings. The Gillette Cup Competition commenced in 1963, followed by the John Player League in 1969 and the Benson and Hedges Cup in 1972.
(*See entries for each competition for winners and records*)

London County

With its home ground at Crystal Palace and under the leadership of W G Grace, the London County Club was promoted as a financial speculation. Its matches were granted first-class status in 1900, its second year, and it continued to play first-class matches until the close of the 1904 season. An application to join the County Championship was refused and this refusal brought an end to the side.

First-class records for London County are:
Highest team total 633 v MCC (*Crystal Palace*) 1901
Lowest team total 55 v MCC (*Lord's*) 1900
Highest individual innings 222 L Walker v MCC (*Crystal Palace*) 1901
Best bowling in innings 9-55 C B Llewellyn v Cambridge U (*Crystal Palace*) 1902

London Club

The first match title involving 'London' is dated July 1, 1707 and London's opponents are Croydon. The first reference to the 'London Club' occurs in 1722 and though cricket references are very scattered during the first half of the 18th century, by 1732 a newspaper carried the notice that London played 13 matches that season and lost none. The London Club was at this time established on the Artillery Ground off City Road, London, and for the next 35 years was the principal Cricket Club in England.

Of the first 40 matches which involved London and whose existence is known not even the team totals have survived – in most cases only the result and the amount of money at stake are given in the press.

The reason for the demise of important matches on the Artillery Ground and the disappearance of the London Club was most probably the unsavoury reputation which grew up through the gambling that was the feature of the Ground. Perhaps the Hambledon Club was formed out of London in order to get away from cricket's disreputable past – at least the rise of Hambledon coincided with the end of the London Club.

Lord's Cricket Ground

The principal ground in the world was established by Thomas Lord in May 1787 at the suggestion of the Earl of Winchilsea, a member of the White Conduit Club, which played in Islington. The ground was laid out where Dorset Square now stands, but Lord moved in 1809–10 to Lisson Grove and in 1813 to the present site in St John's Wood.

The principal records in first-class matches at Lord's are:

Highest team total 729–6d Australia *v* England 1930
Lowest team total 15 MCC *v* Surrey 1839
Highest individual innings 316* J B Hobbs, Surrey *v* Middlesex 1926
Best bowling in innings 10–36 S E Butler, Oxford U *v* Cambridge U 1871

In any match the highest team total is 735–9, MCC *v* Wiltshire, 1888.

Above   *Lord's cricket ground as it is today, looking at the pavilion from the mound stand.*

Above left   *Lord's as it appeared between 1813 and 1825, when fire destroyed the pavilion on the right.*

Left   *The original Lord's cricket field near White Conduit House (where Dorset Square now is) in 1787.*

Lowest Team Total

The lowest total in a match of importance occurred at Lord's on June 13, 1810, The Bs being dismissed by England for 6. Details of the innings are:

1 H Bentley	*c* Harding	0
2 John Bennett	*st* Lambert	0
3 John Wells	*b* Hammond	4
4 W Beldham	*b* Hammond	0
5 Lord F Beauclerk	*b* Hammond	0
6 – Bridger	*c* Hammond	1
7 C Bentley	*b* Hammond	0
8 J Bentley	*not out*	0
9 J Lawrell Esq	*c* Smith	1
10 J Barton Esq	*b* Hammond	0
11 E H Budd Esq	*absent*	
Byes		0
TOTAL		6

Wells played for the Bs as a 'given man' and Lawrell because he backed the side.

In minor matches it is not uncommon for a side to be dismissed without a run being scored, the first recorded example being in Norfolk, where an Eleven of Fakenham, Walsingham and Hempton were dismissed for 0 by an Eleven of Litcham, Dunham and Brisley in July, 1815.

(*For the lowest total in individual countries and counties, see under appropriate headings*)

Lunch

Most runs by a batsman before lunch on first day It is probable that the record was made by G L Jessop on September 5, 1904 for the South *v* South Africans at Hastings, in so far as English first-class cricket

One of the social events of the season was the Eton v Harrow school match at Lord's, this being the scene in 1895.

is concerned. Despite an attack of lumbago and having a runner, Jessop, who went in with the total 18 for 3, hit his first 50 in an hour and reached 100 in 75 minutes. His score at lunch was about 140*.

The world record in first-class cricket is 197* by W R Endean for Transvaal *v* Orange Free State at Johannesburg in 1954–55, but there three hours' play took place before lunch.

Most runs by a team before lunch on first day On May 17, 1897 Yorkshire hit 217 for 2 by lunch with D Denton 100* and F S Jackson 99* *v* Somerset at Taunton, which is believed to be the record in English first-class cricket.

Maidens

The first use of the term 'maiden' to denote an over from which no runs were scored appears in the 1830s.

In first-class matches the record number of maidens bowled in succession are as follows:

Four-ball Overs
23 A Shaw, North *v* South (*Trent Bridge*) 1876

Five-ball Overs
19 J W Trumble, Victoria *v* NSW (*Melbourne*) 1885–86

Six-ball Overs
21 R G Nadkarni, India *v* England (*Madras*) 1963–64

Eight-ball Overs
16 H J Tayfield, South Africa *v* England (*Durban*) 1956–57

The overall record must belong to Tayfield, who in fact bowled 137 balls without conceding a run.

Above left *The Hon F S Jackson, who shared a stand with D Denton which took Yorkshire's score to 217–2 at lunch, a record.*

Above *Russell Endean, who scored 187 not out before lunch for Transvaal against Orange Free State in 1954–55.*

Left *H J Tayfield, of South Africa, who bowled 16 consecutive eight-ball maidens against England in 1956.*

Malaysia (and Singapore)

The earliest reference to cricket is in Singapore in 1837. The first inter-state match, Perak *v* Penang, took place in 1884 and in 1890–91 Ceylon toured Malaya, a tour returned by Malaya in 1893.

In the 1930s an eleven representative of Malaya was approaching first-class standard, but at the present time Malaysia's team is perhaps about as strong as an English Minor County side.

Malaysia took part in the 1979 ICC Trophy, but failed to win a match.

Matches

The longest first-class match lasted ten days. Known as the 'Timeless Test' it was the Fifth Test of the 1938–39 series between South Africa and England. The game began on March 3, 1939 and continued until March 14, though there were breaks on March 5 and March 12, which were Sundays and, owing to rain, no play was possible on March 11. In the final innings England were set 696 to win, but when 654 for 5 had been scored at the close of play on March 14, the match had to end so that the English side could catch the boat back to England. The game took place on the Kingsmead Ground in Durban.

In the first half of the 18th century most matches were completed in a single day, although being two innings per side. The first known match to last for two days took place in Maidstone on August 21 and 22, 1741. The first match known to last three days was the Bourn Club *v* XXII of Dover at Dover, August 13, 14 and 15, 1771, but only three years later – August 15 to 18, 1774 – came the first known four-day match, Hampshire *v* Kent at Broadhalfpenny Down.

On August 8 to 12, 1786 came the first known five-day match at Bourne in Kent, Kent playing the White Conduit Club.

The first six-day match was a six-a-side single wicket game also at Bourne, Kent *v* Hampshire on August 29 to September 3, 1788.

20th century first-class County matches in England have always been arranged for 3 days, except for the season of 1919, when 2-day matches were tried as an experiment. The last first-class match in England arranged for two days only was Notts *v* Australians at Trent Bridge in 1953.

In Australia, Sheffield Shield matches were 'timeless' until the end of the 1926–27 season and since 1930–31 have been limited to 4 days.

In South Africa, Currie Cup matches were limited to two days until 1921–22 when they were increased to three days, but some matches in South Africa of first-class status played in later years were restricted to two days.

MCC

'On Mon., July 30, will be played (at Lord's) a match between 11 gentlemen of the Mary-le-bone Club and 11 gentlemen of the Islington Club.' This notice appeared in *The World* for July 27, 1787 and is the first known reference to the 'Mary-le-bone Club'.

The official year of the founding of MCC is taken as 1787, but it would appear that the Mary-le-bone Club of 1787 was in fact the White Conduit Club, the title having merely been altered because the Club now played on Lord's Ground in Marylebone rather than in Islington, as formerly. In 1788 – May 30 – a revised set of Laws were issued by the 'Cricket Club at Marylebone' and this was the beginning of MCC as the body in charge of the Laws of the game.

From its foundation the MCC can be regarded as a 'first-class' team, in that the best eleven drawn from the members was the equal of a first-class County side.

The records for MCC in first-class matches in England are:

Highest team total   607 *v* Cambridge U (*Lord's*)   1902
Lowest team total   15 *v* Surrey (*Lord's*)   1839
Highest individual innings   344 W G Grace *v* Kent (*Canterbury*) 1876
Best bowling in innings   10–49 W G Grace *v* Oxford U (*Oxford*) 1886
Best bowling in match   18–96 H Arkwright *v* Gents of Kent (*Canterbury*)   1861
(the last was 12 a-side)

May

The feat of scoring 1,000 runs in May in first-class matches has been achieved by three batsmen:

		I	NO	Runs	HS	Avge
W G Grace (*Gloucs*)	1895	10	1	1016	288	112.88
W R Hammond (*Gloucs*)	1927	14	0	1042	192	74.42
C Hallows (*Lancs*)	1928	11	3	1000	232	125.00

On five other occasions batsmen have reached 1,000 runs before June, but have required matches in April to reach the target: T W Hayward (*Surrey*) in 1900, D G Bradman (*Australians*) 1930 and 1938, W J Edrich (*Middlesex*) 1938 and G M Turner (*New Zealand*) 1973.

Most wickets in first-class matches in May are 70 by J T Hearne in 1896.

Glenn Turner in 1973 was the last batsman to score 1,000 runs before the end of May, and is shown scoring the actual 1,000th run.

Middlesex

In the Clerkenwell Parish Book of 1668 the proprietor of the Ram Inn, Smithfield, is rated for a cricket-field.

The first known match was played in Lamb's Conduit Fields, near Holborn, on July 3, 1707 between London and Croydon.

Formation of the County Club   The first report of a Middlesex match was on August 5, 1728 against London at Islington. Through the 18th century teams styled 'Middlesex' appear quite frequently, but nothing has yet been discovered regarding any possible organisation controlling these matches, and the famous London Club of the Artillery Ground (see under separate heading) overshadowed Middlesex.

From the formation of Lord's Ground, Middlesex matches become even more frequent, to the extent that it is difficult not to believe that some Club must have been operating, but at the turn of the century it becomes impossible to separate Middlesex matches from those of the Thursday Club which played at Lord's.

The present Middlesex County Club was formed at a meeting at the London Tavern on December 15, 1863.

First-class status   In so far as modern county cricket is concerned the first 'first-class' match played by Middlesex was against Surrey at Lord's on May 20 and 21, 1850. There were in fact eleven 'Middlesex' matches of importance played in the years prior to the formation of the official County Club – see ACS publication 'Middlesex Cricketers 1850–1976' for full details.

The first match organised by the County Club was v Sussex at Islington on June 6 and 7, 1864.

Grounds   The headquarters of Middlesex in 1864 was adjacent to the Cattle Market, Islington, in 1871 the County played at Lillie Bridge, West Brompton for one season only, in 1872 they moved to Prince's Ground, Chelsea and in 1877 to their present headquarters at Lord's. Currently they also play first-class matches at Uxbridge. Other first-class grounds have been: Chiswick Park (1887); Hornsey (1959).

Honours   Middlesex have won the County Championship outright on eight occasions: 1866, 1903, 1920, 1921, 1947, 1976, 1980 and 1982; in addition they tied for the title in 1949 and 1977.

The Gillette Cup has been won in 1977 and 1980.

The best season in the John Player League is 1982, when the County was second and the best in the Benson and Hedges Cup was in 1975 when they were the beaten finalists.

The players   Three players have made over 500 appearances for the County: J T Murray with 508 matches (1952–75), E H Hendren 581 (1907–37) and the only cricketer over 600, F J Titmus with 642 matches between 1949 and 1982.

A J Webbe is the longest serving captain, leading the County for 13 seasons between 1885 and 1897; he began the following season of 1898 still as official captain, but dropped out after a few matches.

F J Titmus, who was 16 years and 7 months on his debut v Somerset in 1949, is the youngest Middlesex cricketer; the oldest is J T Hearne who was 56 years and 2 months on his final appearance v Scotland in 1923.

D C S Compton has obtained most England caps: 78 between 1937 and 1957.

Team performances   Middlesex have reached a total of 600 on seven occasions, but due to declarations in every case have never hit over 650. The County record is 642 for 3 wkts dec against Hampshire at Southampton on June 13, 14 and 15, 1923. The first four Middlesex men all achieved hundreds: H L Dales 103, H W Lee 107, J W Hearne 232 and E H Hendren 177 not out.

The largest total against the County is 665 made by the West Indian tourists on June 3 and 5, 1939 at Lord's.

The lowest Middlesex total came in the County Club's first year of 1864, when they were dismissed for 20 by MCC at Lord's on July 25: G Wootton took 5 for 8 and J Grundy 5 for 10. The two lowest totals against the County both occurred on the County Ground at Bristol. On August 26, 1909 Gloucestershire were all out for 33 and in their second innings 81, and the whole match being completed in a single day, Middlesex won by an innings and 31 runs. Then on August 23, 1924, Gloucestershire were dismissed for 31, but this time W R Hammond hit 174 not out in Gloucester's second innings and Middlesex lost by 61 runs.

E H Hendren (right) in his 581st and last match for Middlesex in 1937, with his captain R W V Robins. Hendren has scored over 10,000 runs more than any other player for Middlesex.

Denis Compton plays a typical stroke to leg. He is Middlesex's most-capped player.

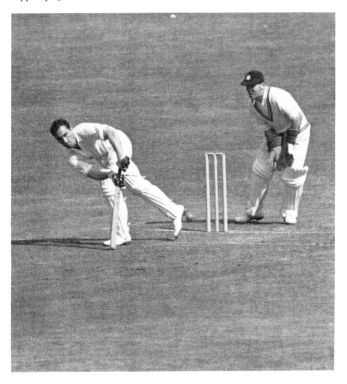

Individual performances E H Hendren hit 301* v Worcestershire at Worcester on July 22 and 24, 1933, but the Middlesex record is held by J D B Robertson, who scored 331* against Worcestershire at Dudley on July 23, 1949. Robertson had played in the Test Match v New Zealand a month earlier, scored a century, and then been dropped by the selectors for the next Test Match, which was played at the same time as the Middlesex match in which he hit his triple hundred; most embarrassing for the England selectors!

Three innings above 300 have been hit against Middlesex; W W Keeton made 312* for Notts in 1939, P Holmes 315* for Yorkshire in 1925, but the record is 316* by J B Hobbs for Surrey at Lord's on August 28 and 30. He batted 415 minutes and hit 41 fours.

Four bowlers have taken all ten wickets in an innings for the County – V E Walker (10–104) v Lancashire at Old Trafford in 1865; G Burton (10–59) v Surrey at the Oval in 1888; A E Trott (10–42) v Somerset at Taunton in 1900, each of which created a new Middlesex record, the last-named being broken at Lord's on June 15, 1929 v Lancashire by G O B Allen, who took 10 for 40 – remarkable figures in that six other bowlers were used in the innings and Lancashire made 241.

No one has taken all ten wickets against the County; the best performance is 9 for 38 by R C Robertson-Glasgow (later the well-known writer) for Somerset at Lord's on June 14 and 16, 1924.

Two bowlers have taken 16 wickets in a match for Middlesex at the same cost. G Burton took 16–114 v Yorkshire at Bramall Lane on August 6, 7 and 8, 1888, then these figures were repeated by J T Hearne on June 27, 28 and 29, 1898 at Old Trafford v Lancashire. Best match figures against the County are 16–109 by C W L Parker for Gloucestershire at Cheltenham on June 25 and 26, 1930.

There is very little to choose between the top four run aggregates in a season for the County. E H Hendren scored 2,669 (av 83.41) in 1923, W J Edrich reached 2,650 (av 85.48) in 1947, Hendren hit 2,623 (av 79.48) in 1928 and J D B Robertson one run less in 1951 (av 62.43).

E H Hendren however has a clear lead when it comes to scoring 1,000 runs in a season, having accomplished the feat 20 times between 1913 and 1937.

Two bowlers have taken 150 wickets in a season for Middlesex, A E Trott performed the feat twice: 150 in 1899 and 154 in 1900; the record holder is F J Titmus with 158 (av 14.63) in 1955. Titmus also holds the record for taking 100 wickets most times – 11 between 1953 and 1971.

Career records are held by E H Hendren with 40,302 runs (av 48.82) between 1907 and 1937 and F J Titmus with 2,361 wickets (av 21.27) between 1949 and 1982. No other batsman exceeds 30,000 runs, but one other bowler reached 2,000 wickets: J T Hearne 2,093 (av 18.24) from 1888 to 1923.

Wicket partnerships

The highest stands in first-class cricket for the County are:

1st 367* G D Barlow, W N Slack v Kent (*Lord's*) 1981
2nd 380 F A Tarrant, J W Hearne v Lancashire (*Lord's*) 1914
3rd 424* W J Edrich, D C S Compton v Somerset (*Lord's*) 1948
4th 325 J W Hearne, E H Hendren v Hampshire (*Lord's*) 1919
5th 338 R S Lucas, T C O'Brien v Sussex (*Hove*) 1895
6th 227 C T Radley, F J Titmus v South Africans (*Lord's*) 1965
7th 271* E H Hendren, F T Mann v Notts (*Trent Bridge*) 1925
8th 182* M H C Doll, H R Murrell v Notts (*Lord's*) 1913
9th 160* E H Hendren, F J Durston v Essex (*Leyton*) 1927
10th 230 R W Nicholls, W Roche v Kent (*Lord's*) 1899

Limited overs cricket records

GILLETTE/NATWEST CUP
Highest team total 280–8 v Sussex (*Lord's*) 1965
Lowest team total 41 v Essex (*Westcliff*) 1972
Highest innings 124* J M Brearley v Bucks (*Lord's*) 1975
Best bowling 6–15 W W Daniel v Sussex (*Hove*) 1980

JOHN PLAYER LEAGUE
Highest team total 256–9 v Worcs (*Worcester*) 1976
Lowest team total 23 v Yorkshire (*Headingley*) 1974
Highest innings 133* C T Radley v Glamorgan (*Lord's*) 1969
Best bowling 6–6 R W Hooker v Surrey (*Lord's*) 1969

BENSON AND HEDGES CUP
Highest team total 303–7 v Northants (*Northampton*) 1977
Lowest team total 97 v Northants (*Lord's*) 1976
Highest innings 129 G D Barlow v Northants (*Northampton*) 1977
Best bowling 7–12 W W Daniel v Minor Counties (East) (*Ipswich*) 1978

Minor Counties Championship

The first attempt to organise a competition between the non-first-class English Counties took place in the 1888 season and was the 'Second Class Counties Competition', the winners being:

1888 Leicestershire
1889 Warwickshire
1890 Somerset
1891 Leicestershire
1892 Warwickshire
1893 Derbyshire, Warwickshire

In 1894 most of the Counties competing in the above Competition were granted first-class status and the following year the present Minor Counties Competition was established.

Championship winners

1895	Norfolk, Durham, Worcestershire	1900	Glamorgan, Durham, Northants
1896	Worcestershire	1901	Durham
1897	Worcestershire	1902	Wiltshire
1898	Worcestershire	1903	Northants
1899	Buckinghamshire, Northants	1904	Northants
		1905	Norfolk

Jack Robertson played the highest innings for Middlesex: 331 not out made on one day against Worcestershire in 1949.

*Best wishes
Jack Robertson*

J T Hearne, whose 16–114 against Lancashire at Old Trafford in 1898 equalled the best match analysis by a Middlesex bowler.

N W Harding, whose 18–100 for Kent II against Wiltshire in 1937 is the best match analysis in the Minor Counties Championship.

1906	Staffordshire	1951	Kent II
1907	Lancashire II	1952	Buckinghamshire
1908	Staffordshire	1953	Berkshire
1909	Wiltshire	1954	Surrey II
1910	Norfolk	1955	Surrey II
1911	Staffordshire	1956	Kent II
1912	In abeyance	1957	Yorkshire II
1913	Norfolk	1958	Yorkshire II
1920	Staffordshire	1959	Warwickshire II
1921	Staffordshire	1960	Lancashire II
1922	Buckinghamshire	1961	Somerset II
1923	Buckinghamshire	1962	Warwickshire II
1924	Berkshire	1963	Cambridgeshire
1925	Buckinghamshire	1964	Lancashire II
1926	Durham	1965	Somerset II
1927	Staffordshire	1966	Lincolnshire
1928	Berkshire	1967	Cheshire
1929	Oxfordshire	1968	Yorkshire II
1930	Durham	1969	Buckinghamshire
1931	Leicestershire II	1970	Bedfordshire
1932	Buckinghamshire	1971	Yorkshire II
1933	Undecided	1972	Bedfordshire
1934	Lancashire II	1973	Shropshire
1935	Middlesex II	1974	Oxfordshire
1936	Hertfordshire	1975	Hertfordshire
1937	Lancashire II	1976	Durham
1938	Buckinghamshire	1977	Suffolk
1939	Surrey II	1978	Devon
1946	Suffolk	1979	Suffolk
1947	Yorkshire II	1980	Durham
1948	Lancashire II	1981	Durham
1949	Lancashire II	1982	Oxfordshire
1950	Surrey II		

Records in Championship matches

Highest team total 621 Surrey II v Devon (*Oval*) 1928

Lowest team total 14 Cheshire v Staffs (*Stoke on Trent*) 1909

Highest individual innings 282 E Garnett, Berks v Wilts (*Reading*) 1908

Best bowling in innings 10–15 G J W Platt, Surrey II v Dorset (*Dorchester*) 1908

M Ashenden, Beds v Salop (*Luton*) 1958

Best bowling in match 18–100 N W Harding, Kent II v Wilts (*Swindon*) 1937

Most runs in season 1212 (av 80.80) A F Brazier (*Surrey II*) 1949

Most wickets in season 119 (av 7.83) S F Barnes (*Staffs*) 1906

Wicket partnerships

1st   323   D F Walker, H E Theobold. Norfolk v Northumberland (*Norwich*) 1939

2nd   388* T H Clark, A F Brazier. Surrey II v Sussex II (*Oval*) 1949

3rd   329   R Harris, J W Murphy. Cornwall v Berkshire (*Camborne*) 1954

4th   293   J L Swann, A W Thompson. Middx II v Surrey II (*Oval*) 1952

5th   271* J A Sutton, G C Hardstaff. Cheshire v Salop (*Northwich*) 1969

6th   333* D J Carnhill, L Bateman. Hertfords v Norfolk (*Norwich*) 1953

7th   274   H S Harrison, W C Smith. Surrey II v Bucks (*Reigate*) 1908

8th   243   L Horridge, W Farrimond. Lancs II v Yorks II (*Old Trafford*) 1930

9th   195   H L Hever, F Phillips. Kent II v Surrey II (*Oval*) 1927

10th 185   G Rogers, F Whiting. Cornwall v Dorset (*Camborne*) 1931

Minor Counties Records

HIGHEST TOTAL

County	Score	Versus	Venue	Year
Bedford	539/7	Oxford	Bedford	1947
Berkshire	537	Devon	Reading	1921
Buckingham	505	Bedford	Bedford	1912
Cambridge	488	Suffolk	Cambridge	1904
Carmarthen	356	Buckingham	Llanelly	1911
Cheshire	415	Northumberland	Jesmond	1956
Cornwall	522/9*	Devon	Devonport	1947
Cumberland	326/9	Northumberland	Jesmond	1955
Denbigh	221	Stafford	Colwyn Bay	1933
Devon	533/7*	Dorset	Sherborne	1902
Dorset	491/6	Wiltshire	Sherborne	1937
Durham	503/6*	Northumberland	Jesmond	1939
Glamorgan	540	Devon	Exeter	1907
Hertford	534/8	Bedford	Stevenage	1924
Lincoln	458/5*	Cambridge	Grantham	1925
Monmouth	479	Carmarthen	Newport	1909
Norfolk	526/7*	Kent	Gravesend	1937
Northants	517/8*	Durham	South Shields	1900
Northumberland	509/7*	Cambridge	Jesmond	1913
Oxford	460/9*	Berkshire	Didcot	1947
Shropshire	349/7*	Somerset	Shrewsbury	1961
Stafford	505/6*	Buckingham	Stone	1948
Suffolk	516/6*	Cambridge	Newmarket	1908
Wiltshire	491	Devon	Exeter	1901
Worcester	397/7*	Hertford	Watford	1897

LOWEST TOTAL

Score	Versus	Venue	Year
19	Cambridge	Chatteris	1971
34	Northants	Northampton	1900
20	Hertford	Aylesbury	1903
37	Suffolk	Bury St Edmunds	1904
32	Glamorgan	Swansea	1910
14	Stafford	Stoke	1909
27	Devon	Plymouth	1965
36	Yorkshire	Workington	1956
19	Stafford	Porthill	1930
29	Berkshire	Reading	1930
28	Wiltshire	Blandford	1973
20	Staffords	Stoke	1907
20	Wiltshire	Chippenham	1905
31	Bucks	High Wycombe	1930
	Northants	Northampton	1902
32	Yorkshire	Keighley	1924
22	Dorset	Poole	1932
28	Worcester	Worcester	1896
56	Worcester	Worcester	1898
23	Stafford	Stoke	1946
52	Buckingham	Aylesbury	1900
30	Warwick	Bridgnorth	1962
20	Lancashire	Stoke	1936
29	Oxford	Felixstowe	1904
29	Oxford	Oxford	1968
79	Northants	Northampton	1896

HIGHEST SCORE

County	Score	Player	Versus	Venue	Year
Bedford	234	A B Poole	Oxford	Banbury	1936
Berkshire	282	E Garnett	Wiltshire	Reading	1908
Buckingham	191	D F V Johns	Bedford	Bedford Sch	1952
Cambridge	221	L J Reid	Hertford	Cambridge	1909
Carmarthen	132	G T Greville	Cornwall	Llanelly	1910
Cheshire	192	R M O Cooke	Yorkshire	Castleford	1971
Cornwall	191	G Rogers	Dorset	Camborne	1931
Cumberland	139	R Entwistle	Lancashire	Kendal	1970
Denbigh	100	A T Ratcliffe	Lancashire	Old Trafford	1931
Devon	235*	D H Cole	Dorset	Blandford	1955
Dorset	203*	G W L Courteney	Oxford	Oxford	1953
Durham	217*	E W Elliott	Lancashire	Sunderland	1906
Glamorgan	254	H E Morgan	Monmouth	Cardiff	1901
Hertford	223	F Golding	Oxford	Oxford	1905
Lincoln	232	R E Frearson	Cambridge	Grantham	1925
Monmouth	247*	L Pitchford	Dorset	Abercorn	1933
Norfolk	222	G A Stevens	Bedford	Norwich	1920
Northants	186	G J Thompson	MCC	Lord's	1900
Northumberland	221	L E Liddell	Lancashire	Jesmond	1949
Oxford	220	C Walters	Bedford	Luton	1924
Shropshire	134*	R Burton	Durham	Oswestry	1976
Stafford	217	A H Heath	Lincoln	Stoke	1889
Suffolk	229	J F Ireland	Cambridge	Newmarket	1911
Wiltshire	196	A E Lloyd	Surrey	Oval	1937
Worcester	176	H K Foster	Hertford	Watford	1897

BEST BOWLING

Analysis	Player	Versus	Venue	Year
10-15	M Ashenden	Shropshire	Luton	1958
10-25	G R Langdale	Dorset	Reading	1953
9-35	F Edwards	Bedford	Bedford	1923
10-37	D Hayward	Norfolk	Norwich	1898
8-76	E Gee	Monmouth	Newport	1908
9-25	H Wilson	Stafford	Wallasey	1926
10-26	F Whiting	Wiltshire	Trowbridge	1921
8-50	D J Lupton	Durham	Millom	1979
7-29	E Davies	Lincoln	Wrexham	1931
10-50	J Kelly	Berkshire	Torquay	1961
10-26	M G Kilvington	Cornwall	Wadebridge	1969
10-130	A Morris	Yorkshire	Barnsley	1910
9-56	H Creber	Carmarthen	Llanelly	1908
9-39	H F White	Bedford	St Albans	1909
9-5	W A Sutton	Leicester	Coalville	1928
10-31	T W Sadler	Dorset	Pantag	1930
10-50	C Shore	Durham	Norwich	1897
8-17	G J Thompson	Berkshire	Northampton	1900
10-52	W Hetherton	Yorkshire	Horsforth	1925
9-30	D J Laitt	Somerset	Taunton	1970
8-42	G V Othan	Bedford	Shrewsbury	1976
10-26	S F Barnes	Yorkshire	Wakefield	1907
10-23	G C Perkins	Hertford	Felixstowe	1960
9-29	J H Merryweather	Berkshire	Salisbury	1968
10-54	E G Arnold	Northants	Northampton	1897

Monopolising the Innings

G M Turner scored 141* out of Worcestershire's all out total of 169 against Glamorgan at Swansea on June 29 and 30, 1977, Turner's portion of the innings being 83.4%. No one else reached double figures and the ten other batsmen made only 14 scoring strokes between them.

NatWest Trophy

The National Westminster Bank took over the sponsorship of the Gillette Cup at the start of the 1981 season.
(See under Gillette Cup for records etc)

Opposite above Bert Sutcliffe *played the highest individual innings in New Zealand, 385 for Otago v Canterbury in 1952-53.*

Opposite below J R Reid, *a captain of New Zealand, whose 296 against Northern Districts in 1962-63 is the highest score for Wellington.*

New Zealand

The first reference in the game occurs in 1832 in the diary of Archdeacon Williams, but it would seem that cricket was played in New Zealand several years prior to this.

First-class cricket The first inter-provincial match took place between Wellington and Auckland at Wellington on March 16, 1860, but this and several matches soon after were only arranged as one-day games and are therefore not considered as first-class. The first inter-provincial match to last for more than a single day was played at Dunedin between Otago and Canterbury on January 27, 28 and 29, 1864 and is considered the start of first-class cricket in New Zealand.

Highest team total New South Wales scored 752 for 8 wkts dec against Otago at Dunedin on February 15, 16 and 18, 1924. This is the only total to exceed 700 in New Zealand first-class cricket. NSW reached 500 in 260 minutes! In any match the record is 922 for 9 by Australians v XV of South Canterbury at Temeka, 1913-14.

Lowest team total In first-class matches the lowest total is 13 by Auckland against Canterbury at Auckland on December 31, 1877 - of the 13 no less than 8 were extras and the highest innings by one of the batsmen was 2. The first recorded instance of a team being all out for 0 was Havelock v Whareti in 1909-10.

Highest individual innings The highest innings in 385 by B Sutcliffe for Otago v Canterbury at Christchurch, December 26 and 27, 1952. He batted 461 minutes and hit 3 sixes and 46 fours - the next highest scorer in the innings was A W Gilbertson with 29, which equalled the extras.

Best bowling in innings A E Moss returned the analysis of 21.3-10-28-10 for Canterbury v Wellington at Christchurch on December 27, 1889, which is not only the first-class New Zealand record, but also the best return on his first-class debut for any bowler in the world.

Best bowling in match S T Callaway took 15 for 60 for Canterbury v Hawke's Bay at Napier on January 14 and 15, 1904, which is the first-class record, no bowler having yet taken 16 wickets.

Record wicket partnerships in first-class matches

1st	373	B Sutcliffe, L Watt. Otago v Auckland (*Auckland*) 1950-51
2nd	252	W A Baler, E M Beechey. Wellington v Auckland (*Wellington*) 1918-19
3rd	445	P E Whitelaw, W N Carson. Auckland v Otago (*Dunedin*) 1936-37
4th	350	Mushtaq Mohammad, Asif Iqbal. Pakistan v New Zealand (*Dunedin*) 1972-73
5th	266	B Sutcliffe, W S Haig. Otago v Auckland (*Dunedin*) 1949-50
6th	269	V T Trumper, C Hill. Australians v NZ XI (*Wellington*) 1904-05
7th	265	J L Powell, N Dorreen. Canterbury v Otago (*Christchurch*) 1929-30
8th	433	V T Trumper, A Sims. Australians v Canterbury (*Christchurch*) 1913-14
9th	239	H B Cave, I B Leggat. Central Districts v Otago (*Dunedin*) 1952-53
10th	184	R C Blunt, W Hawksworth. Otago v Canterbury (*Christchurch*) 1931-32

Team records

The records for first-class New Zealand teams, i.e. those which appear at the present time in the Shell Trophy, are as follows:

AUCKLAND
Highest team total 693-6 dec v Canterbury (*Auckland*) 1939-40
Lowest team total 13 v Canterbury (*Auckland*) 1877-78
Highest innings 290 W N Carson v Otago (*Dunedin*) 1936-37
Best bowling 9-36 A F Wensley v Otago (*Auckland*) 1929-30

CANTERBURY
Highest team total 547-5 dec v Wellington (*Christchurch*) 1953-54
Lowest team total 25 v Otago (*Christchurch*) 1866-67
Highest innings 226 B F Hastings v New Zealand Under 23 (*Christchurch*) 1964-65
Best bowling 10-28 A E Moss v Wellington (*Christchurch*) 1889-90

CENTRAL DISTRICTS
Highest team total   487–5 dec *v* Wellington (*Wellington*)   1964–65
Lowest team total   50 *v* Wellington (*Upper Hutt*)   1979–80
Highest innings   202* B E Congdon *v* Otago (*Nelson*)   1968–69
Best bowling   9–100 B W Yuile *v* Canterbury (*New Plymouth*)
   1965–66

NORTHERN DISTRICTS
Highest team total   384 *v* Wellington (*Hamilton*)   1959–60
Lowest team total   52 *v* Canterbury (*Hamilton*)   1966–67
Highest innings   195 J M Parker *v* Canterbury (*Whangarei*)   1972–73
Best bowling   8–21 M C Langdon *v* Auckland (*Auckland*)   1963–64

OTAGO
Highest team total   602–8 dec *v* Canterbury (*Dunedin*)   1928–29
Lowest team total   34 *v* Wellington (*Hamilton*)   1956–57
Highest innings   385 B Sutcliffe *v* Canterbury (*Christchurch*)
   1952–53
Best bowling   9–50 A H Fisher *v* Queensland (*Dunedin*)   1896–97

WELLINGTON
Highest team total   595 *v* Auckland (*Auckland*)   1927–28
Lowest team total   19 *v* Nelson (*Nelson*)   1885–86
Highest innings   296 J R Reid *v* N Districts (*Wellington*)   1962–63
Best bowling   9–67 A W S Brice *v* Auckland (*Wellington*)   1918–19

North *v* South

The first match in England between the North and South took place at
Lord's on July 11 and 12, 1836 and the series rivalled the Gentlemen *v*
Players as the most important matches of the English cricket season for
many years. The Southern Elevens were selected from Kent, Surrey,
Sussex, Hampshire, Middlesex, Gloucestershire and later Essex and
Glamorgan.

The last first-class North *v* South Match took place at Blackpool on
September 6, 7 and 8, 1961, though in 1971 the fixture was played at
Aspley Lane, Nottingham on July 29 as a limited overs one-day game.

Northamptonshire

The first mention of cricket in Northamptonshire occurs on Tuesday,
August 18, 1741 when the Gentlemen of Northants played Gentlemen
of Buckinghamshire on the Cow Meadow near Northampton for 20
guineas a side.

Formation of the County Club   The town of Northampton had a
Cricket Club in 1775 and, as with other counties, the problem for the
historian is to decide when Northampton Cricket Club becomes
Northamptonshire Cricket Club. 1820 is given frequently as the
founding date of the County Club, but no contemporary evidence has
yet been discovered to support this – the date first appearing in a cricket
annual in 1856. The fact that a newspaper report in 1832 states that it
was proposed to form a County Club the following season would appear
to prove that the 1820 date was incorrect, or if correct then the Club had
vanished by 1832. The 1832 proposal in fact never materialised into a
County Club and the few matches involving 'Northamptonshire' that
took place in the next 40 years seem to have been organised, for the most
part, by the Northampton Town Club. This state of affairs ended on
July 31, 1878 when a meeting at the George Hotel, Kettering decided to
form a County Cricket Club – this Club has continued to the present
time.

First-class status   Northamptonshire arranged six matches home
and away against existing first-class counties for the season of 1905, and
as the MCC reduced the minimum number of matches required to
qualify for the Championship from 16 to 12, Northamptonshire became
a first-class County in 1905 – the first match was against Hampshire at
Southampton on May 18, 19 and 20, 1905.

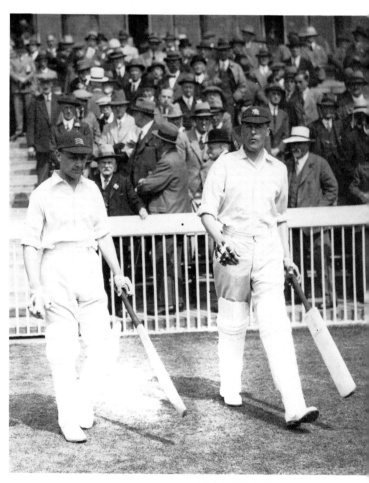

*Above right   Dennis Brookes, with 492 appearances between 1934 and
1959, has played most often for Northamptonshire.*

*Right   G O B Allen and F E Woolley going out to bat for the South
against the North in June 1932, when the match was a Test trial.*

116

Grounds The 1878 County Club played matches on the race-course at Northampton, but in 1886 the present County Ground in Northampton was first used for County matches and has been the Headquarters of the County Club since then. The only other ground used for first-class matches at the present time is the School Ground, Wellingborough (since 1946), but several grounds have been used recently for one-day matches: Luton (since 1973); Tring (since 1974); Milton Keynes (since 1977); Horton (since 1976); Brackley (since 1972); Bletchley (1976).

The following grounds have staged first-class County games: Town Ground, Peterborough (1906–66); Town Ground, Kettering (1923–71); Town Ground, Rushden (1924–63); Town Ground, Wellingborough (1929); Baker Perkins Ground, Peterborough (1967–69).

Honours The County won the Gillette Cup in 1976; the Benson and Hedges Cup in 1980. The best position attained in the John Player League is 4th in 1974 and in the County Championship 2nd in 1912, 1957, 1965 and 1976.

The players Three cricketers have played in more than 400 matches for the County: D Brookes 492 from 1934 to 1959; J E Timms 468 from 1925 to 1949; B L Reynolds 426 from 1950 to 1970.

The County has suffered from an alarming rate of change in its captain, the longest serving leader being P J Watts with 7 years, 1971–4 and 1978–80.

The youngest cricketer to appear is T B G Welch, who was 16 years and 12 days old on his debut v Warwickshire in 1922. The oldest cricketer is J Mercer who last appeared v Hampshire in 1947 aged 52 years and 1 month.

P Willey has obtained most England caps with 20.

Team performances The only instance of Northants reaching 550 runs in an innings occurred against Sussex at Hove on July 30 and 31, 1914 – the innings was given a good start by W H Denton and J S Denton (twin brothers) who added 145 for the first wicket – the side's total was 557 for 6 wkt dec.

Peter Willey, seen sweeping against the Australians at Arundel, is Northamptonshire's most capped player.

J E Timms, on his way to a century against Sussex in 1949, his last season, played 468 times for Northants from 1925.

117

There have been seven totals over 600 against the County, but the only one to exceed 650 is 670 for 9 wkts dec, for Sussex, also at Hove, on July 13 and 14, 1921. On the first day Sussex scored 563 for 8 and on the second morning added a further 107 runs for the loss of one more wicket before declaring.

The lowest total for the County is 12 made on the Spa Ground, Gloucester on June 11, 1907 – rain caused the match to be drawn.

The only side to be dismissed under 40 by Northants is Lancashire, who were all out for 33 on August 10, 1977. Lancashire, who were 350 behind on the first innings, then hit 501 in their second innings. The match was drawn.

Individual performances   R Subba Row made the highest score for Northants, 300, against his previous County Club, Surrey, at the Oval on June 5 and 6, 1958. Subba Row batted 566 minutes and hit 42 fours – Surrey's three main bowlers, Loader, Laker and Lock were all absent, playing for England.

The single triple hundred against the County was hit by K S Duleepsinhji – 333 for Sussex at Hove on May 7, 1930 – he batted 330 minutes and hit a six and 34 fours.

With 10–127, V W C Jupp is the only Northants cricketer to take all ten wickets in an innings for the County, a feat he achieved against Kent at Tunbridge Wells on July 6 and 7, 1932. Kent hit 360 and Jupp registered the highest score for his County in both innings, making 34 out of 97 and 32 out of 75. Despite his great all-round effort Northants lost by an innings and 188 runs.

The only example of ten wickets against the County is C Blythe's 10–30 for Kent. Blythe went on to take 17–48 in the match, another record. The game was played at Northampton on May 30, 31 and June 1, 1907.

Best bowling in a match for the County is 15–31 by G E Tribe against Yorkshire at Northampton on July 3 and 4, 1958. Yorkshire were dismissed for 67 and 65 and Northants won the game by 9 wickets.

2,000 runs in a season for the County have been hit six times, three of which were by D Brookes, whose 2,198 (av 51.06) in 1952 is the record. N Oldfield hit 2,192 (av 49.81) in 1949 and L Livingston reached the milestone twice – in 1954 and 1955. Brookes hit 1,000 runs in a season on 17 occasions between 1937 and 1959, easily the record.

Most wickets in a season are 175 by G E Tribe in 1955 – he is the only bowler to top 150 for the County. He achieved 100 wickets in 8 seasons from 1952 to 1959 – these were the only years in which he played Championship cricket for Northants.

D Brookes holds the record for most runs in a career, making 28,980 for Northants from 1934 to 1959 (av 36.13). J E Timms with 20,384 runs is the other batsman to exceed 20,000.

Four bowlers took between 1,000 and 1,100 wickets in their County career – G E Tribe 1,021; V W C Jupp 1,078; G J Thompson 1,078 and E W Clark with a record 1,097 between 1922 and 1947 (av 21.32).

Wicket partnerships

The highest stands in first-class cricket for the County are:

1st 361 N Oldfield, V Broderick v Scotland (*Peterborough*) 1953
2nd 322 W Larkins, R G Williams v Leics (*Grace Rd, Leicester*) 1980
3rd 320 L Livingston, F Jakeman v South Africans (*Northampton*) 1951
4th 370 R T Virgin, P Willey v Somerset (*Northampton*) 1976
5th 347 D Brookes, D W Barrick v Essex (*Northampton*) 1952
6th 376 R Subba Row, A Lightfoot v Surrey (*Oval*) 1958
7th 229 W W Timms, F I Walden v Warwickshire (*Northampton*) 1926
8th 155 F R Brown, A E Nutter v Glamorgan (*Northampton*) 1952
9th 156 R Subba Row, S Starkie v Lancashire (*Northampton*) 1955
10th 148 B Bellamy, J V Murdin v Glamorgan (*Northampton*) 1925

Limited overs cricket records

GILLETTE/NATWEST CUP
Highest team total   275–5 v Notts (*Trent Bridge*)   1976
Lowest team total   62 v Leics (*Grace Rd, Leicester*)   1974
Highest innings   114* G Cook v Surrey (*Northampton*)   1979
Best bowling   5–24 J D F Larter v Leics (*Grace Rd, Leicester*)   1964

JOHN PLAYER LEAGUE
Highest team total   282–4 v Yorkshire (*Middlesbrough*)   1982
Lowest team total   41 v Middlesex (*Northampton*)   1972
Highest innings   158 W Larkins v Worcestershire (*Luton*)   1982
Best bowling   7–39 A Hodgson v Somerset (*Northampton*)   1976

BENSON AND HEDGES CUP
Highest team total   259–5 v Scotland (*Glasgow*)   1982
Lowest team total   85 v Sussex (*Northampton*)   1978
Highest innings   132 W Larkins v Warwickshire (*Edgbaston*)   1982
Best bowling   5–21 Sarfraz Nawaz v Middlesex (*Lord's*)   1980

No Ball

The first known Laws stated 'If he delivers ye Ball with his hinder foot over ye Bowling crease the Umpire Shall Call no Ball.'

It was not until 1816 that a Law was introduced allowing the umpires to call 'No Ball' for 'throwing'. In the same year a 'No Ball' was counted as an Extra, rather than a 'dead' ball, but the first known score sheet with 'No Balls' given in the Extras only dates from 1830 – MCC v Middlesex at Lord's, May 17 and 18.

Most no-balls in a first-class match is at least 103: West Indies v Pakistan (*Bridgetown*) 1976–77. None of these 103 were scored off. It is not known how many other no-balls were bowled in this match.

Most no-balls (not scored off) in an innings are 35: West Indies v India (*Bridgetown*) 1975–76.

(*See also Throwing*)

Richard Daft, an early stalwart of Nottinghamshire, who at 55 years and 9 months in 1891 was their oldest player.

Nottinghamshire

On August 26 and 27, 1771, Nottingham played Sheffield on the Forest Race-course near Nottingham, the first mention of cricket in the county.

Formation of the County Club The first specific mention of a meeting to form a County Cricket Club appears in the local press in April, 1841. Before this county matches were organised by the Nottingham Old Club, whose history goes back probably to 1771, though few details of the Club are known. The County Club was organised with an elected Committee from 1860.

First-class status The first genuine inter-county match was played against Sussex on August 27, 28 and 29, 1835 on Brown's Ground, Brighton. All important matches can be regarded as 'first-class' from this date. Before 1835, Nottingham played a regular series of matches against Sheffield. Details of these early matches can be found in the ACS 'Guide'.

Grounds In 1835 the principal cricket ground in Nottingham was on the Race-course on the Forest, Nottingham. The first inter-county match was staged on the Trent Bridge Ground in 1840, since when this has been the county headquarters. The other grounds currently used by the County are: Central Avenue, Worksop (since 1921) and Cleethorpes (since 1980). Grounds used for first-class matches previously are: Kelham Rd, Newark (1855); Elm Rd, Newark (1966–78); Welbeck Abbey (1901–04); Shireoaks (1961). The Aspley Lane Ground, Nottingham has been used for a few John Player League matches.

Honours The County has won the Championship outright in 1853, 1862, 1865, 1868, 1871, 1872, 1875, 1880, 1883, 1884, 1885, 1886, 1907, 1929 and 1981 and has tied for the title in 1869, 1873, 1879, 1882 and 1889.

Best position in the John Player League is 4th in 1982. The County reached the semi-final of the Gillette Cup in 1969 and were beaten finalists in the Benson and Hedges Cup in 1982.

The players G Gunn is the only cricketer to play in over 500 matches for the County; his total, between 1902 and 1932, is 583.

The only batsman to score over 300 for Nottinghamshire is W W Keeton, who made 312 not out against Middlesex in 1939.

Longest serving captain is A W Carr with 16 seasons between 1919 and 1934 – W Clarke led the County for 21 seasons from first to last (1835 to 1855), but in some years there were no County matches of importance.

The youngest cricketer to play for Nottinghamshire is B N French, who was 16 years and 9 months when he played against Cambridge University in 1976, though in limited overs cricket this is beaten by P Johnson, who was 16 years and 4 months when he played against Warwickshire in 1981.

The oldest cricketer is Richard Daft, whose final appearance was v Middlesex in 1891 when he was 55 years and 9 months.

The record for the most England Test appearances by a Notts player is 33 held by D W Randall to the end of the 1982 season.

Team performances Nottinghamshire have exceeded 700 in an innings twice, the record being 739 for 7 wkts dec against Leicestershire at Trent Bridge on May 25 and 26, 1903 – the major contributor to this total was J R Gunn, who hit 294 in 265 minutes. The other total over 700 was 726 v Sussex at Trent Bridge in 1895.

Surrey are the only team to exceed 700 against Notts. They hit 706 for 4 wkts dec at Trent Bridge on May 26 and 27, 1947. D G W Fletcher, in only his second first-class match, was the highest scorer with 194 in 320 minutes.

Lowest total by the County is 13 against Yorkshire at Trent Bridge on June 20 and 21, 1901. W Rhodes had figures of 7.5-4-4-6. Against the County two teams have been dismissed for 16. The first was Derbyshire at Trent Bridge on July 10 and 11, 1879 – F Morley took 7 for 7 – and the second was Surrey at the Oval on July 27, 1880 – F Morley took 7 for 9.

Individual performances W W Keeton hit 312 not out (the only Notts score above 300) against Middlesex at the Oval on July 15 and 17, 1939. Keeton batted 435 minutes and hit a five and 28 fours. The match was played at the Oval because Lord's was required for the Eton v Harrow match.

Two triple hundreds have been hit against the County. W R Hammond hit 317 for Gloucester on the Wagon Works Grd, Gloucester on August 31 and September 1, 1936, but the record is 345 by C G Macartney for the Australian touring side at Trent Bridge on June 25, 1921. Macartney batted 235 minutes and hit 4 sixes and 47 fours. The match was the most disastrous ever experienced by Notts, for the County lost in two days by an innings and 517 runs.

Ten wickets in an innings has been performed twice for the County; the first occasion however was in a match against an England Eleven at Eastwood Hall in 1870, when Notts fielded 16 men. J C Shaw took 10 for 20. On June 9 and 11, 1956, K Smales took 10 for 66 against Gloucestershire at Stroud, the only time the feat has been accomplished in inter-county matches for Notts.

The best analysis against the County is 10 for 10 by H Verity for Yorkshire at Headingley on July 12, 1932. Two other bowlers to obtain ten wickets against the County are G C Collins (10–65) for Kent at Dover in 1922 and W E Hollies (10–49) for Warwickshire at Edgbaston in 1946.

By coincidence the best bowling in a match is 17–89 both for and against the County. F C Matthews performed the feat for Notts v Northants at Trent Bridge on June 20 and 21, 1923, whilst Dr W G Grace returned the same figures for Gloucestershire at Cheltenham on August 14 and 15, 1877. In the second innings Grace actually ended with 7 wickets in 17 balls and conceded no runs.

Over 2,500 runs have been scored twice for the County, W W Whysall being the successful batsman on both occasions. In 1928 he hit 2,573 runs (av 52.51) and the following year broke his record with 2,620 runs (av 53.47) – he again exceeded 2,000 runs in 1930, then tragically died following an accident in November of the same year.

G Gunn reached 1,000 runs in a season 20 times between 1905 and 1931 – easily a record for the County.

Most wickets in a season are 181 by B Dooland (av 14.96) in 1954 and T G Wass holds the record for reaching 100 wickets in a season on most occasions, namely 10 between 1900 and 1912.

G Gunn with 31,592 runs (av 35.70) is the only batsman to score over 25,000 runs for the County. His career ran from 1902 to 1932.

T G Wass is the only bowler to take over 1,500 wickets, with 1,653 (av 20.34) between 1896 and 1920.

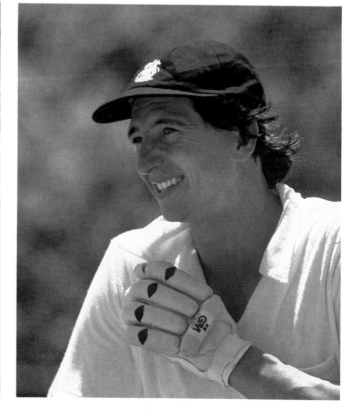

Above   *The famous ground at Trent Bridge, the home of Nottinghamshire since 1840.*

Right   *W W Whysall, who twice scored over 2,500 runs in a season for Notts.*

Far right   *Derek Randall is Notts' most capped player, with 33 to the end of the 1982 season.*

Wicket partnerships

The highest stands in first-class cricket for the County are:

1st   391   A O Jones, A Shrewsbury v Gloucestershire (*Bristol*) 1899
2nd   398   W Gunn, A Shrewsbury v Sussex (*Trent Bridge*) 1890
3rd   369   W Gunn, J R Gunn v Leicestershire (*Trent Bridge*) 1903
4th   361   A O Jones, J R Gunn v Essex (*Leyton*) 1905
5th   266   A Shrewsbury, W Gunn v Sussex (*Hove*) 1884
6th   303* F H Winrow, P F Harvey v Derbyshire (*Trent Bridge*) 1947
7th   204   M J Smedley, R A White v Surrey (*Oval*) 1967
8th   220   G F H Heane, R Winrow v Somerset (*Trent Bridge*) 1935
9th   165   G Wootton, W McIntyre v Kent (*Trent Bridge*) 1869
10th 152   E B Alletson, W Riley v Sussex (*Hove*) 1911

In the 10th wkt stand above the 152 runs were hit in 40 minutes, with Alletson making 142 of them and Riley 10.

Limited overs cricket records

GILLETTE/NATWEST CUP
Highest team total   271 v Gloucestershire (*Trent Bridge*) 1968
Lowest team total   123 v Yorkshire (*Scarborough*) 1969
Highest innings   107 M Hill v Somerset (*Taunton*) 1964
Best bowling   6–18 C E B Rice v Sussex (*Hove*) 1982

JOHN PLAYER LEAGUE
Highest team total   260–5 v Warwickshire (*Edgbaston*) 1976
Lowest team total   66 v Yorkshire (*Bradford*) 1969
Highest innings   120* C E B Rice v Glamorgan (*Swansea*) 1978
Best bowling   6–12 R J Hadlee v Lancs (*Trent Bridge*) 1980

BENSON AND HEDGES CUP
Highest team total   269–5 v Derbyshire (*Trent Bridge*) 1980
Lowest team total   94 v Lancashire (*Trent Bridge*) 1975
Highest innings   130* C E B Rice v Scotland (*Glasgow*) 1982
Best bowling   6–22 M K Bore v Leics (*Grace Rd, Leicester*) 1980
        C E B Rice v Northants (*Northampton*) 1981

Obstructing Field

There have only been 14 examples of a batsman being dismissed 'obstructing field' in first-class cricket:

C A Absolom   Cambridge University v Surrey (*Oval*)   1868
T Straw   Worcestershire v Warwickshire (*Worcester*)   1899
T Straw   Worcestershire v Warwickshire (*Edgbaston*)   1901
J P Whiteside   Leicestershire v Lancashire (*Leicester*)   1901
L Hutton   England v South Africa (*Oval*)   1951
J A Hayes   Canterbury v Central Districts (*Christchurch*)   1954–55
D D Deshpande   Madhya Pradesh v Uttar Pradesh (*Benares*) 1956–57
*M Mehra   Railways v Delhi (*Delhi*)   1959–60
K Ibadulla   Warwickshire v Hampshire (*Coventry*)   1963
Kaiser   Dera Ismail Khan v Railways (*Lahore*)   1964–65
Ejaz Ahmad   Lahore A v Lahore D (*Lahore*)   1973–74
Qasim Feroze   Bahawalpur v Universities (*Lahore*)   1974–75
T Quirk   Northern Transvaal v Border (*East London*)   1978–79
Mahmood Rashid   United Bank v MCB (*Bahawalpur*)   1981–82
In another version Mehra is shown as dismissed 'handled ball'.

Oldest Cricketers

The oldest cricketer to take part in a first-class match is Raja Maharaj Singh who was believed to be 72 when he played for Bombay Governor's XI v Commonwealth in Bombay on November 25, 26 and 27, 1950.

In South African first-class cricket A W Nourse was 58 when he appeared for Western Province v Australians on March 14, 16 and 17, 1936.

The oldest Australian first-class cricketer is believed to be J Marshall who was 58 when appearing for Tasmania v Victoria in 1853–54, but his date of birth has not been verified.

Born in January 1774, B Aislabie was 67 years and 5 months when he appeared for MCC v Cambridge University at Lord's on July 1 and 2, 1841, being the oldest cricketer to appear in English first-class matches – though according to a contemporary he was never much of a player:

The Worcestershire eleven in 1899. The batsman seated bottom left is T Straw, the only cricketer to be dismissed 'obstructing field' twice in first-class cricket.

'He doats on the game, has played many a year,
Weighs at least seventeen stones, on his pins rather queer,
But he still takes the bat, and there's no better fun,
Than to see him when batting attempting a run.'

Overs

In English first-class cricket the number of balls per over have been:
Four balls   to 1888
Five balls   1889 to 1899
Six balls   1900 to date (except 1939 when eight balls were used)

In overseas first-class cricket the situation is much more complex, with the number of balls varying even from match to match – a detailed article appeared in *The Cricket Statistician* No. 7 (Oct 1974).

In the United States, ten-ball overs were used in competition matches before the First World War.

Playing for Warwickshire *v* Worcestershire at Dudley on June 1, 3 and 4, 1946 J M A Marshall bowled an over of 11 balls – the umpire inadvertently allowing five extra deliveries after Marshall had taken a wicket with his sixth ball.

Most overs in an innings

Four-ball overs
123 by D Buchanan for Gentlemen *v* Cambridge University at Fenner's in 1880.

Five-ball overs
100.1 by A Shaw for Sussex *v* Notts at Trent Bridge in 1895.

Six-ball overs
98 by S Ramadhin for West Indies *v* England at Edgbaston in 1957.

Eight-ball overs
69 by Shahid Aziz for Punjab B *v* P I A at Karachi in 1975–76.

Most overs in an English season

Four-ball overs
2631.2 by A Shaw for Notts and MCC in 1876.

Five-ball overs
2003.1 by J T Hearne for Middlesex in 1896.

Six-ball overs
2039 by A P Freeman for Kent in 1933.

Eight-ball overs
936.3 by H Verity for Yorkshire in 1939.

Most runs off an over   In first-class matches, G St A Sobers holds the record with 36 (6 sixes) for Notts *v* Glamorgan at Swansea on August 31, 1968 – the bowler was M A Nash.

In all matches the record is believed to be 62 by H Morley off R Grubb, Tourists *v* Gargett (Gargett) 1968–69.

Oxford University

The first reference to cricket at the University occurred in 1727, but the first match score which is extant involving Oxford cricketers is dated 1795, when the Bullingdon Club of Oxford played MCC on Bullingdon Common, June 15. The direct forerunner of Oxford University Cricket Club was the Magdalen Club which was established about 1800, but 'Oxford University' does not appear in a match title until the first inter-university match of 1827 and Oxford University are regarded as a 'first-class' side from that date, though like Cambridge the side was not the equal of the best County Elevens until the 1860s.

The records for the University in first-class matches are:
Highest team total   651 *v* Sussex (*Hove*) 1895
Lowest team total   12 *v* MCC (*Oxford*) 1877
Highest individual innings   281 K J Key *v* Middx (*Chiswick Park*) 1887
Best bowling in innings   10–38 S E Butler *v* Cambr U (*Lord's*) 1871
Best bowling in match   15–65 B J T Bosanquet *v* Sussex (*Oxford*) 1900
Most runs in season   1307 (av 93.35) Nawab of Pataudi snr 1931
Most runs in career   3319 (av 47.41) N S Mitchell-Innes 1934–37
Most wickets in season   70 (av 18.15) I A R Peebles 1930
Most wickets in career   182 (av 19.32) R H B Bettington 1920–23

K J Key, later to captain Surrey, holds the record for the highest score for Oxford University, 281 against Middlesex in 1887.

I A R Peebles took 70 wickets for Oxford University in 1930, the most successful season for an Oxford bowler.

Wicket partnerships

1st	338	T Bowring, H Teesdale v Gents of Eng (*Oxford*)	1908
2nd	226	W G Keighley, H A Pawson v Cambr U (*Lord's*)	1947
3rd	273	F C de Saram, N S Mitchell-Innes v Gloucs (*Oxford*) 1934	
4th	276	P G T Kingsley, N M Ford v Surrey (*Oval*)	1930
5th	256*	A A Baig, C A Fry v Free Foresters (*Oxford*)	1959
6th	270	D R Walsh, S A Westley v Warwicks (*Oxford*)	1969
7th	340	K J Key, H Philipson v Middx (*Chiswick Park*)	1887
8th	160	H Philipson, A C M Croome v MCC (*Lord's*)	1889
9th	157	H M Garland-Wells, C F H Hill-Wood v Kent (*Oxford*) 1928	
10th	149	F H Hollins, B A Collins v MCC (*Oxford*)	1901

(*See also University Match*)

Pakistan

The State of Pakistan was set up as a result of the Partition of India in 1947 and the first first-class match to be played in Pakistan was Punjab University v Governor's XI at Lahore on February 6, 7 and 8, 1948 – this was the only first-class game in the 1947–48 season and owing to the disruption caused by the Partition only 15 first-class matches took place in the seasons 1948–49 to 1952–53 inclusive and almost all these were against overseas touring teams. The first Pakistan internal first-class Competition – Qaid-i-Azam Trophy – was established for the 1953–54 season. (See under 'Qaid-i-Azam' for list of winners.)

Records in Pakistan in first-class cricket

Highest team total 951–7 dec Sind v Baluchistan (*Karachi*) 1973–74
Lowest team total 27 Dera Ismail Khan v Railways (*Lahore*) 1964–65
Highest individual innings 499 Hanif Mohammad, Karachi v Bahawalpur (*Karachi*) 1958–59
Best bowling in innings 10–58 Shahid Mahmood, Karachi Whites v Khairpur (*Karachi*) 1969–70
Best bowling in match 15–76 Fazal Mahmood, Punjab v Services (*Lahore*) 1956–57

Wicket partnerships

1st	561	Waheed Mirza, Mansoor Akhtar. Karachi Whites v Quetta (*Karachi*) 1976–77
2nd	426	Arshad Pervez, Mohsin Khan. Habib Bank v Income Tax (*Lahore*) 1977–78
3rd	456	Khalid Irtiza, Aslam Ali. United Bank v Multan (*Karachi*) 1975–76
4th	346	Zafar Altaf, Majid Khan. Lahore Greens v Bahawalpur (*Lahore*) 1965–66
5th	355	Altaf Shah, Tariq Bashir. HBFC v Multan (*Multan*) 1976–77
6th	353	Salahuddin, Zaheer Abbas. Karachi v East Pakistan (*Karachi*) 1968–69
7th	308	Waqar Hassan, Imtiaz Ahmed. Pakistan v New Zealand (*Lahore*) 1955–56
8th	240	Gulfraz Khan, Raja Sarfraz. Railways v Universities (*Lahore*) 1976–77
9th	181	Rashid Israr, Abdul Raqib. Habib Bank v National Bank (*Lahore*) 1976–77
10th	196*	Noheen Yousuf, Maqsood Kundi. Muslim Commercial Bank v National Bank (*Lahore*) 1981–82

There have been a number of other first-class domestic competitions in Pakistan, namely The Ayub Trophy 1960–70; The BCCP Trophy 1970–72; The Patron's Trophy 1972 to date; Pentangular Tournament 1973–77; Invitation Tournament 1977–80; S A Bhutto Memorial Tournament 1972–77; A S Pirzada Memorial Tournament 1974–76; Punjab Tournament 1973–76.

Papua-New Guinea

The first organised cricket was in Port Moresby in 1937, though some cricket had been played in Papua since the 1890s. The Papua-New Guinea Cricket Board of Control was established in 1972 and admitted to the ICC in 1973. The West Indian Tourists to Pakistan, India and Sri Lanka in 1974–75 played one match there.

Papua-New Guinea took part in the 1979 ICC Trophy and won one match – v Singapore.

In 1982 they fared much better in the competition and beat Bangladesh to achieve third place, after losing to Bermuda in the semi-finals.

Parsis

The first Cricket Club formed by the Parsis was in Bombay in 1848 and for some years the Parsis were the leading Indian community so far as cricket was concerned. In 1879 it was intended to send a Parsi Team to tour England, but the plans were abandoned. In 1886 the Parsi Gentlemen became the first Indian side to tour England and a second side came in 1888.

The first match between the Bombay Europeans and the Parsis took place in 1877 and from this match and its immediate successors came the Bombay Presidency Matches, the first of which was on August 26 and 27, 1892 at Bombay. This game is by many authorities regarded as the start of domestic first-class cricket in India.

Partnerships

(*See under Wicket Partnerships*)

Philadelphia

The major centre of cricket in the United States from the 1870s to the First World War, Philadelphia, was the scene of the only major domestic Competitive cricket competition in America – the Halifax Cup, which was the Trophy for which the principal Philadelphian Clubs competed. The standard of cricket was such that the Gentlemen of Philadelphia were able to send teams to England to play first-class cricket against the major Counties. Five tours in all were undertaken – in 1884, 1888, 1897, 1903 and 1908 – and the last three involved first-class matches.

Until recently there has been little attempt to study the matches played in Philadelphia in the period between 1870 and 1914 and decide if any of the domestic cricket there should be regarded as first-class.

The Manheim cricket grounds at Philadelphia in 1894, when a touring team under Lord Hawke played two matches against Gentlemen of Philadelphia.

Pitch

The distance between the two wickets was laid down as 22 yards in the earliest known Laws and has remained constant ever since, except for matches involving youngsters.

Originally the choice of pitch was given to the side winning the toss. In 1774, the visiting side was allowed to choose, providing it was within 30 yards of a spot chosen by the home side. From 1811 the choice of pitch was decided by the umpires and from 1947 the ground authorities have decided the pitch.

John Player League

Inaugurated in 1969 as a single innings a side match of 40 overs each, this League is sponsored by John Player and Sons and is played by the first-class English Counties on Sundays. The first games took place on April 27, 1969.

The principal records in the competition are:

Highest team total 307–4 Worcestershire v Derbys (*Worcester*) 1975
Lowest team total 23 Middlesex v Yorkshire (*Headingley*) 1974
Highest individual innings 163* C G Greenidge, Hants v Warwicks (*Edgbaston*) 1979
Best bowling 8–26 K D Boyce, Essex v Lancs (*Old Trafford*) 1971

Wicket partnerships

1st 224 J A Ormrod, D N Patel. Worcs v Hants (*Southampton*) 1982
2nd 179 B W Luckhurst, M H Denness. Kent v Somerset (*Canterbury*) 1973
3rd 215 W Larkins, R G Williams. Northants v Worcs (*Luton*) 1982
4th 188 A J Lamb, R G Williams. Northants v Worcs (*Worcester*) 1981
5th 179 I V A Richards, I T Botham. Somerset v Hants (*Taunton*) 1981
6th 121 C P Wilkins, A J Borrington. Derbys v Warwicks (*Chesterfield*) 1972

Pages from the 'New Articles of the Game of Cricket' published in 1774, giving the choice of pitch to the visitors. There have been two subsequent changes, and now the ground authorities decide the pitch.

7th 101 S J Windybank, D A Graveney. Gloucs v Notts (*Trent Bridge*) 1981
8th 95* D Breakwell, K F Jennings. Somerset v Notts (*Trent Bridge*) 1976
9th 88 S N Hartley, A Ramage. Yorks v Middlesex (*Lord's*) 1982
10th 57 D A Graveney, J B Mortimore. Gloucs v Lancs (*Tewkesbury*) 1973

(For records for each County see under appropriate heading)

John Player League Championship Tables

1969	P	W	L	T	NR	Pts
1 Lancashire	16	12	3	0	1	49
2 Hampshire	16	12	4	0	0	48
3 Essex	16	11	4	0	1	45
4 Kent	16	9	6	1	0	38
5 Surrey	16	9	6	0	1	37
6 Gloucestershire	16	8	8	0	0	32
7 Middlesex	16	7	7	0	2	30

A happy Richard Gilliat holding aloft the John Player Trophy as Hampshire took the Sunday league title for the first time in 1975.

1969 continued	P	W	L	T	NR	Pts
8 Yorkshire	16	7	7	0	2	30
9 Warwickshire	16	6	6	0	4	28
10 Glamorgan	16	7	9	0	0	28
11 Leicestershire	16	6	7	0	3	27
12 Worcestershire	16	6	7	0	3	27
13 Nottinghamshire	16	5	9	1	1	23
14 Northamptonshire	16	5	9	0	2	22
15 Derbyshire	16	5	10	0	1	21
16 Somerset	16	5	10	0	1	21
17 Sussex	16	3	11	0	2	14

Teams obtained 4 pts for a win, 2 pts for a tie and 1 pt for a no result match. If two teams were equal on points the team with a higher run rate per over was given preference

Matches were limited to 40 overs per side, but if bad weather delayed the match a minimum of 10 overs per side had to be bowled to obtain a result

1970	P	W	L	NR	Pts
1 Lancashire	16	13	2	1	53
2 Kent	16	12	4	0	48
3 Derbyshire	16	11	5	0	44
4 Essex	16	8	5	3	35
5 Warwickshire	16	8	6	2	34
6 Worcestershire	16	8	7	1	33
7 Leicestershire	16	7	7	2	30
8 Gloucestershire	16	7	7	2	30
9 Surrey	16	7	7	2	30
10 Nottinghamshire	16	7	9	0	28
11 Middlesex	16	6	8	2	26
12 Hampshire	16	6	10	0	24
13 Northamptonshire	16	6	10	0	24
14 Yorkshire	16	5	9	2	22
15 Somerset	16	5	9	2	22
16 Glamorgan	16	5	9	2	22
17 Sussex	16	3	10	3	15

1971	P	W	L	NR	Pts
1 Worcestershire	16	11	5	0	44
2 Essex	16	11	5	0	44
3 Lancashire	16	10	6	0	40
4 Leicestershire	16	10	6	0	40
5 Somerset	16	9	5	2	38
6 Hampshire	16	9	7	0	36
7 Sussex	16	8	8	0	32
8 Kent	16	8	8	0	32
9 Surrey	16	8	8	0	32
10 Glamorgan	16	7	7	2	30
11 Derbyshire	16	7	8	1	29
12 Nottinghamshire	16	6	9	1	25
13 Middlesex	16	6	10	0	24
14 Northamptonshire	16	6	10	0	24
15 Yorkshire	16	5	9	2	22
16 Gloucestershire	16	5	9	2	22
17 Warwickshire	16	5	11	0	20

Worcestershire won the title having a run rate of 4.522 per over against 4.519 by Essex

1972	P	W	L	T	NR	Pts
1 Kent	16	11	4	0	1	45
2 Leicestershire	16	11	5	0	0	44
3 Essex	16	10	5	0	1	41
4 Yorkshire	16	10	5	0	1	41
5 Middlesex	16	8	6	0	2	34
6 Hampshire	16	7	5	1	3	33
7 Somerset	16	8	7	0	1	33
8 Lancashire	16	8	7	0	1	33
9 Derbyshire	16	7	7	0	2	30
10 Surrey	16	7	7	0	2	30
11 Worcestershire	16	7	8	0	1	29
12 Warwickshire	16	7	8	0	1	29
13 Nottinghamshire	16	6	10	0	0	24
14 Northamptonshire	16	5	8	1	2	24
15 Sussex	16	5	8	0	3	23
16 Gloucestershire	16	3	10	2	1	17
17 Glamorgan	16	2	12	0	2	10

1973	P	W	L	T	NR	Pts
1 Kent	16	12	2	0	2	50
2 Yorkshire	16	11	5	0	0	44
3 Hampshire	16	9	4	0	3	39
4 Lancashire	16	8	4	0	4	36
5 Leicestershire	16	8	6	0	2	34
6 Gloucestershire	16	7	6	0	3	31
7 Sussex	16	7	7	0	2	30
8 Middlesex	16	7	7	0	2	30
9 Surrey	16	6	6	1	3	29
10 Essex	16	7	8	0	1	29
11 Somerset	16	5	7	0	4	24
12 Derbyshire	16	5	8	0	3	23

1973 continued	P	W	L	T	NR	Pts
13 Nottinghamshire	16	5	9	0	2	22
14 Glamorgan	16	5	9	0	2	22
15 Worcestershire	16	4	9	1	2	20
16 Warwickshire	16	4	8	0	4	20
17 Northamptonshire	16	4	9	0	3	19

If two teams lead the table with equal points, a 'play off' match will henceforth decide the title – this replaced the higher run rate rule

1974	P	W	L	T	NR	Pts
1 Leicestershire	16	12	1	1	2	54
2 Somerset	16	12	2	0	2	52
3 Kent	16	10	4	0	2	44
4 Northamptonshire	16	10	6	0	0	40
5 Hampshire	16	9	5	0	2	40
6 Sussex	16	8	6	1	1	36
7 Yorkshire	16	8	6	0	2	36
8 Middlesex	16	7	7	1	1	32
9 Worcestershire	16	7	7	0	2	32
10 Surrey	16	7	8	0	1	30
11 Warwickshire	16	7	8	0	1	30
12 Lancashire	16	5	9	1	1	24
13 Gloucestershire	16	4	8	0	4	24
14 Glamorgan	16	5	10	0	1	22
15 Derbyshire	16	4	11	0	1	18
16 Essex	16	4	11	0	1	18
17 Nottinghamshire	16	3	13	0	0	12

The number of points awarded for a 'no Result' match was increased from 1 to 2 pts

1975	P	W	L	T	NR	Pts
1 Hampshire	16	13	3	0	0	52
2 Worcestershire	16	12	3	1	0	50
3 Kent	16	12	4	0	0	48
4 Essex	16	10	6	0	0	40
5 Nottinghamshire	16	9	7	0	0	36
Warwickshire	16	9	7	0	0	36
Yorkshire	16	9	7	0	0	36
8 Lancashire	16	8	7	1	0	34
9 Derbyshire	16	7	8	0	1	30
10 Middlesex	16	7	9	0	0	28
11 Sussex	16	6	9	0	1	26
12 Leicestershire	16	6	10	0	0	24
Surrey	16	6	10	0	0	24
14 Somerset	16	5	10	1	0	22
15 Gloucestershire	16	5	11	0	0	20
Northamptonshire	16	5	11	0	0	20
17 Glamorgan	16	4	11	1	0	18

If two teams lead the table with equal points, henceforth most wins will decide the title, if they are still equal then most away wins, if still equal then highest run rate. This rule does not apply to other positions in the table

1976	P	W	L	Pts
1 Kent	16	10	6	40
2 Essex	16	10	6	40
3 Leicestershire	16	10	6	40
Somerset	16	10	6	40
Sussex	16	10	6	40
6 Nottinghamshire	16	9	7	36
Warwickshire	16	9	7	36
8 Hampshire	16	8	8	32
Lancashire	16	8	8	32
Surrey	16	8	8	32
Worcestershire	16	8	8	32
12 Derbyshire	16	7	9	28
Middlesex	16	7	9	28
Northamptonshire	16	7	9	28
15 Yorkshire	16	6	10	24
16 Glamorgan	16	5	11	20
17 Gloucestershire	16	4	12	16

Both Kent and Essex had 5 away wins, but Kent won the title with a run rate of 4.98 against 4.56. Leics, Somerset and Sussex all had 4 away wins and were equal third

1977	P	W	L	NR	Pts
1 Leicestershire	16	13	3	0	52
2 Essex	16	12	2	2	52
3 Middlesex	16	9	5	2	40
4 Sussex	16	9	6	1	38
Hampshire	16	8	5	3	38
6 Kent	16	7	6	3	34
Gloucestershire	16	6	5	5	34
8 Glamorgan	16	7	7	2	32
9 Derbyshire	16	6	8	2	28
Somerset	16	6	8	2	28
Warwickshire	16	5	7	4	28
12 Nottinghamshire	16	6	9	1	26
13 Surrey	16	5	9	2	24
Worcestershire	16	5	9	2	24
Yorkshire	16	3	7	6	24
16 Lancashire	16	5	10	1	22
17 Northamptonshire	16	4	10	2	20

Leics won the title having 13 wins against 12 by Essex

The rule which decided the title, if teams were equal on points, by wins, away wins, then higher run rate, was extended to operate for the first three positions in the table

1978	P	W	L	NR	Pts
1 Hampshire	16	11	3	2	48
2 Somerset	16	11	3	2	48
3 Leicestershire	16	11	3	2	48
4 Worcestershire	16	10	5	1	42
5 Lancashire	16	9	6	1	38
6 Essex	16	7	6	3	34
7 Yorkshire	16	7	7	2	32
8 Derbyshire	16	6	7	3	30
Sussex	16	6	7	3	30
10 Glamorgan	16	6	8	2	28
Kent	16	6	8	2	28
Surrey	16	6	8	2	28
13 Nottinghamshire	16	4	7	5	26
Northamptonshire	16	5	8	3	26
15 Middlesex	16	5	9	2	24
16 Warwickshire	16	4	11	1	18
17 Gloucestershire	16	3	11	2	16

Hants, Leics and Somerset were equal on points, wins and away wins; the title was decided on higher run rate: Hants had 5.35, Som 4.58 and Leics 4.26

1979	P	W	L	NR	Pts
1 Somerset	16	12	3	1	50
2 Kent	16	11	3	2	48
3 Worcestershire	16	9	4	3	42
4 Middlesex	16	9	5	2	40
Yorkshire	16	8	4	4	40
6 Essex	16	8	6	2	36
Leicestershire	16	7	5	4	36
8 Gloucestershire	16	7	7	2	32
Nottinghamshire	16	6	6	4	32
10 Hampshire	16	7	8	1	30
Lancashire	16	6	7	3	30
12 Glamorgan	16	6	10	0	24
Northamptonshire	16	5	9	2	24
Surrey	16	5	9	2	24
Sussex	16	6	10	0	24
16 Derbyshire	16	4	9	3	22
17 Warwickshire	16	2	13	1	10

1980	P	W	L	T	NR	Pts
1 Warwickshire	16	11	4	1	0	46
2 Somerset	16	11	5	0	0	44
3 Middlesex	16	10	5	0	1	42
4 Leicestershire	16	9	6	0	1	38
5 Surrey	16	8	6	0	2	36
6 Derbyshire	16	8	7	0	1	34
Northamptonshire	16	8	7	0	1	34
Worcestershire	16	8	7	0	1	34

1980 continued		P	W	L	T	NR	Pts
9	Sussex	16	6	6	0	4	32
10	Gloucestershire	16	7	8	0	1	30
11	Hampshire	16	6	8	0	2	28
	Kent	16	6	8	1	1	28
13	Lancashire	16	6	9	0	1	26
14	Essex	16	6	10	0	0	24
	Nottinghamshire	16	6	10	0	0	24
	Yorkshire	16	6	10	0	0	24
17	Glamorgan	16	4	10	0	2	20

1981		P	W	L	T	NR	Pts
1	Essex	16	12	3	0	1	50
2	Somerset	16	11	5	0	0	44
3	Warwickshire	16	10	4	0	2	44
4	Derbyshire	16	10	5	0	1	42
5	Sussex	16	8	5	0	3	38
6	Hampshire	16	8	7	0	1	34
7	Kent	16	7	7	1	1	32
	Surrey	16	7	7	0	2	32
	Yorkshire	16	6	6	0	4	32
10	Glamorgan	16	6	8	0	2	28
	Lancashire	16	6	8	1	1	28
	Nottinghamshire	16	6	8	0	2	28
	Worcestershire	16	7	9	0	0	28
14	Leicestershire	16	5	9	0	2	24
15	Middlesex	16	4	9	0	3	22
16	Gloucestershire	16	3	9	0	4	20
17	Northamptonshire	16	4	11	0	1	18

Somerset gained second place over Warwickshire, having won more matches

1982		P	W	L	T	NR	Pts
1	Sussex	16	14	1	0	1	58
2	Middlesex	16	11	4	0	1	46
3	Leicestershire	16	9	6	0	1	38
4	Kent	16	9	7	0	0	36
5	Essex	16	9	7	0	0	36
	Hampshire	16	8	6	2	0	36
	Nottinghamshire	16	8	6	1	1	36
8	Northamptonshire	16	8	7	0	1	34
9	Somerset	16	8	8	0	0	32
10	Glamorgan	16	6	7	0	3	30
	Lancashire	16	6	7	1	2	30
12	Surrey	16	6	9	1	0	26
	Derbyshire	16	6	9	0	1	26
14	Gloucestershire	16	5	9	0	2	24
15	Worcestershire	16	5	10	0	1	22
16	Yorkshire	16	3	10	1	2	18
17	Warwickshire	16	3	11	0	2	16

Plunket Shield

This Challenge Shield was presented by Lord Plunket, Governor-General of New Zealand, for Competition among the major New Zealand Cricket Associations – Auckland, Wellington, Canterbury and Otago – and initially awarded in 1906–07 to Canterbury. The holders of the Shield have been:

Canterbury   1906–07 to December 1907
Auckland   December 1907 to February 1911
Canterbury   February 1911 to February 1912
Auckland   February 1912 to January 1913
Canterbury   January 1913 to December 1918
Wellington   December 1918 to January 1919
Canterbury   January 1919 to January 1920
Auckland   January 1920 to January 1921
Wellington   January 1921

In 1921 it was decided to abandon the challenge system and run a competition on a league basis. The winners of the League have been:

1921–22	Auckland	1951–52	Canterbury
1922–23	Canterbury	1952–53	Otago
1923–24	Wellington	1953–54	Central Districts
1924–25	Otago	1954–55	Wellington
1925–26	Wellington	1955–56	Canterbury
1926–27	Auckland	1956–57	Wellington
1927–28	Wellington	1957–58	Otago
1928–29	Auckland	1958–59	Auckland
1929–30	Wellington	1959–60	Canterbury
1930–31	Canterbury	1960–61	Wellington
1931–32	Wellington	1961–62	Wellington
1932–33	Otago	1962–63	Northern Districts
1933–34	Auckland	1963–64	Auckland
1934–35	Canterbury	1964–65	Canterbury
1935–36	Wellington	1965–66	Wellington
1936–37	Auckland	1966–67	Central Districts
1937–38	Auckland	1967–68	Central Districts
1938–39	Auckland	1968–69	Auckland
1939–40	Auckland	1969–70	Otago
1945–46	Canterbury	1970–71	Central Districts
1946–47	Auckland	1971–72	Otago
1947–48	Otago	1972–73	Wellington
1948–49	Canterbury	1973–74	Wellington
1949–50	Wellington	1974–75	Otago
1950–51	Otago		

The last season of Plunket Shield Cricket was 1974–75. In 1975–76 a new Competition sponsored by Shell Oil was inaugurated (see Shell Series).

The Plunket Shield is now used for the match between North and South Islands.

Prudential Cup

A World Cup Tournament based on single innings a side matches of 60 overs each and on a knock-out principle, the Prudential Cup is sponsored by the Prudential Assurance Co Ltd. The first Tournament was held in England in 1975 between eight countries – England, Australia, West Indies, New Zealand, Pakistan, India, Sri Lanka and East Africa.

The match results were:

Group A
England 334–4 (D L Amiss 137) beat India 132–3 by 202 runs
New Zealand 309–5 (G M Turner 171*) beat East Africa 128–8 by 181 runs
England 266–6 (K W R Fletcher 131) beat New Zealand 186 by 80 runs
East Africa 120 lost to India 123–0 by 10 wkts
England 290–5 beat East Africa 94 (J A Snow 4–11) by 196 runs
India 230 lost to New Zealand 233–6 (G M Turner 114*) by 4 wkts

Group B
Australia 278–7 beat Pakistan 205 (D K Lillee 5–34) by 73 runs
Sri Lanka 86 (B D Julien 4–20) lost to West Indies 87–1 by 9 wkts
Australia 328–5 (A Turner 101) beat Sri Lanka 276–4 by 52 runs
Pakistan 266–7 lost to West Indies 267–9 by 1 wkt
Australia 192 lost to West Indies 195–3 by 7 wkts
Pakistan 330–6 beat Sri Lanka 138 by 192 runs

Semi Finals
England 93 (G J Gilmour 6–14) lost to Australia 94–6 by 4 wkts
New Zealand 158 (B D Julien 4–27) lost to West Indies 159–5 by 5 wkts

Final
West Indies 291–8 (C H Lloyd 102) beat Australia 274 (K D Boyce 4–50) by 17 runs

The Second Tournament was held in England in 1979, with the six Test playing countries plus the two finalists of the preliminary I C C Trophy.

The results were:

Group A

Australia 159–9 lost to England 160–4 by 6 wkts

Canada 139–9 lost to Pakistan 140–2 by 8 wkts

Pakistan 286–7 beat Australia 197 by 89 runs

Canada 45 (C M Old 4–8, R G D Willis 4–11) lost to England 46–2 by 8 wkts

England 165–9 beat Pakistan 151 (M Hendrick 4–15) by 14 runs

Canada 105 (A G Hurst 5–21) lost to Australia 106–3 by 7 wkts

Group B

India 190 (M A Holding 4–33) lost to West Indies 194–1 (C G Greenidge 106*) by 9 wkts

Sri Lanka 189 lost to New Zealand 190–1 by 9 wkts

India 182 lost to New Zealand 183–2 by 8 wkts

West Indies *v* Sri Lanka – no play: rain

West Indies 244–7 beat New Zealand 212–9 by 32 runs

Sri Lanka 238–5 beat India 191 by 47 runs

Semi Finals

England 221–8 beat New Zealand 212–9 by 9 runs

West Indies 293–6 (Asif Iqbal 4–56) beat Pakistan 250 by 43 runs

Final

West Indies 286–9 (I V A Richards 138*) beat England 194 (J Garner 5–38) by 92 runs

Clive Lloyd, the captain of the West Indies, with the Prudential Cup won for the second time in 1979, when England were beaten by 92 runs. The West Indies were the only winners to 1983.

The eight finalists for the Prudential World Cup photographed at Lord's in 1979. The teams are Sri Lanka, Pakistan, West Indies, England, Australia, New Zealand, India and Canada.

Prudential Trophy

In 1972 the Prudential Assurance Co Ltd sponsored a series of three one-day internationals between England and the tourists to England that summer, Australia. The results of these matches were:

At Old Trafford	Australia 222–8 lost to England 226–4 (D L Amiss 103) by 6 wkts
At Lord's	England 236–9 lost to Australia 240–5 by 5 wkts
At Edgbaston	Australia 179–9 (G G Arnold 4–27) lost to England 180–8 by 2 wkts

In 1973 two matches each were played against New Zealand and West Indies:

At Swansea	New Zealand 158 (J A Snow 4–32) lost to England 159–3 (D L Amiss 100) by 7 wkts
At Old Trafford	England 167–8 drew with New Zealand – did not bat
At Headingley	West Indies 181 lost to England 182–9 by 1 wkt
At The Oval	England 189–9 lost to West Indies 190–2 (R C Fredericks 105) by 8 wkts

In 1974 two matches each were played against India and Pakistan:

At Headingley	India 265 lost to England 266–6 by 4 wkts
At The Oval	India 171 lost to England 172–4 by 6 wkts
At Trent Bridge	England 244–4 (D Lloyd 116*) lost to Pakistan 246–3 (Majid J Khan 109) by 7 wkts
At Edgbaston	England 81 lost to Pakistan 84–2 by 8 wkts

In 1976 three matches were played v West Indians:

At Scarborough	England 202–8 (A M E Roberts 4–32) lost to West Indies 207–3 (I V A Richards 119*) by 6 wkts
At Lord's	West Indies 221 beat England 185 (A M E Roberts 4–27) by 36 runs
At Edgbaston	West Indies 223–9 beat England 173 (V A Holder 5–50) by 50 runs

In 1977 three matches were played against Australia:

At Old Trafford	Australia 169–9 lost to England 173–8 by 2 wkts
At Edgbaston	England 171 (G S Chappell 5–20, G J Cosier 5–18) beat Australia 70 (J K Lever 4–29) by 101 runs
At The Oval	England 242 (D L Amiss 108) lost to Australia 246–8 (G S Chappell 125*) by 2 wkts

In 1978 two matches each were played against Pakistan and New Zealand:

At Old Trafford	England 217–7 beat Pakistan 85 (R G D Willis 4–15) by 132 runs
At The Oval	England 248–6 (D I Gower 114*) beat Pakistan 154–8 by 94 runs
At Scarborough	England 206–8 (B L Cairns 5–28) beat New Zealand 187–8 by 19 runs
At Old Trafford	England 278–5 (C T Radley 117*) beat New Zealand 152 by 126 runs

In 1980 two matches were played against West Indies and Australia:

At Headingley	West Indies 198 beat England 174 by 24 runs
At Lord's	West Indies 235–9 lost to England 236–7 by 3 wkts
At The Oval	England 248–6 (D K Lillee 4–35) beat Australia 225–8 (M Hendrick 5–31) by 23 runs
At Edgbaston	England 320–8 (G A Gooch 108) beat Australia 273–5 by 47 runs

In 1981 three matches were played against Australia:

At Lord's	Australia 210–7 lost to England 212–4 by 6 wkts
At Edgbaston	Australia 249–8 beat England 247 by 2 runs
At Headingley	Australia 236–8 (G M Wood 108) beat England 165 (R M Hogg 4–29) by 71 runs

In 1982 two matches each were played against India and Pakistan:

At Headingley	India 193 (I T Botham 4–56) lost to England 194–1 by 9 wkts
At The Oval	England 276–9 beat India 162–8 by 114 runs
At Trent Bridge	Pakistan 250–6 lost to England 252–3 (A J Lamb 118) by 7 wkts
At Old Trafford	England 295–8 beat Pakistan 222 by 73 runs

Public Schools

The first recorded inter-school match was played at Lord's on August 5, 1794 between Charterhouse and Westminster. The match was played in the holidays and under the title 'City of London v City of Westminster'. It is not certain whether the title was used as a joke or a ruse – when Eton played Westminster two years later, the Eton headmaster flogged the whole Eton Eleven on their return, for defying his ruling that the match should not take place (presumably because of the unsavoury reputation attached to cricket at that time).

The records in inter-schools matches are:

Highest individual innings 278 J L Guise, Winchester v Eton 1921
Best bowling in innings 9–10 A W Duncan, Merchiston v Watson's 1899
Most runs in season 1443 (av 60.12) H C Tebbutt (*The Leys*) 1904
Most wickets in season 123 (av 7.23) G H Francis (*Chatham House, Ramsgate*) 1908

Qaid-I-Azam Trophy

The first first-class competition established in Pakistan, the Qaid-I-Azam Trophy, has been decided on various systems.

Finals

1953–54	Bahawalpur beat Punjab by 8 wkts	Karachi
1954–55	Karachi beat Services by 9 wkts	Karachi
1956–57	Punjab beat Karachi Whites by 43 runs	Lahore
1957–58	Bahawalpur beat Karachi C by 211 runs	Bahawalpur
1958–59	Karachi beat Services by 279 runs	Karachi
1959–60	Karachi beat Lahore by 99 runs	Karachi
1961–62	Karachi Blues beat Services by 4 wkts	Karachi
1962–63	Karachi A beat Karachi B by an inns and 163 runs	Karachi
1963–64	Karachi Blues beat Karachi Whites by 18 runs	Karachi
*1964–66	Karachi Blues beat Lahore Greens by 105 runs	Karachi
*1966–68	Karachi beat Railways by 10 wkts	Karachi
1968–69	Lahore beat Karachi on first innings	Lahore
1969–70	PIA beat PWD by 195 runs	Karachi
1970–71	Karachi Blues beat Punjab University on first innings	Lahore
1972–73	Railways beat Sind by an inns and 69 runs	Karachi
1973–74	Railways beat Sind by 274 runs	Lahore
1974–75	Punjab A beat Sind by an inns and 249 runs	Karachi
1975–76	National Bank beat Punjab by 9 wkts	Lahore
1976–77	United Bank beat National Bank on first innings	Lahore
1977–78	Habib Bank beat National Bank by 127 runs	Lahore
1978–79	National Bank beat Habib Bank by 384 runs	Karachi
1979–80	PIA beat National Bank and Habib Bank	Lahore

Competition spread over two seasons

Since 1980–81 the Trophy has been run on a league basis.

Championship winners

1980–81	United Bank
1981–82	National Bank

Ranji Trophy

The National Championship of India for the Ranji Trophy, to give the competition its correct title, was established in 1934 to commemorate K S Ranjitsinji, who died on April 2, 1933.

India was divided into four zones – North, East, South and West – each zone finding their best team on a knock-out basis with matches of four days' duration. The winners then played in the semi-finals and final to decide the Champion, these matches being timeless.

For the season 1948–49 only, the zones were abolished and an open draw experimented with. In 1953–54 a fifth zone – Central – was introduced.

From 1957–58 the zones have been played on a league instead of knock-out basis and from 1970–71 each zonal runner-up as well as the winner competes in the final knock-out rounds.

Results of the finals

1934–35 Bombay 266 and 300 (V M Merchant 120, D R Puri 6–101) beat Northern India 219 and 139 (H J Vajifdar 8–40) by 208 runs

1935–36 Bombay 384 and 199 (A G Ram Singh 5–92) beat Madras 268 (B K Kalapesi 5–92) and 125 by 190 runs

1936–37 Nawanagar 424 (M H Mankad 185) and 383 beat Bengal 315 and 236 (A G Skinner 125) by 256 runs

1937–38 Nawanagar 152 and 270 (Hyder Ali 5–92) lost to Hyderabad 113 and 310–9 (E B Aibara 137*) by 1 wkt

1938–39 Bengal 222 (Amir Elahi 5–73) and 418 beat Southern Punjab 328 (S Wazir Ali 222*, K Bhattacharjee 5–100) and 134 by 178 runs

1939–40 United Provinces 237 and 355 (P E Palia 216) lost to Maharashtra 581 (K V Bhandarkar 132) and 12–0 by 10 wkts

1940–41 Madras 145 and 347 (C T Sarwate 6–83) lost to Maharashtra 284 (V S Hazare 137) and 210–4 (S W Sohoni 104) by 6 wkts

1941–42 Mysore 68 (J B Khot 6–19) and 157 (J B Khot 5–40, A K Bhalerao 5–46) lost to Bombay 506–9 dec (K C Ibrahim 117) by an inns and 281 runs

1942–43 Baroda 308 (Ghulam Ahmed 6–114) and 321 (S R Mehta 5–103) beat Hyderabad 215 (C S Nayudu 6–60) and 107 (C S Nayudu 5–21) by 307 runs

1943–44 Bengal 234 (Shantilal 6–50) and 176 lost to Western India 433 (G Kishenchand 111) by an inns and 23 runs

1944–45 Bombay 462 (C S Nayudu 6–153) and 764 (V M Merchant 278, R S Modi 151, R S Cooper 104) beat Holkar 360 (S Mushtaq Ali 109, D G Phadkar 5–75) and 492 (D C S Compton 249*, S Mushtaq Ali 130) by 374 runs

1945–46 Holkar 342 (C K Nayudu 200) and 273 beat Baroda 198 (C S Nayudu 5–55) and 361 (C S Nayudu 5–148) by 56 runs

1946–47 Holkar 202 (V S Hazare 6–85) and 173 (Amir Elahi 6–62) lost to Baroda 784 (Gul Mahomed 319, V S Hazare 288) by an inns and 409 runs

1947–48 Bombay 191 and 261 (H G Gaekwad 6–90) lost to Holkar 361 and 95–1 by 9 wkts

1948–49 Bombay 620 (K C Ibrahim 219, M M Dalvi 110) and 361 (S W Sohoni 5–86) beat Baroda 268 (D G Phadkar 6–49) and 245 (V S Hazare snr 115) by 468 runs

1949–50 Holkar 419 (S Mushtaq Ali 140) and 272 lost to Baroda 437 (V S Hazare snr 130, C S Nayudu 5–182) and 258–6 (V S Hazare jun 101) by 4 wkts

1950–51 Holkar 429 (S Mushtaq Ali 187, M H Mankad 6–132) and 443 (C T Sarwate 234) beat Gujerat 327 and 356 (J M Patel 152) by 189 runs

1951–52 Bombay 596 (G S Ramchand 149, M H Mankad 141) and 442–5 dec (M K Mantri 152) beat Holkar 410 (D G Phadkar 7–109) and 97 by 531 runs

1952–53 Bengal 479 (P B Dutta 141) and 320–5 dec lost to Holkar 496 (B B Nimbalkar 219) and 177–9 on first innings

1953–43 Holkar 292 and 193 lost to Bombay 376 (R S Modi 141) and 111–2 by 8 wkts

1954–55 Madras 478 (C D Gopinath 133) and 311 beat Holkar 417 and 326 (M K Murugesh 5–114) by 46 runs

1955–56 Bengal 255 (M S Hardikar 8–39) and 179 (B P Gupte 5–80) lost to Bombay 308 (P R Umrigar 112, P M Chatterjee 7–101) and 129–2 by 8 wkts

1956–57 Services 171 and 150 (K R Panjri 5–57) lost to Bombay 359–7 dec (Y K Rele 162*) by an inns and 38 runs

1957–58 Baroda 495 (V S Hazare snr 203, D K Gaekwad 132) beat Services 239 and 205 by an inns and 51 runs

1958–59 Bombay 294 (H D Amroliwalla 139, P M Chatterjee 6–76) and 536–9 dec (M L Apte 157, R B Kenny 111) beat Bengal 176 and 234 by 420 runs

1959–60 Bombay 504 (M S Hardikar 145, G S Ramchand 106) beat Mysore 221 (G Guard 5–66) and 261 (V Subramanyam 103) by an inns and 22 runs

1960–61 Rajasthan 140 (R B Desai 7–46) and 249 lost to Bombay 346 (G S Ramchand 118, S A Durani 8–99) and 44–3 by 7 wkts

1961–62 Bombay 539 (A L Wadekar 235, G S Ramchand 100) beat Rajasthan 157 (S J Diwadkar 5–68) and 95 by an inns and 287 runs

1962–63 Bombay 551–6 dec (R G Nadkarni 219, R B Desai 107, G S Ramchand 102*) beat Rajasthan 196 (C Stayers 6–36) and 336 (V L Manjrekar 108) by an inns and 19

1963–64 Bombay 526 (S J Diwadkar 177) and 21–1 beat Rajasthan 108 and 438 (Hanumant Singh 128, S A Durani 118, V L Manjrekar 105) by 9 wkts

1964–65 Bombay 596 (R G Nadkarni 194) beat Hyderabad 235 (B P Gupte 5–62) and 235 by an inns and 126 runs

1965–66 Rajasthan 165 (M S Hardikar 6–25) and 268 lost to Bombay 362 (A L Wadekar 185, C G Joshi 6–96) and 32–2 by 8 wkts

1966–67 Rajasthan 282 (Hanumant Singh 109) and 445–7 dec (Hanumant Singh 213*, Suryaveer Singh 132) lost to Bombay 586–7 dec (D N Sardesai 199, M S Hardikar 108*, R G Nadkarni 103) and 54–2 on first innings

1967–68 Madras 258 and 302 lost to Bombay 312 (A V Mankad 112) and 225–5 on first innings

1968–69 Bengal 387 and 261–7 dec lost to Bombay 469 (A L Wadekar 133) and 77–3 on first innings

1969–70 Rajasthan 217 and 255 lost to Bombay 531 (A V Mankad 171, S M Gavaskar 114) by an inns and 59 runs

1970–71 Bombay 287 (R D Parkar 108, N F Saldana 6–66) and 196 (V Joshi 5–62) beat Maharashtra 230 and 205 (P K Shivalkar 6–56) by 48 runs

1971–72 Bombay 377 (S M Gavaskar 157) and 254 beat Bengal 279 and 106 (P K Shivalkar 6–43) by 246 runs

1972–73 Bombay 151 (V V Kumar 5–48, S Venkataraghavan 5–60) and 146 beat Tamil Nadu 113 (P K Shivalkar 8–16) and 61 (E D Solkar 5–23) by 123 runs

1973–74 Karnataka 276 and 212 beat Rajasthan 176 and 127 (E A S Prasanna 5–45) by 185 runs

1974–75 Karnataka 240 (G R Viswanath 144, K D Ghavri 5–66) and 215 lost to Bombay 305 (E A S Prasanna 6–123) and 151–3 by 7 wkts

1975–76 Bihar 161 (A M Ismail 5–48) and 240 (A M Ismail 5–58) lost to Bombay 352 and 50–0 by 10 wkts

1976–77 Bombay 317 and 224 (B S Bedi 5–90) beat Delhi 291 (K D Ghavri 6–105) and 121 (P K Shivalkar 6–55) by 129 runs

1977–78 Uttar Pradesh 129 (B S Chandrasekhar 6–57) and 112 (B S Chandrasekhar 6–24) lost to Karnataka 434 (G R Viswanath 247, B P Patel 100, R S Hans 9–152) by an inns and 193 runs

1978–79 Delhi 516 (S Amarnath 132, S C Khanna 111) and 416–8 dec (M Amarnath 178*, S C Khanna 128) beat Karnataka 399 (B P Patel 166*) and 122 (S Madan Lal 5–30) by 399 runs

1979-80   Delhi 547 (M Amarnath 191, Kirti Azad 102, P K Shivalkar 5-125) and 177 (Ravi Shastri 6-61) beat Bombay 245 and 239 (B S Bedi 5-60) by 240 runs

1980-81   Delhi 251 (R C Shukla 120, B S Sandu 6-72) and 220 (S V Nayak 6-65) lost to Bombay 517 (A V Mankad 265, G Parker 121, S Madan Lal 8-118) by an inns and 46 runs

1981-82   Karnataka 705 (R M H Binny 115, B P Patel 124, S M H Kirmani 116, R Kanvilkar 113) lost to Delhi 707-8 (M Amarnath 185, G Singh 101) on first innings

Rhodesia (Zimbabwe)

The first recorded match in Rhodesia took place near Fort Victoria on August 16, 1890. In the mid-1890s the principal match in the country was Salisbury v Bulawayo, but first-class cricket was not established until Rhodesia joined the Currie Cup Competition – the first match being v Transvaal on March 15 and 16, 1905 at Johannesburg. This was however a brief encounter, for after one season Rhodesia was not again seen in the Currie Cup until 1929-30. They played also in 1931-32, but after than did not return until 1946-47. In 1979-80 they played as Zimbabwe-Rhodesia and left the Competition at the close of that season.

The only first-class matches in the country since the 1980-81 season involved the Zimbabwe side against tourists.

Zimbabwe toured England in 1982 and played first-class matches.

Competing in the 1982 ICC Trophy, Zimbabwe won the competition.

Riots

Riots on cricket grounds are associated today with the West Indies and to a lesser extent Pakistan, but unruly behaviour by the crowd was quite a feature of English cricket in the 18th and 19th centuries and indeed prior to that – there is a reference in 1693 to spectators at a cricket match in Sussex being fined for 'riot and battery'.

The best known riot in Australian first-class cricket occurred on February 8, 1879 when the English touring team were playing New South Wales at Sydney. The crowd stormed on to the field when an umpiring decision went against a home batsman 'The English team soon found themselves in the centre of a surging, gesticulating and shouting mob and one rowdy struck Lord Harris (the English captain) across the body with a whip or stick.' Play ended for the day, but the match continued on the Monday (the third day).

The run out of McWatt on the 4th day of the West Indies v England Test at Georgetown, February 27, 1954 resulted in the crowd hurling bottles, packing cases and anything to hand on to the field and some of the English team were fortunate not to be injured. The England captain – L Hutton – refused to leave the field and play eventually continued.

A similar incident occurred on the 3rd day of the West Indies v England match at Port of Spain, January 30, 1960 – the England team under P B H May left the field and no further play took place that day. The second Test of the 1967-68 series, England v West Indies at Kingston was also stopped on the third afternoon through a riot – the time lost was added on to the last day.

The worst-hit tour of all was the visit in 1968-69 to Pakistan by the MCC. The country was in a state of political upheaval and the Test matches between Pakistan and England were used by the agitators as a focal point for their demands. There was rioting on the first day of the first Test at Lahore, then at Dacca in the second Test, when the police and military withdrew to leave matters in control of the students. The tour was finally abandoned in the middle of the third Test at Karachi and the English side came home.

Above *Players leave the field with police escort during the riot at Sabina Park, Kingston, Jamaica, in February 1968, which followed the dismissal of Basil Butcher.*

Left *Umpires and players watch while bottles and boxes are thrown on to the pitch during the third Test at Georgetown, British Guiana, in 1954.*

Players running for safety as riots erupted during the third and final Test between Pakistan and England in Karachi in 1969. The tour was abandoned.

The match between West Indies and Australia at Kingston on April 28–May 3, 1978 was abandoned after crowd disturbances on the final day – the West Indies Board suggested that the match should be continued an extra day, but the umpires refused to allow this, claiming it was against the Laws.

During the World Series West Indies *v* Australia match at Bridgetown on March 14, 1979 the dismissal of R C Fredericks – lbw – led to bottle throwing and matters got so bad that the match was abandoned.

Royal Air Force

Although inter-service matches had been played for some years it was not until 1927 that the match between the Royal Navy and the RAF was considered first-class – it was played at the Oval on August 10, 11 and 12 and was the first time the RAF had beaten the Navy.

The final first-class match played by the RAF took place on June 19, 20 and 21, 1946 *v* Worcestershire at Worcester.

The highest individual innings in first-class matches for the RAF is 115 by E A Fawcus *v* Royal Navy at the Oval in 1927 and the best bowling in an innings 7–25 by R E G Fulljames *v* Army at the Oval in 1928.

Royal Navy

There is a reference to crews of British ships playing cricket at Lisbon in 1736 and the Navy had much to do with spreading the game throughout the world. It is believed that the annual match between the Royal Navy and the Army was first staged at Lord's in 1908. In 1912 it was extended from a two-day to three-day match and accorded first-class status, the first first-class match involving the Royal Navy. The Navy however have always found it difficult to put their strongest team into the field and have not been too successful in matches against the Army. The last first-class match by the Navy was against the Army on July 24, 25 and 26, 1929 and the highest score in first-class matches is 143 by R A D Brooks against the Army in 1920, the same player also attained the best bowling figures: 8 for 90 against RAF at the Oval in 1927.

Schweppes Championship

The English County Championship has been sponsored by Schweppes since 1977.

(*See County Championship*)

Scotland

There is a mention of military cricket in Perth about 1750, but a more definite reference occurs in 1785 when a match was played on the estate of the Earl of Cathcart. In 1860 Col Buchanan's Scottish Team played Ireland in the first match between the two countries.

After the formation of the present Scottish Cricket Union in 1908, matches by Scotland became more organised, though Scottish Elevens had played many matches prior to that date, including games against Yorkshire, Nottinghamshire, Gloucestershire and Surrey. The first match to be generally regarded as 'first-class' was *v* Australians at Edinburgh, July 17, 18 and 19, 1905 and the matches with Ireland are first-class from 1909.

Second Eleven Championship

This Competition was inaugurated in 1959 and the Champions have been:

1959	Gloucestershire	1971	Hampshire
1960	Northamptonshire	1972	Nottinghamshire
1961	Kent	1973	Essex
1962	Worcestershire	1974	Middlesex
1963	Worcestershire	1975	Surrey
1964	Lancashire	1976	Kent
1965	Glamorgan	1977	Yorkshire
1966	Surrey	1978	Sussex
1967	Hampshire	1979	Warwickshire
1968	Surrey	1980	Glamorgan
1969	Kent	1981	Hampshire
1970	Kent	1982	Worcestershire

Sheffield Shield

Lord Sheffield took an English team to Australia in 1891–92 and donated 150 guineas to promote cricket in Australia. This gift was used by the Australian Cricket Council to inaugurate an official competition between the first-class colonies in Australia, the winning colony to be awarded the 'Sheffield Shield'. In the first season, 1892–93 only New South Wales, Victoria and South Australia competed, but the Competition has gradually expanded to include all the states – see year-by-year tables.

The major records in the Competition are:

Highest team total 1107 Victoria *v* New South Wales (*Melbourne*) 1926–27
Lowest team total 27 South Australia *v* N S W (*Sydney*) 1955–56
Highest individual innings 452* D G Bradman, N S W *v* Queensland (*Sydney*) 1929–30
Best bowling in innings 10–36 T W Wall, S Australia *v* N S W (*Sydney*) 1932–33

Sheffield Shield championship tables

1892–93

		P	W	L	D
1	Victoria	4	4	0	0
2	South Australia	4	2	2	0
3	New South Wales	4	0	4	0

1893–94

		P	W	L	D
1	South Australia	4	3	1	0
2	New South Wales	4	2	2	0
3	Victoria	4	1	3	0

1894–95

		P	W	L	D
1	Victoria	4	3	1	0
2	South Australia	4	2	2	0
3	New South Wales	4	1	3	0

1895–96

		P	W	L	D
1	New South Wales	4	3	1	0
2	Victoria	4	2	2	0
3	South Australia	4	1	3	0

1896–97

		P	W	L	D
1	New South Wales	4	4	0	0
2	South Australia	4	1	3	0
3	Victoria	4	1	3	0

1897–98

		P	W	L	D
1	Victoria	4	3	1	0
2	South Australia	4	2	2	0
3	New South Wales	4	1	3	0

1898–99

		P	W	L	D
1	Victoria	4	3	1	0
2	New South Wales	4	2	2	0
3	South Australia	4	1	3	0

1899–1900

		P	W	L	D
1	New South Wales	4	3	1	0
2	Victoria	4	2	2	0
3	South Australia	4	1	3	0

1900–01

		P	W	L	D
1	Victoria	4	4	0	0
2	New South Wales	4	1	3	0
	South Australia	4	1	3	0

1901–02

		P	W	L	D
1	New South Wales	4	4	0	0
2	Victoria	3	1	2	0
3	South Australia	3	0	3	0

(*S Australia v Victoria match not played*)

1902–03

		P	W	L	D
1	New South Wales	4	4	0	0
2	Victoria	4	2	2	0
3	South Australia	4	0	4	0

1903–04

		P	W	L	D	Pts
1	New South Wales	4	3	1	0	2
2	South Australia	3	1	2	0	−1
	Victoria	3	1	2	0	−1

(*S Australia v Victoria match not played*)

1904–05

		P	W	L	D	Pts
1	New South Wales	4	4	0	0	4
2	South Australia	4	1	3	0	−2
	Victoria	4	1	3	0	−2

1905–06

		P	W	L	D	Pts
1	New South Wales	4	4	0	0	4
2	South Australia	4	1	3	0	−2
	Victoria	4	1	3	0	−2

1906–07

		P	W	L	D	Pts
1	New South Wales	4	4	0	0	4
2	South Australia	4	1	3	0	−2
	Victoria	4	1	3	0	−2

1907–08

		P	W	L	D	Pts
1	Victoria	3	2	1	0	1
2	South Australia	2	1	1	0	0
3	New South Wales	3	1	2	0	−1

(*South Australia did not play any home matches*)

1908–09

		P	W	L	D	Pts
1	New South Wales	4	3	1	0	2
2	South Australia	4	2	2	0	0
3	Victoria	4	1	3	0	−2

1909–10

		P	W	L	D	Pts
1	South Australia	4	3	1	0	2
2	New South Wales	4	2	2	0	0
3	Victoria	4	1	3	0	−2

1910–11

		P	W	L	D	Pts
1	New South Wales	3	2	1	0	1
2	South Australia	3	2	1	0	1
3	Victoria	4	1	3	0	−2

(*N S W were awarded the title, having better average. The second match between N S W and S Australia not played*)

1911–12

		P	W	L	D	Pts
1	New South Wales	4	4	0	0	4
2	Victoria	4	2	2	0	0
3	South Australia	4	0	4	0	−4

1912–13

		P	W	L	D	Pts
1	South Australia	4	3	1	0	2
2	New South Wales	4	2	2	0	0
3	Victoria	4	1	3	0	−2

1913–14

		P	W	L	D	Pts
1	New South Wales	4	3	1	0	2
2	South Australia	4	2	2	0	0
3	Victoria	4	1	3	0	−2

1914–15

		P	W	L	D	Pts
1	Victoria	4	3	1	0	2
2	New South Wales	4	3	1	0	2
3	South Australia	4	0	4	0	−4

(*Victoria were awarded the title, having better average*)

1919–20

		P	W	L	D	Pts
1	New South Wales	4	3	1	0	2
2	Victoria	4	3	1	0	2
3	South Australia	4	0	4	0	−4

(*N S W were awarded the title, having better average*)

1920–21

		P	W	L	D	Pts
1	New South Wales	4	4	0	0	4
2	Victoria	4	2	2	0	0
3	South Australia	4	0	4	0	−4

(*The match at Sydney between N S W and S Australia was abandoned at the request of S Australia and credited to N S W as a win*)

1921–22

		P	W	L	D	Pts
1	Victoria	4	4	0	0	4
2	New South Wales	4	2	2	0	0
3	South Australia	4	0	4	0	−4

1922–23

		P	W	L	D	Pts
1	New South Wales	4	3	1	0	2
2	Victoria	4	3	1	0	2
3	South Australia	4	0	4	0	−4

(*N S W were awarded the title, having better average*)

1923–24

	P	W	L	D	Pts
1 Victoria	4	4	0	0	4
2 New South Wales	4	2	2	0	0
3 South Australia	4	0	4	0	−4

1924–25

	P	W	L	D	Pts
1 Victoria	4	3	1	0	2
2 New South Wales	4	2	2	0	0
3 South Australia	4	1	3	0	−2

1925–26

	P	W	L	D	Pts
1 New South Wales	4	4	0	0	4
2 South Australia	4	1	3	0	−2
3 Victoria	4	1	3	0	−2

1926–27

	P	W	L	D	%
1 South Australia	5	3	2	0	60.00
2 New South Wales	6	3	3	0	50.00
3 Victoria	6	3	3	0	50.00
4 Queensland	5	2	3	0	40.00

(S Australia and Queensland only played each other once)

1927–28

	P	W	Won on 1st inns	Lost on 1st inns	L	Pts
1 Victoria	6	4	0	2	0	18
2 South Australia	6	3	0	0	3	12
3 New South Wales	6	1	2	1	2	11
4 Queensland	6	0	2	1	3	7

A points system was introduced as follows: a win 4 pts, a win on 1st innings 3 pts; a tie 2 pts; a loss on 1st innings 1 pt. Matches were now limited to 5 days

1928–29

	P	W	Won on 1st inns	Lost on 1st inns	L	Pts
1 New South Wales	6	3	3	0	0	24
2 Victoria	6	2	0	4	0	14
3 Queensland	6	1	1	1	3	9
4 South Australia	6	1	1	0	4	8

The points system was altered as follows: a win 5 pts, win on first innings 3 pts, draw or tie 2 pts, loss on first innings 1 pt

If two States have equal points then the position is determined by the best batting and bowling averages

1929–30

	P	W	Won on 1st inns	Lost on 1st inns	L	D	Pts
1 Victoria	6	4	0	1	0	1	23
2 New South Wales	6	3	1	0	1	1	20
3 South Australia	6	2	1	0	3	0	13
4 Queensland	6	0	0	1	5	0	1

1930–31

	P	W	Won on 1st inns	Lost on 1st inns	L	D	Pts
1 Victoria	6	1	2	1	0	2	16
2 New South Wales	6	2	0	3	0	1	15
3 Queensland	6	1	2	0	2	1	13
4 South Australia	6	1	1	1	3	0	9

1931–32

	P	W	Won on 1st inns	Lost on 1st inns	L	D	Pts
1 New South Wales	6	4	0	0	2	0	20
2 South Australia	6	4	0	0	2	0	20
3 Queensland	6	2	0	0	4	0	10
4 Victoria	6	2	0	0	4	0	10

NSW won the title with a better average than S Australia

1932–33

	P	W	Won on 1st inns	Lost on 1st inns	L	D	Pts
1 New South Wales	6	5	1	0	0	0	28
2 Victoria	6	3	0	1	2	0	16
3 South Australia	6	3	0	0	3	0	15
4 Queensland	6	0	0	0	6	0	0

1933–34

	P	W	Won on 1st inns	Lost on 1st inns	L	D	Pts
1 Victoria	6	3	1	2	0	0	20
2 New South Wales	6	3	1	1	1	0	19
3 South Australia	6	2	0	0	4	0	10
4 Queensland	6	1	1	0	4	0	8

1934–35

	P	W	Won on 1st inns	Lost on 1st inns	L	D	Pts
1 Victoria	6	5	0	0	1	0	25
2 New South Wales	6	3	0	1	2	0	16
3 South Australia	6	2	0	0	4	0	10
4 Queensland	6	1	1	0	4	0	8

1935–36

	P	W	Won on 1st inns	Lost on 1st inns	L	D	Pts
1 South Australia	6	4	1	0	0	1	25
2 New South Wales	6	2	0	1	2	1	13
3 Victoria	6	1	2	1	2	0	12
4 Queensland	6	0	1	2	3	0	5

Match between S Australia and NSW abandoned due to death of King George V – each state awarded a draw

1936–37

	P	W	Won on 1st inns	Lost on 1st inns	L	D	Pts
1 Victoria	6	3	3	0	0	0	24
2 South Australia	6	3	0	2	1	0	17
3 New South Wales	6	1	1	2	2	0	10
4 Queensland	6	1	0	0	5	0	5

1937–38

	P	W	Won on 1st inns	Lost on 1st inns	L	D	Pts
1 New South Wales	6	3	1	1	0	1	21
2 South Australia	6	2	1	1	2	0	14
3 Victoria	6	1	2	1	1	1	14
4 Queensland	6	0	0	1	3	2	5

S Australia took second place, having better average

1938–39

	P	W	Won on 1st inns	Lost on 1st inns	L	D	Pts
1 South Australia	6	3	1	1	0	1	21
2 Victoria	6	3	1	0	1	1	20
3 Queensland	6	2	1	0	3	0	13
4 New South Wales	6	0	0	2	4	0	2

1939–40

	P	W	Won on 1st inns	Lost on 1st inns	L	Pts
1 New South Wales	6	4	0	0	2	20
2 South Australia	6	3	1	0	2	18
3 Victoria	6	3	0	1	2	16
4 Queensland	6	1	0	0	5	5

1946–47

	P	W	Won on 1st inns	Lost on 1st inns	L	D	Pts
1 Victoria	6	5	0	0	0	1	27
2 New South Wales	6	3	0	1	2	0	16
3 Queensland	6	1	1	0	4	0	8
4 South Australia	6	0	1	1	3	1	6

1947–48

	P	W	Won on 1st inns	Lost on 1st inns	L	D	Pts
1 Western Australia	4	2	1	0	1	0	13
2 New South Wales	7	3	1	0	2	1	20
3 South Australia	7	3	0	1	3	0	16
4 Queensland	7	2	0	0	3	2	14
5 Victoria	7	2	0	1	3	1	13

Western Australia were awarded the title on average

1948–49

	P	W	Won on 1st inns	Lost on 1st inns	l	D	Pts	%
1 New South Wales	7	4	3	0	0	0	29	82.85
2 Victoria	7	3	2	1	1	0	22	62.85
3 Queensland	7	2	0	2	3	0	12	34.28
4 South Australia	7	2	0	2	3	0	12	34.28
5 Western Australia	4	0	0	0	4	0	0	—

1949–50

	P	W	Won on 1st inns	Lost on 1st inns	l	D	Pts	%
1 New South Wales	7	5	1	0	1	0	28	80.00
2 Victoria	7	3	2	0	2	0	21	60.00
3 Western Australia	4	2	0	0	2	0	10	50.00
4 Queensland	7	2	0	2	3	0	12	34.00
5 South Australia	7	0	1	2	4	0	5	14.00

1950–51

	P	W	Won on 1st inns	Lost on 1st inns	l	D	Pts	%
1 Victoria	7	5	1	1	0	0	29	82.85
2 New South Wales	7	4	2	1	0	0	27	77.14
3 Western Australia	4	1	1	0	2	0	8	40.00
4 Queensland	7	1	1	0	5	0¹	8	22.85
5 South Australia	7	0	0	3	4	0	3	8.57

1951–52

	P	W	Won on 1st inns	Lost on 1st inns	l	D	Pts	%
1 New South Wales	7	3	4	0	0	0	27	77.14
2 Queensland	7	2	1	2	2	0	15	42.85
3 Victoria	7	2	1	2	2	0	15	42.85
4 South Australia	7	2	0	3	2	0	13	37.14
5 Western Australia	4	0	1	0	3	0	3	15.00

1952–53

	P	W	Won on 1st inns	Lost on 1st inns	l	D	Pts	%
1 South Australia	7	4	3	0	0	0	29	82.85
2 New South Wales	7	2	2	2	1	0	18	51.42
3 Victoria	7	3	0	2	2	0	17	48.57
4 Western Australia	4	1	1	0	2	0	8	40.00
5 Queensland	7	0	0	2	5	0	2	5.71

1953–54

	P	W	Won on 1st inns	Lost on 1st inns	l	D	Pts	%
1 New South Wales	7	4	2	0	1	0	26	74.28
2 Victoria	7	4	1	1	1	0	24	68.57
3 Queensland	7	1	2	2	2	0	13	37.14
4 South Australia	7	1	0	3	3	0	8	22.85
5 Western Australia	4	0	1	0	3	0	3	15.00

1954–55

	P	W	Won on 1st inns	Lost on 1st inns	l	D	Pts	%
1 New South Wales	4	2	1	0	1	0	13	65.00
2 Victoria	4	1	2	0	1	0	11	55.00
3 Western Australia	2	0	1	0	0	1	5	50.00
4 Queensland	4	1	0	2	1	0	7	35.00
5 South Australia	4	0	0	2	1	1	4	20.00

(Matches reduced to limit financial losses, but experiment proved a false economy)

1955–56

	P	W	Won on 1st inns	Lost on 1st inns	l	D	Pts	%
1 New South Wales	7	2	3	1	0	1	22	62.85
2 Victoria	7	2	2	2	0	1	20	57.14
3 Queensland	7	1	2	3	1	0	14	40.00
4 Western Australia	4	0	1	2	1	0	5	25.00
5 South Australia	7	0	2	2	3	0	8	22.85

1956–57

	P	W	Won on 1st inns	T	Lost on 1st inns	L	Pts
1 New South Wales	8	3	2	1	2	0	25
2 Queensland	8	2	4	0	2	0	24
3 Victoria	8	3	1	1	1	2	21
4 Western Australia	8	1	1	0	3	3	11
5 South Australia	8	0	2	0	2	4	8

(W Australia played all the other States home and away, so that the percentage system was no longer required)

1957–58

	P	W	Won on 1st inns	D	Lost on 1st inns	L	Pts
1 New South Wales	8	4	1	0	2	1	48
2 Victoria	8	2	3	1	0	2	34
3 Queensland	8	1	3	1	2	1	24
Western Australia	8	2	1	0	2	3	24
5 South Australia	8	1	1	0	3	3	10

The points system was altered as follows: 10 pts for win with 1st innings lead; 6 pts for win without 1st innings lead; 4 pts for win on 1st innings; 2 pts for a draw

N S W lost to S Australia but gained first innings lead and 4 pts, S Australia receiving 6 pts

1958–59

	P	W	Won on 1st inns	D	Lost on 1st inns	L	Pts
1 New South Wales	8	4	3	0	1	0	52
2 Queensland	8	2	2	1	3	0	30
3 Victoria	8	1	2	1	1	3	20
4 Western Australia	8	1	2	0	2	3	18
5 South Australia	8	1	1	0	3	3	14

1959–60

	P	W	Won on 1st inns	D	Lost on 1st inns	L	Pts
1 New South Wales	8	5	0	0	1	2	50
2 Victoria	8	4	2	0	1	1	48
3 Western Australia	8	3	1	0	2	2	34
4 Queensland	8	2	1	0	2	3	24
5 South Australia	8	0	2	0	0	6	8

1960–61

	P	W	Won on 1st inns	D	Lost on 1st inns	L	Pts
1 New South Wales	8	4	2	0	1	1	44
2 Victoria	8	4	1	0	2	1	40
3 Western Australia	8	2	0	0	2	4	32
4 Queensland	8	2	2	0	2	2	24
5 South Australia	8	1	2	0	0	5	18

W Australia lost to N S W, Victoria and Queensland, but gained first innings lead in each match and 4 pts, their opponents received 6 pts

1961–62

	P	W	Won on 1st inns	D	Lost on 1st inns	L	Pts
1 New South Wales	8	6	1	0	0	1	64
2 Queensland	8	3	2	1	0	2	36
3 South Australia	8	3	0	0	0	5	30
4 Victoria	8	2	0	0	1	5	24
5 Western Australia	8	2	0	1	2	3	22

S Australia, Victoria, W Australia and N S W received 4 pts for 1st innings on a match lost and W Australia, Queensland, N S W and S Australia received 6 pts for a win, after losing on 1st innings

1962–63

	P	W	Won on 1st inns	D	Lost on 1st inns	L	Pts
1 Victoria	8	4	2	0	1	1	48
2 South Australia	8	3	2	0	1	2	38
3 New South Wales	8	3	1	0	1	3	34
4 Western Australia	8	2	0	0	0	6	24
5 Queensland	8	2	1	0	3	2	20

W Australia received 4 pts for leading on first innings of a match lost, Queensland received 6 pts for winning that match

1963–64

	P	W	Won on 1st inns	D	Lost on 1st inns	L	Pts
1 South Australia	8	4	1	0	1	2	53
2 Victoria	8	3	3	0	0	2	46
3 New South Wales	8	3	2	0	2	1	30
4 Queensland	8	1	2	0	3	2	14
5 Western Australia	8	0	1	0	3	4	4

S Australia received 4 pts on two occasions for first innings lead on a match lost and Victoria 4 pts once; N S W received 6 pts on two occasions for winning a match, having lost on first innings and Queensland received 6 pts once

1964–65

		P	W	Won on 1st inns	D	Lost on 1st inns	L	Pts
1	New South Wales	8	3	2	0	3	0	34
2	Victoria	8	2	2	0	3	1	32
	South Australia	8	2	1	0	2	3	32
4	Western Australia	8	2	2	0	1	3	24
5	Queensland	8	1	3	0	1	3	18

N S W, W Australia and Queensland received 6 pts each for a win, after losing on first innings, S Australia received 4 pts twice and Victoria 4 pts once for first innings lead on a match lost

1965–66

		P	W	Won on 1st inns	D	Lost on 1st inns	L	Pts
1	New South Wales	8	4	0	0	1	3	40
2	Western Australia	8	2	4	0	2	0	36
3	South Australia	8	2	1	0	3	2	28
4	Victoria	8	2	3	0	2	1	24
5	Queensland	8	1	1	0	1	5	18

Victoria received 6 pts twice, N S W and Queensland 6 pts once for a win after losing on first innings; Queensland received 4 pts twice, N S W and S Australia 4 pts once for first innings lead in a match lost

1966–67

		P	W	Won on 1st inns	D	Lost on 1st inns	L	Pts
1	Victoria	8	2	5	0	0	1	40
2	South Australia	8	3	1	0	2	2	34
3	New South Wales	8	3	1	0	4	0	30
4	Western Australia	8	1	2	0	1	4	22
5	Queensland	8	1	1	0	3	3	14

N S W received 6 pts for a win after losing on first innings, W Australia received 4 pts in the same match

1967–68

		P	W	Won on 1st inns	D	Lost on 1st inns	L	Pts
1	Western Australia	8	5	1	0	0	2	54
2	Victoria	8	4	1	1	0	2	46
3	South Australia	8	5	0	0	0	3	42
4	New South Wales	8	2	0	0	2	4	20
5	Queensland	8	0	1	1	1	5	14

S Australia received 6 pts twice for a win, after losing on first innings. Queensland received 4 pts twice for first innings lead in matches lost

1968–69

		P	W	Won on 1st inns	D	Lost on 1st inns	L	Pts
1	South Australia	8	5	0	1	1	1	52
2	Western Australia	8	4	0	0	1	3	44
3	Queensland	8	5	0	0	0	3	38
4	Victoria	8	1	3	1	0	3	28
5	New South Wales	8	1	0	0	1	6	14

Queensland received 6 pts twice for a win, after losing on first innings

1969–70

		P	W	Won on 1st inns	D	Lost on 1st inns	L	Pts
1	Victoria	8	4	1	0	2	1	48
2	Western Australia	8	3	2	0	3	0	38
3	New South Wales	8	2	1	0	1	4	24
	Queensland	8	2	2	0	0	4	24
	South Australia	8	2	1	0	1	4	24

Queensland received 6 pts for a win after losing on first innings, Victoria received 4 pts in the same match

1970–71

		P	W	Won on 1st inns	D	Lost on 1st inns	L	Pts
1	South Australia	8	3	3	0	2	0	42
2	Victoria	8	2	3	2	1	0	32
3	Western Australia	8	2	1	0	3	2	24
4	New South Wales	8	1	3	1	1	2	20
5	Queensland	8	0	0	1	3	4	10

Victoria and N S W each received 6 pts for a win after losing on first innings; Queensland received 4 pts twice for first innings lead in a match lost

1971–72

		P	W	D	L	Match Pts	Bonus Pts	Pts
1	Western Australia	8	4	3	1	40	53	93
2	South Australia	8	4	1	3	40	52	92
3	New South Wales	8	2	3	3	20	48	68
4	Victoria	8	3	2	3	32	35	67
5	Queensland	8	1	3	4	12	27	39

The match between Queensland and Victoria was abandoned, each State received 2 pts

The new points system was 10 pts for a win and bonus points awarded in the first 65 overs of each first innings – 1 pt for every 25 runs over 150 and 1 pt for every two wickets taken

1972–73

		P	W	D	L	Bonus Pts Bat	Bonus Pts Bwl	Pts
1	Western Australia	8	4	2	2	26	29	95
2	South Australia	8	3	4	1	23	26	79
3	New South Wales	8	3	1	4	12	30	72
4	Victoria	8	1	4	3	29	25	64
5	Queensland	8	2	3	3	8	31	59

1973–74

		P	W	D	L	Match Pts	Bonus Pts	Pts
1	Victoria	8	5	1	2	50	55	105
2	Queensland	8	4	2	2	40	58	98
3	New South Wales	8	4	2	2	40	50	90
4	Western Australia	8	3	1	4	30	53	83
5	South Australia	8	1	0	7	10	52	62

1974–75

		P	W	D	L	Match Pts	Bonus Bat	Bonus Bwl	Pts
1	Western Australia	8	3	3	2	30	34	32	96
2	Queensland	8	4	2	2	40	16	35	91
3	Victoria	8	4	1	3	40	27	21	88
4	New South Wales	8	3	3	2	30	24	31	85
5	South Australia	8	1	1	6	10	15	28	53

1975–76

		P	W	D	L	Match Pts	Bonus Pts	Pts
1	South Australia	8	5	2	1	50	55	105
2	Queensland	8	4	3	1	40	44	84
3	Western Australia	8	4	1	3	40	38	78
4	New South Wales	8	2	1	5	20	51	71
5	Victoria	8	1	1	6	10	50	60

1976–77

		P	W	T	D	L	Bonus Pts Bat	Bonus Pts Bwl	Match Pts	Pts
1	Western Australia	8	6	0	2	0	39	39	60	138
2	Victoria	8	3	0	1	4	31	30	30	91
3	Queensland	8	3	1	1	3	21	27	35	83
4	New South Wales	8	3	0	3	2	19	33	30	82
5	South Australia	8	0	1	1	6	28	29	5	62

Queensland and South Australia received 5 pts each for a tie

1977–78

		P	W	D	L	Bonus Pts Bat	Bonus Pts Bwl	Match Pts	Pts
1	Western Australia	9	7	2	0	37	40	70	147
2	Queensland	9	4	4	1	43	38	40	121
3	Victoria	9	3	2	4	45	42	30	117
4	South Australia	9	2	3	4	30	32	20	82
5	New South Wales	9	1	2	6	32	38	10	80
6	Tasmania	5	0	3	2	$32\frac{2}{5}$	$21\frac{3}{5}$	0	54

Tasmania played each State once and its points are multiplied by 9 and divided by 5

1978–79

		P	W	D	L	Bonus Pts Bat	Bonus Pts Bwl	Match Pts	Pts
1	Victoria	9	4	3	2	32	38	40	110
2	Western Australia	9	3	5	1	28	36	30	94
3	New South Wales	9	3	4	2	30	32	30	92
4	Queensland	9	3	3	3	21	33	30	84
5	South Australia	9	1	3	5	18	29	10	57
6	Tasmania	5	1	2	2	18	19.8	18	55

1979–80		P	W	D	L	Bonus Pts Match			
						Bat	Bwl	Pts	Pts
1	Victoria	9	6	2	1	34	36	60	130
2	South Australia	9	4	2	3	43	38	40	121
3	New South Wales	9	4	3	2	45	33	40	118
4	Queensland	9	3	3	3	37	33	30	100
5	Western Australia	9	1	2	6	33	38	10	81
6	Tasmania	5	0	2	3	34.2	32.4	0	66

1980–81		P	W	D	L	Bonus Pts Match			
						Bat	Bwl	Pts	Pts
1	Western Australia	9	5	2	2	39	36	50	125
2	New South Wales	9	4	4	1	45	37	40	122
3	Queensland	9	3	6	0	51	37	30	118
4	Victoria	9	3	4	2	32	29	30	91
5	Tasmania	5	0	0	5	37.8	32.4	0	70.2
6	South Australia	9	1	2	6	28	31	10	69

1981–82		P	W	1st inns	NR	L	Pts
1	South Australia	9	4	6	1	1	74
2	New South Wales	9	4	6	2	1	72
3	Western Australia	9	3	4	1	1	54
4	Tasmania	5	1	2	0	3	36
5	Queensland	9	1	2	2	2	20
6	Victoria	9	0	4	0	5	16

The Shell Series

Shell Oil Company sponsored two Competitions in New Zealand commencing with the 1975–76 season. The first was the Shell Cup in which each major Association played the others on a league basis and the team with most points won the Cup. The winners have been:

1975–76	Canterbury
1976–77	Northern Districts
1977–78	Canterbury
1978–79	Otago – discontinued after this season.

(Cup now used for one-day competition.)

The other Competition is the Shell Trophy, which has been played under various rules. The winners have been:

1975–76	Canterbury
1976–77	Otago
1977–78	Auckland
1978–79	Otago
1979–80	Northern Districts
1980–81	Auckland
1981–82	Wellington

The matches in both competitions are all first-class and supersede the Plunket Shield (*q.v.*).

The Shell Shield

Sponsored by the Shell Oil Company, 'The Shell Shield for Caribbean Regional Cricket Tournament' was first instituted in 1965–66 season. All matches are first-class and the competing teams are Barbados, British Guiana (Guyana), Jamaica, Trinidad, Leeward and Windward Islands, the last two previously playing as a Combined Team.

Shield Winners

1965–66	Barbados	1974–75	Guyana
1966–67	Barbados	1975–76	Barbados, Trinidad
1968–69	Jamaica	1976–77	Barbados
1969–70	Trinidad	1977–78	Barbados
1970–71	Trinidad	1978–79	Barbados
1971–72	Barbados	1979–80	Barbados
1972–73	Guyana	1980–81	Combined Islands
1973–74	Barbados	1981–82	Barbados

Shortest Player

The shortest player to appear in first-class county cricket is believed to be T W Gunn, who played for Surrey in six matches between 1863 and 1869. He was 5ft 1½in tall.

Sides

Although it is generally recognised that cricket matches are staged between two sides of eleven players, this fact was not stated in the Laws until 1884 and even the present Laws (1980) still allow for any number to play, though only eleven may field.

The most players recorded on a side are 56, the match being Earl of Winterton's Eleven v 56 Labourers at Shillinglee Park on August 23, 1846.

In strictly first-class matches, 12 players on each side were fairly common in England until the 1920s – usually in matches involving Oxford or Cambridge University.

Too many men Sussex went on to the field v Hampshire at Hove on June 14, 1880 with 12 players in an eleven-a-side match, but the error was discovered after one over and W A Tester withdrew from the field. After further discussion however, G G S Grundy retired and Tester returned.

Too few men The only instance in a County Championship match of a county playing throughout the match with only nine men occurred at Southampton on August 20 and 21, 1885, when Somerset lacked two players in their match v Hampshire.

Odds matches The idea of one team having more members than the other probably originated to even up the teams for the purposes of betting. The most common Odds Matches were Eleven v Twenty-Two and the annual County Trials between the County Eleven and the Colts of the County usually had these odds. Even as late as 1932–33, the M C C played an odds match on their tour of Australia.

Sixes

Most Sixes in an innings It is believed that the most sixes hit in a single innings are 36 by D Hope in a club game in Durban, South Africa in 1939–40.

In first-class cricket the record is 15 by J R Reid for Wellington v Northern Districts in Wellington, 1962–63. Two cricketers have hit 13 in English first-class cricket, Majid J Khan for Pakistanis v Glamorgan at Swansea in 1967 and C G Greenidge twice, for D H Robins' XI v Pakistanis at Eastbourne in 1974 and for Hampshire v Sussex at Southampton in 1975.

Most sixes off consecutive balls G St A Sobers hit all six deliveries in one over off M A Nash for six, playing for Notts v Glamorgan at Swansea, September 2, 1968.

Gary Sobers, who scored most consecutive sixes when hitting all six balls in one over for six in 1968.

Most sixes in a match W J Stewart with 17, holds the first-class record, playing for Warwickshire v Lancashire at Blackpool, July 29, 30 and 31, 1959.

Most sixes in a first-class season It is believed that A W Wellard of Somerset is the only cricketer to exceed 50 sixes in a season, a feat he accomplished 4 times, namely 1935 with 72, 1936 with 57, 1938 with 57 and 1933 with 51.

Slowest Innings

Longest time before scoring first run T G Evans playing for England v Australia at Adelaide on February 5 and 6, 1947 was at the wicket 95 minutes before scoring, which is a record in first-class cricket.

Longest time without adding to score Mohsin Khan, playing for Punjab v England XI at Bahawalpur, January 9, 1978, batted 93 minutes without adding to his score.

Slowest fifty T E Bailey took 357 minutes to make 50 for England v Australia at Brisbane, December 8 and 9, 1959.

Slowest hundred Mudassar Nazar batted 557 minutes to reach his 100, December 14 and 15, 1977, for Pakistan v England at Lahore. When he reached 99, an error on the scoreboard led the crowd to believe he had made 100 and they swarmed onto the pitch causing a 25 minutes break in play.

The slowest 100 in English first-class cricket took 458 minutes by K W R Fletcher for England v Pakistan at the Oval in 1974.

Slowest innings (discounting no score) Taken as runs per hour, the slowest first-class innings is 1 scored in 102 minutes by G E Vivian for Auckland v Canterbury at Christchurch in 1977–78.

Godfrey Evans' first 95 minutes at the crease for England v Australia in 1947 is the longest time taken for a batsman to open his score.

Somerset

The earliest known reference to cricket in Somerset is to a match in 1751.

Formation of the County Club Although there is mention of Somerset playing on September 4, 1798, the first reference to a County Club comes in 1864 when the Yeovil Club changed its title to the Yeovil and County of Somerset Cricket Club. This title did not survive for very long and the present Somerset County Club was formed at Sidmouth in Devon on August 18, 1875. A team of Gentlemen from Somerset were playing Gentlemen of Devonshire at Sidmouth and after the match held a meeting at which it was resolved that a County Club be formed.

First-class status Wisden's Almanack first designates Somerset as first-class in 1882 – the initial first-class match being at Old Trafford v Lancashire on June 8, 9 and 10. In 1886 however the County ceased playing against any other first-class county and Somerset do not return to first-class status until 1891, when they arranged sufficient matches against other first-class Counties to take part in the County Championship. The first match after their return to first-class status was v Middlesex at Lord's on May 18, 19 and 20, 1891

Grounds The County Ground at Taunton has been the headquarters of Somerset since first-class matches began in 1882. Other current first-class grounds are Lansdown, Bath (since 1884); Clarence Park, Weston-super-mare (since 1914). Grounds on which the County has staged first-class matches include: Knowle (1926–28); Imperial Ground, Bristol (1957–64); Frome (1932–61); Downside School (1934); Wells (1935–51); Yeovil (1935–67); Glastonbury)1952–73); Millfield School (1961).

Honours The County's best position in the Championship is third, attained in the following years: 1892, 1958, 1963, 1966 and 1981.

The County won the Gillette Cup in 1979, the John Player League in the same year and the Benson and Hedges Cup in 1981 and 1982.

The players B A Langford with 504 matches between 1953 and 1974 is the cricketer with most appearances for the County and the longest serving Captain is S M J Woods, who led the County for 13 seasons between 1894 and 1906.

The youngest player is C E Winter, who was 15 years and 9 months when he played against Hampshire in 1882. The oldest player is E Robson, aged 53 years and 2 months on his farewell appearance v Warwickshire in 1923.

The cricketer to obtain most caps for England is I T Botham with 54 to the end of 1982.

Team performances Somerset have hit over 600 runs in an innings twice; against Yorkshire in 1901 they scored 630 at Headingley, but the record is 675 for 9 wkts dec against Hampshire at Bath on July 14 and 15, 1924, the only man to hit a hundred in the innings being A Young with 198. There have been nine totals over 600 against the County and indeed two over 800, the record being 811 by Surrey at the Oval on May 29 and 30, 1899; the innings lasted over 510 minutes and R Abel carried his bat right through for 357.

There have been two totals below 30 both for and against the County, three of the matches involving neighbouring Gloucestershire. Lancashire dismissed Somerset for 29 at Old Trafford in 1882, but Gloucestershire hold the record, having dismissed them for 25 on the County Ground, Bristol, August Bank Holiday Monday, 1947. T W J Goddard had figures of 3-1-4-5. This was revenge for a similar total inflicted on Gloucestershire by Somerset at Cheltenham in 1891, then on August Bank Holiday 1920, Somerset dismissed Gloucestershire for 22 in their first innings, giving Somerset a lead of 149, but J Daniell the County captain, made a very generous declaration in Somerset's second innings and Gloucestershire hit off the 274 required to win the game by 4 wickets.

Individual performances H Gimblett with 310 against Sussex at Eastbourne on August 19 and 20, 1948 is the only County batsman to hit over 300. He batted 465 minutes and hit 2 sixes and 37 fours. The record against the County is 424 by A C MacLaren at Taunton, July 15 and 16, 1895 for Lancashire, but three other innings over 300 have been hit against Somerset – 357* by R Abel for Surrey at the Oval in 1899; 304 in the same year by R M Poore for Hampshire at Taunton and 303* by W W Armstrong in 1905 for the Australians at Taunton.

Two bowlers have taken all ten wickets in an innings for Somerset, the

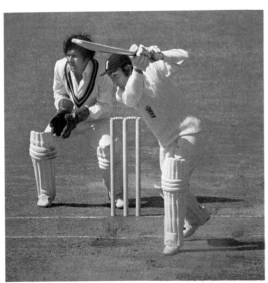

Top   *Mudassar Nazar has the slowest hundred in first-class cricket – 557 minutes for Pakistan v England in 1977.*

Above   *Keith Fletcher batting during the slowest hundred in English first-class cricket – 448 minutes for England v Pakistan in 1974.*

Right   *Somerset playing the Australians in 1977 at their ground in the old city of Bath.*

record being 10–49 by E J Tyler against Surrey at Taunton on August 22 and 23, 1895 – a feat which was of great importance since it nearly prevented Surrey becoming County Champions. J C White with 10–76 is the other bowler taking all ten wickets – against Worcestershire at Worcester on June 18 and 20, 1921.

Two years previously, also against Worcestershire, but at Bath, J C White beame the only Somerset cricketer to take 16 wickets in a match – 16–83 on July 22. This was not a County Championship game and the record in the Competition is 15–54 by B A Langford v Lancashire at Weston-super-Mare in 1958. The record against the County is 17–137 by W Brearley for Lancashire at Old Trafford on July 3 and 4, 1905.

W E Alley is the only County cricketer to exceed 2,500 runs in a season – his record being 2,761 (av 58.74) in 1961. H Gimblett hit 1,000 runs on the most occasions with 12 between 1936 and 1953. P B Wight (1954–63) and W E Alley (1957–68) both performed the feat 10 times.

Leading wicket-taker in a season is A W Wellard with 169 (av 19.24) in 1938, but J C White holds the record for passing 100 wickets most times, with 14 between 1919 and 1932.

H Gimblett is the only batsman to exceed 20,000 runs in his career, totalling 21,142 (av 39.96) between 1935 and 1954. Similarly J C White is the only bowler to take 2,000 wickets, with 2,166 (av 18.02) between 1909 and 1937.

Wicket partnerships

The highest stands in first-class cricket for the County are:

1st	346	H T Hewett, L C H Palairet v Yorkshire (*Taunton*) 1892	
2nd	286	J C W MacBryan, M D Lyon v Derbyshire (*Buxton*) 1924	
3rd	300	G Atkinson, P B Wight v Glamorgan (*Bath*)	1960
4th	310	P W Denning, I T Botham v Gloucestershire (*Taunton*) 1980	
5th	235	J C White, C C C Case v Gloucestershire (*Taunton*) 1927	
6th	265	W E Alley, K E Palmer v Northants (*Northampton*) 1961	
7th	240	S M J Woods, V T Hill v Kent (*Taunton*)	1898
8th	153*	I V A Richards, C H Dredge v Pakistan (*Taunton*)	1982
9th	183	C M H Greetham, H W Stephenson v Leicestershire (*Weston-Super-Mare*) 1963	
10th	143	J Bridges, H Gibbs v Surrey (*Weston-super-Mare*) 1919	

Limited overs cricket records

GILLETTE/NATWEST CUP

Highest team total 330–4 v Glamorgan (*Sophia Gdns, Cardiff*) 1978
Lowest team total 59 v Middlesex (*Lord's*) 1977
Highest innings 145 P W Denning v Glamorgan (*Sophia Gdns, Cardiff*) 1978
Best bowling 6–29 J Garner v Northants (*Lord's*) 1979

JOHN PLAYER LEAGUE

Highest team total 286–7 v Hampshire (*Taunton*) 1981
Lowest team total 58 v Essex (*Chelmsford*) 1977
Highest innings 131 D B Close v Yorkshire (*Bath*) 1974
Best bowling 6–25 G I Burgess v Glamorgan (*Glastonbury*) 1972

BENSON AND HEDGES CUP

Highest team total 307–6 Gloucestershire (*Taunton*) 1982
Lowest team total 98 v Middlesex (*Lord's*) 1982
Highest innings 137* B C Rose v Kent (*Canterbury*) 1980
Best bowling 5–14 J Garner v Surrey (*Lord's*) 1981

South Africa

The first definite reference to cricket in South Africa occurs in 1808 when, on January 5, a match was played between the Officers of the Artillery and Officers of the Colony. It is however believed that cricket was played in the 1795–97 period when an English Garrison was first stationed at the Cape.

In 1862 the annual match Mother Country v Colonial Born was staged for the first time – January 22 at Cape Town. In 1876 Port Elizabeth presented the 'Champion Bat' for competition between towns in South Africa.

E J Tyler has Somerset's best bowling analysis for an innings – 10 for 49 against Surrey in 1895.

The winners of the 'Champion Bat' were:

1875–76	Kingwilliamstown	Played 3, Won 3
1879–80	Kingwilliamstown	Played 4, Won 3
1884–85	Port Elizabeth	Played 3, Won 3
1887–88	Kimberley	Played 3, Won 3
1890–91	Western Province	Played 2, Won 2

In 1888–89, Sir Donald Currie presented a Cup for Competition and the Currie Cup (see under separate heading) superceded the Champion Bat Competition.

First First-class Match in South Africa The match between the English touring team of 1888–89 and a South African side, played at Port Elizabeth on March 12 and 13, 1889, is regarded as the first first-class match in South Africa, the first first-class domestic match being Port Elizabeth v Natal at Port Elizabeth on December 27 and 28, 1889.

Records in South African matches, with the first-class record following the outright record, if different are:

Highest team total 714–9 by Natal v Rhodesia in 1955–56
676 MCC v Griqualand West (*Kimberley*) 1938–39
Lowest team total 16 Border v Natal (*East London*) 1959–60
(Border were then dismissed for 18 in their second innings)
Highest individual innings 412* M I Yusuf, Govt Indian Schools v Star Club (*Bulawayo*) 1936–37
306* E A B Rowan, Transvaal v Natal (*Johannesburg*) 1939–40
Best bowling in innings 10–26 A E E Vogler, E Province v W Province (*Johannesburg*) 1906–07
Best bowling in match 17–54 W P Howell, Australia v W Province (*Cape Town*) 1902–03

First-class record Wicket Partnerships

1st	424	J F W Nicolson, I J Siedle. Natal v O F S (*Bloemfontein*) 1926–27
2nd	374	R B Simpson, R M Cowper. Australians v N E Transvaal (*Pretoria*) 1966–67
3rd	399	R T Simpson, D C S Compton. MCC v N E Transvaal (*Benoni*) 1948–49
4th	342	E A B Rowan, P J M Gibb. Transvaal v N E Transvaal (*Johannesburg*) 1952–53
5th	338	R G Pollock, A L Wilmot. E Province v Natal (*P Elizabeth*) 1975–76
6th	244*	J M M Commaille, A W Palm. W Province v Griqualand West (*Johannesburg*) 1923–24
7th	299	B Mitchell, A Melville. Transvaal v Griqualand West (*Kimberley*) 1946–47
8th	222	S S L Steyn, D P B Morkel. W Province v Border (*Cape Town*) 1929–30
9th	221	N V Lindsay, G R McCubbin. Transvaal v Rhodesia (*Bulawayo*) 1922–23
10th	174	H R Lance, D Mackay-Coghill. Transvaal v Natal (*Johannesburg*) 1965–66

Records in First-Class Cricket for South African Teams

BOLAND

Highest team total 378–6 dec v E Province B (*Vitenhage*) 1981–82
Lowest team total 110 v W Province B (*Cape Town*) 1981–81
Highest individual innings 202* E J Barlow v E Province B (*Vitenhage*) 1981–82
Best bowling in innings 6–58 J Hendricks v E Province B (*Port Elizabeth*) 1980–81

BORDER

Highest team total 509 v O F S (*Bloemfontein*) 1969–70
Lowest team total 16 v Natal (*East London*) 1959–60
Highest individual innings 222 I D Harty v N Transvaal (*East London*) 1959–60
Best bowling in innings 9–32 A F Hagemann v Griqualand W (*Kimberley*) 1960–61

EASTERN PROVINCE

Highest team total 594–6 dec v W Province (*Cape Town*) 1962–63
Lowest team total 34 v Natal (*Port Elizabeth*) 1980–81
Highest individual innings 284 E A B Rowan v Griqualand W (*Port Elizabeth*) 1945–46
Best bowling in innings 10–26 A E E Vogler v Griqualand W (*Johannesburg*) 1906–07

GRIQUALAND WEST

Highest team total 603 v Western Province (*Kimberley*) 1929–30
Lowest team total 29 v Transvaal (*Johannesburg*) 1950–51
Highest individual innings 215 K G Viljoen v W Province (*Kimberley*) 1929–30
Best bowling in innings 9–54 K McLaren v Natal B (*Umzinto*) 1973–74

NATAL

Highest team total 664–6 dec v Western Province (*Durban*) 1936–37
Lowest team total 45 v A I F (*Pietermaritzburg*) 1919–20
Highest individual innings 304* A W Nourse v Transvaal (*Johannesburg*) 1919–20
Best bowling in innings 9–88 V I Smith v Border (*Pietermaritzburg*) 1946–47

NORTHERN TRANSVAAL (inc. N E Transvaal)

Highest team total 552–8 dec v O F S (*Bloemfontain*) 1955–56
Lowest team total 41 v Eastern Province (*Benoni*) 1967–68
Highest individual innings 237 P L Corbett v Transvaal B (*Johannesburg*) 1962–63
Best bowling in innings 9–23 J T Botten v Griqualand W (*Pretoria*) 1958–59

ORANGE FREE STATE

Highest team total 552 v Natal (*Bloemfontein*) 1926–27
Lowest team total 37 v Transvaal (*Bloemfontain*) 1936–37
Highest individual innings 258 C Richardson v Transvaal B (*Johannesburg*) 1959–60
Best bowling in innings 8–32 L Tuckett v Griqualand W (*Kimberley*) 1951–52

TRANSVAAL

Highest team total 609 v O F S (*Johannesburg*) 1934–35
Lowest team total 53 v Australians (*Johannesburg*) 1949–50
Highest individual innings 306* E A B Rowan v Natal (*Johannesburg*) 1939–40
Best bowling in innings 9–19 A M B Rowan v Australians (*Johannesburg*) 1949–50

WESTERN PROVINCE

Highest team total 601 v Border (*Cape Town*) 1929–30
Lowest team total 55 v O F S (*Cape Town*) 1926–27
Highest individual innings 271* J E Cheetham v O F S (*Bloemfontein*) 1950–51
Best bowling in innings 9–52 M H Bowditch v Natal (*Cape Town*) 1965–66

Sri Lanka (formerly Ceylon)

The first reference to cricket in Sri Lanka appears on September 5, 1832 in the *Colombo Journal* calling for the formation of a Cricket Club. In the same year the Colombo Cricket Club was duly formed and the first reported match took place v 97th Regiment in November 1832.

The first important match took place on November 27, 29 and 30, 1889 between G F Vernon's Team and All Ceylon at Kandy. The first major domestic competition was established in 1938 for the *Daily News* Trophy with 12 teams competing.

The records in Sri Lankan cricket are as follows, the best in any class of cricket being given first, followed by the first-class record if this differs:

Highest team total 925 Municipality v Irrigation Dept (*Colombo*) 1959
549–8 dec West Indies v All Ceylon (*Colombo*) 1966–67
Lowest team total 2 Ceylon Tobacco v C V Bhatto Co 1967
32 Madras v All Ceylon 1892
Highest individual innings 352* F Pereira, Port Commission v Excise Dept 1957
285 F M M Worrell, Commonwealth v All Ceylon 1950–51
Best bowling in innings 10–8 D S Jayasundera, Coas Co v Judicial Dept 1933
9–18 R K Oxenham, Australians v All Ceylon 1934–35
Best bowling in match 18–53 Col Churchill, Garrison v D A C C 1890
15–43 D L Underwood, International XI v Board President's XI 1967–68

Highest partnership for any wicket

3rd	470	T D Rajapakse, W W Fernando. Army v Peradeniya University 1975–76
5th	310	F M M Worrell, W H H Sutcliffe. Commonwealth v All Ceylon 1950–51

Sri Lanka took part in the ICC Trophy of 1979 and won that Trophy. They were subsequently granted Test match status and played their first Test in the 1981–82 season.

Stumpings

The record number of stumpings in a single innings in first-class cricket is 6 by H Yarnold for Worcestershire v Scotland at Broughty Ferry on July 2, 1951. In any match the record in an innings is 8 by H W P Middleton in a house match at Repton in 1930.

The record number of stumpings in a season in first-class cricket is 64 by L E G Ames (Kent) in 1932.
(*See also Wicket Keeping.*)

Strikes

The only instance in English first-class cricket of the majority of a County team going on strike against the County Committee occurred in 1881, when the seven principal Notts cricketers went on strike for most of the summer. The players' demands included equal pay for all seven players and a guaranteed benefit after ten years' service with the County. The dispute was amicably settled the following year.

Substitutes

The earliest Laws are quite specific in stating 'In case of a real hurt to a Striker, they are to allow another to come inn, and the Person hurt to come inn again; but are not to allow a fresh Man to play, on either Side, on any Account.'

Despite this Law there have been numerous instances of substitutes batting and/or bowling even in first-class cricket, the last occasion being on July 29, 1982 when D J Brown, acting as substitute for G C Small, bowled for Warwickshire v Lancashire at Southport. Small was called to Edgbaston for the England squad for the first Test v Pakistan, but not being required for the final Eleven, rejoined his county match on the third day, having missed the second. Prior to this the last example in English first-class cricket was at Oxford June 7, 8 and 9, 1939. F W Wilkinson was injured whilst bowling for Minor Counties XI v Oxford University on the first day and D J F Watson, an Oxford undergraduate, batted for Wilkinson and in fact virtually won the match for the Minor Counties with a partnership of 101 with A H Parnaby in the second innings. Recent T C C B Regulations now supersede the official laws and permit the use of substitutes in certain instances.

Sunday Cricket

In the 17th Century there are several instances of people being prosecuted for playing cricket on a Sunday – the first recorded occurred in Boxgrove, Sussex in 1622. In 1640 cricketers were prosecuted in Maidstone for playing on Sunday, although having previously been allowed to do so without interference from the authorities.

Sunday cricket seems to have started just after the First World War, in England, but it was unpopular in some influential circles and received very little publicity – some clubs even played under disguised titles.

The first inter-county first-class match to include play on Sunday took place at Ilford on Sat, Sun, Mon, May 14, 15 and 16, 1966 between Essex and Somerset. It was illegal to charge an entrance fee, but the 6,000 spectators paid nearly £500 through scorecard sales, collections etc.

In Australia the first first-class Sunday play had occurred in the 1964–65 season between Western Australia and Queensland.

The first Test match in England to include Sunday play took place at Trent Bridge in June 1981.

Surrey

On January 17, 1597, in a court case in Guildford, John Derrick deposed that he had played at 'kreckett' on a plot of ground in the town when he was a boy – Derrick was aged 59 in 1597, which would put the reference to cricket in the county at about 1550.

Formation of the County Club The first so-called County match was v Kent on June 29, 1709 at Dartford Brent, and between 1730 and 1810, there are very few years when Surrey did not play a match. The Surrey Eleven were at their height for about 20 years starting around 1790, and often played matches against the Rest of England in this period. Surrey matches are indeed so frequent that it is probable that some sort of County Club existed, but no details have yet come to light. For about 30 years from around 1810 to 1840 Surrey County Cricket was almost extinct, and the present County Club was formed at a meeting which took place during the match between the Gentlemen and the Players of Surrey on August 21 and 22, 1845.

First-class status As one of the oldest Counties to place an eleven in the field, Surrey has always been regarded as a 'great' or first-class County. Disregarding the match of 1709, Surrey began in recorded

The Essex team pictured before the start of play on Sunday. Back row (l-r): Saville, Cass, Jordan, Pritchard (12th man), East, Hobbs, Fletcher. Front row (l-r) Knight, Taylor, Bailey, Barker, Bear.

SUNDAY CRICKET PACKS THEM IN

IT was standing room only when county cricket came to Ilford on Sunday. Over 6,000 people crammed into Valentines Park to watch the second day's play in the match between Essex and Somerset and county official could not conceal their delight at the success of the experiment, writes JACK STEGGLES.

BARRY KNIGHT ... fine performance

Left A report of the first Sunday play in an inter-county first-class match, at Ilford, Essex, in 1966.

Below Bobby Abel, whose 357 not out against Somerset in 1899 is the highest innings played for Surrey.

Above left *Ken Barrington is the Surrey player who won the most England caps – 82 between 1955 and 1968.*

Above *The famous gasholders which overlook the Oval, the home of Surrey C C C.*

Left *The Surrey squad in 1952, beginning the run of seven consecutive championships. Back, left to right: Lock, Brazier, Pratt, Clark, Whittaker, Bedser (E), Laker, Loader, Kirby, McIntyre, Cox, Strudwick (scorer). Front: Fletcher, Bedser (A), Fishlock, Surridge, May, Parker, Constable.*

matches in 1730 with three matches against London and one against Middlesex.

Grounds Kennington Oval has been the headquarters of the County Club since its formation, except briefly in 1854. The only other current first-class ground is at Guildford (since 1938). Other grounds which have been used for first-class matches are: Kingston-on-Thames (1946), Reigate (1909) and Broadwater, Godalming (1854).

Honours As noted previously, the County was the best in England between about 1790 and 1810; it briefly regained its supremacy in 1830 and 1831 and later in 1850, 1851, 1854, 1856, 1857 and 1858. Since 1864 Surrey have been County Champions as follows: 1864, 1887, 1888, 1890, 1891, 1892, 1894, 1895, 1899, 1914, 1952, 1953, 1954, 1955, 1956, 1957, 1958 and 1971; they were also joint-Champions in 1889 and 1950.

The County won the NatWest Trophy in 1982 and the Benson and Hedges Cup in 1974. The best place in the John Player League is 5th in 1969 and 1980.

The players Six players have appeared in 500 matches for the County. J B Hobbs played in 598 matches (1905–34); T W Hayward in 593 (1893–1914); H Strudwick 555 (1902–27); A Sandham 525 (1911–37); R Abel 514 (1881–1914); E G Hayes 500 (1896–1919).

The longest serving captain is J Shuter, who led Surrey for 14 seasons from 1880 to 1893.

The youngest player to represent the County is G A R Lock, aged 17 years and 8 days when appearing v Kent (Oval) 1946.

The oldest player is J Shuter, who was 54 years and 4 months when he made his final appearance v Oxford University in 1909.

K F Barrington is the Surrey cricketer with the most England caps, having appeared in 82 Test matches between 1955 and 1968.

Team performances The highest team total for the County is 811 against Somerset at the Oval on May 29 and 30, 1899 and the County have scored over 700 on two other occasions: 742 v Hampshire at the Oval in 1909 and 706 for 4 wkts dec v Notts at Trent Bridge in 1947.

The two totals over 700 against the County are 705 for 8 wkts dec by Sussex at Hastings on July 14 and 15, 1902, to which Surrey replied with 552 and at the close of play on the second day no less than 980 runs had been made in the match, only 9 wickets having fallen, and 704 by Yorkshire at the Oval on August 10 and 11, 1899; again Surrey were equal to the challenge and hit 551 in their innings.

Lowest totals both for and against the County and the only ones under 20 are 16. Surrey were dismissed by Notts for that total at the Oval on July 27, 1880, with F Morley taking 7–9 and Surrey dismissed M C C for 16 on May 14, 1872; in this match Surrey themselves were all out for 49 and the whole match was completed in a single day, Surrey winning by 5 wickets.

Individual performances More double centuries have been scored for Surrey than any other first-class County. At the end of the 1982 season, the total stood at 87. Five of these innings have topped the 300 mark. The highest innings is 357 not out by R Abel against Somerset at the Oval on May 29 and 30, 1899 (also see Highest Team Total), Abel hit a six, seven 5s and thirty-eight 4s. W W Read scored 338 v Oxford University at the Oval in 1888; J B Hobbs 316* v Middlesex at Lord's in 1926, T W Hayward 315* v Lancashire at the Oval in 1898 and A Ducat 306* v Oxford University at the Oval in 1919.

Two triple hundreds have been hit against Surrey, both innings being exactly 300. F B Watson scored the first for Lancashire at Old Trafford on June 4 and 5, 1928. Watson batted 510 minutes and hit 37 fours. He was not out when the game ended, Lancashire having just taken first innings lead by scoring 588 for 4 wkts in reply to Surrey's 567. R Subba Row also hit 300 – for Northants v Surrey at the Oval in 1958.

Five bowlers have taken all ten wickets in an innings for the County, the best analysis being obtained by T Rushby (10–43) v Somerset at Taunton on July 6 and 7, 1921. Other bowlers to perform the feat are T Richardson (10–45) v Essex at the Oval, 1894; G A R Lock (10–54) v Kent at Blackheath, 1956; E A Watts (10–67) v Warwickshire at Edgbaston, 1939; J C Laker (10–88) v Australians at the Oval, 1956.

Ten wickets in an innings has been accomplished 4 times against the County, the best analysis being by W P Howell (10–28) for the Australians on May 15, 1899; other instances are by V E Walker (10–74) for England at the Oval, 1859; E J Tyler (10–49) for Somerset at Taunton, 1895; G Burton (10–59) for Middlesex at the Oval, 1888.

Above *John* (left) *and James Langridge. James Langridge holds the record of most appearances for Sussex, brother John is fourth. John Langridge has the highest aggregate of runs for Sussex.*

Opposite *A E R Gilligan, who also captained England, is the longest-serving Sussex captain.*

G A R Lock is the only bowler to take 16 wkts in a match for the County, his record of 16–83 being obtained at the expense of Kent at Blackheath on July 9 and 10, 1956. Surrey completely outplayed Kent and won by an innings and 173.

Against Surrey, the best match figures were by W P Howell, who went on from his 10 wkts in the first innings of the Australians match in 1899 to return a match analysis of 15 for 57 – it was his first first-class match in England.

T W Hayward is the only Surrey player to top 3,000 runs in a season for the County – his record is 3,246 (av 72.13) in 1906. He also hit 2,734 in 1904. The other player to score more than 2,500 runs is R Abel with 2,849 in 1901. J B Hobbs scored more than 1,000 runs in a season on 24 occasions between 1905 and 1933; T W Hayward performed the feat 20 times between 1895 and 1914 – Hayward did not miss a single season in his sequence.

200 wickets in a season has been taken for Surrey four times, three times by T Richardson, whose record year was 1895 with 252 (av 13.94). The other bowler to reach 200 was W C Smith with 225 (av 12.83) in 1910.

T Richardson took 100 wickets in a season ten times between 1893 and 1903; he is followed by G A R Lock with 9 seasons between 1952 and 1961.

J B Hobbs is the leading run-scorer in a career, hitting 43,554 runs (av 49.71) between 1905 and 1934. Two others have exceeded 30,000 – T W Hayward with 36,175 (av 42.40) from 1893 to 1914 and A Sandham with 33,312 (av 43.88) from 1911 to 1937.

Three bowlers have topped the 1,500 mark in their career. The leader is T Richardson with 1,775 (av 17.87) between 1892 and 1904, second comes G A R Lock with 1,713 (av 17.41) from 1946 to 1963 and third is P G H Fender with 1,586 (av 24.07) from 1914 to 1935.

Wicket partnerships

The highest stands in first-class cricket for the County are:

1st	428	J B Hobbs, A Sandham	v Oxford U	(*Oval*)	1926
2nd	371	J B Hobbs, E G Hayes	v Hampshire	(*Oval*)	1909
3rd	353	A Ducat, E G Hayes	v Hampshire	(*Southampton*)	1919
4th	447	R Abel, T W Hayward	v Yorkshire	(*Oval*)	1899
5th	308	J N Crawford, F C Holland	v Somerset	(*Oval*)	1908
6th	298	A Sandham, H S Harrison	v Sussex	(*Oval*)	1913
7th	200	T F Shepherd, J W Hitch	v Kent	(*Blackheath*)	1921
8th	204	T W Hayward, L C Braund	v Lancashire	(*Oval*)	1898
9th	168	E R T Holmes, E W J Brooks	v Hampshire	(*Oval*)	1936
10th	173	A Ducat, A Sandham	v Essex	(*Leyton*)	1921

Limited Overs Cricket Records

GILLETTE/NATWEST CUP
Highest team total 280–5 v Middlesex (*Oval*) 1970
Lowest team total 74 v Kent (*Oval*) 1967
Highest innings 129 M A Lynch v Durham (*Oval*) 1982
Best bowling 7–33 R D Jackman v Yorkshire (*Harrogate*) 1970

JOHN PLAYER LEAGUE
Highest team total 248–2 v Gloucestershire (*Oval*) 1976
Lowest team total 64 v Worcestershire (*Worcester*) 1978
Highest innings 122 G P Howarth v Gloucestershire ((*Oval*) 1976
Best bowling 6–25 Intikhab Alam v Derbyshire (*Oval*) 1974

BENSON AND HEDGES CUP
Highest team total 276–6 v Essex (*Oval*) 1982
Lowest team total 125 v Sussex (*Hove*) 1972
Highest innings 115 G R J Roope v Essex (*Chelmsford*) 1973
Best bowling 5–21 P H L Wilson v Combined Univ (*Oval*) 1979

Sussex

In the Easter Presentments of 1622 is the following first mention of cricket in the county:

'Boxgrove. I present Raphe West, Edward Hartley, Richard Slaughter, William Martin, Richard Martin junior together with others in their company whose names I have no notice of for playing at cricket in the churchyard on Sunday the fifte of May after sufficient Warning to the contrary, for three speciall reasons: first for that it is contrary to the 7th article: secondly for that they use to breake the church-windows with the ball: and thirdly for that a little childe had like to have her braines beaten out with a cricket batt.'

Formation of the County Club The second Duke of Richmond was a great supporter of cricket in the first half of the 18th century and was responsible for organising a number of matches – his team was probably representative of the main strength of the County, and although Sussex teams appear in matches through the 18th century, commencing about 1728, they are no where near as frequent as those of Kent and Surrey. In the 19th century Sussex were prominent from 1815 onwards, but the first inkling of a County Club does not appear until June 17, 1836, when a meeting in Brighton instituted a 'Sussex Cricket Fund' to support county matches. It would appear that the present County Club was formed directly out of this on March 1, 1839.

First-class status The County has been regarded as 'important' or first-class throughout recorded cricket history.

Grounds In 1864 the main ground used by Sussex was Brunswick Rd, Hove, but in 1872 the County moved to the present County Ground in Hove. Other grounds currently used for first-class matches are: Hastings (since 1865) and Eastbourne (since 1867). Towns staging first-class matches in the past include: Chichester (1906–50); Horsham (1908–79); Worthing (1935–64) and Pagham (1976–79).

Honours Sussex were the Champion County in 1826, 1827, 1833, 1845, 1848 and 1855 and jointly in 1852.

The County won the Gillette Cup in 1963, 1964 and 1978 and the John Player League in 1982. In the Benson and Hedges Cup Sussex reached the semi-finals in 1982.

The players Three cricketers have played in 600 matches for the County: James Langridge 622 matches between 1924 and 1953; G R Cox snr 618 matches between 1895 and 1928; K G Suttle 600 between 1949 and 1971. A further five players have exceeded 500 matches: John G Langridge 567, J M Parks 561, M W Tate 524, H R Butt 518 and J Vine 506.

The longest serving captain is A E R Gilligan with 8 seasons from 1922 to 1928.

The youngest player to represent the County is J M Mare who was 16 years and 6 months when playing v Surrey in 1870. The oldest cricketer is G R Cox snr who was 54 years and 6 months in his final appearance v Hampshire in 1928.

E R Dexter holds most England caps with 62 between 1958 and 1968.

Team performances The highest total by Sussex is 705 for 8 wkts dec against Surrey at Hastings on July 14 and 15, 1902, K S Ranjitsinhji hit 234* in 205 minutes in this match, whilst C B Fry contributed 159. Second highest total is 686 for 8 wkts against Leicestershire at Grace Rd, Leicester on July 13 and 14, 1899 – despite fine weather not even the two first innings were completed in this match, Leicestershire making 609 for 8 wkts dec and 19 of the twenty-two players bowled.

The County have been dismissed for under 20 once, when they scored 19 against Notts at Hove on August 14, 1873 – the wicket-keeper, H Phillips, was absent, having missed his train. There is also one total under 20 against Sussex – Kent were all out for 18 at Gravesend on June 7, 1867 – again one player did not bat, G M Kelson was absent injured.

Individual performances The highest innings for Sussex and only score over 300 is 333 by K S Duleepsinhji against Northants at Hove on May 6, 1930, the second highest innings was made by his uncle, K S Ranjitsinhji with 285* v Somerset at Taunton on August 9 and 10, 1901 – he batted 320 minutes.

Two bowlers have claimed ten wickets in an innings for the County. C H G Bland (10–48) performed the feat against Kent at Tonbridge on June 7, 1899 and unexpectedly won the game for his County. N I Thomson (10–49) bowled out Warwickshire at Worthing on June 6, 1964, but his team lost by 182 runs, being bowled out in their second innings for 23.

The best match analysis is returned by G R Cox snr, also against Warwickshire, at Horsham, on June 5, 7 and 8, 1926. Cox was aged 52 and bowled 75.3 overs to accomplish his figures of 17 for 106 – Sussex won the match. A P Freeman, with 17 for 67, is the only bowler to take 17 wickets against Sussex. The match was against Kent at Hove on August 30, 31 and September 1, 1922. In the first innings Freeman returned the remarkable figures of 10-4-11-9.

Left *The Sussex county ground at Hove, the headquarters since 1872.*

Below left *K S Ranjitsinhji and C B Fry, two great Sussex batsmen who each scored over 2,800 runs in a season.*

Opposite above *Ted Dexter is the most-capped Sussex player, with 62 caps between 1958 and 1968.*

Opposite below *The stroke which brought Geoffrey Boycott his hundredth hundred in a Test match. His aggregate of 8,114 Test match runs is a record.*

Only 26 runs separate the first four batsmen heading the list of Sussex men with most runs in a season. John G Langridge is top with 2,850 (av 64.77) in 1949, J H Parks hit 2,847 runs (51.76) in 1937, C B Fry 2,842 (av 83.58) in 1901 and K S Ranjitsinhji 2,824 (av 88.25) in 1900. James Langridge has reached 1,000 tuns on the most occasions – 20 between 1927 and 1952; J M Parks performed the feat 18 times between 1953 and 1972.

M W Tate heads the most wickets in a season table with 198 (av 13.45) in 1925 and he comes second in the list as well with 179 in 1923. Tate also achieved 100 wickets in a season on most occasions – 13 between 1922 and 1935. N I Thomson reached 100 wickets 12 times between 1953 and 1964.

John G Langridge is the only player to hit 30,000 runs for Sussex, his total being 34,152 (av 37.70) between 1928 and 1955. The bowler with most wickets is M W Tate with 2,211 (av 17.41) between 1912 and 1937. No one else topped 2,000, G R Cox snr being second with 1,810 (av 22.82) between 1895–1928.

Wicket partnerships

The highest stands in first-class cricket for the County are:

1st	490	E H Bowley, John G Langridge *v* Middlesex (*Hove*) 1933
2nd	385	E H Bowley, M W Tate *v* Northants (*Hove*) 1921
3rd	298	K S Ranjitsinhji, E H Killick *v* Lancashire (*Hove*) 1901
4th	326*	James Langridge, G Cox jnr *v* Yorkshire (*Headingley*) 1949
5th	297	J H Parks, H W Parks *v* Hampshire (*Portsmouth*) 1937
6th	255	K S Duleepsinhji, M W Tate *v* Northants (*Hove*) 1930
7th	344	K S Ranjitsinhji, W Newham *v* Essex (*Leyton*) 1902
8th	229*	C L A Smith, G Brann *v* Kent (*Hove*) 1902
9th	178	A F Wensley, H W Parks *v* Derbyshire (*Horsham*) 1930
10th	156	H R Butt, G R Cox snr *v* Cambridge Univ (*Fenner's*) 1908

Limited overs cricket records

GILLETTE/NATWEST CUP
Highest team total   314–7 v Kent (*Tunbridge Wells*)   1963
Lowest team total   49 v Derbyshire (*Chesterfield*)   1969
Highest innings   141* G D Mendis v Warwickshire (*Hove*)   1980
Best bowling   6–30 D L Bates v Gloucestershire (*Hove*)   1968

JOHN PLAYER LEAGUE
Highest team total   293–4 v Worcestershire (*Horsham*)   1980
Lowest team total   61 v Derbyshire (*Derby*)   1978
Highest innings   129 A W Greig v Yorks (*Scarborough*)   1976
Best bowling   6–14 M A Buss v Lancashire (*Hove*)   1973

BENSON AND HEDGES CUP
Highest team total   305–6 v Kent (*Hove*)   1974
Lowest team total   61 v Middlesex (*Hove*)   1978
Highest Innings   114* P J Graves v Cambridge U (*Hove*)   1974
Best bowling   5–8 Imran Khan v Northants (*Northampton*)   1978

Tallest players
It is believed that the tallest cricketer to play for a first-class county is A T C Allom who appeared in one match for Surrey in 1960. His height is 6ft 10½in.

Test Cricket
The first 'Test Match' in the present generally accepted list of such matches was staged at Melbourne on March 15, 16, 17 and 19, 1877 between England, represented by the team taken to Australia by James Lillywhite, and Australia. In the 1890s there were two conflicting lists of 'Test Matches' one drawn up in England and the other in Australia, but in the early years of the present century the Australian list became the accepted one. The principal reason why some matches are of debatable Test Match status is that all the English teams to visit Australia before 1903–04 – there were 13 which played 'Test Matches' – were private speculations and the sides were selected by whoever organised the tour or his nominees and not by a body representative of English cricket. In this publication however the present list of all matches is used for all record purposes.

The first matches against South Africa are by no means up to the standard of the England v Australia matches, the England side being nothing like representative, and later on the rather ludicrous situation is reached when England play two Test series simultaneously – in 1929–30 – one in West Indies and the other in New Zealand and even with England putting two 'Test' teams in the field, several of the best English players remained at home!

Following the 1877 Test, the years of the Test debut of each of the present Test playing countries are:

South Africa   1888–89
West Indies   1928
New Zealand   1929–30
India   1932
Pakistan   1954
Sri Lanka   1981–82

All the countries made their Test debut against England.
(For debut seasons for each Test country v the others, see the details of each match series, which follow this general summary of Test records.)

Test records

Highest team total   903–7 dec England v Australia (*Oval*)   1938
Lowest team total   26 New Zealand v England (Auckland)   1954–55
Highest individual innings   365* G St A Sobers, West Indies v Pakistan (*Kingston*)   1957–58
Best bowling in innings   10–53 J C Laker, England v Australia (*Old Trafford*)   1956
Best bowling in match   19–90 J C Laker, England v Australia (*Old Trafford*)   1956
Most runs in career   8,114 G Boycott (*England*)   1964–82
Most wickets in career   321 D K Lillee (*Australia*)   1970/1–1981/2
Most runs in series   974 D G Bradman, Australia v England   1930
Most wickets in series   49 S F Barnes, England v S Africa   1913–14

Record wicket partnerships

1st   413   M H Mankad, P Roy, India *v* New Zealand (*Madras*) 1955–56
2nd   451   W H Ponsford, D G Bradman, Australia *v* England (*Oval*)   1934
3rd   370   W J Edrich, D C S Compton, England *v* South Africa (*Lord's*)   1947
4th   411   P B H May, M C Cowdrey, England *v* West Indies (*Edgbaston*)   1957
5th   405   S G Barnes, D G Bradman, Australia *v* England (*Sydney*)   1946–47
6th   346   J H W Fingleton, D G Bradman, Australia *v* England (*Melbourne*)   1936–37
7th   347   D St E Atkinson, C C Depiza, West Indies *v* Australia (*Bridgetown*)   1954–55
8th   246   L E G Ames, G O B Allen, England *v* New Zealand (*Lord's*)   1931
9th   190   Asif Iqbal, Intikhab Alam, Pakistan *v* England (*Oval*) 1967
10th   151   B F Hastings, R O Collinge, New Zealand *v* Pakistan (*Auckland*)   1972–73

Other notable Test records

Highest individual innings on debut   287 R E Foster, England *v* Australia (*Sydney*)   1903–04
'Double' in a match   114; 13–106 I T Botham, England *v* India (*Bombay*)   1979–80
Fastest fifty   28 mins J T Brown, England *v* Australia (*Melbourne*) 1894–95
Fastest hundred   70 mins J M Gregory, Australia *v* South Africa (*Johannesburg*)   1921–22
Fastest double hundred   214 mins D G Bradman, Australia *v* England (*Headingley*)   1930
Slowest hundred   557 mins Mudassar Nazar, Pakistan *v* England (*Lahore*)   1977–78
Most consecutive appearances   85 G St A Sobers (West Indies) 1954–55 to 1971–72
Youngest player   17 yrs 122 days, J E D Sealey (West Indies) 1929–30
(Four Pakistani players, Mushtaq Mohammad, Aftab Baloch, Nasim-ul-Ghani and Khalid Hassan are listed as younger than Sealy, but their years of birth have yet to be verified.)
Oldest player   52 yrs 165 days, W Rhodes (England)   1929–30

Above *The scorer of the fastest Test match 50 is J T Brown, who took 28 minutes in 1894–95.*

Right *J M Gregory of Australia holds the record for the fastest Test match century: 70 minutes against South Africa in 1894–95.*

Above *Jim Laker leaves the field at Old Trafford after achieving one of the safest of Test match records – 19 wickets in a match against Australia in 1956.*

Far left *D G Bradman, whose 974 runs in a Test series in 1934 is a record.*

Left *J H W Fingleton, holder with D G Bradman of the record sixth-wicket Test match partnership.*

Above   *Ian Botham, who performed the 'match double' of a century and ten wickets against India in 1979–80.*

Above right   *The most Test match wickets have been taken by Dennis Lillee, of Australia – 321 up to the end of the 1981–82 season.*

Right   *Asif Iqbal, the Pakistan captain and all-rounder, who shares with Intikhab Alam the ninth-wicket partnership record in Tests.*

Test Match Results

1 England *v* Australia

1876–77 1st Series Aus 1, Eng 1
1 MELBOURNE Australia won by 45 runs
Australia 245 (C Bannerman 165*) and 104 (A Shaw 5–38, G Ulyett 4–39)
England 196 (H Jupp 63, W E Midwinter 5–78) and 108 (T Kendall 7–55)
2 MELBOURNE England won by 4 wkts
Australia 122 (A Hill 4–27) and 259 (J Southerton 4–46, J Lillywhite 4–70)
England 261 (G Ulyett 52, T Kendall 4–82) and 122–6 (G Ulyett 63)

1878–79 2nd Series Aus 1, Eng 0
1 MELBOURNE Australia won by 10 wkts
England 113 (C A Absolom 52, F R Spofforth 6–48) and 160 (F R Spofforth 7–62)
Australia 256 (A C Bannerman 73, T Emmett 7–68) and 19–0

1880 3rd Series Eng 1, Aus 0
1 THE OVAL England won by 5 wkts
England 420 (W G Grace 152, A P Lucas 55, Lord Harris 52) and 57–5
Australia 149 (F Morley 5–56) and 327 (W L Murdoch 153*)

1881–82 4th Series Aus 2, Eng 0, Drawn 2
1 MELBOURNE Match Drawn
England 294 (G Ulyett 87, W Bates 58, J Selby 55) and 308 (J Selby 70, W H Scotton 50*, W H Cooper 6–120)
Australia 320 (T P Horan 124) and 127–3
2 SYDNEY Australia won by 5 wkts
England 133 (G E Palmer 7–68) and 232 (G Ulyett 67, R G Barlow 62, T W Garrett 4–62, G E Palmer 4–97)
Australia 197 (W Bates 4–52) and 169–5
3 SYDNEY Australia won by 6 wkts
England 188 (A Shrewsbury 82, G E Palmer 5–46) and 134 (T W Garrett 6–78, G E Palmer 4–44)
Australia 260 (P S McDonnell 147, A C Bannerman 70, E Peate 5–43) and 66–4
4 MELBOURNE Match Drawn
England 309 (G Ulyett 149, T W Garrett 5–80) and 234–2 (G Ulyett 64, R G Barlow 56, W Bates 52*)
Australia 300 (W L Murdoch 85, P S McDonnell 52, W E Midwinter 4–81)

1882 5th Series Aus 1, Eng 0
1 THE OVAL Australia won by 7 runs
Australia 63 (R G Barlow 5–19, E Peate 4–31) and 122 (H H Massie 55, E Peate 4–40)
England 101 (F R Spofforth 7–46) and 77 (F R Spofforth 7–44)

1882–83 6th Series Aus 2, Eng 2
1 MELBOURNE Australia won by 9 wkts
Australia 291 (G J Bonnor 85) and 58–1
England 177 (G E Palmer 7–65) and 169 (G Giffen 4–38)
2 MELBOURNE England won by an innings and 27 runs
England 294 (W W Read 75, W Bates 55, C F H Leslie 54, G E Palmer 5–103, G Giffen 4–89)
Australia 114 (W Bates 7–28) and 153 (W Bates 7–74)
W Bates performed the hat-trick in the first innings
3 SYDNEY England won by 69 runs
England 247 (W W Read 66, E F S Tylecote 66, F R Spofforth 4–73) and 123 (F R Spofforth 7–44)
Australia 218 (A C Bannerman 94, F Morley 4–47) and 83 (R G Barlow 7–40)
4 SYDNEY Australia won by 4 wkts
England 263 (A G Steel 135*) and 197
Australia 262 (G J Bonnor 87, J McC Blackham 57) and 199–6 (A C Bannerman 63, J McC Blackham 58*)

1884 7th Series Eng 1, Aus 0, Drawn 2
1 OLD TRAFFORD Match Drawn
England 95 (H F Boyle 6–42, F R Spofforth 4–42) and 180–9 (G E Palmer 4–47)
Australia 182
2 LORD'S England won by an innings and 5 runs
Australia 229 (H J H Scott 75, G Giffen 63, E Peate 6–85) and 145 (G Ulyett 7–36)
England 379 (A G Steel 148, G E Palmer 6–111)
3 THE OVAL Match Drawn
Australia 551 (W L Murdoch 211, P S McDonnell 103, H J H Scott 102, A Lyttelton 4–19)
England 346 (W W Read 117, W H Scotton 90, G E Palmer 4–90) and 85–2
All eleven of England bowled in Australia's innings – Lyttelton, the wicket-keeper, bowling under-arm, had the best figures

1884–85 8th Series Eng 3, Aus 2
1 ADELAIDE England won by 8 wkts
Australia 243 (P S McDonnell 124, J McC Blackham 66, W Bates 5–31) and 191 (P S McDonnell 83, R Peel 5–51)
England 369 (W Barnes 134, W H Scotton 82, G Ulyett 68, G E Palmer 5–81) and 67–2
2 MELBOURNE England won by 10 wkts
England 401 (J Briggs 121, A Shrewsbury 72, W Barnes 58, S P Jones 4–47) and 7–0
Australia 279 (A H Jarvis 82, T P Horan 63, J W Trumble 59) and 126 (W Barnes 6–31)
3 SYDNEY Australia won by 6 runs
Australia 181 (T W Garrett 51*, W Flowers 5–46, W Attewell 4–53) and 165 (W Bates 5–24)
England 133 (T P Horan 6–40, F R Spofforth 4–54) and 207 (W Flowers 56, J M Read 56, F R Spofforth 6–90)
4 SYDNEY Australia won by 8 wkts
England 269 (W Bates 64, W Barnes 50, G Giffen 7–117) and 77 (F R Spofforth 5–30, G E Palmer 4–32)
Australia 309 (G J Bonnor 128, A C Bannerman 51, W Barnes 4–61) and 40–2
5 MELBOURNE England won by an innings and 98 runs
Australia 163 (F R Spofforth 50, G Ulyett 4–52) and 125
England 386 (A Shrewsbury 105*, W Barnes 74, W Bates 61)

1886 9th Series Eng 3, Aus 0
1 OLD TRAFFORD England won by 4 wkts
Australia 205 (S P Jones 87, G Ulyett 4–46) and 123 (R G Barlow 7–44)
England 223 (W W Read 51, F R Spofforth 4–82) and 107–6
2 LORD'S England won by an innings and 106 runs
England 353 (A Shrewsbury 164, W Barnes 58, F R Spofforth 4–73)
England 121 (J Briggs 5–29) and 126 (J Briggs 6–45)
3 THE OVAL England won by an innings and 217 runs
England 434 (W G Grace 170, W W Read 94, J Briggs 53, F R Spofforth 4–65)
Australia 68 (G A Lohmann 7–36) and 149 (G A Lohmann 5–68)

1886–87 10th Series Eng 2, Aus 0
1 SYDNEY England won by 13 runs
England 45 (C T B Turner 6–15, J J Ferris 4–27) and 184 (J J Ferris 5–76)
Australia 119 and 97 (W Barnes 6–28)
2 SYDNEY England won by 71 runs
England 151 (J J Ferris 5–71, C T B Turner 5–41) and 154 (J J Ferris 4–69, C T B Turner 4–52)
Australia 84 (G A Lohmann 8–35) and 150 (W Bates 4–26)

1887–88 11th Series Eng 1, Aus 0
1 SYDNEY England won by 126 runs
England 113 (C T B Turner 5–44, J J Ferris 4–60) and 137 (C T B Turner 7–43)
Australia 42 (R Peel 5–18, G A Lohmann 5–17) and 82 (R Peel 5–40, G A Lohmann 4–35)

1888 12th Series Eng 2, Aus 0
1 LORD'S Australia won by 61 runs
Australia 116 (R Peel 4–36) and 60 (R Peel 4–14, G A Lohmann 4–33)
England 53 (C T B Turner 5–27) and 62 (C T B Turner 5–36, J J Ferris 5–26)
2 THE OVAL England won by an innings and 137 runs
Australia 80 (J Briggs 5–25) and 100 (W Barnes 5–32, R Peel 4–49)
England 317 (R Abel 70, W Barnes 62, G A Lohmann 62*, C T B Turner 6–112)
3 OLD TRAFFORD England won by an innings and 21 runs
England 172 (C T B Turner 5–86)
Australia 81 (R Peel 7–31) and 70 (R Peel 4–37)

1890 13th Series Eng 2, Aus 0
1 LORD'S England won by 7 wkts
Australia 132 (J J Lyons 55, W Attewell 4–42) and 176 (J E Barrett 67*)
England 173 (G Ulyett 74, J J Lyons 5–30) and 137–3 (W G Grace 75*)
2 THE OVAL England won by 2 wkts
Australia 92 (F Martin 6–50) and 102 (F Martin 6–52)
England 100 (J J Ferris 4–25) and 95–8 (J J Ferris 5–49)
(The match arranged to be played at Old Trafford was abandoned without a ball being bowled)

1891–92 14th Series Aus 2, Eng 1
1 MELBOURNE Australia won by 54 runs
Australia 240 (W Bruce 57, J W Sharpe 6–84) and 236 (J J Lyons 51)
England 264 (W G Grace 50, G Bean 50, R W McLeod 5–55) and 158 (C T B Turner 5–51)
2 SYDNEY Australia won by 72 runs
Australia 145 (G A Lohmann 8–58) and 391 (J J Lyons 134, A C Bannerman 91, W Bruce 72, J Briggs 4–69)
England 307 (R Abel 132*, G Giffen 4–88) and 156 (A E Stoddart 69, G Giffen 6–72, C T B Turner 4–46)
3 ADELAIDE England won by an innings and 230 runs
England 499 (A E Stoddart 134, R Peel 83, W G Grace 58, J M Read 57)
Australia 100 (J Briggs 6–49) and 169 (J Briggs 6–87)

1893 15th Series Eng 1, Aus 0, Drawn 2
1 LORD'S Match Drawn
England 334 (A Shrewsbury 106, F S Jackson 91, C T B Turner 6–67) and 234–8 dec (A Shrewsbury 81, W Gunn 77, G Giffen 5–43)
Australia 269 (H Graham 107, S E Gregory 57, W H Lockwood 6–101)
2 THE OVAL England won by an innings and 43 runs
England 483 (F S Jackson 103, A E Stoddart 83, W G Grace 68, A Shrewsbury 66, A Ward 55, W W Read 52, G Giffen 7–128)
Australia 91 (J Briggs 5–34, W H Lockwood 4–37) and 349 (G H S Trott 92, A C Bannerman 55, G Giffen 53, J Briggs 5–114, W H Lockwood 4–96)
3 OLD TRAFFORD Match Drawn
Australia 204 (W Bruce 68, T Richardson 5–49, J Briggs 4–81) and 236 (A C Bannerman 60, T Richardson 5–107)
England 243 (W Gunn 102*, G Giffen 4–113) and 118–4

1894–95 16th Series Eng 3, Aus 2
1 SYDNEY England won by 10 runs
Australia 586 (S E Gregory 201, G Giffen 161, F A Iredale 81, J McC Blackham 74, T Richardson 5–181) and 166 (J Darling 53, R Peel 6–67)
England 325 (A Ward 75, J Briggs 57, G Giffen 4–75) and 437 (A Ward 117, J T Brown 53, G Giffen 4–164)
2 MELBOURNE England won by 94 runs
England 75 (C T B Turner 5–32) and 475 (A E Stoddart 173, R Peel 53, G Giffen 6–155)
Australia 123 (T Richardson 5–57) and 333 (F A Iredale 68, G H S Trott 95, W Bruce 54, R Peel 4–77)
3 ADELAIDE Australia won by 382 runs
Australia 238 (G Giffen 58, T Richardson 5–75) and 411 (F A Iredale 140, W Bruce 80, A E Trott 72*, R Peel 4–96)
England 124 (G Giffen 5–76, S T Callaway 5–37) and 143 (A E Trott 8–43)
4 SYDNEY Australia won by an innings and 147 runs
Australia 284 (H Graham 105, A E Trott 85*, J Briggs 4–65)
England 65 and 72 (G Giffen 5–26, C T B Turner 4–33)
5 MELBOURNE England won by 6 wkts
Australia 414 (J Darling 74, S E Gregory 70, G Giffen 57, J J Lyons 55, R Peel 4–114) and 267 (G Giffen 51, J Darling 50, T Richardson 6–104)
England 385 (A C MacLaren 120, R Peel 73, A E Stoddart 68, G H S Trott 4–71, G Giffen 4–130) and 298–4 (J T Brown 140, A Ward 93)

1896 17th Series Eng 2, Aus 1
1 LORD'S England won by 6 wkts
Australia 53 (T Richardson 6–39) and 347 (G H S Trott 143, S E Gregory 103, J T Hearne 5–76, T Richardson 5–134)
England 292 (R Abel 94, W G Grace 66) and 111–4
2 OLD TRAFFORD Australia won by 3 wkts
Australia 412 (F A Iredale 108, G Giffen 80, G H S Trott 53, T Richardson 7–168) and 125–7 (T Richardson 6–76)
England 231 (A F A Lilley 65*, K S Ranjitsinhji 62) and 305 (K S Ranjitsinhji 154*)
3 THE OVAL England won by 66 runs
England 145 (H Trumble 6–59) and 84 (H Trumble 6–30)
Australia 119 (J T Hearne 6–41) and 44 (R Peel 6–32, J T Hearne 4–19)

1897–98 18th Series Aus 4, Eng 1
1 SYDNEY England won by 9 wkts
England 551 (K S Ranjitsinhji 175, A C MacLaren 109, T W Hayward 72, G H Hirst 62) and 96–1 (A C MacLaren 50*)
Australia 237 (H Trumble 70, C E McLeod 50*, J T Hearne 5–42) and 408 (J Darling 101, C Hill 96, J T Hearne 4–99)
2 MELBOURNE Australia won by an innings and 55 runs
Australia 520 (C E McLeod 112, F A Iredale 89, G H S Trott 79, S E Gregory 71, C Hill 58)
England 315 (K S Ranjitsinhji 71, W Storer 51, H Trumble 4–54) and 150 (M A Noble 6–49, H Trumble 4–53)
3 ADELAIDE Australia won by an innings and 13 runs
Australia 573 (J Darling 178, F A Iredale 84, C Hill 81, S E Gregory 52, T Richardson 4–164)
England 278 (G H Hirst 85, T W Hayward 70, W P Howell 4–70) and 282 (A C MacLaren 124, K S Ranjitsinhji 77, C E McLeod 5–65, M A Noble 5–84)
4 MELBOURNE Australia won by 8 wkts
Australia 323 (C Hill 188, J T Hearne 6–98) and 115–2 (C E McLeod 64*)
England 174 (E Jones 4–56) and 263 (K S Ranjitsinhji 55)
5 SYDNEY Australia won by 6 wkts
England 335 (A C MacLaren 65, N F Druce 64, E Jones 6–82) and 178 (H Trumble 4–37)
Australia 239 (C E McLeod 64, T Richardson 8–94) and 276–4 (J Darling 160, J Worrall 62)

1899 19th Series Aus 1, Eng 0, Drawn 4
1 TRENT BRIDGE Match Drawn
Australia 252 (C Hill 52, W Rhodes 4–58, J T Hearne 4–71) and 230–8 dec (C Hill 80)
England 193 (C B Fry 50, E Jones 5–88) and 155–7 (K S Ranjitsinhji 93*)
2 LORD'S Australia won by 10 wkts
England 206 (F S Jackson 73, G L Jessop 51, E Jones 7–88) and 240 (A C MacLaren 88*, T W Hayward 77)
Australia 421 (C Hill 135, V T Trumper 135*, M A Noble 54) and 28–0
3 HEADINGLEY Match Drawn
Australia 172 (J Worrall 76, H I Young 4–30) and 224 (H Trumble 56, J T Hearne 4–50)
England 220 (A F A Lilley 55, H Trumble 5–60) and 19–0
4 OLD TRAFFORD Match Drawn
England 372 (T W Hayward 130, A F A Lilley 58) and 94–3
Australia 196 (M A Noble 60*, W M Bradley 5–67, H I Young 4–79) and 346–7 dec (M A Noble 89, V T Trumper 63, J Worrall 53)
5 THE OVAL Match drawn
England 576 (T W Hayward 137, F S Jackson 118, C B Fry 60, K S Ranjitsinhji 54, E Jones 4–164)
Australia 352 (S E Gregory 117, J Worrall 55, J Darling 71, W H Lockwood 7–71) and 254–5 (C E McLeod 77, J Worrall 75, M A Noble 69*)

1901–02 20th Series Aus 4, Eng 1
1 SYDNEY England won by an innings and 124 runs
England 464 (A C MacLaren 116, A F A Lilley 84, T W Hayward 69, L C Braund 58, C E McLeod 4–84)
Australia 168 (S F Barnes 5–65) and 172 (L C Braund 5–61, C Blythe 4–30)

2 MELBOURNE Australia won by 229 runs
Australia 112 (S F Barnes 6–42, C Blythe 4–64) and 353 (R A Duff 104, C Hill 99, S F Barnes 7–121)
England 61 (M A Noble 7–17) and 175 (J T Tyldesley 66, M A Noble 6–60, H Trumble 4–49)
3 ADELAIDE Australia won by 4 wkts
England 388 (L C Braund 103*, T W Hayward 90, W G Quaife 68, A C MacLaren 67) and 247 (H Trumble 6–74)
Australia 321 (C Hill 98, V T Trumper 65, S E Gregory 55, J R Gunn 5–76) and 315–6 (C Hill 97, J Darling 69, H Trumble 62*)
4 SYDNEY Australia won by 7 wkts
England 317 (A C MacLaren 92, J T Tyldesley 79, J V Saunders 4–119) and 99 (M A Noble 5–54, J V Saunders 5–43)
Australia 299 (M A Noble 56, W W Armstrong 55, G L Jessop 4–68, L C Braund 4–118) and 121–3 (R A Duff 51*)
5 MELBOURNE Australia won by 32 runs
Australia 144 (T W Hayward 4–22, J R Gunn 4–38) and 255 (C Hill 87, L C Braund 5–95)
England 189 (H Trumble 5–62) and 178 (M A Noble 6–98)

1902 21st Series Aus 2, Eng 1, Drawn 2
1 EDGBASTON Match Drawn
England 376–9 dec (J T Tyldesley 138, F S Jackson 53, W H Lockwood 52*)
Australia 36 (W Rhodes 7–17) and 46–2
2 LORD'S Match Drawn
England 102–2 (F S Jackson 55*)
Australia did not bat
3 BRAMALL LANE, SHEFFIELD Australia won by 143 runs
Australia 194 (S F Barnes 6–49) and 289 (C Hill 119, V T Trumper 62, W Rhodes 5–63)
England 145 (J V Saunders 5–50, M A Noble 5–51) and 195 (A C MacLaren 63, G L Jessop 55, M A Noble 6–52, H Trumble 4–49)
4 OLD TRAFFORD Australia won by 3 runs
Australia 299 (V T Trumper 104, C Hill 65, R A Duff 54, J Darling 51, W H Lockwood 6–48, W Rhodes 4–104) and 86 (W H Lockwood 5–28)
England 262 (F S Jackson 128, L C Braund 65, H Trumble 4–75) and 120 (H Trumble 6–53, J V Saunders 4–52)
5 THE OVAL England won by 1 wkt
Australia 324 (H Trumble 64*, M A Noble 52, G H Hirst 5–77) and 121 (W H Lockwood 5–45)
England 183 (H Trumble 8–65) and 263–9 G L Jessop 104, G H Hirst 58, H Trumble 4–108, J V Saunders 4–105)

1903–04 22nd Series Eng 3, Aus 2
1 SYDNEY England won by 5 wkts
Australia 285 (M A Noble 133, E G Arnold 4–76) and 485 (V T Trumper 185*, R A Duff 84, C Hill 51, W Rhodes 5–94)
England 577 (R E Foster 287, L C Braund 102, J T Tyldesley 53) and 194–5 (T W Hayward 91, G H Hirst 60*)
2 MELBOURNE England won by 185 runs
England 315 (J T Tyldesley 97, P F Warner 68, T W Hayward 58, H Trumble 4–107) and 103 (J T Tyldesley 62, H Trumble 5–34)
Australia 122 (V T Trumper 74, W Rhodes 7–56) and 111 (W Rhodes 8–68)
3 ADELAIDE Australia won by 216 runs
Australia 388 (V T Trumper 113, C Hill 88, R A Duff 79, M A Noble 59) and 351 (S E Gregory 112, M A Noble 65, V T Trumper 59, B J T Bosanquet 4–73)
England 245 (G H Hirst 58) and 278 (P F Warner 79, T W Hayward 67, A J Hopkins 4–81)
4 SYDNEY England won by 157 runs
England 249 (A E Knight 70*, M A Noble 7–100) and 210 (T W Hayward 54)
Australia 131 (E G Arnold 4–28, W Rhodes 4–33) and 171 (M A Noble 53*, B J T Bosanquet 6–51)
5 MELBOURNE Australia won by 218 runs
Australia 247 (V T Trumper 88, L C Braund 8–81) and 133 (G H Hirst 5–48)
England 61 (A Cotter 6–40, M A Noble 4–19) and 101 (H Trumble 7–28)

1905 23rd Series Eng 2, Aus 0, Drawn 3
1 TRENT BRIDGE England won by 213 runs
England 196 (J T Tyldesley 56, F Laver 7–64) and 426–5 dec (A C MacLaren 140, F S Jackson 82*, J T Tyldesley 61)
Australia 221 (C Hill 54, M A Noble 50, F S Jackson 5–52) and 188 (S E Gregory 51, B J T Bosanquet 8–107)
2 LORD'S Match Drawn
England 282 (C B Fry 73, A C MacLaren 56) and 151–5 (A C MacLaren 79)
Australia 181 (F S Jackson 4–50)
3 HEADINGLEY Match Drawn
England 301 (F S Jackson 144*) and 295–5 dec (J T Tyldesley 100, T W Hayward 60, W W Armstrong 5–122)
Australia 195 (W W Armstrong 66, A Warren 5–57) and 224–7 (M A Noble 62)
4 OLD TRAFFORD England won by an innings and 80 runs
England 446 (F S Jackson 113, T W Hayward 82, R H Spooner 52, C E McLeod 5–125)
Australia 197 (J Darling 73, W Brearley 4–72) and 169 (R A Duff 60, W Brearley 4–54)
5 THE OVAL Match Drawn
England 430 (C B Fry 144, F S Jackson 76, T W Hayward 59, A Cotter 7–148) and 261–6 dec (J T Tyldesley 112*, R H Spooner 79)
Australia 363 (R A Duff 146, J Darling 57, W Brearley 5–110) and 124–4

1907–08 24th Series Aus 4, Eng 1
1 SYDNEY Australia won by 2 wkts
England 273 (G Gunn 119, A Cotter 6–101) and 300 (G Gunn 74, J Hardstaff 63, J V Saunders 4–68)
Australia 300 (C Hill 87, A Fielder 6–82) and 275–8 (H Carter 61)
2 MELBOURNE England won by 1 wkt
Australia 266 (M A Noble 61, J N Crawford 5–79) and 397 (W W Armstrong 77, C G Macartney 54, M A Noble 64, V T Trumper 63, H Carter 53, S F Barnes 5–72)
England 382 (K L Hutchings 126, J B Hobbs 83, A Cotter 5–142) and 282–9 (F L Fane 50)
3 ADELAIDE Australia won by 245 runs
Australia 285 (C G Macartney 75, A Fielder 4–80) and 506 (C Hill 160, R J Hartigan 116, M A Noble 65)
England 363 (G Gunn 65, J N Crawford 62, J Hardstaff 61) and 183 (J Hardstaff 72, J V Saunders 5–65, J D A O'Connor 5–40)
4 MELBOURNE Australia won by 308 runs
Australia 214 (V S Ransford 51, J N Crawford 5–48, A Fielder 4–54) and 385 (W W Armstrong 133*, H Carter 66, V S Ransford 54, A Fielder 4–91)
England 105 (J B Hobbs 57, J V Saunders 5–28) and 186 (J V Saunders 4–76)
5 SYDNEY Australia won by 49 runs
Australia 137 (S F Barnes 7–60) and 422 (V T Trumper 166, S E Gregory 56, J N Crawford 5–141, W Rhodes 4–102)
England 281 (G Gunn 122*, J B Hobbs 72) and 229 (W Rhodes 69, J V Saunders 5–82)

1909 25th Series Aus 2, Eng 1, Drawn 2
1 EDGBASTON England won by 10 wkts
Australia 74 (C Blythe 6–44, G H Hirst 4–28) and 151 (C Blythe 5–58, G H Hirst 5–58)
England 121 (W W Armstrong 5–27) and 105–0 (J B Hobbs 62*)
2 LORD'S Australia won by 9 wkts
England 269 (J H King 60, A Cotter 4–80) and 121 (W W Armstrong 6–35)
Australia 350 (V S Ransford 143*, A E Relf 5–85) and 41–1
3 HEADINGLEY Australia won by 126 runs
Australia 188 (W Rhodes 4–38) and 207 (S F Barnes 6–63)
England 182 (J Sharp 61, J T Tyldesley 55, C G Macartney 7–58) and 87 (A Cotter 5–38, C G Macartney 4–27)
4 OLD TRAFFORD Match Drawn
Australia 147 (S F Barnes 5–56, C Blythe 5–63) and 279–9 dec (V S Ransford 54*, C G Macartney 51, W Rhodes 5–83)
England 119 (F Laver 8–31) and 108–3 (R H Spooner 58)
5 THE OVAL Match Drawn
Australia 325 (W Bardsley 136, V T Trumper 73, C G Macartney 50, D W Carr 5–146) and 339–5 dec (W Bardsley 130, S E Gregory 74, M A Noble 55)
England 352 (J Sharp 105, W Rhodes 66, C B Fry 62, K L Hutchings 59, A Cotter 6–95) and 104–3 (W Rhodes 54)

1911–12 26th Series Eng 4, Aus 1
1 SYDNEY Australia won by 146 runs
Australia 447 (V T Trumper 113, R B Minnett 90, W W Armstrong 60) and 308 (C Kelleway 70, C Hill 65, F R Foster 5–92, J W H T Douglas 4–50)
England 318 (J W Hearne 76, J B Hobbs 63, F R Foster 56, H V Hordern 5–85) and 291 (G Gunn 62, H V Hordern 7–90)
2 MELBOURNE England won by 8 wkts
Australia 184 (S F Barnes 5–44) and 299 (W W Armstrong 90, F R Foster 6–91)
England 265 (J W Hearne 114, W Rhodes 61, A Cotter 4–73, H V Hordern 4–66) and 219–2 (J B Hobbs 126*)
3 ADELAIDE England won by 7 wkts
Australia 133 (F R Foster 5–36) and 476 (C Hill 98, H Carter 72, W Bardsley 63, T J Matthews 53, S F Barnes 5–105)
England 501 (J B Hobbs 187, F R Foster 71, W Rhodes 59, A Cotter 4–125) and 112–3 (W Rhodes 57*)
4 MELBOURNE England won by an innings and 225 runs
Australia 191 (R B Minnett 56, S F Barnes 5–74, F R Foster 4–77) and 173 (J W H T Douglas 5–46)
England 589 (W Rhodes 179, J B Hobbs 178, G Gunn 75, F E Woolley 56, F R Foster 50)
5 SYDNEY England won by 70 runs
England 324 (F E Woolley 133*, G Gunn 52, H V Hordern 5–95) and 214 (G Gunn 61, H V Hordern 5–66)
Australia 176 and 292 (R B Minnett 61, V T Trumper 50, F R Foster 4–43, S F Barnes 4–106)

1912 27th Series Eng 1, Aus 0, Drawn 2
1 LORD'S Match Drawn
England 310–7 dec (J B Hobbs 107, W Rhodes 59)
Australia 282–7 (C G Macartney 99, C Kelleway 61)
2 OLD TRAFFORD Match Drawn
England 203 (W Rhodes 92, G R Hazlitt 4–77, W J Whitty 4–43)
Australia 14–0
3 THE OVAL England won by 244 runs
England 245 (J B Hobbs 66, F E Woolley 62, R B Minnett 4–34, W J Whitty 4–69) and 175 (C B Fry 79, G R Hazlitt 7–25)
Australia 111 (S F Barnes 5–30, F E Woolley 5–29) and 65 (H Dean 4–19, F E Woolley 5–20)

1920–21 28th Series Aus 5, Eng 0
1 SYDNEY Australia won by 377 runs
Australia 267 (H L Collins 70) and 581 (W W Armstrong 158, H L Collins 104, C Kelleway 78, C G Macartney 69, W Bardsley 57, J M Taylor 51)
England 190 (F E Woolley 52) and 281 (J B Hobbs 59, J W Hearne 57, E H Hendren 56)
2 MELBOURNE Australia won by an innings and 91 runs
Australia 499 (C E Pellew 116, J M Gregory 100, J M Taylor 68, H L Collins 64, W Bardsley 51)
England 251 (J B Hobbs 122, E H Hendren 67, J M Gregory 7–69) and 157 (F E Woolley 50, W W Armstrong 4–26)
3 ADELAIDE Australia won by 119 runs
Australia 453 (H L Collins 162, W A S Oldfield 50, C H Parkin 5–60) and 582 (C Kelleway 147, W W Armstrong 121, C E Pellew 104, J M Gregory 78*, H Howell 4–115)
England 447 (C A G Russell 135*, F E Woolley 79, J W H Makepeace 60, J W H T Douglas 60, A A Mailey 5–160) and 370 (J B Hobbs 123, C A G Russell 59, E H Hendren 51, A A Mailey 5–142)
4 MELBOURNE Australia won by 8 wkts
England 284 (J W H Makepeace 117, J W H T Douglas 50, A A Mailey 4–115) and 315 (W Rhodes 73, J W H T Douglas 60, P G H Fender 59, J W H Makepeace 54, A A Mailey 9–121)
Australia 389 (W W Armstrong 123*, J M Gregory 77, H L Collins 59, W Bardsley 56, P G H Fender 5–122) and 211–2 (J M Gregory 76*, J Ryder 52*)
5 SYDNEY Australia won by 9 wkts
England 204 (F E Woolley 53, C Kelleway 4–27) and 280 (J W H T Douglas 68, A A Mailey 5–119)
Australia 392 (C G Macartney 170, J M Gregory 93, P G H Fender 5–90) and 93–1 (W Bardsley 50*)

1921 29th Series Aus 3, Eng 0, Drawn 2
1 TRENT BRIDGE Australia won by 10 wkts
England 112 (J M Gregory 6–58) and 147 (E A McDonald 5–32)
Australia 232 (W Bardsley 66) and 30–0
2 LORD'S Australia won by 8 wkts
England 187 (F E Woolley 95, A A Mailey 4–55) and 283 (F E Woolley 93, L H Tennyson 74*, J M Gregory 4–76, E A McDonald 4–89)
Australia 342 (W Bardsley 88, J M Gregory 52, F J Durston 4–102) and 131–2 (W Bardsley 63*)
3 HEADINGLEY Australia won by 219 runs
Australia 407 (C G Macartney 115, W W Armstrong 77, C E Pellew 52, J M Taylor 50, C H Parkin 4–106) and 273–7 dec (T J E Andrews 92)
England 259 (J W H T Douglas 75, L H Tennyson 63, G Brown 57, E A McDonald 4–105) and 202
4 OLD TRAFFORD Match Drawn
England 362–4 dec (C A G Russell 101, G E Tyldesley 78*) and 44–1
Australia 175 (C H Parkin 5–38)
5 THE OVAL Match Drawn
England 403–8 dec (C P Mead 182*, L H Tennyson 51, E A McDonald 5–143) and 244–2 (C A G Russell 102*, G Brown 84, J W Hitch 51*)
Australia 389 (T J E Andrews 94, J M Taylor 75, C G Macartney 61)

1924–25 30th Series Aus 4, Eng 1
1 SYDNEY Australia won by 195 runs
Australia 450 (H L Collins 114, W H Ponsford 110, M W Tate 6–130) and 452 (J M Taylor 108, A J Richardson 98, H L Collins 60, M W Tate 5–98)
England 298 (J B Hobbs 115, H Sutcliffe 59, E H Hendren 74*, J M Gregory 5–115, A A Mailey 4–129) and 411 (F E Woolley 123, H Sutcliffe 115, J B Hobbs 57, A P Freeman 50*)
2 MELBOURNE Australia won by 81 runs
Australia 600 (V Y Richardson 138, W H Ponsford 128, A E V Hartkopf 80, J M Taylor 72) and 250 (J M Taylor 90, M W Tate 6–99, F E Woolley 4–84)
England 479 (H Sutcliffe 176, J B Hobbs 154) and 290 (H Sutcliffe 127, F E Woolley 50, A A Mailey 5–92, J M Gregory 4–87)
3 ADELAIDE Australia won by 11 runs
Australia 489 (J Ryder 201*, A J Richardson 69, T J E Andrews 72, R Kilner 4–127) and 250 (J Ryder 88, R Kilner 4–51, F E Woolley 4–77)
England 365 (J B Hobbs 119, E H Hendren 92) and 363 (W W Whysall 75, H Sutcliffe 59, A P F Chapman 58)
4 MELBOURNE England won by an innings and 29 runs
England 548 (H Sutcliffe 143, W W Whysall 76, R Kilner 74, J B Hobbs 66, E H Hendren 65, A A Mailey 4–186)
Australia 269 (J M Taylor 86) and 250 (J M Taylor 68, M W Tate 5–75)
5 SYDNEY Australia won by 307 runs
Australia 295 (W H Ponsford 80, M W Tate 4–92, R Kilner 4–97) and 325 (T J E Andrews 80, C Kelleway 73, W A S Oldfield 65*, M W Tate 5–115)
England 167 (C V Grimmett 5–45) and 146 (C V Grimmett 6–37)

1926 31st Series Eng 1, Aus 0, Drawn 4
1 TRENT BRIDGE Match Drawn
England 32–0 Australia did not bat
2 LORD'S Match Drawn
Australia 383 (W Bardsley 193*, R Kilner 4–70) and 194–5 (C G Macartney 133*)
England 475–3 dec (E H Hendren 127*, J B Hobbs 119, F E Woolley 87, H Sutcliffe 82, A P F Chapman 50*)
3 HEADINGLEY Match Drawn
Australia 494 (C G Macartney 151, W M Woodfull 141, A J Richardson 100, M W Tate 4–99)
England 294 (G G Macaulay 76, C V Grimmett 5–88) and 254–3 (H Sutcliffe 94, J B Hobbs 88)
4 OLD TRAFFORD Match Drawn
Australia 335 (W M Woodfull 117, C G Macartney 109, C F Root 4–84)
England 305–5 (G E Tyldesley 81, J B Hobbs 74, F E Woolley 58)
5 THE OVAL England won by 289 runs
England 280 (H Sutcliffe 76, A A Mailey 6–138) and 436 (H Sutcliffe 161, J B Hobbs 100)
Australia 302 (J M Gregory 73, H L Collins 61) and 125 (W Rhodes 4–44)

1928–29 32nd Series Eng 4, Aus 1
1 BRISBANE England won by 675 runs
England 521 (E H Hendren 169, H Larwood 70, A P F Chapman 50) and 342–8 dec (C P Mead 73, D R Jardine 65*, C V Grimmett 6–131)
Australia 122 (H Larwood 6–32) and 66 (J C White 4–7)
2 SYDNEY England won by 8 wkts
Australia 253 (W M Woodfull 68, G Geary 5–35) and 397 (H S T L Hendry 112, W M Woodfull 111, J Ryder 79, M W Tate 4–99)
England 636 (W R Hammond 251, E H Hendren 74, G Geary 66, D D Blackie 4–148) and 16–2
3 MELBOURNE England won by 3 wkts
Australia 397 (J Ryder 112, A F Kippax 100, D G Bradman 79) and 351 (D G Bradman 112, W M Woodfull 107, J C White 5–107)
England 417 (W R Hammond 200, D R Jardine 62, H Sutcliffe 58, D D Blackie 6–94) and 332–7 (H Sutcliffe 135)
4 ADELAIDE England won by 12 runs
England 334 (W R Hammond 119*, J B Hobbs 74, H Sutcliffe 64, C V Grimmett 5–102) and 383 (W R Hammond 177, D R Jardine 98, R K Oxenham 4–67)
Australia 369 (A Jackson 164, J Ryder 63, J C White 5–130, M W Tate 4–77) and 336 (J Ryder 87, D G Bradman 58, A F Kippax 51, J C White 8–126)
5 MELBOURNE Australia won by 5 wkts
England 519 (J B Hobbs 142, M Leyland 137, E H Hendren 95) and 257 (J B Hobbs 65, M W Tate 54, M Leyland 53*, T W Wall 5–66)
Australia 491 (D G Bradman 123, W M Woodfull 102, A G Fairfax 65, G Geary 5–105) and 287–5 (J Ryder 57*)

1930 33rd Series Aus 2, Eng 1, Drawn 2
1 TRENT BRIDGE England won by 93 runs
England 270 (J B Hobbs 78, A P F Chapman 52, R W V Robins 50, C V Grimmett 5–107) and 302 (J B Hobbs 74, E H Hendren 72, H Sutcliffe 58*, C V Grimmett 5–94)
Australia 144 (A F Kippax 64*, R W V Robins 4–51) and 335 (D G Bradman 131)
2 LORD'S Australia won by 7 wkts
England 425 (K S Duleepsinhji 173, M W Tate 54, A G Fairfax 4–101) and 375 (A P F Chapman 121, G O B Allen 57, C V Grimmett 6–167)
Australia 729–6 dec (D G Bradman 254, W M Woodfull 155, A F Kippax 83, W H Ponsford 81) and 72–3
3 HEADINGLEY Match Drawn
Australia 566 (D G Bradman 334, A F Kippax 77, W M Woodfull 50, M W Tate 5–124)
England 391 (W R Hammond 113, C V Grimmett 5–135) and 95–3
4 OLD TRAFFORD Match Drawn
Australia 345 (W H Ponsford 83, W M Woodfull 54, A F Kippax 51, C V Grimmett 50)
England 251–8 (H Sutcliffe 74, K S Duleepsinhji 54, S J McCabe 4–41)
5 THE OVAL Australia won by an innings and 39 runs
England 405 (H Sutcliffe 161, R E S Wyatt 64, K S Duleepsinhji 50, C V Grimmett 4–135) and 251 (W R Hammond 60, H Sutcliffe 54, P M Hornibrook 7–92)
Australia 695 (D G Bradman 232, W H Ponsford 110, A Jackson 73, W M Woodfull 54, S J McCabe 54, A G Fairfax 53*, I A R Peebles 6–204)

1932–33 34th Series Eng 4, Aus 1
1 SYDNEY England won by 10 wkts
Australia 360 (S J McCabe 187*, H Larwood 5–96, W Voce 4–110) and 164 (H Larwood 5–28)
England 524 (H Sutcliffe 194, W R Hammond 112, Nawab of Pataudi 102) and 1–0
2 MELBOURNE Australia won by 111 runs
Australia 228 (J H W Fingleton 83) and 191 (D G Bradman 103*)
England 169 (H Sutcliffe 52, W J O'Reilly 5–63, T W Wall 4–52) and 139 (W J O'Reilly 5–66, H Ironmonger 4–26)
3 ADELAIDE England won by 338 runs
England 341 (M Leyland 83, R E S Wyatt 78, E Paynter 77, T W Wall 5–72) and 412 (W R Hammond 85, L E G Ames 69, D R Jardine 56, W J O'Reilly 4–79)
Australia 222 (W H Ponsford 85, G O B Allen 4–71) and 193 (W M Woodfull 73*, D G Bradman 66, G O B Allen 4–50, H Larwood 4–71)
4 BRISBANE England won by 6 wkts
Australia 340 (V Y Richardson 83, D G Bradman 76, W M Woodfull 67, H Larwood 4–101) and 175
England 356 (H Sutcliffe 86, E Paynter 83, W J O'Reilly 4–120) and 162–4 (M Leyland 86)
5 SYDNEY England won by 8 wkts
Australia 435 (L S Darling 85, S J McCabe 73, L P J O'Brien 61, W A S Oldfield 52, H Larwood 4–98) and 182 (D G Bradman 71, W M Woodfull 67, H Verity 5–33)
England 454 (W R Hammond 101, H Larwood 98, H Sutcliffe 56, R E S Wyatt 51, P K Lee 4–111) and 168–2 (W R Hammond 75*, R E S Wyatt 61*)

1934 35th Series Aus 2, Eng 1, Drawn 2
1 TRENT BRIDGE Australia won by 238 runs
Australia 374 (A G Chipperfield 99, S J McCabe 65, W H Ponsford 53, K Farnes 5–102) and 273–8 dec (S J McCabe 88, W A Brown 73, K Farnes 5–77)
England 268 (E H Hendren 79, H Sutcliffe 62, G Geary 53, C V Grimmett 5–81, W J O'Reilly 4–75) and 141 (W J O'Reilly 7–54)
2 LORD'S England won by an innings and 38 runs
England 440 (L E G Ames 120, M Leyland 109, C F Walters 82, T W Wall 4–108)
Australia 284 (W A Brown 105, H Verity 7–61) and 118 (H Verity 8–43)
3 OLD TRAFFORD Match Drawn
England 627–9 dec (M Leyland 153, E H Hendren 132, L E G Ames 72, H Sutcliffe 63, G O B Allen 61, H Verity 60, C F Walters 52, W J O'Reilly 7–189) and 123–0 (H Sutcliffe 69*, C F Walters 50*)
Australia 491 (S J McCabe 137, W M Woodfull 73, W A Brown 72, H Verity 4–78) and 66–1
4 HEADINGLEY Match Drawn
England 200 (C V Grimmett 4–57) and 229–6
Australia 584 (D G Bradman 304, W H Ponsford 181, W E Bowes 6–142)
5 THE OVAL Australia won by 562 runs
Australia 701 (W H Ponsford 266, D G Bradman 244, W E Bowes 4–164, G O B Allen 4–170) and 327 (D G Bradman 77, S J McCabe 70, W E Bowes 5–55, E W Clark 5–98)
England 321 (M Leyland 110, C F Walters 64) and 145 (C V Grimmett 5–64)

1936–37 36th Series Aus 3, Eng 2
1 BRISBANE England won by 322 runs
England 358 (M Leyland 126, C J Barnett 69, W J O'Reilly 5–102) and 256 (G O B Allen 68, F A Ward 6–102)
Australia 234 (J H W Fingleton 100, S J McCabe 51, W Voce 6–41) and 58 (G O B Allen 5–36, W Voce 4–16)
2 SYDNEY England won by an innings and 22 runs
England 426–6 dec (W R Hammond 231*, C J Barnett 57)
Australia 80 (W Voce 4–10) and 324 (S J McCabe 93, D G Bradman 82, J H W Fingleton 73)
3 MELBOURNE Australia won by 365 runs
Australia 200–9 dec (S J McCabe 63) and 564 (D G Bradman 270, J H W Fingleton 136)
England 76–9 dec (M W Sievers 5–21) and 323 (M Leyland 111*, R W V Robins 61, W R Hammond 51, L O'B Fleetwood-Smith 5–124)
4 ADELAIDE Australia won by 148 runs
Australia 288 (S J McCabe 88, A G Chipperfield 57*) and 433 (D G Bradman 212, S J McCabe 55, R G Gregory 50, W R Hammond 5–57)
England 330 (C J Barnett 129, L E G Ames 52, W J O'Reilly 4–51, L O'B Fleetwood-Smith 4–129) and 243 (R E S Wyatt 50, L O'B Fleetwood-Smith 6–110)
5 MELBOURNE Australia won by an innings and 200 runs
Australia 604 (D G Bradman 169, C L Badcock 118, S J McCabe 112, R G Gregory 80, K Farnes 6–96)
England 239 (J Hardstaff jun 83, W J O'Reilly 5–51, L J Nash 4–70) and 165 (W R Hammond 56)

1938 37th Series Aus 1, Eng 1, Drawn 2
1 TRENT BRIDGE Match Drawn
England 658–8 dec (E Paynter 216*, C J Barnett 126, D C S Compton 102, L Hutton 100, L O'B Fleetwood-Smith 4–153)
Australia 411 (S J McCabe 232, D G Bradman 51, K Farnes 4–106, D V P Wright 4–153) and 427–6 (D G Bradman 144*, W A Brown 133)
2 LORD'S Match Drawn
England 494 (W R Hammond 240, E Paynter 99, L E G Ames 83, W J O'Reilly 4–93, E L McCormick 4–101) and 242–8 dec (D C S Compton 76*)
Australia 422 (W A Brown 206*, A L Hassett 56, H Verity 4–103) and 204–6 (D G Bradman 102)
3 HEADINGLEY Australia won by 5 wkts
England 223 (W R Hammond 76, W J O'Reilly 5–66) and 123 (W J O'Reilly 5–56, L O'B Fleetwood-Smith 4–34)
Australia 242 (D G Bradman 103, B A Barnett 57, K Farnes 4–77) and 107–5
4 THE OVAL England won by an innings and 579 runs
England 903–7 dec (L Hutton 364, M Leyland 187, J Hardstaff jun 169*, W R Hammond 59, A Wood 53)
Australia 201 (W A Brown 69, W E Bowes 5–49) and 123 (K Farnes 4–63)
D G Bradman and J H W Fingleton were absent injured in both innings
(The match arranged to be played at Old Trafford was abandoned without a ball being bowled)

1946–47 38th Series Aus 3, Eng 0, Drawn 2
1 BRISBANE Australia won by an innings and 332 runs
Australia 645 (D G Bradman 187, A L Hassett 128, C L McCool 95, K R Miller 79, D V P Wright 5–167)
England 141 (K R Miller 7–60) and 172 (E R H Toshack 6–82)
2 SYDNEY Australia won by an innings and 33 runs
England 255 (W J Edrich 71, J T Ikin 60, I W Johnson 6–42) and 371 (W J Edrich 119, D C S Compton 54, C L McCool 5–109)
Australia 659–8 dec (S G Barnes 234, D G Bradman 234)
3 MELBOURNE Match Drawn
Australia 365 (C L McCool 104*, D G Bradman 79) and 536 (A R Morris 155, R R Lindwall 100, D Tallon 92)
England 351 (W J Edrich 89, C Washbrook 62, N W D Yardley 61, B Dooland 4–69) and 310–7 (C Washbrook 112, N W D Yardley 53*)
4 ADELAIDE Match Drawn
England 460 (D C S Compton 147, L Hutton 94, J Hardstaff jun 67, C Washbrook 65, R R Lindwall 4–52) and 340–8 dec (D C S Compton 103*, L Hutton 76, E R H Toshack 4–76)
Australia 487 (K R Miller 141*, A R Morris 122, A L Hassett 78, I W Johnson 52) and 215–1 (A R Morris 124*, D G Bradman 56*)
5 SYDNEY Australia won by 5 wkts
England 280 (L Hutton 122*, W J Edrich 60, R R Lindwall 7–63) and 186 (D C S Compton 76, C L McCool 5–44)
Australia 253 (S G Barnes 71, A R Morris 57, D V P Wright 7–105) and 214–5 (D G Bradman 63)

1948 39th Series Aus 4, Eng 0, Drawn 1
1 TRENT BRIDGE Australia won by 8 wkts
England 165 (J C Laker 63, W A Johnston 5–36) and 441 (D C S Compton 184, L Hutton 74, T G Evans 50, K R Miller 4–125, W A Johnston 4–147)
Australia 509 (D G Bradman 138, A L Hassett 137, S G Barnes 62, J C Laker 4–138) and 98–2 (S G Barnes 64*)
2 LORD'S Australia won by 409 runs
Australia 350 (A R Morris 105, D Tallon 53, A V Bedser 4–100) and 460–7 dec (S G Barnes 141, D G Bradman 89, K R Miller 74, A R Morris 62)
England 215 (D C S Compton 53, R R Lindwall 5–70) and 186 (E R H Toshack 5–40)
3 OLD TRAFFORD Match Drawn
England 363 (D C S Compton 145*, R R Lindwall 4–99) and 174–3 dec (C Washbrook 85*, W J Edrich 53)
Australia 221 (A R Morris 51, A V Bedser 4–81) and 92–1 (A R Morris 54*)
4 HEADINGLEY Australia won by 7 wkts
England 496 (C Washbrook 143, W J Edrich 111, L Hutton 81, A V Bedser 79) and 365–8 dec (D C S Compton 66, C Washbrook 65, L Hutton 57, W J Edrich 54, W A Johnston 4–95)
Australia 458 (R N Harvey 112, S J E Loxton 93, R R Lindwall 77, K R Miller 58) and 404–3 (A R Morris 182, D G Bradman 173*)
5 THE OVAL Australia won by an innings and 149 runs
England 52 (R R Lindwall 6–20) and 188 (L Hutton 64, W A Johnston 4–40)
Australia 389 (A R Morris 196, S G Barnes 61, W E Hollies 5–131)

1950–51 40th Series Aus 4, Eng 1
1 BRISBANE Australia won by 70 runs
Australia 228 (R N Harvey 74, A V Bedser 4–45) and 32–7 dec (T E Bailey 4–22)
England 68–7 dec (W A Johnston 5–35) and 122 (L Hutton 62*, J B Iverson 4–43)
2 MELBOURNE Australia won by 28 runs
Australia 194 (A L Hassett 52, A V Bedser 4–37, T E Bailey 4–40) and 181 (F R Brown 4–26)
England 197 (F R Brown 62, J B Iverson 4–37) and 150 (W A Johnston 4–26)
3 SYDNEY Australia won by an innings and 13 runs
England 290 (F R Brown 79, L Hutton 62, K R Miller 4–37) and 123 (J B Iverson 6–27)
Australia 426 (K R Miller 145*, I W Johnson 77, A L Hassett 70, A V Bedser 4–107, F R Brown 4–153)
4 ADELAIDE Australia won by 274 runs
Australia 371 (A R Morris 206, D V P Wright 4–99) and 403–8 dec (J W Burke 101*, K R Miller 99, R N Harvey 68)
England 272 (L Hutton 156*) and 228 (R T Simpson 61, W A Johnston 4–73)
5 MELBOURNE England won by 8 wkts
Australia 217 (A L Hassett 92, A R Morris 50, A V Bedser 5–46, F R Brown 5–49) and 197 (G B Hole 63, R N Harvey 52, A V Bedser 5–59)
England 320 (R T Simpson 156*, L Hutton 79, K R Miller 4–76) and 95–2 (L Hutton 60*)

1953 41st Series Eng 1, Aus 0, Drawn 4
1 TRENT BRIDGE Match Drawn
Australia 249 (A L Hassett 115, A R Morris 67, K R Miller 55, A V Bedser 7–55) and 123 (A R Morris 60, A V Bedser 7–44)
England 144 (R R Lindwall 5–57) and 120–1 (L Hutton 60*)
2 LORD'S Match Drawn
Australia 346 (A L Hassett 104, A K Davidson 76, R N Harvey 59, J H Wardle 4–77, A V Bedser 5–105) and 368 (K R Miller 109, A R Morris 89, R R Lindwall 50, F R Brown 4–82)
England 372 (L Hutton 145, T W Graveney 78, D C S Compton 57, R R Lindwall 5–66) and 282–7 (W Watson 109, T E Bailey 71)
3 OLD TRAFFORD Match Drawn
Australia 318 (R N Harvey 122, G B Hole 66, A V Bedser 5–115) and 35–8 (J H Wardle 4–7)
England 276 (L Hutton 66)
4 HEADINGLEY Match Drawn
England 167 (T W Graveney 55, R R Lindwall 5–54) and 275 (W J Edrich 64, D C S Compton 61, K R Miller 4–63)
Australia 266 (R N Harvey 71, G B Hole 53, A V Bedser 6–95) and 147–4
5 THE OVAL England won by 8 wkts
Australia 275 (R R Lindwall 62, A L Hassett 53, F S Trueman 4–86) and 162 (G A R Lock 5–45, J C Laker 4–75)
England 306 (L Hutton 82, T E Bailey 64, R R Lindwall 4–70) and 132–2 (W J Edrich 55*)

1954–55 42nd Series Eng 3, Aus 1, Drawn 1
1 BRISBANE Australia won by an innings and 154 runs
Australia 601–8 dec (R N Harvey 162, A R Morris 153, R R Lindwall 64*, G B Hole 57)
England 190 (T E Bailey 88) and 257 (W J Edrich 88)
2 SYDNEY England won by 38 runs
England 154 and 296 (P B H May 104, M C Cowdrey 54)
Australia 228 (F H Tyson 4–45, T E Bailey 4–59) and 184 (R N Harvey 92*, F H Tyson 6–85)
3 MELBOURNE England won by 128 runs
England 191 (M C Cowdrey 102, R G Archer 4–33) and 279 (P B H May 91, W A Johnston 5–85)
Australia 231 (J B Statham 5–60) and 111 (F H Tyson 7–27)
4 ADELAIDE England won by 5 wkts
Australia 323 (L V Maddocks 69) and 111
England 341 (L Hutton 80, M C Cowdrey 79, R Benaud 4–120) and 97–5
5 SYDNEY Match Drawn
England 371–7 dec (T W Graveney 111, D C S Compton 84, P B H May 79, T E Bailey 72)
Australia 221 (C C McDonald 72, J H Wardle 5–79) and 118–6

1956 43rd Series Eng 2, Aus 1, Drawn 2
1 TRENT BRIDGE Match Drawn
England 217–8 dec (P E Richardson 81, P B H May 73, K R Miller 4–69) and 188–3 dec (M C Cowdrey 81, P E Richardson 73)
Australia 148 (R N Harvey 64, J C Laker 4–58) and 120–3 (J W Burke 58*)
2 LORD'S Australia won by 185 runs
Australia 285 (C C McDonald 78, J W Burke 65) and 257 (R Benaud 97, F S Trueman 5–90, T E Bailey 4–64)
England 171 (P B H May 63, K R Miller 5–72) and 186 (P B H May 53, K R Miller 5–80, R G Archer 4–71)
3 HEADINGLEY England won by an innings and 42 runs
England 325 (P B H May 101, C Washbrook 98)
Australia 143 (J C Laker 5–58, G A R Lock 4–41) and 140 (R N Harvey 69, J C Laker 6–55)
4 OLD TRAFFORD England won by an innings and 170 runs
England 459 (D S Sheppard 113, P E Richardson 104, M C Cowdrey 80, I W Johnson 4–151)
Australia 84 (J C Laker 9–37) and 205 (C C McDonald 89, J C Laker 10–53)
5 THE OVAL Match Drawn
England 247 (D C S Compton 94, P B H May 83*, R G Archer 5–53, K R Miller 4–91) and 182–3 dec (D S Sheppard 62)
Australia 202 (K R Miller 61, J C Laker 4–80) and 27–5

1958–59 44th Series Aus 4, Eng 0, Drawn 1
1 BRISBANE Australia won by 8 wkts
England 134 and 198 (T E Bailey 68, R Benaud 4–66)
Australia 186 (P J Loader 4–56) and 147–2 (N C O'Neill 71*)
2 MELBOURNE Australia won by 8 wkts
England 259 (P B H May 113, A K Davidson 6–64) and 87 (Meckiff 6–38)
Australia 308 (R N Harvey 167, J B Statham 7–57) and 42–2
3 SYDNEY Match Drawn
England 219 (R Benaud 5–83) and 287–7 dec (M C Cowdrey 100*, P B H May 92, R Benaud 4–94)
Australia 357 (N C O'Neill 77, A K Davidson 71, K D Mackay 57, L E Favell 54, J C Laker 5–107, G A R Lock 4–130) and 54–2
4 ADELAIDE Australia won by 10 wkts
Australia 476 (C C McDonald 170, J W Burke 66, N C O'Neill 56, F S Trueman 4–90) and 36–0
England 240 (M C Cowdrey 84, R Benaud 5–91) and 270 (P B H May 59, T W Graveney 53*, R Benaud 4–82)
5 MELBOURNE Australia won by 9 wkts
England 205 (P E Richardson 68, R Benaud 4–43) and 214 (T W Graveney 54)
Australia 351 (C C McDonald 133, A T W Grout 74, R Benaud 64, F S Trueman 4–92) and 69–1 (C C McDonald 51*)

1961 45th Series Aus 2, Eng 1, Drawn 2
1 EDGBASTON Match Drawn
England 195 (R Subba Row 59, K D Mackay 4–57) and 401–4 (E R Dexter 180, R Subba Row 112)
Australia 516 (R N Harvey 114, N C O'Neill 82, R B Simpson 76, K D Mackay 64, W M Lawry 57)
2 LORD'S Australia won by 5 wkts
England 206 (A K Davidson 5–42) and 202 (K F Barrington 66, G D McKenzie 5–37)
Australia 340 (W M Lawry 130, K D Mackay 54, F S Trueman 4–118) and 71–5
3 HEADINGLEY England won by 8 wkts
Australia 237 (R N Harvey 73, C C McDonald 54, F S Trueman 5–58) and 120 (R N Harvey 53, F S Trueman 6–30)
England 299 (M C Cowdrey 93, G Pullar 53, A K Davidson 5–63) and 62–2
4 OLD TRAFFORD Australia won by 54 runs
Australia 190 (W M Lawry 74, J B Statham 5–53) and 432 (W M Lawry 102, A K Davidson 77*, N C O'Neill 67, R B Simpson 51, D A Allen 4–58)
England 367 (P B H May 95, K F Barrington 78, G Pullar 63, R B Simpson 4–23) and 201 (E R Dexter 76, R Benaud 6–70)
5 THE OVAL Match Drawn
England 256 (P B H May 71, K F Barrington 53, A K Davidson 4–83) and 370–8 (R Subba Row 137, K F Barrington 83, K D Mackay 5–121)
Australia 494 (P J P Burge 181, N C O'Neill 117, B C Booth 71, D A Allen 4–133)

1962–63 46th Series Eng 1, Aus 1, Drawn 3
1 BRISBANE Match Drawn
Australia 404 (B C Booth 112, K D Mackay 86*, R Benaud 51, R B Simpson 50) and 362–4 dec (W M Lawry 98, R B Simpson 71, R N Harvey 57, N C O'Neill 56)
England 389 (P H Parfitt 80, K F Barrington 78, E R Dexter 70, R Benaud 6–115) and 278–6 (E R Dexter 99, G Pullar 56, D S Sheppard 53)
2 MELBOURNE England won by 7 wkts
Australia 316 (W M Lawry 52, F J Titmus 4–43) and 248 (B C Booth 103, W M Lawry 57, F S Trueman 5–62)
England 331 (M C Cowdrey 113, E R Dexter 93, A K Davidson 6–75) and 237–3 (D S Sheppard 113, M C Cowdrey 58*, E R Dexter 52)
3 SYDNEY Australia won by 8 wkts
England 279 (M C Cowdrey 85, G Pullar 53, R B Simpson 5–57, A K Davidson 4–54) and 104 (A K Davidson 5–25)
Australia 319 (R B Simpson 91, B K Shepherd 71*, R N Harvey 64, F J Titmus 7–79) and 67–2
4 ADELAIDE Match Drawn
Australia 393 (R N Harvey 154, N C O'Neill 100) and 293 (B C Booth 77, R B Simpson 71, F S Trueman 4–60)
England 331 (K F Barrington 63, E R Dexter 61, F J Titmus 59*, G D McKenzie 5–89) and 223–4 (K F Barrington 132*)
5 SYDNEY Match Drawn
England 321 (K F Barrington 101) and 268–8 dec (K F Barrington 94, D S Sheppard 68, M C Cowdrey 53)
Australia 349 (P J P Burge 103, N C O'Neill 73, R Benaud 57, F J Titmus 5–103) and 152–4 (P J P Burge 52*)

1964 47th Series Aus 1, Eng 0, Drawn 4
1 TRENT BRIDGE Match Drawn
England 216–8 dec and 193–9 dec (E R Dexter 68, G D McKenzie 5–53)
Australia 168 (R B Simpson 50) and 40–2
2 LORD'S Match Drawn
Australia 176 (T R Veivers 54, F S Trueman 5–48) and 168–4 (P J P Burge 59)
England 246 (J H Edrich 120, G E Corling 4–60)
3 HEADINGLEY Australia won by 7 wkts
England 268 (J M Parks 68, E R Dexter 66, N J N Hawke 5–75, G D McKenzie 4–74) and 229 (K F Barrington 85)
Australia 389 (P J P Burge 160, W M Lawry 78, F J Titmus 4–69) and 111–3 (I R Redpath 58*)
4 OLD TRAFFORD Match Drawn
Australia 656–8 dec (R B Simpson 311, W M Lawry 106, B C Booth 98) and 4–0
England 611 (K F Barrington 256, E R Dexter 174, J M Parks 60, G Boycott 58, G D McKenzie 7–153)
5 THE OVAL Match Drawn
England 182 (N J N Hawke 6–47) and 381–4 (G Boycott 113, M C Cowdrey 93*, F J Titmus 56, K F Barrington 54)
Australia 379 (W M Lawry 94, B C Booth 74, T R Veivers 67*, F S Trueman 4–87)

1965–66 48th Series Eng 1, Aus 1, Drawn 3
1 BRISBANE Match Drawn
Australia 443–6 dec (W M Lawry 166, K D Walters 155, T R Veivers 46*)
England 280 (F J Titmus 60, K F Barrington 53, J M Parks 52, P I Philpott 5–90) and 186–3 (G Boycott 63*)
2 MELBOURNE Match Drawn
Australia 358 (R M Cowper 99, W M Lawry 88, R B Simpson 59, B R Knight 4–84) and 426 (P J P Burge 120, K D Walters 115, W M Lawry 78, R B Simpson 67)
England 558 (J H Edrich 109, M C Cowdrey 104, J M Parks 71, K F Barrington 63, F J Titmus 56*, G Boycott 51, G D McKenzie 5–134) and 5–0
3 SYDNEY England won by an innings and 93 runs
England 488 (R W Barber 185, J H Edrich 103, G Boycott 84, D A Allen 50*, N J N Hawke 7–105)
Australia 221 (R M Cowper 60, G Thomas 51, D J Brown 5–63) and 174 (F J Titmus 4–40, D A Allen 4–47)
4 ADELAIDE Australia won by an innings and 9 runs
England 241 (K F Barrington 60, G D McKenzie 6–48) and 266 (K F Barrington 102, F J Titmus 53, N J N Hawke 5–54)
Australia 516 (R B Simpson 225, W M Lawry 119, G Thomas 52, I J Jones 6–118)
5 MELBOURNE Match Drawn
England 485–9 dec (K F Barrington 115, J M Parks 89, J H Edrich 85, M C Cowdrey 79, K D Walters 4–53) and 69–3
Australia 543–8 dec (R M Cowper 307, W M Lawry 108, K D Walters 60)

1968 49th Series Aus 1, Eng 1, Drawn 3
1 OLD TRAFFORD Australia won by 159 runs
Australia 357 (A P Sheahan 88, W M Lawry 81, K D Walters 81, I M Chappell 73, J A Snow 4–97) and 220 (K D Walters 86, P I Pocock 6–79)
England 165 (R M Cowper 4–48) and 253 (B L d'Oliveira 87*)
2 LORD'S Match Drawn
England 351–7 dec (C Milburn 83, K F Barrington 75)
Australia 78 (D J Brown 5–42) and 127–4 (I R Redpath 53)
3 EDGBASTON Match Drawn
England 409 (M C Cowdrey 104, T W Graveney 96, J H Edrich 88, E W Freeman 4–78) and 142–3 dec (J H Edrich 64)
Australia 222 (I M Chappell 71, R M Cowper 57) and 68–1
4 HEADINGLEY Match Drawn
Australia 315 (I R Redpath 92, I M Chappell 65, D L Underwood 4–41) and 312 (I M Chappell 81, K D Walters 56, R Illingworth 6–87)
England 302 (R M Prideaux 64, J H Edrich 62, A N Connolly 5–72) and 230–4 (J H Edrich 65)
5 THE OVAL England won by 226 runs
England 494 (J H Edrich 164, B L d'Oliveira 158, T W Graveney 63) and 81 (A Connolly 4–65)
Australia 324 (W M Lawry 135, I R Redpath 67) and 125 (R J Inverarity 56, D L Underwood 7–50)

1970–71 50th Series Eng 2, Aus 0, Drawn 4
1 BRISBANE Match Drawn
Australia 433 (K R Stackpole 207, K D Walters 112, I M Chappell 59, J A Snow 6–114) and 214 (W M Lawry 84, K Shuttleworth 5–47)
England 464 (J H Edrich 79, B W Luckhurst 74, A P E Knott 73, B L d'Oliveira 57) and 39–1
2 PERTH Match Drawn
England 397 (B W Luckhurst 131, G Boycott 70, G D McKenzie 4–66) and 287–6 dec (J H Edrich 115*, G Boycott 50)
Australia 440 (I R Redpath 171, G S Chappell 108, I M Chappell 50, J A Snow 4–143) and 100–3
3 SYDNEY England won by 299 runs
England 332 (G Boycott 77, J H Edrich 55, A A Mallett 4–40, J W Gleeson 4–83) and 319–5 dec (G Boycott 142*, B L d'Oliveira 56, R Illingworth 53)
Australia 236 (I R Redpath 64, K D Walters 55, D L Underwood 4–66) and 116 (W M Lawry 60*, J A Snow 7–40)
4 MELBOURNE Match Drawn
Australia 493–9 dec (I M Chappell 111, R W Marsh 92*, W M Lawry 56, I R Redpath 72, K D Walters 55) and 169–4 dec
England 392 (B W Luckhurst 109, B L d'Oliveira 117) and 161–0 (G Boycott 76*, J H Edrich 74*)
5 ADELAIDE Match Drawn
England 470 (J H Edrich 130, K W R Fletcher 80, G Boycott 58, J H Hampshire 55, D K Lillee 5–84) and 233–4 dec (G Boycott 119*)
Australia 235 (K R Stackpole 87, P Lever 4–49) and 328–3 (K R Stackpole 136, I M Chappell 104)
6 SYDNEY England won by 62 runs
England 184 and 302 (B W Luckhurst 59, J H Edrich 57)
Australia 264 (G S Chappell 65, I R Redpath 59) and 160 (K R Stackpole 67)
After the match at Perth, the next Test should have been played at Melbourne, but bad weather prevented a ball being bowled and the match was re-arranged

1972 51st Series Eng 2, Aus 2, Drawn 1
1 OLD TRAFFORD England won by 89 runs
England 249 (A W Greig 57) and 234 (A W Greig 62, D K Lillee 6–66)
Australia 142 (K R Stackpole 53, J A Snow 4–41, G G Arnold 4–62) and 252 (R W Marsh 91, K R Stackpole 67, A W Greig 4–53, J A Snow 4–87)
2 LORD'S Australia won by 8 wkts
England 272 (A W Greig 54, R A L Massie 8–84) and 116 (R A L Massie 8–53)
Australia 308 (G S Chappell 131, I M Chappell 56, R W Marsh 50, J A Snow 5–57) and 81–2 (K R Stackpole 57*)
3 TRENT BRIDGE Match Drawn
Australia 315 (K R Stackpole 114, D J Colley 54, J A Snow 5–92) and 324–4 dec (R Edwards 170*, G S Chappell 72, I M Chappell 50)
England 189 (D K Lillee 4–35, R A L Massie 4–43) and 290–4 (B W Luckhurst 96, B L d'Oliveira 50*)
4 HEADINGLEY England won by 9 wkts
Australia 146 (K R Stackpole 52, D L Underwood 4–37) and 136 (D L Underwood 6–45)
England 263 (R Illingworth 57, A A Mallett 5–114) and 21–1
5 THE OVAL Australia won by 5 wkts
England 284 (A P E Knott 92, P H Parfitt 51, D K Lillee 5–58) and 356 (B Wood 90, A P E Knott 63, D K Lillee 5–123)
Australia 399 (I M Chappell 118, G S Chappell 113, R Edwards 79, D L Underwood 4–90) and 242–5 (K R Stackpole 79)

1974–75 52nd Series Aus 4, Eng 1, Drawn 1
1 BRISBANE Australia won by 166 runs
Australia 309 (I M Chappell 90, G S Chappell 58, R G D Willis 4–56) and 288–5 dec (G S Chappell 71, K D Walters 62*, R Edwards 53)
England 265 (A W Greig 110, M H N Walker 4–73) and 166 (J R Thomson 6–46)
2 PERTH Australia won by 9 wkts
England 208 (A P E Knott 51) and 293 (F J Titmus 61, J R Thomson 5–93)
Australia 481 (R Edwards 115, K D Walters 103, G S Chappell 62) and 23–1
3 MELBOURNE Match Drawn
England 242 (A P E Knott 52, J R Thomson 4–72) and 244 (D L Amiss 90, A W Greig 60, A A Mallett 4–60, J R Thomson 4–72)
Australia 241 (I R Redpath 55, R G D Willis 5–61) and 238–8 (G S Chappell 61, A W Greig 4–56)
4 SYDNEY Australia won by 171 runs
Australia 405 (G S Chappell 84, R B McCosker 80, I M Chappell 53, G G Arnold 5–86, A W Greig 4–104) and 289–4 dec (G S Chappell 144, I R Redpath 105)
England 295 (A P E Knott 82, J H Edrich 50, J R Thomson 4–74) and 228 (A W Greig 54, A A Mallett 4–21)
5 ADELAIDE Australia won by 163 runs
Australia 304 (T J Jenner 74, K D Walters 55, D L Underwood 7–113) and 273–5 dec (K D Walters 71*, R W Marsh 55, I R Redpath 52, D L Underwood 4–102)
England 172 (M H Denness 51, D K Lillee 4–49) and 241 (A P E Knott 106*, K W R Fletcher 63, D K Lillee 4–69)
6 MELBOURNE England won by an innings and 4 runs
Australia 152 (I M Chappell 65, P Lever 6–38) and 373 (G S Chappell 102, I R Redpath 83, R B McCosker 76, I M Chappell 50, A W Greig 4–88)
England 529 (M H Denness 188, K W R Fletcher 146, A W Greig 89, J H Edrich 70, M H N Walker 8–143)

1975 53rd Series Aus 1, Eng 0, Drawn 3
1 EDGBASTON Australia won by an innings and 85 runs
Australia 359 (R W Marsh 61, R B McCosker 59, R Edwards 56, I M Chappell 52)
England 101 (D K Lillee 5–15, M H N Walker 5–48) and 173 (K W R Fletcher 51, J R Thomson 5–38)
2 LORD'S Match Drawn
England 315 (A W Greig 96, A P E Knott 69, D S Steele 50, D K Lillee 4–84) and 436–7 dec (J H Edrich 175, B Wood 52)
Australia 268 (R Edwards 99, J A Snow 4–66) and 329–3 (I M Chappell 86, R B McCosker 79, G S Chappell 73*, R Edwards 52*)
3 HEADINGLEY Match Drawn
England 288 (D S Steele 73, J H Edrich 62, A W Greig 51, G J Gilmour 6–85) and 291 (D S Steele 92)
Australia 135 (P H Edmonds 5–28) and 220–3 (R B McCosker 95*, I M Chappell 62)
4 THE OVAL Match Drawn
Australia 532–9 dec (I M Chappell 192, R B McCosker 127, K D Walters 65) and 40–2

England 191 (J R Thomson 4–50, M H N Walker 4–63) and 538 (R A Woolmer 149, J H Edrich 96, G R J Roope 77, D S Steele 66, A P E Knott 64, K D Walters 4–34, D K Lillee 4–91)

1976–77 54th Series (Centenary Test) Aus 1, Eng 0
MELBOURNE Australia won by 45 runs
Australia 138 and 419–9 dec (R W Marsh 110*, I C Davis 68, K D Walters 66, D W Hookes 56, C M Old 4–104)
England 95 (D K Lillee 6–26, M H N Walker 4–54) and 417 (D W Randall 174, D L Amiss 64, D K Lillee 5–139)

1977 55th Series Eng 3, Aus 0, Drawn 2
1 LORD'S Match Drawn
England 216 (R A Woolmer 79, D W Randall 53, J R Thomson 4–41) and 305 (R A Woolmer 120, A W Greig 91, J R Thomson 4–86)
Australia 296 (C S Serjeant 81, G S Chappell 66, K D Walters 53, R G D Willis 7–78) and 114–6 (D W Hookes 50)
2 OLD TRAFFORD England won by 9 wkts
Australia 297 (K D Walters 88) and 218 (G S Chappell 112, D L Underwood 6–66)
England 437 (R A Woolmer 137, D W Randall 79, A W Greig 76) and 82–1
3 TRENT BRIDGE England won by 7 wkts
Australia 243 (R B McCosker 51, I T Botham 5–74) and 309 (R B McCosker 107, R G D Willis 5–88)
England 364 (A P E Knott 135, G Boycott 107, L S Pascoe 4–80) and 189–3 (J M Brearley 81, G Boycott 80*)
4 HEADINGLEY England won by an innings and 85 runs
England 436 (G Boycott 191, A P E Knott 57, L S Pascoe 4–91, J R Thomson 4–113)
Australia 103 (I T Botham 5–21, M Hendrick 4–41) and 248 (R W Marsh 63, M Hendrick 4–54)
5 THE OVAL Match Drawn
England 214 (M F Malone 5–63, J R Thomson 4–87) and 57–2
Australia 385 (D W Hookes 85, M H N Walker 78*, R W Marsh 57, R G D Willis 5–102)

1978–79 56th Series Eng 5, Aus 1
1 BRISBANE England won by 7 wkts
Australia 116 (R G D Willis 4–44) and 339 (K J Hughes 129, G N Yallop 102)
England 286 (D W Randall 75, R M Hogg 6–74, A G Hurst 4–93) and 170–3 (D W Randall 74*)
2 PERTH England won by 166 runs
England 309 (D I Gower 102, G Boycott 77, R M Hogg 5–65) and 208 (R M Hogg 5–57)
Australia 190 (P M Toohey 81*, R G D Willis 5–44) and 161 (G M Wood 64, J K Lever 4–28)
3 MELBOURNE Australia won by 103 runs
Australia 258 (G M Wood 100) and 167
England 143 (R M Hogg 5–30) and 179 (R M Hogg 5–36)
4 SYDNEY England won by 93 runs
England 152 (I T Botham 59, A G Hurst 5–28) and 346 (D W Randall 150, J M Brearley 53, J D Higgs 5–148, R M Hogg 4–67)
Australia 294 (W M Darling 91, A R Border 60*) and 111 (J E Emburey 4–46)
5 ADELAIDE England won by 205 runs
England 169 (I T Botham 74, R M Hogg 4–26) and 360 (R W Taylor 97, G Miller 64, A G Hurst 4–97)
Australia 164 (I T Botham 4–42) and 160
6 SYDNEY England won by 9 wkts
Australia 198 (G N Yallop 121, I T Botham 4–57) and 143 (B Yardley 61*, G Miller 5–44, J E Emburey 4–52)
England 308 (G A Gooch 74, D I Gower 65, J D Higgs 4–69) and 35–1

1979–80 57th Series Aus 3, Eng 0
1 PERTH Australia won by 138 runs
Australia 244 (K J Hughes 99, I T Botham 6–78) and 337 (A R Border 115, J M Wiener 58, I T Botham 5–98)
England 228 (J M Brearley 64, D K Lillee 4–73) and 215 (G Boycott 99*, G Dymock 6–34)
2 SYDNEY Australia won by 6 wkts
England 123 (D K Lillee 4–40, G Dymock 4–42) and 237 (D I Gower 98*)
Australia 145 (I T Botham 4–29) and 219–4 (G S Chappell 98*)
3 MELBOURNE Australia won by 8 wkts
England 306 (G A Gooch 99, J M Brearley 60*, D K Lillee 6–60) and 273 (I T Botham 119*, G A Gooch 51, D K Lillee 5–78, L S Pascoe 4–80)
Australia 477 (G S Chappell 114, I M Chappell 75, B M Laird 74, A R Border 63, J K Lever 4–111) and 103–2

1980 58th Series (Centenary Test) Drawn 1
LORD'S Match Drawn
Australia 385–5 dec (K J Hughes 117, G M Wood 112, A R Border 56*) and 189–4 dec (K J Hughes 84, G S Chappell 59)
England 205 (G Boycott 62, L S Pascoe 5–59, D K Lillee 4–43) and 244–3 (G Boycott 128*, M W Gatting 51*)

1981 59th Series Eng 3, Aus 1, Drawn 2
1 TRENT BRIDGE Australia won by 4 wkts
England 185 (M W Gatting 52, T M Alderman 4–68) and 125 (D K Lillee 5–46, T M Alderman 5–62)
Australia 179 (A R Border 63) and 132–6 (G R Dilley 4–24)
2 LORD'S Match Drawn
England 311 (P Willey 82, M W Gatting 59, G F Lawson 7–81) and 265–8 dec (D I Gower 89, G Boycott 60)
Australia 345 (A R Border 64) and 90–4 (G M Wood 62*)
3 HEADINGLEY England won by 18 runs
Australia 401–9 dec (J Dyson 102, K J Hughes 89, G N Yallop 58, I T Botham 6–95) and 111 (R G D Willis 8–43)
England 174 (I T Botham 50, D K Lillee 4–49) and 356 (I T Botham 149*, G R Dilley 56, T M Alderman 6–135)
4 EDGBASTON England won by 29 runs
England 189 (T M Alderman 5–42) and 219 (R J Bright 5–68)
Australia 258 (J E Emburey 4–43) and 121 (I T Botham 5–11)
5 OLD TRAFFORD England won by 103 runs
England 231 (C J Tavare 69, P J W Allott 52*, D K Lillee 4–55, T M Alderman 4–88) and 404 (I T Botham 118, C J Tavare 78, A P E Knott 59, J E Emburey 57, T M Alderman 5–109)
Australia 130 (M F Kent 52, R G D Willis 4–63) and 402 (A R Border 123*, G N Yallop 114)
6 THE OVAL Match Drawn
Australia 352 (A R Border 106*, G M Wood 66, M F Kent 54, I T Botham 6–125, R G D Willis 4–91) and 344–9 dec (D M Wellham 103, A R Border 84, R W Marsh 52, M Hendrick 4–82, I T Botham 4–128)
England 314 (G Boycott 137, M W Gatting 53, D K Lillee 7–89) and 261–7 (A P E Knott 70*, M W Gatting 56, J M Brearley 51, D K Lillee 4–70)

2 England *v* South Africa

1888–89 1st Series Eng 2, SA 0
1 PORT ELIZABETH England won by 8 wkts
South Africa 84 (C A Smith 5–19, J Briggs 4–39) and 129 (A J Fothergill 4–19)
England 148 (A Rose-Innes 5–43) and 67–2
2 CAPE TOWN England won by an innings and 202 runs
England 292 (R Abel 120, H Wood 59, W H Ashley 7–95)
South Africa 47 (J Briggs 7–17) and 43 (J Briggs 8–11)

1891–92 2nd Series Eng 1, SA 0
1 CAPE TOWN England won by an innings and 189 runs
England 369 (H Wood 134*)
South Africa 97 (J J Ferris 6–54) and 83 (J J Ferris 7–37)

1895–96 3rd Series Eng 3, SA 0
1 PORT ELIZABETH England won by 288 runs
England 185 (J Middleton 5–64) and 226 (S M J Woods 53, J Middleton 4–66)
South Africa 93 (G A Lohmann 7–38) and 30 (G A Lohmann 8–7)
2 JOHANNESBURG England won by an innings and 197 runs
South Africa 151 (G A Lohmann 9–28) and 134 (C Heseltine 5–38)
England 482 (T W Hayward 122, H R Bromley-Davenport 84, C W Wright 71, A J L Hill 65, C B Fry 64, G A Rowe 5–115, J H Sinclair 4–118)
3 CAPE TOWN England won by an innings and 32 runs
South Africa 115 (G A Lohmann 7–42) and 117 (A J L Hill 4–8)
England 265 (A J L Hill 124)

1898–99 4th Series Eng 2, SA 0
1 JOHANNESBURG England won by 32 runs
England 145 and 237 (P F Warner 132*, J Middleton 5–51)
South Africa 251 (J H Sinclair 86, A E Trott 4–61) and 99 A E Trott 5–49)
2 CAPE TOWN England won by 210 runs
England 92 (J H Sinclair 6–26, J Middleton 4–18) and 330 (J T Tyldesley 112)
South Africa 177 (J H Sinclair 106, A E Trott 4–69) and 35 (S Haigh 6–11, A E Trott 4–19)

1905–06 5th Series SA 4, Eng 1
1 JOHANNESBURG South Africa won by 1 wkt
England 184 and 190 (P F Warner 51, G A Faulkner 4–26)
South Africa 91 (W S Lees 5–34) and 287–9 (A W Nourse 93*, G C White 81)
2 JOHANNESBURG South Africa won by 9 wkts
England 148 and 160 (F L Fane 65, R O Schwarz 4–30)
South Africa 277 (J H Sinclair 66, S Haigh 4–64) and 33–1
3 JOHANNESBURG South Africa won by 243 runs
South Africa 385 (C M H Hathorn 102, A W Nourse 61*, W S Lees 6–78) and 349–5 dec (G C White 147, L J Tancred 73, A W Nourse 55)
England 295 (F L Fane 143, S J Snooke 4–57, R O Schwarz 4–67) and 196 (D Denton 61, S J Snooke 8–70)
4 CAPE TOWN England won by 4 wkts
South Africa 218 (C Blythe 6–68) and 138 (G C White 73, C Blythe 5–50, W S Lees 4–27)
England 198 (J H Sinclair 4–41, G A Faulkner 4–49) and 160–6 (F L Fane 66*)
5 CAPE TOWN South Africa won by an innings and 16 runs
England 187 (J N Crawford 74, J H Sinclair 4–45) and 130 (A W Nourse 4–25)
South Africa 333 (A E E Vogler 62*, S J Snooke 60)

1907 6th Series Eng 1, SA 0, Drawn 2
1 LORD'S Match Drawn
England 428 (L C Braund 104, G L Jessop 93, J T Tyldesley 52, A E E Vogler 7–128)
South Africa 140 (A W Nourse 62, E G Arnold 5–37) and 185–3 (P W Sherwell 115)
2 HEADINGLEY England won by 53 runs
England 76 (G A Faulkner 6–17) and 162 (C B Fry 54, G C White 4–47)
South Africa 110 (C Blythe 8–59) and 75 (C Blythe 7–40)
3 THE OVAL Match Drawn
England 295 (C B Fry 129, R E Foster 51) and 138 (A E E Vogler 4–49)
South Africa 178 (S J Snooke 63, C Blythe 5–61) and 159–5

1909–10 7th Series SA 3, Eng 2
1 JOHANNESBURG South Africa won by 19 runs
South Africa 208 (G A Faulkner 78, A W Nourse 53, G H T Simpson-Hayward 6–43) and 345 (A W Nourse 123, C P Buckenham 4–110)
England 310 (J B Hobbs 89, W Rhodes 66, A E E Vogler 5–87, G A Faulkner 5–120) and 224 (G J Thompson 63, A E E Vogler 7–94)
2 DURBAN South Africa won by 95 runs
South Africa 199 (G H T Simpson-Hayward 4–42) and 347 (G C White 118, A W Nourse 69, S J Snooke 53)
England 199 (J B Hobbs 53, A E E Vogler 5–83) and 252 (J B Hobbs 70, G A Faulkner 6–87)
3 JOHANNESBURG England won by 3 wkts
South Africa 305 (G A Faulkner 76, G C White 72, A E E Vogler 65, C P Buckenham 5–115) and 237 (S J Snooke 52, G H T Simpson-Hayward 5–69)
England 322 (D Denton 104, F E Woolley 58*, G A Faulkner 4–89, A E E Vogler 4–98) and 221–7 (J B Hobbs 93*, A E E Vogler 4–109)
4 CAPE TOWN South Africa won by 4 wkts
England 203 (F E Woolley 69, M C Bird 57) and 178 (F E Woolley 64, A E E Vogler 5–72)
South Africa 207 (G J Thompson 4–50) and 175–6
5 CAPE TOWN England won by 9 wkts
England 417 (J B Hobbs 187, W Rhodes 77, G J Thompson 51, N O Norton 4–47) and 16–1
South Africa 103 (C Blythe 7–46) and 327 (G A Faulkner 99)

1912 8th Series Eng 3, SA 0
1 LORD'S England won by an innings and 62 runs
South Africa 58 (F R Foster 5–16, S F Barnes 5–25) and 217 (C B Llewellyn 75, S F Barnes 6–85)
England 337 (R H Spooner 119, F E Woolley 73, S J Pegler 7–65)
2 HEADINGLEY England won by 174 runs
England 242 (F E Woolley 57, A W Nourse 4–52) and 238 (R H Spooner 82, J B Hobbs 55, G A Faulkner 4–50)
South Africa 147 (S F Barnes 6–52) and 159 (S F Barnes 4–63)
3 THE OVAL England won by 10 wkts
South Africa 95 (S F Barnes 5–28, F E Woolley 5–41) and 93 (S F Barnes 8–29)
England 176 (J B Hobbs 68, G A Faulkner 7–84) and 14–0

1913–14 9th Series Eng 4, SA 0, Drawn 1
1 DURBAN England won by an innings and 157 runs
South Africa 182 (H W Taylor 109, S F Barnes 5–57) and 111 (S F Barnes 5–48)
England 450 (J W H T Douglas 119, J B Hobbs 82, M C Bird 61, L H Tennyson 52)
2 JOHANNESBURG England won by an innings and 12 runs
South Africa 160 (G P D Hartigan 51, S F Barnes 8–56) and 231 (A W Nourse 56, S F Barnes 9–103)
England 403 (W Rhodes 152, C P Mead 102, A E Relf 63, J M Blanckenberg 5–83)
3 JOHANNESBURG England won by 91 runs
England 238 (J B Hobbs 92) and 308 (C P Mead 86, J W H T Douglas 77, C Newberry 4–72)
South Africa 151 (J W Hearne 5–49) and 304 (J W Zulch 82, H W Taylor 70, J M Blanckenberg 59, S F Barnes 5–102)
4 DURBAN Match Drawn
South Africa 170 (P A M Hands 51, S F Barnes 7–56) and 305–9 dec (H W Taylor 93, S F Barnes 7–88)
England 163 (J B Hobbs 64, C P Carter 6–50) and 154–5 (J B Hobbs 97)
5 PORT ELIZABETH England won by 10 wkts
South Africa 193 (P A M Hands 83, J W H T Douglas 4–14) and 228 (H W Taylor 87, J W Zulch 60, M W Booth 4–49)
England 411 (C P Mead 117, F E Woolley 54, E B Lundie 4–101) and 11–0

1922–23 10th Series Eng 2, SA 1, Drawn 2
1 JOHANNESBURG South Africa won by 168 runs
South Africa 148 (A S Kennedy 4–37, V W C Jupp 4–59) and 420 (H W Taylor 176, W H Brann 50, A S Kennedy 4–132)
England 182 (J M Blanckenberg 6–76) and 218 (E P Nupen 5–53)
2 CAPE TOWN England won by 1 wkt
South Africa 113 (P G H Fender 4–29) and 242 (R H Catterall 76, H W Taylor 68, G G Macaulay 5–64, A S Kennedy 4–58)
England 183 (J M Blanckenberg 5–61, A E Hall 4–49) and 173–9 (A E Hall 7–63)
3 DURBAN Match Drawn
England 428 (C P Mead 181, F T Mann 84, P G H Fender 60, A E Hall 4–105) and 11–1
South Africa 368 (H W Taylor 91, C M Francois 72, A W Nourse 52, R H Catterall 52, A S Kennedy 5–88)
4 JOHANNESBURG Match Drawn
England 244 (A W Carr 63, A E Hall 6–82) and 376–6 dec (F E Woolley 115*, C A G Russell 96, F T Mann 59, A Sandham 58)
South Africa 295 (T A Ward 64, A W Nourse 51, L E Tapscott 50*) and 247–4 (H W Taylor 101, A W Nourse 63)
5 DURBAN England won by 109 runs
England 281 (C A G Russell 140, C P Mead 66) and 241 (C A G Russell 111)
South Africa 179 and 234 (H W Taylor 102, A S Kennedy 5–76)

1924 11th Series Eng 3, SA 0, Drawn 2
1 EDGBASTON England won by an innings and 18 runs
England 438 (J B Hobbs 76, E H Hendren 74, H Sutcliffe 64, F E Woolley 64, R Kilner 59, G M Parker 6–152)
South Africa 30 (A E R Gilligan 6–7, M W Tate 4–12) and 390 (R H Catterall 120, J M Blanckenberg 56, M J Susskind 51, A E R Gilligan 5–83, M W Tate 4–103)
2 LORDS England won by an innings and 18 runs
South Africa 273 (R H Catterall 120, M J Susskind 64) and 240 (M J Susskind 53)
England 531–2 dec (J B Hobbs 211, F E Woolley 134*, H Sutcliffe 122, E H Hendren 50*)
3 HEADINGLEY England won by 9 wkts
England 396 (E H Hendren 132, H Sutcliffe 83, S J Pegler 4–116) and 60–1

South Africa 132 (H W Taylor 59*, M W Tate 6–42) and 323 (H W Taylor 56, R H Catterall 56)
4 OLD TRAFFORD Match Drawn
South Africa 116–4 (T A Ward 50)
England did not bat
5 THE OVAL Match Drawn
South Africa 342 (R H Catterall 95, M J Susskind 65)
England 421–8 (E H Hendren 142, F E Woolley 51, M W Tate)

1927–28 12th Series Eng 2, SA 2, Drawn 1
1 JOHANNESBURG England won by 10 wkts
South Africa 196 (R H Catterall 86, G Geary 7–70) and 170 (C L Vincent 53, W R Hammond 5–36, G Geary 5–60)
England 313 (G E Tyldesley 122, H Sutcliffe 102, W R Hammond 51, H L E Promnitz 5–58) and 57–0
2 CAPE TOWN England won by 87 runs
England 133 (G F Bissett 5–37, C L Vincent 4–22) and 428 (H Sutcliffe 99, R E S Wyatt 91, P Holmes 88, G E Tyldesley 87)
South Africa 250 (H W Taylor 68, A P Freeman 4–58) and 224 (H W Taylor 71)
3 DURBAN Match Drawn
South Africa 246 (H G Deane 77, E P Nupen 51) and 464–8 dec (J F W Nicolson 78, R H Catterall 76, H G Deane 73, E P Nupen 69, H W Taylor 60)
England 430 (W R Hammond 90, G E Tyldesley 78, G T S Stevens 69, C L Vincent 6–131, E P Nupen 4–94) and 132–2 (G E Tyldesley 62*, P Holmes 56)
4 JOHANNESBURG South Africa won by 4 wkts
England 265 (R E S Wyatt 58, A E Hall 6–100, G F Bissett 4–43) and 215 (P Holmes 63, G F Bissett 4–70)
South Africa 328 (H W Taylor 101, H B Cameron 64) and 156–6
5 DURBAN South Africa won by 8 wkts
England 282 (G E Tyldesley 100, W R Hammond 66, H Sutcliffe 51, E P Nupen 5–83) and 118 (G F Bissett 7–29)
South Africa 332–7 dec (R H Catterall 119, H B Cameron 53) and 69–2

1929 13th Series Eng 2, SA 0, Drawn 3
1 EDGBASTON Match Drawn
England 245 (E H Hendren 70, A L Ochse 4–79) and 308–4 dec (W R Hammond 138*, H Sutcliffe 114)
South Africa 250 (B Mitchell 88, R H Catterall 67, H Larwood 5–57) and 171–1 (R H Catterall 98, B Mitchell 61*)
2 LORD'S Match Drawn
England 302 (H Sutcliffe 100, M Leyland 73, A J Bell 6–99, D P B Morkel 4–93) and 312–8 dec (M Leyland 102, M W Tate 100*, A L Ochse 4–99)
South Africa 322 (D P B Morkel 88, J A J Christy 70, H G Owen-Smith 52*) and 90–5
3 HEADINGLEY England won by 5 wkts
South Africa 236 (R H Catterall 74, C L Vincent 60, A P Freeman 7–115) and 275 (H G Owen-Smith 129)
England 328 (F E Woolley 83, W R Hammond 65, N A Quinn 6–92) and 186–5 (F E Woolley 95*)
4 OLD TRAFFORD England won by an innings and 32 runs
England 427–7 dec (F E Woolley 154, R E S Wyatt 113, M Leyland 55)
South Africa 130 (D P B Morkel 63, A P Freeman 7–71) and 265 (H B Cameron 83, H W Taylor 70, A P Freeman 5–100)
5 THE OVAL Match Drawn
England 258 (H Sutcliffe 104, C L Vincent 5–105) and 264–1 (H Sutcliffe 109*, W R Hammond 101*, J B Hobbs 52)
South Africa 492–8 dec (H W Taylor 121, H G Deane 93, D P B Morkel 81, H B Cameron 62, Q McMillan 50*)

1930–31 14th Series SA 1, Eng 0, Drawn 4
1 JOHANNESBURG South Africa won by 28 runs
South Africa 126 (I A R Peebles 4–43, W Voce 4–45) and 306 (B Mitchell 72, R H Catterall 54, H B Cameron 51, W Voce 4–59, W R Hammond 4–63)
England 193 (E P Nupen 5–63) and 211 (W R Hammond 63, M J L Turnbull 61, E P Nupen 6–87)
2 CAPE TOWN Match Drawn
South Africa 513–8 dec (I J Siedle 141, B Mitchell 123, H W Taylor 117, R H Catterall 56)
England 350 (E H Hendren 93, W R Hammond 57, M Leyland 52) and 252 (E H Hendren 86, W R Hammond 65)
3 DURBAN Match Drawn
South Africa 177 (W Voce 5–58) and 145–8 (H W Taylor 64*)
England 223–1 dec (W R Hammond 136*, R E S Wyatt 54)
4 JOHANNESBURG Match Drawn
England 442 (M Leyland 91, W R Hammond 75, E H Hendren 64, A E Hall 4–105) and 169–9 dec (E P Nupen 6–46)
South Africa 295 (H W Taylor 72, B Mitchell 68, I J Siedle 62, I A R Peebles 6–63) and 280–7 (B Mitchell 74, H B Cameron 69*, W Voce 4–87)
5 DURBAN Match Drawn
South Africa 252 (B Mitchell 73, I J Siedle 57, I A R Peebles 4–67) and 219–7 dec
England 230 (M W Tate 50, C L Vincent 6–51) and 72–4

1935 15th Series SA 1, Eng 0, Drawn 4
1 TRENT BRIDGE Match Drawn
England 384–7 dec (R E S Wyatt 149, M Leyland 69, H Sutcliffe 61)
South Africa 220 (I J Siedle 59, H B Cameron 52, M S Nichols 6–35) and 17–1
2 LORD'S South Africa won by 157 runs
South Africa 228 (H B Cameron 90) and 278–7 dec (B Mitchell 164*)
England 198 (R E S Wyatt 53, X C Balaskas 5–49) and 151 (A B C Langton 4–31, X C Balaskas 4–54)
3 HEADINGLEY Match Drawn
England 216 (W R Hammond 63, A Mitchell 58, C L Vincent 4–45, A B C Langton 4–59) and 294–7 dec (W R Hammond 87*, A Mitchell 72, D Smith 57, C L Vincent 4–104)
South Africa 171 (E A B Rowan 62) and 194–5 (B Mitchell 58)
4 OLD TRAFFORD Match Drawn
England 357 (R W V Robins 108, A H Bakewell 63, M Leyland 53, R J Crisp 5–99) and 231–6 dec (W R Hammond 63*, A H Bakewell 54, C L Vincent 4–78)
South Africa 318 (K G Viljoen 124, H B Cameron 53, W E Bowes 5–100) and 169–2 (A D Nourse 53*)
5 THE OVAL Match drawn
South Africa 476 (B Mitchell 128, E L Dalton 117, A B C Langton 73*, K G Viljoen 60, H D Read 4–136) and 287–6 (E L Dalton 57*)
England 534–6 dec (M Leyland 161, L E G Ames 148*, W R Hammond 65)

1938–39 16th Series Eng 1, SA 0, Drawn 4
1 JOHANNESBURG Match Drawn
England 422 (E Paynter 117, B H Valentine 97, P A Gibb 93, N Gordon 5–103) and 291–4 dec (P A Gibb 106, E Paynter 100, W R Hammond 58)
South Africa 390 (E L Dalton 102, B Mitchell 73, A D Nourse 73, A B C Langton 64*, K G Viljoen 50, H Verity 4–61) and 108–1
2 CAPE TOWN Match Drawn
England 449–9 dec (W R Hammond 181, L E G Ames 115, B H Valentine 112, P A Gibb 58, N Gordon 5–157)
South Africa 286 (A D Nourse 120, H Verity 5–70) and 201–2 (E A B Rowan 89*, P G V van der Bijl 87)
3 DURBAN England won by an innings and 13 runs
England 469–4 dec (E Paynter 243, W R Hammond 120)
South Africa 103 (K Farnes 4–29) and 353 (B Mitchell 109, E A B Rowan 67, K G Viljoen 61)
4 JOHANNESBURG Match Drawn
England 215 (L Hutton 92, A B C Langton 5–58) and 203–4 (W R Hammond 61*)
South Africa 349–8 dec (E A B Rowan 85, A Melville 67, B Mitchell 63)
5 DURBAN Match Drawn
South Africa 530 (P G V van der Byl 125, A D Nourse 103, A Melville 78, R E Grieveson 75, E L Dalton 57, R T D Perks 5–100) and 481 (A Melville 103, P G V van der Bijl 97, B Mitchell 89, K G Viljoen 74, K Farnes 4–74)
England 316 (L E G Ames 84, E Paynter 62, E L Dalton 4–59) and 654–5 (W J Edrich 219, W R Hammond 140, P A Gibb 120, E Paynter 75, L Hutton 55)

1947 17th Series Eng 3, SA 0, Drawn 2
1 TRENT BRIDGE Match Drawn
South Africa 533 (A Melville 189, A D Nourse 149, T A Harris 60, W E Hollies 5–123) and 166–1 (A Melville 104*, K G Viljoen 51*)
England 208 (D C S Compton 65, W J Edrich 57, L Tuckett 5–68) and 551 (D C S Compton 163, N W D Yardley 99, T G Evans 74, C Washbrook 59, W J Edrich 50, V I Smith 4–143)
2 LORD'S England won by 10 wkts
England 554–8 dec (D C S Compton 208, W J Edrich 189, C Washbrook 65, L Tuckett 5–115) and 26–0
South Africa 327 (A Melville 117, A D Nourse 61, D V P Wright 5–95) and 252 (B Mitchell 80, A D Nourse 58, D V P Wright 5–80)
3 OLD TRAFFORD England won by 7 wkts
South Africa 339 (K G Viljoen 93, B Mitchell 80, D V Dyer 62, W J Edrich 4–95) and 267 (A D Nourse 115, A Melville 59, W J Edrich 4–77)
England 478 (W J Edrich 191, D C S Compton 115, L Tuckett 4–108) and 130–3
4 HEADINGLEY England won by 10 wkts
South Africa 175 (B Mitchell 53, A D Nourse 51, H J Butler 4–34) and 184 (A D Nourse 57, K Cranston 4–12)
England 317–7 dec (L Hutton 100, C Washbrook 75, N B F Mann 4–68) and 47–0
5 THE OVAL Match Drawn
England 427 (L Hutton 83, N W D Yardley 59, D C S Compton 53, C Gladwin 51*, N B F Mann 4–93) and 325 (D C S Compton 113)
South Africa 302 (B Mitchell 120, O C Dawson 55) and 423–7 (B Mitchell 189*, A D Nourse 97)

1948–49 18th Series Eng 2, SA 0, Drawn 3
1 DURBAN England won by 2 wkts
South Africa 161 (A V Bedser 4–39) and 219 (W W Wade 63, D V P Wright 4–72)
England 253 (L Hutton 83, D C S Compton 72, N B F Mann 6–59, A M B Rowan 4–108) and 128–8 (C N McCarthy 6–43)
2 JOHANNESBURG Match Drawn
England 608 (C Washbrook 195, L Hutton 158, D C S Compton 114, J F Crapp 56)
South Africa 315 (B Mitchell 86, W W Wade 85) and 270–2 (E A B Rowan 156*, A D Nourse 56*)
3 CAPE TOWN Match Drawn
England 308 (C Washbrook 74, A M B Rowan 5–80) and 276–3 dec (L Hutton 87, A J Watkins 64*, J F Crapp 54, D C S Compton 51*)
South Africa 356 (B Mitchell 120, A D Nourse 112, O E Wynne 50, D C S Compton 5–70) and 142–4 (R O Jenkins 4–48)
4 JOHANNESBURG Match Drawn
England 379 (A J Watkins 111, C Washbrook 97, J F Crapp 51, C N McCarthy 5–114) and 253–7 dec (L Hutton 123, A M B Rowan 4–69)
South Africa 257–9 dec (A D Nourse 129*, W W Wade 54) and 194–4 (E A B Rowan 86*, K G Viljoen 63)
5 PORT ELIZABETH England won by 3 wkts
South Africa 379 (W W Wade 125, B Mitchell 99, A D Nourse 73, A V Bedser 4–61) and 187–3 dec (B Mitchell 56)
England 395 (F G Mann 136*, A M B Rowan 5–167) and 174–7 (N B F Mann 4–65)

1951 19th Series Eng 3, SA 1, Drawn 1
1 TRENT BRIDGE South Africa won by 71 runs
South Africa 483–9 dec (A D Nourse 208, J H B Waite 76, G M Fullerton 54) and 121 (A V Bedser 6–37)
England 419–9 dec (R T Simpson 137, D C S Compton 112, L Hutton 63, W Watson 58, C N McCarthy 4–104, G W A Chubb 4–146) and 114 (A M B Rowan 5–68, N B F Mann 4–24)
2 LORD'S England won by 10 wkts
England 311 (D C S Compton 79, W Watson 79, J T Ikin 51, G W A Chubb 5–77, C N McCarthy 4–76) and 16–0
South Africa 115 (R Tattersall 7–52) and 211 (G M Fullerton 60, J E Cheetham 54, R Tattersall 5–49)
3 OLD TRAFFORD England won by 9 wkts
South Africa 158 (A V Bedser 7–58) and 191 (E A B Rowan 57, A V Bedser 5–54)
England 211 (G W A Chubb 6–51) and 142–1 (L Hutton 98*)
4 HEADINGLEY Match Drawn
South Africa 538 (E A B Rowan 236, P N F Mansell 90, C B van Ryneveld 83, R A McLean 67) and 87–0 (E A B Rowan 60*)
England 505 (P B H May 138, L Hutton 100, T E Bailey 95, F A Lowson 58, A M B Rowan 5–174)
5 THE OVAL England won by 4 wkts
South Africa 202 (E A B Rowan 55, J C Laker 4–64) and 154 (J C Laker 6–55)
England 194 (D C S Compton 73, M G Melle 4–9) and 164–6

1955 20th Series Eng 3, SA 2
1 TRENT BRIDGE England won by an innings and 5 runs
England 334 (D Kenyon 87, P B H May 83)
South Africa 181 (D J McGlew 68, J E Cheetham 54, J H Wardle 4–24) and 148 (D J McGlew 51, F H Tyson 6–28)
2 LORD'S England won by 71 runs
England 133 (P S Heine 5–60, T L Goddard 4–59) and 353 (P B H May 112, D C S Compton 69, T W Graveney 60, H J Tayfield 5–80)
South Africa 304 (R A McLean 142, H J Keith 57, J H Wardle 4–65) and 111 (J B Statham 7–39)
3 OLD TRAFFORD South Africa won by 3 wkts
England 284 (D C S Compton 158) and 381 (P B H May 117, D C S Compton 71, M C Cowdrey 50, P S Heine 5–86)
South Africa 521–8 dec (J H B Waite 113, P L Winslow 108, D J McGlew 104*, T L Goddard 62) and 145–7 (R A McLean 50)
4 HEADINGLEY South Africa won by 224 runs
South Africa 171 (P J Loader 4–52) and 500 (D J McGlew 133, W R Endean 116*, T L Goddard 74, H J Keith 73, J H Wardle 4–100)
England 191 (D C S Compton 61, P S Heine 4–70, H J Tayfield 4–70) and 256 (P B H May 97, T L Goddard 5–69, H J Tayfield 5–94)
5 THE OVAL England won by 92 runs
England 151 (T L Goddard 5–31) and 204 (P B H May 89*, H J Tayfield 5–60)
South Africa 112 (G A R Lock 4–39) and 151 (J H B Waite 60, J C Laker 5–56, G A R Lock 4–62)

1956–57 21st Series Eng 2, SA 2, Drawn 1
1 JOHANNESBURG England won by 131 runs
England 268 (P E Richardson 117, M C Cowdrey 59, N A T Adcock 4–36) and 150
South Africa 215 and 72 (T E Bailey 5–20)
2 CAPE TOWN England won by 312 runs
England 369 (M C Cowdrey 101, T G Evans 62, D C S Compton 58, H J Tayfield 5–130) and 220–6 dec (D C S Compton 64, M C Cowdrey 61)
South Africa 205 (J H Wardle 5–53) and 72 (J H Wardle 7–36)
3 DURBAN Match Drawn
England 218 (T E Bailey 80, P E Richardson 68, N A T Adcock 4–39) and 254 (D J Insole 110*, H J Tayfield 8–69)
South Africa 283 (R A McLean 100, T L Goddard 69, J H Wardle 5–61) and 142–6
4 JOHANNESBURG South Africa won by 17 runs
South Africa 340 (R A McLean 93, T L Goddard 67, J H B Waite 61) and 142
England 251 (P B H May 61, H J Tayfield 4–79) and 214 (D J Insole 68, M C Cowdrey 55, H J Tayfield 9–113)
5 PORT ELIZABETH South Africa won by 58 runs
South Africa 164 (W R Endean 70) and 134 (F H Tyson 6–40)
England 110 (P S Heine 4–22, N A T Adcock 4–20) and 130 (H J Tayfield 6–78)

1960 22nd Series Eng 3, SA 0, Drawn 2
1 EDGBASTON England won by 100 runs
England 292 (R Subba Row 56, M J K Smith 54, E R Dexter 52, N A T Adcock 5–62) and 203 (H J Tayfield 4–62)
South Africa 186 (J H B Waite 58, F S Trueman 4–58) and 209 (R A McLean 68, J H B Waite 56*)
2 LORD'S England won by an innings and 73 runs
England 362–8 dec (M J K Smith 99, R Subba Row 90, E R Dexter 56, P M Walker 52, G M Griffin 4–87)
South Africa 152 (J B Statham 6–63, A E Moss 4–35) and 137 (J B Statham 5–34)
3 TRENT BRIDGE England won by 8 wkts
England 287 (K F Barrington 80, M C Cowdrey 67, T L Goddard 5–80) and 49–2
South Africa 88 (F S Trueman 5–27) and 247 (S O'Linn 98, J H B Waite 60, F S Trueman 4–77)

4 OLD TRAFFORD Match Drawn
England 260 (K F Barrington 76, N A T Adcock 4–66) and 153–7 dec
South Africa 229 (R A McLean 109, D A Allen 4–58) and 46–0
5 THE OVAL Match Drawn
England 155 (G Pullar 59, N A T Adcock 6–65, J E Pothecary 4–58) and 479–9 dec (G Pullar 175, M C Cowdrey 155)
South Africa 419 (T L Goddard 99, J H B Waite 77, S O'Linn 55) and 97–4

1964–65 23rd Series Eng 1, SA 0, Drawn 4
1 DURBAN England won by an innings and 104 runs
England 485–5 dec (K F Barrington 148*, J M Parks 108*, R W Barber 74, G Boycott 73)
South Africa 155 (D A Allen 5–41) and 226 (K C Bland 68, F J Titmus 5–66)
2 JOHANNESBURG Match Drawn
England 531 (E R Dexter 172, K F Barrington 121, R W Barber 97, P H Parfitt 52, P M Pollock 5–129)
South Africa 317 (A J Pithey 85, E J Barlow 71, F J Titmus 4–73) and 336–6 (K C Bland 144*, R G Pollock 55, T L Goddard 50, D A Allen 4–87)
3 CAPE TOWN Match Drawn
South Africa 501–7 dec (A J Pithey 154, E J Barlow 138, K C Bland 78) and 346 (E J Barlow 78, R G Pollock 73, K C Bland 64, D T Lindsay 50)
England 442 (M J K Smith 121, E R Dexter 61, R W Barber 58, J M Parks 59, H D Bromfield 5–88) and 15–0
4 JOHANNESBURG Match Drawn
South Africa 390–6 dec (E J Barlow 96, A J Pithey 95, J H B Waite 64, T L Goddard 60, K C Bland 55) and 307–3 dec (T L Goddard 112, R G Pollock 65*)
England 384 (P H Parfitt 122*, K F Barrington 93, R W Barber 61, A H McKinnon 4–128) and 153–6 (G Boycott 76*)
5 PORT ELIZABETH Match Drawn
South Africa 502 (R G Pollock 137, E J Barlow 69, P L van der Merwe 66, T L Goddard 61) and 178–4 dec (R G Pollock 77*)
England 435 (G Boycott 117, K F Barrington 72) and 29–1

1965 24th Series SA 1, Eng 0, Drawn 2
1 LORD'S Match Drawn
South Africa 280 (R G Pollock 56) and 248 (K C Bland 70, E J Barlow 52)
England 338 (K F Barrington 91, R W Barber 56, F J Titmus 59) and 145–7 (R Dumbrill 4–30)
2 TRENT BRIDGE South Africa won by 94 runs
South Africa 269 (R G Pollock 125, T W Cartwright 6–94) and 289 (E J Barlow 76, A Bacher 67, R G Pollock 59, J D F Larter 5–68)
England 240 (M C Cowdrey 105, P M Pollock 5–53) and 224 (P H Parfitt 86, P M Pollock 5–34)
3 THE OVAL Match Drawn
South Africa 208 (H R Lance 69, J B Statham 5–40, K Higgs 4–47) and 392 (K C Bland 127, A Bacher 70, H R Lance 53, K Higgs 4–96)
England 202 (M C Cowdrey 58, P M Pollock 5–43) and 308–4 (M C Cowdrey 78*, K F Barrington 73, W E Russell 70)

1970 25th Series
Five Tests were arranged – at Lord's, Trent Bridge, Edgbaston, Headingley and The Oval – but the visit was cancelled at the request of the British Government

3 England *v* West Indies

1928 1st Series Eng 3, WI 0
1 LORD'S England won by an innings and 58 runs
England 401 (G E Tyldesley 122, A P F Chapman 50, L N Constantine 4–82)
West Indies 177 (V W C Jupp 4–37) and 166 (J A Small 52, A P Freeman 4–37)
2 OLD TRAFFORD England won by an innings and 30 runs
West Indies 206 (C A Roach 50, A P Freeman 5–54) and 115 (A P Freeman 5–39)
England 351 (D R Jardine 83, W R Hammond 63, H Sutcliffe 54, J B Hobbs 53)
3 THE OVAL England won by an innings and 71 runs
West Indies 238 (C A Roach 53, M W Tate 4–59) and 129 (A P Freeman 4–47)
England 438 (J B Hobbs 159, G E Tyldesley 73, H Sutcliffe 63, M W Tate 54, H C Griffith 6–103, G N Francis 4–112)

1929–30 2nd Series Eng 1, WI 1, Drawn 2
1 BRIDGETOWN Match Drawn
West Indies 369 (C A Roach 122, F I de Caires 80, J E D Sealey 58, G T S Stevens 5–105) and 384 (G A Headley 176, C A Roach 77, F I de Caires 70, G T S Stevens 5–90)
England 467 (A Sandham 152, E H Hendren 80) and 167–3 (A Sandham 51)
2 PORT OF SPAIN England won by 167 runs
England 208 (E H Hendren 77, H C Griffith 5–63) and 425–8 dec (E H Hendren 205*, L E G Ames 105, L N Constantine 4–165)
West Indies 254 (E A C Hunte 58, L N Constantine 52, W E Astill 4–58, W Voce 4–79) and 212 (W Voce 7–70)
3 GEORGETOWN West Indies won by 289 runs
West Indies 471 (C A Roach 209, G A Headley 114, E A C Hunte 53) and 290 (G A Headley 112, C R Browne 70*, W E Astill 4–70)
England 145 (E H Hendren 56, L N Constantine 4–35, G N Francis 4–40) and 327 (E H Hendren 123, L N Constantine 5–87)
4 KINGSTON Match Drawn
England 849 (A Sandham 325, L E G Ames 149, G Gunn 85, E H Hendren 61, R E S Wyatt 58, J O'Connor 51, O C Scott 5–266) and 272–9 dec (E H Hendren 55, A Sandham 50, O C Scott 4–108)
West Indies 286 (R K Nunes 66) and 408–5 (G A Headley 223, R K Nunes 92)

1933 3rd Series Eng 2, WI 0, Drawn 1
1 LORD'S England won by an innings and 27 runs
England 296 (L E G Ames 83*, C F Walters 51, E A Martindale 4–85)
West Indies 97 (R W V Robins 6–32) and 172 (G A Headley 50, H Verity 4–45, G G Macaulay 4–57)
2 OLD TRAFFORD Match Drawn
West Indies 375 (G A Headley 169*, I Barrow 105, E W Clark 4–99) and 225 (C A Roach 64, L N Constantine 64, Jas Langridge 7–56)
England 374 (D R Jardine 127, R W V Robins 55, E A Martindale 5–73)
3 THE OVAL England won by an innings and 17 runs
England 312 (A H Bakewell 107, C J Barnett 52, E A Martindale 5–93)
West Indies 100 (C S Marriott 5–37) and 195 (C A Roach 56, C S Marriott 6–59)

1934–35 4th Series WI 2, Eng 1, Drawn 1
1 BRIDGETOWN England won by 4 wkts
West Indies 102 (K Farnes 4–40) and 51–6 dec (C I J Smith 5–16)
England 81–7 dec and 75–6 (E A Martindale 5–22)
1 PORT OF SPAIN West Indies won by 217 runs
West Indies 302 (J E D Sealey 92, L N Constantine 90, C I J Smith 4–100) and 280–6 dec (G A Headley 93)
England 258 (E R T Holmes 85*, J Iddon 73) and 107
3 GEORGETOWN Match Drawn
England 226 (L G Hylton 4–27) and 160–6 dec (R E S Wyatt 71)
West Indies 184 (G A Headley 53, K L Wishart 52, W E Hollies 7–50) and 104–5
4 KINGSTON West Indies won by an innings and 161 runs
West Indies 535–7 dec (G A Headley 270*, J E D Sealey 91, R S Grant 77, G A E Paine 5–168)
England 271 (L E G Ames 126, J Iddon 54) and 103 (E A Martindale 4–28)

1939 5th Series Eng 1, WI 0, Drawn 2
1 LORD'S England won by 8 wkts
West Indies 277 (G A Headley 106, J B Stollmeyer 59, W H Copson 5–85) and 225 (G A Headley 107, W H Copson 4–67)
England 404–5 dec (L Hutton 196, D C S Compton 120) and 100–2
2 OLD TRAFFORD Match Drawn
England 164–7 dec (J Hardstaff jun 76) and 128–6 dec (L N Constantine 4–42)
West Indies 133 (G A Headley 51, W E Bowes 6–33) and 43–4
3 THE OVAL Match Drawn
England 352 (J Hardstaff jun 94, N Oldfield 80, L Hutton 73, L N Constantine 5–75) and 366–3 (L Hutton 165*, W R Hammond 138)
West Indies 498 (K H Weekes 137, V H Stollmeyer 96, L N Constantine 79, G A Headley 65, J B Stollmeyer 59, R T D Perks 5–156)

1947–48 6th Series WI 2, Eng 0, Drawn 2
1 BRIDGETOWN Match Drawn
West Indies 296 (G E Gomez 86, J B Stollmeyer 78, J C Laker 7–103) and 351–9 dec (R J Christiani 99, E A V Williams 72, W Ferguson 56*, R Howorth 6–124)
England 253 (J Hardstaff jun 98, J D B Robertson 80, P E Jones 4–54) and 86–4 (J D B Robertson 51*)
2 PORT OF SPAIN Match Drawn
England 362 (S C Griffith 140, J C Laker 55, W Ferguson 5–137) and 275 (J D B Robertson 133, W Ferguson 6–92)
West Indies 497 (A G Ganteaume 112, G M Carew 107, F M M Worrell 97, G E Gomez 62) and 72–3
3 GEORGETOWN West Indies won by 7 wkts
West Indies 297–8 dec (F M M Worrell 131*, R J Christiani 51, K Cranston 4–78) and 78–3
England 111 (J D C Goddard 5–31) and 263 (J Hardstaff jun 63, W Ferguson 5–116)
4 KINGSTON West Indies won by 10 wkts
England 227 (J D B Robertson 64, L Hutton 56, H H H Johnson 5–41) and 336 (W Place 107, J Hardstaff jun 64, L Hutton 60, H H H Johnson 5–55)
West Indies 490 (E de C Weekes 141, W Ferguson 75, K R Rickards 67) and 76–0

1950 7th Series WI 3, Eng 1
1 OLD TRAFFORD England won by 202 runs
England 312 (T G Evans 104, T E Bailey 82*, A L Valentine 8–104) and 288 (W J Edrich 71)
West Indies 215 (E de C Weekes 52, R Berry 5–63) and 183 (J B Stollmeyer 78, W E Hollies 5–63, R Berry 4–53)
2 LORD'S West Indies won by 326 runs
West Indies 326 (A F Rae 106, E de C Weekes 63, F M M Worrell 52, R O Jenkins 5–116) and 425–6 dec (C L Walcott 168*, G E Gomez 70, E de C Weekes 63, R O Jenkins 4–174)
England 151 (S Ramadhin 5–66, A L Valentine 4–48) and 274 (C Washbrook 114, S Ramadhin 6–86)
3 TRENT BRIDGE West Indies won by 10 wkts
England 223 and 436 (C Washbrook 102, R T Simpson 94, W G A Parkhouse 69, J G Dewes 67, T G Evans 63, S Ramadhin 5–135)
West Indies 558 (F M M Worrell 261, E de C Weekes 129, A F Rae 68, A V Bedser 5–127) and 103–0 (J B Stollmeyer 52*)
4 THE OVAL West Indies won by an innings and 56 runs
West Indies 503 (F M M Worrell 138, A F Rae 109, G E Gomez 74, J D C Goddard 58*, D V P Wright 5–141)
England 344 (L Hutton 202*, J D C Goddard 4–25, A L Valentine 4–121) and 103 (A L Valentine 6–39)

1953–54 8th Series WI 2, Eng 2, Drawn 1
1 KINGSTON West Indies won by 140 runs
West Indies 417 (J K Holt 94, C L Walcott 65, J B Stollmeyer 60, E de C Weekes 55, C A McWatt 54, J B Statham 4–90) and 209–6 dec (E de C Weekes 90*)
England 170 (S Ramadhin 4–65) and 316 (W Watson 116, P B H May 69, L Hutton 56, E S M Kentish 5–49)
2 BRIDGETOWN West Indies won by 181 runs
West Indies 383 (C L Walcott 220, B H Pairaudeau 71, D St E Atkinson 53, J C Laker 4–81) and 292–2 dec (J K Holt 166, F M M Worrell 76*)
England 181 (L Hutton 72, S Ramadhin 4–50) and 313 (D C S Compton 93, L Hutton 70, T W Graveney 64*, P B H May 62)
3 GEORGETOWN England won by 9 wkts
England 435 (L Hutton 169, D C S Compton 64, S Ramadhin 6–113) and 75–1
West Indies 251 (E de C Weekes 94, C A McWatt 54, J B Statham 4–64) and 256 (J K Holt 64)
4 PORT OF SPAIN Match Drawn
West Indies 681–8 dec (E de C Weekes 206, F M M Worrell 167, C L Walcott 124, D St E Atkinson 74) and 212–4 dec (F M M Worrell 56, D St E Atkinson 53*, C L Walcott 51*)
England 537 (P B H May 135, D C S Compton 133, T W Graveney 92) and 98–3
5 KINGSTON England won by 9 wkts
West Indies 139 (C L Walcott 50, T E Bailey 7–34) and 346 (C L Walcott 116, J B Stollmeyer 64, J C Laker 4–71)
England 414 (L Hutton 205, J H Wardle 66, G St A Sobers 4–75) and 72–1

1957 9th Series Eng 3, WI 0, Drawn 2
1 EDGBASTON Match Drawn
England 186 (S Ramadhin 7–49) and 583–4 dec (P B H May 285*, M C Cowdrey 154)
West Indies 474 (O G Smith 161, C L Walcott 90, F M M Worrell 81, G St A Sobers 53, J C Laker 4–119) and 72–7
2 LORD'S England won by an innings and 36 runs
West Indies 127 (T E Bailey 7–44) and 261 (E de C Weekes 90, G St A Sobers 66, T E Bailey 4–54)
England 424 (M C Cowdrey 152, T G Evans 82, P E Richardson 76, R Gilchrist 4–115)
3 TRENT BRIDGE Match Drawn
England 619–6 dec (T W Graveney 258, P E Richardson 126, P B H May 104, M C Cowdrey 55) and 64–1
West Indies 372 (F M M Worrell 191*, F S Trueman 5–63) and 367 (O G Smith 168, J D C Goddard 61, J B Statham 5–118, F S Trueman 4–80)
4 HEADINGLEY England won by an innings and 5 runs
West Indies 142 (P J Loader 6–36) and 132
England 279 (P B H May 69, M C Cowdrey 68, D S Sheppard 68, F M M Worrell 7–70)
5 THE OVAL England won by an innings and 237 runs
England 412 (T W Graveney 164, P E Richardson 107, S Ramadhin 4–107)
West Indies 89 (G A R Lock 5–28) and 86 (G A R Lock 6–20)

1959–60 10th Series Eng 1, WI 0, Drawn 4
1 BRIDGETOWN Match Drawn
England 482 (E R Dexter 136*, K F Barrington 128, G Pullar 65) and 71–0
West Indies 563–8 dec (G St A Sobers 226, F M M Worrell 197*, F S Trueman 4–93)
2 PORT OF SPAIN England won by 256 runs
England 382 (K F Barrington 121, M J K Smith 108, E R Dexter 77) and 230–9 dec
West Indies 112 (F S Trueman 5–35) and 244 (R B Kanhai 110)
3 KINGSTON Match Drawn
England 277 (M C Cowdrey 114, W W Hall 7–69) and 305 (M C Cowdrey 97, G Pullar 66, C D Watson 4–62)
West Indies 353 (G St A Sobers 147, E D A St J McMorris 73, S M Nurse 70) and 175–6 (R B Kanhai 57, F S Trueman 4–54)
4 GEORGETOWN Match Drawn
England 295 (M C Cowdrey 65, D A Allen 55, W W Hall 6–90) and 334–8 (E R Dexter 119, R Subba Row 100, F M M Worrell 4–49)
West Indies 402–8 dec (G St A Sobers 145, R B Kanhai 55)
5 PORT OF SPAIN Match Drawn
England 393 (M C Cowdrey 119, E R Dexter 76, K F Barrington 69, S Ramadhin 4–73) and 350–7 dec (J M Parks 101*, M J K Smith 96, G Pullar 54)
West Indies 338–8 dec (G St A Sobers 92, C C Hunte 72*, C L Walcott 53) and 209–5 (F M M Worrell 61)

1963 11th Series WI 3, Eng 1, Drawn 1
1 OLD TRAFFORD West Indies won by 10 wkts
West Indies 501–6 dec (C C Hunte 182, R B Kanhai 90, F M M Worrell 74*, G St A Sobers 64) and 1–0
England 205 (E R Dexter 73, L R Gibbs 5–59) and 296 (M J Stewart 87, L R Gibbs 6–98)
2 LORD'S Match Drawn
West Indies 301 (R B Kanhai 73, J S Solomon 56, F S Trueman 6–100) and 229 (B F Butcher 133, F S Trueman 5–52, D Shackleton 4–72)
England 297 (K F Barrington 80, E R Dexter 70, C C Griffith 5–91) and 228–9 (K F Barrington 60, D B Close 70, W W Hall 4–93)

3 EDGBASTON England won by 217 runs
England 216 (D B Close 55, G St A Sobers 5–60) and 278–9 dec (P J Sharpe 85*, E R Dexter 57, G A R Lock 56, L R Gibbs 4–49)
West Indies 186 (F S Trueman 5–75, E R Dexter 4–38) and 91 (F S Trueman 7–44)
4 EADINGLEY West Indies won by 221 runs
West Indies 397 (G St A Sobers 102, R B Kanhai 92, J S Solomon 62, F S Trueman 4–117) and 229 (B F Butcher 78, G St A Sobers 52, F J Titmus 4–44)
England 174 (G A R Lock 53, C C Griffith 6–36) and 231 (J M Parks 57, D B Close 56, L R Gibbs 4–76)
5 THE OVAL West Indies won by 8 wkts
England 275 (P J Sharpe 63, C C Griffith 6–71) and 223 (P J Sharpe 83, W W Hall 4–39)
West Indies 246 (C C Hunte 80, B F Butcher 53) and 255–2 (C C Hunte 108*, R B Kanhai 77)

1966 12th Series WI 3, Eng 1, Drawn 1
1 OLD TRAFFORD West Indies won by an innings and 40 runs
West Indies 484 (G St A Sobers 161, C C Hunte 135, F J Titmus 5–83)
England 167 (L R Gibbs 5–37) and 277 (C Milburn 94, M C Cowdrey 69, L R Gibbs 5–69)
2 LORD'S Match Drawn
West Indies 269 (S M Nurse 64, K Higgs 6–91) and 369–5 dec (G St A Sobers 163*, D A J Holford 105*)
England 355 (T W Graveney 96, J M Parks 91, G Boycott 60, W W Hall 4–106) and 197–4 (C Milburn 126*)
3 TRENT BRIDGE West Indies won by 139 runs
West Indies 235 (S M Nurse 93, K Higgs 4–71, J A Snow 4–82) and 482–5 dec (B F Butcher 209*, G St A Sobers 94, R B Kanhai 63, S M Nurse 53)
England 325 (T W Graveney 109, M C Cowdrey 96, B L d'Oliveira 76, G St A Sobers 4–90, W W Hall 4–105) and 253 (G Boycott 71, B L d'Oliveira 54, C C Griffith 4–34)
4 HEADINGLEY West Indies won by an innings and 55 runs
West Indies 500–9 dec (G St A Sobers 174, S M Nurse 137, K Higgs 4–94)
England 240 (B L d'Oliveira 88, G St A Sobers 5–41) and 205 (R W Barber 55, L R Gibbs 6–39)
5 THE OVAL England won by an innings and 34 runs
West Indies 268 (R B Kanhai 104, G St A Sobers 81) and 225 (S M Nurse 70, B F Butcher 60)
England 527 (T W Graveney 165, J T Murray 112, K Higgs 63, J A Snow 59*)

1967–68 13th Series Eng 1, WI 0, Drawn 4
1 PORT OF SPAIN Match Drawn
England 568 (K F Barrington 143, T W Graveney 118, M C Cowdrey 72, G Boycott 68, C C Griffith 5–69)
West Indies 363 (C H Lloyd 118, R B Kanhai 85) and 243–8 (B F Butcher 52)
2 KINGSTON Match Drawn
England 376 (M C Cowdrey 101, J H Edrich 96, K F Barrington 63, W W Hall 4–63) and 68–8
West Indies 143 (J A Snow 7–49) and 391–9 dec (G St A Sobers 113*, S M Nurse 73)
3 BRIDGETOWN Match Drawn
West Indies 349 (B F Butcher 86, G St A Sobers 68, G S Camacho 57, J A Snow 5–86) and 284–6 (C H Lloyd 113*, B F Butcher 60)
England 449 (J H Edrich 146, G Boycott 90, T W Graveney 55, B L d'Oliveira 51)
4 PORT OF SPAIN England won by 7 wkts
West Indies 526–7 dec (R B Kanhai 153, S M Nurse 136, G S Camacho 87) and 92–2 dec
England 404 (M C Cowdrey 148, A P E Knott 69*, G Boycott 62, B F Butcher 5–34) and 215–3 (G Boycott 80*, M C Cowdrey 71)
5 GEORGETOWN Match Drawn
West Indies 414 (G St A Sobers 152, R B Kanhai 150, J A Snow 4–82) and 264 (G St A Sobers 95*, J A Snow 6–60)
England 371 (G Boycott 116, G A R Lock 89, M C Cowdrey 59) and 206–9 (M C Cowdrey 82, A P E Knott 73*, L R Gibbs 6–60)

1969 14th Series Eng 2, WI 2, Drawn 1
1 OLD TRAFFORD England won by 10 wkts
England 413 (G Boycott 128, T W Graveney 75, J H Edrich 58, B L d'Oliveira 57, J N Shepherd 5–104) and 12–0
West Indies 147 (D J Brown 4–39, J A Snow 4–54) and 275 (R C Fredericks 64)
2 LORD'S Match Drawn
West Indies 380 (C A Davis 103, G S Camacho 67, R C Fredericks 63, J A Snow 5–114) and 295–9 dec (C H Lloyd 70, R C Fredericks 60, G St A Sobers 50*)
England 344 (R Illingworth 113, J H Hampshire 107, A P E Knott 53) and 295–7 (G Boycott 106, P J Sharpe 86)
3 HEADINGLEY England won by 30 runs
England 223 (J H Edrich 79, V A Holder 4–48) and 240 (G St A Sobers 5–42)
West Indies 161 (B R Knight 4–63) and 272 (B F Butcher 91, G S Camacho 71, D L Underwood 4–55)

1973 15th Series Eng 0, WI 2, Drawn 1
1 THE OVAL West Indies won by 158 runs
West Indies 415 (C H Lloyd 132, A I Kallicharran 80, K D Boyce 72, G G Arnold 5–113) and 255 (A I Kallicharran 80, G St A Sobers 51)
England 257 (G Boycott 97, K D Boyce 5–70) and 255 (F C Hayes 106*, K D Boyce 6–77)
2 EDGBASTON Match Drawn
West Indies 327 (R C Fredericks 150, B D Julien 54) and 302 (C H Lloyd 94, G St A Sobers 74, R B Kanhai 54, G G Arnold 4–43)
England 305 (G Boycott 56*, D L Amiss 56, K W R Fletcher 52) and 182–2 (D L Amiss 86*)
3 LORD'S West indies won by an innings and 226 runs
West Indies 652–8 dec (R B Kanhai 157, G St A Sobers 150*, B D Julien 121, C H Lloyd 63, R C Fredericks 51, R G D Willis 4–118)
England 233 (K W R Fletcher 68, K D Boyce 4–50, V A Holder 4–56) and 193 (K W R Fletcher 86*, K D Boyce 4–50)

1973–74 16th Series WI 1, Eng 1, Drawn 3
1 PORT OF SPAIN West Indies won by 7 wkts
England 131 (K D Boyce 4–42) and 392 (D L Amiss 174, G Boycott 93, L R Gibbs 6–108)
West Indies 392 (A I Kallicharran 158, B D Julien 86*, P I Pocock 5–110) and 132–3 (R C Fredericks 65*)
2 KINGSTON Match Drawn
England 353 (G Boycott 68, M H Denness 67) and 432–9 (D L Amiss 262*)
West Indies 583–9 dec (L G Rowe 120, R C Fredericks 94, A I Kallicharran 93, B D Julien 66, G St A Sobers 57)
3 BRIDGETOWN Match Drawn
England 395 (A W Greig 148, A P E Knott 87, B D Julien 5–57) and 277–7 (K W R Fletcher 129*, A P E Knott 67)
West Indies 596–8 dec (L G Rowe 302, A I Kallicharran 119, D L Murray 53*, A W Greig 6–164)
4 GEORGETOWN Match Drawn
England 448 (A W Greig 121, D L Amiss 118, A P E Knott 61)
West Indies 198–4 (R C Fredericks 98)
5 PORT OF SPAIN England won by 26 runs
England 267 (G Boycott 99) and 263 (G Boycott 112)
West Indies 305 (L G Rowe 123, R C Fredericks 67, C H Lloyd 52, A W Greig 8–86) and 199 (A W Greig 5–70)

1976 17th Series WI 3, Eng 0, Drawn 2
1 TRENT BRIDGE Match Drawn
West Indies 494 (I V A Richards 232, A I Kallicharran 97, D L Underwood 4–82) and 176–5 dec (I V A Richards 63, J A Snow 4–53)
England 332 (D S Steele 106, R A Woolmer 82, W W Daniel 4–53) and 156–2 (J H Edrich 76*)
2 LORD'S Match Drawn
England 250 (D B Close 60, A M E Roberts 5–60) and 254 (D S Steele 64, A M E Roberts 5–63)
West Indies 182 (C G Greenidge 84, C H Lloyd 50, J A Snow 4–68, D L Underwood 5–39) and 241–6 (R C Fredericks 138)
3 OLD TRAFFORD West Indies won by 425 runs
West Indies 211 (C G Greenidge 134, M W W Selvey 4–41) and 411–5 dec (I V A Richards 135, C G Greenidge 101, R C Fredericks 50)
England 71 (M A Holding 5–17) and 126 (A M E Roberts 6–37)
4 HEADINGLEY West Indies won by 55 runs
West Indies 450 (C G Greenidge 115, R C Fredericks 109, I V A Richards 66, L G Rowe 50, J A Snow 4–77) and 196 (C L King 58, R G D Willis 5–42)
England 387 (A W Greig 116, A P E Knott 116) and 204 (A W Greig 76*)
5 THE OVAL West Indies won by 231 runs
West Indies 687–8 dec (I V A Richards 291, C H Lloyd 84, R C Fredericks 71, L G Rowe 70, C L King 63) and 182–0 dec (R C Fredericks 86*, C G Greenidge 85*)
England 435 (D L Amiss 203, A P E Knott 50, M A Holding 8–92) and 203 (A P E Knott 57, M A Holding 6–57)

1980 18th Series WI 1, Eng 0, Drawn 4
1 TRENT BRIDGE West Indies won by 2 wkts
England 263 (I T Botham 57, A M E Roberts 5–72) and 252 (G Boycott 75, J Garner 4–30)
West Indies 308 (I V A Richards 64, D L Murray 64, C G Greenidge 53, R G D Willis 4–82) and 209–8 (D L Haynes 62, R G D Willis 5–65)
2 LORD'S Match Drawn
England 269 (G A Gooch 123, M A Holding 6–67, J Garner 4–36) and 133–2
West Indies 518 (D L Haynes 184, I V A Richards 145, C H Lloyd 56)
3 OLD TRAFFORD Match Drawn
England 150 (B C Rose 70) and 391–7 (G Boycott 86, P Willey 62*, M W Gatting 56)
West Indies 260 (C H Lloyd 101, I V A Richards 65)
4 THE OVAL Match Drawn
England 370 (G A Gooch 83, G Boycott 53, B C Rose 50) and 209–9 dec (P Willey 100*, M A Holding 4–79)
West Indies 265 (S F A Bacchus 61, G R Dilley 4–57)
5 HEADINGLEY Match Drawn
England 143 and 227–6 (G A Gooch 55)
West Indies 245 (G R Dilley 4–79)

1980–81 19th Series WI 2, Drawn 2
1 PORT OF SPAIN West Indies won by an innings and 79 runs
West Indies 426–9 dec (D L Haynes 96, C G Greenidge 84, C H Lloyd 64, A M E Roberts 50*, J M Emburey 5–124)
England 178 (C E H Croft 5–40) and 169 (G Boycott 70)
2 BRIDGETOWN West Indies won by 298 runs
West Indies 265 (C H Lloyd 100, H A Gomes 58, I T Botham 4–77) and 379–7 dec (I V A Richards 182*, C H Lloyd 66)
England 122 (C E H Croft 4–39) and 224 (G A Gooch 116, D I Gower 54)
3 ST JOHN'S Match Drawn
England 271 (P Willey 102*, C E H Croft 6–74) and 234–3 (G Boycott 104*, G A Gooch 83)
West Indies 468–9 dec (I V A Richards 114, E H Mattis 71, C G Greenidge 63, C H Lloyd 58, M A Holding 58*, I T Botham 4–127)
4 KINGSTON Match Drawn
England 285 (G A Gooch 153, M A Holding 5–56) and 302–6 (D I Gower 154*, P Willey 67)
West Indies 442 (C H Lloyd 95, H A Gomes 90, D L Haynes 84, C G Greenidge 62, G R Dilley 4–116)
The Test arranged for Georgetown was cancelled for political reasons.

4 England *v* New Zealand

1929–30 1st Series Eng 1, NZ 0, Drawn 3
1 CHRISTCHURCH England won by 8 wkts
New Zealand 112 (M J C Allom 5–38, M S Nichols 4–28) and 131
England 181 and 66–2
2 WELLINGTON Match Drawn
New Zealand 440 (C S Dempster 136, J E Mills 117, M L Page 67, F E Woolley 7–76) and 164–4 dec (C S Dempster 80*)
England 320 (M S Nichols 78*, F T Badcock 4–80) and 107–4 (K S Duleepsinhji 56*)
3 AUCKLAND Match Drawn
England 330–4 dec (K S Duleepsinhji 117, E H Bowley 109, F E Woolley 59)
New Zealand 96–1 (C S Dempster 62*)
4 AUCKLAND Match Drawn
England 540 (G B Legge 196, M S Nichols 75, K S Duleepsinhji 63, E W Dawson 55) and 22–3
New Zealand 387 (T C Lowry 80, G L Weir 63, H M McGirr 51, M J C Allom 4–42)

1931 2nd Series Eng 1, NZ 0, Drawn 2
1 LORD'S Match Drawn
New Zealand 224 (C S Dempster 53, I A R Peebles 5–77) and 469–9 dec (C S Dempster 120, M L Page 104, R C Blunt 96, I A R Peebles 4–150)
England 454 (L E G Ames 137, G O B Allen 122, F E Woolley 80, W E Merritt 4–104) and 146–5
2 THE OVAL England won by an innings and 26 runs
England 416–4 dec (K S Duleepsinhji 109, W R Hammond 100*, H Sutcliffe 117)
New Zealand 193 (T C Lowry 62, G O B Allen 5–14) and 197 (H G Vivian 51, I A R Peebles 4–63)
3 OLD TRAFFORD Match Drawn
England 224–3 (H Sutcliffe 109, K S Duleepsinhji 63)
New Zealand did not bat

1932–33 3rd Series Drawn 2
1 CHRISTCHURCH Match Drawn
England 560–8 dec (W R Hammond 227, L E G Ames 103, F R Brown 74, W Voce 66)
New Zealand 223 (G L Weir 66, J L Kerr 59) and 35–0
2 AUCKLAND Match Drawn
New Zealand 158 (C S Dempster 83*, W E Bowes 6–34) and 16–0
England 548–7 dec (W R Hammond 336*, R E S Wyatt 60)

1937 4th Series Eng 1, NZ 0, Drawn 2
1 LORD'S Match Drawn
England 424 (W R Hammond 140, J Hardstaff jun 114, E Paynter 74, A W Roberts 4–101, J Cowie 4–118) and 226–4 dec (C J Barnett 83*, J Hardstaff 64)
New Zealand 295 (A W Roberts 66*, D A R Moloney 64, W M Wallace 52) and 175–8 (W M Wallace 56)
2 OLD TRAFFORD England won by 130 runs
England 358–9 dec (L Hutton 100, C J Barnett 62, J Hardstaff jun 58, J Cowie 4–73) and 187 (F R Brown 57, J Cowie 6–67)
New Zealand 281 (W A Hadlee 93, H G Vivian 58, A W Wellard 4–81) and 134 (H G Vivian 50, T W J Goddard 6–29)
3 THE OVAL Match Drawn
New Zealand 249 (M P Donnelly 58, M L Page 53, A W Roberts 50, R W V Robins 4–40) and 187 (H G Vivian 57)
England 254–7 dec (J Hardstaff jun 103, D C S Compton 65) and 31–1

1946–47 5th Series Drawn 1
1 CHRISTCHURCH Match Drawn
New Zealand 345–9 dec (W A Hadlee 116, B Sutcliffe 58, A V Bedser 4–95)
England 265–7 dec (W R Hammond 79, J Cowie 6–83)

1949 6th Series Drawn 4
1 HEADINGLEY Match Drawn
England 372 (D C S Compton 114, L Hutton 101, T B Burtt 5–97, J Cowie 5–127) and 267–4 dec (C Washbrook 103*, W J Edrich 70)
New Zealand 341 (F B Smith 96, M P Donnelly 64, T E Bailey 6–118) and 195–2 (B Sutcliffe 82, F B Smith 54*)
2 LORD'S Match Drawn
England 313–9 dec (D C S Compton 116, T E Bailey 93, T B Burtt 4–102) and 306–5 (J D B Robertson 121, L Hutton 66)
New Zealand 484 (M P Donnelly 206, B Sutcliffe 57, W E Hollies 5–133)
3 OLD TRAFFORD Match Drawn
New Zealand 293 (M P Donnelly 75, J R Reid 50, T E Bailey 6–84) and 348–7 (B Sutcliffe 101, M P Donnelly 80)
England 440–9 dec (R T Simpson 103, L Hutton 73, W J Edrich 78, T E Bailey 72*, T B Burtt 6–162)
4 THE OVAL Match Drawn
New Zealand 345 (B Sutcliffe 88, V J Scott 60, W M Wallace 55, A V Bedser 4–74) and 308–9 dec (J R Reid 93, W M Wallace 58, B Sutcliffe 54, J C Laker 4–78)

England 482 (L Hutton 206, W J Edrich 100, R T Simpson 68, G F Cresswell 6–168, J Cowie 4–123)

1950–51 7th Series Eng 1, NZ 0, Drawn 1
1 CHRISTCHURCH Match Drawn
New Zealand 417–8 dec (B Sutcliffe 116, W M Wallace 66, W A Hadlee 50, J R Reid 50) and 46–3
England 550 (T E Bailey 134*, R T Simpson 81, D C S Compton 79, F R Brown 62, C Washbrook 58, A M Moir 6–155)
2 WELLINGTON England won by 6 wkts
New Zealand 125 (D V P Wright 5–48) and 189 (V J Scott 60, R Tattersall 6–44)
England 227 (L Hutton 57) and 91–4

1954–55 8th Series Eng 2, NZ 0
1 DUNEDIN England won by 8 wkts
New Zealand 125 (B Sutcliffe 74, J B Statham 4–24) and 132 (F H Tyson 4–16)
England 209–8 dec (J R Reid 4–36) and 49–2
2 AUCKLAND England won by an innings and 20 runs
New Zealand 200 (J R Reid 73, J B Statham 4–28) and 26 (R Appleyard 4–7)
England 246 (L Hutton 53, A M Moir 5–62)

1958 9th Series Eng 4, NZ 0, Drawn 1
1 EDGBASTON England won by 205 runs
England 221 (P B H May 84, M C Cowdrey 81, A R MacGibbon 5–64, J C Alabaster 4–46) and 215–6 dec (P E Richardson 100, M C Cowdrey 70)
New Zealand 94 (F S Trueman 5–31) and 137
2 LORD'S England won by an innings and 148 runs
England 269 (M C Cowdrey 65, J A Hayes 4–36, A R MacGibbon 4–86)
New Zealand 47 (G A R Lock 5–17, J C Laker 4–13) and 74 (G A R Lock 4–12)
3 HEADINGLEY England won by an innings and 71 runs
New Zealand 67 (J C Laker 5–17, G A R Lock 4–14) and 129 (G A R Lock 7–51)
England 267–2 dec (P B H May 113*, C A Milton 104*)
4 OLD TRAFFORD England won by an innings and 13 runs
New Zealand 267 (A R MacGibbon 66, J T Sparling 50, J B Statham 4–71) and 85 (G A R Lock 7–35)
England 365–9 dec (P B H May 101, P E Richardson 74, W Watson 66, E R Dexter 52)
5 THE OVAL Match Drawn
New Zealand 161 and 91–3 (J R Reid 51*)
England 219–9 dec (A R MacGibbon 4–65)

1958–59 10th Series Eng 1, NZ 0, Drawn 1
1 CHRISTCHURCH England won by an innings and 99 runs
England 374 (E R Dexter 141, P B H May 71)
New Zealand 142 (G A R Lock 5–31) and 133 (J W Guy 56, G A R Lock 6–53)
2 AUCKLAND Match Drawn
New Zealand 181 (B Sutcliffe 61)
England 311–7 (P B H May 124*, P E Richardson 67)

1962–63 11th Series Eng 3, NZ 0
1 AUCKLAND England won by an innings and 215 runs
England 562–7 dec (P H Parfitt 131*, K F Barrington 126, B R Knight 125, M C Cowdrey 86, F J Cameron 4–118)
New Zealand 258 (B W Yuile 64, R C Motz 60, J R Reid 59) and 89 (J D F Larter 4–26, R Illingworth 4–34)
2 WELLINGTON England won by an innings and 47 runs
New Zealand 194 (R W Blair 64, F S Trueman 4–46) and 187 (W R Playle 65, F J Titmus 4–50)
England 428–8 dec (M C Cowdrey 128*, K F Barrington 76, A C Smith 69*)
3 CHRISTCHURCH England won by 7 wkts
New Zealand 266 (J R Reid 74, F S TRueman 7–75) and 159 (J R Reid 100, F J Titmus 4–46)
England 253 and 173–3

1965 12th Series Eng 3, NZ 0
1 EDGBASTON England won by 9 wkts
England 435 (K F Barrington 137, M C Cowdrey 85, E R Dexter 57, R C Motz 5–108) and 96–1 (R W Barber 51)
New Zealand 116 (F J Titmus 4–18) and 413 (V Pollard 81, B Sutcliffe 53, R W Barber 4–132)
2 LORD'S England won by 7 wkts
New Zealand 175 (V Pollard 55, B R Taylor 51, F E Rumsey 4–25) and 347 (B W Sinclair 72, G T Dowling 66, F J Titmus 5–19)
England 307 (M C Cowdrey 119, E R Dexter 62, R O Collinge 4–85) and 218–3 (E R Dexter 80*, G Boycott 76)
3 HEADINGLEY England won by an innings and 187 runs
England 546–4 dec (J H Edrich 310*, K F Barrington 163)
New Zealand 193 (J R Reid 54, R Illingworth 4–42, J D F Larter 4–66) and 166 (V Pollard 53, F J Titmus 5–19)

1965–66 13th Series Drawn 3
1 CHRISTCHURCH Match Drawn
England 342 (D J Allen 88, P H Parfitt 54, M J K Smith 54) and 201–5 dec (M J K Smith 87)
New Zealand 347 (B E Congdon 104, R C Motz 58, E C Petrie 55, I J Jones 4–71) and 48–8 (K Higgs 4–5)
2 DUNEDIN Match Drawn
New Zealand 192 (R C Motz 57) and 147–9 (D A Allen 4–46)
England 254–8 dec (M C Cowdrey 89*, J T Murray 50)
3 AUCKLAND Match Drawn
New Zealand 296 (B W Sinclair 114, B E Congdon 64, D A Allen 5–123) and 129
England 222 (M C Cowdrey 59, W E Russell 56) and 159–4

1969 14th Series Eng 2, NZ 0, Drawn 1
1 LORD'S England won by 230 runs
England 190 (R Illingworth 53) and 340 (J H Edrich 115)
New Zealand 169 (R Illingworth 4–37, D L Underwood 4–38) and 131 (D L Underwood 7–32)
2 TRENT BRIDGE Match Drawn
New Zealand 294 (B F Hastings 83, B E Congdon 66, A Ward 4–61) and 66–1
England 451–8 dec (J H Edrich 155, P J Sharpe 111, D R Hadlee 4–88)
3 THE OVAL England won by 8 wkts
New Zealand 150 (G M Turner 53, D L Underwood 6–41) and 229 (B F Hastings 61, D L Underwood 6–60)
England 242 (J H Edrich 68, B R Taylor 4–47) and 138–2 (M H Denness 55)

1970–71 15th Series Eng 1, NZ 0, Drawn 1
1 CHRISTCHURCH England won by 8 wkts
New Zealand 65 (D L Underwood 6–12) and 254 (G M Turner 76, B E Congdon 55, D L Underwood 6–85)
England 231 (B L d'Oliveira 100, H J Howarth 4–46) and 89–2 (J H Hampshire 51*)
2 AUCKLAND Match Drawn
England 321 (A P E Knott 101, P Lever 64, B L d'Oliveira 58, M C Cowdrey 54, R S Cunis 6–76) and 237 (A P E Knott 96, R O Collinge 4–41)
New Zealand 313–7 dec (M G Burgess 104, G M Turner 65, G T Dowling 53, D L Underwood 5–108) and 40–0

1973 16th Series Eng 2, NZ 0, Drawn 1
1 TRENT BRIDGE England won by 38 runs
England 250 (G Boycott 51, B R Taylor 4–53, D R Hadlee 4–42) and 325–8 dec (A W Greig 139, D L Amiss 138*)
New Zealand 97 (A W Greig 4–33) and 440 (B E Congdon 176, V Pollard 116, G G Arnold 5–131)
2 LORD'S Match Drawn
England 253 (A W Greig 63, G R J Roope 56, G Boycott 61) and 463–9 (K W R Fletcher 178, G Boycott 92, D L Amiss 53, G R J Roope 51, H J Howarth 4–144)
New Zealand 551–9 dec (B E Congdon 175, M G Burgess 105, V Pollard 105, B F Hastings 86, C M Old 5–113)
3 HEADINGLEY England won by an innings and 1 run
New Zealand 276 (M G Burgess 87, V Pollard 62, C M Old 4–71) and 142 (G M Turner 81, G G Arnold 5–27)
England 419 (G Boycott 115, K W R Fletcher 81, R Illingworth 65, R O Collinge 5–74)

1974–75 17th Series Eng 1, NZ 0, Drawn 1
1 AUCKLAND England won by an innings and 83 runs
England 593–6 dec (K W R Fletcher 216, M H Denness 181, J H Edrich 64, A W Greig 51)
New Zealand 326 (J M Parker 121, J F M Morrison 58, K J Wadsworth 58, A W Greig 5–98) and 184 (J F M Morrison 58, G P Howarth 51*, A W Greig 5–51)
2 CHRISTCHURCH Match Drawn
New Zealand 342 (G M Turner 98, K J Wadsworth 58)
England 272–2 (D L Amiss 164*, M H Denness 59*)

1977–78 18th Series Eng 1, NZ 1, Drawn 1
1 WELLINGTON New Zealand won by 72 runs
New Zealand 228 (J G Wright 55, C M Old 6–54) and 123 (R G D Willis 5–32)
England 215 (G Boycott 77, R J Hadlee 4–74) and 64 (R J Hadlee 6–26)
2 CHRISTCHURCH England won by 174 runs
England 418 (I T Botham 103, G Miller 89, G R J Roope 50, P H Edmonds 50, R J Hadlee 4–147) and 96–4 dec
New Zealand 235 (R W Anderson 62, J M Parker 53*, I T Botham 5–73, P H Edmonds 4–38) and 105 (R G D Willis 5–14)
3 AUCKLAND Match Drawn
New Zealand 315 (G P Howarth 122, G N Edwards 55, M G Burgess 50, I.T Botham 5–109) and 382–8 (G P Howarth 102, R W Anderson 55, G N Edwards 54)
England 429 (C T Radley 158, G R J Roope 68, G Boycott 54, I T Botham 53, S L Boock 5–67, R O Collinge 4–98)

1978 19th Series Eng 3, NZ 0
1 THE OVAL England won by 7 wkts
New Zealand 234 (G P Howarth 94, J G Wright 62, R G D Willis 5–42) and 182 (P H Edmonds 4–20)
England 279 (D I Gower 111) and 138–3 (G A Gooch 91*)
2 TRENT BRIDGE England won by an innings and 119 runs
England 429 (G Boycott 131, C T Radley 59, G A Gooch 55, J M Brearley 50, R J Hadlee 4–94)
New Zealand 120 (I T Botham 6–34) and 190 (B A Edgar 60, P H Edmonds 4–44)
3 LORD'S England won by 7 wkts
New Zealand 339 (G P Howarth 123, M G Burgess 68, I T Botham 6–101) and 67 (I T Botham 5–39, R G D Willis 4–16)
England 289 (C T Radley 77, D I Gower 71, R J Hadlee 5–84) and 118–3

5 England v India

1932 1st Series Eng 1, India 0
1 LORD'S England won by 158 runs
England 259 (D R Jardine 79, L E G Ames 65, Mahomed Nissar 5–93) and 275–8 dec (D R Jardine 85*, E Paynter 54, M Jahangir Khan 4–60)
India 189 (W E Bowes 4–49) and 187 (L Amar Singh 51)

1933–34 2nd Series Eng 2, India 0, Drawn 1
1 BOMBAY England won by 9 wkts
India 219 and 258 (L Amarnath 118, C K Nayudu 67, M S Nichols 5–55)
England 438 (B H Valentine 136, C F Walters 78, D R Jardine 60, Mahomed Nissar 5–90) and 40–1
2 CALCUTTA Match Drawn
England 403 (Jas Langridge 70, D R Jardine 61, H Verity 55*, L Amar Singh 4–106) and 7–2
India 247 (Dilawar Hussain 59, V M Merchant 54, H Verity 4–64) and 237 (Dilawar Hussain 57, H Verity 4–76)
3 MADRAS England won by 202 runs
England 335 (A H Bakewell 85, D R Jardine 65, C F Walters 59, L Amar Singh 7–86) and 261–7 dec (C F Walters 102, S Nazir Ali 4–83)
India 145 (H Verity 4–49) and 249 (Yuvraj of Patiala 60, Jas Langridge 5–63, H Verity 4–104)

1936 3rd Series Eng 2, India 0, Drawn 1
1 LORD'S England won by 9 wkts
India 147 (G O B Allen 5–35) and 93 (G O B Allen 5–43, H Verity 4–17)
England 134 (M Leyland 60, L Amar Singh 6–35) and 108–1 (H Gimblett 67*)
2 OLD TRAFFORD Match Drawn
India 203 (H Verity 4–41) and 390–5 (V M Merchant 114, S Mushtaq Ali 112, C Ramaswami 60)
England 571–8 dec (W R Hammond 167, J Hardstaff jun 94, T S Worthington 87, R W V Robins 76, H Verity 66*)
3 THE OVAL England won by 9 wkts
England 471–8 dec (W R Hammond 217, T S Worthington 128, Mahoded Nissar 5–120) and 64–1
India 222 (V M Merchant 52, S Mushtaq Ali 52, J M Sims 5–73) and 312 (C K Nayudu 81, Dilawar Hussain 54, G O B Allen 7–80)

1946 4th Series Eng 1, India 0, Drawn 2
1 LORD'S England won by 10 wkts
India 200 (R S Modi 57*, A V Bedser 7–49) and 275 (M H Mankad 63, L Amarnath 50, A V Bedser 4–96)
England 428 (J Hardstaff jun 205*, P.A Gibb 60, L Amarnath 5–118) and 48–0
2 OLD TRAFFORD Match Drawn
England 294 (W R Hammond 69, L Hutton 67, C Washbrook 52, D C S Compton 51, L Amarnath 5–96, M H Mankad 5–101) and 153–5 dec (D C S Compton 71*)
India 170 (V M Merchant 78, R Pollard 5–24, A V Bedser 4–41) and 152–9 (A V Bedser 7–52)
3 THE OVAL Match Drawn
India 331 (V M Merchant 128, S Mushtaq Ali 59, W J Edrich 4–68)
England 95–3

1951–52 5th Series Eng 1, India 1, Drawn 3
1 NEW DELHI Match Drawn
England 203 (J D B Robertson 50, S G Shinde 6–91) and 368–6 (A J Watkins 138*, D B Carr 76, F A Lowson 68, M H Mankad 4–58)
India 418–6 dec (V S Hazare 164*, V M Merchant 154)
2 BOMBAY Match Drawn
India 485–9 dec (V S Hazare 155, P Roy 140, C D Gopinath 50*, J B Statham 4–96) and 208
England 456 (T W Graveney 175, A J Watkins 80, M H Mankad 4–91) and 55–2
3 CALCUTTA Match Drawn
England 342 (R T Spooner 71, A J Watkins 68, C J Poole 55, M H Mankad 4–89) and 252–5 dec (R T Spooner 92, C J Poole 69*)
India 344 (D G Phadkar 115, M H Mankad 59, F Ridgway 4–83, R Tattersall 4–104) and 103–0 (M H Mankad 71*)
4 KANPUR India won by an innings and 8 runs
India 121 (R Tattersall 6–48, M J Hilton 4–32) and 157 (H R Adhikari 60, M J Hilton 5–61)
England 203 (A J Watkins 66, Ghulam Ahmed 5–70, M H Mankad 4–54) and 76–2
5 MADRAS India won by an innings and 8 runs
England 266 (J D B Robertson 77, R T Spooner 66, M H Mankad 8–55) and 183 (J D B Robertson 56, M H Mankad 4–53, Ghulam Ahmed 4–77)
India 457–9 dec (P R Umrigar 130, P Roy 111, D G Phadkar 61)

1952 6th Series Eng 3, India 0, Drawn 1
1 HEADINGLEY England won by 7 wkts
India 293 (V L Manjrekar 133, V S Hazare 89, J C Laker 4–39) and 165 (D G Phadkar 64, V S Hazare 56, F S Trueman 4–27, R O Jenkins 4–50)
England 334 (T W Graveney 71, T G Evans 66, Ghulam Ahmed 5–100) and 128–3 (R T Simpson 51)
2 LORD'S England won by 8 wkts
India 235 (M H Mankad 72, V S Hazare 69*, F S Trueman 4–72) and 378 (M H Mankad 184, J C Laker 4–102, F S Trueman 4–110)

England (L Hutton 150, T G Evans 104, P B H May 74, T W
Graveney 73, R T Simpson 53, M H Mankad 5–196)
3 OLD TRAFFORD England won by an innings and 207 runs
England 347–9 dec (L Hutton 104, T G Evans 71, P B H May 69)
India 58 (F S Trueman 8–31) and 82 (A V Bedser 5–27, G A R
Lock 4–41)
4 THE OVAL Match Drawn
England 326–6 dec (D S Shepherd 119, L Hutton 86, J T Ikin 53)
India 98 (A V Bedser 5–41, F S Trueman 5–48)

1959 7th Series Eng 5, India 0
1 TRENT BRIDGE England won by an innings and 59 runs
England 422 (P B H May 106, T G Evans 73, M J Horton 58, K F
Barrington 56, S P Gupte 4–102)
India 206 (P Roy 54, F S Trueman 4–45) and 157 (J B Statham
5–31)
2 LORD S England won by 8 wkts
India 168 (N J Contractor 81, T Greenhough 5–35) and 165 (V L
Manjrekar 61)
England 226 (K F Barrington 80, R B Desai 5–89) and 108–2 (M C
Cowdrey 63*)
3 HEADINGLEY England won by an innings and 173 runs
India 161 (H J Rhodes 4–50) and 149 (D B Close 4–35)
England 483–8 dec (M C Cowdrey 160, K F Barrington 80,
W G A Parkhouse 78, G Pullar 75, S P Gupte 4–111)
4 OLD TRAFFORD England won by 171 runs
England 490 (G Pullar 131, M J K Smith 100, K F Barrington 87,
M C Cowdrey 67, R Surendranath 5–115) and 265–8 dec (S P
Gupte 4–76)
India 208 (C G Borde 75) and 376 (P R Umrigar 118, A A Baig
112, N J Contractor 56)
5 THE OVAL England won by an innings and 27 runs
India 140 (F S Trueman 4–24) and 194 (R G Nadkarni 76)
England 361 (M J K Smith 98, R Subba Row 94, R Swetman 65, R
Illingworth 50, R Surendranath 5–75)

1961–62 8th Series India 2, Eng 0, Drawn 3
1 BOMBAY Match Drawn
England 500–8 dec (K F Barrington 151*, E R Dexter 85, G Pullar
83, P E Richardson 71, V B Ranjane 4–76) and 184–5 dec (K F
Barrington 52*)
India 390 (S A Durani 71, C G Borde 69, V L Manjrekar 84, M L
Jaisimha 51)
2 KANPUR Match Drawn
India 467–8 dec (P R Umrigar 147*, V L Manjrekar 96, M L
Jaisimha 70)
England 244 (R W Barber 69*, S P Gupte 5–90) and 497–5 (K F
Barrington 172, E R Dexter 126*, G Pullar 119)
3 NEW DELHI Match Drawn
India 466 (V L Manjrekar 189*, M L Jaisimha 127, D A Allen
4–87)
England 256–3 (K F Barrington 113*, G Pullar 89)
4 CALCUTTA India won by 187 runs
India 380 (C G Borde 68, M A K Pataudi 64, V L Mehra 62, D A
Allen 5–67) and 252 (C G Borde 61, D A Allen 4–95, G A R
Lock 4–111)
England 212 (P E Richardson 62, E R Dexter 57, S A Durani 5–47,
C G Borde 4–65) and 233 (E R Dexter 62)
5 MADRAS India won by 128 runs
India 428 (M A K Pataudi 103, N J Contractor 86, F M Engineer
65, R G Nadkarni 63) and 190 (V L Manjrekar 85, G A R Lock
6–65)
England 281 (M J K Smith 73, S A Durani 6–105) and 209 (S A
Durani 4–72)

1963–64 9th Series Drawn 5
1 MADRAS Match Drawn
India 457–7 dec (B K Kunderan 192, V L Manjrekar 108, D N
Sardesai 65, M L Jaisimha 51, F J Titmus 5–116) and 152–9 dec
(F J Titmus 4–46)
England 317 (J B Bolus 88, K F Barrington 80, C G Borde 5–88)
and 241–5 (J B Mortimore 73*, M J K Smith 57)
2 BOMBAY Match Drawn
India 300 (S A Durani 90, C G Borde 84) and 249–8 dec (D N
Sardesai 66, M L Jaisimha 66)
England 233 (F J Titmus 84*, B S Chandrasekhar 4–67) and 206–3
(J B Bolus 57, J G Binks 55)
3 CALCUTTA Match Drawn
India 241 (D N Sardesai 54, J S E Price 5–73) and 300–7 dec
(M L Jaisimha 129)
England 267 (M C Cowdrey 107, R B Desai 4–62) and 145–2
(M J K Smith 75*)
4 NEW DELHI Match Drawn
India 344 (Hanumant Singh 105) and 463–4 (M A K Pataudi
203*, B K Kunderan 100, C G Borde 67*, M L Jaisimha 50)
England 451 (M C Cowdrey 151, P H Parfitt 67, J B Bolus 58)
5 KANPUR Match Drawn
England 559–8 dec (B R Knight 127, P H Parfitt 121, J B Bolus 58,
J M Parks 51*)
India 266 (D N Sardesai 79, R G Nadkarni 52*, F J Titmus 6–73)
and 347–3 (R G Nadkarni 122*, D N Sardesai 87, S A
Durani 61*, B K Kunderan 55)

1967 10th Series India 3, Eng 0
1 HEADINGLEY England won by 6 wkts
England 550–4 dec (G Boycott 246*, B L d'Oliveira 109, K F
Barrington 93, T W Graveney 59) and 126–4

India 164 (M A K Pataudi 64) and 510 (M A K Pataudi 148, A L
Wadekar 91, F M Engineer 87, Hanumant Singh 73, R
Illingworth 4–100)
2 LORD'S England won by an innings and 124 runs
India 152 (A L Wadekar 57) and 110 (R Illingworth 6–29)
England 386 (T W Graveney 151, K F Barrington 97, B S
Chandrasekhar 5–127)
3 EDGBASTON England won by 132 runs
England 298 (J T Murray 77, K F Barrington 75) and 203 (E A S
Prasanna 4–60)
India 92 and 277 (A L Wadekar 70, D B Close 4–68, R Illingworth
4–92)

1971 11th Series India 1, Eng 0, Drawn 2
1 LORD'S Match Drawn
England 304 (J A Snow 73, A P E Knott 67, B S Bedi 4–70) and
191 (J H Edrich 62, S Venkataraghavan 4–52)
India 313 (A L Wadekar 85, G R Viswanath 68, E D Solkar 67, N
Gifford 4–84) and 145–8 (S M Gavaskar 53, N Gifford 4–43)
2 OLD TRAFFORD Match Drawn
England 386 (R Illingworth 107, P Lever 88*, B W Luckhurst 78,
S Abid Ali 4–64) and 245–3 dec (B W Luckhurst 101, J H
Edrich 59)
India 212 (S M Gavaskar 57, E D Solkar 50, P Lever 5–70) and
65–3
3 THE OVAL India won by 4 wkts
England 355 (A P E Knott 90, J A Jameson 82, R A Hutton 81)
and 101 (B S Chandrasekhar 6–38)
India 284 (F M Engineer 59, D N Sardesai 54, R Illingworth 5–70)
and 174–6

1972–73 12th Series India 2, Eng 1, Drawn 2
1 NEW DELHI England won by 6 wkts
India 173 (S Abid Ali 58, G G Arnold 6–45) and 233 (E D Solkar
75, F M Engineer 63, D L Underwood 4–56)
England 200 (A W Greig 68*, B S Chandrasekhar 8–79) and 208–4
(A R Lewis 70*)
2 CALCUTTA India won by 28 runs
India 210 (F M Engineer 75) and 155 (S A Durani 53, A W Greig
5–24, C M Old 4–43)
England 174 (B S Chandrasekhar 5–65) and 163 (A W Greig 67,
B S Bedi 5–63, B S Chandrasekhar 4–42)
3 MADRAS India won by 4 wkts
England 242 (K W R Fletcher 97*, B S Chandrasekhar 6–90) and
159 (M H Denness 76, E A S Prasanna 4–16, B S Bedi 4–38)
India 316 (M A K Pataudi 73, P I Pocock 4–114) and 86–6 (P I
Pocock 4–28)
4 KANPUR Match Drawn
India 357 (A L Wadekar 90, S M Gavaskar 69, M A K Pataudi 54,
C M Old 4–69) and 186–6 (B S Chandrasekhar 75*)
England 397 (A R Lewis 125, J Birkenshaw 64, K W R Fletcher 58,
B S Chandrasekhar 4–86)
5 BOMBAY Match Drawn
India 448 (F M Engineer 121, G R Viswanath 113, A L Wadekar
87, S A Durani 73) and 244–5 dec (S M Gavaskar 67, F M
Engineer 66)
England 480 (A W Greig 148, K W R Fletcher 113, A P E Knott
56, B S Chandrasekhar 5–135) and 67–2

1974 13th Series Eng 3, India 0
1 OLD TRAFFORD England won by 113 runs
England 328–9 dec (K W R Fletcher 123*, D L Amiss 56, A W
Greig 53) and 213–3 dec (J H Edrich 100*)
India 246 (S M Gavaskar 101, S Abid Ali 71, R G D Willis 4–64)
and 182 (S M Gavaskar 58, G R Viswanath 50, C M Old 4–20)
2 LORD'S England won by an innings and 285 runs
England 629 (D L Amiss 188, M H Denness 118, A W Greig 106,
J H Edrich 96, B S Bedi 6–226)
India 302 (F M Engineer 86, G R Viswanath 52, C M Old 4–67)
and 42 (C M Old 5–21, G G Arnold 4–19)
3 EDGBASTON England won by an innings and 78 runs
India 165 (F M Engineer 64*, M Hendrick 4–28) and 216 (S S
Naik 77)
England 459–2 dec (D Lloyd 214*, M H Denness 100, D L Amiss
79, K W R Fletcher 51*)

1976–77 14th Series Eng 3, India 1, Drawn 1
1 NEW DELHI England won by an innings and 25 runs
England 381 (D L Amiss 179, A P E Knott 75, J K Lever 53, B S
Bedi 4–92)
India 122 (J K Lever 7–46) and 234 (S M Gavaskar 71, D L
Underwood 4–78)
2 CALCUTTA England won by 10 wkts
India 155 (R G D Willis 5–27) and 181 (B P Patel 56)
England 321 (A W Greig 103, R W Tolchard 67, C M Old 52,
B S Bedi 5–110, E A S Prasanna 4–93) and 16–0
3 MADRAS England won by 200 runs
England 262 (J M Brearley 59, A W Greig 54, B S Bedi 4–72) and
185–9 dec (B S Chandrasekhar 5–50, E A S Prasanna 4–55)
India 164 (J K Lever 5–59) and 83 (D L Underwood 4–28)
4 BANGALORE India won by 140 runs
India 253 (S Amarnath 63, S M H Kirmani 52, R G D Willis
6–53) and 259–9 dec (G R Viswanath 79*, S M Gavaskar 50,
D L Underwood 4–76)
England 195 (D L Amiss 82, B S Chandrasekhar 6–76) and 177
(A P E Knott 81*, B S Bedi 6–71)

5 BOMBAY Match Drawn
India 338 (S M Gavaskar 108, B P Patel 83, D L Underwood 4–89)
and 192 (S Amarnath 63, D L Underwood 5–84)
England 317 (J M Brearley 91, A W Greig 76, D L Amiss 50,
E A S Prasanna 4–73, B S Bedi 4–109) and 152–7 (K W R
Fletcher 58*, K D Ghavri 5–33)

1979 15th Series England 1, India 0, Drawn 3
1 EDGBASTON England won by an innings and 83 runs
England 633–5 dec (D I Gower 200*, G Boycott 155, G A Gooch
83, G Miller 63*, Kapil Dev 5–146)
India 297 (G R Viswanath 78, S M Gavaskar 61) and 253 (S M
Gavaskar 68, C P S Chauhan 56, G R Viswanath 51, I T Botham
5–70, M Hendrick 4–45)
2 LORD'S Match Drawn
India 96 (I T Botham 5–35) and 318–4 (G R Viswanath 113, D B
Vengsarkar 103, S M Gavaskar 59)
England 419–9 dec (D I Gower 82, R W Taylor 64, G Miller 62,
D W Randall 57)
3 HEADINGLEY Match Drawn
England 270 (I T Botham 137)
India 223–6 (S M Gavaskar 78, D B Vengsarkar 65*)
4 THE OVAL Match Drawn
England 305 (G A Gooch 79, P Willey 52) and 334–8 dec (G
Boycott 125, D L Bairstow 59)
India 202 (G R Viswanath 62, I T Botham 4–65) and 429–8 (S M
Gavaskar 221, C P S Chauhan 80, D B Vengsarkar 52)

1979–80 16th Series (Jubilee Match) Eng 1, India 0
BOMBAY England won by 10 wkts
India 242 (I T Botham 6–58) and 149 (I T Botham 7–48)
England 296 (I T Botham 114, K D Ghavri 5–52) and 98–0

1981–82 17th Series India 1, Eng 0, Drawn 5
1 BOMBAY India won by 138 runs
India 179 (S M Gavaskar 55, I T Botham 4–72, G R Dilley 4–47)
and 227 (I T Botham)
England 166 (G Boycott 60, C J Tavare 56, D R Doshi 5–39) and
102 (Kapil Dev 5–70, S Madan Lal 5–23)
2 BANGALORE Match Drawn
England 400 (D I Gower 82, G A Gooch 58, I T Botham 55, G R
Dilley 52, R J Shastri 4–83) and 174–3 dec (G Boycott 50)
India 428 (S M Gavaskar 172, K Srikkanth 65, Kapil Dev 59, J K
Lever 5–100)
3 NEW DELHI Match Drawn
England 476–9 dec (C J Tavare 149, G Boycott 105, G A Gooch
71, K W R Fletcher 51, S Madan Lal 5–85, Kapil Dev 4–68)
India 487 (G R Viswanath 107, R J Shastri 93, S M H Kirmani 67)
4 CALCUTTA Match Drawn
England 248 (K W R Fletcher 69, I T Botham 58, Kapil Dev 6–91)
and 265–5 dec (D I Gower 74, G A Gooch 63, K W R Fletcher
60*)
India 208 (D B Vengsarkar 70) and 170–3 (S M Gavaskar 83*)
5 MADRAS Match Drawn
India 481–4 dec (G R Viswanath 222, Yashpal Sharma 140) and
160–3 dec (P Roy 60*)
England 328 (G A Gooch 127, D I Gower 64, I T Botham 52, D R
Doshi 4–69)
6 KANPUR Match Drawn
England 378–9 dec (I T Botham 142, D I Gower 85, G A Gooch
58, D R Doshi 4–81)
India 377–7 (Kapil Dev 116, G R Viswanath 74, Yashpal Sharma
55*, S M Gavaskar 52).

1982 18th Series Eng 1, India 0, Drawn 2
1 LORD'S England won by 7 wkts
England 455 (D W Randall 126, I T Botham 67, P H Edmonds
64, Kapil Dev 5–125) and 67–3
India 128 (I T Botham 5–46) and 369 (D B Vengsarkar 157, Kapil
Dev 89, R G D Willis 6–101)
2 OLD TRAFFORD Match Drawn
England 425 (I T Botham 128, G Miller 98, J K Cook 66, C J
Tavare 67, D R Doshi 6–102)
India 379–8 (S M Patil 129*, Kapil Dev 65, S M H Kirmani 58,
G R Viswanath 54)
3 THE OVAL Match Drawn
England 594 (I T Botham 208, A J Lamb 107, D W Randall 95, G
Cook 50) and 191–3 dec (C J Tavare 75*)
India 410 (Kapil Dev 97, R J Shastri 66, S M Patil 62, G R
Viswanath 56) and 111–3 (G R Viswanath 75*)

6 England v Pakistan

1954 1st Series Eng 1, Pak 1, Drawn 2
1 LORD'S Match Drawn
Pakistan 87 (J B Statham 4–18, J H Wardle 4–33) and 121–3
(Waqar Hassan 53)
England 117–9 dec (Khan Mohammad 5–61, Fazal Mahmood 4–54)
2 TRENT BRIDGE England won by an innings and 129 runs
Pakistan 157 (R Appleyard 5–51) and 272 (Maqsood Ahmed 69,
Hanif Mohammad 51)
England 558–6 dec (D C S Compton 278, R T Simpson 101, T W
Graveney 84)
3 OLD TRAFFORD Match Drawn
England 359–8 dec (D C S Compton 93, T W Graveney 65, J H
Wardle 54, Fazal Mahmood 4–107)
Pakistan 90 (J H Wardle 4–19) and 25–4

4 THE OVAL Pakistan won by 24 runs
Pakistan 133 (F H Tyson 4–35) and 164 (J H Wardle 7–56)
England 130 (D C S Compton 53, Fazal Mahmood 6–53, Mahmood Hussain 4–58) and 143 (P B H May 53, Fazal Mahmood 6–46)

1961–62 2nd Series Eng 1, Pak 0, Drawn 2
1 LAHORE England won by 5 wkts
Pakistan 387–9 dec (Javed Burki 138, Mushtaq Mohammad 76, Saeed Ahmed 74) and 200
England 380 (K F Barrington 139, M J K Smith 99, Mohammad Munaf 4–42) and 209–5 (E R Dexter 66*)
2 DACCA Match Drawn
Pakistan 393–9 dec (Javed Burki 140, Hanif Mohammad 111, Saeed Ahmed 69, G A R Lock 4–155) and 216 (Hanif Mohammad 104, Alim-ud-Din 50, D A Allen 5–30, G A R Lock 4–70)
England 439 (G Pullar 165, R W Barber 86, K F Barrington 84, Antao d'Souza 4–94) and 38–0
3 KARACHI Match Drawn
Pakistan 253 (Alim-ud-Din 109, Hanif Mohammad 67, B R Knight 4–66) and 404–8 (Hanif Mohammad 89, Imtiaz Ahmed 86, Alim-ud-Din 53)
England 507 (E R Dexter 205, P H Parfitt 111, G Pullar 60, M J K Smith 56, Antao d'Souza 5–112)

1962 3rd Series Eng 4, Pak 0, Drawn 1
1 EDGBASTON England won by an innings and 24 runs
England 544–5 dec (M C Cowdrey 159, P H Parfitt 101*, T W Graveney 97, D A Allen 79*, E R Dexter 72)
Pakistan 246 (Mushtaq Mohammad 63, J B Statham 4–54) and 274 (Saeed Ahmed 65)
2 LORD'S England won by 9 wkts
Pakistan 100 (F S Trueman 6–31) and 355 (Javed Burki 101, Nasim-ul-Ghani 101, L J Coldwell 6–85)
England 370 (T W Graveney 153, E R Dexter 65, Mohammad Farooq 4–70) and 86–1
3 HEADINGLEY England won by an innings and 117 runs
England 428 (P H Parfitt 119, M J Stewart 86, D A Allen 62, Munir Malik 5–128)
Pakistan 131 (Alim-ud-Din 50, E R Dexter 4–10) and 180 (Alim-ud-Din 60, Saeed Ahmed 54, J B Statham 4–50)
4 TRENT BRIDGE Match Drawn
England 428–5 dec (T W Graveney 114, P H Parfitt 101*, E R Dexter 85, D S Sheppard 83)
Pakistan 219 (Mushtaq Mohammad 55, B R Knight 4–38, F S Trueman 4–71) and 216–6 (Mushtaq Mohammad 100*, Saeed Ahmed 64)
5 THE OVAL England won by 10 wkts
England 480–5 dec (M C Cowdrey 182, E R Dexter 172, D S Sheppard 57, K F Barrington 50*) and 27–0
Pakistan 183 (J D F Larter 5–57) and 323 (Imtiaz Ahmed 98, Mushtaq Mohammad 72, J D F Larter 4–88)

1967 4th Series Eng 2, Pak 0, Drawn 1
1 LORD'S Match Drawn
England 369 (K F Barrington 148, T W Graveney 81, B L d'Oliveira 59) and 241–9 dec (B L d'Oliveira 81*)
Pakistan 354 (Hanif Mohammad 187*, Asif Iqbal 76) and 88–3
2 TRENT BRIDGE England won by 10 wkts
Pakistan 140 (K Higgs 4–35) and 114 (Saeed Ahmed 68, D L Underwood 5–52)
England 252–8 dec (K F Barrington 109*) and 3–0
3 THE OVAL England won by 8 wkts
Pakistan 216 (Mushtaq Mohammad 66, G G Arnold 5–58) and 255 (Asif Iqbal 146, Intikhab Alam 51, K Higgs 5–58)
England 440 (K F Barrington 142, T W Graveney 77, F J Titmus 65, G G Arnold 59, Mushtaq Mohammad 4–80) and 34–2

1968–69 5th Series Drawn 3
1 LAHORE Match Drawn
England 306 (M C Cowdrey 100, J H Edrich 54, A P E Knott 52, Saeed Ahmed 4–64, Intikhab Alam 4–117) and 225–9 dec (K W R Fletcher 83)
Pakistan 209 (Asif Iqbal 70, R M H Cottam 4–50) and 203–5 (Majid Jahangir 68)
2 DACCA Match Drawn
Pakistan 246 (Mushtaq Mohammad 52, J A Snow 4–70) and 195–6 dec (D L Underwood 5–94)
England 274 (B L d'Oliveira 114*, Pervez Sajjad 4–75) and 33–0
3 KARACHI Match Drawn
England 502–7 (C Milburn 139, T W Graveney 105, A P E Knott 96*)
Pakistan did not bat

1971 6th Series Eng 1, Pak 0, Drawn 2
1 EDGBASTON Match Drawn
Pakistan 608–7 dec (Zaheer Abbas 274, Asif Iqbal 104*, Mushtaq Mohammad 100)
England 353 (A P E Knott 116, B L d'Oliveira 73, Asif Masood 5–111) and 229–5 (B W Luckhurst 108*, Asif Masood 4–49)
2 LORDS Match Drawn
England 241–2 dec (G Boycott 121*) and 117–0 (R A Hutton 58*, B W Luckhurst 53*)
Pakistan 148
3 HEADINGLEY England won by 25 runs
England 316 (G Boycott 112, B L d'Oliveira 74) and 264 (B L d'Oliveira 72, D L Amiss 56, Saleem Altaf 4–11)
Pakistan 350 (Zaheer Abbas 72, Wasim Bari 63, Mushtaq Mohammad 57) and 205 (Sadiq Mohammad 91)

1972–73 7th Series Drawn 3
1 LAHORE Match Drawn
England 355 (D L Amiss 112, K W R Fletcher 55, M H Denness 50) and 306–7 dec (A R Lewis 74, A W Greig 72, M H Denness 68, Intikhab Alam 4–80)
Pakistan 422 (Sadiq Mohammad 119, Asif Iqbal 102, Mushtaq Mohammad 66, A W Greig 4–86) and 124–3 (Talaat Ali 57)
2 HYDERABAD Match Drawn
England 487 (D L Amiss 158, K W R Fletcher 78, A P E Knott 71, Mushtaq Mohammad 4–93, Intikhab Alam 4–137) and 218–6 (A W Greig 64, A P E Knott 63*)
Pakistan 569–9 dec (Mushtaq Mohammad 157, Intikhab Alam 138, Asif Iqbal 68, P I Pocock 5–169)
3 KARACHI Match Drawn
Pakistan 445–6 dec (Majid Khan 99, Mushtaq Mohammad 99, Sadiq Mohammad 89, Intikhab Alam 61) and 199 (N Gifford 5–55, J Birkenshaw 5–57)
England 386 (D L Amiss 99, A R Lewis 88, K W R Fletcher 54, Intikhab Alam 4–105) and 30–1

1974 8th Series Drawn 3
1 HEADINGLEY Match Drawn
Pakistan 285 (Majid Kahn 75, Sarfraz Nawaz 53) and 179
England 183 and 238–6 (J H Edrich 70, K W R Fletcher 67*, Sarfraz Nawaz 4–56)
2 LORD'S Match Drawn
Pakistan 130–9 dec (D L Underwood 5–20) and 226 (Mushtaq Mohammad 76, Wasim Raja 53, D L Underwood 8–51)
England 270 (A P E Knott 83) and 27–0
3 THE OVAL Match Drawn
Pakistan 600–7 dec (Zaheer Abbas 240, Majid Khan 98, Mushtaq Mohammad 76) and 94–4
England 545 (D L Amiss 183, K W R Fletcher 122, C M Old 65, Intikhab Alam 5–116)

1977–78 9th Series Drawn 3
1 LAHORE Match Drawn
Pakistan 407–9 dec (Haroon Rashid 122, Mudassar Nazar 114, Javed Miandad 71) and 106–3
England 288 (G K Miller 98*, G Boycott 63, Sarfraz Nawaz 4–68)
2 HYDERABAD Match Drawn
Pakistan 275 (Haroon Rashid 108, Javed Miandad 88*) and 259–4 dec (Mudassar Nazar 66, Javed Miandad 61*)
England 191 (G Boycott 79, Abdul Qadir 6–44) and 186–1 (G Boycott 100*, J M Brearley 74)
3 KARACHI Match Drawn
England 266 (G R J Roope 56, Abdul Qadir 4–81) and 222–5 (G Boycott 56, D W Randall 55)
Pakistan 281 (Mudassar Nazar 76, P H Edmonds 7–66)

1978 10th Series Eng 2, Pak 0, Drawn 1
1 EDGBASTON England won by an innings and 57 runs
Pakistan 164 (C M Old 7–50) and 231 (Sadiq Mohammad 79, P H Edmonds 4–44)
England 452–8 dec (C T Radley 106, I T Botham 100, D I Gower 58, Sikander Bakht 4–132)
2 LORD'S England won by an innings and 120 runs
England 364 (I T Botham 108, G R J Roope 69, D I Gower 56, G A Gooch 54)
Pakistan 105 (R G D Willis 5–47, P H Edmonds 4–6) and 139 (I T Botham 8–34)
3 HEADINGLEY Match Drawn
Pakistan 201 (Sadiq Mohammad 97, C M Old 4–41, I T Botham 4–59)
England 119–7 (Sarfraz Nawaz 5–39)

1982 11th Series Eng 2, Pak 1
1 EDGBASTON England won by 113 runs
England 272 (D I Gower 74, C J Tavare 54, Imran Khan 7–52) and 291 (D W Randall 105, R W Taylor 54, Tahir Naqqash 5–40)
Pakistan 251 (Mansoor Akhtar 58) and 199 (Imran Khan 65)
2 LORD'S Pakistan won by 10 wkts
Pakistan 428–8 dec (Mohsin Khan 200, Zaheer Abbas 75, Mansoor Akhtar 57) and 77–0
England 227 and 276 (C J Tavare 82, I T Botham 69, Mudassar Nazar 6–32)
3 HEADINGLEY England won by 4 wkts
Pakistan 275 (Imran Khan 67*, Mudassar Nazar 65, Javed Miandad 54) and 199 (Javed Miandad 52, I T Botham 5–74)
England 256 (D I Gower 74, I T Botham 57, Imran Khan 5–49) and 190–6 (G Fowler 86)

7 England *v* Sri Lanka

1981–82 1st Series Eng 1, Sri Lanka 0
1 COLOMBO England won by 7 wkts
Sri Lanka 218 (R S Madugalle 65, A Ranatunge 54, D L Underwood 5–28) and 175 (R L Dias 77, J E Emburey 6–33)
England 223 (D I Gower 89, A L F de Mel 4–70) and 171–3 (C J Tavare 85)

8 Australia *v* South Africa

1902–03 1st Series Aus 2, SA 0, Drawn 1
1 JOHANNESBURG Match Drawn
South Africa 454 (L J Tancred 97, C B Llewellyn 90, A W Nourse 72, E A Halliwell 57) and 101–4
Australia 296 (R A Duff 82*, C Hill 76, V T Trumper 63, C B Llewellyn 6–92, J H Sinclair 4–129) and 372–7 dec (C Hill 142, W W Armstrong 59, M A Noble 53*)
2 JOHANNESBURG Australia won by 159 runs
Australia 175 (C B Llewellyn 5–43) and 309 (W W Armstrong 159*, C B Llewellyn 5–73)
South Africa 240 (J H Sinclair 101) and 85 (J V Saunders 7–34)
3 CAPE TOWN Australia won by 10 wkts
Australia 252 (C Hill 91*, V T Trumper 70, C B Llewellyn 6–97) and 59–0
South Africa 85 (W P Howell 4–18, J V Saunders 4–37) and 225 (J H Sinclair 104, W P Howell 5–81)

1910–11 2nd Series Aus 4, SA 1
1 SYDNEY Australia won by an innings and 114 runs
Australia 528 (C Hill 191, W Bardsley 132, D R A Gehrs 67, R O Schwarz 5–102)
South Africa 174 (G A Faulkner 62, R O Schwarz 61, A Cotter 6–69, W J Whitty 4–33) and 240 (A W Nourse 64*, P W Sherwell 60, W J Whitty 4–75)
2 MELBOURNE Australia won by 89 runs
Australia 348 (W Bardsley 85, W W Armstrong 75, V S Ransford 58) and 327 (V T Trumper 159, R O Schwarz 4–76, C B Llewellyn 4–81)
South Africa 506 (G A Faulkner 204, S J Snooke 77, J H Sinclair 58*, W W Armstrong 4–134) and 80 (W J Whitty 6–17, A Cotter 4–47)
3 ADELAIDE South Africa won by 38 runs
South Africa 482 (J W Zulch 105, S J Snooke 103, G A Faulkner 56, W W Armstrong 4–103) and 360 (G A Faulkner 115, C B Llewellyn 80, W J Whitty 6–104)
Australia 465 (V T Trumper 214*, W Bardsley 54, V S Ransford 50, C B Llewellyn 4–107) and 339 (C Kelleway 65, W Bardsley 58, C Hill 55, R O Schwarz 4–48)
4 MELBOURNE Australia won by 530 runs
Australia 328 (W Bardsley 82, V S Ransford 75, C Kelleway 59) and 578 (W W Armstrong 132, C Hill 100, V S Ransford 95, V T Trumper 87, D R A Gehrs 58)
South Africa 205 (A W Nourse 92*, W J Whitty 4–78) and 171 (G A Faulkner 80, H V Hordern 5–66)
5 SYDNEY Australia won by 7 wkts
Australia 364 (C G Macartney 137, W Bardsley 94, H V Hordern 50, R O Schwarz 6–47) and 198–3 (V T Trumper 74*, C G Macartney 56)
South Africa 160 (G A Faulkner 52, H V Hordern 4–73) and 401 (J W Zulch 150, G A Faulkner 92, W J Whitty 4–66)

1912 3rd Series Aus 2, SA 0, Drawn 1
1 OLD TRAFFORD Australia won by an innings and 88 runs
Australia 448 (W Bardsley 121, C Kelleway 114, S J Pegler 6–105)
South Africa 265 (G A Faulkner 122*, W J Whitty 5–55) and 95 (C Kelleway 5–33)
2 LORD'S Australia won by 10 wkts
South Africa (H W Taylor 93, W J Whitty 4–68) and 173 (C B Llewellyn 59, T J Matthews 4–29)
Australia 390 (W Bardsley 164, C Kelleway 102, S J Pegler 4–79) and 48–0
3 TRENT BRIDGE Match Drawn
South Africa 329 (A W Nourse 64, G C White 59*)
Australia 219 (W Bardsley 56, S J Pegler 4–80)

1921–22 4th Series Aus 1, SA 0, Drawn 2
1 DURBAN Match Drawn
Australia 299 (J. Ryder 78*, C G Macartney 59, J M Gregory 51, J M Blanckenberg 5–78) and 324–7 dec (C G Macartney 116, J Ryder 58)
South Africa (J W Zulch 80, J M Gregory 6–77) and 184–7
2 JOHANNESBURG Match Drawn
Australia 450 (H L Collins 203, J M Gregory 119, J Ryder 56, C P Carter 6–91) and 7–0
South Africa 243 (A W Nourse 64, J M Gregory 4–71) and 472–8 dec (C N Frank 152, A W Nourse 111, H W Taylor 80)
3 CAPE TOWN Australia won by 10 wkts
South Africa 180 (J W Zulch 50, A A Mailey 4–40) and 216 (C G Macartney 5–44)
Australia 396 (J Ryder 142, H L Collins 54, J M Blanckenberg 4–82) and 1–0

1931–32 5th Series Aus 5, SA 0
1 BRISBANE Australia won by an innings and 163 runs
Australia 450 (D G Bradman 226, W M Woodfull 76, W A S Oldfield 56*, A J Bell 4–120)
South Africa 170 (B Mitchell 58, H Ironmonger 5–42) and 117 (T W Wall 5–14, H Ironmonger 4–44)
2 SYDNEY Australia won by an innings and 155 runs
South Africa 153 (S J McCabe 4–13, C V Grimmett 4–28) and 161 (C V Grimmett 4–44)
Australia 469 (K E Rigg 127, D G Bradman 112, S J McCabe 79, W M Woodfull 58, A J Bell 5–140)
3 MELBOURNE Australia won by 169 runs
Australia 198 (K E Rigg 68, A F Kippax 52, A J Bell 5–69, N A Quinn 4–42) and 554 (D G Bradman 167, W M Woodfull 161, S J McCabe 71, A F Kippax 67, Q McMillan 4–150, C L Vincent 4–154)
South Africa 358 (K G Viljoen 111) and 225 (J A J Christy 63, C V Grimmett 6–92, H Ironmonger 4–54)
4 ADELAIDE Australia won by 10 wkts
South Africa 308 (H W Taylor 78, B Mitchell 75, H B Cameron 52, C V Grimmett 7–116) and 274 (B Mitchell 95, H W Taylor 84, J A J Christy 51, C V Grimmett 7–83)
Australia 513 (D G Bradman 299*, W M Woodfull 82, A J Bell 5–142) and 73–0

5 MELBOURNE Australia won by an innings and 72 runs
South Africa 36 (H Ironmonger 5–6, L J Nash 4–18) and 45 (H Ironmonger 6–18)
Australia 153

1935–36 6th Series Aus 4, SA 0, Drawn 1
1 DURBAN Australia won by 9 wkts
South Africa 248 (E A B Rowan 66, L O'B Fleetwood-Smith 4–64) and 282 (A D Nourse 91, I J Siedle 59, W J O'Reilly 5–49)
Australia 429 (S J McCabe 149, A G Chipperfield 109, W A Brown 66, L S Darling 60, A B C Langton 4–113) and 102–1 (W A Brown 55)
2 JOHANNESBURG Match Drawn
South Africa 157 (W J O'Reilly 4–54) and 491 (A D Nourse 231)
Australia 250 (J H W Fingleton 62, W A Brown 51, B Mitchell 4–26, A B C Langton 4–85) and 274–2 (S J McCabe 189*)
3 CAPE TOWN Australia won by an innings and 78 runs
Australia 362–8 dec (W A Brown 121, J H W Fingleton 112, X C Balaskas 4–126)
South Africa 102 (C V Grimmett 5–32) and 182 (I J Siedle 59, C V Grimmett 5–56, W J O'Reilly 4–35)
4 JOHANNESBURG Australia won by an innings and 184 runs
South Africa 157 (W J O'Reilly 5–20) and 98 (C V Grimmett 7–40)
Australia 439 (J H W Fingleton 108, L P J O'Brien 59, W J O'Reilly 56*, E Q Davies 4–75, X C Balaskas 4–165)
5 DURBAN Australia won by an innings and 6 runs
South Africa 222 (K G Viljoen 56, A D Nourse 50, C V Grimmett 7–100) and 227 (B Mitchell 72, C V Grimmett 6–73, W J O'Reilly 4–47)
Australia 455 (J H W Fingleton 118, W A Brown 84, L S Darling 62, B Mitchell 5–87)

1949–50 7th Series Aus 4, SA 0, Drawn 1
1 JOHANNESBURG Australia won by an innings and 85 runs
Australia 413 (A L Hassett 112, S J E Loxton 101, I W Johnson 66)
South Africa 137 (E A B Rowan 60, K R Miller 5–40) and 191 (W A Johnston 6–44)
2 CAPE TOWN Australia won by 8 wkts
Australia 526–7 dec (R N Harvey 178, J R Moroney 87, K R Miller 58, A L Hassett 57, N B F Mann 4–105) and 87–2
South Africa 278 (E A B Rowan 67, A D Nourse 65, C L McCool 5–41) and 333 (A D Nourse 114, H J Tayfield 75, R R Lindwall 5–32)
3 DURBAN Australia won by 5 wkts
South Africa 311 (E A B Rowan 143, A D Nourse 66, W A Johnston 4–75) and 99 (I W Johnson 5–34, W A Johnston 4–39)
Australia 75 (H J Tayfield 7–23) and 336–5 (R N Harvey 151*, S J E Loxton 54)
4 JOHANNESBURG Match Drawn
Australia 465–8 dec (J R Moroney 118, A R Morris 111, K R Miller 84, R N Harvey 56*, A L Hassett 53, M G Melle 5–113) and 259–2 (J R Moroney 101*, R N Harvey 100)
South Africa 352 (G M Fullerton 88, E A B Rowan 55, N B F Mann 52)
5 PORT ELIZABETH Australia won by an innings and 259 runs
Australia 549–7 dec (A L Hassett 167, A R Morris 157, R N Harvey 116)
South Africa 158 (K R Miller 4–42) and 132 (A D Nourse 55)

1952–53 8th Series Aus 2, SA 2, Drawn 1
1 BRISBANE Australia won by 96 runs
Australia 280 (R N Harvey 109, A L Hassett 55, M G Melle 6–71, J C Watkins 4–41) and 277 (A R Morris 58, R N Harvey 52, H J Tayfield 4–116)
South Africa 221 (D T Ring 6–72) and 240 (D J McGlew 69, K J Funston 65, R R Lindwall 5–60)
2 MELBOURNE South Africa won by 82 runs
South Africa 227 (A R A Murray 51, K R Miller 4–62) and 388 (W R Endean 162*, J H B Waite 62)
Australia 243 (C C McDonald 82, K R Miller 52, H J Tayfield 6–84) and 290 (R N Harvey 60, D T Ring 53, H J Tayfield 7–81)
3 SYDNEY Australia won by an innings and 38 runs
South Africa 173 (K J Funston 56, R R Lindwall 4–40) and 232 (W R Endean 71, R A McLean 65, R R Lindwall 4–72)
Australia 443 (R N Harvey 190, C C McDonald 67, D T Ring 58, K R Miller 55, A R A Murray 4–169)
4 ADELAIDE Match Drawn
Australia 530 (A L Hassett 163, C C McDonald 154, R N Harvey 84, G B Hole 59, H J Tayfield 4–142) and 233–3 dec (R N Harvey 116, A R Morris 77)
South Africa 387 K J Funston 92, J C Watkins 76, W R Endean 56, W A Johnston 5–110, R Benaud 4–118) and 177–6 (D J McGlew 54)
5 MELBOURNE South Africa won by 6 wkts
Australia 520 (R N Harvey 205, A R Morris 99, I D Craig 53) and 209 (E R H Fuller 5–66)
South Africa 435 (J C Watkins 92, R A McLean 81, J E Cheetham 66, J H B Waite 64, P N F Mansell 52, W A Johnston 6–152) and 297–4 (R A McLean 76*, W R Endean 70, J C Watkins 50)

1957–58 9th Series Aus 3, SA 0, Drawn 2
1 JOHANNESBURG Match Drawn
South Africa 470–9 dec (J H B Waite 115, D J McGlew 108, T L Goddard 90, W R Endean 50, R A McLean 50, I. Meckiff 5–125) and 201 (W R Endean 77, J H B Waite 59, A K Davidson 6–34)
Australia 368 (R. Benaud 122, C C McDonald 75, R B Simpson 60, P S Heine 6–58) and 162–3 (K D Mackay 65*)
2 CAPE TOWN Australia won by an innings and 141 runs
Australia 449 (J W Burke 189, C C McDonald 99, K D Mackay 63, H J Tayfield 5–120)
South Africa 209 (R Benaud 4–95) and 99 (T L Goddard 56*, R Benaud 5–49)
3 DURBAN Match Drawn
Australia 163 (I D Craig 52, N A T Adcock 6–43) and 292–7 (J W Burke 83, R N Harvey 68, K D Mackay 52*)
South Africa 384 (J H B Waite 134, D J McGlew 105, R Benaud 5–114)
4 JOHANNESBURG Australia won by 10 wkts
Australia 401 (R Benaud 100, K D Mackay 83*, J W Burke 81, A K Davidson 62, P S Heine 6–96) and 1–0
South Africa 203 (K J Funston 70, R Benaud 4–70) and 198 (D J McGlew 70, K J Funston 64*, R Benaud 5–84)
5 PORT ELIZABETH Australia won by 8 wkts
South Africa 214 (H J Tayfield 66, L F Kline 4–33, A K Davidson 4–44) and 144 (A K Davidson 5–38, R Benaud 5–82)
Australia 291 (K D Mackay 77*, C C McDonald 58) and 68–2

1963–64 10th Series Aus 1, SA 1, Drawn 3
1 BRISBANE Match Drawn
Australia 435 (B C Booth 169, N C O'Neill 82, P M Pollock 6–95) and 144–1 dec (W M Lawry 87*)
South Africa 346 (E J Barlow 114, J H B Waite 66, T L Goddard 52, R Benaud 5–68) and 13–1
2 MELBOURNE Australia won by 8 wkts
South Africa 274 (E J Barlow 109, K C Bland 50, G D McKenzie 4–82) and 306 (J H B Waite 77, A J Pithey 76, E J Barlow 54)
Australia 447 (W M Lawry 157, I R Redpath 97, B K Shepherd 96, J T Partridge 4–108) and 136–2 (R B Simpson 55*)
3 SYDNEY Match Drawn
Australia 260 (B C Booth 75, R B Simpson 58, P M Pollock 5–83, J T Partridge 4–88) and 450–9 dec (R Benaud 90, W M Lawry 89, N C O'Neill 88, G D McKenzie 76, J T Partridge 5–123)
South Africa 302 (R G Pollock 122, T L Goddard 80, K C Bland 51) and 326–5 (K C Bland 85, T L Goddard 84, A J Pithey 53*)
4 ADELAIDE South Africa won by 10 wkts
Australia 345 (P J P Burge 91, R B Simpson 78, B K Shepherd 70, B C Booth 58, T L Goddard 5–60) and 331 (B K Shepherd 78, N C O'Neill 66)
South Africa 595 (E J Barlow 201, R G Pollock 175, N J N Hawke 6–139) and 82–0
5 SYDNEY Match Drawn
Australia 311 (B C Booth 102*, P J P Burge 56, J T Partridge 7–91) and 270 (B C Booth 87)
South Africa 411 (K C Bland 126, T L Goddard 93, D T Lindsay 65, R Benaud 4–118) and 76–0

1966–67 11th Series SA 3, Aus 1, Drawn 1
1 JOHANNESBURG South Africa won by 233 runs
South Africa 199 (D T Lindsay 69, G D McKenzie 5–46) and 620 (D T Lindsay 182, R G Pollock 90, P L van der Merwe 76, H R Lance 70, A Bacher 63, E J Barlow 50)
Australia 325 (W M Lawry 98, R B Simpson 65) and 261 (T R Veivers 55, T L Goddard 6–53)
2 CAPE TOWN Australia won by 6 wkts
Australia 542 (R B Simpson 153, K R Stackpole 134, I R Redpath 54, G D Watson 50, E J Barlow 5–85) and 180–4 (I R Redpath 69*)
South Africa 353 (R G Pollock 209, P L van der Merwe 50, G D McKenzie 5–65) and 367 (D T Lindsay 81, P M Pollock 75*, D B Pithey 55, H R Lance 53)
3 DURBAN South Africa won by 8 wkts
South Africa 300 (D T Lindsay 137) and 185–2 (R G Pollock 67*, A Bacher 60*)
Australia 147 and 334 (R B Simpson 94, I R Redpath 80, M J Procter 4–71)
4 JOHANNESBURG Match Drawn
Australia 143 (M J Procter 4–32) and 148–8
South Africa 332–9 dec (D T Lindsay 131, D A Renneberg 5–97)
5 PORT ELIZABETH South Africa won by 7 wkts
Australia 173 (R M Cowper 60) and 278 (R M Cowper 54)
South Africa 276 (R G Pollock 105, T L Goddard 74, G D McKenzie 5–65) and 179–3 (T L Goddard 59)

1969–70 12th Series SA 4, Aus 0
1 CAPE TOWN South Africa won by 170 runs
South Africa 382 (E J Barlow 127, A Bacher 57, A A Mallett 5–126) and 232 (R G Pollock 50, A N Connolly 5–47, J W Gleeson 4–70)
Australia 164 (K D Walters 73, P M Pollock 4–20) and 280 (W M Lawry 83, M J Procter 4–47)
2 DURBAN South Africa won by an innings and 129 runs
South Africa 622–9 dec (R G Pollock 274, B A Richards 140, H R Lance 61)
Australia 157 (A P Sheahan 62) and 336 (I R Redpath 74*, K D Walters 74, K R Stackpole 71)
3 JOHANNESBURG South Africa won by 307 runs
South Africa 279 (B L Irvine 79, B A Richards 65, R G Pollock 52) and 408 (E J Barlow 110, B L Irvine 73, R G Pollock 87, J W Gleeson 5–127)
Australia 202 (K D Walters 64, P M Pollock 5–39) and 178 (I R Redpath 66)
4 PORT ELIZABETH South Africa won by 323 runs
South Africa 311 (B A Richards 81, E J Barlow 73, A N Connolly 6–47) and 470–8 dec (B A Richards 126, B L Irvine 102, A Bacher 73, D T Lindsay 60)
Australia 212 (A P Sheahan 67, I R Redpath 55) and 246 (M J Procter 6–73)

9 Australia *v* West Indies

1930–31 1st Series Aus 4, WI 1
1 ADELAIDE Australia won by 10 wkts
West Indies 296 (E L Bartlett 84, C A Roach 56, G C Grant 53*, C V Grimmett 7–87) and 249 (G C Grant 71*, L S Birkett 64, A Hurwood 4–86, C V Grimmett 4–96)
Australia 376 (A F Kippax 146, S J McCabe 90, O C Scott 4–83) and 172–0 (W H Ponsford 92*, A Jackson 70*)
2 SYDNEY Australia won by an innings and 172 runs
Australia 369 (W H Ponsford 183, W M Woodfull 58, O C Scott 4–66)
West Indies 107 (C V Grimmett 4–54) and 90 (A Hurwood 4–22)
3 BRISBANE Australia won by an innings and 217 runs
Australia 558 (D G Bradman 223, W H Ponsford 109, A F Kippax 84, H C Griffith 4–133)
West Indies 193 (G A Headley 102*, R K Oxenham 4–39, C V Grimmett 4–95) and 148 (C V Grimmett 5–49)
4 MELBOURNE Australia won by an innings and 122 runs
West indies 99 (H Ironmonger 7–23) and 107 (A G Fairfax 4–31, H Ironmonger 4–56)
Australia 328–8 dec (D G Bradman 152, W M Woodfull 83)
5 SYDNEY West indies won by 30 runs
West indies 350–6 dec (F R Martin 123*, G A Headley 105, G C Grant 62) and 124–5 dec
Australia 224 (A G Fairfax 54, G N Francis 4–48) and 220 (A G Fairfax 60*, H C Griffith 4–50)

1951–52 2nd Series Aus 4, WI 1
1 BRISBANE Australia won by 3 wkts
West Indies 216 (R R Lindwall 4–62) and 245 (E D Weekes 70, G E Gomez 55, D T Ring 6–80)
Australia 226 (R R Lindwall 61, A L Valentine 5–99) and 236–7 (S Ramadhin 5–90)
2 SYDNEY Australia won by 7 wkts
West Indies 362 (R J Christiani 76, F M M Worrell 64, C L Walcott 60, G E Gomez 54, R R Lindwall 4–66) and 290 (J D C Goddard 57*, E de C Weekes 56)
Australia 517 (A L Hassett 132, K R Miller 129, D T Ring 65, A L Valentine 4–111) and 137–3
3 ADELAIDE West Indies won by 6 wkts
Australia 82 (F M M Worrell 6–38) and 255 (D T Ring 67, A L Valentine 6–102)
West Indies 105 (W A Johnston 6–62) and 233–4
4 MELBOURNE Australia won by 1 wkt
West Indies 272 (F M M Worrell 108, K R Miller 5–60) and 203 (J B Stollmeyer 54, G E Gomez 52)
Australia 216 (R N Harvey 83, J Trim 5–34) and 260–9 (A L Hassett 102, A L Valentine 5–88)
5 SYDNEY Australia won by 202 runs
Australia 116 (G E Gomez 7–55) and 377 (K R Miller 69, A L Hassett 64, C C McDonald 62, G B Hole 62, F M M Worrell 4–95)
West Indies 78 (K R Miller 5–26) and 213 (J B Stollmeyer 104, R R Lindwall 5–52)

1954–55 3rd Series Aus 3, WI 0, Drawn 2
1 KINGSTON Australia won by 9 wkts
Australia 515–9 dec (K R Miller 147, R N Harvey 133, A R Morris 65, C C McDonald 50) and 20–1
West Indies 259 (C L Walcott 108, R R Lindwall 4–61) and 275 (O G Smith 104, J K Holt 60)
2 PORT OF SPAIN Match Drawn
West Indies 382 (E de C Weekes 139, C L Walcott 126, R R Lindwall 6–95) and 273–4 (C L Walcott 110, E de C Weekes 87*)
Australia 600–9 dec (R N Harvey 133, A R Morris 111, C C McDonald 110, R G Archer 84, I W Johnson 66)
3 GEORGETOWN Australia won by 8 wkts
West Indies 182 (E de C Weekes 81, R Benaud 4–15) and 207 (C L Walcott 73, F M M Worrell 56, I W Johnson 7–44)
Australia 257 (R Benaud 68, C C McDonald 61) and 133–2
4 BRIDGETOWN Match Drawn
Australia 668 (K R Miller 137, R R Lindwall 118, R G Archer 98, R N Harvey 74, L E Favell 72, G R A Langley 53, D T Dewdney 4–125) and 249 (I W Johnson 57, L E Favell 53, D St E Atkinson 5–56)
West Indies 510 (D St E Atkinson 219, C C Depeiaza 122) and 234–6 (C L Walcott 83)
5 KINGSTON Australia won by an innings and 82 runs
West Indies 357 (C L Walcott 155, F M M Worrell 61, E de C Weekes 56, K R Miller 6–107) and 319 (C L Walcott 110, G St A Sobers 64)
Australia 758–8 dec (R N Harvey 204, R G Archer 128, C C McDonald 127, R Benaud 121, K R Miller 109)

1960–61 4th Series Aus 2, WI 1, Tied 1, Drawn 1
1 BRISBANE Match Tied
West Indies 453 (G St A Sobers 132, F M M Worrell 65, J S Solomon 65, F C M Alexander 60, W W Hall 50, A K Davidson 5–135) and 284 (F M M Worrell 65, R B Kanhai 54, A K Davidson 6–87)
Australia 505 (N C O'Neill 181, R B Simpson 92, C C McDonald 57, W W Hall 4–140) and 232 (A K Davidson 80, R Benaud 52, W W Hall 5–63)
2 MELBOURNE Australia won by 7 wkts
Australia 348 (K D Mackay 74, J W Martin 55, L E Favell 51, W W Hall 4–51) and 70–3
West Indies 181 (R B Kanhai 84, S M Nurse 70, A K Davidson 6–53) and 233 (C C Hunte 110, F C M Alexander 72)
3 SYDNEY West Indies won by 222 runs
West Indies 339 (G St A Sobers 168, A K Davidson 5–80, R Benaud 4–86) and 326 (F C M Alexander 108, F M M Worrell 82, C W Smith 55, R Benaud 4–113)
Australia 202 (N C O'Neill 71, A L Valentine 4–67) and 241 (R N Harvey 85, N C O'Neill 70, L R Gibbs 5–66, A L Valentine 4–86)
4 ADELAIDE Match Drawn
West Indies 393 (R B Kanhai 117, F M M Worrell 71, F C M Alexander 63*, R Benaud 5–96) and 432–6 dec (R B Kanhai 115, F C M Alexander 87*, C C Hunte 79, F M M Worrell 53)

Australia 366 (R B Simpson 85, R Benaud 77, C C McDonald 71, L R Gibbs 5–97) and 273–9 (N C O'Neill 65, K D Mackay 62*)

5 MELBOURNE Australia won by 2 wkts

West Indies 292 (G St A Sobers 64, F M Misson 4–58) and 321 (F C M Alexander 73, C C Hunte 52, A K Davidson 5–84)

Australia 356 (C C McDonald 91, R B Simpson 75, P J P Burge 68, G St A Sobers 5–120, L R Gibbs 4–74) and 258–8 (R B Simpson 92, P J P Burge 53)

1964–65 5th Series WI 2, Aus 1, Drawn 2

1 KINGSTON West Indies won by 179 runs

West Indies 239 (W A White 57*, L C Mayne 4–43) and 373 (C C Hunte 81, J S Solomon 76, B F Butcher 71, L C Mayne 4–56, P I Philpott 4–109)

Australia 217 (W W Hall 5–60) and 216 (B C Booth 56, W W Hall 4–45)

2 PORT OF SPAIN Match Drawn

West Indies 429 (B F Butcher 117, C C Hunte 89, G St A Sobers 69, B A Davis 54, N C O'Neill 4–41) and 386 (B A Davis 58, C C Hunte 53, R B Kanhai 53, R B Simpson 4–83)

Australia 516 (R M Cowper 143, B C Booth 117, G Thomas 61)

3 GEORGETOWN West Indies won by 212 runs

West Indies 355 (R B Kanhai 89, N J N Hawke 6–72) and 180 (N J N Hawke 4–43, P I Philpott 4–49)

Australia 179 and 144 (L R Gibbs 6–29)

4 BRIDGETOWN Match Drawn

Australia 650–6 dec (W M Lawry 210, R B Simpson 201, R M Cowper 102, N C O'Neill 51) and 175–4 dec (N C O'Neill 74*, W M Lawry 58*)

West Indies 573 (S M Nurse 201, R B Kanhai 129, C C Hunte 75, G St A Sobers 55, C C Griffith 54, G D McKenzie 4–114) and 242–5 (C C Hunte 81, B A Davis 68)

5 PORT OF SPAIN Australia won by 10 wkts

West Indies 224 (R B Kanhai 121) and 131 (C C Hunte 60*, G D McKenzie 5–33)

Australia 294 (R B Simpson 72, R M Cowper 69, C C Griffith 6–46) and 63–0

1968–69 6th Series Aus 3, WI 1, Drawn 1

1 BRISBANE West Indies won by 125 runs

West Indies 296 (R B Kanhai 94, M C Carew 83, A N Connolly 4–60) and 353 (C H Lloyd 129, M C Carew 71*, J W Gleeson 5–122)

Australia 284 (I M Chappell 117, W M Lawry 105, L R Gibbs 5–88) and 240 (I M Chappell 50, G St A Sobers 6–73)

2 MELBOURNE Australia won by an innings and 30 runs

West Indies 200 (R C Fredericks 76, G D McKenzie 8–71) and 280 (S M Nurse 74, G St A Sobers 67, J W Gleeson 5–61)

Australia 510 (W M Lawry 205, I M Chappell 165, K D Walters 76, G St A Sobers 4–97, L R Gibbs 4–139)

3 SYDNEY Australia won by 10 wkts

West Indies 264 (C H Lloyd 50, G D McKenzie 4–85) and 324 (B F Butcher 101, R B Kanhai 69, J W Gleeson 4–91)

Australia 547 (K D Walters 118, I R Redpath 80, E W Freeman 76, K R Stackpole 58) and 42–0

4 ADELAIDE Match Drawn

West Indies 276 (G St A Sobers 110, B F Butcher 52, E W Freeman 4–52) and 616 (B F Butcher 118, M C Carew 90, R B Kanhai 80, D A J Holford 80, G St A Sobers 52, A N Connolly 5–122)

Australia 533 (K D Walters 110, I M Chappell 76, W M Lawry 62, K R Stackpole 62, G D McKenzie 59, A P Sheahan 51, L R Gibbs 4–145) and 339–9 (I M Chappell 96, W M Lawry 89, K R Stackpole 50, K D Walters 50)

5 SYDNEY Australia won by 382 runs

Australia 619 (K D Walters 242, W M Lawry 151, E W Freeman 56) and 394–8 dec (I R Redpath 132, K D Walters 103)

West Indies 279 (M C Carew 64, C H Lloyd 53, A N Connolly 4–61) and 352 (S M Nurse 137, G St A Sobers 113)

1972–73 7th Series Aus 2, WI 0, Drawn 3

1 KINGSTON Match Drawn

Australia 428–7 dec (R W Marsh 97, K D Walters 72, R Edwards 63, L R Gibbs 4–85) and 260–2 dec (K R Stackpole 142, I R Redpath 60)

West Indies 428 (M L C Foster 125, R B Kanhai 84, L G Rowe 76, A I Kallicharran 50, M H N Walker 6–114, J R Hammond 4–79) and 67–3

2 BRIDGETOWN Match Drawn

Australia 324 (G S Chappell 106, R W Marsh 78, I M Chappell 72) and 300–2 dec (I M Chappell 106*, K D Walters 102*, K R Stackpole 53)

West Indies 391 (R B Kanhai 105, R C Fredericks 98, D L Murray 90, M H N Walker 5–97) and 36–0

3 PORT OF SPAIN Australia won by 44 runs

Australia 332 (K D Walters 112, I R Redpath 66, G S Chappell 56) and 281 (I M Chappell 97, L R Gibbs 5–102)

West Indies 280 (R B Kanhai 56, A I Kallicharran 53, T J Jenner 4–98) and 289 (A I Kallicharran 91, R C Fredericks 76, K J O'Keeffe 4–57)

4 GEORGETOWN Australia won by 10 wkts

West Indies 366 (C H Lloyd 178, R B Kanhai 57, K D Walters 5–66) and 109 (J R Hammond 4–38, M H N Walker 4–45)

Australia 341 (I M Chappell 109, K D Walters 81, G S Chappell 51) and 135–0 (K R Stackpole 76*, I R Redpath 57*)

5 PORT OF SPAIN Match Drawn

Australia 419–8 dec (R Edwards 74, K D Walters 70, I M Chappell 56, R W Marsh 56) and 218–7 dec (L R Gibbs 4–66)

West Indies 319 (R C Fredericks 73, C H Lloyd 59, M H N Walker 5–75, T J Jenner 5–90) and 135–5

1975–76 8th Series Aus 5, WI 1

1 BRISBANE Australia won by 8 wkts

West Indies 214 (D L Murray 66, G J Gilmour 4–42) and 370 (L G Rowe 107, A I Kallicharran 101, D L Murray 55)

Australia 366 (G S Chappell 123, A Turner 81, L R Gibbs 5–102) and 219–2 (G S Chappell 109*, I M Chappell 74*)

2 PERTH West Indies won by an innings and 87 runs

Australia 329 (I M Chappell 156, M A Holding 4–88) and 169 (A M E Roberts 7–54)

West Indies 585 (R C Fredericks 169, C H Lloyd 149, D L Murray 63, A I Kallicharran 57)

3 MELBOURNE Australia won by 8 wkts

West Indies 224 (R C Fredericks 59, J R Thomson 5–62, D K Lillee 4–56) and 312 (C H Lloyd 102)

Australia 485 (G J Cosier 109, I R Redpath 102, R W Marsh 56, G S Chappell 52, A M E Roberts 4–126) and 55–2

4 SYDNEY Australia won by 7 wkts

West Indies 355 (L G Rowe 67, C H Lloyd 51, M H N Walker 4–70) and 128 (D L Murray 50, J R Thomson 6–50)

Australia 405 (G S Chappell 182*, A Turner 53) and 82–3

5 ADELAIDE Australia won by 190 runs

Australia 418 (I R Redpath 103, G J Gilmour 95, V A Holder 5–108) and 345–7 dec (A Turner 136, I R Redpath 65)

West Indies 274 (K D Boyce 95*, A I Kallicharran 76, J R Thomson 4–68) and 299 (I V A Richards 101, K D Boyce 69, A I Kallicharran 67)

6 MELBOURNE Australia won by 165 runs

Australia 351 (I R Redpath 101, G S Chappell 68, G N Yallop 57) and 300–3 dec (R B McCosker 109*, I R Redpath 70, G S Chappell 54*)

West Indies 160 (I V A Richards 50, G J Gilmour 5–34, D K Lillee 5–63) and 326 (I V A Richards 98, C H Lloyd 91*, J R Thomson 4–80)

1977–78 9th Series WI 3, Aus 1, Drawn 1

1 PORT OF SPAIN West Indies won by an innings and 106 runs

Australia 90 (C E H Croft 4–15) and 209 (G N Yallop 81, A M E Roberts 5–56)

West Indies 405 (A I Kallicharran 127, C H Lloyd 86, D L Haynes 61, J D Higgs 4–91)

2 BRIDGETOWN West Indies won by 9 wkts

Australia 250 (B Yardley 74, G M Wood 69, C E H Croft 4–47, J Garner 4–65) and 178 (G M Wood 56, A M E Roberts 4–50, J Garner 4–56)

West Indies 288 (D L Haynes 66, D L Murray 60, J R Thomson 6–77) and 141–1 (C G Greenidge 80*, D L Haynes 55)

3 GEORGETOWN Australia won by 3 wkts

West Indies 205 (A T Greenidge 56, S Shivnarine 53, J R Thomson 4–56, W M Clark 4–65) and 439 (H A Gomes 101, A B Williams 100, S Shivnarine 63, D R Parry 51, W M Clark 4–124)

Australia 286 (R B Simpson 67, S J Rixon 54, G M Wood 50, N Phillip 4–75) and 362–7 (G M Wood 126, C S Serjeant 124)

4 PORT OF SPAIN West indies won by 198 runs

West indies 292 (A I Kallicharran 92, A B Williams 87) and 290 (A E Greenidge 69, D R Parry 65, B Yardley 4–40)

Australia 290 (G N Yallop 75, V A Holder 6–28) and (D R Parry 5–15)

5 KINGSTON Match Drawn

Australia 343 (P M Toohey 122, G N Yallop 57, R R Jumadeen 4–72) and 305–3 dec (P M Toohey 97, G M Wood 90)

West Indies 280 (H A Gomes 115, S Shivnarine 53, T J Laughlin 5–101) and 258–9 (A I Kallicharran 126, B Yardley 4–35)

1979–80 10th Series WI 2, Aus 0, Drawn 1

1 BRISBANE Match Drawn

Australia 268 (B M Laird 92, G S Chappell 74, J Garner 4–55) and 448–6 dec (K J Hughes 130*, G S Chappell 124, B M Laird 75)

West Indies 441 (I V A Richards 140, J Garner 60, L G Rowe 50, D K Lillee 4–104) and 40–3

2 MELBOURNE West Indies won by 10 wkts

Australia 156 (M A Holding 4–40) and 259 (K J Hughes 70, B M Laird 69)

West Indies 397 (I V A Richards 96, A M E Roberts 54, G Dymock 4–106) and 22–0

3 ADELAIDE West Indies won by 408 runs

West Indies 328 (C H Lloyd 121, I V A Richards 76, D K Lillee 5–78) and 448 (A I Kallicharran 106, C G Greenidge 76, I V A Richards 74, G Dymock 5–104)

Australia 203 (A R Border 54, B M Laird 52, C E H Croft 4–57) and 165 (M A Holding 4–40)

1981–82 11th Series Aus 1, WI 1, Drawn 1

1 MELBOURNE Australia won by 58 runs

Australia 198 (K J Hughes 100*, M A Holding 5–45) and 222 (A R Border 66, B M Laird 64, M A Holding 6–62)

West Indies 201 (H A Gomes 55, D K Lillee 7–83) and 161 (B Yardley 4–38)

2 SYDNEY Match Drawn

West Indies 384 (H A Gomes 126, C G Greenidge 66, D K Lillee 4–119) and 255 (C H Lloyd 57, D L Haynes 51, B Yardley 7–98)

Australia 267 (G M Wood 63, A R Border 53*, M A Holding 5–64) and 200–4 (J Dyson 127*)

3 ADELAIDE West Indies won by 5 wkts

Australia 238 (A R Border 78, G S Chappell 61, M A Holding 5–72, A M E Roberts 4–43) and 386 (A R Border 126, K J Hughes 84, B M Laird 78, J Garner 5–56)

West Indies 389 (H A Gomes 124*, C H Lloyd 53, P J Dujon 51, B Yardley 5–132, J R Thomson 4–112) and 239–5 (C H Lloyd 77*, C G Greenidge 52, I V A Richards 50)

10 Australia *v* New Zealand

1945–46 1st Series Aus 1, NZ 0

1 WELLINGTON Australia won by an innings and 103 runs

New Zealand 42 (W J O'Reilly 5–14, E R H Toshack 4–12) and 54

Australia 199–8 dec (W A Brown 67, S G Barnes 54, J Cowie 6–40)

1973–74 2nd Series Aus 2, NZ 0, Drawn 1

1 MELBOURNE Australia won by an innings and 25 runs

Australia 462–8 dec (K R Stackpole 122, K D Walters 79, G S Chappell 60, I M Chappell 54, G J Gilmour 52, D R Hadlee 4–102)

New Zealand 237 (K J Wadsworth 80, G J Gilmour 4–75) and 200 (A A Mallett 4–63)

2 SYDNEY Match Drawn

New Zealand 312 (J M Parker 108, K J Wadsworth 54, K D Walters 4–39) and 305–9 dec (J F M Morrison 117, B F Hastings 83)

Australia 162 (R J Hadlee 4–33) and 30–2

3 ADELAIDE Australia won by an innings and 57 runs

Australia 477 (R W Marsh 132, K D Walters 94, K J O'Keeffe 85, D R O'Sullivan 5–148)

New Zealand 218 and 202 (B E Congdon 71*, G Dymock 5–58)

1973–74 3rd Series Aus 1, NZ 1, Drawn 1

1 WELLINGTON Match Drawn

Australia 511–6 dec (G S Chappell 247*, I M Chappell 145) and 460–8 (G S Chappell 133, I M Chappell 121, I R Redpath 93)

New Zealand 484 (B E Congdon 132, B F Hastings 101, G M Turner 79, J F M Morrison 66)

2 CHRISTCHURCH New Zealand won by 5 wkts

Australia 223 (I R Redpath 71) and 259 (K D Walters 65, I R Redpath 58, I C Davis 50, R J Hadlee 4–71, D R Hadlee 4–75)

New Zealand 255 (G M Turner 101, M H N Walker 4–60) and 230–5 (G M Turner 110*)

3 AUCKLAND Australia won by 297 runs

Australia 221 (K D Walters 104*, R O Collinge 5–82, B E Congdon 4–46) and 346 (I R Redpath 159*, R O Collinge 4–84)

New Zealand 112 (G J Gilmour 5–64, A A Mallett 4–22) and 158 (G M Turner 72, M H N Walker 4–39)

1976–77 4th Series Aus 1, NZ 0, Drawn 1

1 CHRISTCHURCH Match Drawn

Australia 552 (K D Walters 250, G J Gilmour 101) and 154–4 dec (R B McCosker 77*)

New Zealand 357 (M G Burgess 66, H J Howarth 61, K J O'Keeffe 5–101) and 293–8 (B E Congdon 107*, M H N Walker 4–65)

2 AUCKLAND Australia won by 10 wkts

New Zealand 229 (G P Howarth 59, G N Edwards 51, D K Lillee 5–51) and 175 (R J Hadlee 81, D K Lillee 6–72)

Australia 377 (R B McCosker 84, G J Gilmour 64, G S Chappell 58, E J Chatfield 4–100) and 28–0

1980–81 5th Series Aus 2, NZ 0, Drawn 1

1 BRISBANE Australia won by 10 wkts

New Zealand 225 (G P Howarth 65, J M Parker 52, J D Higgs 4–59) and 142 (B A Edgar 51, R J Hadlee 51ç, D K Lillee 6–53)

Australia 305 (G M Wood 111, B L Cairns 5–87) and 63–0

2 PERTH Australia won by 8 wkts

New Zealand 196 (J V Coney 71, D K Lillee 5–63) and 121 (J D Higgs 4–25)

Australia 265 (R W Marsh 91, K D Walters 55, R J Hadlee 5–87, B L Cairns 4–88) and 55–2

3 MELBOURNE Match Drawn

Australia 321 (K D Walters 107, K J Hughes 51) and 188 (G S Chappell 78, R J Hadlee 6–57)

New Zealand 317 (G P Howarth 65, J M Parker 56, J V Coney 55*, R M Hogg 4–60) and 128–6

1981–82 6th Series Aus 1, NZ 1, Drawn 1

1 WELLINGTON Match Drawn

New Zealand 266–7 dec (G P Howarth 58*, B A Edgar 55)

Australia 85–1

2 AUCKLAND New Zealand won by 5 wkts

Australia 210 (G B Troup 4–82) and 280 (G M Wood 100, R J Hadlee 5–63)

New Zealand 387 (B A Edgar 161, J M Coney 73, G P Howarth 56, B Yardley 4–142) and 109–5

3 CHRISTCHURCH Australia won by 8 wkts

Australia 353 (G S Chappell 176, G M Wood 64, R J Hadlee 6–100) and 63–2

New Zealand 149 (J R Thomson 4–51) and 272 (J G Wright 141, B Yardley 4–80)

11 Australia *v* India

1947–48 1st Series Aus 4, India 0, Drawn 1

1 BRISBANE Australia won by an innings and 226 runs

Australia 382–8 dec (D G Bradman 185, K R Miller 58, L Amarnath 4–84)

India 58 (E R H Toshack 5–2) and 98 (E R H Toshack 6–29)

2 SYDNEY Match Drawn

India 188 (D G Phadkar 51) and 61–7

Australia 107 (V S Hazare 4–29)

3 MELBOURNE Australia won by 233 runs

Australia 394 (D G Bradman 132, A L Hassett 80, L Amarnath 4–78, M H Mankad 4–135) and 255–4 dec (D G Bradman 127*, A R Morris 100*)

India 291–9 dec (M H Mankad 116, D G Phadkar 55*, I W Johnson 4–59) and 125 (I W Johnson 4–35, W A Johnston 4–44)

4 ADELAIDE Australia won by an innings and 16 runs

Australia 674 (D G Bradman 201, A L Hassett 198*, S G Barnes 112, K R Miller 67, C R Rangachari 4–141)

India 381 (V S Hazare 116, D G Phadkar 123, I W Johnson 4–64) and 277 (V S Hazare 145, H R Adhikari 51, R R Lindwall 7–38)
5 MELBOURNE Australia won by an innings and 177 runs
Australia 575–8 dec (R N Harvey 153, W A Brown 99, S J E Loxton 80, D G Bradman 57*)
India 331 (M H Mankad 111, V S Hazare 74, D G Phadkar 56*) and 67

1956–57 2nd Series Aus 2, India 0, Drawn 1
1 MADRAS Australia won by an innings and 5 runs
India 161 (R Benaud 7–72) and 153 (R R Lindwall 7–43)
Australia 319 (I W Johnson 73, M H Mankad 4–90)
2 BOMBAY Match Drawn
India 251 (G S Ramchand 109, V L Manjrekar 55) and 250–5 (P Roy 79, P R Umrigar 78)
Australia 523–7 dec (J W Burke 161, R N Harvey 140, P J P Burge 83)
3 CALCUTTA Australia won by 94 runs
Australia 177 (P J P Burge 58, Ghulam Ahmed 7–49) and 189–9 dec (R N Harvey 69, M H Mankad 4–49)
India 136 (R Benaud 6–52) and 136 (R Benaud 5–53, J W Burke 4–37)

1959–60 3rd Series Aus 2, India 1, Drawn 2
1 NEW DELHI Australia won by an innings and 127 runs
India 135 and 206 (P Roy 99, R Benaud 5–76, L F Kline 4–42)
Australia 468 (R N Harvey 114, K D Mackay 78, P R Umrigar 4–49)
2 KANPUR India won by 119 runs
India 152 (A K Davidson 5–31, R Benaud 4–63) and 291 (N J Contractor 74, R B Kenny 51, A K Davidson 7–93)
Australia 219 (C C McDonald 53, R N Harvey 51, J M Patel 9–69) and 105 (J M Patel 5–55, P R Umrigar 4–27)
3 BOMBAY Match Drawn
India 289 (N J Contractor 108, A A Baig 50, A K Davidson 4–62, I Meckiff 4–79) and 226–5 dec (A A Baig 58, P Roy 57, R B Kenny 55*)
Australia 387–8 dec (N C O'Neill 163, R N Harvey 102, R G Nadkarni 6–105) and 34–1
4 MADRAS Australia won by an innings and 55 runs
Australia 342 (L E Favell 101, K D Mackay 89, R B Desai 4–93)
India 149 (B K Kunderan 71, R Benaud 5–43) and 138
5 CALCUTTA Match Drawn
India 194 and 339 (M L Jaisimha 74, R B Kenny 62, C G Borde 50, R Benaud 4–103)
Australia 331 (N C O'Neill 113, P J P Burge 60, A T W Grout 50, R B Desai 4–111) and 121–2 (L E Favell 62*)

1964–65 4th Series Aus 1, India 1, Drawn 1
1 MADRAS Australia won by 139 runs
Australia 211 (W M Lawry 62, R G Nadkarni 5–31) and 397 (R B Simpson 77, T R Veivers 74, P J P Burge 60, R G Nadkarni 6–91)
India 276 (M A K Pataudi 128*, G D McKenzie 6–58) and 193 (Hanumant Singh 94, G D McKenzie 4–33)
2 BOMBAY India won by 2 wkts
Australia 320 (P J P Burge 80, B N Jarman 78, T R Veivers 67, B S Chandrasekhar 4–50) and 274 (R M Cowper 81, B C Booth 74, W M Lawry 68, R G Nadkarni 4–33, B S Chandrasekhar 4–73)
India 341 (M A K Pataudi 86, M L Jaisimha 66, V L Manjrekar 59, T R Veivers 4–68) and 256–8 (D N Sardesai 56, M A K Pataudi 53)
3 CALCUTTA Match Drawn
Australia 174 (R B Simpson 67, W M Lawry 50, S A Durani 6–73) and 143–1 (R B Simpson 71)
India 235 (C G Borde 68*, M L Jaisimha 57, R B Simpson 4–45)

1967–68 5th Series Aus 4, India 0
1 ADELAIDE Australia won by 146 runs
Australia 335 (R M Cowper 92, A P Sheahan 81, R B Simpson 55, S Abid Ali 6–55) and 369 (R M Cowper 108, R B Simpson 103, R F Surti 5–74)
India 307 (F M Engineer 89, R F Surti 70, C G Borde 69, A N Connolly 4–54) and 251 (V Subramanya 75, R F Surti 53, D A Renneberg 5–39)
2 MELBOURNE Australia won by an innings and 4 runs
India 173 (M A K Pataudi 75, G D McKenzie 7–66) and 352 (A L Wadekar 99, M A K Pataudi 85)
Australia 529 (I M Chappell 151, R B Simpson 109, W M Lawry 100, B N Jarman 65, E A S Prasanna 6–141)
3 BRISBANE Australia won by 39 runs
Australia 379 (K D Walters 93, W M Lawry 64, A P Sheahan 58, R M Cowper 51) and 294 (I R Redpath 79, K D Walters 62*, E A S Prasanna 6–104)
India 279 (M A K Pataudi 74, M L Jaisimha 74, R F Surti 52) and 355 (M L Jaisimha 101, R F Surti 64, C G Borde 63, R M Cowper 4–104)
4 SYDNEY Australia won by 144 runs
Australia 317 (K D Walters 94*, A P Sheahan 72, W M Lawry 66) and 292 (R M Cowper 165, W M Lawry 52, E A S Prasanna 4–96)
India 268 (S Abid Ali 78, M A K Pataudi 51, E W Freeman 4–86) and 197 (S Abid Ali 81, R B Simpson 5–59, R M Cowper 4–49)

1969–70 6th Series Aus 3, India 1, Drawn 1
1 BOMBAY Australia won by 8 wkts
India 271 (M A K Pataudi 95, A V Mankad 74, G D McKenzie 5–69) and 137 (J W Gleeson 4–56)
Australia 345 (K R Stackpole 103, I R Redpath 77, E A S Prasanna 5–121) and 67–2
2 KANPUR Match Drawn
India 320 (F M Engineer 77, A V Mankad 64, A N Connolly 4–91) and 312–7 dec (G R Viswanath 137, A V Mankad 68)
Australia 348 (A P Sheahan 114, I R Redpath 70, K D Walters 53) and 95–0 (W M Lawry 56*)
3 NEW DELHI India won by 7 wkts
Australia 296 (I M Chappell 138, K R Stackpole 61, B S Bedi 4–71, E A S Prasanna 4–111) and 107 (B S Bedi 5–37, E A S Prasanna 5–42)
India 223 (A V Mankad 97, A A Mallett 6–64) and 181–3 (A L Wadekar 91*)
4 CALCUTTA Australia won by 10 wkts
India 212 (G R Viswanath 54, G D McKenzie 6–67) and 161 (A L Wadekar 62, A N Connolly 4–31, E W Freeman 4–54)
Australia 335 (I M Chappell 99, K D Walters 56, B S Bedi 7–98) and 42–0
5 MADRAS Australia won by 77 runs
Australia 258 (K D Walters 102, S Venkataraghavan 4–71, E A S Prasanna 4–100) and 153 (I R Redpath 63, E A S Prasanna 6–74)
India 163 (M A K Pataudi 59, A A Mallett 5–91) and 171 (G R Viswanath 59, A L Wadekar 55, A A Mallett 5–53)

1977–78 7th Series Aus 3, India 2
1 BRISBANE Australia won by 16 runs
Australia 166 (P M Toohey 82, B S Bedi 5–55) and 327 (R B Simpson 89, P M Toohey 57, S Madan Lal 5–72)
India 153 (W M Clark 4–46) and 324 (S M Gavaskar 113, S M H Kirmani 55, J R Thomson 4–76, W M Clark 4–101)
2 PERTH Australia won by 2 wkts
India 402 (M Amarnath 90, C P S Chauhan 88, J R Thomson 4–101) and 330–9 dec (S M Gavaskar 127, M Amarnath 100, J B Gannon 4–77)
Australia 394 (R B Simpson 176, J Dyson 53, S J Rixon 50, B S Bedi 5–89) and 342–8 (A L Mann 105, P M Toohey 83, B S Bedi 5–105)
3 MELBOURNE India won by 222 runs
India 256 (M Amarnath 72, G R Viswanath 59, W M Clark 4–73) and 343 (S M Gavaskar 118, G R Viswanath 54, W M Clark 4–96)
Australia 213 (C S Serjeant 85, G J Cosier 67, B S Chandrasekhar 6–52) and 164 (B S Chandrasekhar 6–52, B S Bedi 4–58)
4 SYDNEY India won by an innings and 2 runs
Australia 131 (B S Chandrasekhar 4–30) and 263 (P M Toohey 85, G J Cosier 68, E A S Prasanna 4–51)
India 386–8 dec (G R Viswanath 79, K D Ghavri 64, J R Thomson 4–83)
5 ADELAIDE Australia won by 47 runs
Australia 505 (G N Yallop 121, R B Simpson 100, W M Darling 65, P M Toohey 60, B S Chandrasekhar 5–136) and 256 (W M Darling 56, R B Simpson 51, K D Ghavri 4–45, B S Bedi 4–53)
India 269 (G R Viswanath 89, W M Clark 4–62) and 445 (M Amarnath 86, D B Vengsarkar 78, G R Viswanath 73, S M H Kirmani 51, B Yardley 4–134)

1979–80 8th Series India 2, Aus 0, Drawn 4
1 MADRAS Match Drawn
Australia 390 (A R Border 162, K J Hughes 100, D R Doshi 6–103) and 212–7 (A M J Hilditch 55, A R Border 50)
India 425 (Kapil Dev 83, D B Vengsarkar 65, Yashpal Sharma 52, S M H Kirmani 57, S M Gavaskar 50, J D Higgs 7–143)
2 BANGALORE Match Drawn
Australia 333 (K J Hughes 86, A M J Hilditch 62, N S Yadav 4–49) and 77–3
India 457–5 dec (G R Viswanath 161*, D B Vengsarkar 112, B Yardley 4–107)
3 KANPUR India won by 153 runs
India 271 (S M Gavaskar 76, C P S Chauhan 58, D B Vengsarker 52, G Dymock 5–99, R M Hogg 4–66) and 311 (C P S Chauhan 84, G R Viswanath 52, G Dymock 7–67)
Australia 304 (G N Yallop 89, W M Darling 59, K J Hughes 50) and 125 (Kapil Dev 4–30, N S Yadav 4–35)
4 NEW DELHI Match Drawn
India 510–7 dec (G R Viswanath 131, S M Gavaskar 115, Yashpal Sharma 100*, G Dymock 4–135)
Australia 298 (D F Whatmore 77, K J Wright 55*, Kapil Dev 5–82) and 413 (A M J Hilditch 85, P R Sleep 64, D F Whatmore 54)
5 CALCUTTA Match Drawn
Australia 442 (G N Yallop 167, K J Hughes 92, B Yardley 61*, A R Border 54, Kapil Dev 5–74, D R Doshi 4–92) and 151–6 dec (K J Hughes 64*)
India 347 (G R Viswanath 96, D B Vengsarkar 89, B Yardley 4–91) and 200–4 (Yashpal Sharma 85*, C P S Chauhan 50, G Dymock 4–63)
6 BOMBAY India won by an innings and 100 runs
India 458–8 dec (S M Gavaskar 123, S M H Kirmani 101*, K D Ghavri 86, C P S Chauhan 73)
Australia 160 (G N Yallop 60, D R Doshi 5–43, N S Yadav 4–40) and 198 (K J Hughes 80, A R Border 61, Kapil Dev 4–39)

1980–81 9th Series Aus 1, India 1, Drawn 1
1 SYDNEY Australia won by an innings and 4 runs
India 201 (S M Patil 65*, D K Lillee 4–86, L S Pascoe 4–61) and 201 (J D Higgs 4–45)
Australia 406 (G S Chappell 204, K D Walters 67, Kapil Dev 5–97, K D Ghavri 5–107)
2 ADELAIDE Match Drawn
Australia 528 (K J Hughes 213, G M Wood 125, A R Border 57, N S Yadav 4–143) and 221–7 dec (K J Hughes 53, G S Chappell 52)
India 419 (S M Patil 174, C P S Chauhan 97, D K Lillee 4–80) and 135–8
3 MELBOURNE India won by 59 rums
India 237 (G R Viswanath 114, D K Lillee 4–65) and 324 (C P S Chauhan 70, D K Lillee 4–104)
Australia 419 (A R Border 124, K D Walters 78, G S Chappell 76) and 83 (Kapil Dev 5–28)

12 Australia *v* Pakistan

1956–57 1st Series Pak 1, Aus 0
1 KARACHI Pakistan won by 9 wkts
Australia 80 (Fazal Mahmood 6–34, Kham Mohammad 4–43) and 187 (R Benaud 56, Fazal Mahmood 7–80)
Pakistan 199 (A H Kardar 69, Wazir Mohammad 67, I W Johnson 4–50) and 69–1

1959–60 2nd Series Aus 2, Pak 0, Drawn 1
1 DACCA Australia won by 8 wkts
Pakistan 200 (Hanif Mohammad 66, D Sharpe 56, A K Davidson 4–42, R Benaud 4–69) and 134 (K D Mackay 6–42, R Benaud 4–42)
Australia 225 (R N Harvey 96, A T W Grout 66*, Fazal Mahmood 5–71) and 112–2
2 LAHORE Australia won by 7 wkts
Pakistan 146 (A K Davidson 4–48) and 366 (Saeed Ahmed 166, Imtiaz Ahmed 54, L F Kline 7–75)
Australia 391–9 dec (N C O'Neill 134) and 123–3
3 KARACHI Match Drawn
Pakistan 287 (Saeed Ahmed 91, Ijaz Butt 58, Hanif Mohammad 51, R Benaud 5–93) and 194–8 dec (Hanif Mohammad 101*)
Australia 257 (R N Harvey 54, Fazal Mahmood 5–74) and 83–2

1964–65 3rd Series Drawn 1
1 KARACHI Match Drawn
Pakistan 414 (Khalid Ibadulla 166, Abdul Kadir 95, Intikhab Alam 53, G D McKenzie 6–69) and 279–8 dec (Javed Burki 62)
Australia 352 (R B Simpson 153, P J P Burge 54) and 227–2 (R B Simpson 115)

1964–65 4th Series Drawn 1
1 MELBOURNE Match Drawn
Pakistan 287 (Hanif Mohammad 104, Saeed Ahmed 80) and 326 (Hanif Mohammad 93, Intikhab Alam 61, N J N Hawke 4–72, G D McKenzie 4–74)
Australia 448 (T R Veivers 88, R M Cowper 83, B C Booth 57, B K Shepherd 55, Arif Butt 6–89) and 88–2

1972–73 5th Series Aus 3, Pak 0
1 ADELAIDE Australia won by an innings and 114 runs
Pakistan 257 (Wasim Bari 72, Intikhab Alam 64, D K Lillee 4–49, R A L Massie 4–70) and 214 (Sadiq Mohammad 81, A A Mallett 8–59)
Australia 585 (I M Chappell 196, R W Marsh 118, R Edwards 89)
2 MELBOURNE Australia won by 92 runs
Australia 441–5 dec (I R Redpath 135, G S Chappell 116*, R W Marsh 74, I M Chappell 66) and 425 (J Benaud 142, A P Sheahan 127, G S Chappell 62)
Pakistan 574–8 dec (Majid Khan 158, Sadiq Mohammad 137, Intikhab Alam 68, Mushtaq Mohammad 60, Zaheer Abbas 51, Saeed Ahmed 50) and 200
3 SYDNEY Australia won by 52 runs
Australia 334 (I R Redpath 79, R Edwards 69, Sarfraz Nawaz 4–53) and 184 (Sarfraz Nawaz 4–56, Saleem Altaf 4–60)
Pakistan 360 (Mushtaq Mohammad 121, Asif Iqbal 65, Nasim-ul-Ghani 64, G S Chappell 5–61) and 106 (M H N Walker 6–15)

1976–77 6th Series Pak 1, Aus 1, Drawn 1
1 ADELAIDE Match Drawn
Pakistan 272 (Zaheer Abbas 85) and 466 (Asif Iqbal 152*, Zaheer Abbas 101, Javed Miandad 54, D K Lillee 5–163)
Australia 454 (K D Walters 107, I C Davis 105, R B McCosker 65, G S Chappell 52, Mushtaq Mohammad 4–58) and 261–6 (G S Chappell 70, K D Walters 51, Iqbal Qasim 4–84)
2 MELBOURNE Australia won by 348 runs
Australia 517–8 dec (G J Cosier 168, G S Chappell 121, A Turner 82, I C Davis 56, Iqbal Qasim 4–111) and 315–8 dec (R B McCosker 105, I C Davis 88, G S Chappell 67, Imran Khan 5–122)
Pakistan 333 (Sadiq Mohammad 105, Zaheer Abbas 90, Majid Khan 76, D K Lillee 6–82) and 151 (Zaheer Abbas 58, K J O'Keeffe 4–38, D K Lillee 4–53)
3 SYDNEY Pakistan won by 8 wkts
Australia 211 (G J Cosier 50, Imran Khan 6–102) and 180 (Imran Khan 6–63)
Pakistan 360 (Asif Iqbal 120, Javed Miandad 64, Haroon Rashid 57, M H N Walker 4–112) and 32–2

1978–79 7th Series Pak 1, Aus 1
1 MELBOURNE Pakistan won by 71 runs
Pakistan 196 (R M Hogg 4–49) and 353–9 dec (Majid Khan 108, Zaheer Abbas 59)
Australia 168 (Imran Khan 4–26) and 310 (A R Border 105, K J Hughes 84, A M J Hilditch 62, Sarfraz Nawaz 9–86)
2 PERTH Australia won by 7 wkts
Pakistan 277 (Javed Miandad 129*, A G Hurst 4–61) and 285 (Asif Iqbal 134*, A G Hurst 5–94)
Australia 327 (A R Border 85, W M Darling 75) and 236–3 (W M Darling 79, A R Border 66*)

1979–80 8th Series Pak 1, Aus 0, Drawn 2
1 KARACHI Pakistan won by 7 wkts
Australia 225 (K J Hughes 85, Tausif Ahmed 4–64, Iqbal Qasim 4–69) and 140 (A R Border 58*, Iqbal Qasim 7–49)
Pakistan 292 (Majid Khan 89, Taslim Arif 58, R J Bright 7–87) and 76–3
2 FAISALABAD Match Drawn
Australia 617 (G S Chappell 235, G N Yallop 172, K J Hughes 88, R W Marsh 71)
Pakistan 382–2 (Taslim Arif 210*, Javed Miandad 106*)
3 LAHORE Match Drawn
Australia 407–7 dec (A R Border 150*, J M Wiener 93, G S Chappell 56, Iqbal Qasim 4–90) and 391–8 (A R Border 153, B M Laird 63, G S Chappell 57)

Pakistan 420–9 dec (Majid Khan 110*, Mudassar Nazar 59, Wasim Raja 55, Imran Khan 56, R J Bright 5–172)

1981–82 9th Series Aus 2, Pak 1
1 PERTH Australia won by 286 runs
Australia 180 (Imran Khan 4–66) and 424–8 dec (K J Hughes 106, B M Laird 85)
Pakistan 62 (D K Lillee 5–18, T M Alderman 4–36) and 256 (Javed Miandad 79, B Yardley 6–84)
2 BRISBANE Australia won by 10 wkts
Pakistan 291 (Zaheer Abbas 80, D K Lillee 5–81) and 223 (D K Lillee 4–51, B Yardley 4–77)
Australia 512–9 dec (G S Chappell 201, G M Wood 72, Imran Khan 4–92) and 3–0
3 MELBOURNE Pakistan won by an inns and 82 runs
Pakistan 500–8 dec (Mudassar Nazar 95, Zaheer Abbas 90, Majid Khan 74, Imran Khan 70*, Wasim Raja 50, B Yardley 7–187)
Australia 293 (G M Wood 100) and 125 (B M Laird 52, Iqbal Qasim 4–44)

13 South Africa *v* New Zealand

1931–32 1st Series SA 2, NZ 0
1 CHRISTCHURCH South Africa won by an innings and 12 runs
New Zealand 293 (F T Badcock 64, A W Roberts 54, Q McMillan 4–61) and 146 (G L Weir 74*, Q McMillan 5–66)
South Africa 451 (B Mitchell 113, J A J Christy 103, E L Dalton 82, D P B Morkel 51)
2 WELLINGTON South Africa won by 8 wkts
New Zealand 364 (H G Vivian 100, C S Dempster 64, F T Badcock 53, I B Cromb 51*, Q McMillan 5–125) and 193 (H G Vivian 73, N A Quinn 4–37)
South Africa 410 (X C Balaskas 122*, K G Viljoen 81, J A J Christy 62, H G Vivian 4–58) and 150–2 (B Mitchell 53, J A J Christy 53)

1952–53 2nd Series SA 1, NZ 0, Drawn 1
1 WELLINGTON South Africa won by an innings and 180 runs
South Africa 524–8 dec (D J McGlew 255*, A R A Murray 109, R W Blair 4–98)
New Zealand 172 (B Sutcliffe 62) and 172 (J C Watkins 4–22)
2 AUCKLAND Match Drawn
South Africa 377 (W R Endean 116, J H B Waite 72, J E Cheetham 54) and 200–5 dec (D J McGlew 50)
New Zealand 245 (H J Tayfield 5–62) and 31–2

1953–54 3rd Series SA 4, NZ 0, Drawn 1
1 DURBAN South Africa won by an innings and 58 runs
South Africa 437–9 dec (R A McLean 101, D J McGlew 84, C B van Ryneveld 68*)
New Zealand 230 (G O Rabone 107, H J Tayfield 6–62) and 149 (G O Rabone 68)
2 JOHANNESBURG South Africa won by 132 runs
South Africa 271 (W R Endean 93, C B van Ryneveld 65) and 148 (J R Reid 4–34, A R MacGibbon 4–62)
New Zealand 187 (B Sutcliffe 80*, D E J Ironside 5–51) and 100 (N A T Adcock 5–43)
3 CAPE TOWN Match Drawn
New Zealand 505 (J R Reid 135, J E F Beck 99, M E Chapple 76, B Sutcliffe 66, G O Rabone 56, D E J Ironside 4–117)
South Africa 326 (J E Cheetham 89, D J McGlew 86, G O Rabone 6–68, A R MacGibbon 4–71) and 159–3 (R J Westcott 62)
4 JOHANNESBURG South Africa won by 9 wkts
South Africa 243 (D J McGlew 61, J H B Waite 52) and 25–1
New Zealand 79 (H J Tayfield 6–13) and 188 (N A T Adcock 5–45)
5 PORT ELIZABETH South Africa won by 5 wkts
New Zealand 226 (J C Watkins 4–34, N A T Adcock 4–86) and 222 (J R Reid 73, B Sutcliffe 52, C B van Ryneveld 4–67)
South Africa 237 (J R Reid 4–51) and 215–5 (W R Endean 87)

1961–62 4th Series SA 2, NZ 2, Drawn 1
1 DURBAN South Africa won by 30 runs
South Africa 292 (D J McGlew 127*, R A McLean 63, J C Alabaster 4–59) and 149 (J H B Waite 63)
New Zealand 245 (P G Z Harris 74, P T Barton 54, K A Walter 4–63) and 166 (S N McGregor 55, P M Pollock 6–38)
2 JOHANNESBURG Match Drawn
South Africa 322 (J H B Waite 101, M K Elgie 56, F J Cameron 5–83) and 178–6 dec (R C Motz 4–68)
New Zealand 223 (G T Dowling 74, G B Lawrence 8–53) and 165–4 (J R Reid 75*, G T Dowling 58)
3 CAPE TOWN New Zealand won by 72 runs
New Zealand 385 (P G Z Harris 101, J R Reid 92, M E Chapple 69, S N McGregor 68, S F Burke 6–128) and 212–9 dec (A E Dick 50*, S F Burke 5–68)
South Africa 190 (E J Barlow 51, F J Cameron 5–48, J C Alabaster 4–61) and 335 (R A McLean 113, D J McGlew 63, J C Alabaster 4–119)
4 JOHANNESBURG South Africa won by an innings and 51 runs
New Zealand 164 (J R Reid 60, G B Lawrence 5–52) and 249 (J R Reid 142, G B Lawrence 4–57)
South Africa 464 (D J McGlew 120, R A McLean 78, E J Barlow 67)
5 PORT ELIZABETH New Zealand won by 40 runs
New Zealand 275 (P T Barton 109) and 228 (G T Dowling 78, J R Reid 69, G B Lawrence 4–85)
South Africa 190 and 273 (E J Barlow 59, P M Pollock 54*, J r Reid 4–44)

1963–64 5th Series Drawn 3
1 WELLINGTON Match Drawn
South Africa 302 and 218–2 dec (E J Barlow 92)
New Zealand 253 (M E Chapple 59, P M Pollock 6–47) and 138–6 (S G Gedye 52)
2 DUNEDIN Match Drawn
New Zealand 149 (B W Sinclair 52, J T Partridge 4–51) and 138 (D B Pithey 6–58)
South Africa 223 (T L Goddard 63, J R Reid 6–60) and 42–3
3 AUCKLAND Match Drawn
South Africa 371 (K C Bland 83, T L Goddard 73, E J Barlow 61, R W Blair 4–85) and 200–5 dec (E J Barlow 58)
New Zealand 263 (B W Sinclair 138, S N McGregor 62, J T Partridge 6–86) and 191–8 (S G Gedye 55, T L Goddard 4–18)

14 West Indies *v* New Zealand

1951–52 1st Series WI 1, NZ 0, Drawn 1
1 CHRISTCHURCH West indies won by 5 wkts
New Zealand 236 (S Ramadhin 5–86) and 189 (S Ramadhin 4–39)
West Indies 287 (F M M Worrell 71, C L Walcott 65, S C Guillen 54, T B Burtt 5–69) and 142–5 (F M M Worrell 62*)
2 AUCKLAND Match Drawn
West indies 546–6 dec (C L Walcott 115, J B Stollmeyer 152, F M M Worrell 100, A F Rae 99, E de C Weekes 51)
New Zealand 160 (V J Scott 84) and 17–1

1955–56 2nd Series WI 3, NZ 1
1 DUNEDIN West Indies won by an innings and 71 runs
New Zealand 74 (S Ramadhin 6–23) and 208 (J E F Beck 66)
West Indies 353 (E de C Weekes 123, O G Smith 64, R W Blair 4–90)
2 CHRISTCHURCH West indies won by an innings and 64 runs
West Indies 386 (E de C Weekes 103, D St E Atkinson 85, J D C Goddard 83*)
New Zealand 158 (S Ramadhin 5–46) and 164 (A L Valentine 5–32, O G Smith 4–75)
3 WELLINGTON West Indies won by 9 wkts
West Indies 404 (E de C Weekes 156, B H Pairaudeau 68, D St E Atkinson 60) and 13–1
New Zealand 208 (J E F Beck 55) and 208 (D D Taylor 77, D St E Atkinson 5–66)
4 AUCKLAND New Zealand won by 190 runs
New Zealand 255 (J R Reid 84, D T Dewdney 5–21) and 157–9 dec (D St E Atkinson 7–53)
West Indies 145 (H A Furlonge 64, H B Cave 4–22, A R MacGibbon 4–44) and 77 (H B Cave 4–21)

1968–69 3rd Series WI 1, NZ 1, Drawn 1
1 AUCKLAND West Indies won by 5 wkts
New Zealand 323 (B R Taylor 124, B E Congdon 85) and 297–8 dec (G T Dowling 71, V Pollard 51*)
West Indies 276 (M C Carew 109, S M Nurse 95) and 348–5 (S M Nurse 168, B F Butcher 78*)
2 WELLINGTON New Zealand won by 6 wkts
West Indies 297 (J L Hendricks 54*, B F Butcher 50, R C Motz 6–69) and 148 (B F Butcher 59)
New Zealand 282 (G M Turner 74, B E Congdon 52, R M Edwards 5–84) and 166–4 (B F Hastings 62*)
3 CHRISTCHURCH Match Drawn
West Indies 417 (S M Nurse 258, M C Carew 91, R C Motz 5–113)
New Zealand 217 (D A J Holford 4–66) and 367–6 (B F Hastings 117*, G T Dowling 76)

1971–72 4th Series Drawn 5
1 KINGSTON Match Drawn
West Indies 508–4 dec (L G Rowe 214, R C Fredericks 163) and 218–3 dec (L G Rowe 100*)
New Zealand 386 (G M Turner 223*, K J Wadsworth 78) and 236–6 (M G Burgess 101, D A J Holford 4–55)
2 PORT OF SPAIN Match Drawn
New Zealand 348 (B E Congdon 166*, R S Cunis 51, V A Holder 4–60) and 288–3 dec (G M Turner 95, B E Congdon 82, M G Burgess 62*)
West Indies 341 (C A Davis 90, R C Fredericks 69, B R Taylor 4–41) and 121–5
3 BRIDGETOWN Match Drawn
West Indies 133 (B R Taylor 7–74) and 564–8 (C A Davis 183, G St A Sobers 142, L G Rowe 51, D A J Holford 50)
New Zealand 422 (B E Congdon 126, B F Hastings 105, G St A Sobers 4–64)
4 GEORGETOWN Match Drawn
West Indies 365–7 dec (A I Kallicharran 100*, G A Greenidge 50) and 86–0
New Zealand 543–3 dec (G M Turner 259, T W Jarvis 182, B E Congdon 61*)
5 PORT OF SPAIN Match Drawn
West Indies 368 (A I Kallicharran 101, R C Fredericks 60) and 194 (B R Taylor 5–41)
New Zealand 162 (Inshan Ali 5–59) and 253–7 (B E Congdon 58, G M Turner 50, V A Holder 4–41)

1979–80 5th Series NZ 1, WI 0, Drawn 2
1 DUNEDIN New Zealand won by 1 wkt
West Indies 140 (D L Haynes 55, R J Hadlee 5–34) and 212 (D L Haynes 105, R J Hadlee 6–68)
New Zealand 249 (B A Edgar 65, R J Hadlee 51, C E H Croft 4–64) and 104–9 (J Garner 4–36)
2 CHRISTCHURCH Match Drawn
West Indies 228 (C G Greenidge 91, A I Kallicharran 75, B L Cairns 6–85) and 447–5 (D L Haynes 122, L G Rowe 100, C L King 100*, C G Greenidge 97)
New Zealand 460 (G P Howarth 147, R J Hadlee 103, J V Coney 80)
3 AUCKLAND Match Drawn
West indies 220 (L G Rowe, 50, G B Troup 4–71, R J Hadlee 4–75) and 264–9 dec (C G Greenidge 74, G B Troup 6–95)
New Zealand 305 (B A Edgar 127, J Garner 6–56) and 73–4

15 West Indies *v* India

1948–49 1st Series WI 1, India 0, Drawn 4
1 NEW DELHI Match Drawn
West Indies 631 (C L Walcott 152, E de C Weekes 128, R J Christiani 107, G E Gomez 101, C R Rangachari 5–107)
India 454 (H R Adhikari 114*, K C Ibrahim 85, R S Modi 63, L Amarnath 62) and 220–6
2 BOMBAY Match Drawn
West Indies 629–6 dec (E de C Weekes 194, A F Rae 104, F J Cameron 75*, R J Christiani 74, C L Walcott 68, J B Stollmeyer 66)
India 273 (D G Phadkar 74, W Ferguson 4–126) and 333–3 (V S Hazare 134*, R S Modi 112, L Amarnath 58*)
3 CALCUTTA Match Drawn
West Indies 366 (E de C Weekes 162, C L Walcott 54, Ghulam Ahmed 4–94, S A Banerjee 4–120) and 336–9 dec (C L Walcott 108, E de C Weekes 101)
India 272 (R S Modi 80, V S Hazare 59, S Mushtaq Ali 54) and 325–3 (S Mushtaq Ali 106, R S Modi 87, V S Hazare 58*)
4 MADRAS West Indies won by an innings and 193 runs
West Indies 582 (J B Stollmeyer 160, A F Rae 109, E de C Weekes 90, G E Gomez 50, D G Phadkar 7–159)
India 245 (R S Modi 56, J Trim 4–48) and 144 (V S Hazare 52, P E Jones 4–30)
5 BOMBAY Match Drawn
West Indies 286 (J B Stollmeyer 85, E de C Weekes 56, D G Phadkar 4–74) and 267 (A F Rae 97, S N Banerjee 4–54)
India 193 and 355–8 (V S Hazare 122, R S Modi 86, P E Jones 5–85)

1952–53 2nd Series WI 1, India 0, Drawn 4
1 PORT OF SPAIN Match Drawn
India 417 (P R Umrigar 130, M L Apte 64, G S Ramchand 61) and 294 (P R Umrigar 69, D G Phadkar 65, M L Apte 52)
West Indies 438 (E de C Weekes 207, B H Pairaudeau 115, S P Gupte 7–162) and 142–0 (J B Stollmeyer 76*, A F Rae 63*)
2 BRIDGETOWN West Indies won by 142 runs
West Indies 296 (C L Walcott 98) and 228 (J B Stollmeyer 54, D G Phadkar 5–64)
India 253 (M L Apte 64, V S Hazare 63, P R Umrigar 56, A L Valentine 4–58) and 129 (S Ramadhin 5–26)
3 PORT OF SPAIN Match Drawn
India 279 (G S Ramchand 62, P R Umrigar 61, F M King 5–74) and 362–7 dec (M L Apte 163*, M H Mankad 96, P R Umrigar 67)
West Indies 315 (E de C Weekes 161, S P Gupte 5–107) and 192–2 (J B Stollmeyer 104*, E de C Weekes 55*)
4 GEORGETOWN Match Drawn
India 262 (M H Mankad 66, C V Gadkari 50*, A L Valentine 5–127) and 190–5
West Indies 364 (C L Walcott 125, E de C Weekes 86, F M M Worrell 56, S P Gupte 4–122)
5 KINGSTON Match Drawn
India 312 (P R Umrigar 117, P Roy 85, A L Valentine 5–64) and 444 (P Roy 150, V L Manjrekar 118, G E Gomez 4–72, A L Valentine 4–149)
West Indies 576 (F M M Worrell 237, C L Walcott 118, E de C Weekes 109, B H Pairaudeau 58, S P Gupte 5–180, M H Mankad 5–228) and 92–4

1958–59 3rd Series WI 3, India 0, Drawn 2
1 BOMBAY Match Drawn
West Indies 227 (R B Kanhai 66, O G Smith 63, S P Gupte 4–86) and 323–4 dec (G St A Sobers 142*, B F Butcher 64*, O G Smith 58)
India 152 (P R Umrigar 55, R Gilchrist 4–39) and 289–5 (P Roy 90, G S Ramchand 67*)
2 KANPUR West Indies won by 203 runs
West Indies 222 (F C M Alexander 70, S P Gupte 9–103) and 443–7 dec (G St A Sobers 198, J S Solomon 86, B F Butcher 60)
India 222 (P R Umrigar 57, W W Hall 6–50) and 240 (N J Contractor 50, W W Hall 5–76)
3 CALCUTTA West Indies won by an innings and 336 runs
West Indies 614–5 dec (R B Kanhai 256, G St A Sobers 106*, B F Butcher 103, J S Solomon 69*)
India 124 and 154 (V L Manjrekar 58*, R Gilchrist 6–55)
4 MADRAS West Indies won by 295 runs
West Indies 500 (B F Butcher 142, R B Kanhai 99, J K Holt 63, M H Mankad 4–95) and 168–5 dec (J K Holt 81*, S P Gupte 4–78)
India 222 (A G Kripal Singh 53, G St A Sobers 4–26) and 151 (C G Borde 56)
5 NEW DELHI Match Drawn
India 415 (C G Borde 109, N J Contractor 92, P R Umrigar 76, H R Adhikari 63, W W Hall 4–66) and 275 (C G Borde 96, P Roy 58, D K Gaekwad 52, O G Smith 5–90)
West Indies 644–8 dec (J K Holt 123, O G Smith 100, J S Solomon 100*, C C Hunte 92, B F Butcher 71, R B Desai 4–169)

1961–62 4th Series WI 5, India 0
1 PORT OF SPAIN West Indies won by 10 wkts
India 203 (R F Surti 57, S A Durani 56) and 98 (G St A Sobers 4–22)
West Indies 289 (J L Hendricks 64, C C Hunte 58, S A Durani 4–82) and 15–0
2 KINGSTON West Indies won by an innings and 18 runs
India 395 (C G Borde 93, R G Nadkarni 78*, F M Engineer 53, P R Umrigar 50, G St A Sobers 4–75) and 218 (W W Hall 6–49)
West Indies 631–8 dec (G St A Sobers 153, R B Kanhai 138, E D A St J McMorris 125, I L Mendonca 78, F M M Worrell 58)

3 BRIDGETOWN West Indies won by an innings and 30 runs
India 258 and 187 (D N Sardesai 60, V L Manjrekar 51, L R Gibbs 8–38)
West Indies 475 (J S Solomon 96, R B Kanhai 89, F M M Worrell 77, C C Hunte 59)
4 PORT OF SPAIN West Indies won by 7 wkts
West Indies 444–9 dec (R B Kanhai 139, F M M Worrell 73*, E D A St J McMorris 50, W V Rodriguez 50, W W Hall 50*, P R Umrigar 5–107) and 176–3 (E D A St J McMorris 56)
India 197 (P R Umrigar 56, W W Hall 5–20) and 422 (P R Umrigar 172*, S A Durani 104, V L Mehra 62, L R Gibbs 4–112)
5 KINGSTON West Indies won by 123 runs
West Indies 253 (G St A Sobers 104, V B Ranjane 4–72) and 283 (F M M Worrell 98*, G St A Sobers 50)
India 178 (R G Nadkarni 61, L A King 5–46) and 235 (P R Umrigar 60, G St A Sobers 5–63)

1966–67 5th Series WI 2, India 0, Drawn 1
1 BOMBAY West Indies won by 6 wkts
India 296 (C G Borde 121, S A Durani 55) and 316 (B K Kunderan 79, M A K Pataudi 51, L R Gibbs 4–67)
West Indies 421 (C C Hunte 101, C H Lloyd 82, D A J Holford 80, G St A Sobers 50, B S Chandrasekhar 7–157) and 192–4 (C H Lloyd 78*, G St A Sobers 53*)
2 CALCUTTA West Indies won by an innings and 45 runs
West Indies 390 (R B Kanhai 90, G St A Sobers 70, S M Nurse 56)
India 167 (L R Gibbs 5–51) and 178 (G St A Sobers 4–56)
3 MADRAS Match Drawn
India 404 (C G Borde 125, F M Engineer 109, R F Surti 50*) and 323 (A L Wadekar 67, V Subramanyam 61, Hanumant Singh 50, C C Griffith 4–61, L R Gibbs 4–96)
West Indies 406 (G St A Sobers 95, R B Kanhai 77, B S Chandrasekhar 4–130) and 270–7 (G St A Sobers 74*, B S Bedi 4–81)

1970–71 6th Series India 1, WI 0, Drawn 4
1 KINGSTON Match Drawn
India 387 (D N Sardesai 212, E D Solkar 61, V A Holder 4–60)
West Indies 217 (R B Kanhai 56, E A S Prasanna 4–65) and 385–5 (R B Kanhai 158*, G St A Sobers 93, C H Lloyd 57)
2 PORT OF SPAIN India won by 7 wkts
West Indies 214 (C A Davis 71*, E A S Prasanna 4–54) and 261 (R C Fredericks 80, C A Davis 74*, S Venkataraghavan 5–95)
India 352 (D N Sardesai 112, S M Gavaskar 65, E D Solkar 55, J M Noreiga 9–95) and 125–3 (S M Gavaskar 67*)
3 GEORGETOWN Match Drawn
West Indies 363 (D M Lewis 81*, C H Lloyd 60) and 307–3 dec (C A Davis 125*, G St A Sobers 108*)
India 376 (S M Gavaskar 116, G R Viswanath 50, S Abid Ali 50*) and 123–0 (S M Gavaskar 64*, A V Mankad 53*)
4 BRIDGETOWN Match Drawn
West Indies 501–5 dec (G St A Sobers 178*, D M Lewis 88, R B Kanhai 85, C A Davis 79) and 180–6 dec
India 347 (D N Sardesai 150, E D Solkar 65, U G Dowe 4–69) and 221–5 (S M Gavaskar 117*)
5 PORT OF SPAIN Match Drawn
India 360 (S M Gavaskar 124, D N Sardesai 75, S Venkataraghavan 51) and 427 (S M Gavaskar 220, A L Wadekar 54, J M Noreiga 5–129)
West Indies 526 (G St A Sobers 132, C A Davis 105, M L C Foster 99, D M Lewis 72, S Venataraghavan 4–100) and 165–8 (C H Lloyd 64)

1974–75 7th Series WI 3, India 2
1 BANGALORE West Indies won by 267 runs
West Indies 289 (A I Kallicharran 124, C G Greenidge 93, S Venkataraghavan 4–75, B S Chandrasekhar 4–112) and 356–6 dec (C H Lloyd 163, C G Greenidge 107)
India 260 (H S Kanitkar 65) and 118
2 NEW DELHI West Indies won by an innings and 17 runs
India 220 (P Sharma 54) and 256 (F M Engineer 75, L R Gibbs 6–76)
West Indies 493 (I V A Richards 192*, C H Lloyd 71, K D Boyce 68, E A S Prasanna 4–147)
3 CALCUTTA India won by 85 runs
India 233 (G R Viswanath 52, A M E Roberts 5–50) and 316 (G R Viswanath 139, F M Engineer 61)
West Indies 240 (R C Fredericks 100, S Madan Lal 4–22) and 224 (A I Kallicharran 57, B S Bedi 4–52)
4 MADRAS India won by 100 runs
India 190 (G R Viswanath 97*, A M E Roberts 7–64) and 256 (A D Gaekwad 80, A M E Roberts 5–57)
West Indies 192 (I V A Richards 50, E A S Prasanna 5–70) and 154 (A I Kallicharran 51, E A S Prasanna 4–41)
5 BOMBAY West Indies won by 201 runs
West Indies 604–6 dec (C H Lloyd 242*, R C Fredericks 104, A I Kallicharran 98, D L Murray 91, K D Ghavri 4–140) and 205–3 dec (C G Greenidge 54)
India 406 (E D Solkar 102, G R Viswanath 95, S M Gavaskar 86, A D Gaekwad 51, L R Gibbs 7–98) and 202 (B P Patel 73*, V A Holder 6–39)

1975–76 8th Series WI 2, India 1, Drawn 1
1 BRIDGETOWN West Indies won by an innings and 97 runs
India 177 (D A J Holford 5–23) and 214 (G R Viswanath 62, S Madan Lal 55*)
West Indies 488–9 dec (I V A Richards 142, C H Lloyd 102, A I Kallicharran 93, R C Fredericks 54, B S Chandrasekhar 4–163)
2 PORT OF SPAIN Match Drawn
West Indies 241 (I V A Richards 130, B S Bedi 5–82) and 215–8 (C H Lloyd 70)
India 402–5 dec (S M Gavaskar 156, B P Patel 115*)
3 PORT OF SPAIN India won by 6 wkts
West Indies 359 (I V A Richards 177, C H Lloyd 68, B S Chandrasekhar 6–120, B S Bedi 4–73) and 271–6 dec (A I Kallicharran 103*)
India 228 (M A Holding 6–65) and 406–4 (G R Viswanath 112, S M Gavaskar 102, M Amarnath 85)
4 KINGSTON West Indies won by 10 wkts
India 306–6 dec (A D Gaekwad 81, S M Gavaskar 66, M A Holding 4–82) and 97 (M Amarnath 60)
West Indies 391 (R C Fredericks 82, D L Murray 71, I V A Richards 64, M A Holding 55, B S Chandrasekhar 5–153) and 13–0

1978–79 9th Series India 1, WI 0, Drawn 5
1 BOMBAY Match Drawn
India 424 (S M Gavaskar 205, C P S Chauhan 52, G R Viswanath 52, V A Holder 4–94, S T Clarke 4–98) and 224–2 (C P S Chauhan 84, S M Gavaskar 73)
West Indies 493 (A I Kallicharran 187, D A Murray 84, H A Gomes 63, D R Parry 55, B S Chandrasekhar 5–116)
2 BANGALORE Match Drawn
West Indies 437 (S F A Bacchus 96, A I Kallicharran 71, S Shivnarine 62, H A Gomes 51) and 200–8 (H A Gomes 82, K D Ghavri 5–51)
India 371 (A D Gaekwad 87, D B Vengsarkar 73, G R Viswanath 70, S T Clarke 5–126)
3 CALCUTTA Match Drawn
India 300 (S M Gavaskar 107, Kapil Dev 61, N Phillip 4–64) and 361–1 dec (S M Gavaskar 182*, D B Vengsarkar 157*)
West Indies 327 (A B Williams 111, A I Kallicharran 55, S Venkataraghavan 4–55) and 197–9 (D A Murray 66, K D Ghavri 4–46)
4 MADRAS India won by 3 wkts
West Indies 228 (A I Kallicharran 98, Kapil Dev 4–38) and 151 (H A Gomes 91, S Venkataraghavan 4–43)
India 255 (G R Viswanath 124, N Phillip 4–48, S T Clarke 4–75) and 125–7
5 NEW DELHI Match Drawn
India 566 (Kapil Dev 126, S M Gavaskar 120, D B Vengsarkar 109, C P S Chauhan 60)
West Indies 172 and 179–3 (S F A Bacchus 61)
6 KANPUR Match Drawn
India 644–7 dec (G R Viswanath 179, A D Gaekwad 102, M Amarnath 101*, C P S Chauhan 79, Kapil Dev 62)
West Indies 452–8 (S F A Bacchus 250, R R Jumadeen 56, K D Ghavri 4–118)

16 West Indies *v* Pakistan

1957–58 1st Series WI 3, Pak 1, Drawn 1
1 BRIDGETOWN Match Drawn
West Indies 579–9 dec (E de C Weekes 197, C C Hunte 142, O G Smith 78, G St A Sobers 52, Mahmood Hussain 4–153) and 28–0
Pakistan 106 (R Gilchrist 4–32) and 657–8 dec (Hanif Mohammad 337, Imtiaz Ahmed 91, Saeed Ahmed 65)
2 PORT OF SPAIN West Indies won by 120 runs
West Indies 325 (R B Kanhai 96, E de C Weekes 78, G St A Sobers 52) and 312 (G St A Sobers 80, F C M Alexander 57, O G Smith 51, Fazal Mahmood 4–89)
Pakistan 282 (Wallis Mathias 73, Fazal Mahmood 60, O G Smith 4–71) and 235 (Hanif Mohammad 81, Saeed Ahmed 64, R Gilchrist 4–61)
3 KINGSTON West Indies won by an innings and 174 runs
Pakistan 328 (Imtiaz Ahmed 122, Wallis Mathias 77, Saeed Ahmed 52, E St E Atkinson 5–42) and 288 (Wazir Mohammad 106, A H Kardar 57)
West Indies 790–3 dec (G St A Sobers 365*, C C Hunte 260, C L Walcott 88*)
4 GEORGETOWN West Indies won by 8 wkts
Pakistan 408 (Saeed Ahmed 150, Hanif Mohammad 79, R Gilchrist 4–102) and 318 (Wazir Mohammad 97*, A H Kardar 56, L R Gibbs 5–80)
West Indies 410 (C L Walcott 145, G St A Sobers 125, Nasim-ul-Ghani 5–116) and 317–2 (C C Hunte 114, G St A Sobers 109*, R B Kanhai 62)
5 PORT OF SPAIN Pakistan won by an innings and 1 run
West Indies 268 (O G Smith 86, E de C Weekes 51, Fazal Mahmood 6–83) and 227 (C L Walcott 62, Nasim-ul-Ghani 6–67)
Pakistan 496 (Wazir Mohammad 189, Saeed Ahmed 97, Hanif Mohammad 54, J Taylor 5–109, L R Gibbs 4–108)

1958–59 2nd Series Pak 2, WI 1
1 KARACHI Pakistan won by 10 wkts
West Indies 146 (Fazal Mahmood 4–35, Nasim-ul-Ghani 4–35) and 245 (J S Solomon 66, B F Butcher 61)
Pakistan 304 (Hanif Mohammad 103, Saeed Ahmed 78) and 88–0
2 DACCA Pakistan won by 41 runs
Pakistan 145 (Wallis mathias 64, W W Hall 4–28) and 144 (E St E Atkinson 4–42, W W Hall 4–49)
West Indies 76 (Fazal Mahmood 6–34) and 172 (Fazal Mahmood 6–66, Mahmood Hussain 4–48)
3 LAHORE West Indies won by an innings and 156 runs
West Indies 469 (R B Kanhai 217, G St A Sobers 72, J S Solomon 56)
Pakistan 209 (W W Hall 5–87) and 104 (S Ramadhin 4–25)

1974–75 3rd Series Drawn 2
1 LAHORE Match Drawn
Pakistan 199 (A M E Roberts 5–66) and 373–7 dec (Mushtaq Mohammad 123, Aftab Baloch 60*, Asif Iqbal 52, A M E Roberts 4–121)
West Indies 214 (A I Kallicharran 92*, Sarfraz Nawaz 6–89) and 258–4 (L Baichan 105*, C H Lloyd 83)
2 KARACHI Match Drawn
Pakistan 406–8 dec (Wasim Raja 107*, Majid Khan 100, Wasim Bari 58) and 256 (Sadiq Mohammad 98*, Asif Iqbal 77)
West Indies 493 (A I Kallicharran 115, B D Julien 101, R C Fredericks 77, C H Lloyd 73) and 1–0

1976–77 4th Series WI 2, Pak 1, Drawn 2
1 BRIDGETOWN Match Drawn
Pakistan 435 (Wasim Raja 117*, Majid Khan 88, J Garner 4–130) and 291 (Wasim Raja 71, Wasim Bari 60*, C E H Croft 4–47)
West Indies 421 (C H Lloyd 157, D L Murray 52) and 251–9 (I V A Richards 92, R C Fredericks 52, Sarfraz Nawaz 4–79)
2 PORT OF SPAIN West Indies won by 6 wkts
Pakistan 180 (Wasim Raja 65, C E H Croft 9–29) and 340 (Wasim Raja 84, Sadiq Mohammad 81, Majid Khan 54, A M E Roberts 4–85)
West Indies 316 (R C Fredericks 120, Mushtaq Mohammad 4–50) and 206–4 (C G Greenidge 70, R C Fredericks 57)
3 GEORGETOWN Match Drawn
Pakistan 194 (J Garner 4–48) and 540 (Majid Khan 167, Zaheer Abbas 80, Haroon Rashid 60, J Garner 4–100)
West Indies 448 (I T Shillingford 120, C G Greenidge 91, A I Kallicharran 72, I V A Richards 50, Maijd Khan 4–45) and 154–1 (C G Greenidge 96, R C Fredericks 52*)
4 PORT OF SPAIN Pakistan won by 266 runs
Pakistan 341 (Mushtaq Mohammad 121, Majid Khan 92) and 301–9 dec (Wasim Raja 70, Mushtaq Mohammad 56, Sarfraz Nawaz 51)
West Indies 154 (Mushtaq Mohammad 5–28, Imran Khan 4–64) and 222
5 KINGSTON West Indies won by 140 runs
West Indies 280 (C G Greenidge 100, Imran Khan 6–90) and 359 (R C Fredericks 83, C G Greenidge 82)
Pakistan 198 (Haroon Rashid 72, C E H Croft 4–49) and 301 (Asif Iqbal 135, Wasim Raja 64)

1980–81 5th Series WI 1, Pak 0, Drawn 3
1 LAHORE Match Drawn
Pakistan 369 (Imran Khan 123, Wasim Raja 76, Sarfraz Nawaz 55) and 156–7 (Majid Khan 62*)
West Indies 297 (I V A Richards 75, D A Murray 50, Abdul Qadir 4–132)
2 FAISALABAD West Indies won by 156 runs
West Indies 235 (I V A Richards 72, Mohammad Nazir 5–44) and 242 (I V A Richards 67, Iqbal Qasim 6–89)
Pakistan 176 (Javed Miandad 50) and 145 (M D Marshall 4–25)
3 KARACHI Match Drawn
Pakistan 128 (Javed Miandad 60, S T Clarke 4–27) and 204–9 (Wasim Raja 77*)
West Indies 169 (H A Gomes 61, Imran Khan 4–66, Iqbal Qasim 4–48)
4 MULTAN Match Drawn
West Indies 249 (I V A Richards 120, Imran Khan 5–62) and 116–5
Pakistan 166 (Javed Miandad 57, J Garner 4–38)

17 New Zealand *v* India

1955–56 1st Series India 2, NZ 0, Drawn 3
1 HYDERABAD Match Drawn
India 498–4 dec (P R Umrigar 223, V L Manjrekar 118, A G Kripal Singh 100*)
New Zealand 326 (J W Guy 102, A R MacGibbon 59, J R Reid 54, S P Gupte 7–128) and 212–2 (B Sutcliffe 137*)
2 BOMBAY India won by an innings and 27 runs
India 421–8 dec (M H Mankad 223, A G Kripal Singh 63)
New Zealand 258 (B Sutcliffe 73) and 136 (S P Gupte 5–45)
3 NEW DELHI Match Drawn
New Zealand 450–2 dec (B Sutcliffe 230*, J R Reid 119*, J W Guy 52) and 112–1 (J G Leggat 50*)
India 531–7 dec (V L Manjrekar 177, G S Ramchand 72, R G Nadkarni 68*, N J Contractor 62)
4 CALCUTTA Match Drawn
India 132 and 438–7 dec (G S Ramchand 106*, P Roy 100, V L Manjrekar 90, N J Contractor 61)
New Zealand 336 (J R Reid 120, J W Guy 91, S P Gupte 6–90) and 75–6
5 MADRAS India won by an innings and 109 runs
India 537–3 dec (M H Mankad 231, P Roy 173, P R Umrigar 79*)
New Zealand 209 (S P Gupte 5–72) and 219 (J G Leggat 61, J R Reid 63, M H Mankad 4–65, S P Gupte 4–73)

1964–65 2nd Series India 1, NZ 0, Drawn 3
1 MADRAS Match Drawn
India 397 (F M Engineer 90, R G Nadkarni 75, C G Borde 68, M L Jaisimha 51) and 199–2 dec (V L Manjrekar 102*)
New Zealand 315 (B Sutcliffe 56) and 62–0
2 CALCUTTA Match Drawn
New Zealand 462–9 dec (B Sutcliffe 151*, B R Taylor 105, J R Reid 82, R B Desai 4–128) and 191–9 dec
India 380 (M A K Pataudi 153, C G Borde 62, B R Taylor 5–86) and 92–3
3 BOMBAY Match Drawn
New Zealand 297 (G T Dowling 129, R W Morgan 71, R B Desai 6–56) and 80–8
India 88 (B R Taylor 5–26) and 463–5 dec (D N Sardesai 200*, C G Borde 109, Hanumant Singh 75*)
4 NEW DELHI India won by 7 wkts
New Zealand 262 (R W Morgan 82, S Venkataraghavan 8–72) and 272 (T W Jarvis 77, B Sutcliffe 54, R O Collinge 54, S Venkataraghavan 4–80)
India 465–8 dec (M A K Pataudi 113, D N Sardesai 106, C G Borde 87, Hanumant Singh 82, R O Collinge 4–89) and 73–3

1967–68 3rd Series India 3, NZ 1
1 DUNEDIN India won by 5 wkts
New Zealand 350 (G T Dowling 143, B E Congdon 58, M G Burgess 50, S Abid Ali 4–26) and 208 (B A G Murray 54, E A S Prasanna 6–94)
India 359 (A L Wadekar 80, F M Engineer 63, R C Motz 5–86) and 200–5 (A L Wadekar 71)
2 CHRISTCHURCH New Zealand won by 6 wkts
New Zealand 502 (G T Dowling 239, B A G Murray 74, K Thomson 69, B S Bedi 6–127) and 88–4 (B E Congdon 61*)
India 288 (R F Surti 67, C G Borde 57, M A K Pataudi 52, R C Motz 6–63) and 301 (F M Engineer 63, G A Bartlett 6–38)
3 WELLINGTON India won by 8 wkts
New Zealand 186 (M G Burgess 66, E A S Prasanna 5–32) and 199 (M G Burgess 60, B E Congdon 51, R G Nadkarni 6–43)
India 327 (A L Wadekar 143) and 59–2
4 AUCKLAND India won by 272 runs
India 252 (M A K Pataudi 51, R C Motz 4–51) and 261–5 dec (R F Surti 99, C G Borde 65*)
New Zealand 140 (E A S Prasanna 4–44) and 101 (E A S Prasanna 4–40)

1969–70 4th Series India 1, NZ 1, Drawn 1
1 BOMBAY India won by 60 runs
India 156 and 260 (M A K Pataudi 67)
New Zealand 229 (B E Congdon 78, E A S Prasanna 4–97) and 127 (B S Bedi 6–42, E A S Prasanna 4–74)
2 NAGPUR New Zealand won by 167 runs
New Zealand 319 (M G Burgess 89, G T Dowling 69, B E Congdon 64, B S Bedi 4–98) and 214 (G M Turner 57, S Venkataraghavan 6–74)
India 257 (S Abid Ali 63, H J Howarth 4–66) and 109 (H J Howarth 5–34)
3 HYDERABAD Match Drawn
New Zealand 181 (B A G Murray 80, E A S Prasanna 5–51) and 175–8 dec (G T Dowling 60)
India 89 (D R Hadlee 4–30) and 76–7

1975–76 5th Series India 1, NZ 1, Drawn 1
1 AUCKLAND India won by 8 wkts
New Zealand 266 (B E Congdon 54, B S Chandrasekhar 6–94) and 215 (J M Parker 70, B E Congdon 54, E A S Prasanna 8–76)
India 414 (S Amarnath 124, S M Gavaskar 116, M Amarnath 64, B E Congdon 5–65) and 71–2
2 CHRISTCHURCH Match Drawn
India 270 (G R Viswanath 83, R O Collinge 6–63) and 255–6 (G R Viswanath 79, S M Gavaskar 71)
New Zealand 403 (G M Turner 117, B E Congdon 58, S Madan Lal 5–134, M Amarnath 4–63)
3 WELLINGTON New Zealand won by an innings and 33 runs
India 220 (B P Patel 81, R J Hadlee 4–35) and 81 (R J Hadlee 7–23)
New Zealand 334 (M G Burgess 95, G M Turner 64, B E Congdon 52)

1976–77 6th Series India 2, NZ 0, Drawn 1
1 BOMBAY India won by 162 runs
India 399 (S M Gavaskar 119, S M H Kirmani 88, R J Hadlee 4–95) and 202–4 dec (B P Patel 82)
New Zealand 298 (J M Parker 104, G M Turner 65, B S Chandrasekhar 4–77) and 141 (B S Bedi 5–27)
2 KANPUR Match Drawn
India 524–9 dec (M Amarnath 70, G R Viswanath 68, S M H Kirmani 64, S M Gavaskar 66, A V Mankad 50, B S Bedi 50*) and 208–2 dec (G R Viswanath 103*, A D Gaekwad 77*)
New Zealand 350 (G M Turner 113, A D G Roberts 84*, M G Burgess 54) and 193–7
3 MADRAS India won by 216 runs
India 298 (G R Viswanath 87, S Venkataraghavan 64, B L Cairns 5–55) and 201–5 dec (M Amarnath 55)
New Zealand 140 (B S Bedi 5–48) and 143 (B S Bedi 4–22)

1980–81 7th Series NZ 1, India 0, Drawn 2
1 WELLINGTON New Zealand won by 62 runs
New Zealand 375 (G P Howarth 137*) and 100 (Kapil Dev 4–34)
India 223 (S M Patil 64, B C Cairns 5–33) and 190 (R J Hadlee 4–65)
2 CRISTCHURCH Match Drawn
India 223 (S M Patil 64, B L Cairns 5–33) and 190 (R J Hadlee 4–65)
New Zealand 286–5 (J F Reid 123*)
3 AUCKLAND Match Drawn
India 238 (S M H Kirmani 78, J G Bracewell 4–61) and 284 (S M Patil 57, D B Vengsarkar 52*, J G Bracewell 5–75)
New Zealand 366 (J G Wright 110, J F Reid 74, J V Coney 65, R J Shastri 5–125) and 95–5

18 New Zealand *v* Pakistan

1955–56 1st Series Pak 2, NZ 0, Drawn 1
1 KARACHI Pakistan won by an innings and 1 run
New Zealand 164 (Zulfiqar Ahmed 5–37) and 124 (Zulfiqar Ahmed 6–42)
Pakistan 289 (Imtiaz Ahmed 64, A R MacGibbon 4–98)
2 LAHORE Pakistan won by 4 wkts
New Zealand 348 (S N McGregor 111, N S Harford 93, A R MacGibbon 61, Khan Mohammad 4–78) and 328 (J R Reid 86, N S Harford 64, Zulfiqar Ahmed 4–114)
Pakistan 561 (Imtiaz Ahmed 209, Waqar Hassan 189, A M Moir 4–114) and 117–6 (J R Reid 4–38)
3 DACCA Match Drawn
New Zealand 70 (Khan Mohammad 6–21) and 69–6
Pakistan 195–6 dec (Hanif Mohammad 103)

1964–65 2nd Series Drawn 3
1 WELLINGTON Match Drawn
New Zealand 266 (J R Reid 97, B W Sinclair 65, Asif Iqbal 5–48) and 179–7 dec
Pakistan 187 (R C Motz 4–45) and 140–7 (Asif Iqbal 52*)
2 AUCKLAND Match Drawn
Pakistan 226 (Javed Burki 63, F J Cameron 4–36, B W Yuile 4–43) and 207 (Abdul Kadir 58, F J Cameron 5–34)
New Zealand 214 (R W Morgan 66, J R Reid 52, Asif Iqbal 5–52) and 166–7 (G T Dowling 62, Pervez Sajjid 5–42)
3 CHRISTCHURCH Match Drawn
Pakistan 206 (Mohammad Ilyas 88) and 309–8 dec (Hanif Mohammad 100*, Saeed Ahmed 87)
New Zealand 202 (Asif Iqbal 4–46) and 223–5 (R W Morgan 97)

1964–65 3rd Series Pak 2, NZ 0, Drawn 1
1 RAWALPINDI Pakistan won by an innings and 64 runs
New Zealand 175 (B R Taylor 76, Pervez Sajjid 4–42) and 79 (Pervez Sajjid 4–5)
Pakistan 318 (Saeed Ahmed 68, Mohammad Ilyas 56, Asif Iqbal 51)
2 LAHORE Match Drawn
Pakistan 385–7 dec (Hanif Mohammad 203*, Majid Khan 80, F J Cameron 4–90) and 194–8 dec
New Zealand 482–6 dec (B W Sinclair 130, J R Reid 88, G T Dowling 83, T W Jarvis 55, R W Morgan 50)
3 KARACHI Pakistan won by 8 wkts
New Zealand 285 (J R Reid 128) and 223 (J R Reid 76, B E Congdon 57, Intikhab Alam 4–39)
Pakistan 307–8 dec (Saeed Ahmed 172) and 202–2 (Mohammad Ilyas 126)

1969–70 4th Series NZ 1, Pak 0, Drawn 2
1 KARACHI Match Drawn
Pakistan 220 (Sadiq Mohammad 69, H J Howarth 5–80) and 283–8 dec (Younis Ahmed 62)
New Zealand 274 (D R Hadlee 56, B A G Murray 50, Mohammad Nazir 7–99) and 112–5 (Pervez Sajjad 5–33)
2 LAHORE New Zealand won by 5 wkts
Pakistan 114 and 208 (Shafqat Rana 95)
New Zealand 241 (B A G Murray 90, B F Hastings 80*, Pervez Sajjad 7–74) and 82–5
3 DACCA Match Drawn
New Zealand 273 (G M Turner 110, M G Burgess 59, Intikhab Alam 5–91) and 200 (M G Burgess 119*, Intikhab Alam 5–91, Pervez Sajjad 4–60)
Pakistan 290–7 dec (Asif Iqbal 92, Shafqat Rana 65, H J Howarth 4–85) and 51–4 (R S Cunis 4–21)

1972–73 5th Series Pak 1, NZ 0, Drawn 2
1 WELLINGTON Match Drawn
Pakistan 357 (Sadiq Mohammad 166, Majid Khan 79, B R Taylor 4–110) and 290–6 dec (Majid Khan 79, Sadiq Mohammad 68, Intikhab Alam 53*, H J Howarth 4–99)
New Zealand 325 (M G Burgess 79, B F Hastings 72, Sarfraz Nawaz 4–126) and 78–3
2 DUNEDIN Pakistan won by an innings and 166 runs
Pakistan 507–6 dec (Mushtaq Mohammad 201, Asif Iqbal 175, Sadiq Mohammad 61)
New Zealand 156 (Intikhab Alam 7–52) and 185 (V Pollard 61, Mushtaq Mohammad 5–49, Intikhab Alam 4–78)
3 AUCKLAND Match Drawn
Pakistan 402 (Majid Khan 110, Mushtaq Mohammad 61, Saleem Altaf 53*, B R Taylor 4–86) and 271 (Mushtaq Mohammad 52)
New Zealand 402 (B F Hastings 110, R E Redmond 107, R O Collinge 68*, G M Turner 58, Intikhab Alam 6–127) and 92–3 (R E Redmond 56)

1976–77 6th Series Pak 2, NZ 0, Drawn 1
1 LAHORE Pakistan won by 6 wkts
Pakistan 417 (Asif Iqbal 166, Javed Miandad 163, R J Hadlee 5–121) and 105–4
New Zealand 157 (Intikhab Alam 4–35) and 360 (M G Burgess 111, R W Anderson 92, Imran Khan 4–59)
2 HYDERABAD Pakistan won by 10 wkts
Pakistan 473–3 dec (Sadoq Mohammad 103*, Mushtaq Mohammad 101, Majid Khan 98, Asif Iqbal 73) and 4–0
New Zealand 219 and 254 (J M Parker 82, Intikhab Alam 4–44)
3 KARACHI Match Drawn
Pakistan 565–9 dec (Javed Miandad 206, Majid Khan 112, Mushtaq Mohammad 107, Imran Khan 59, R J Hadlee 4–138) and 290–5 dec (Javed Miandad 85, Mushtaq Mohammad 67*, Majid Khan 50)
New Zealand 468 (W K Lees 152, R J Hadlee 87, B L Cairns 52*) and 262–7

1978–79 7th Series Pak 1, NZ 0, Drawn 2
1 CHRISTCHURCH Pakistan won by 128 runs
Pakistan 271 (Javed Miandad 81, R J Hadlee 5–62) and 323–6 dec (Javed Miandad 160*, Talaat Ali 61)
New Zealand 290 (B A Edgar 129, Mushtaq Mohammad 4–60) and 176 (Mushtaq Mohammad 5–59, Wasim Raja 4–68)
2 NAPIER Match Drawn
Pakistan 360 (Asif Iqbal 104, Wasim Raja 74, R J Hadlee 4–101) and 234–3 dec (Majid Khan 119*)
New Zealand 402 (G P Howarth 114, J G Wright 88, J V Coney 69, Imran Khan 5–106, Sikander Bakht 4–67)
3 AUCKLAND Match Drawn
New Zealand 254 (J V Coney 82, R J Hadlee 53*) and 281–8 dec (M G Burgess 71, Sarfraz Nawaz 4–61)
Pakistan 359 (Zaheer Abbas 135, R J Hadlee 5–104) and 8–0

19 India *v* Pakistan

1952–53 1st Series India 2, Pak 1, Drawn 2
1 NEW DELHI India won by an innings and 70 runs
India 372 (H R Adhikari 81*, V S Hazare 76, Ghulam Ahmed 50, Amir Elahi 4–134)
Pakistan 150 (Hanif Mohammad 51, M H Mankad 8–52) and 152 (M H Mankad 5–79, Ghulam Ahmed 4–35)
2 LUCKNOW Pakistan won by an innings and 43 runs
India 106 (Fazal Mahmood 5–52) and 182 (L Amarnath 61*, Fazal Mahmood 7–42)
Pakistan 331 (Nazar Mohammad 124*)
3 BOMBAY India won by 10 wkts
Pakistan 186 (Waqar Hassan 81, L Amarnath 4–40) and 242 (Hanif Mohammad 96, Waqar Hassan 65, M H Mankad 5–72)
India 387–4 dec (V S Hazare 146*, P R Umrigar 102) and 45–0
4 MADRAS Match Drawn
Pakistan 344 (A H Kardar 79, Zulfiqar Ahmed 63*)
India 175–6 (P R Umrigar 62)
5 CALCUTTA Match Drawn
Pakistan 257 (Imtiaz Ahmed 57, Hanif Mohammad 56, Nazar Mohammad 55, D G Phadkar 5–72) and 236–7 dec (Waqar Hassan 97)
India 397 (R H Shodhan 110, D G Phadkar 57, Fazal Mahmood 4–141) and 28–0

1954–55 2nd Series Drawn 5
1 DACCA Match Drawn
Pakistan 257 (Imtiaz Ahmed 54, Waqar Hassan 52, Ghulam Ahmed 5–109) and 158 (Alim-ul-Din 51, Waqar Hassan 51, S P Gupte 5–18)
India 148 (Mahmood Hussain 6–67, Khan Mohammad 4–42) and 147–2 (V L Manjrekar 74*, P Roy 67*)
2 BAHAWALPUR Match Drawn
India 235 (N S Tamhane 54*, G S Ramchand 53, V L Manjrekar 50, Khan Mohammad 5–74, Fazal Mahmood 4–86) and 209–5 (P Roy 77, V L Manjrekar 59)
Pakistan 312–9 dec (Hanif Mohammad 142, Alim-un-Din 64, P R Umrigar 6–74)
3 LAHORE Match Drawn
Pakistan 328 (Maqsood Ahmed 99, Wazir Mohammad 55, Imtiaz Ahmed 55, S P Gupte 5–133) and 136–5 dec (Alim-ud-Din 58)
India 251 (P R Umrigar 78, Mahmood Hussain 4–70) and 74–2
4 PESHAWAR Match Drawn
Pakistan 188 (S P Gupte 5–63) and 182 (Imtiaz Ahmed 69, M H Mankad 5–64)
India 245 (P R Umrigar 108, Khan Mohammad 4–79) and 23–1
5 KARACHI Match Drawn
Pakistan 162 (G S Ramchand 6–49) and 241–5 dec (Alim-ud-Din 103*, A H Kardar 93)
India 145 (Fazal Mahmood 5–49, Khan Mohammad 5–72) and 69–2

1960–61 3rd Series Drawn 5
1 BOMBAY Match Drawn
Pakistan 350 (Hanif Mohammad 160, Saeed Ahmed 121, S P Gupte 4–43) and 166–4 (Imtiaz Ahmed 69)
India 449–9 dec (R B Desai 85, V L Manjrekar 73, N J Contractor 62, P G Joshi 52*, Mahmood Hussain 5–129, Mohammad Farooq 4–139)
2 KANPUR Match Drawn
Pakistan 335 (Javed Burki 79, Nasim-ul-Ghani 70*, P R Umrigar 4–71) and 140–3
India 404 (P R Umrigar 115, M L Jaisimha 99, V L Manjrekar 52, Haseeb Ahsan 5–121)
3 CALCUTTA Match Drawn
Pakistan 301 (Mushtaq Mohammad 61, Intikhab Alam 56, Hanif Mohammad 56, C G Borde 4–21, R Surendranath 4–93) and 146–3 dec (Hanif Mohammad 63*)
India 180 (Fazal Mahmood 5–26) and 127–4
4 MADRAS Match Drawn
Pakistan 448–8 dec (Imtiaz Ahmed 135, Saeed Ahmed 103, Hanif Mohammad 62, R B Desai 4–66) and 59–0
India 539–9 dec (C G Borde 177*, P R Umrigar 117, N J Contractor 81, Haseeb Ahsan 6–202)
5 NEW DELHI Match Drawn
India 463 (P R Umrigar 112, N J Contractor 92, R F Surti 64) and 16–0
Pakistan 286 (Mushtaq Mohammad 101, Javed Burki 61, V V Kumar 5–64, R B Desai 4–103) and 250 (Imtiaz Ahmed 53, R G Nadkarni 4–43, R B Desai 4–88)

1978–79 4th Series Pak 2, India 0, Drawn 1
1 FAISALABAD Match Drawn
Pakistan 503–8 dec (Javed Miandad 154, Zaheer Abbas 176, B S Chandrasekhar 4–130) and 264–4 dec (Asif Iqbal 104, Zaheer Abbas 96)
India 462–9 dec (G R Viswanath 145, S M Gavaskar 89, D B Vengsarkar 83, Mushtaq Mohammad 4–55) and 43–0
2 LAHORE Pakistan won by 8 wkts
India 199 (D B Vengsarkar 76, Sarfraz Nawaz 4–46, Imran Khan 4–54) and 465 (S M Gavaskar 97, C P S Chauhan 93, G R Viswanath 83, S Amarnath 60)
Pakistan 539–6 dec (Zaheer Abbas 235*, Wasim Bari 85, Mushtaq Mohammad 67) and 128–2
3 KARACHI Pakistan won by 8 wkts
India 344 (S M Gavaskar 111, Kapil Dev 59, Sarfraz Nawaz 4–89) and 300 (S M Gavaskar 137, M Amarnath 53, Sarfraz Nawaz 5–70)
Pakistan 481–9 dec (Javed Miandad 100, Mushtaq Mohammad 78, Mudassar Nazar 57) and 164–2 (Javed Miandad 62*)

Throwing – No balled for

In the copies of the Laws published during the 18th century there is no mention of the method to be used when bowling the ball, but it was by tradition bowled under-arm and any attempt to contravene this unwritten Law was frowned on – 'About a couple of years after Walker had been with us, he began the system of throwing instead of bowling, now so much the fashion. At that time it was esteemed foul play and so it was decided by a council of the Hambledon Club which was called for the purpose.' The quotation is from *The Cricketers of My Time* by John Nyren published in 1833 and describing the bowling of Tom Walker of Hambledon about 1786.

John Willes seems to have been the next major bowler to ignore the unwritten under-arm code. He played for Gentlemen v Players in 1806, but it is not known when he started bowling round-arm instead of under-arm, though it would appear that round-arm bowling was becoming quite commonplace by 1810. In 1816 the Laws were amended to include a clause stating that the hand should not be higher than the elbow when bowling but not until 1822 was a bowler no-balled for delivering the ball above the elbow, this occurring on July 15, 1822 in the match between MCC and Kent at Lord's, the offending bowler being John Willes – he left the match in protest.

In 1835 the Law was altered to permit round-arm bowling, i.e. the hand must not be above the shoulder. It was however only a few years before bowlers began to bowl with their hand above the shoulder and in 1862 E Willsher was no-balled for bowling with his hand above the shoulder in the match between England and Surrey at the Oval, August 26, but John Lillywhite, the umpire responsible, was replaced the next day and Willsher continued to bowl. The Law was changed to permit over-arm bowling on June 10, 1864.

Since 1864 the Law regarding 'throwing' has been concerned with the straightening of the bowling arm just prior to the delivery of the ball, rather than the height of the arm.

The first bowler to be no-balled in first-class matches was T W S Wills for Victoria v New South Wales at Melbourne, March 30, 1872 – he only bowled 2 overs and was no-balled 3 times. In English first-class cricket, the first example is G E Jowett who bowled 2 overs in the Lancashire v Surrey match at Liverpool on July 17, 1885. The first major bowler to be accused of throwing was however J Crossland of Lancashire in the 1880s, though he was never no-balled (except by the spectators). Several bowlers were no-balled in the period 1898–1903 in England, but until the 1950s instances have been rare. Notable examples in recent years have been G A R Lock, G M Griffin, I Meckiff and H J Rhodes.

Throwing – Longest distance for

The longest recorded distance for throwing the cricket ball is 140 yards and 2 feet by Robert Percival on Durham Sands Racecourse in 1882 (incorrectly given as 1884 in some sources).

Tied Matches

The first recorded tie match was London v Richmond, Fulham and Barnes on Lamb's Conduit Fields in 1736. The first first-class tied match was played at Lord's, June 20 and 21, 1839, the sides being MCC and a Combined Oxford and Cambridge University XI.

Timed out

The only definite occasion in first-class English County cricket in which a batsman was given out because he did not reach the crease within two minutes of the fall of the previous wicket took place at Taunton on May 22, 1919 in the match between Somerset and Sussex, the batsman being H J Heygate, who was crippled with rheumatism and unable to take his place at the wicket when the 9th Sussex wicket fell in the second innings.

The phrase 'timed out' was not included as such in the Laws until 1980 and Heygate is shown on the scorecard simply as 'absent'.

Tours

Through the English ambassador in Paris it was arranged that a party of English cricketers should go to France in 1789. The party arrived at Dover *en route* for Paris on August 10, 1789, only to meet the

The first cricket tourists from England, George Parr's side to America in 1859, photographed on board ship at Liverpool on 7 September 1859. Back row: R Carpenter, W Caffyn, T Lockyer, J Wisden, H H Stephenson, G Parr, J Grundy, J Caesar, T Hayward, J Jackson. Front row: A J Diver, John Lillywhite.

ambassador – the Duke of Dorset – fleeing from France owing to the Revolution having broken out. The tour was promptly cancelled.

So far as can be discovered the next attempt to take an English team abroad was not made until 1859, when George Parr captained an all-professional side to North America.

The records in first-class matches for English teams overseas are:

Highest team total 849 England v West Indies (*Kingston*) 1929–30
Lowest team total 33 A Priestley's Team v Trinidad (*Port of Spain*) 1896–97

Highest individual innings 336* W R Hammond, England v New Zealand (*Auckland*) 1932–33
Best bowling in innings 9–28 G A Lohmann, England v South Africa (*Johannesburg*) 1895–96

The records in first-class matches for teams touring England are:

Highest team total 843 Australians v OU and CU Past and Present (*Portsmouth*) 1893
Lowest team total 18 Australians v MCC (*Lord's*) 1896
Highest individual innings 345 C G Macartney, Australians v Notts (*Trent Bridge*) 1921
Best bowling in innings 10–28 W P Howell, Australians v Surrey (*Oval*) 1899

Tours Abroad by English teams

The following list contains all the major overseas tours undertaken by English teams.

	To	Organiser	Captain	P	W	L	D	P	W	L	D
					All matches				**First class**		
1859	North America	W P Pickering	G Parr	5	5	0	0		Nil		
1861–62	Australia	Spiers and Pond	H H Stephenson	12	6	2	4		Nil		
1863–64	Australia and New Zealand	Melbourne CC	G Parr	16	10	0	6		Nil		
1868	North America	North American Cricket	E Willsher	6	5	0	1		Nil		
1872	North America	MCC	R A FitzGerald	8	7	0	1		Nil		
1873–74	Australia	Melbourne CC	W G Grace	15	10	3	2		Nil		
*1876–77	Australia and New Zealand	J Lillywhite	J Lillywhite	23	11	4	8	3	1	1	1
*1878–79	Australia, New Zealand and USA	Melbourne CC	Lord Harris	15	6	3	6	5	2	3	0
1879	North America	J P Ford	R Daft	12	9	0	3		Nil		
*1881–82	USA, Australia and	Lillywhite/Shaw/Shrewsbury	A Shaw	30	15	3	12	7	3	2	2
*1882–83	Ceylon, Australia	Melbourne CC	Hon Ivo Bligh	18	9	3	6	7	4	3	0
*1884–85	Egypt, Australia	Lillywhite/Shaw/Shrewsbury	A Shrewsbury	34	16	2	16	8	6	2	0
1885	North America	E J Sanders	R T Thornton	8	6	1	1	4	3	1	0
1886	North America	E J Sanders	W E Roller	9	8	0	1	3	3	0	0
*1886–87	Australia	Lillywhite/Shaw/Shrewsbury	A Shrewsbury	29	12	2	15	10	6	2	2
1887–88	Australia	Melbourne CC (known as G F Vernon's Team)	Lord Hawke	26	11	1	14	8	6	1	1
1887–88	Australia and New Zealand	Lillywhite/Shaw/Shrewsbury	C A Smith	25	14	2	9	7	5	2	0
*1887–88	Australia	Combined Teams	W W Read	1	1	0	0	2	2	0	0
*1888–89	South Africa	Major R G Warton	C A Smith	19	13	4	2	2	2	0	0
1889–90	Ceylon, India	G F Vernon	G F Vernon	13	10	1	2		Nil		
1891	North America	Lord Hawke	Lord Hawke	8	6	1	1	2	1	1	0
*1891–92	Malta, Ceylon, Australia	Lord Sheffield	W G Grace	29	12	2	15	8	6	2	0
*1891–92	South Africa	W W Read	W W Read	21	14	0	7	1	1	0	0
1892–93	Ceylon, India	Lord Hawke	Lord Hawke	23	15	2	6	8	4	2	2
1894	North America	Philadelphia	Lord Hawke	5	3	0	2	3	2	1	1
*1894–95	Ceylon, Australia	Australia	A E Stoddart	24	10	4	10	12	8	4	0
1894–95	West Indies	Lord Stamford	R S Lucas	16	10	4	2	7	3	3	1
1895	North America	Philadelphia	F Mitchell	5	2	1	2	4	2	2	0
1895–96	South Africa	South Africa	Lord Hawke	18	7	3	8	4	3	0	1
1896–97	West Indies	West Indies	Lord Hawke	14	9	2	3	7	3	2	2
1896–97	West Indies	Jamaica	A Priestley	16	10	5	1	9	4	5	0
1897	USA	Philadelphia	P F Warner	6	2	1	3	3	2	1	0
*1897–98	Australia	Australia	A E Stoddart	22	6	5	11	12	4	5	3
1898	North America	Philadelphia	P F Warner	8	6	0	2	3	3	0	0
*1898–99	South Africa	J D Logan	Lord Hawke	17	15	0	2	5	5	0	0
1899	North America	Philadelphia	K S Ranjitsinhji	5	3	0	2	2	2	0	0
1901	North America	Philadelphia	B J T Bosanquet	5	3	2	0	2	1	1	0
*1901–02	Australia	Australia	A C MacLaren	22	8	6	8	11	5	6	0
1901–02	West Indies	West Indies	R A Bennett	19	13	5	1	13	8	5	0
1902–03	USA, New Zealand and Australia	New Zealand CC (known as Lord Hawke's Team)	P F Warner	22	19	2	1	10	7	2	1
1902–03	India	OUA and Calcutta	K J Key	19	12	2	5	6	2	2	2
1903	USA	Kent CCC	J R Mason	4	4	0	0	2	2	0	0
*1903–04	Australia	MCC	P F Warner	20	10	2	8	14	9	2	3
1904–05	West Indies	Lord Brackley	Lord Brackley	20	11	3	6	10	6	3	1
1905	North America	MCC	E W Mann	8	5	1	2	2	1	1	0

To	Organiser	Captain	All matches				First class			
			P	W	L	D	P	W	L	D
*1905–06 South Africa	MCC	P F Warner	26	17	5	4	12	7	5	0
1906–07 South Africa, New Zealand	MCC	E G Wynyard	17	11	2	4	11	6	2	3
1907 North America	MCC	H V Hesketh-Prichard	5	1	0	4	2	0	0	2
*1907–08 Australia	MCC	A O Jones	19	7	4	8	18	7	4	7
1909 Egypt	MCC	G H T Simpson-Hayward	8	7	1	0	Nil			
*1909–10 South Africa	MCC	H D G Leveson-Gower	18	9	4	5	13	7	4	2
1910–11 West Indies	MCC	A W F Somerset	12	4	4	4t	11	3	4	4t
*1911–12 Ceylon, Australia	MCC	P F Warner	19	13	1	5	14	11	1	2
1911–12 Argentine	MCC	Lord Hawke	9	6	1	2	3	2	1	0
1912–13 West Indies	MCC	A W F Somerset	9	5	3	1	9	5	3	1
1913 USA	Incogniti	C E Greenway	6	4	1	1	2	1	1	0
*1913–14 South Africa	MCC	J W H T Douglas	22	12	1	9	18	9	1	8
1920 North America	Incogniti	E J Metcalfe	9	7	0	2	Nil			
*1920–21 Ceylon, Australia	MCC	J W H T Douglas	23	9	6	8	13	5	6	2
*1922–23 South Africa	MCC	F T Mann	22	14	1	7	14	10	1	3
1922–23 Ceylon, Australia and New Zealand	MCC	A C MacLaren	23	11	3	9	15	6	3	6
1923 Canada	Free Foresters	E G Wynyard	7	6	0	1	Nil			
1924 USA	Incogniti	E J Metcalfe	7	2	0	5	Nil			
*1924–25 Ceylon, Australia	MCC	A E R Gilligan	24	8	6	10	17	7	6	4
1924–25 South Africa	S B Joel	Hon L H Tennyson	21	8	2	11	14	5	2	7
1925–26 West Indies	MCC	Hon F S Gough-Calthorpe	13	2	1	10	12	2	1	9
1926–27 India, Burma, Ceylon	MCC	A E R Gilligan	34	11	0	23	30	10	0	20
1926–27 South America	MCC	P F Warner	10	6	1	3	5	3	1	1
1926–27 Jamaica	Hon L H Tennyson	Hon L H Tennyson	7	1	0	6	3	0	0	3
*1927–28 South Africa	MCC	R T Stanyforth	18	7	2	9	16	7	2	7
1927–28 Jamaica	Hon L H Tennyson	Hon L H Tennyson	5	1	2	2	3	0	2	1
*1928–29 Ceylon, Australia	MCC	A P F Chapman	25	11	1	13	17	8	1	8
1928–29 Jamaica	J Cahn	J Cahn	6	1	2	3	3	0	2	1
1929 Egypt	H M Martineau	H M Martineau	5	1	0	4	2	1	0	1
*1929–30 Ceylon, Australia and New Zealand	MCC	A H H Gilligan	23	11	2	10	13	4	2	7
*1929–30 West Indies	MCC	Hon F S Gough-Calthorpe	13	4	2	7	12	4	2	6
1929–30 Argentine	Sir J Cahn	Sir J Cahn	6	2	1	3	3	1	0	2
1930 Egypt	H M Martineau	H M Martineau	5	1	1	3	2	1	0	1
*1930–31 South Africa	MCC	A P F Chapman	20	7	1	12	16	5	1	10
1931 Egypt	H M Martineau	H M Martineau	5	3	0	2	2	2	0	0
1931–32 Jamaica	Lord Tennyson	Lord Tennyson	6	1	3	2	3	0	3	0
1932 Egypt	H M Martineau	H M Martineau	7	3	4	0	2	0	2	0
*1932–33 Ceylon, Australia and New Zealand	MCC	D R Jardine	26	10	1	15t	20	10	1	9t
1933 Egypt	H M Martineau	H M Martineau	8	4	1	3	2	2	0	0
1933 N America, Bermuda	Sir J Cahn	Sir J Cahn	20	16	0	4	Nil			
*1933–34 India, Ceylon	MCC	D R Jardine	34	17	1	16	18	10	1	7
1934 Egype	H M Martineau	H M Martineau	10	9	1	0	2	2	0	0
*1934–35 West Indies	MCC	R E S Wyatt	12	2	2	8	12	2	2	8
1935 Egypt	H M Martineau	H M Martineau	10	3	4	3	2	0	2	0
1935–36 Ceylon, Australia and New Zealand	MCC	E R T Holmes	25	8	2	15	14	5	2	7
1935–36 Jamaica	Yorkshire CCC	P A Gibb	6	1	0	5	3	1	0	2
1936 Egypt	H M Martineau	H M Martineau	10	8	1	1	2	2	0	0
*1936–37 Ceylon, Australia and New Zealand	MCC	G O B Allen	29	9	5	15	20	6	5	9
1936–37 Ceylon, Malaya	Sir J Cahn	Sir J Cahn	9	3	0	6	1	1	0	0
1937 Egypt	H M Martineau	H M Martineau	11	6	1	4	2	1	1	0
1937 Canada	MCC	G C Newman	19	12	1	6	Nil			
1937–38 India	Lord Tennyson	Lord Tennyson	24	8	5	11	15	4	5	6
1937–38 South America	Sir T E W Brinckman	Sir T E W Brinckman	11	5	1	5	3	1	1	1
1938 Egypt	H M Martineau	H M Martineau	12	10	1	1	2	2	0	0
1938–39 Jamaica	Universities	E J H Dixon	7	2	1	4	2	0	1	1
*1938–39 South Africa	MCC	W R Hammond	18	9	0	9	17	8	0	9
1938–39 New Zealand	Sir J Cahn	Sir J Cahn	10	4	0	6	1	0	0	1
1939 Egypt	H M Martineau	H M Martineau	10	7	0	3	2	2	0	0
*1946–47 Australia and New Zealand	MCC	W R Hammond	29	6	3	20	21	3	3	15
*1947–48 West Indies	MCC	G O B Allen	11	0	2	9	11	0	2	9
*1948–49 South Africa	MCC	F G Mann	23	11	0	12	20	9	0	11

To	Organiser	Captain	All matches				First class			
			P	W	L	D	P	W	L	D
*1950–51 Ceylon, Australia and New Zealand	MCC	F R Brown	30	10	4	16	20	8	4	8
1951 Canada	MCC	R W V Robins	22	18	2	2	1	1	0	0
*1951–52 India, Pakistan, Ceylon	MCC	N D Howard	27	10	3	14	23	7	3	13
*1953–54 West Indies, Bermuda	MCC	L Hutton	17	8	2	7	10	6	2	2
*1954–55 Ceylon, Australia and New Zealand	MCC	L Hutton	28	17	2	9	21	12	2	7
1955–56 Pakistan	MCC	D B Carr	16	7	2	7	14	7	2	5
1955–56 West Indies, Bermuda	E W Swanton	M J Cowdrey	7	3	2	2	4	1	2	1
*1956–57 South Africa	MCC	P B H May	22	13	3	6	20	11	3	6
1956–57 Jamaica	Duke of Norfolk	E D R Eager	10	4	0	6	3	2	0	1
1956–57 India	C G Howard	W J Edrich	2	1	1	0	2	1	1	0
1957–58 Tanganyika, Kenya, Uganda	MCC	F R Brown	9	3	1	5	Nil			
*1958 Ceylon, Ausgralia and New Zealand	MCC	P B H May	26	10	4	12	22	7	4	11
1958–59 South America	MCC	G H G Doggart	11	9	0	2	Nil			
1959 North America	MCC	D R W Silk	25	21	0	4	Nil			
1959–60 Rhodesia	Surrey CCC	W S Surridge	2	0	1	1	2	0	1	1
*1959–60 West Indies, Honduras	MCC	P B H May	17	6	1	10	13	4	1	8
1960–61 New Zealand	MCC	D R W Silk	21	12	1	8	10	4	1	5
1961 Bermuda	Bermuda CA	W S Surridge	12	5	0	7	Nil			
1961 Tanganyika, Kenya, Uganda	F R Brown	F R Brown	7	4	0	3	Nil			
*1961–62 Pakistan, India, Ceylon	MCC	E R Dexter	24	8	2	14	22	7	2	13
1962 Bermuda	Gloucestershire CCC	C T M Pugh	9	3	3	3	Nil			
*1962–63 Ceylon, Australia and New Zealand	MCC	E R Dexter	32	16	3	13	20	8	3	9
1963–64 Tanganyika, Kenya, Uganda	MCC	M J K Smith	11	7	0	4	2	1	0	1
*1963–64 India	MCC	M J K Smith	10	1	0	9	10	1	0	9
1963–64 Jamaica	Cavaliers	D C S Compton	5	3	0	2	3	2	0	1
1964 N America, Bermuda	Yorkshire	D B Close	12	9	0	3	Nil			
1964–65 West Indies	Cavaliers	T E Bailey	7	1	1	5	4	0	1	3
1964–54 World Tour	Worcestershire CCC	D Kenyon	14	8	1	5	2	1	1	0
1964–65 South America	MCC	A C Smith	15	14	0	1	Nil			
*1964–65 South Africa	MCC	M J K Smith	19	11	0	8	17	10	0	7
*1965–66 Ceylon, Australia, New Zealand, Hong Kong	MCC	M J K Smith	31	14	2	15	19	5	2	12
1965–66 Jamaica	Worcestershire CCC	D Kenyon	5	0	0	5	1	0	0	1
1966–67 Pakistan	MCC	J M Brearley	8	4	0	4	7	4	0	3
1966–67 Barbados	Arabs CC	A C D Ingleby-Mackenzie	9	4	4	1	Nil			
1967 N America	MCC	D R W Silk	25	21	0	4	Nil			
*1967–68 West Indies	MCC	M C Cowdrey	16	4	0	12	12	3	0	9
1967–68 Africa, Asia	International	M J Stewart	21	15	0	6	5	4	0	1
1967–68 Kenya, Uganda	Warwickshire CC	M J K Smith	9	2	0	7	1	0	0	1
*1968–69 Ceylon, Pakistan	MCC	M C Cowdrey	10	2	1	7	7	0	0	7
1968–69 South Africa	R J McAlpine	R J McAlpine	14	4	5	5	Nil			
1969–70 West Indies	Duke of Norfolk	M C Cowdrey	9	5	2	2	3	1	1	1
1969–70 West Indies	Glamorgan CCC	A R Lewis	6	1	1	4	2	0	0	2
1969–70 Ceylon, Far East	MCC	A R Lewis	8	6	0	2	1	1	0	0
*1970–71 Australia and New Zealand	MCC	R Illingworth	29	13	3	13	16	4	1	11
1971–72 Zambia	Gloucestershire CCC	A S Brown	5	3	0	2	Nil			
1972–73 West Indies	Kent CCC	B W Luckhurst	11	4	0	7	Nil			
1972–73 South Africa	D H Robins	D J Brown	10	4	4	2	6	1	3	2
1972–73 Malaysia, Singapore	Oxford and Cambridge Universities	P C H Jones	10	8	0	2	Nil			
*1972–73 India, Pakistan, Sri Lanka	MCC	A R Lewis	17	4	2	11	16	3	2	11
1973–74 South Africa	D H Robins	D B Close	13	8	1	4	7	2	1	4
1973–74 Kenya, Zambia, Tanzania	MCC	J M Brearley	8	5	0	3	1	1	0	0
*1973–74 West Indies	MCC	M H Denness	16	3	3	10	12	2	2	8
1973–74 Barbados	Arabs CC	A R Lewis	9	3	1	5	Nil			
*1974–75 Australia, New Zealand, Hong Kong	MCC	M H Denness	30	11	6	13	18	6	5	7
1974–75 West Indies	English Counties	J H Hampshire	7	3	0	4	Nil			
1974–75 South Africa	D H Robins	D B Close	8	2	3	3	5	0	2	3
1974–75 West Indies	D H Robins	J A Jameson	12	6	4	2	Nil			
1975–76 South Africa	D H Robins	D Lloyd	11	5	3	3	4	2	2	0
1975–76 West Africa	MCC	E A Clark	10	8	0	2	Nil			
1976 Canada	D H Robins	P H Parfitt	15	14	0	1	Nil			

	To	Organiser	Captain	All matches				First class			
				P	W	L	D	P	W	L	D
*1976–77	India, Sri Lanka, Australia	MCC	A W Greig	19	5	3	11	16	4	2	10
1976–77	Bangladesh	MCC	E A Clark	4	1	0	3		Nil		
1977–78	Far East	D H Robins	M H Denness	13	7	0	6	1	0	0	1
*1977–78	Pakistan, New Zealand	England	J M Brearley	21	8	3	10t	15	4	1	10t
1977–78	Kenya	Minor Counties	D Bailey	6	5	1	0		Nil		
1978–79	Bangladesh	MCC	E A Clark	6	2	0	4		Nil		
*1978–79	Australia	England	J M Brearley	26	17	4	5	13	8	2	3
1978–79	South America	D H Robins	C S Cowdrey	13	13	0	0		Nil		
1979–80	Australia, New Zealand	D H Robins	C S Cowdrey	15	7	2	6	2	0	0	2
*1979–80	Australia, India	England	J M Brearley	21	11	7	3	9	4	3	2
*1980–81	West Indies	England	I T Botham	14	5	4	5	9	2	2	5
1980–81	Zimbabwe	Middlesex	J M Brearley	6	3	1	2t	3	1	1	1
1980–81	Zimbabwe	Leicestershire CCC	R W Tolchard	5	1	1	3	3	0	0	3
*1981–82	India, Sri Lanka	England	K W R Fletcher	22	6	5	11	15	3	1	11
1981–82	South Africa	SAB	G A Gooch	8	0	4	4	4	0	1	3

t Denotes tied match included in draws

*Tours with Test matches. Matches with no play at all are not included

Above *The unbeaten Australian team in England in 1948. Left to right, back: I Johnson, A R Morris, E Toshack, K R Miller, D Tallon, R R Lindwall, R N Harvey. Front: W A Brown, A L Hassett, D G Bradman, C McCool, S G Barnes.*

Left *Lord Harris' team to Australia in 1878–79. Left to right, back: F Penn, A J Webbe, C A Absalom, S S Schultz, L Hone. Centre: F Mackinnon, A N Hornby, Lord Harris, H C Maul, G Ulyett. Front: A P Lucas, V Royle, T Emmett.*

Touring Teams in England

The following list contains all the major teams that have toured England.

		All matches				First class			
		P	W	L	D	P	W	L	D
1868	Australian Aborigines	47	14	14	19	Nil			
1874	American Baseball	7	4	0	3	Nil			
1878	1st Australians	37	18	7	12	15	7	4	4
1880	1st Canadians	17	5	6	6	Nil			
	2nd Australians	37	21	4	12	10	5	2	3
1882	3rd Australians	38	23	4	11	32	17	4	11
1884	4th Australians	32	18	7	7	31	17	7	7
	1st Philadelphians	18	8	5	5	Nil			
1886	1st Parsis	27	1	17	9	Nil			
	(plus one match, score unknown)								
	5th Australians	39	9	8	22	27	9	7	21
1887	2nd Canadians	19	5	5	9	Nil			
1888	6th Australians	40	19	14	7	37	17	13	7
	2nd Parsis	31	8	11	12	Nil			
1889	2nd Philadelphians	12	4	3	5	Nil			
1890	7th Australians	38	13	16	9	34	10	16	8
1893	8th Australians	36	18	10	8	31	14	10	7
1894	1st South Africans	24	12	5	7	Nil			
1896	9th Australians	34	19	6	9	34	19	6	9
1897	3rd Philadelphians	15	2	9	4	15	2	9	4
1899	10th Australians	35	16	3	16	35	16	3	16
1900	1st West Indians	17	5	8	4	Nil			
1901	2nd South Africans	25	13	9	2t	15	5	9	0t
1902	11th Australians	39	23	2	14	37	21	2	14
1903	4th Philadelphians	20	10	6	4	15	6	6	3
1904	3rd South Africans	26	13	3	9t	22	10	2	9t
1905	12th Australians	38	16	3	19	35	15	3	17
1906	2nd West Indians	19	7	10	2	13	3	8	2
1907	4th South Africans	31	12	4	6	27	17	4	6
1908	5th Philadelphians	16	7	6	3	9	3	6	0
1909	13th Australians	39	13	4	22	37	11	4	22
1910	Toronto Zingari	17	9	3	5	Nil			
1911	1st Indians	23	6	15	2	14	2	10	2
1912	14th Australians	37	9	8	20	36	9	8	19
	5th South Africans	37	13	8	16	37	13	8	16
	Philadelphia CC	10	4	3	3	Nil			
1919	Australian Imperial Forces	32	13	4	15	28	12	4	12
1921	15th Australians	39	23	2	14	34	21	2	11
	Philadelphian Pilgrims	12	5	2	5	Nil			
1922	3rd Canadians	11	0	4	7	Nil			
1923	3rd West Indians	28	13	7	8	20	6	7	7
1924	6th South Africans	38	8	9	21	35	8	9	19
1926	16th Australians	40	12	1	27	33	9	1	23
1927	1st New Zealanders	38	13	5	20	26	7	5	14
1928	4th West Indians	41	7	12	22	30	5	12	13
1929	7th South Africans	37	11	7	19	34	9	7	18
1930	17th Australians	33	12	1	19t	31	11	1	18t
1931	2nd New Zealanders	36	7	3	26	32	6	3	23
1932	2nd Indians	36	13	9	14	26	9	8	9
	South Americans	18	2	5	11	6	2	3	1
1933	5th West Indians	44	9	9	26	30	5	9	16
1934	18th Australians	34	15	1	18	30	13	1	16
1935	8th South Africans	39	22	2	15	31	17	2	12
1936	3rd Indians	31	5	13	13	28	4	12	12
	4th Canadians	15	7	1	7	Nil			
1937	3rd New Zealanders	37	13	9	15	32	9	9	14
1938	19th Australians	35	20	2	13	29	15	2	12
1939	6th West Indians	33	10	6	17	25	8	6	11
1945	Australian Services	48	24	9	15	6	3	2	1
	New Zealand Services	19	3	7	9	1	0	1	0
1946	4th Indians	33	13	4	16	29	11	4	14
1947	9th South Africans	33	16	5	12	28	14	5	9
1948	20th Australians	34	25	0	9	31	23	0	8
1949	4th New Zealanders	35	14	1	20	32	13	1	18
1950	7th West Indians	38	19	3	16	31	17	3	11
1951	10th South Africans	34	8	5	21	30	5	5	20
1952	5th Indians	34	6	5	23	29	4	5	20
1953	21st Australians	35	16	1	18	33	16	1	16
1954	1st Pakistanis	32	10	3	19	30	9	3	18
	5th Canadians	15	4	3	8	4	0	2	2
1955	11th South Africans	31	16	4	11	28	15	4	9
1956	22nd Australians	34	11	3	20	31	9	3	19
1957	8th West Indians	35	16	3	16	31	14	3	14
1958	5th New Zealanders	35	7	6	21t	31	7	6	17t
1959	6th Indians	35	7	11	17	33	6	11	16
1960	12th South Africans	31	15	5	11	30	14	5	11
1961	23rd Australians	37	14	2	21	32	13	1	18
	South African Fezelas	21	14	0	7	3	3	0	0
1962	2nd Pakistanis	35	6	8	21	29	4	8	17
1963	9th West Indians	38	19	3	16	30	15	2	13
	Pakistan Eaglets	20	11	2	7	8	2	2	4
1964	24th Australians	35	14	3	18	30	11	3	16
	Mashonaland (Rhodesia)	27	15	2	10	Nil			
1965	6th New Zealanders	21	4	6	11	19	3	6	10
	13th South Africans	19	5	3	11	18	5	2	11
1966	10th West Indians	34	13	5	16	27	8	4	15
	South Africa (W Isaacs)	17	9	0	8	Nil			
1967	7th Indians	21	4	7	10	18	2	7	9
	3rd Pakistanis	22	3	6	13	17	3	3	11
	South African Universities	21	10	1	10	2	1	0	3
	Zambia Eagles	18	9	4	5	Nil			
1968	25th Australians	29	10	3	16	25	8	3	14
	USA	21	2	6	13	Nil			
1969	11th West Indians	23	3	4	16	19	2	3	14
	7th New Zealanders	18	4	3	11	18	4	3	11
	South Africa (W Isaacs)	16	9	1	6	1	0	0	1
	Barbados	7	3	3	1	2	0	1	1
1970	Rest of World	5	4	1	0	5	4	1	0
	Israel	9	4	2	3	Nil			
	Jamaica	12	2	2	8	4	1	0	3
1971	4th Pakistanis	19	5	4	10	19	5	4	10
	8th Indians	19	7	1	11	19	7	1	11
1972	26th Australians	37	14	10	13	26	11	5	10
1973	8th New Zealanders	23	4	3	16	19	3	2	14
	12th West Indians	23	10	2	11	18	7	1	10
1974	9th Indians	21	5	5	11	18	4	3	11
	5th Pakistanis	23	16	0	7	16	9	0	7
1975	27th Australians*	21	12	4	5	15	8	2	5
1976	13th West Indians	35	26	2	7	26	18	2	6
1977	28th Australians	31	8	8	15	22	5	4	13
1978	6th Pakistanis	16	1	4	11	13	1	2	10
	9th New Zealanders	20	5	8	7	16	5	4	7
1979	1st Sri Lankans	16	6	3	7	9	1	1	7
	10th Indians*	19	1	6	12	16	1	3	12
1980	14th West Indians	29	16	2	11	16	8	0	8
	29th Australians	8	1	4	3	5	1	2	2
1981	30th Australians	25	7	6	12	17	3	3	11
	2nd Sri Lankans	15	3	1	11	13	1	1	11
1982	11th Indians*	18	2	4	12	12	1	1	10
	7th Pakistanis*	21	7	6	8	15	6	3	6
	Zimbabwe†	4	0	2	2	2	0	0	2

*For scores of Prudential Cup matches, see Prudential Cup
†Not including ICC Trophy games

Triple centuries

The first recorded triple century was made by W E W Collins for Northwood v Freshwater at Cowes on the Isle of Wight, August 27, 1874, his score being 338 not out. The first first-class triple century came in 1876, when W G Grace hit 344 on August 11 and 12 for Gentlemen of MCC v Kent. On August 17 and 18, Grace hit a second first-class triple century – 318 not out v Yorkshire at Cheltenham.

The most triple centuries in a first-class career are 6 by D G Bradman: 452*, 369, 357, 340*, 334, and 304.

Twins

The following sets of twins have played in English first-class cricket:

A V and E A Bedser (*Surrey*)
J S and W H Denton (*Northamptonshire*)
A D E and A E S Rippon (*Somerset*)
F G and G W Stephens (*Warwickshire*)
M N S Taylor (*Notts and Hants*) and D J S Taylor (*Somerset*)
G J and O Spencer-Smith (*Hampshire*)
J G Varey (*Oxford U*) and D W Varey (*Cambridge U*)
A and A F Payne (*Oxford U*)
C and H Pigg (*Cambridge U*)
C C Garthwaite (*Army*) and P F Garthwaite (*Oxford U*)
S A Westley (*Oxford U and Gloucs*) and R B Westley (*Oxford U*)
H G Phipps (*MCC*) and W T Phipps (*Southgate*)
G M Ede and E L Ede (*Hampshire*)

Ubiquitous cricketers

Since 1873 only two cricketers have appeared in first-class cricket for four Counties. A A Jones played for Sussex 1966–69, Somerset 1970–75, Middlesex 1976–79 and Glamorgan 1980 and 1981 – in addition he appeared in first-class matches overseas for Northern Transvaal in 1972–73 and Orange Free State in 1976–77. In 1982 J Cumbes joined A A Jones. Cumbes has played for Lancashire 1963–67 and 1971; Surrey 1968–69; Worcestershire 1972–81; Warwickshire 1982.

Before the rule preventing players from appearing for more than one County in any one year (passed in 1873), there were a number of examples of cricketers playing both for their county of birth and the county in which they resided. J Southerton however managed to appear in inter-county matches for three counties in a single summer – Sussex, Hampshire and Surrey in 1867.

Under-arm bowling

Although still within the Laws, except in certain limited overs matches, under-arm bowling is rarely seen even in minor matches today. The most recent occurrence of any note took place at Melbourne on February 1, 1981 during the Benson and Hedges World Series Cup when Australia played New Zealand. The latter required six to win off the final delivery and the bowler, T M Chappell, changed to under-arm to prevent the six being scored. This action led to much controversy.

On several occasions in post-war cricket bowlers have delivered an over of under-arm balls as a form of protest, usually over slow run scoring, but the last occasion on which a cricketer was chosen to play in a County Championship match purely on his ability as an under-arm bowler took place at Trent Bridge on May 14, 16 and 17, 1921. The cricketer was T J Molony appearing for Surrey v Notts and his analysis for the two innings was 14-1-30-3.

The original under-arm bowlers had more or less disappeared from important cricket in the 1830s, though W A Humphreys (*Sussex*) went to Australia with the 1894–95 English team mainly on the strength of his lob bowling and G H T Simpson-Hayward bowled under-arm with success against the South Africans in the Tests of 1909–10.

Under 25 County competition

Sponsored by the Warwickshire CC Supporters' Association the Competition is organised on a regional league basis of four Leagues with the four winners playing the semi-finals and final at Edgbaston. The matches are one-day limited over games.

Championship winners

1972	Middlesex	1978	Yorkshire
1973	Middlesex	1979	Undecided
1974	Middlesex	1980	Sussex
1975	Leicestershire	1981	Glamorgan
1976	Yorkshire	1982	Kent
1977	Undecided		

A V and E A Bedser, probably the most famous twins to play first class cricket, were members of the triumphant Surrey side of the 1950s.

The last and most controversial incident involving underarm bowling. Trevor Chappell bowling the last ball of a Benson and Hedges World Series Cup match in 1981.

University match

The first meeting between Oxford and Cambridge took place at Lord's on June 4, 1827 – rain limited the fixture to a single day. The match was for many years one of the events of the Social season and thus huge crowds gathered at Lord's – over 20,000 would attend a single day's play in the 1880s. The match has been played every year since 1838, except 1915 to 1918, 1940 and 1941.

1827	Drawn	1874	Oxford won by inns and 92 runs
1829	Oxford won by 115 runs	1875	Oxford won by 6 runs
1836	Oxford won by 121 runs	1876	Cambridge won by 9 wkts
1838	Oxford won by 98 runs	1877	Oxford won by 10 wkts
1839	Cambridge won by inns and 125 runs	1878	Cambridge won by 238 runs
1840	Cambridge won by 63 runs	1879	Cambridge won by 9 wkts
1841	Cambridge won by 8 runs	1880	Cambridge won by 115 runs
1842	Cambridge won by 162 runs	1881	Oxford won by 135 runs
1843	Cambridge won by 54 runs	1882	Cambridge won by 7 wkts
1844	Drawn	1883	Cambridge won by 7 wkts
1845	Cambridge won by 6 wkts	1884	Oxford won by 7 wkts
1846	Oxford won by 3 wkts	1885	Cambridge won by 7 wkts
1847	Cambridge won by 138 runs	1886	Oxford won by 133 runs
1848	Oxford won by 23 runs	1887	Oxford won by 7 wkts
1849	Cambridge won by 3 wkts	1888	Drawn
1850	Oxford won by 127 runs	1889	Cambridge won by inns and 105 runs
1851	Cambridge won by inns and 4 runs	1890	Cambridge won by 7 wkts
1852	Oxford won by inns and 77 runs	1891	Cambridge won by 2 wkts
1853	Oxford won by inns and 19 runs	1892	Oxford won by 5 wkts
1854	Oxford won by inns and 8 runs	1893	Cambridge won by 266 runs
1855	Oxford won by 3 wkts	1894	Oxford won by 8 wkts
1856	Cambridge won by 3 wkts	1895	Cambridge won by 134 runs
1857	Oxford won by 81 runs	1896	Oxford won by 4 wkts
1858	Oxford won by inns and 38 runs	1897	Cambridge won by 179 runs
1859	Cambridge won by 28 runs	1898	Oxford won by 9 wkts
1860	Cambridge won by 3 wkts	1899	Drawn
1861	Cambridge won by 133 runs	1900	Drawn
1862	Cambridge won by 8 wkts	1901	Drawn
1863	Oxford won by 8 wkts	1902	Cambridge won by 5 wkts
1864	Oxford won by 4 wkts	1903	Oxford won by 268 runs
1865	Oxford won by 114 runs	1904	Drawn
1866	Oxford won by 12 runs	1905	Cambridge won by 40 runs
1867	Cambridge won by 5 wkts	1906	Cambridge won by 94 runs
1868	Cambridge won by 168 runs	1907	Cambridge won by 5 wkts
1869	Cambridge won by 58 runs	1908	Oxford won by 2 wkts
1870	Cambridge won by 2 runs	1909	Drawn
1871	Oxford won by 8 wkts	1910	Oxford won by inns and 126 runs
1872	Cambridge won by inns and 166 runs	1911	Oxford won by 74 runs
1873	Oxford won by 3 wkts	1912	Cambridge won by 3 wkts
		1913	Cambridge won by 4 wkts
		1914	Oxford won by 194 runs

1919	Oxford won by 45 runs	1950	Drawn
1920	Drawn	1951	Oxford won by 21 runs
1921	Cambridge won by inns and 24 runs	1952	Drawn
1922	Cambridge won by inns and 100 runs	1953	Cambridge won by 2 wkts
1923	Oxford won by inns and 227 runs	1954	Drawn
1924	Cambridge won by 9 wkts	1955	Drawn
1925	Drawn	1956	Drawn
1926	Cambridge won by 34 runs	1957	Cambridge won by inns and 186 runs
1927	Cambridge won by 116 runs	1958	Cambridge won by 99 runs
1928	Drawn	1959	Oxford won by 85 runs
1929	Drawn	1960	Drawn
1930	Cambridge won by 205 runs	1961	Drawn
1931	Oxford won by 8 wkts	1962	Drawn
1932	Drawn	1963	Drawn
1933	Drawn	1964	Drawn
1934	Drawn	1965	Drawn
1935	Cambridge won by 195 runs	1966	Oxford won by inns and 9 runs
1936	Cambridge won by 8 wkts	1967	Drawn
1937	Oxford won by 7 wkts	1968	Drawn
1938	Drawn	1969	Drawn
1939	Oxford won by 45 runs	1970	Drawn
1942	Cambridge won by 77 runs	1971	Drawn
1943	Drawn	1972	Cambridge won by inns and 25 runs
1944	Cambridge won by 6 wkts	1973	Drawn
1945	Cambridge won by 10 wkts	1974	Drawn
1946	Oxford won by 6 wkts	1975	Drawn
1947	Drawn	1976	Oxford won by 10 wkts
1948	Oxford won by inns and 8 runs	1977	Drawn
1949	Cambridge won by 7 wkts	1978	Drawn
		1979	Cambridge won by inns and 52 runs
		1980	Drawn
		1981	Drawn
		1982	Cambridge won by 7 wkts

Cambridge have won 53 matches and Oxford 45 (the 1942–45 matches are not counted in the regular series).

Records

Highest team total: Oxford, 503, 1900 Cambridge, 432–9 dec, 1936
Lowest team total: Oxford, 32, 1878 Cambirdge, 39, 1858
Highest individual innings: Oxford, 238* Nawab of Pataudi snr 1931 Cambridge, 211 G Goonesena 1957
Best bowling in innings: Oxford, 10–38 S E Butler Cambridge 8–44 G E Jefferey

Highest wicket partnerships in match

1st	243	K J Key, W Rashleigh for Oxford 1886
2nd	226	W G Keighley, H A Pawson for Oxford 1947
3rd	183	A T Barber, E R T Holmes for Oxford 1927
4th	230	D C H Townsend, F G H Chalk for Oxford 1934
5th	191	J E Raphael, E L Wright for Oxford 1905
6th	178	M R Jardine, V T Hill for Oxford 1892
7th	289	G Goonesena, G W Cook for Cambridge 1957
8th	112	H E Webb, A W H Mallett for Oxford 1948
9th	97*	J F Marsh, F J V Hopley for Cambridge 1904
10th	90	W J H Curwen, E G Martin for Oxford 1906

All matches have taken place at Lords except 1829, 1843, 1846, 1848 and 1850, which were played at Oxford.

Only two players have represented both Universities: D W Jarrett and S M Wookey. In the early years some players appeared in five University matches, but in the 1860s players were restricted to four, and this restriction has now been removed.

United States of America

Although there is a possible reference to cricket in America as early as 1656, the earliest certain mention is in 1709 in Virginia – the diary of William Byrd of Westover, Virginia, contains many references to playing cricket, the earliest being on April 25, 1709.

The international match with Canada commenced in 1844 and the results in this series are:

1844	Canada won by 33 runs	1902	US won by inns and 104 runs
1845	Canada won by 61 runs		
1845	Canada won by 2 wkts	1903	US won by 147 runs
1846	Drawn	1904	US won by 7 wkts
1853	US won by 34 runs	1905	Canada won by inns and 29 runs
1854	Canada won by 10 wkts		
1856	US won by 9 wkts	1906	US won by 253 runs
1857	Canada won by 7 wkts	1907	US won by 80 runs
1858	US won by 4 wkts	1908	US won by inns and 21 runs
1859	US won by 4 wkts		
1860	US won by 5 wkts	1909	Canada won by 143 runs
1865	US won by 1 wkt	1911	Drawn
1879	US won by 5 wkts	1912	US won by 8 wkts
1880	Drawn	1963	Canada won by inns and 164 runs
1881	US won by 10 wkts		
1882	US won by 8 wkts	1964	Canada won by inns and 94 runs
1883	US won by inns and 49 runs		
		1965	Drawn
1884	Canada won by 100 runs	1966	US won by 58 runs
1885	Canada won by 39 runs	1967	Canada won by 7 wkts
1886	Canada won by 97 runs	1968	Drawn
1888	US won by inns and 87 runs	1969	US won by 131 runs
		1970	Drawn
1890	US won by inns and 31 runs	1971	Canada won by 1 wkt
		1972	US won by inns and 34 runs
1891	US won by 36 runs		
1892	US won by inns and 222 runs	1973	Drawn
		1974	US won by 176 runs
1893	US won by 4 wkts	1975	Drawn
1894	Drawn	1976	US won by 2 wkts
1895	Canada won by 141 runs	1977	Canada won by inns and 187 runs
1896	Canada won by 40 runs		
1897	Canada won by 8 wkts	1978	US won by 25 runs
1898	US won by inns and 1 run	1979	Canada won by 6 wkts
		1980	Canada won by 136 runs
1899	US won by 34 runs	1981	Not played
1900	US won by 1 wkt	1982	Not played
1901	US won by 94 runs		

Records in the series are:

Highest team total: Canada 403–6 dec in Toronto 1963
  United States 352 in Manheim 1892
Lowest team total: Canada 28 in New York 1846
  United States 32 in Toronto 1854
Highest individual innings Canada 176 R Nascimento in Toronto 1963
  US 129 A M Wood in Manheim 1892
Best bowling in innings Canada 9–? Bradbury in Toronto 1854
  US 8–17 J B King in Manheim 1906

Competing in both the 1979 and 1982 I C C Trophy competitions, U S A won two matches in the former year, but only one in the latter.
(see also under Philadelphia)

Village championship

Inaugurated by John Haig and Co in 1972 on a knock-out basis with nearly 800 English villages competing, the National Village Championship has been sponsored by Samuel Whitbread since 1979. The final has taken place at Lord's each year, except in 1974, when rain caused caused a postponement and the match took place at Edgbaston.

The results of the finals have been:

1972 Astwood Bank 165–8 (P Johns 5–27) lost to Troon 170–3 (T Carter 79*) by 7 wkts
1973 Troon 176–3 (G B Carter 70*) beat Gowerton 164–5 (A Daniel 50) by 12 runs
1974 Collingham 109 lost to Bomarsund Welfare 112–7 by 3 wkts
1975 Isleham 120 lost to Gowerton 124–4 (H E D Bevan 57*) by 6 wkts
1976 Troon 113–7 beat Sessay 95 (B Moyle 4–23) by 18 runs
1977 Cookley 138 (R Coulsson 6–24) beat Lindal Moor 110 by 28
1978 Toft 130–8 lost to Linton Park 131–6 (N Thirkell 51*) by 4 wkts
1979 East Bierley 216–4 (C Defoe 61) beat Ynysygerwyn 124 by 92 runs
1980 Marchwiel 161–8 beat Longparish 82–9 by 79 runs
1981 St Fagan's 149 beat Broad Oak 127 by 22 runs
1982 Collingham 148–9 (G Driscoll 63*) lost to St Fagan's 149–4 by 6 wkts

Warwickshire

The earliest reference to the game in the County occurs in 1751, when an announcement of a match between two Gentlemen's Clubs at Aston, near Birmingham, was published in Aris's Gazette on July 15.

Formation of the County Club The present County Cricket Club was formed at a meeting at Coventry on April 8, 1882.

First-class status The County were granted first-class status for the first time at the start of the 1894 season, their first first-class match being against Notts at Trent Bridge on May 3, 4 and 5, 1894.

Grounds The County Club has used Edgbaston Cricket Ground, Birmingham, as its headquarters since the ground was laid out for use in the 1886 season.

Other grounds currently used by the County are: Courtaulds Grd, Coventry (since 1946); Griff and Coton Grd, Nuneaton (since 1930).

Grounds that have been used for first-class matches by the County are: Mitchell and Butler's Grd, Birmingham (1931–61); Bulls Head Grd, Coventry (1903–19); Rover Grd, Coventry (1925–30); Morris Motors Grd, Coventry (1931–32); Leamington Spa (1905–10); Nuneaton CC Grd (1912–14); Stratford-on-Avon (1951).

Honours The County have won the Championship in 1911, 1951 and 1972; the John Player League in 1980; Gillette Cup in 1966 and 1968. The best years in the Benson and Hedges Cup are 1972, 1975, 1976 and 1978, when they were semi-finalists.

The players The only cricketer to appear in more than 500 matches for the County is William Quaife, who represented the County 665 times between 1894 and 1928. Second on the list is F R Santall with 496 matches between 1919 and 1939.

The longest serving captain is M J K Smith who led the County for 11 seasons between 1957 and 1967.

Youngest cricketer to represent the County is F R Santall, who was 16 years and 23 days on his debut v Worcestershire in 1919.

William Quaife is the oldest cricketer, being 56 years and 4 months on his final appearance v Derbyshire in 1928.

R G D Willis is the Warwickshire Cricketer with most England caps, having a total of 69 to the end of the 1982 season (this total does not include the 5 matches when he was registered as a Surrey player).

Team performances The County have made one total over 650 – 657 for 6 wkts dec against Hampshire at Edgbaston on July 24, 25 and 26, 1899; William Quaife hit 207*, A C S Glover 119* and T S Fishwick 109. Hampshire needed 232 to avoid an innings defeat, but rain ended the match early.

887 by Yorkshire on May 7 and 8, 1896 at Edgbaston is the highest against the County, the only other total over 650 being 656 for 3 wkts dec by Notts on the Rover Grd, Coventry on June 23 and 25, 1928. Notts scored their runs in 400 minutes. Warwickshire replied with 371 for 9 wkts, then rain washed out the last day.

The County has been dismissed for under 20 once – 16 v Kent at Tonbridge on June 21, 1913. Warwickshire have dismissed another County for under 20 once – Hampshire were all out for 15 on June 14, 1922 at Edgbaston; Hampshire made a remarkable recovery and won the match (see Hants section).

Individual performances F R Foster hit 305* against Worcestershire at Dudley on June 2, 1914. This is the only triple hundred for the County. Foster batted 260 minutes and hit a five and 44 fours. Worcestershire collapsed in their second innings and Warwickshire won by an innings and 321 runs. F E Field the Warwickshire bowler returned remarkable figures: 8.4–6–2–6.

Edgbaston, the home of Warwickshire CCC since 1886, and a regular Test match venue.

W G Quaife, whose 33,862 runs is Warwickshire's highest aggregate.

F R Foster's 305 not out in 1914 is the only triple century for Warwickshire.

R G D Willis, England captain, is Warwickshire's most-capped player.

The highest score against the County is 316 by R H Moore for Hampshire on July 28, 1937. Moore batted 380 minutes and hit 3 sixes and 43 fours.

Three bowlers have taken all ten wickets in an innings for Warwickshire. J D Bannister has the best figures (10–41) v Combined Services on Mitchell and Butler's Ground, Birmingham on May 27 and 28, 1959; W E Hollies took 10–49 v Notts at Edgbaston on July 24 and 25, 1946; H Howell took 10–51 v Yorkshire at Edgbaston on May 23 and 24, 1923. There have also been three instances of 10 wickets in an innings against the County, 10 for 36 by H Verity for Yorkshire at Headingley on May 18, 1931 being the best analysis. N I Thomson took 10 for 49 for Sussex at Worthing on June 6, 1964 and E A Watts 10 for 67 for Surrey at Edgbaston on August 21 and 22, 1939 – curiously Watts took no wickets in the Warwickshire first innings and the bowler principally involved in dismissing Warwickshire then, of course, took no wickets in the second innings, despite the fact that Warwickshire followed on.

Best bowling in a match belongs to S Hargreave, who took 15 for 76 against Surrey at the Oval on May 5 and 6, 1903. Hargreave had been on tour with the English side in New Zealand in the winter of 1902–03 and arrived back on Monday, May 4, which should have been the first day of the above match; rain however prevented a start until Tuesday and Hargreave was drafted into the Warwickshire Eleven with startling results – Warwickshire won the match by 126 runs.

A P Freeman has the best match figures against the County, taking 17 for 92 for Kent at Folkestone on June 29 and 30, 1932. Freeman bowled unchanged through both innings.

Most runs in a season are 2,417 by M J K Smith (av 60.43) in 1959. Smith scored 1,000 runs in a season 16 times between 1957 and 1974, but the record is 20 times by William Quaife between 1898 and 1926.

W E Hollies holds the record for most wickets in a season with 180 (av 15.13) in 1946. He also took 100 wickets in a season on most occasions – 14 between 1935 and 1957.

Only William Quaife has exceeded 30,000 runs for the County, his total being 33,862 (av 36.18) between 1894 and 1928.

W E Hollies is almost 1,000 wickets ahead of the next bowler (S Santall with 1,207) in the bowling career records. Hollies took 2,201 (av 20.45) between 1932 and 1957.

Wicket partnerships

The highest stands in first-class cricket for the County are:

1st	377*	N F Horner, K Ibadulla v Surrey (*Oval*)		1960
2nd	465*	J A Jameson, R B Kanhai v Gloucestershire (*Edgbaston*)		1974
3rd	327	S Kinneir, William Quaife v Lancashire (*Edgbaston*)		1901
4th	470	A I Kallicharran, G W Humpage v Lancashire (*Southport*)		1982
5th	268	William Quaife, Walter Quaife v Essex (*Leyton*)		1900
6th	220	H E Dollery, J Buckingham v Derbyshire (*Derby*)		1938
7th	250	H E Dollery, J S Ord v Kent (*Maidstone*)		1953
8th	228	A J W Croom, R E S Wyatt v Worcestershire (*Dudley*)		1925
9th	154	G W Stephens, A J W Croom v Derbyshire (*Edgbaston*)		1925
10th	128	F R Santall, W Sanders v Yorkshire (*Edgbaston*)		1930

Limited overs cricket records

GILLETTE/NATWEST CUP
Highest team total 314–6 v Oxfordshire (*Edgbaston*) 1980
Lowest team total 109 v Kent (*Canterbury*) 1971
Highest innings 141* A I Kallicharran v Somerset (*Taunton*) 1982
Best bowling 6–32 K Ibadulla v Hants (*Edgbaston*) 1965

JOHN PLAYER LEAGUE
Highest team total 301–6 v Essex (*Colchester*) 1982
Lowest team total 65 v Kent (*Maidstone*) 1979
Highest innings 123* J A Jameson v Notts (*Trent Bridge*) 1973
Best bowling 5–13 D J Brown v Worcs (*Edgbaston*) 1970

BENSON AND HEDGES CUP
Highest team total 291–5 v Lancashire (*Old Trafford*) 1981

Lowest team total 96 v Leicestershire (*Grace Rd, Leicester*) 1972
Highest innings 119* R B Kanhai v Northants (*Northampton*) 1975
Best bowling 7–32 R G D Willis v Yorkshire (*Edgbaston*) 1981

West Indies

The first mention of cricket in the West Indies occurs in Barbados in 1806, where there is a meeting of St Anne's Cricket Club – it would seem therefore that cricket was played in Barbados for some time before 1806.

The first inter-colonial match was played on February 15 and 16, 1865 between Barbados and Demerara at Bridgetown and this is regarded as the first first-class match in the West Indies. For cricketing purposes the term 'West Indies' includes Barbados, Demerara (later called British Guiana, now Guyana), Jamaica, Trinidad, Leewards Islands and Windward Islands.

From 1892 to 1939 Barbados, Demerara and Trinidad competed in a Tournament held in turn in each colony – because of distance Jamaica did not compete. The results were:

1892–93	Barbados (*Port of Spain*)
1895–96	Demerara (*Georgetown*)
1897–98	Barbados (*Bridgetown*)
1899–1900	Barbados (*Port of Spain*)
1901–02	Trinidad (*Georgetown*)
1903–04	Trinidad (*Bridgetown*)
1905–06	Barbados (*Port of Spain*)
1907–08	Trinidad (*Georgetown*)
1908–09	Barbados (*Bridgetown*)
1909–10	Trinidad (*Port of Spain*)
1910–11	Barbados (*Georgetown*)
1911–12	Barbados (*Bridgetown*)
1921–22	No Result (*Port of Spain*)
1922–23	Barbados (*Georgetown*)
1923–24	Barbados (*Bridgetown*)
1924–25	Trinidad (*Port of Spain*)
1925–26	Trinidad (*Georgetown*)
1926–27	Barbados (*Bridgetown*)
1928–29	Trinidad (*Port of Spain*)
1929–30	British Guiana (*Georgetown*)
1931–32	Trinidad (*Bridgetown*)
1933–34	Trinidad (*Port of Spain*)
1934–35	British Guiana (*Georgetown*)
1935–36	British Guiana (*Bridgetown*)
1936–37	Trinidad (*Port of Spain*)
1937–38	British Guiana (*Georgetown*)
1938–39	Trinidad (*Bridgetown*)

In 1956–57 a Tournament was held in Georgetown with Jamaica competing for the first time, British Guiana winning the final on first innings. In 1961–62 the Combined Islands of Leewards and Windwards also competed in a tournament held in Georgetown, British Guiana again winning. In 1963–64 a league championship was tried, British Guiana proving to be champions. The present Shell Shield started in 1965–66 (*see under 'Shell Shield'*).

The first-class records in the West Indies are:
Highest team total 849 England v West Indies (*Kingston*) 1929–30
Lowest team total 16 Trinidad v Barbados (*Bridgetown*) 1941–42
Highest individual innings 365* G St A Sobers, West Indies v Pakistan (*Kingston*) 1956–57
Best bowling in innings 10–36 F Hinds, A B Hill's XII v Trinidad (*Port of Spain*) 1900–01
Best bowling in match 16–58 E M Dowson, R A Bennett's XI v Jamaica (*Kingston*) 1901–02

Record wicket partnerships in first-class cricket

1st	390	G L Wight, G L Gibbs, British Guiana v Barbados (*Georgetown*) 1951–52
2nd	446	C C Hunte, G St A Sobers, West Indies v Pakistan (*Kingston*) 1957–58
3rd	434	J B Stollmeyer, G E Gomez, Trinidad v British Guiana (*Port of Spain*) 1946–47

4th 574* C L Walcott, F M M Worrell, Barbados v Trinidad
     (*Port of Spain*) 1945–46
5th 327 P Holmes, W E Astill, MCC v Jamaica (*Kingston*)
     1925–26
6th 487* G A Headley, C C Passailaigue, Jamaica v Ld
     Tennyson's XI (*Kingston*) 1931–32
7th 347 D St E Atkinson, C C Depeiza, West Indies v Australia
     (*Bridgetown*) 1954–55
8th 255 E A V Williams, E A Martindale, Barbados v Trinidad
     (*Bridgetown*) 1935–36
9th 168 L G Crawley, F B Watson, MCC v Jamaica (*Kingston*)
     1925–26
10th 167 A W F Somerset, W C Smith, MCC v Barbados
     (*Bridgetown*) 1912–13

Team records in first-class matches

BARBADOS
Highest team total 753 v Jamaica (*Bridgetown*) 1951–52
Lowest team total 47 v Demerara (*Georgetown*) 1887–88
Highest individual innings 314* C L Walcott v Trinidad (*Port of
Spain*) 1945–46
Best bowling in innings 8–8 J E D Sealy v Trinidad (*Bridgetown*)
  1942–43

GUYANA (formerly Demerara and British Guiana)
Highest team total 692–9 dec v Barbados (*Georgetown*) 1951–52
Lowest team total 47 v Demerara (*Georgetown*) 1887–88
Highest individual innings 268 H P Bayley v Barbados (*Georgetown*)
  1937–38
Best bowling in innings 9–19 O H Layne v Shepherd's XI
  (*Georgetown*) 1909–10

JAMAICA
Highest team total 702–5 dec v Tennyson's XI (*Kingston*) 1931–32
Lowest team total 33 v Bennett's XI (*Kingston*) 1901–02
Highest individual innings 344* G A Headley v Tennyson's XI
  (*Kingston*) 1931–32
Best bowling in innings 8–67 O C Scott v Tennyson's XI (*Kingston*)
  1927–28

Above *The great
West Indian batsman
George Headley (seen
batting against Essex)
added 487 for the sixth
wicket with C C
Passailaigue for
Jamaica against Lord
Tennyson's XI in
1931–32.*

Left *Clyde Walcott,
whose stand of 574
with Frank Worrell,
Barbados v Trinidad,
1945–46, is a West
Indies record.*

LEEWARD ISLANDS
Highest team total 462 v Windward Is (*Nevis*) 1976–77
Lowest team total 92 v Windward Is (*Castries*) 1969–70
Highest individual innings 167 I V A Richards v Trinidad (*St Johns*)
  1981–82
Best bowling in innings 6–33 N C Guishard v Windward Is (*Roseau*)
  1981–82

TRINIDAD
Highest team total 750–8 dec v British Guiana (*Port of Spain*)
  1946–47
Lowest team total 16 Barbados (*Bridgetown*) 1941–42
Highest individual innings 324 J B Stollmeyer v British Guiana
  (*Port of Spain*) 1946–47
Best bowling in innings 9–97 B D Julien v Jamaica (*Port of Spain*)
  1981–82

Above *Gary Sobers, whose 365 not out in 1956–57 is the highest score made in the West Indies.*

Vivian Richards, among whose achievements is the highest innings for the Leeward Isles.

WINDWARD ISLANDS

Highest team total 468 *v* Leeward Is (*Antigua*) 1974–75
Lowest team total 69 *v* MCC (*Grenada*) 1959–60
Highest individual innings 238 I T Shillingford *v* Leeward Is (*Castries*) 1977–78
Best bowling in innings 7–33 N Phillip *v* Leeward Is (*Roseau*) 1981–82

Wicket partnerships

The first recorded partnership exceeding 100 occurred on September 28, 1769 on Broadhalfpenny Down. T Sueter and G Brown put on 128 for the 1st Hampshire wicket against Surrey; this record has been broken as follows:

200	1st	W Harding, R Purchase, Frencham *v* c1780
275	3rd	W S Church, J P Gundry, Oxford XI *v* Purton (*Purton*) 1859
305	5th	T Hayward, R Carpenter, A E E *v* Radcliffe-on-Trent (*Radcliffe*) 1870
322	1st	T S Pearson, E F S Tylecote, Free Foresters *v* Newark (*Newark*) 1874
356	1st	L K Scott, Hon M G Talbot, Royal Engineers *v* IZ (*Chatham*) 1875
391*	1st	S H Meek, F C Pollitt, F C Hoare's XI *v* Fenton Hall (*Fenton Hall*) 1877
404	1st	W F Forbes, Lord Throwley, A E Fellowes' XI *v* Hunts (*Huntingdon*) 1881
454	3rd	W Barnes, W E Midwinter, MCC *v* Leics (*Lord's*) 1882
603	2nd	G F Vernon, A H Trevor, Orleans Club *v* Rickling Green (*Rickling Green*) 1882
623*	2nd	W C Oates, F Fitzgerald, 1st Royal Munster Fusiliers *v* Army Service Corps (*Curragh*) 1895
641	3rd	T Patton, N Rippon, Buffalo River *v* Whorouly (*Gapsted, Victoria*) 1913–14

The record for each wicket at the present time is as follows (where the record is in a minor match it is followed by the first-class record):

561	1st	Waheed Mirza, Mansoor Akhtar, Karachi Whites *v* Quetta (*Karachi*) 1976–77
623*	2nd	W C Oates, F Fitzgerald (see list above)
465*		J A Jameson, R B Kanhai, Warwicks *v* Gloucs (*Edgbaston*) 1974
641	3rd	T Patton, N Rippon (see list above)
456		Khalid Irtiza, Aslam Ali, United Bank *v* Multan (*Karachi*) 1975–76
577	4th	Gul Mahomed, V S Hazare, Baroda *v* Holkar (*Baroda*) 1946–47
433	5th	W W Armstrong, E Monfries, Melbourne *v* University (*Melbourne*) 1903–04
405		S G Barnes, D G Bradman, Australia *v* England (*Sydney*) 1946–47
487*	6th	G A Headley, C C Passailaigue, Jamaica *v* Ld Tennyson's XI (*Kingston*) 1931–32
429	7th	C J Eady, W Abbott, Break o' Day *v* Wellington (*Hobart*) 1901–02
347		D St Atkinson, C C Depeiza, West Indies *v* Australia (*Bridgetown*) 1954–55
442	8th	E G Noble, S E Gregory, Sydney *v* Warwick (*Sydney*) 1890–91
433		V T Trumper, A Sims, Australians *v* Canterbury (*Christchurch*) 1913–14
293	9th	E A C Druce, V P Johnstone, Trinity Wanderers *v* Eastbourne (*Eastbourne*) 1900
283		A Warren, J Chapman, Derbyshire *v* Warwickshire (*Blackwell*) 1910
307	10th	A F Kippax, J E H Hooker, NSW *v* Victoria (*Melbourne*) 1928–29
299	11th	E V Sale,—Robson, New Zealand club match 1905–06

(*For record wicket partnerships for major countries and counties see appropriate headings.*)

Wicket keeping

In 1833 John Nyren in 'The Young Cricketer's Tutor' notes: 'It is the duty of the bowler to be the wicket-keeper at his own wicket, during the intervals of his bowling.' Not long after this however the idea of having a player specialising as wicket-keeper came into vogue and as early as 1820 there is a mention of the use of wicket-keeping gloves, though these did not come into general use until the 1850s.

The ultimate achievement of a wicket-keeper is to have a hand in the dismissal of all ten batsmen in an innings. So far as is known this has only occurred once: W J Bennette stumped 6 and caught 4 in a schools match in Ceylon in 1954. The best performance in England is 9 by H W P Middleton (stumped 8, caught 1) in a house match at Repton School in 1930.

In first-class cricket the record stands at 8 (all caught) by A T W Grout for Queensland v Western Australia at Brisbane, February 13 and 15, 1960. The English first-class record is 7 achieved on 9 occasions, the earliest being by E J Smith (4 caught, 3 stumped) Warwickshire v Derbyshire, Edgbaston 1926.

The record number of dismissals in a match is 12; the earliest, and the only instance in England, is by E Pooley (caught 8, stumped 4) for Surrey v Sussex at the Oval, July 6, 1868. The other two both happened in Australia: D Tallon, Queensland v NSW at Sydney in 1938–39 and H B Taber, NSW v South Australia at Adelaide in 1968–69.

The record number of catches by a wicket-keeper in a match is 11, achieved on three occasions: A Long, Surrey v Sussex, Hove, 1964; R W Marsh, W Australia v Victoria, Perth, 1965–66; D L Bairstow, Yorkshire v Derbyshire, Scarborough, 1982.

The first-class record in a season is held by L E G Ames for Kent in 1928; he caught 79 and stumped 49, a total of 128.

The only wicket-keeper to exceed 1,500 dismissals in a first-class career is J T Murray of Middlesex, whose total is 1,527 (caught 1,270, stumped 257) between 1952 and 1975.
(see also Stumpings)

A T W Grout, whose eight wickets in an innings is a wicket-keeping record.

J T Murray, whose aggregate of 1,527 dismissals is a record for a wicket-keeper.

Don Tallon is one of three wicket-keepers to have taken twelve wickets in a match, Queensland v New South Wales, 1938–39.

Wickets in match

In an Eleven-a-side match the most wickets obtainable by a bowler are 20. The following is a complete list of bowlers known to have accomplished this feat:

20–48   F R Spofforth, Local match (*Bendigo, NSW*)   1881–82
20–80   J Martin, Stockbridge v Abbots Ann (*Stockbridge*)   1883
20–56   J Bryant, Erskine v Deaf Mutes (*Melbourne*)   1887–88
20–?   J R Painter, Bourton Vale v MCC (*Bourton-in-the-Water*) 1887–88
20–24   C Bashford, Reynards Rd Methodists v St Augustine's Church (*Coburg, Victoria*)   1903–04
20–?   T W Dyson, Asylum v Gordon Macleary (*Toronto*)   1905
20–37   W White, Hughenden v Woodcroft (*Bristol*)   1921
20–65   L R Benaud, Penrith Waratah v St Mary's (*Penrith, NSW*) 1922–23
20–16   A Rimmer, 7th Grade v Cathedral GS (*Christchurch, NZ*) 1925–26
20–31   Y S Ramswami, Marimallappa HS v Bangalore Wesleyan HS (*Bangalore*)   1932–33
20–21   W Doig, East Freemantle v ? (*Perth, W Austr*)   1935–36
20–54   J E Pothecary, Sea Point v Lansdowne School (*Cape Town*) 1950–51

In a first-class match the record is:
19–90   J C Laker, England v Australia (*Old Trafford*)   1956

Wickets in innings

In an eleven-a-side match the best possible bowling figures are 10 wickets for no runs. The following is a complete list of bowlers known to have accomplished this feat:
A Dartnell, Broad Green v Thornton Heath (*Norbury*)   1867
R T P Tearne, Pershore v Rev G Swinton's XI (*Pershore*)   1879
A Hipgrave, Heathcote v ? (*Sydney, NSW*)   1882–83
F Rae, Alliance v Granville (*Drayton Park*)   1885
J Cottrell, St Benedict's v Pupil Teachers (*Liverpool*)   1885

H S Thynne, A C Bell's XI v Melksham Choir (*Seend*)   1892
J Watts, Castle v Junior Hawks (*Clapham Common*)   1902
S N Priestley, Tewkesbury GS v Eldersfield Sch (*Tewkesbury*)   1904
E P Martin, Camberwell GS 2nd XI v Manor House Sch 2nd XI (*Clapham*)   1906
J Tune, Cliff v Eastringham (*Cliff, Yks*)   1922
S Tucker, Homesdale British Sch v Horley Council Sch (*Reigate*) 1924
J Burr, Strathmore v Strathmore North (*Strathmore, Vict*)   1962–63
N Doherty, Panania-Easts v Regents Park (*Sydney, NSW*)   1965–66
D Poole, Taunton School v Glen Eyre (*Taunton*)   1966
D Norquay, Seaforth v Pittwater (*Sydney, NSW*)   1966–67
R Morgan, Beachport Colts v Cellulose (*Millicent, S Austr*) 1968–69

The bowler to take 10 wkts at least cost in first-class cricket is:
10–10   H Verity, Yorkshire v Notts (*Headingley*)   1932

Hedley Verity, whose ten wickets for ten runs for Yorkshire against Notts at Headingley in 1932 is the best analysis by any bowler taking all ten wickets.

Wickets in successive balls
The world record is believed to be 9 wickets in successive balls; this has been achieved twice:

P Hugo, Smithfield v Aliwal North (*Johannesburg*) 1930–31
S Fleming, Marlborough College v Bohally Intermediate School (*Blenheim, NZ*) 1967–68
In England the records stands at 8 wickets:
J Walker, Ashbombe Park v Tunstall (*Leek*) 1882
J Stebbing, Frindsbury v Rainham (*Kent*) 1902

In first-class matches no bowler has obtained more than 4 wickets with consecutive deliveries, but of the 27 who have performed this feat three went on to take 5 wickets in 6 balls:

W H Copson, Derbyshire v Warwickshire (*Derby*) 1937
W A Henderson, N E Transvaal v OFS (*Bloemfontein*) 1937–38
P I Pocock, Surrey v Sussex (*Eastbourne*) 1972

Amir Elahi took 5 wkts in 5 balls for Muslims v The Rest (*Surat*) 1944–45. It is possible that this will be ranked as a first-class match and thus provides a new first-class record.
(*see also Hat-tricks and Four in Four*)

Wides
Wide balls were first noted in the Laws in 1816, but until 1827 they were included among the 'byes' in the team total. The first note of wides as a separate item in a printed scoresheet comes in 1827 – Sussex v Kent at Brighton on September 17. The introduction of 'round-arm' bowling at this time caused a considerable increase in the number of wides bowled.

The most in an innings are 46, Cambridge U v Oxford U (*Lord's*) 1839.

Wins
Most wins in a season in first-class matches by a County are 27 by Surrey in 1955.

In County Championship matches only, Yorkshire hold the record with 25 in 1923.

Worcestershire
The first mention of cricket in Worcestershire dates from 1829.

Formation of the County Club The first known match involving a side called Worcestershire took place on August 28, 1844 when Worcestershire played Shropshire on Hartlebury Common.

A Worcestershire County Club was formed in 1847 and on May 5, 1855 a meeting at the Star Hotel, Worcester agreed to the merging of the County Club with the Worcester City Club to form the Worcester City and County Cricket Club. This Club lasted until about 1863 and on March 3, 1865 the present County Club was formed.

First-class status Having won the Minor Counties Competition in 1898, Worcestershire arranged the minimum of fixtures with existing first-class counties in order to qualify for inclusion in the County Championship and then applied to MCC for first-class status. This was granted on December 12, 1898 and the County played its first first-class match v Yorkshire on May 4, 5 and 6, 1899.

Grounds The New Road Ground, Worcester, has been the County headquarters since it was promoted to first-class status.

Grounds which the County have used are: Recreation Grd, Bournville (1910–11); County Ground, Dudley (1911–71); Evesham (1951); Halesowen (1964–69); Racecourse Grd, Hereford (1919–); Chester Rd, Kidderminster (1921–73); Stourbridge (1905–); Stourport-on-Severn (1980–).

Honours The County won the Championship in 1964, 1965 and 1974; the John Player League in 1971 and were the losing finalists in the Gillette Cup in 1963 and 1966 and in the Benson and Hedges Cup in 1973 and 1976.

The players D Kenyon and R T D Perks stand alone amongst the County's players with over 500 first-class matches each to their names. Kenyon appeared 589 times between 1946 and 1967, whilst Perks played in 560 matches between 1930 and 1955.

H K Foster captained Worcestershire for 10 consecutive seasons (1901–10), a record which has recently been equalled by N Gifford between 1971 and 1980, but H K Foster also led the County in 1913.

Youngest cricketer to represent the County is M F W Passey, who was 16 years and 63 days on his debut v Glamorgan in 1953.

Oldest player is R H Moss, who was 57 years and 2 months on his solitary appearance for the County in 1925 v Gloucestershire.

B L d'Oliveira with 44 caps is the Worcestershire player with most England Test appearances.

Team performances The County have exceeded 600 twice, both times at Worcester. In 1905 627–9 dec was scored v Kent, but this was beaten on August 6 and 7 of the following summer with a total of 633 v Warwickshire. The County's bowlers have conceded more than 600 runs on six separate occasions and the record against them was also compiled in 1906 at Worcester – Leicestershire batted 465 minutes to make 701 for 4 dec, with C J B Wood hitting 255 in 330 minutes.

Leicester batted on all three days – July 19, 20 and 21 – and after their innings closed Worcester hit 344 for 2 in 270 minutes.

The lowest scores both for and against the county were made in 1903 – on June 18 at Worcester, Hampshire were dismissed for 30 in 70 minutes, but a month later, on July 17, Yorkshire bowled out Worcester at Huddersfield for 24, with W Rhodes returning the remarkable analysis of 9-6-4-5.

Individual performances The highest score for the County is 311* made by G M Turner in 342 minutes against Warwickshire at Worcester on May 29, 1982. Worcester made 501 for 1 dec. The best score against the County is 331*, being hit by J D B Robertson for Middlesex on July 23, 1949.

On fourteen occasions a bowler has taken nine wickets in an innings for the County, but the feat of taking all ten has still to be achieved. The best analysis is 18.4-7-23-9 by C F Root v Lancashire on May 19, 1931 at Worcester. Worcestershire dismissed Lancashire for 75 and 85 in this game – a remarkable feat considering that Lancashire had been the Champion County in 1930.

Five bowlers have taken all ten wickets against the County; J Briggs for Lancashire in 1900, J C White for Somerset in 1921, T W J Goddard for Gloucestershire in 1937 and R Berry for Lancashire in 1953 are four, but the best figures are by J Mercer for Glamorgan on July 29, 1936, with 26-10-51-10 at Worcester.

Only one batsman has exceeded 2,500 runs in a season for the County – the record belonging to H H I Gibbons with 2,654 (av 52.03) in 1934. D Kenyon however exceeded 2,000 runs in a year on most occasions with six, and he holds the record for attaining 1,000 runs on most occasions with 19 between 1947 and 1967.

Most wickets in a season are 207 (av 17.52) taken by C F Root in 1925. R T D Perks took at least 100 wickets in a season on 15 occasions which is the Worcestershire record, his first 100 being in 1934 and his last in 1955.

Career records are held by D Kenyon with 33,490 runs (av 33.19) between 1946 and 1967 and R T D Perks 2,143 wickets (av 23.73) between 1930 and 1955. Kenyon is over 12,000 runs above the next batsman, whilst Perks has a lead of over 500 in the bowling career table.

Wicket partnerships

The highest stands in first-class cricket for the County are:

1st	309	F L Bowley, H K Foster v Derbyshire (*Derby*)	1901
2nd	274	H H I Gibbons, Nawab of Pataudi v Kent (*Worcester*) 1933	
	274	H H I Gibbons, Nawab of Pataudi v Glamorgan (*Worcester*) 1934	
3rd	314	M J Horton, T W Graveney v Somerset (*Worcester*) 1962	
4th	281	J A Ormrod, Younis Ahmed v Notts (*Trent Bridge*)	1979
5th	393	E G Arnold, W B Burns v Warwicks (*Edgbaston*)	1909
6th	227	E J O Hemsley, D N Patel v Oxford Univ (*Oxford*) 1976	
7th	197	H H I Gibbons, R Howorth v Surrey (*Oval*)	1938
8th	145*	F Chester, W H Taylor v Essex (*Worcester*)	1914
9th	181	J A Cuffe, R D Burrows v Gloucs (*Worcester*)	1907
10th	119	W B Burns, G A Wilson v Somerset (*Worcester*)	1906

The remarkable point on the records above is the 2nd wicket record – two identical partnerships by the same batsmen – curiously on both occasions the Nawab hit an undefeated double century.

Limited overs cricket records

GILLETTE/NATWEST CUP
Highest team total 286–5 v Yorkshire (*Headingley*) 1982
Lowest team total 98 v Durham (*Chester-le-Street*) 1975
Highest innings 117* G M Turner v Lancs (*Worcester*) 1971
Best bowling 6–14 J A Flavell v Lancs (*Worcester*) 1963

JOHN PLAYER LEAGUE
Highest team total 307–4 v Derbys (*Worcester*) 1975
Lowest team total 86 v Yorkshire (*Headingley*) 1969
Highest innings 147 G M Turner v Sussex (*Horsham*) 1980
Best bowling 6–26 A P Pridgeon v Surrey (*Worcester*) 1978

BENSON AND HEDGES CUP
Highest team total 314–5 v Lancashire (*Old Trafford*) 1980
Lowest team total 92 v Oxf and Cambr Univs (*Fenner's*) 1975
Highest innings 143* G M Turner v Warwicks (*Edgbaston*) 1976
Best bowling 6–8 N Gifford v Minor Counties (S) (*High Wycombe*) 1979

World series cricket

In the winter of 1976–77, the Australian Commercial Television Company run by Kerry Packer put in a bid against the ABC for the rights to televise the Test matches of 1977–78. Despite the fact that Mr Packer's bid was higher than the ABC's, the Australian Board of Control accepted ABC's tender. Mr Packer's company then proceeded to set up a series of cricket matches in Australia for the 1977–78 season in rivalry to the matches arranged by the Australian Board of Control. To feature in Mr Packer's 'World Series Cricket' about 40 players were signed up to play in three teams – Australia, West Indies and Rest of the World.

The World Series matches were divided into three types, the Super-Tests, which were 5-day games, and two types of one-day limited overs matches, one being floodlit, and the other played mainly at minor cricket centres in Australia.

The ICC reacted by banning all the players from both Test and County cricket. A W Greig, J A Snow and M J Procter, all of whom had signed contracts to play in World Series Cricket took the ICC to the High Court and the High Court ruled that the bans by the ICC and the TCCB were a restraint of trade and therefore void.

The World Series Cricket matches went ahead during the Australian season of 1977–78 and again in 1978–79, when matches were also played in West Indies and New Zealand.

Mr Packer's rival cricket ended on April 24, 1979 when the Australian Board of Control gave Mr Packer's television company exclusive rights for three years.

The leading records in the Super-Tests were:

Highest team total 625 World v Australia (*Perth*) 1977–78
Lowest team total 85 World v Australia (*Auckland*) 1978–79
Highest individual innings 246 G S Chappell, Australia v World (*Melbourne*) 1977–78
Best bowling in innings 7–23 D K Lillee, Australia v West Indies (*Sydney*) 1978–79

Yorkshire

At Stanwick near Richmond during the week commencing August 5, 1751 a match was played between Duke of Cleveland's XI v Earl of Northumberland's XI. This is the first known game played in the County. In the same year, there is also reference to cricket in Sheffield. **Formation of the County Club** As early as 1798 there were several matches played involving 'All Yorkshire', but it would appear that these games were between various military sides. The main centre of cricket in the County in the 19th Century was Sheffield, and the Yorkshire matches of the 1830s against Norfolk and Sussex were organised by the Sheffield Club. A Match Fund Committee to run County matches was formed in Sheffield on March 7, 1861 and in 1863 this was reconstituted as the Yorkshire County Cricket Club – this is the start of the present County Club. A rival County Club flourished from York at various times, but never superseded the Sheffield-based organisation.

Left *Norman Gifford, Worcestershire captain from 1971 to 1980.*

The New Road Ground at Worcester with its famous cathedral, has been the headquarters of Worcestershire CCC since the county became first-class.

World Series Cricket led to some innovations, including the use of coloured flannels for the players – here the 'reds' are West Indies and the 'yellows' Australia.

First-class status With the full strength Sheffield Club being very nearly representative of the County as a whole in the 1820s through to the 1850s, Sheffield was to Yorkshire what Nottingham was to Nottinghamshire. The findings of the Association of Cricket Statisticians were that Sheffield/Yorkshire should rank as 'first-class' from 1827.

Grounds The ground used in 1827 was that of the Sheffield Club at Darnall. This was last used in 1829 and in 1830 the Club played at the Hyde Park Ground, Sheffield. The final match here was in 1851 and in 1855 the Bramall Lane Ground was first used for County Cricket. Bramall Lane was closed as a cricket ground in 1973. The present Sheffield ground is at Abbeydale Park. The present headquarters of the County is Headingley, Leeds – first County match 1891.

Other grounds to stage first-class Yorkshire matches are: Easby Road, Bradford (1863–74); Horton Park Ave, Bradford (1881 to date); Saville Town, Dewsbury (1867–1933); Thrum Hall, Halifax (1888–97); St George's Ground, Harrogate (1894 to date); Hall Park, Horsforth (1885); Recreation Ground, Holbeck (1868–86); Hunslet (1869); Argyle St, Hull (1879); Anlaby Road, Hull (1899 to date); Albert Rd, Middlesbrough (1864–1867); Linthorpe Rd, Middlesbrough (1882); Acklam Park, Middlesbrough (1956 to date); Castle Hill, Scarborough (1874–77); North Marine Rd, Scarborough (1878 to date); Fartown, Huddersfield (1873 to date); College Ground, Wakefield (1878); Bootham Cres, York (1890).

Honours The County won the Championship in the following seasons: 1867, 1869, 1870, 1893, 1896, 1898, 1900, 1901, 1902, 1905, 1908, 1912, 1919, 1922, 1923, 1924, 1925, 1931, 1932, 1933, 1935, 1937, 1938, 1939, 1946, 1949, 1959, 1960, 1962, 1963, 1966, 1967, 1968 – a total of 33 titles, more than any other county. Yorkshire won the Gillette Cup in 1965 and 1969. The best position obtained in the John Player League is 2nd in 1973 and in the Benson and Hedges Cup is being beaten in the Final in 1972.

The players Nine cricketers have made over 500 appearances each for the County, but W Rhodes with 881 matches is over 150 matches ahead of his nearest rival (G H Hirst, 715). Rhodes' career lasted from 1898 to 1930.

Longest serving captain is Lord Hawke who led the County for 28 years between 1883 and 1910.

The youngest cricketer to represent the County in a first-class match is D E V Padgett who was 16 yrs and 320 days when making his debut *v* Somerset in 1951, but in 1981 P W Jarvis played *v* Sussex aged 16 yrs and 75 days in a John Player League match.

The oldest cricketer to appear for the County is G H Hirst who was 58 yrs and 4 days on his last outing *v* MCC in 1929.

The Yorkshire cricketer with most England Test caps is G Boycott with 108.

Team performances The highest score for the County is 887 against Warwickshire at Edgbaston on May 7 and 8, 1896. Yorkshire had scored 452 for 7 by close of play on the first day, so there was really nothing to suggest that the total would nearly double on the second day with only the last three batsmen to be dismissed; the overnight batsmen however, Peel 37* and Lord Hawke 3*, took their individual scores to 210 and 166 and with G H Hirst at No 10 making 85, the new record was created. Yorkshire have exceeded 600 on five occasions, but only once has that figure been achieved against the County – the record is 630 by Somerset at Headingley on July 16 and 17, 1901. This match is perhaps one of the most remarkable ever to be played in the County Championship. Somerset were dismissed for 87 in their first innings to which Yorkshire replied with 325. Somerset then hit 630 and went on to dismiss Yorkshire for 113, thus winning the game by 279 runs. It was the sole defeat inflicted on Yorkshire during the season and whilst Yorkshire won the County Championship, Somerset ended third from bottom.

Yorkshire have on ten occasions dismissed their opponents for 25 or

Night matches were also a feature of WSC cricket. This match is at the VFL Park, Melbourne, in 1977.

Left *Kerry Packer (left), the instigator of World Series cricket, and Tony Greig, who supported him, outside the High Court in London.*

The Scarborough Festival. The ground at North Marine Road has staged Yorkshire matches since 1878.

less, but have only suffered this indignity once. The records are: 13 by Notts at Trent Bridge on June 20 and 21, 1901 and 23 by Yorkshire v Hampshire at Middlesbrough on May 19 and 20, 1965, D W White taking 6 for 10.

Individual performances Six triple hundreds have been made for the County, two each by P Holmes (315* and 302*) and J T Brown (311 and 300), one by H Sutcliffe (313), and the record of 341 by G H Hirst, scored v Leicestershire at Aylestone Road on May 19 and 20, 1905. Hirst batted seven hours and hit a six and 53 fours. The single triple hundred against the County was scored by W G Grace on the College Ground, Cheltenham, August 17 and 18, 1876. Grace hit 318* in eight hours and five minutes, his innings including a seven, two 6s, two 5s and 28 fours. He gave one chance when 201.

Of the four occasions on which a bowler took all ten wickets in an innings for Yorkshire, two were by H Verity, his best and the County record being 19.4-16-10-10 v Notts at Headingley on July 12, 1932. The other two bowlers to take all ten are A Drake (10–35) and T F Smailes (10–47).

Three bowlers have taken all ten wickets against the County, the best analysis being obtained by C V Grimmett (22.3-8-37-10) for the Australians at Bramall Lane on May 10, 1930. The other two successful bowlers are G Wootton (10–51) in 1865 and H Howell (10–51) 1923.

H Verity (17–91) is the only bowler to obtain 17 wickets in a match for the County, achieving his feat v Essex at Leyton on July 14, 1933 – Essex being dismissed twice in a single day. The record against Yorkshire is also 17 for 91, performed by H Dean for Lancashire at Liverpool on July 10, 11 and 12, 1913. This match was not a Championship game, but a special contest arranged to celebrate the visit of George V to the City.

H Sutcliffe hit 2,883 runs (av 80.08) for Yorkshire in 1932, which is the County record, the only other batsman to exceed 2,500 being L Hutton with 2,640 (av 69.47) in 1949. H Sutcliffe hit over 1,000 runs in 21 seasons (1919–39) which is also the County record.

W Rhodes has taken most wickets in a season, reaching 240 (av 12.72) in 1900 – the following year he took 233 (av 15.00), which is the second highest total. Rhodes reached 100 wickets in a season no less than 22 times (between 1898 and 1929), easily the County record.

Batting and bowling career records are held by H Sutcliffe with 38,561 runs (av 50.20) and W Rhodes 3,608 wickets (av 16.00), both totals being well in excess of the second best. Sutcliffe's career spanned 1919 to 1945 and Rhodes' 1898 to 1930.

Wicket partnerships

The highest stands in first-class cricket for the County are:

1st	555	P Holmes, H Sutcliffe v Essex (*Leyton*)	1932	
2nd	396	W Barber, M Leyland v Middlesex (*Bramall Lane*)	1932	
3rd	323*	H Sutcliffe, M Leyland v Glamorgan (*Huddersfield*) 1928		
4th	312	D Denton, G H Hirst v Hants (*Southampton*)	1914	
5th	340	E Wainwright, G H Hirst v Surrey (*Oval*)	1899	
6th	276	M Leyland, E Robinson v Glamorgan (*Swansea*)	1926	
7th	254	D C F Burton, W Rhodes v Hampshire (*Dewsbury*)	1919	
8th	292	R Peel, Lord Hawke v Warwickshire (*Edgbaston*)	1896	
9th	192	G H Hirst, S Haigh v Surrey (*Bradford*)	1898	
10th	149	G Boycott, G B Stevenson v Warwickshire (*Edgbaston*) 1982		

Limited overs cricket records

GILLETTE/NATWEST CUP
Highest team total   317-4 v Surrey (*Lord's*) 1965
Lowest team total   76 v Surrey (*Harrogate*) 1970
Highest innings 146 G Boycott v Surrey (*Lord's*) 1965
Best bowling 6–15 F S Trueman v Somerset (*Taunton*) 1965

JOHN PLAYER LEAGUE
Highest team total 248-5 v Derbyshire (*Chesterfield*) 1979
Lowest team total 74 v Warwickshire (*Edgbaston*) 1972
Highest innings 119 J H Hampshire v Leics (*Hull*) 1971
Best bowling 7–15 R A Hutton v Worcs (*Headingley*) 1969

BENSON AND HEDGES CUP
Highest team total 269-6 v Worcs (*Worcester*) 1980
Lowest team total   114 v Kent (*Canterbury*) 1978
Highest innings 142 G Boycott v Worcs (*Worcester*) 1980
Best bowling 6–27 A G Nicholson v Minor Counties (N) (*Middlesbrough*) 1972

Yorkshire League

Championship winners

1936	Hull	1963	Rotherham Town
1937	Hull	1964	Scarborough
1938	Hull	1965	Sheffield Utd
1939	Sheffield Utd	1966	Scarborough
1940	Hull	1967	Harrogate
1947	Hull	1968	Leeds
1948	Hull	1969	Scarborough
1949	Hull	1970	York
1950	Rawmarsh	1971	Scarborough
1951	York	1972	Hull
1952	Hull	1973	Scarborough
1953	Hull	1974	York
1954	Sheffield Utd	1975	Leeds
1955	Rotherham Town	1976	Scarborough
1956	Sheffield Utd	1977	York
1957	Scarborough	1978	Scarborough
1958	Leeds	1979	Harrogate
1959	Scarborough	1980	Scarborough
1960	Scarborough	1981	Scarborough
1961	Castleford	1982	Bradford
1962	Castleford		

Youngest cricketers

The youngest player to appear in an English first-class match since 1864 is C R Young who was aged 15 years and 131 days when he represented Hampshire v Kent at Gravesend on June 13, 1867. Young in fact appeared for Gentlemen of South v Players of South on October 1, 1866 at Southampton, when he was 14, but the match cannot be regarded as first-class – the Gentlemen of South being in reality Gentlemen of Hampshire and a most inferior team.

In Australian first-class matches the youngest is L J Junor, who appeared for Victoria v Western Australia in 1929–30 aged 15 yrs and 265 days.

The records in India and Pakistan are stated to be: *in India* 12 yrs 73 days, Alimuddin, Rajputana v Delhi, Ajmer, 1942–43; *in Pakistan* 12 yrs 363 days, Qasim Feroze, for Bahawalpur, 1970–71.

Left *Wilfred Rhodes has most appearances and most wickets for Yorkshire.*

Index